To my wife Bonni – it's a privilege to share my business, life, and love with you.

Philip Yaeger, PhD, MBA, CPA, CGMA   Owner, Editor-in-chief
Megan Lewczyk, MAcc, CPA   Production Editor

This book was set in Calibri font designed by Lucas de Groot.
Cover Design: Larissa Jaster Design Studio
Cover Photography: Travis Rieth

The following items, copyright © the American Institute of Certified Professional Accountants, Inc., New York, NY 10036, are reprinted and/or adapted with permission:

1. Material from Uniform CPA Exam Selected Questions and Unofficial Answers © 2000–2017
2. Definitions, examples, etc. from The Code of Professional Conduct
3. Material from the Preparation, Compilation and Review Standards
4. Material from the Clarified Statements on Auditing Standards
5. Material from the AICPA Audit Guide over Audit Sampling

Material from the Certified Management Accountant Examinations, copyright © 2011–2014 by the Institute of Certified Management Accountants, Montvale, New Jersey 07645, are reprinted and/or adapted with permission.

The FASB material is copyrighted by the Financial Accounting Foundation, 401 Merritt 7, Norwalk, CT 06856, and is used with permission.

The information disclosed in this document, including all designs and related materials, is the property of Yaeger CPA Review. Yaeger CPA Review and/or its licensors, as appropriate, reserve all patent, copyright and other proprietary rights to this document, including all design, reproduction, use, and sales rights thereto. You may not reproduce or transmit in any form or by any means, electronic or mechanical, including photocopying, recording, and storage in an information retrieval system, nor may you modify or create derivative works based on the text of any file, or any part thereof, without the prior written permission of Yaeger CPA Review.

Limit of Liability/Disclaimer of Warranty: While the content development team has used their best efforts in preparing this book, they make no representations or warranties with respect to the accuracy or completeness of the contents of this book and specifically disclaim any implied warranties of merchantability or fitness for a particular purpose. No warranty may be created or extended by sales representatives or written sales materials. The advice and strategies contained herein may not be suitable for your situation. You should consult with a professional where appropriate. Neither the publisher nor author shall be liable for any loss of profit or any other commercial damages, including but not limited to special, incidental, consequential, or other damages.

Solicitation or disclosure of CPA Examination questions and answers is strictly prohibited.

ISBN: 978-0-9987002-4-3   *Yaeger CPA Review 2018 - Auditing and Attestation*
           978-0-9987002-5-0   *Yaeger CPA Review 2018 - Business Environment and Concepts*
           978-0-9987002-6-7   *Yaeger CPA Review 2018 - Regulation*
           978-0-9987002-7-4   *Yaeger CPA Review 2018 - Financial Accounting and Reporting*

Copyright © 2018 Yaeger CPA Review. ALL RIGHTS RESERVED.

Second Edition: December 2017 (Version 2.8)

For additional information on our other products or for customer service, please call 1.800.824.2811.

Introduction:
Preparing for the CPA Exam

A. Message from Phil Yaeger

On behalf of YAEGER CPA REVIEW, I thank you for purchasing our program, and I wish you the best success with the CPA EXAM! If you have questions during your studies, I will be very happy to speak with you personally at any time. I am here to help you and motivate you during your journey.

With warmest regards,

Philip S. Yaeger

B. CPA Exam Basics

The CPA (Certified Public Accountant) exam is a computer-based exam that according to the American Institute of Certified Public Accountants (AICPA), tests the knowledge and skills typically possessed by a person with two years of accounting experience, to protect the public interest. Experience requirements may be obtained before or after passing the CPA exam with some time limitations dependent on your state. Even though many students take the CPA Exam after graduating college, the AICPA has stated that this should not, and will not, impact the standard established regarding required knowledge and skills necessary for licensure as a CPA.

The CPA Exam must be passed to qualify for licensure as a CPA. The licensure can be obtained in any of the 55 U.S. jurisdictions, which includes all 50 states, Puerto Rico, Guam, District of Columbia, Commonwealth of Northern Mariana Islands, and the U.S. Virgin Islands.

Apply to take the exam through your state board of accountancy or NASBA (nasba.org), as applicable. It is best to apply to take the exam when you have met the educational requirements of the jurisdiction you plan to apply for the exam in. It is recommended to check the jurisdiction you plan to take the exam in to ensure you have met the requirements before commencing your CPA Exam preparation. Most states offer a self-assessment education evaluation worksheet which you can complete to determine your status.

The Uniform CPA Exam consists of four sections: Auditing and Attestation(AUD), Business Environment and Concepts (BEC), Financial Accounting and Reporting (FAR), and Regulation (REG). Each exam section is four hours, for a total of 16 hours of testing.

Examination Structure by Section				
Section	Item Type	Item Weighting	Testlet and Time Allocation Recommendation	
Auditing and Attestation (AUD)	72 MCQs 8 TBSs	50% 50%	No.1 36 MCQs - 1 hour No.2 36 MCQs - 1 hour No.3 2 TBSs - 30 min. No.4 3 TBSs - 45 min. No.5 3 TBSs - 45 min.	Time to complete – 4 hours
Business Environment and Concepts (BEC)	62 MCQs 4 TBSs 3 Written Communications	50% 35% 15%	No.1 31 MCQs - 1 hour No.2 31 MCQs - 1 hour No.3 2 TBSs - 30 min. No.4 2 TBSs - 30min. No.5 3 Written Communications - 60 min.	Time to complete – 4 hours

Financial Accounting and Reporting (FAR)	66 MCQs 8 TBSs	50% 50%	No.1 No.2 No.3 No.4 No.5	33 MCQs - 1 hour 33 MCQs - 1 hour 2 TBSs - 30 min. 3 TBSs - 45 min. 3 TBSs - 45 min.	Time to complete – 4 hours
Regulation (REG)	76 MCQs 8 TBSs	50% 50%	No.1 No.2 No.3 No.4 No.5	38 MCQs - 1 hour 38 MCQs - 1 hour 2 TBSs - 30 min. 3 TBSs - 45 min. 3 TBSs - 45 min.	Time to complete – 4 hours

Sections may be taken in any order; however, you must complete all four sections within 18 months of passing the first section. The passing score is 75 for each section.

The exam is administered at Prometric testing centers in the USA (and some international locations): https://www.prometric.com/en-us/clients/cpa/Pages/landing.aspx.The exam can be physically sat for in a different state to that in which you apply for your license in. Some states allow for candidates to sit the exam internationally in Japan, Brazil, Bahrain, Kuwait, Lebanon and the United Arab Emirates. Check your state board for more information.

Testing "windows" represent available months when a candidate can take the exam. The testing windows are the first two months of each calendar quarter (e.g., January and February). To accommodate candidate demand for more opportunities to take the exam, the testing windows have been extended through the 10th of the third month of each testing window and are applicable for all testing windows through December 2018. Additional information will be posted as it is announced by the AICPA.

Types of questions on the CPA Exam include:
1) **Multiple-choice questions**: These questions are in all four sections and are based on the content/topics outlined in the AICPA blueprint (discussed below).

2) **Task-based simulations:** These questions utilize the type of activities that replicate real-life work situations. The simulations may include tasks such as editing a document, searching databases, or completing worksheets. Task-based simulations appear in all four sections of the exam.

    Document Review Simulations (DRS) and *Research* simulations are two specialized types of task-based simulations. A *DRS* will present a primary document, as well as related source materials, for the candidate to review. Highlighted words, phrases, sentences or paragraphs in the DRS document may or may not be correct, requiring the candidate to select appropriate edits based on relevant source materials.

    Research simulations require candidates to locate authoritative guidance to answer the prompt and cite the location where he/she found the information.

3) **Written communications tasks**: Written Communication questions are found only in the BEC sections. They are like a case study that includes a writing skill exercise. The candidate must review a description of a situation and will then be asked to write a constructed response relating to the situation. The instructions will require that the CPA candidate write a letter or a memorandum providing the correct information about the situation in a clear, complete, and professional manner.

C. **CPA Candidate Checklist**
   ☐ Complete your state's education requirements to sit for the CPA Exam
   ☐ Start studying with YAEGER CPA REVIEW
   ☐ Apply for your exam:

   Option A (NASBA-supported state – see NASBA.org):
   ☐ Apply at https://cpacentral.nasba.org/ to sit for the exam
   ☐ Your application, fees, and transcripts must be sent to NASBA
   ☐ NASBA will send your authorization to test (ATT) to the National Candidate Database (NCD)
   ☐ If approved by NCD, you will receive a notice to schedule (NTS)

   Option B (non NASBA-supported state):
   ☐ Apply to your State Board of Accountancy directly to sit for the exam
   ☐ Your application, fees, and transcripts must be sent to the State Board
   ☐ The State Board will send your ATT to the NCD
   ☐ If approved by NCD, NCD will issue a Payment Coupon to notify you of remaining exam fees that must be paid to NASBA if you only were required to send the application fee to the State Board
   ☐ Once all fees are paid, you will receive your NTS

   After you receive your NTS:
   ☐ Visit www.prometric.com to schedule your exam
   ☐ Sit for the scheduled exam (*you MUST bring NTS and two forms of ID or you can't take exam*)
   ☐ Wait patiently and receive your scores
   ☐ Complete the experience requirements for your state and submit application for licensure to state board

D. **Exam Day**

	Testlet 1	Testlet 2	Testlet 3	Scheduled 15 Minute Break	Testlet 4	Testlet 5
AUD	36 MCQ	36 MCQ	2 TBS		3 TBS	3 TBS
BEC	31 MCQ	31 MCQ	2 TBS		2 TBS	3 WC
FAR	33 MCQ	33 MCQ	2 TBS		3 TBS	3 TBS
REG	38 MCQ	38 MCQ	2 TBS		3 TBS	3 TBS

Candidates must work each testlet in order and complete/submit the current testlet before access to the next testlet is permitted. Once you submit, you are **not** permitted to return and reopen a completed/submitted testlet.

E. **Current Version of the CPA Exam**

Beginning April 1 2017, an updated version of the CPA Exam will be administered to CPA candidates. According to the AICPA, professional content knowledge will remain fundamental to protecting the public interest. Also, the candidates must be competent in the following skills:
- Remembering and understanding: The perception and comprehension of the significance of an area utilizing knowledge gained.
- Application: The use of demonstration of knowledge, concepts or techniques.

- Analysis: The examination and study of the interrelationships of separate areas in order to identify causes and find evidence to support inferences.
- Evaluation: Examination of assessment of problems and use of judgment to draw conclusions.

To test these competencies, the new CPA Exam has increased the number of task-based simulations and the length of the CPA Exam increased from 14 to 16 hours (four hours for each section).

The material that the candidate should learn is now based on the **AICPA Blueprints**. In 2018, the CPA Exam is no longer based on content specification outlines (CSOs). The AICPA Blueprints can be found at https://www.aicpa.org/becomeacpa/cpaexam/examinationcontent.html

These are the maps that tell the candidate the areas that are tested and what tasks are required for the candidate to master the information. *If you just follow the blueprints, you will know exactly the required information to be successful on the exam.*

There are hundreds of specific "representative tasks" that indicate what a new CPA would typically be responsible for performing on the job.

> **Hint: At a glance -- what is the AICPA blueprint?**
> - Serves as an essential study tool for CPA candidates
> - Replaces OLD Content Specific Outline (CSO)
> - Demonstrates what is tested on exams (including specific tasks)
> - Outlines skills and knowledge needed for licensure (typically possessed by a person with two years of experience)

YAEGER CPA REVIEW textbooks, and all videos, follow the AICPA Blueprints. Each blueprint is mentioned, and the relevant material is discussed, along with any relevant journal entries. Not all courses in CPA REVIEW follow the blueprints, but YAEGER DOES!

YAEGER CPA REVIEW has aligned its review content with the blueprints and shows each representative task with this icon:

CPA Exam
Blueprint
Representative Task

For example, below is a representative task from the AUDITING AND ATTESTATION (AUD) section blueprint, under:
- Area I — Ethics, Professional Responsibilities and General Principles
- Content Group/Topic: A. NATURE AND SCOPE
- 1. Nature and scope: audit engagements
- Representative Task: Identify the nature, scope and objectives of the different types of audit engagements, including issuer and nonissuer audits.

In the auditing and attestation YAEGER CPA REVIEW book, this representative task will look like this:

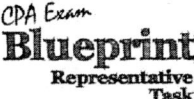 Identify the nature, scope and objectives of the different types of audit engagements, including issuer and nonissuer audits.

F. Exam Schedule

The CPA Exam schedule for 2018 will be posted on the AICPA website when announced. The AICPA website is www.aicpa.org. Candidates should **definitely** visit this site before scheduling their exam for the most recent updates and information.

G. **AICPA Tutorial and Sample Tests**
On the AICPA website (https://www.aicpa.org/becomeacpa/cpaexam/forcandidates/tutorialandsampletest.html) candidates can experience the user interface that they will see on exam day. It is also the best place to see AICPA constructed examples of multiple-choice and task-based simulations with full functionality. YAEGER CPA REVIEW highly recommends all CPA candidates complete the sample test prior to taking their exam.

H. **Access to Professional Literature**
A commonly tested task-based simulation involves answering a research question, where the candidate must search through professional literature databases to answer the question.

Candidates who have applied to take the exam and have received their NTS can access a **free six-month subscription to the professional literature** used in the computerized CPA Exam. The professional literature includes the AICPA Professional Standards, FASB Original Pronouncements, and FASB Accounting Standards Codification. Access to this authoritative literature will familiarize candidates with the use of online accounting resources with full search functionality. Candidates should test the use of the keyword search to make the best use of their time in the exam.

The following link will take you to the National Association of State Boards of Accountancy (NASBA) website where you can apply for the free six-month subscription to the professional literature package: https://nasba.org/proflit/

I. **Examination Scoring**
A score of 75 is required to pass each section of the exam. A score of 75, however, is not indicative of the percent of correct answers. Rather, the score represents the weighted combination of multiple-choice questions, task-based simulations and written communications (for BEC only). Each section uses a scoring scale from 0 to 99. The scaled scores take into consideration whether the question was answered correctly and the level of difficulty of each question. The CPA exam score was obtained using Item Response Theory (IRT) scoring and was calculated as a whole, taking into account all of your responses.

Fifty percent of a candidate's score in the AUD, FAR, and REG sections comes from multiple-choice questions with the remaining 50% from task-based simulations. In the BEC section, 50% of a candidate's score comes from multiple-choice questions, 35% comes from task-based simulations, and 15% from written communication tasks.

A Candidate Performance Report will be provided if you receive a non-passing score. An example of this report is below.

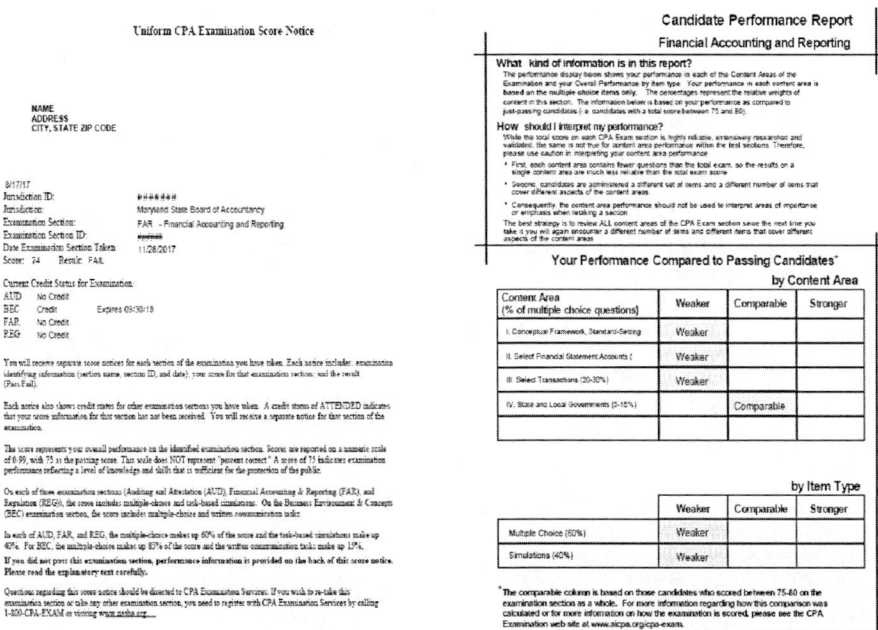

The Candidate Performance Report helps you determine what areas to focus on when you prepare to re-take an exam section. The Candidate Performance Report shows performance in each of the content areas of the exam and overall performance by item type and provides a comparison of your exam results to candidates who passed with a score between 75 and 80. According to the AICPA:

> *The relative performance scale (stronger, comparable, weaker) on the Candidate Performance Report is derived from the range between one-half of one standard deviation above and below the average score of candidates who earned scores between 75 and 80. Performance within the range is considered "comparable," below the range "weaker," and above the range "stronger."*

Candidates who received a weaker assessment for a particular content area should not focus only on that area when reviewing the material. It is always best to study everything. As no two exams are identical, if a candidate only studies their areas of weakness, they may do better in those areas, but worse on others when re-testing.

J. Yaeger's AdaptaPASS Technology

Since 1977, YAEGER CPA REVIEW has been following the philosophy that conceptual learning trumps memorization every time. And today is no different! YAEGER CPA REVIEW takes learning to the next level. With the most advanced technology in the CPA Exam Review industry, YAEGER CPA REVIEW combines traditional teaching and learning with an adaptive technology that determines what learning style works best for each individual CPA Exam candidate.

What is AdaptaPASS? It is an adaptive learning program that YAEGER developed to determine what learning style works best for each CPA candidate. Some students are visual learners, or auditory learners; others prefer to read and work a great deal of multiple-choice and/or simulation problems to reinforce a concept. Some have more time than others to prepare. It makes no difference. AdaptaPASS accounts for all different learning styles and creates a study program just for each individual candidate! The candidate begins by answering a few qualifying questions, then AdaptaPASS will deliver the optimal learning environment. This will include a blend of all study formats and content served in a way that takes the guesswork out of how the candidate is doing and what study method/format works best for them to succeed.

AdaptaPASS is not a "results" based platform like all others in the market. AdaptaPASS is the only program that creates a prescribed learning environment that adapts simultaneously with the candidate's progress. Proactively, the candidate will benefit from the "best" learning environment for them. Fully utilize the study plan that you will establish with YAEGER CPA REVIEW to stay on track for success on the CPA Exam.

K. Partnership with Dr. Marc Schoen

YAEGER CPA REVIEW is very excited to partner with Dr. Marc Schoen, a UCLA professor and leading performance psychologist to bring his expertise to you with a customized program designed specifically for CPA candidates.

The Performance under Pressure Audio Bundle teaches you how to properly control your fear response when faced with CPA Exam stress to boost your test score! Perform at your very best on exam day and tap into your brain's ability to problem solve with higher-order processing.

How? Using a gentle, but powerful technique that will reshape the way your brain responds to pressure. Train both your mind and body for CPA Exam success with an integrated study experience. Be reminded while using our AdaptaPASS software when to practice these research-based techniques founded in cutting-edge neuroscience.

We look forward to helping you on your CPA Exam journey. Best wishes for CPA Exam success from YAEGER CPA REVIEW!

AUD 1 – Ethics, Professional Responsibilities and General Principles

A. Nature and Scope of Engagements	**1A-2 – 1A-6**
1. Nature and scope: audit engagement	2
2. Nature and scope: engagements conducted under Government Accountability Office Government Auditing Standards	3
3. Nature and scope: non-audit engagements	5
B. Ethics, Independence, and Professional Conduct	**1B-1 – 1B-28**
1. AICPA Code of Professional Conduct	1
2. Requirements of the SEC and the PCAOB	23
3. Requirements of the Government Accountability Office and the Department of Labor	26
C. Terms of Engagement	**1C-1 – 1C-5**
1. Preconditions for an Engagement	1
2. Terms of Engagement and Engagement Letter	2
D. Requirements for Engagement Documentation	**1D-1 – 1D-4**
E. Communication with Management and Those Charged with Governance	**1E-1 – 1E-6**
1. Planned scope and timing of an engagement	1
2. Internal control related matters	2
3. All other matters	4
F. Communication with Component Auditors and Parties Other Than Management and Those Charged with Governance	**1F-1 – 1F-3**
G. A Firm's System of Quality Control, Including Quality Control at The Engagement Level	**1G-1 – 1G-5**
Glossary: Ethics, Professional Responsibilities and General Principles	Glossary 1-1 – 1-6
Multiple Choice – Questions	MCQ 1-1 – 1-9
Multiple Choice – Solutions	MCQ 1-10 – 1-18

Ethics, Professional Responsibilities and General Principles

Performing audit and attestation engagements are primary functions of a CPA. All CPAs must be well versed in how to properly preform audit procedures, use the findings to issue an audit opinion. In addition, CPAs must understand their role in the larger business landscape, including the ethics and responsibilities of CPAs in public practice.

> **Hint:** Audit and Attestation section of the CPA Exam is the only part of the exam to require CPA candidates to evaluate a scenario and formulate recommendations, using their assessment of the situation to draw conclusions (5-15% of AUD requires this level of skill).

This first chapter serves as an introduction and covers the nature and scope of both audit and non-audit engagements, ethics, independence, terms of engagements, documentation and communication requirements, and quality control.

A summary of the players is as follows:

GAAP (Private Sector)	FASB [ASC]
	IASB [IFRS] (Previously IAS for IASC)
	GASB
	FASAB
	SASB
AICPA	SAS (Non-issuers) [AU-C]
	SSAE [AT]
	SSARS [AR]
	ET, QC, PFP, CS
U.S. Government	SEC
	SOX – PCAOB (Issuers) [AS]
	GAO
	DOL
IFAC	IAASB [ISA]
	IESBA

> **Hint:** Don't forget –
> Independence **required**: audits, reviews, attestations
> Independence **not required**: compilations (must disclose if not independent), tax, consulting

Areas of emphasis and overview of important AUD topics:
1. Generally accepted auditing standards (GAAS)
2. New client
    a. Decision to accept
        i. Evaluate independence and ability to handle
        ii. Evaluate communications with predecessor auditor – permission of client
    b. If accepted, understand the client and industry
        i. Engagement letter
        ii. Determine materiality levels [qualitative and quantitative]
        iii. Evaluate risk: AR = IR x CR x DR [RMM x DR]
        iv. Must do risk assessment procedures and further audit procedures (test of controls, substantive tests)
3. Auditor's responsibility
    a. Errors and fraud – reasonable assurance
    b. Direct effect laws and regulations
    c. Other laws and regulations

4. Management assertions [PERCV]

P	Presentation and disclosure
E	Existence and occurrence
R	Rights and obligations
C	Completeness
V	Valuation or allocation

A. Nature and Scope of Engagements

1. Nature and scope: audit engagement

Identify the nature, scope and objectives of the different types of audit engagements, including issuer and nonissuer audits.

a. Nature
Understand the type of audit:
- Audit of a public company (an issuer) – Use auditing standards promulgated by the PCAOB (ASs).
- Audit of a nonissuer (a private company) – Use auditing standards promulgated by the AICPA (AU-Cs)

b. Scope and objectives

1) **For public companies** (per PCAOB AS 1001.01):
The objective of the ordinary audit of financial statements by the independent auditor is the expression of an opinion on the fairness with which they present, in all material respects, financial position, results of operations, and its cash flows in conformity with generally accepted accounting principles (GAAP).

The auditor's report is the medium through which he/she expresses his/her opinion or, if circumstances require, disclaims an opinion.

In either case, he states whether his audit has been made in accordance with the standards of the PCAOB. These standards require him to state whether, in his opinion, the financial statements, including footnotes [notes], are presented in conformity with generally accepted accounting principles and to identify those circumstances in which such principles have not been consistently observed in the preparation of the financial statements of the current period in relation to those of the preceding period.

2) **For non-public companies** (per AICPA AU-C 200.04):
The purpose of an audit is to provide financial statement users with an opinion by the auditor on whether the financial statements are presented fairly, in all material respects, in accordance with an applicable financial reporting framework, which enhances the degree of confidence that intended users can place in the financial statements.

An audit conducted in accordance with GAAS and relevant ethical requirements enables the auditor to form that opinion.

Per AU-C 200.12-13:
The overall objectives of the auditor, in conducting an audit of financial statements, are to:
i. Obtain reasonable assurance about whether the financial statements, as a whole, are free from material misstatement, whether due to fraud or error, thereby enabling the auditor to express an opinion on whether the financial statements are presented fairly, in all material respects, in accordance with an applicable financial reporting framework; and,
ii. Report on the financial statements and communicate, as required by GAAS, in accordance with the auditor's findings.

In all cases, when reasonable assurance cannot be obtained, and a qualified opinion in the auditor's **report** is insufficient in the circumstances for purposes of reporting to the intended users of the financial statements, GAAS require that the auditor disclaim an opinion or withdraw from the engagement, when withdrawal is possible under applicable law or regulation.

The AICPA's scope and objectives (see AU-C 200.15-20) impose certain requirements on auditors, including the following:
i. Ethical requirements: (1) The auditor must be independent of the client and (2) The auditor should comply with the AICPA's Code of Professional Conduct (see review in Area I B.1.).
ii. The auditor should plan and perform an audit with professional skepticism.
iii. The auditor should exercise professional judgment in planning and performing an audit.
iv. To obtain reasonable assurance, the auditor should obtain sufficient appropriate audit evidence to reduce audit risk to an acceptably low level and thereby enable the auditor to draw reasonable conclusions on which to base the auditor's opinion.
v. The auditor should comply with all AU-C sections relevant to the audit.

Hint: The SEC eliminated the auditor attestation requirement for non-accelerated filers pursuant to requirements of the Dodd-Frank Act.

Multiple Choice
AUD 1-Q1

2. Nature and scope: engagements conducted under Government Accountability Office Government Auditing Standards

Identify the nature, scope and objectives of engagements performed in accordance with Government Accountability Office Government Auditing Standards.

Hint: Government Accountability Office Government Auditing Standards (GAGAS) is commonly referred to as the Yellow Book.

Per GAGAS 2.03 (Yellow Book):
All audits begin with objectives, and those objectives determine the type of audit to be performed and the applicable standards to be followed.

The types of audits that are covered by GAGAS, as defined by their objectives, are classified in GAGAS as
- financial audits,
- attestation engagements, and
- performance audits.

Per GAGAS 2.07-.08:

a. **Financial audits** provide an independent assessment of whether an entity's reported financial information (e.g., financial condition, results, and use of resources) are presented fairly in accordance with recognized criteria.

Financial audits performed in accordance with GAGAS include financial statement audits and other related financial audits:
1) **Financial statement audits**: The primary purpose of a financial statement audit is to provide an opinion about whether an entity's financial statements are presented fairly in all material respects in conformity with an applicable financial reporting framework. Reporting on financial statement audits performed in accordance with GAGAS also includes reports on internal control over financial reporting and on compliance with provisions of laws, regulations, contracts, and grant agreements that have a material effect on the financial statements.

2) **Other types of financial audits**: Other types of financial audits conducted in accordance with GAGAS entail various scopes of work, including: (1) obtaining sufficient, appropriate evidence to form an opinion on single financial statements, specified elements, accounts, or items of a financial statement; (2) issuing letters for underwriters and certain other requesting parties; and (3) auditing compliance with applicable compliance requirements relating to one or more government programs.

GAGAS incorporates by reference the American Institute of Certified Public Accountants (AICPA) Statements on Auditing Standards (SAS). Additional requirements for performing financial audits in accordance with GAGAS are contained in chapter 4 (of GAGAS). For financial audits performed in accordance with GAGAS, auditors should also comply with chapters 1 through 3 (of GAGAS).

Per GAGAS 2.09:

b. **Attestation engagements** can cover a broad range of financial or nonfinancial objectives about the subject matter or assertion depending on the users' needs. GAGAS incorporates by reference the AICPA's Statements on Standards for Attestation Engagements (SSAE). Additional requirements for performing attestation engagements in accordance with GAGAS are contained in chapter 5 (of GAGAS). The AICPA's standards recognize attestation engagements that result in an examination, a review, or an agreed-upon procedures report on a subject matter or on an assertion about a subject matter that is the responsibility of another party.

Per GAGAS 2.10:

c. **Performance audits** are defined as audits that provide findings or conclusions based on an evaluation of sufficient, appropriate evidence against criteria. Performance audits provide objective analysis to assist management, and those charged with governance and oversight, in using the information to improve program performance and operations, reduce costs, facilitate decision making by parties with responsibility to oversee or initiate corrective action, and contribute to public accountability.

Multiple Choice

AUD 1-Q2

3. Nature and scope: non-audit engagements

Identify the nature, scope and objectives of the different types of non-audit engagements, including engagements conducted in accordance with the attestation standards and the accounting and review services standards.

a. **Nature, scope and objectives**
Similar to the auditing standards, the AICPA undertook a project to clarify the professional standards relating to accounting and review engagements.
Accounting and review engagements refer to compilations and reviews of financial statements. The professional standards for compilations and reviews of financial statements are called **Statements on Standards for Accounting and Review Services** (SSARS) and are issued by the Accounting and Review Services Committee of the AICPA. SSARS are only for nonissuers.

Compilations and reviews provide less assurance that audits and the relationships between type of service, level of assurance, and evidence requirements are summarized in the following table.

	Compilation	Review	Audit
Evidence Requirements	Minimal	Significant	Extensive
Assurance	None	Limited	High

1) Defining Professional Responsibilities in SSARSs
AR-C 60.15-16 discuss the accountant's required compliance with SSARS.

SSARSs use the following two categories of professional requirements, identified by specific terms, to describe the degree of responsibility they impose on accountants:
   i. **Unconditional requirements**. The accountant must comply with an unconditional requirement in all cases in which such requirement is relevant. SSARSs use the word **"must"** to indicate an unconditional requirement.

   ii. **Presumptively mandatory requirements**. The accountant must comply with a presumptively mandatory requirement in all cases in which such a requirement is relevant, except in rare circumstances, discussed in paragraph .16. SSARSs use the word **"should"** to indicate a presumptively mandatory requirement. In other words, if an AR-C section provides that a procedure or action is one that the accountant "should consider," consideration of the procedure or action is presumptively required. Whether the accountant performs the procedure or action is based upon the outcome of the accountant's consideration and the accountant's professional judgment.

   In rare circumstances, the accountant may judge it necessary to depart from a relevant presumptively mandatory requirement. In such circumstances, the accountant should perform alternative procedures to achieve the intent of the requirement. The need for an accountant to depart from a relevant, presumptively mandatory requirement is expected to arise only when the requirement is for a specific procedure to be performed and, in the specific circumstances of the engagement, that procedure would be ineffective in achieving the intent of the requirement.

b. **Preparation of financial statements (not a compilation or a review) (AR-C 70)**
   The main source of professional guidance that serves as the basis for this subsection is obtained from AR-C 70, Preparation of Financial Statements (see SSARS No. 21), AICPA.

   1) Generally, AR-C 70 applies when an accountant in public practice is engaged to prepare financial statements, but he or she **does not** perform a compilation, review, or audit of the financial statements. AR-C 70 does not apply to financial statements used for:
      i. submission to taxing authorities,
      ii. for inclusion in written personal financial plans prepared by the accountant,
      iii. in conjunction with litigation services that involve pending or potential legal or regulatory proceedings, or
      iv. in conjunction with business valuation services.

   An engagement to prepare financial statements is a non-attest service and does not require a determination about whether the accountant is independent of the entity.

   An engagement to prepare financial statements does not require the accountant to verify the accuracy or completeness of the information provided by management, or otherwise gather evidence, to express an opinion or a conclusion on the financial statements or otherwise report on the financial statements.

c. **Compilation engagements (AR-C 80)**
   The main source of professional guidance that serves as the basis for compilation engagements is obtained from AR-C 80, Compilation Engagements (see SSARS No. 21), AICPA.

   A compilation engagement is one in which accountants assist management in the presentation of financial statements without providing any assurance about those statements.

d. **Review of financial statements (AR-C 90)**
   The main source of professional guidance that serves as the basis for reviews of financial statements is obtained from AR-C 90, Review of Financial Statements (see SSARS No. 21), AICPA.

   A review of financial statements requires an accountant to obtain limited assurance as a basis for reporting whether the accountant is aware of any material modifications that should be made to the financial statements for them to be in accordance with the applicable financial reporting framework (often GAAP), primarily through the performance of inquiry and analytical procedures.

Multiple Choice

AUD 1-Q3

B. Ethics, Independence, and Professional Conduct
1. AICPA Code of Professional Conduct

> Understand the principles, rules and interpretations included in the AICPA Code of Professional Conduct.

The AICPA Code of Professional Conduct is organized as follows:
    Preface (Applicable to All Members)
    Part 1 – Members in Public Practice
    Part 2 – Members in Business
    Part 3 – Other Members
    Appendices (A, B, C, and D)

The AICPA Code of Professional Conduct covers **all** professional engagements.

> **Hint**: You can access a copy of the AICPA's Code of Professional Conduct using the following web address: http://www.aicpa.org/Research/Standards/CodeofConduct/Pages/default.aspx

a. **Preface**
The AICPA membership adopted the Code of Professional Conduct (the code) to provide guidance and rules to all members in the performance of their professional responsibilities. The code consists of **principles** and **rules** as well as **interpretations** and other guidance. The principles provide the framework for the rules that govern the performance of their professional responsibilities.

The AICPA bylaws require that members adhere to the rules of the code. Compliance with the rules depends primarily on members' understanding and voluntary actions; secondarily on reinforcement by peers and public opinion; and ultimately on disciplinary proceedings, when necessary, against members who fail to comply with the rules. Members must be prepared to justify departures from these rules.

Interpretations of the rules of conduct are adopted after exposure to the membership, state societies, state boards, and other interested parties. The interpretations of the rules of conduct provide guidelines about the scope and application of the rules but are not intended to limit such scope or application. A member who departs from the interpretations shall have the burden of justifying such departure in any disciplinary hearing.

A member should also consult the following, if applicable:
- The ethical requirements of the member's state CPA society and authoritative regulatory bodies such as state board(s) of accountancy
- The Securities and Exchange Commission (SEC)
- The Public Company Accounting Oversight Board (PCAOB)
- The Government Accountability Office (GAO)
- The Department of Labor (DOL)
- Federal, state and local taxing authorities

b. **Principles of Professional Conduct**
Membership in the American Institute of Certified Public Accountants is voluntary. By accepting membership, a member assumes an obligation of self-discipline above and beyond the requirements of laws and regulations.

These Principles of the Code of Professional Conduct of the AICPA express the profession's recognition of its responsibilities to the public, to clients, and to colleagues. They guide members in the performance of their professional responsibilities and express the basic tenets of ethical and professional conduct. The Principles call for an unswerving commitment to honorable behavior, even at the sacrifice of personal advantage. The 6 principles include the following:

1) Responsibilities principle
   In carrying out their responsibilities as professionals, members should exercise sensitive professional and moral judgments in all their activities.

2) The public interest principle
   Members should accept the obligation to act in a way that will serve the public interest, honor the public trust, and demonstrate a commitment to professionalism.

3) Integrity principle
   To maintain and broaden public confidence, members should perform all professional responsibilities with the highest sense of integrity.

4) Objectivity and independence principle
   A member should maintain objectivity and be free of conflicts of interest in discharging professional responsibilities. A member in public practice should be independent in fact and appearance when providing auditing and other attestation services.

5) Due care principle
   A member should observe the profession's technical and ethical standards, strive continually to improve competence and the quality of services, and discharge professional responsibility to the best of the member's ability.

   Due care requires a member to plan and supervise adequately any professional activity for which he or she is responsible.

6) Scope and nature of services principle
   A member in public practice should observe the Principles of the Code of Professional Conduct in determining the scope and nature of services to be provided.

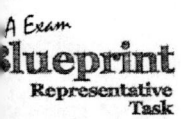

Recognize situations that present threats to compliance with the AICPA Code of Professional Conduct, including threats to independence.

Situations that could present a threat to compliance with the AICPA Code of Professional Conduct includes situations where the member is not objective or independent, or otherwise engages in performing services that do not abide by the Code's guidelines.

By understanding the requirements of the AICPA Code of Professional Conduct, CPA candidates can then identify situations that don't comply with the Code's principles and rules. For example, situations involving the solicitation of services with contingent fees or situations when a member has performed an act discreditable (e.g., solicitation or disclosure of CPA Examinations questions and answers) would be against the Code of Professional Conduct and therefore a threat to compliance. As such, the requirements for compliance are discussed below.

> Apply the principles, rules and interpretations included in the AICPA Code of Professional Conduct to given situations.

c. Independence

1) **Independence Rule:** A member in public practice shall be independent in the performance of professional services as required by standards promulgated by bodies designated by Council.

2) The following definitions are very important to the concept of independence. As such, we present them here for convenience:
   i. **Close relative.** A close relative is a parent, sibling, or nondependent child.

   ii. **Covered member.** A covered member is
      a) An individual on the attest engagement team.
      b) An individual in a position to influence the attest engagement.
      c) A partner, partner equivalent, or manager who provides more than 10 hours of non-attest services to the attest client within any fiscal year. Designation as covered member ends on the later of (i) the date that the firm signs the report on the financial statements for the fiscal year during which those services were provided or (ii) the date he or she no longer expects to provide 10 or more hours of non-attest services to the attest client on a recurring basis.
      d) A partner or partner equivalent in the office in which the lead attest engagement partner primarily practices in connection with the attest engagement.
      e) The firm, including the firm's employee benefit plans.
      f) An entity whose operating, financial, or accounting policies can be controlled (as defined by generally accepted accounting principles [GAAP] for consolidation purposes) by any of the individuals or entities described in (a) through (e) or by two or more such individuals or entities if they act together.

   In summary, covered members include (a) engagement team members, (b) individuals who may influence the audit (e.g., partners above the engagement partner), (c) all partners in the lead attest engagement partner's office, and (d) certain other persons or entities.

   iii. **Direct financial interest.** A personal investment under the direct control of the investor. For example, owning stock or debt securities of an audit client.

   iv. **Immediate family.** Immediate family is a spouse, spousal equivalent, or dependent (whether or not related).

   v. **Impair independence.** To eliminate ("extinguish" per Code) independence. When a member's independence is impaired, the member is not independent.

   vi. **Independence.** Consists of two elements, defined as follows:
      a) **Independence of mind** is the state of mind that permits a member to perform an attest service without being affected by influences that compromise professional judgment, thereby allowing an individual to act with integrity and exercise objectivity and professional skepticism.
      b) **Independence in appearance** is the avoidance of circumstances that would cause a reasonable and informed third party, who has knowledge of all relevant information, including the safeguards applied, to reasonably conclude that the integrity, objectivity, or professional skepticism of a firm or member of the attest engagement team is compromised.

This definition should not be interpreted as an absolute. For example, the phrase "without being affected by influences that compromise professional judgment" is not intended to convey that the member must be free of any and all influences that might compromise objective judgment. Instead, the member should determine whether such influences, if present, create a threat that is not at an acceptable level that a member would not act with integrity and exercise objectivity and professional skepticism in the conduct of a particular engagement or would be perceived as not being able to do so by a reasonable and informed third party with knowledge of all relevant information.

vii. **Indirect financial interest.** An investment in which the specific investment decisions are not under the control of the investor. For example, an investment in a professionally managed mutual fund.

viii. **Individual in a position to influence the attest engagement.** An individual in a position to influence the attest engagement is one who
   a) Evaluates the performance or recommends the compensation of the attest engagement partner;
   b) Directly supervises or manages the attest engagement partner, including all successively senior levels above that individual through the firm's chief executive;
   c) Consults with the attest engagement team regarding technical or industry-related issues specific to the attest engagement; or
   d) Participates in or oversees, at all successively senior levels, quality control activities, including internal monitoring, with respect to the specific attest engagement.

ix. **Joint closely held investment.** An investment in an entity or a property by the member and client (or the client's officers or directors or any owner who has the ability to exercise significant influence over the client) that enables them to control the entity or property.

x. **Key position.** A key position is an audit sensitive position

xi. **Partner equivalent.** A partner equivalent is a professional employee who is not a partner but has the ultimate responsibility for an attest engagement or has the authority to bind the CPA firm to conduct an attest engagement without partner approval. For example, assume a CPA firm employee is a manager who functions as a partner in that she has ultimate responsibility for several engagements—this employee is a partner equivalent.

xii. **Period of the professional engagement.** The period of the professional engagement begins when a member either signs an initial engagement letter or other agreement to perform attest services or begins to perform an attest engagement for a client, whichever is earlier. The period lasts for the entire duration of the professional relationship (which could cover many periods) and ends with the formal or informal notification, either by the member or the client, of the termination of the professional relationship or by the issuance of a report, whichever is later. Accordingly, the period does not end with the issuance of a report and recommence with the beginning of the following year's attest engagement.

d. Overall independence concepts
Independence questions not answered directly by the Code are addressed using the independence conceptual framework. The framework uses "threats" and "safeguards" as do the other frameworks, but tailors them to specifically address independence. The independence conceptual framework is reviewed shortly.

1) Scope of independence
It is particularly important to realize that impaired independence concerns exist both at the individual accountant and the public accounting firm level; the independence of one, both, or neither may be impaired with respect to a client or potential client. When the firm's independence is impaired with respect to a client, it may not provide attest services for that client.

When an individual's independence is impaired, the CPA firm in some circumstances retains its independence. Frequently, a key for the firm is to make staffing decisions on attestation engagements that assure firm independence (e.g., in some situations it is as simple as keeping a non-independent staff person off the engagement).

i. **Covered members** (defined earlier) have the highest level of independence requirements since, in most circumstances, when a covered member's independence is impaired, the CPA firm's independence is also ordinarily impaired.

ii. **Basic Independence Requirements**
The following three sections discuss independence requirements and situations in which an individual accountant's impaired independence may also lead to impaired firm independence
   a) All partners and professional staff
   b) Additional independence requirements for covered members
   c) Overall CPA firm independence requirements

Independence requirements for all partners and staff. The following situations lead to impaired CPA firm independence (in addition to impaired member independence). Thus, a CPA firm is unable to provide attestation services due to impaired independence if any of the following relationships exist:
1. A partner or professional employee of the CPA firm or immediate family owns more than five percent of an attest client's outstanding equity securities during the period of the professional engagement. Also, no group of such persons acting together may own that amount; that is, for example, the aggregation of all such partner and staff investments (including family) may not exceed the five percent threshold.
2. A partner or professional employee of the CPA firm is simultaneously associated with both, the CPA firm and the client, as a director, officer, employee, promoter, trustee, etc.
3. A CPA now employed by the CPA firm, but previously associated with an attest client, has not disassociated himself/herself from that client and/or participates in audits of any periods during which they were employed by the client.

Recall that if firm independence is impaired, no attestation services may be performed for that client.

Additional independence requirements for covered members. The independence requirements are more stringent for covered members as compared to partners and staff who are not covered members—if a covered member's independence is impaired, the CPA firm's independence is impaired.

1. Financial relationships of a covered member which impair the independence of both the member and the firm include:
   a. All direct financial interests

   > **Example**: A covered member may not own any stock (or debt) of an attest client on which he or she is a covered member without impairing both that covered member's and the firm's independence.

   b. Material indirect financial interests

   > **Example**: A covered member owns a material amount of stock in a mutual fund that is heavily invested in the stock of an attest client.

   > **Hint**: Details on determining materiality are included in the Code, but generally beyond the scope of the CPA Exam.

   c. A material "joint closely held investment" held with an attest client (or one of the client's officers or directors, or any owner with significant influence over the attest client).

Multiple Choice

AUD 1-Q4

2. Financial interests of relatives and friends
   a. Immediate family (spouse, spousal equivalent, dependents). Overall, immediate family members are subject to the same requirements as the covered member. For example, if the covered member cannot own common stock of a client, neither can that covered member's spouse or dependent children.

   Exceptions (allowable situations) include:
   (i) An individual in a covered member's immediate family is employed by the client in a position other than a key position (a position in which the individual has primary responsibility for, or influence over, accounting or financial statement reporting decisions).
   (ii) Certain circumstances when an immediate family member holds a financial interest in an attest client through his/her employer's benefit plan.

   b. Close relatives (e.g., parents, siblings, or nondependent children). Overall, CPA firm independence is impaired if close relative has:
   (i) A key position with the client, or
   (ii) An investment in a client that is material to the close relative and the accountant has knowledge.

   c. Other considerations for all relatives and friends. Independence is only impaired when a reasonable person, aware of all relevant facts relating to a situation, would conclude that there is an unacceptable threat to independence (based on the conceptual framework for independence).

    d. Recall that ordinarily, if a covered member's independence is impaired, the firm's independence is also impaired. A non-covered member's independence impairment by situations such as the above, ordinarily will not impair firm independence.

3. Future employment with a client
   a. Covered members must report to the public accounting firm any specific offer or the intention to seek employment with an audit client.
      (i) CPA firm should remove the covered member from all engagements for that client until the offer has been rejected or employment is no longer being sought.
      (ii) CPA firm should also consider whether additional procedures are necessary to obtain reasonable assurance that all work of that CPA was performed with objectivity and integrity.
   b. When a public accounting firm professional accepts employment with the audit client, the engagement team should consider the need to modify future engagement procedures to adjust for the risk that audit effectiveness could be reduced due to the professional's knowledge of the audit plan
      (i) For public companies, the Sarbanes-Oxley Act requires that one year pass before a member of the audit team may accept employment with an SEC registrant for certain designated positions (e.g., chief executive officer, controller, chief financial or accounting officer).

4. Gifts and entertainment. Any gifts accepted from a client must be clearly insignificant in value to the recipient; entertainment accepted must be reasonable in the circumstances.

Multiple Choice

AUD 1-Q5

Overall CPA firm independence requirements

1. **Past due fees.** Firm independence is impaired if a covered member has unpaid fees from an attest client for any previously rendered professional service provided more than one year prior to the date of the current-year report.

2. **Litigation.** There are situations regarding litigation between covered members and attest clients in which threats to the covered member's compliance with the Independence Rule would not be at an acceptable level and could not be reduced to an acceptable level by safeguards, therefore independence would be impaired. Examples of these situations are:
   a. An attest client's present management commences litigation alleging deficiencies in audit work performed for the attest client or expresses its intention to commence such litigation, and the covered member concludes that it is probable that such a claim will be filed.
   b. A covered member commences litigation against an attest client's present management alleging management fraud or deceit.

3. **Network firms.** A firm member of a network of firms is required to be independent of financial statement audit and review clients of the other members of the network for such clients for which the use of an audit report is not restricted. Characteristics of a network include having a brand name, common control, profits/costs, common business strategy, significant professional resources, and common quality controls.

4. **Financial institution (e.g., banks) attest clients.** The following are allowed and **do not impair either individual CPA or firm independence**.
   a. Maintaining state or federally insured deposits (e.g., checking accounts, savings accounts, certificates of deposit); uninsured deposits do not impair independence if the uninsured amounts are immaterial.
   b. Certain loans, including:
      (i) Automobile loans and leases collateralized by the automobile
      (ii) Loans fully collateralized by the cash surrender value of an insurance policy
      (iii) Loans fully collateralized by cash deposits at the same lending institution (for example, passbook loans)
      (iv) Aggregate outstanding balances from credit cards and overdraft reserve accounts that have a balance of $10,000 or less, after payment of the most recent monthly statement made by the due date or within any available grace period.

Multiple Choice

> AUD 1-Q6

5. **Non-attest services.** When a CPA performs non-attest services for an attest client it **may** or **may not** impair independence.
   a. Depending upon the nature of their practice, CPAs must be in compliance with independence rules of a number of regulators (e.g., Securities and Exchange Commission, General Accounting Office, and the Department of Labor).
   b. CPAs should not assume management responsibility for attest clients. Independence is not impaired if non-attest services are performed prior to the period of the professional audit engagement and relate to periods before the current audit. Independence ordinarily is not impaired by attest related communications between the CPA and management regarding:
      (i) Client's selection and application of accounting policies and disclosures.
      (ii) Appropriateness of client's accounting methods.
      (iii) Adjusting journal entries that member prepares or proposes.
      (iv) Form or content of the financial statements.
      (v) Financial statement preparation, cash-to-accrual conversions, and reconciliations.
   c. When non-attest services are provided, the client must:
      (i) Assume all management responsibilities.
      (ii) Oversee the service by designating an individual, preferably in senior management, who possesses suitable skill, knowledge and/or experience. The member should assess and be satisfied that such individual can perform the role.
      (iii) Evaluate adequacy and results.
      (iv) Accept responsibility for results.
      (v) Establish and maintain internal controls.

d. Activities that impair independence:
   (i) Setting policies or strategic direction for the client.
   (ii) Directing or accepting responsibility for actions of client employees (except as allowed for using the work of internal auditors).
   (iii) Authorizing, executing, or consummating transactions.
   (iv) Preparing source documents.
   (v) Having custody of assets.
   (vi) Deciding which recommendations are to be implemented or given priority.
   (vii) Reporting to those charged with governance on behalf of management.
   (viii) Accepting responsibility for managing a client's project.
   (ix) Accepting responsibility for preparing client financial statements.
   (x) Serving as stock transfer agent, registrar, or general counsel.
   (xi) Accepting responsibility for designing, implementing or maintaining internal control.
   (xii) Performing evaluations of internal control as part of the company's monitoring activities.

e. Self-review or management participation threats to compliance with the Independence Rule [1.200.001] may exist when a **member performs appraisal, valuation, or actuarial service** for an attest client. Threats to compliance with the Independence Rule [1.200.001] **would not be at an acceptable level and could not be reduced to an acceptable level by the application of safeguards** if the member performs an appraisal, a valuation, or an actuarial service for an attest client when (a) the services involve a significant degree of subjectivity and (b) the results of the service, individually or when combined with other valuation, appraisal, or actuarial services, are material to the attest client's financial statements. Accordingly, independence would be impaired under these circumstances.

f. **Internal audit services** involve assisting the attest client in the performance of its internal audit activities, sometimes referred to as "internal audit outsourcing." When a member provides internal audit services to an attest client, self-review and management participation threats to the covered member's compliance with the Independence Rule [1.200.001] may exist. The attest client's management is responsible for directing the internal audit function, including the management thereof. Such responsibilities include, but are not limited to, designing, implementing and maintaining internal control. **Threats to compliance with the Independence Rule [1.200.001] would not be at an acceptable level, and cannot be reduced to an acceptable level by the application of safeguards, and independence would be impaired if the attest client outsources the internal audit function to the member,** whereby the member, in effect, manages the attest client's internal audit activities.

6. **Bookkeeping, Payroll, and Other Disbursements (1.295.120)**
   When a member provides bookkeeping, payroll, and other disbursement services to an attest client, self- review and management participation threats to the covered member's compliance with the "Independence Rule" [1.200.001] may exist.

Without impairing independence, a member may:
a. record transactions to an attest client's general ledger when management has determined or approved the account classifications for the transaction.
b. post client-coded transactions to an attest client's general ledger.
c. prepare financial statements based on information in the attest client's trial balance.
d. post client-approved journal or other entries to an attest client's trial balance.
e. propose standard, adjusting, or correcting journal entries or other changes affecting the financial statements to the attest client. Prior to the member posting these journal entries or changes, the member should be satisfied that management has reviewed the entries and understands the nature of the proposed entries and the effect the entries will have on the attest client's financial statements.
f. generate unsigned checks using source documents or other records provided and approved by the attest client.
g. process an attest client's payroll using payroll time records that the attest client has provided and approved.
h. transmit client-approved payroll or other disbursement information to a bank or similar entity subsequent to the attest client's review and authorization for the member to make the transmission. Prior to such transmission, the attest client is responsible for making the arrangements with the bank or similar entity to limit the corresponding individual payments regarding the amount and payee. In addition, once transmitted, the attest client must authorize the bank or similar entity to process the payroll information.
i. prepare a reconciliation (for example, bank and accounts receivable) that identifies reconciling items for the client's evaluation. **However, threats to compliance with the "Independence Rule" [1.200.001] would not be at an acceptable level and could not be reduced to an acceptable level by the application of safeguards, and independence would be impaired, if, for example, a member:**
   (i) determines or changes journal entries, any account coding or classification of transactions, or any other accounting records without first obtaining the attest client's approval.
   (ii) authorizes or approves transactions.
   (iii) prepares source documents.
   (iv) makes changes to source documents without the attest client's approval.
   (v) accepts responsibility to authorize payment of attest client funds, electronically or otherwise, except for electronic payroll tax payments when the member complies with the requirements of the "Tax Services" interpretation [1.295.160] of the "Independence Rule."
   (vi) accepts responsibility to sign or cosign an attest client's checks, even if only in emergency situations.
   (vii) maintains an attest client's bank account or otherwise has custody of an attest client's funds or makes credit or banking decisions for the attest client.
   (viii) approves vendor invoices for payment.

Multiple Choice

AUD 1-Q7

e. Other Code of Professional Conduct Issues
   1) Conflicts of interest
      A conflict of interest creates **adverse interest** and **self-interest threats** to the member's compliance with the Integrity and Objectivity rules.

      > **Hint**: Independence impairments (on audits, reviews, and other attest services requiring independence) cannot be eliminated by the safeguards provided in this interpretation or by disclosure and consent.

      When an actual conflict of interest has been identified, the member should evaluate the significance of the threat created by the conflict of interest. Members should consider both qualitative and quantitative factors when evaluating the significance of the threat, considering both of the following:
      i. The significance of relevant interests or relationships.
      ii. The significance of the threats created by performing the professional service or services. (i.e., the more direct the connection between the professional service and the matter on which the parties' interests are in conflict, the more significant the threat.)

      If the member concludes that the threat is not at an acceptable level, the member should apply safeguards to eliminate the threat or reduce it to an acceptable level.

      In cases where an identified threat may be too significant, the member should (a) decline to perform or discontinue the professional services that would result in the conflict of interest; or (b) terminate the relevant relationships or dispose of the relevant interests to eliminate the threat or reduce it to an acceptable level.

      When a conflict of interest exists, the member should disclose the nature of the conflict of interest to clients and other appropriate parties affected by the conflict and obtain their consent to perform the professional services. Disclosure is required even if a member concludes that threats are reduced to acceptable level.

   2) Director positions
      When a member serves as a director of an entity, such as a bank, the member's fiduciary responsibilities to the entity may create threats to the member's compliance with the Integrity and Objectivity rules and the Confidential Client Information rule.

      > **Example:** An adverse interest threat to the member's objectivity may exist if the member's clients are customers of the entity or likely to engage in significant transactions with the entity. While a member's general knowledge and experience may be very helpful to an entity in formulating policies and making business decisions, it would be more appropriate for the member to serve as a consultant to the board.

   3) Gifts and entertainment
      A member should evaluate the significance of any threats to determine if they are at an acceptable level. **Threats are at an acceptable level when gifts or entertainment are reasonable in the circumstances.** The member should exercise judgment in determining whether gifts or entertainment would be considered reasonable in the circumstances.

Multiple Choice

AUD 1-Q8

4) Knowing misrepresentations in the preparation of financial statements or records
   Threats to compliance with the Integrity and Objectivity Rules [1.100.001] would not be at an acceptable level and could not be reduced to an acceptable level by the application of safeguards and the member would be considered to have knowingly misrepresented facts in violation of the Integrity and Objectivity Rules, if the member:
   i. makes, or permits or directs another to make, materially false and misleading entries in an entity's financial statements or records;
   ii. fails to correct an entity's financial statements or records that are materially false and misleading when the member has the authority to record the entries; or
   iii. signs, permits or directs another to sign, a document containing materially false and misleading information.

5) Subordination of judgment
   The Integrity and Objectivity Rules [1.100.001] prohibits a member from knowingly misrepresenting facts or subordinating his or her judgment when performing professional services for a client, or an employer, even on a volunteer basis.

   Safeguards would include discussion with one's supervisor, firm policies for resolving differences of opinion, advice of legal counsel, documenting the difference of opinion, and leaving the firm (i.e., quit).

6) Acts discreditable
   A member shall not commit an act discreditable to the profession.

   Acts discreditable to the profession include the following:
   i. Discrimination and harassment in employment practices.
   ii. Solicitation or disclosure of CPA Examinations questions and answers.
   iii. Failure to file a tax return or pay a tax liability.
   iv. Negligence in the preparation of financial statements or records.
   v. Departure from the requirements of governmental bodies, commissions, or other regulatory agencies (such as PCAOB auditing standards).
   vi. Disclose confidential employer information.
   vii. False, misleading, or deceptive acts in promoting or marketing professional services.
   viii. A CPA's retention of a client's records as a means of enforcing payment of an overdue audit fee.

Multiple Choice

AUD 1-Q9 through AUD 1-Q10

7) Contingent fees
   A member in public practice shall **not**:
   i. Perform, for a contingent fee, any professional services, or receive such a fee from a client for whom the member or the member's firm performs,
      a) an audit or review of a financial statement; or
      b) a compilation of a financial statement when the member expects, or reasonably might expect, that a third party will use the financial statement and the member's compilation report, without disclosing a lack of independence; or
      c) an examination of prospective financial information; or
      d) Prepare an original or amended tax return, or claim for a tax refund for a contingent fee for any client.

ii. Allowable contingent fees
The following are examples of **circumstances in which a contingent fee is permitted** under the "Contingent Fees Rule" [1.510.001]:
   a) Representing a client in connection with a revenue agent's examination of the client's federal or state income tax return
   b) Filing an amended federal or state income tax return claiming a tax refund based on a tax issue that is the subject of a test case involving a different taxpayer or with respect to which the taxing authority is developing a position
   c) Filing an amended federal or state income tax return (or refund claim) claiming a tax refund in an amount greater than the threshold for review by the Joint Committee on Taxation or state taxing authority
   d) Requesting a refund of either overpayments of interest or penalties charged to a client's account or tax deposits that a federal or state taxing authority improperly accounted for in circumstances in which the taxing authority has established procedures for the substantive review of such refund requests
   e) Requesting, by means of a protest or similar document, the state or local taxing authority's consideration of a reduction in a property's assessed value under an established taxing authority's review process for hearing all taxpayer arguments relating to assessed value
   f) Representing a client in connection with obtaining a private letter ruling or influencing the drafting of a regulation or statute

Multiple Choice

AUD 1-Q11

8) Commissions and referral fees
   i. Prohibited commissions. A member in public practice shall not, for a commission, recommend or refer to a client any product or service, or for a commission, recommend or refer any product or service to be supplied by a client, or receive a commission, when the member or member's firm also performs for that client:
      a) an audit or review of a financial statement; or
      b) a compilation of a financial statement when the member expects, or reasonably might expect, that a third party will use the financial statement and the member's compilation report without disclosing a lack of independence; or
      c) an examination of prospective financial information.

   ii. Referral fees. Any member who accepts a referral fee for recommending or referring any service of a CPA to any person or entity or who pays a referral fee to obtain a client shall disclose such acceptance or payment to the client.

9) Advertising and other forms of solicitation
   A member in public practice shall not seek to obtain clients by advertising or other forms of solicitation in a manner that is false, misleading, or deceptive. Solicitation by the use of coercion, over-reaching, or harassing conduct is prohibited.

10) Confidential client information
    A member in public practice shall not disclose any confidential client information without the specific consent of the client.

    However, this rule shall not be construed (1) to relieve a member of his or her professional obligations of the Compliance With Standards Rule [1.310.001] or the Accounting Principles Rule [1.320.001], (2) to affect in any way the member's obligation to comply with a validly issued and enforceable subpoena or summons, or to prohibit a member's compliance with applicable laws and government regulations, (3) to prohibit review of a member's professional practice under AICPA or state CPA society or Board of Accountancy authorization, or (4) to preclude a member from initiating a complaint with, or responding to any inquiry made by, the professional ethics division or trial board of the Institute or a duly constituted investigative or disciplinary body of a state CPA society or Board of Accountancy.

11) Form of practice and name
A member may practice public accounting only in a form of organization permitted by law or regulation whose characteristics conform to resolutions of Council.

A member shall not practice public accounting under a firm name that is misleading.

Names of one or more past owners may be included in the firm name of a successor organization.

A firm may not designate itself as "Members of the American Institute of Certified Public Accountants" unless all its CPA owners are members of the AICPA.

A majority of the ownership of the member's firm, in terms of financial interests and voting rights, must belong to CPAs. Any non-CPA owner would have to be actively engaged as a member of the firm or its affiliates. Ownership by investors or commercial enterprises, not actively engaged as members of the firm or its affiliates, is against the public interest and continues to be prohibited.

There must be a CPA who has ultimate responsibility for all the following services: (1) any audit or other engagement performed in accordance with the Statements on Auditing Standards, (2) any review of a financial statement performed in accordance with the Statements on Standards for Accounting and Review Services ,any examination of prospective financial information performed in accordance with the Statements on Standards for Attestation Engagements, (4) any engagement to be performed in accordance with the standards of the Public Company Accounting Oversight Board (PCAOB), or (5) any examination, review, or agreed upon procedures engagement to be performed in accordance with the SSAE; compilation services and other engagements governed by Statements on Auditing Standards or Statements on Standards for Accounting and Review Services; and non-CPA owners could not assume ultimate responsibility for any such services or engagements.

Non-CPA owners would be permitted to use the title "principal," "owner," "officer," "member" or "shareholder" or any other title permitted by state law, but not hold themselves out to be CPAs.

f. Conceptual Framework Approach

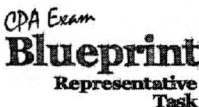

Apply the Conceptual Framework for Members in Public Practice included in the AICPA Code of Professional Conduct to situations that could present threats to compliance with the rules included in the Code.

The AICPA Code of Professional Conduct operates in a manner that can be summarized using the following flowchart:

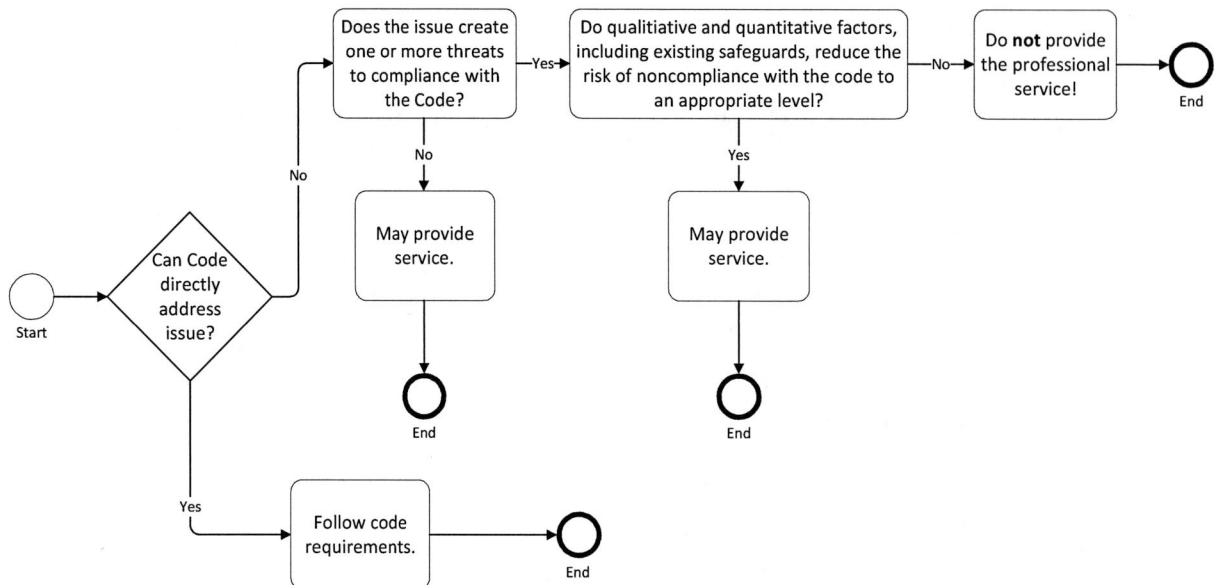

You should understand how to apply the conceptual framework approach for analyzing ethical issues.

Hint: The following definitions are listed here, instead of the Glossary, because of their importance to this section.

- **Acceptable level** – A level at which a reasonable and informed third party, who is aware of the relevant information, would be expected to conclude that a member's compliance with the rules is not compromised.
- **Safeguards** – Actions or other measures that may eliminate a threat or reduce a threat to an acceptable level.
- **Threats** – Relationships or circumstances that could compromise a member's compliance with the rules.

Under the conceptual framework approach, members should identify threats to compliance with the rules and evaluate the significance of those threats. Members should evaluate identified threats both individually and in the aggregate, because threats can have a cumulative effect on a member's compliance with the rules. Members should perform **three main steps** in applying the conceptual framework approach:

Step 1 – Identify threats.
The relationships or circumstances that a member encounters in various engagements and work assignments will often create different threats to complying with the rules. When a member encounters a relationship or circumstance that is not specifically addressed by a rule or an

interpretation, under this approach, the member should determine whether the relationship or circumstance creates one or more threats, such as those identified below. The existence of a threat does not mean that the member is in violation of the rules; however, the member should evaluate the significance of the threat.

Step 2 – Evaluate the significance of a threat.
In evaluating the significance of an identified threat, the member should determine whether a threat is at an acceptable level.

A threat is at an acceptable level when a reasonable and informed third party, who is aware of the relevant information, would be expected to conclude that the threat would not compromise the member's compliance with the rules. Members should consider both qualitative and quantitative factors when evaluating the significance of a threat, including the extent to which existing safeguards already reduce the threat to an acceptable level. If the member evaluates the threat and concludes that a reasonable and informed third party, who is aware of the relevant information, would be expected to conclude that the threat does not compromise a member's compliance with the rules, the threat is at an acceptable level, and the member is not required to evaluate the threat any further under this conceptual framework approach.

Step 3 – Identify and apply safeguards.
If, in evaluating the significance of an identified threat, the member concludes that the threat is not at an acceptable level, the member should apply safeguards to eliminate the threat or reduce it to an acceptable level. The member should apply judgment in determining the nature of the safeguards to be applied, because the effectiveness of safeguards will vary, depending on the circumstances. When identifying appropriate safeguards to apply, one safeguard may eliminate or reduce multiple threats. In some cases, the member should apply multiple safeguards to eliminate or reduce one threat to an acceptable level. In other cases, an identified threat may be so significant that no safeguards will eliminate the threat or reduce it to an acceptable level, or the member will be unable to implement effective safeguards. Under such circumstances, providing the specific professional services would compromise the member's compliance with the rules, and the member should determine whether to decline or discontinue the professional services or resign from the engagement.

1) **Threats**
   Many threats fall into one or more of the following seven broad categories: adverse interest, advocacy, familiarity, management participation, self-interest, self-review, and undue influence.

   i. **Adverse interest threat.** The threat that a member will not act with objectivity because the member's interests are opposed to the client's interests.

      Examples of adverse interest threats include the following:
      a) The client has expressed an intention to commence litigation against the member.
      b) A client or officer, director, or significant shareholder of the client participates in litigation against the firm.
      c) A subrogee asserts a claim against the firm for recovery of insurance payments made to the client.
      d) A class action lawsuit is filed against the client and its officers and directors and the firm and its professional accountants.

ii. **Advocacy threat.** The threat that a member will promote a client's interests or position to the point that his or her objectivity or independence is compromised.

   Examples of advocacy threats include the following:
   a) A member provides forensic accounting services to a client in litigation or a dispute with third parties.
   b) A firm acts as an investment adviser for an officer, a director, or a 10 percent shareholder of a client.
   c) A firm underwrites or promotes a client's shares.
   d) A firm acts as a registered agent for a client.
   e) A member endorses a client's services or products.

iii. **Familiarity threat.** The threat that, due to a long or close relationship with a client, a member will become too sympathetic to the client's interests or too accepting of the client's work or product.

   Examples of familiarity threats include the following:
   a) A member's immediate family or close relative is employed by the client.
   b) A member's close friend is employed by the client.
   c) A former partner or professional employee joins the client in a key position and has knowledge of the firm's policies and practices for the professional services engagement.
   d) Senior personnel have a long association with a client.
   e) A member has a significant close business relationship with an officer, a director, or a 10 percent shareholder of a client.

iv. **Management participation threat.** The threat that a member will take on the role of client management or otherwise assume management responsibilities, such may occur during an engagement to provide non-attest services.

v. **Self-interest threat.** The threat that a member could benefit, financially or otherwise, from an interest in, or relationship with, a client or persons associated with the client.

   Examples of self-interest threats include the following:
   a) The member has a financial interest in a client, and the outcome of a professional services engagement may affect the fair value of that financial interest.
   b) The member's spouse enters into employment negotiations with the client.
   c) A firm enters into a contingent fee arrangement for a tax refund claim that is not a predetermined fee.
   d) Excessive reliance exists on revenue from a single client.

vi. **Self-review threat.** The threat that a member will not appropriately evaluate the results of a previous judgment made or service performed or supervised by the member or an individual in the member's firm and that the member will rely on that service in forming a judgment as part of another service.

   Examples of self-review threats include the following:
   a) The member relies on the work product of the member's firm.
   b) The member performs bookkeeping services for a client.
   c) A partner in the member's office was associated with the client as an employee, an officer, a director, or a contractor.

vii. **Undue influence threat.** The threat that a member will subordinate his or her judgment to an individual associated with a client or any relevant third party, due to that individual's reputation or expertise, aggressive or dominant personality, or attempts to coerce or exercise excessive influence over the member.

Examples of undue influence threats include the following:
   a) The firm is threatened with dismissal from a client engagement.
   b) The client indicates that it will not award additional engagements to the firm if the firm continues to disagree with the client on an accounting or tax matter.
   c) An individual associated with a client or any relevant third party threatens to withdraw or terminate a professional service unless the member reaches certain judgments or conclusions.

2) **Safeguards**
Safeguards may partially or completely eliminate a threat or diminish the potential influence of a threat. The nature and extent of the safeguards applied will depend on many factors. To be effective, safeguards should eliminate the threat or reduce it to an acceptable level.

Safeguards that may eliminate a threat or reduce it to an acceptable level fall into **three broad categories**:
1. Safeguards created by the profession, legislation, or regulation.
2. Safeguards implemented by the client. It is not possible to rely solely on safeguards implemented by the client to eliminate or reduce significant threats to an acceptable level.
3. Safeguards implemented by the firm, including policies and procedures to implement professional and regulatory requirements.

The **effectiveness of a safeguard depends on many factors**, including those listed here:
   a) The facts and circumstances specific to a particular situation
   b) The proper identification of threats
   c) Whether the safeguard is suitably designed to meet its objectives
   d) The party(ies) who will be subject to the safeguard
   e) How the safeguard is applied
   f) The consistency with which the safeguard is applied
   g) Who applies the safeguard
   h) How the safeguard interacts with a safeguard from another category
   i) Whether the client is a public interest entity

Examples of safeguards within each category are presented in the following paragraphs. Because these are only examples and are not intended to be all inclusive, it is possible that threats may be sufficiently mitigated through the application of other safeguards not specifically identified herein.

The following are **examples of safeguards created by the profession, legislation, or regulation**:
   a) Education and training requirements on independence and ethics rules
   b) Continuing education requirements on independence and ethics
   c) Professional standards and the threat of discipline
   d) External review of a firm's quality control system
   e) Legislation establishing prohibitions and requirements for a firm or a firm's professional employees
   f) Competency and experience requirements for professional licensure

g) Professional resources, such as hotlines, for consultation on ethical issues

Examples of safeguards implemented by the client that would operate in combination with other safeguards are as follows:

a) The client has personnel with suitable skill, knowledge, or experience who make managerial decisions about the delivery of professional services and makes use of third-party resources for consultation as needed.
b) The tone at the top emphasizes the client's commitment to fair financial reporting and compliance with the applicable laws, rules, regulations, and corporate governance policies.
c) Policies and procedures are in place to achieve fair financial reporting and compliance with the applicable laws, rules, regulations, and corporate governance policies.
d) Policies and procedures are in place to address ethical conduct.
e) A governance structure, such as an active audit committee, is in place to ensure appropriate decision making, oversight, and communications regarding a firm's services.
f) Policies are in place that bar the entity from hiring a firm to provide services that do not serve the public interest or that would cause the firm's independence or objectivity to be considered impaired.

The following are **examples of safeguards implemented by the firm:**
a) Firm leadership that stresses the importance of complying with the rules and the expectation that engagement teams will act in the public interest.
b) Policies and procedures that are designed to implement and monitor engagement quality control.
c) Documented policies regarding the identification of threats to compliance with the rules, the evaluation of the significance of those threats, and the identification and application of safeguards that can eliminate identified threats or reduce them to an acceptable level.
d) Internal policies and procedures that are designed to monitor compliance with the firm's policies and procedures.
e) Policies and procedures that are designed to identify interests or relationships between the firm or its partners and professional staff and the firm's clients.
f) The use of different partners, partner equivalents, and engagement teams from different offices or that report to different supervisors.
g) Training on, and timely communication of, a firm's policies and procedures and any changes to them for all partners and professional staff.
h) Policies and procedures that are designed to monitor the firm's, partner's, or partner equivalent's reliance on revenue from a single client and that, if necessary, trigger action to address excessive reliance.
i) Designation of someone from senior management as the person responsible for overseeing the adequate functioning of the firm's quality control system.
j) A means for informing partners and professional staff of attest clients and related entities from which they must be independent.
k) A disciplinary mechanism that is designed to promote compliance with policies and procedures.
l) Policies and procedures that are designed to empower staff to communicate to senior members of the firm any engagement issues that concern them without fear of retribution.

- m) Policies and procedures relating to independence and ethics communications with audit committees or others charged with client governance.
- n) Discussion of independence and ethics issues with the audit committee or others responsible for the client's governance.
- o) Disclosures to the audit committee or others responsible for the client's governance regarding the nature of the services that are or will be provided and the extent of the fees charged or to be charged.
- p) The involvement of another professional accountant who (a) reviews the work that is done for a client or (b) otherwise advises the engagement team. This individual could be someone from outside the firm or someone from within the firm who is not otherwise associated with the engagement.
- q) Consultation on engagement issues with an interested third party, such as a committee of independent directors, a professional regulatory body, or another professional accountant.
- r) Rotation of senior personnel who are part of the engagement team.
- s) Policies and procedures that are designed to ensure that members of the engagement team do not make or assume responsibility for management decisions for the client.
- t) The involvement of another firm to perform part of the engagement.
- u) Having another firm to re-perform a non-attest service to the extent necessary for it to take responsibility for that service.
- v) The removal of an individual from an attest engagement team when that individual's financial interests or relationships pose a threat to independence or objectivity.
- w) A consultation function that is staffed with experts in accounting, auditing, independence, ethics, and reporting matters, who can help engagement teams assess issues when guidance is unclear or when the issues are highly technical or require a great deal of judgment; and resist undue pressure from a client when the engagement team disagrees with the client about such issues.
- x) Client acceptance and continuation policies that are designed to prevent association with clients that pose a threat that is not at an acceptable level to the member's compliance with the rules.
- y) Policies that preclude audit partners or partner equivalents from being directly compensated for selling non-attest services to the attest client.
- z) Policies and procedures addressing ethical conduct and compliance with laws and regulations.

Multiple Choice

AUD 1-Q12

Apply the Conceptual Framework for Members in Business included in the AICPA Code of Professional Conduct to situations that could present threats to compliance with the rules included in the Code.

See above discussion of the Conceptual Framework approach.

Apply the Conceptual Framework for Independence included in the AICPA Code of Professional Conduct to situations that could present threats to compliance with the rules included in the Code.

The conceptual framework approach entails identifying threats and evaluating the threat that the member would not be independent or would be perceived by a reasonable and informed third party, who is aware of the relevant information, as not being independent. The member must eliminate or reduce that threat to an acceptable level to conclude that the member is independent. Threats are at an acceptable level either because of the types of threats and their potential effect or because safeguards have eliminated or reduced the threat, so that a reasonable and informed third party, who is aware of the relevant information, would perceive that the member's professional judgment is not compromised.

1) Documentation
   When the member applies safeguards to eliminate or reduce significant threats to an acceptable level, the member should document the identified threats and safeguards applied. Failure to prepare the required documentation would be considered a violation of the Compliance With Standards Rule [1.310.001] rather than the Independence Rule [1.200.001] if the member can demonstrate that safeguards were applied that eliminated or reduced significant threats to an acceptable level.

2) Threats
   i. **Adverse interest threat.** The threat that a member will not act with objectivity because the member's interests are in opposition to the interests of an attest client.

      An example is either the attest client or the member commencing litigation against the other or expressing the intent to commence litigation.

   ii. **Advocacy threat.** The threat that a member will promote an attest client's interests or position to the point that his or her independence is compromised.

      Examples of advocacy threats include the following:
      a) A member promotes the attest client's securities as part of an initial public offering.
      b) A member provides expert witness services to an attest client.
      c) A member represents an attest client in U.S. tax court or other public forum.

   iii. **Familiarity threat.** The threat that, because of a long or close relationship with an attest client, a member will become too sympathetic to the attest client's interests or too accepting of the attest client's work or product.

      Examples of familiarity threats include the following:
      a) A member of the attest engagement team has an immediate family member or close relative in a key position at the attest client, such as the attest client's CEO.
      b) A partner or partner equivalent of the firm has been a member of the attest engagement team for a prolonged period.
      c) A member of the firm has recently been a director or an officer of the attest client.
      d) A member of the attest engagement team has a close friend who is in a key position at the attest client.

iv. **Management participation threat.** The threat that a member will take on the role of attest client management or otherwise assume management responsibilities for an attest client.

Examples of management participation threats include the following:
a) A member serves as an officer or a director of the attest client.
b) A member accepts responsibility for designing, implementing, or maintaining internal controls for the attest client.
c) A member hires, supervises, or terminates the attest client's employees.]

v. **Self-interest threat.** The threat that a member could benefit, financially or otherwise, from an interest in, or relationship with, an attest client or persons associated with the attest client.

Examples of self-interest threats include the following:
a) A member has a direct financial interest or material indirect financial interest in the attest client.
b) A member has a loan from the attest client, an officer or a director of the attest client, or an individual who owns 10 percent or more of the attest client's outstanding equity securities.
c) A member or his or her firm relies excessively on revenue from a single attest client.
d) A member or member's firm has a material joint venture or other material joint business arrangement with the attest client.

vi. **Self-review threat.** The threat that a member will not appropriately evaluate the results of a previous judgment made, or service performed or supervised by the member or an individual in the member's firm and that the member will rely on that service in forming a judgment as part of an attest engagement. **Certain self-review threats, such as preparing source documents used to generate the attest client's financial statements, pose such a significant self-review threat that no safeguards can eliminate or reduce the threats to an acceptable level.**

vii. **Undue influence threat.** The threat that a member will subordinate his or her judgment to that of an individual associated with an attest client or any relevant third party due to that individual's reputation or expertise, aggressive or dominant personality, or attempts to coerce or exercise excessive influence over the member.

Examples of undue influence threats include the following:
a) Management threatens to replace the member or member's firm over a disagreement on the application of an accounting principle.
b) Management pressures the member to reduce necessary audit procedures in order to reduce audit fees.
c) The member receives a gift from the attest client, its management, or its significant shareholders.

3) Safeguards
Safeguards may partially or completely eliminate a threat or diminish the potential influence of a threat. The nature and extent of the safeguards applied will depend on many factors, including the size of the firm and whether the attest client is a public interest entity. To be effective, safeguards should eliminate the threat or reduce it to an acceptable level. The following are three broad categories of safeguards:

i. **Safeguards created by the profession, legislation, or regulation.**
ii. **Safeguards implemented by the attest client. It is NOT possible to rely solely on safeguards**
iii. **implemented by the attest client to eliminate or reduce significant threats to an acceptable level.**
iv. **Safeguards implemented by the firm**, including policies and procedures to implement professional and regulatory requirements.

2. Requirements of the SEC and the PCAOB

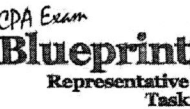

Understand the ethical requirements of the Securities and Exchange Commission and the Public Company Accounting Oversight Board.

Recognize situations that present threats to compliance with the ethical requirements of the Securities and Exchange Commission and the Public Company Accounting Oversight Board.

Apply the ethical requirements and independence rules of the Securities and Exchange Commission and the Public Company Accounting Oversight Board to situations that could present threats to compliance during and audit of an issuer.

a. **PCAOB**
Recall that the PCAOB was established by the Sarbanes-Oxley Act of 2002.

The PCAOB adopted the AICPA Code of Professional Conduct sections relating to independence, integrity and objectivity as interim standards on April 16, 2003. Since then the PCAOB has adopted several additional independence standards. These standards apply to public accounting firms registered with the PCAOB when they are auditing an issuer (a public company).

A registered public accounting firm must comply with all rules and standards of the PCAOB and also those set forth in the rules and regulations of the SEC under the federal securities laws.

1) **Rule 3521.** A registered public accounting firm is not independent of its audit client if the firm provides any service or product to the client for a contingent fee or a commission, or receives from the audit client a contingent fee or commission.

2) **Rule 3522.** A registered public accounting firm is not independent of its audit client if the firm provides any non-audit service to the audit client related to marketing, planning, or opining in favor of:
   i. A confidential transaction (a tax transaction that is offered to a client under conditions of confidentiality and for which the client pays the public accounting firm a fee), or
   ii. Aggressive tax position transaction initially recommended by the public accounting firm.

3) **Rule 3523.** A registered public accounting firm is not independent of its audit client if the firm provides any tax service to a person in a financial reporting oversight role at the audit client, or an immediate family member of such person, unless:
   i. The person is in a financial reporting oversight role only because he or she serves as a member of the board of directors or similar body;
   ii. The person is in a financial reporting oversight role at the audit client only because of the person's relationship to an affiliate of the entity being audited; and

- a) The affiliate's financial statements are not material to the consolidated financial statements, or
- b) The affiliate is audited by another public accounting firm; or
      iii. The person was not in a financial reporting oversight role at the audit client before a hiring or some other change in employment and the tax services were
- a) Provided pursuant to an engagement in process prior to the change in employment, and
- b) Completed on or before 180 days after the change in employment.

4) **Rule 3524.** A registered public accounting firm must get preapproval from the audit committee to perform for an audit client any permissible tax service.

5) **Rule 3525.** In connection with seeking audit committee pre-approval to perform, for an issuer audit client, any permissible non-audit service related to internal control over financial reporting, a registered public accounting firm shall:
   i. describe, in writing, to the audit committee of the issuer the scope of the service;
   ii. discuss with the audit committee of the issuer the potential effects of the service on the independence of the firm; and

> Note: Independence requirements provide that an auditor is not independent of his or her audit client if the auditor is not, or a reasonable investor with knowledge of all relevant facts and circumstances would conclude that the auditor is not, capable of exercising objective and impartial judgment on all issues encompassed within the accountant's engagement. Several principles guide the application of this general standard, including whether the auditor assumes a management role or audits his or her own work. Therefore, an auditor would not be independent if, for example, management had delegated its responsibility for internal control over financial reporting to the auditor or if the auditor had designed or implemented the audit client's internal control over financial reporting.

   iii. document the substance of its discussion with the audit committee of the issuer.

6) **Rule 3526.** A registered public accounting firm must communicate with the audit committee all relationships between the firm and the audit client that may reasonably be thought to bear on independence.

Multiple Choice
AUD 1-Q13 through AUD 1-Q14

b. **SEC**

The SEC requires a "cooling off" period of one year before a member of the audit engagement team can begin working for the registrant in certain key positions. Based on the provisions of the Act, requires that the employment of former audit engagement team members of an accounting firm in a **financial reporting oversight role** (chief executive officer, controller, chief financial officer, chief accounting officer, or any person serving in an equivalent position for the issuer) at an audit client would cause the accounting firm not to be independent, with respect to that registrant, if they were members of the audit engagement team within one year prior to the commencement of procedures for the current audit engagement.

Multiple Choice
AUD 1-Q15 through AUD 1-Q16

The SEC has endeavored to strengthen audit independence through various regulations (some came from the Sarbanes-Oxley Act of 2002). Major items include the following:

1) Issuers must report the nature of disagreements with the former auditors.
   The SEC's Form 8-K requires a registrant to submit written statements on any changes in auditors. The report must state whether there were any disagreements with the former auditor during the previous two-year period on any matter of accounting principle, disclosure, or audit scope or procedure, which could have caused the auditors to make reference in expressing their opinion on the subject matter of the disagreement, regardless of whether the disagreement was resolved to the auditor's satisfaction.

2) Issuers select auditors through audit committees.
   The SEC has adopted the requirement that the audit committee of a listed issuer will need to be directly responsible for the appointment, compensation, retention and oversight of the work of any registered public accounting firm engaged (including resolution of disagreements between management and the auditor regarding financial reporting) for the purpose of preparing or issuing an audit report or performing other audit, review or attest services for the issuer, and the independent auditor will have to report directly to the audit committee. These oversight responsibilities include the authority to retain the outside auditor, which includes the power not to retain (or to terminate) the outside auditor. In addition, in connection with these oversight responsibilities, the audit committee must have ultimate authority to approve all audit engagement fees and terms.

3) Management acknowledges their responsibility for the fairness of the financial statements.
   Section 302 of Sarbanes-Oxley: The SEC shall, by rule, require, for each company filing quarterly and annual reports, **that the principal executive officer or officers and the principal financial officer or officers (or persons performing similar functions) certify in each report that**: (1) the signing officer has reviewed the report; (2) based on the officer's knowledge, the report does not contain any untrue statement of a material fact or omit to state a material fact necessary in order to make the statements made, in light of the circumstances under which such statements were made, not misleading; **(3) based on such officer's knowledge, the financial statements, and other financial information included in the report, fairly present in all material respects the financial condition and results of operations of the issuer as of, and for, the periods presented in the report**; (4) the signing officers: (a) are responsible for establishing and maintaining internal controls; (b) have designed such internal control to ensure that material information relating to the issuer and its consolidated subsidiaries, is made known to such officers by others within those entities, particularly during the period in which the periodic reports are being prepared; (c) have evaluated the effectiveness of the issuer's internal controls as of a date within 90 days prior to the report; and (d) have presented in the report their conclusions about the effectiveness of their internal controls based on their evaluation as of that date. (5) the signing officers have disclosed to the issuer's auditors and the audit committee: (a) all significant deficiencies in the design or operation of internal controls, which could adversely affect the issuer's ability to record, process, summarize, and report financial data and have identified for the issuer's auditors any material weaknesses in internal controls; and (b) any fraud, whether or not material, that involves mgt. or other employees who have a significant role in the issuer's internal controls; (6) the signing officers have indicated in the report whether or not there were significant changes in internal controls or in other factors that could significantly affect internal controls subsequent to the date of their evaluation, including any corrective actions with regard to significant deficiencies and material weaknesses.

4) Services Outside the Scope of Practice of Auditors
Section 201 of Sarbanes-Oxley: The Act makes it unlawful for any registered public accounting firm and prohibits them from providing certain non-audit services contemporaneously with the audit. These non-audit services include the following:
   i. Bookkeeping or other services related to the accounting records or financial statements of the audit client.
   ii. Financial information system design and implementation.
   iii. Appraisal or valuation services, fairness opinions, or contribution-in-kind reports.
   iv. Actuarial services.
   v. Internal audit outsourcing services.
   vi. Management functions or human resources.
   vii. Broker or dealer, investment advisor, or investment banking services.
   viii. Legal services and expert services unrelated to the audit.
   ix. Any other service that the Board determines, by regulation, is impermissible.

5) Audit Partner Rotation
Section 203 Sarbanes-Oxley Act: It shall be unlawful for a registered public accounting firm to provide audit services to an issuer if the lead (or coordinating) audit partner (having primary responsibility for the audit), or the audit partner responsible for reviewing the audit, has performed audit services for that issuer in each of the 5 previous fiscal years of that issuer.

Multiple Choice

AUD 1-Q17 through AUD 1-Q21

3. Requirements of the Government Accountability Office and the Department of Labor
   a. **United States Government Accountability Office (GAO) – Ethics and Independence**
      1) GAO ethics
         The ethical principles that guide the work of auditors who conduct audits in accordance with generally accepted government auditing standards (GAGAS) are: (a) the public interest; (b) integrity; (c) objectivity; (d) proper use of government information, resources, and positions; and (e) professional behavior.

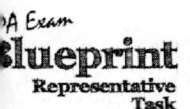

Recognize situations that present threats to compliance with the ethical requirements of the Government Accountability Office Government Auditing Standards.

      2) GAO independence
         In all matters relating to the audit work, the audit organization and the individual auditor, whether government or public, must be independent.

   b. **Department of Labor**

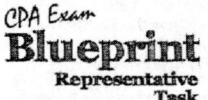

Recognize situations that present threats to compliance with the ethical requirements of the Department of Labor.

Employee benefit plans must be audited in accordance with the Employee Retirement Security Act of 1974 (ERISA), as enforced by DOL. **Independence requirements are in general similar to those of the AICPA**, except that: Accountant or firm may be engaged on a professional basis by the plan sponsor and the accountant may serve as an actuary.

c. **GAGAS Conceptual Framework Approach to Independence**

Apply the ethical requirements and independence rules of the Government Accountability Office Government Auditing Standards to situations that could present threats to compliance during and audit of, or attestation engagement for, a government entity or an entity receiving federal awards.

Many different circumstances, or combinations of circumstances, are relevant in evaluating threats to independence. Therefore, GAGAS establishes a conceptual framework that auditors use to identify, evaluate, and apply safeguards to address threats to independence. The conceptual framework assists auditors in maintaining both independence of mind and independence in appearance. It can be applied to many variations in circumstances that create threats to independence and allows auditors to address threats to independence that result from activities that are not specifically prohibited by GAGAS.

Auditors should apply the conceptual framework at the audit organization, audit, and individual auditor levels to: (1) identify threats to independence; evaluate the significance of the threats identified, both individually and in the aggregate; and (2) apply safeguards as necessary to eliminate the threats or reduce them to an acceptable level.

If no safeguards are available to eliminate an unacceptable threat or reduce it to an acceptable level, independence would be considered impaired.

The GAGAS Conceptual Framework Approach to Independence is very similar to the AICPA's Conceptual Framework for Independence. If you understand the operation of the AICPA's Conceptual Framework for Independence, you can apply the same methodology to GAO independence issues.

Apply the independence rules of the Department of Labor to situations that could present threats to compliance during an audit of employee benefit plans.

The AICPA has prepared the summary, DOL and AICPA Independence Rule Comparison (as of Dec. 15, 2015) to assist members in understanding some of the more common independence rules that affect auditors of employee benefit plans. Information about the DOL rules is excerpted from 29 CFR 2509.75-9, Interpretive Bulletin relating to guidelines on independence of accountant retained by Employee Benefit Plans. Major points from the summary include the following:

1) Immediate Family and Close Relatives
   The AICPA staff could not identify any specific DOL rules addressing application of the independence rules to immediate family members or close relatives.

2) Affiliates of a Plan
   DOL independence guidance extends its independence rules to sponsors of a plan. Per The Act, the sponsor is the entity (or entities in case there is more than one) who established or maintains the plan, such as the employer or employee organization.

3) Financial Interests
   DOL rules would consider independence to be impaired with respect to a plan if during the period of the professional engagement, at the date of the opinion, or during the period covered by the financial statements, the auditor or other member of the firm had a direct or material indirect financial interest in: (1) the plan; or (2) the plan sponsor

4) Simultaneous Employment/Association
   DOL rules would consider independence to be impaired with respect to a plan, if during the period of the professional engagement, at the date of the opinion, or during the period covered by the financial statements, the auditor, his or her firm or a member thereof, was connected as a promoter, underwriter, investment advisor, voting trustee, director, officer, or employee of the plan or of the plan's sponsor.

5) Former Firm Member Now Associated with Plan or Plan Sponsor
   The AICPA staff could not identify any specific DOL rules addressing such association with a plan or a plan sponsor.

6) General Guidance on Non-Attest Services
   DOL rules also state that independence would not be considered to be impaired, if at or during the period of the professional engagement, the accountant or his or her firm is retained or engaged on a professional basis by the plan sponsor.

7) Bookkeeping
   DOL rules would consider independence to be impaired if the audit firm or any of its employees maintain the financial records for an employee benefit plan or for the sponsor of the plan.

8) Actuarial Services
   DOL rules state that the rendering of services by an actuary associated with an accountant or accounting firm would not impair independence. However, the DOL notes that the rendering of services to a plan by an actuary and accountant employed by the same firm may constitute a "prohibited transaction."

9) Benefit Plan Administration
   DOL rules would consider independence to be impaired if the audit firm or any of its employees maintain the financial records for an employee benefit plan or for the sponsor of the plan.

10) Other Non-Attest Services
    The AICPA staff could not identify DOL rules specifically addressing any other non-attest services.

Multiple Choice

AUD 1-Q22

C. Terms of Engagement

The objective of the auditor is to accept an audit engagement for a new or existing audit client only when the basis upon which it is to be performed has been agreed upon through:
- Establishing whether the **preconditions for an audit** are present, and
- Confirming that a **common understanding of the terms of the audit engagement** exists between the auditor and management and, when appropriate, those charged with governance. (AICPA, AU-C 210.02)

1. Preconditions for an Engagement

Identify the preconditions needed for accepting or continuing an audit or non-audit engagement.

Perform procedures to determine whether the preconditions needed for accepting or continuing an audit or non-audit engagement are present.

    a. **Audit – preconditions**
       Preconditions for an audit include the following:
        1) The use by management of an acceptable financial reporting framework in the preparation and fair presentation of the financial statements.
        2) The agreement of management and, when appropriate, those charged with governance, to the premise on which an audit is conducted.

       In order to establish whether the preconditions for an audit are present, the auditor should:
        1) Determine whether the financial reporting framework to be applied in the preparation of the financial statements is acceptable and
        2) Obtain the agreement of management that it acknowledges and understands its responsibility
           i. for the preparation and fair presentation of the financial statements in accordance with the applicable financial reporting framework;
           ii. for the design, implementation, and maintenance of internal control relevant to the preparation and fair presentation of financial statements that are free from material misstatement, whether due to fraud or error; and
           iii. to provide the auditor with
               a) access to all information of which management is aware that is relevant to the preparation and fair presentation of the financial statements, such as records, documentation, and other matters;
               b) additional information that the auditor may request from management for the purpose of the audit; and
               c) unrestricted access to persons within the entity from whom the auditor determines it necessary to obtain audit evidence.

Before accepting an engagement for an initial audit, including a re-audit engagement, the auditor should request management to authorize the predecessor auditor to respond fully to the auditor's inquiries regarding matters that will assist the auditor in determining whether to accept the engagement. If management refuses to authorize the predecessor auditor to respond, or limits the response, the auditor should inquire about the reasons and consider the implications of that refusal in deciding whether to accept the engagement.

Multiple Choice

AUD 1-Q23 through AUD 1-Q25

b. **Non-Audit – preconditions**
General principles for engagements performed in accordance with SSARSs issued by the Accounting and Review Services Committee (ARSC) and codified into AR-C sections.

Per AICPA, AR-C 60.24, the accountant should not accept an engagement to be performed in accordance with SSARSs if:
1) The accountant has reason to believe that relevant ethical requirements will not be satisfied;
2) The accountant's preliminary understanding of the engagement circumstances indicates that information needed to perform the engagement is likely to be unavailable or unreliable; or
3) The accountant has cause to doubt management's integrity such that it is likely to affect the performance of the engagement.

The steps to determine if preconditions are present are similar to those of an audit.

> **Perform procedures to determine whether the financial reporting framework to be applied to an entity's financial statements is acceptable.**

c. **Audit and Non-Audit – financial reporting framework**
Factors that are relevant to the auditor's determination of the acceptability of the financial reporting framework to be applied in the preparation of the financial statements include the following:
1) The nature of the entity (for example, whether it is a business enterprise, a governmental entity, or a not-for-profit organization).
2) The purpose of the financial statements (for example, whether they are prepared to meet the common financial information needs of a wide range of users).
3) The nature of the financial statements (for example, whether the financial statements are a complete set of financial statements or a single financial statement).
4) Whether law or regulation prescribes the applicable financial reporting framework.

> **Perform procedures to obtain the agreement of management that it acknowledges and understands its responsibilities for an audit or non-audit engagement.**

d. **Audit and non-audit – management responsibilities**
Management must agree with their responsibility for the financial statements as stated in the engagement letter.

2. Terms of Engagement and Engagement Letter

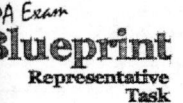

> **Identify the factors affecting the acceptance or continuance of an audit or non-audit engagement.**

a. **Audit (including PCAOB) and Non-audit – acceptance/continuance**
Per AICPA, QC Section 10:
The firm should establish policies and procedures for the acceptance and continuance of client relationships and specific engagements, designed to provide the firm with reasonable assurance that it will undertake or continue relationships and engagements only when the firm
1) is competent to perform the engagement and has the capabilities, including time and resources, to do so;
2) can comply with legal and relevant ethical requirements; and
3) has considered the integrity of the client and does not have information that would lead it to conclude that the client lacks integrity.

Such policies and procedures should
1) require the firm to obtain such information as it considers necessary in the circumstances before accepting an engagement with a new client, when deciding whether to continue an existing engagement, and when considering acceptance of a new engagement with an existing client.
2) require the firm to determine whether it is appropriate to accept the engagement if a potential conflict of interest is identified in accepting an engagement from a new or an existing client.
3) if issues have been identified and the firm decides to accept or continue the client relationship or a specific engagement, require the firm to
   i. consider whether ethical requirements that exist under the "Conflicts of Interest" interpretation (ET sec. 1.110.010) under the "Integrity and Objectivity Rule" (ET sec. 1.100.001) apply, and
   ii. document how the issues were resolved.

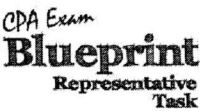

> **Identify the factors to consider when management requests a change in the type of engagement (e.g., from an audit to a review).**

The auditor should not agree to a change in the terms of the audit engagement when no reasonable justification for doing so exists.

A request from management for the auditor to change the terms of the audit engagement may result from a change in circumstances affecting the need for the service, a misunderstanding about the nature of an audit as originally requested, or a restriction on the scope of the audit engagement, whether imposed by management or caused by other circumstances. The auditor, as required by AU-C 210.14, considers the justification given for the request, particularly the implications of a restriction on the scope of the audit engagement.

A change in circumstances that affects management's requirements or a misunderstanding concerning the nature of the service originally requested may be considered a reasonable basis for requesting a change in the audit engagement.

If, prior to completing the audit engagement, the auditor is requested to change the audit engagement to an engagement for which the auditor obtains a lower level of assurance, the auditor should determine whether reasonable justification for doing so exists.

Multiple Choice

AUD 1-Q26 through AUD 1-Q29

> **Perform procedures to confirm that a common understanding of the terms of an engagement exist with management and those charged with governance.**

Generally, this application is accomplished by management (or those charged with governance) signing the engagement letter. See next representative task discussing the terms of a written engagement letter or other suitable form of written agreement.

CPA Exam Blueprint Representative Task

Document the terms of an audit or non-audit engagement in a written engagement letter or other suitable form of written agreement.

b. **Audit – engagement letter**
   The agreed-upon terms of the audit engagement should be documented in an audit engagement letter or other suitable form of written agreement. The agreement should include the following (**required items**):
   1) The objective and scope of the audit of the financial statements
   2) The responsibilities of the auditor
   3) The responsibilities of management
   4) A statement that because of the inherent limitations of an audit, together with the inherent limitations of internal control, an unavoidable risk exists that some material misstatements may not be detected, even though the audit is properly planned and performed in accordance with GAAS
   5) Identification of the applicable financial reporting framework for the preparation of the financial statements
   6) Reference to the expected form and content of any reports to be issued by the auditor and a statement that circumstances may arise in which a report may differ from its expected form and content

Multiple Choice

AUD 1-Q30

An audit engagement letter may also make reference to, for example, the following (**not required items**):
   1) Elaboration of the scope of the audit, including reference to applicable legislation, regulations, GAAS, and ethical and other pronouncements of professional bodies to which the auditor adheres.
   2) The form of any other communication of results of the audit engagement.
   3) Arrangements regarding the planning and performance of the audit, including the composition of the audit team.
   4) The expectation that management will provide written representations.
   5) The agreement of management to make available to the auditor draft financial statements and any accompanying other information in time to allow the auditor to complete the audit in accordance with the proposed timetable.
   6) The agreement of management to inform the auditor of events occurring or facts discovered subsequent to the date of the financial statements, of which management may become aware, that may affect the financial statements.
   7) The basis on which fees are computed and any billing arrangements.
   8) A request for management to acknowledge receipt of the audit engagement letter and to agree to the terms of the engagement outlined therein, as may be evidenced by their signature on the engagement letter.

Multiple Choice

AUD 1-Q31 through AUD 1-Q33

c. **Non-audit – engagement letter**
Similar to an audit engagement, the accountant should agree upon the terms of the engagement with management or those charged with governance, as appropriate. The agreed-upon terms of the engagement should be documented in an **engagement letter** or other suitable form of written agreement.

> *Hint:* In addition, the items listed for an audit engagement, the engagement letter for a non-audit engagement should include: (1) an agreement by management that each page of the financial statements will include a statement indicating that no assurance is provided on the financial statements (financial statement preparation engagement), and/or (2) limitations of the engagement. Clients should be very clear about the level of assurance provided, if any, prior to starting an engagement.

Multiple Choice

AUD 1-Q34 through AUD 1-Q36

D. Requirements for Engagement Documentation

> Identify the elements that comprise sufficient appropriate documentation for an audit or non-audit engagement.

> Identify the requirements for the assembly and retention of documentation for an audit or non-audit engagement.

a. **Audit – documentation requirements**
   Audit documentation provides (AICPA)
   1) evidence of the auditor's basis for a conclusion about the achievement of the overall objectives of the auditor, and
   2) evidence that the audit was planned and performed in accordance with generally accepted auditing standards (GAAS) and applicable legal and regulatory requirements.

Per PCAOB AS 1215.02:
Audit documentation is the written record of the basis for the auditor's conclusions that provides the support for the auditor's representations, whether those representations are contained in the auditor's report or otherwise.

Audit documentation also facilitates the planning, performance, and supervision of the engagement, and is the basis for the review of the quality of the work because it provides the reviewer with written documentation of the evidence supporting the auditor's significant conclusions.

Among other things, audit documentation includes records of the planning and performance of the work, the procedures performed, evidence obtained, and conclusions reached by the auditor.

Audit documentation also may be referred to as work papers or working papers.

The auditor should prepare audit documentation that is sufficient to enable an experienced auditor, having no previous connection with the audit, to understand
   1) the nature, timing, and extent of the audit procedures performed to comply with GAAS and applicable legal and regulatory requirements;
   2) the results of the audit procedures performed, and the audit evidence obtained; and
   3) significant findings or issues arising during the audit, the conclusions reached thereon, and significant professional judgments made in reaching those conclusions.

Multiple Choice

AUD 1-Q37

For audit procedures related to the inspection of significant contracts or agreements, the auditor should include abstracts or copies of those contracts or agreements in the audit documentation.

The auditor should document discussions of significant findings or issues with management, those charged with governance, and others, including the nature of the significant findings or issues discussed, and when and with whom the discussions took place.

If the auditor identified information that is inconsistent with the auditor's final conclusion regarding a significant finding or issue, the auditor should document how the auditor addressed the inconsistency.

Per PCAOB AS 1215.08: In addition to the documentation necessary to support the auditor's final conclusions, audit documentation must include information the auditor has identified relating to significant findings or issues that is inconsistent with or contradicts the auditor's final conclusions

The form, content, and extent of audit documentation depend on factors such as
- the size and complexity of the entity.
- the nature of the audit procedures to be performed.
- the identified risks of material misstatement.
- the significance of the audit evidence obtained.
- the nature and extent of exceptions identified.
- the need to document a conclusion or the basis for a conclusion not readily determinable from the documentation of the work performed or audit evidence obtained.
- the audit methodology and tools used.
- the extent of judgment involved in performing the work and evaluating the results.

Audit documentation may be recorded on paper or on electronic or other media. Examples of audit documentation include the following:
- Audit plans
- Analyses
- Issues memorandums
- Summaries of significant findings or issues
- Letters of confirmation and representation
- Checklists
- Correspondence (including e-mail) concerning significant findings or issues

The auditor should document the report release date in the audit documentation.

The auditor should assemble the audit documentation in an audit file and complete the administrative process of assembling the final audit file on a timely basis, **no later than 60 days** following the report release date.

Per PCAOB AS 1215.15: A complete and final set of audit documentation should be assembled for retention as of a date **not more than 45 days after the report release date** (documentation completion date).

After the documentation completion date, the auditor should not delete or discard audit documentation of any nature before the end of the specified retention period. Such retention period, however, **should not be shorter than five years** from the report release date.

Firms are required to establish policies and procedures for the retention of engagement documentation. Statutes, regulations, or the audit firm's quality control policies may specify a retention period longer than **five years**.

PCAOB requires documentation be retained for **7 years**.

b. **Non-audit – documentation requirements**
The accountant should prepare documentation in connection with each preparation engagement in sufficient detail to provide a clear understanding of the work performed which, at a minimum, includes the following:
1) The engagement letter or other suitable form of written documentation with management.
2) A copy of the financial statements.

3) A copy of the accountant's report (for compilations and reviews)

Documentation may include documentation regarding significant consultations or significant professional judgments made throughout the engagement.

For reviews, per AR-C 90.91, the accountant should prepare review documentation that is sufficient to enable an experienced accountant, having no previous connection to the review, to understand:
1) the nature, timing, and extent of the review procedures performed to comply with SSARSs;
2) the results of the review procedures performed and the review evidence obtained; and
3) significant findings or issues arising during the review, the conclusions reached thereon, and significant professional judgments made in reaching those conclusions.

Hint: This level of documentation is required even if a single engagement partner performs all review work. The review documentation may be subject to review by external parties and must be easily understood by an experienced accountant.

In addition to the requirements above, the review documentation should include the following:
- The engagement letter or other suitable form of written documentation with management
- Communications to management and others regarding fraud or noncompliance with laws and regulations
- Communications with management regarding the accountant's expectation to include an emphasis-of-matter or other-matter paragraph in the accountant's review report
- Communications with other accountants that have audited or reviewed the financial statements of significant components
- The representation letter
- A copy of the reviewed financial statements and the accountant's review report thereon

Prepare documentation that is sufficient to enable an experienced auditor having no previous connection with an audit engagement to understand the nature, timing, extent and results of procedures performed and the significant findings and conclusions reached.

Prepare documentation that is sufficient to enable an accountant having no previous connection with a non-audit engagement to understand the nature, timing, extent and results of procedures performed and the significant findings and conclusions reached.

c. **Audit – sufficient documentation for experienced auditor**
See the previous representative task for an overview of typical audit documentation that is sufficient to enable an experienced auditor with no previous connection with the audit engagement to understand the procedures performed.

The auditor should prepare audit documentation on a timely basis. Preparing sufficient and appropriate audit documentation on a timely basis throughout the audit helps to enhance the quality of the audit and facilitates the effective review and evaluation of the audit evidence obtained and conclusions reached before the auditor's report is finalized.

Documentation prepared at the time such work is performed or shortly thereafter is likely to be more accurate than documentation prepared at a much later time.

d. **Non-audit – sufficient documentation for accountant with no previous connection**
The accountant need not include in review documentation superseded drafts of working papers and financial statements, notes that reflect incomplete or preliminary thinking, previous copies of documents corrected for typographical or other errors, and duplicates of documents.

The accountant is not precluded from supporting the review report by other means in addition to the review documentation. Such other means might include written documentation contained in other engagement files (for example, compilation or non-attest services) or quality control files (for example, consultation files) and, in limited situations, oral explanations. On their own, oral explanations by the accountant do not represent adequate support for the work the accountant performed or conclusions reached, but they may be used to explain or clarify information contained in the review documentation.

Multiple Choice

AUD 1-Q38 through AUD 1-Q39

E. **Communication with Management and Those Charged with Governance**
   1. Planned scope and timing of an engagement

> Identify the matters related to the planned scope and timing of an audit or non-audit engagement that should be communicated to management and those charged with governance.

> Prepare presentation materials and supporting schedules for use in communicating the planned scope and timing of an audit or non-audit engagement to management and those charged with governance.

   a. **Audit – scope and timing**
      1) Matters to Be Communicated to Those Charged with Governance include (see AU-C 260):
         i. Planned Scope and Timing of the Audit
            The auditor should communicate with those charged with governance an overview of the planned scope and timing of the audit.

            Care is required when communicating with those charged with governance about the planned scope and timing of the audit so as not to compromise the effectiveness of the audit, particularly when some or all of those charged with governance are involved in managing the entity.

            Matters communicated may include the following:
            a) How the auditor proposes to address the significant risks of material misstatement, whether due to fraud or error
            b) The auditor's approach to internal control relevant to the audit including, when applicable, whether the auditor will express an opinion on the effectiveness of internal control over financial reporting
            c) The application of materiality in the context of an audit, as discussed in AU-C 320, Materiality in Planning and Performing an Audit
            d) If the entity has an internal audit function, how the auditor and the internal auditors can work together in a constructive and complementary manner, including any planned use of the work of the internal audit function in obtaining audit evidence and the nature and extent of any planned use of internal auditors to provide direct assistance.

Multiple Choice

AUD 1-Q40

   b. **Non-audit – scope and timing**
      The accountant should communicate with management or those charged with governance, as appropriate, on a timely basis during the course of the review engagement, all matters concerning the review engagement that, in the accountant's professional judgment, are of significant importance to merit the attention of management or those charged with governance, as appropriate.

2. Internal control related matters

CPA Exam Blueprint Representative Task

> Identify the matters related to deficiencies and material weaknesses in internal control that should be communicated to those charged with governance and management for an audit or non-audit engagement and the timing of such communications.

> Prepare written communication materials for use in communicating identified internal control deficiencies and material weaknesses for an audit or non-audit engagement to those charged with governance and management.

a. **Audit – internal control matters**
Per AU-C 265:
The auditor should communicate in writing to those charged with governance on a timely basis significant deficiencies and material weaknesses identified during the audit, including those that were remediated during the audit.

The fact that the auditor communicated a significant deficiency or material weakness to those charged with governance and management in a **previous audit** does not eliminate the need for the auditor to repeat the communication if remedial action has not yet been taken. If a previously communicated significant deficiency or material weakness remains, the current year's communication may repeat the description from the previous communication or simply reference the previous communication and the date of that communication.

The level of detail at which to communicate significant deficiencies and material weaknesses is a matter of the auditor's professional judgment in the circumstances. Factors that the auditor may consider in determining an appropriate level of detail for the communication include, for example, the following:
1) The nature of the entity. For example, the communication required for a governmental entity may be different from that for a nongovernmental entity.
2) The size and complexity of the entity. For example, the communication required for a complex entity may be different from that for an entity operating a simple business.
3) The nature of significant deficiencies and material weaknesses that the auditor has identified.
4) The entity's governance composition. For example, more detail may be needed if those charged with governance include members who do not have significant experience in the entity's industry or in the affected areas.
5) Legal or regulatory requirements regarding the communication of specific types of deficiencies in internal control.

The auditor also should communicate to management at an appropriate level of responsibility, on a timely basis
- in writing, significant deficiencies and material weaknesses that the auditor has communicated or intends to communicate to those charged with governance, unless it would be inappropriate to communicate directly to management in the circumstances.
- in writing or orally, other deficiencies in internal control identified during the audit that have not been communicated to management by other parties and that, in the auditor's professional judgment, are of sufficient importance to merit management's attention. If other deficiencies in internal control are communicated orally, the auditor should document the communication.

The communications should be made no later than 60 days following the report release date. However, these communications may be made at an earlier date so that management can evaluate the deficiencies and take the necessary remedial action.

The auditor should include in the auditor's written communication of significant deficiencies and material weaknesses

 i. the definition of the term material weakness and, when relevant, the definition of the term significant deficiency.
 ii. a description of the significant deficiencies and material weaknesses and an explanation of their potential effects.
 iii. sufficient information to enable those charged with governance and management to understand the context of the communication. In particular, the auditor should include in the communication the following elements that explain that (Ref: par. .A30–.A31)
  a) the purpose of the audit was for the auditor to express an opinion on the financial statements.
  b) the audit included consideration of internal control over financial reporting in order to design audit procedures that are appropriate in the circumstances but not for the purpose of expressing an opinion on the effectiveness of internal control.
  c) the auditor is not expressing an opinion on the effectiveness of internal control.
  d) the auditor's consideration of internal control was not designed to identify all deficiencies in internal control that might be material weaknesses or significant deficiencies, and therefore, material weaknesses or significant deficiencies may exist that were not identified.
 iv. an appropriate alert, in accordance with AU-C 905, Alert That Restricts the Use of the Auditor's Written Communication.

The auditor should not issue a written communication stating that no significant deficiencies were identified during the audit.

Multiple Choice

AUD 1-Q41

b. **Non-audit – internal control matters**
Per AR-C 90.A3: A review differs significantly from an audit of financial statements in which the auditor obtains reasonable assurance, which is a high, but not absolute level of assurance, that the financial statements are free of material misstatement.

A review does not contemplate obtaining an understanding of the entity's internal control; assessing fraud risk; testing accounting records by obtaining sufficient appropriate audit evidence through inspection, observation, confirmation, or the examination of source documents; or other procedures ordinarily performed in an audit.

Multiple Choice

AUD 1-Q42

3. All other matters

> Identify matters, other than those related to the planned scope and timing or deficiencies, and material weaknesses in internal control that should be communicated to management and those charged with governance for an audit or non-audit engagement.

a. **Audit – other matters to be communicated to management and those charged with governance**
   Matters that should be communicated to those charged with governance include (AU-C 260):
   - The auditor's responsibilities with regard to the financial statement audit
   - Significant findings or issues from the audit
   - Uncorrected misstatements

   1) The Auditor's Responsibilities with Regard to the Financial Statement Audit
      The auditor should communicate with those charged with governance the auditor's responsibilities with regard to the financial statement audit, including that
      i. the auditor is responsible for forming and expressing an opinion about whether the financial statements that have been prepared by management, with the oversight of those charged with governance, are prepared, in all material respects, in accordance with the applicable financial reporting framework.
      ii. the audit of the financial statements does not relieve management or those charged with governance of their responsibilities. (These may be communicated through the engagement letter.)

   2) Significant Findings or Issues from the Audit
      The auditor should communicate with those charged with governance
      i. the auditor's views about qualitative aspects of the entity's significant accounting practices, including accounting policies, accounting estimates, and financial statement disclosures. When applicable, the auditor should
         a) explain to those charged with governance why the auditor considers a significant accounting practice that is acceptable under the applicable financial reporting framework not to be most appropriate to the particular circumstances of the entity and
         b) determine that those charged with governance are informed about the process used by management in formulating particularly sensitive accounting estimates, including fair value estimates, and about the basis for the auditor's conclusions regarding the reasonableness of those estimates.
      ii. significant difficulties, if any, encountered during the audit; which may include
         a) significant delays in management providing required information.
         b) an unnecessarily brief time within which to complete the audit.
         c) extensive unexpected effort required to obtain sufficient appropriate audit evidence.
         d) the unavailability of expected information.
         e) restrictions imposed on the auditor by management.
         f) management's unwillingness to provide information about management's plans for dealing with the adverse effects of the conditions or events that lead the auditor to believe there is substantial doubt about the entity's ability to continue as a going concern.
         g) disagreements with management, if any.
         h) other findings or issues, if any, arising from the audit that are, in the auditor's professional judgment, significant and relevant to those charged with governance regarding their responsibility to oversee the financial reporting process.

3) Uncorrected Misstatements
   The auditor should communicate with those charged with governance
   i. uncorrected misstatements accumulated by the auditor and the effect that they, individually or in the aggregate, may have on the opinion in the auditor's report. The auditor's communication should identify material uncorrected misstatements individually. The auditor should request that uncorrected misstatements be corrected.
   ii. the effect of uncorrected misstatements related to prior periods on the relevant classes of transactions, account balances or disclosures, and the financial statements as a whole.

Multiple Choice

AUD 1-Q43

4) When Not All of Those Charged with Governance Are Involved in Management
   Unless all of those charged with governance are involved in managing the entity, the auditor also should communicate
   i. material, corrected misstatements that were brought to the attention of management as a result of audit procedures.
   ii. significant findings or issues, if any, arising from the audit that were discussed, or the subject of correspondence, with management.
   iii. the auditor's views about significant matters that were the subject of management's consultations with other accountants on accounting or auditing matters when the auditor is aware that such consultation has occurred.
   iv. written representations the auditor is requesting.

5) The Communication Process
   The auditor should communicate in writing with those charged with governance significant findings or issues from the audit if, in the auditor's professional judgment, oral communication would not be adequate. This communication need not include matters that arose during the course of the audit that were communicated with those charged with governance and satisfactorily resolved.

   The main idea is to create a clear communication channel between the auditor and those charged with governance. If communication is done orally, the auditor should document what was stated, including when and to whom issues were communicated.

6) Restricted Use
   When the auditor communicates matters in accordance with AU-C 260 **in writing**, the communication is considered **a by-product report**. Accordingly, the auditor should indicate in the communication that it is intended solely for the information and use of those charged with governance and, if appropriate, management, and is not intended to be, and should not be, used by anyone other than these specified parties. When matters have been communicated in writing, the auditor should retain a copy of the communication as part of the audit documentation.

7) Timing of Communications
   The auditor should communicate with those charged with governance on a timely basis.

8) Adequacy of the Communication Process
   The auditor should evaluate whether the two-way communication between the auditor and those charged with governance has been adequate for the purpose of the audit. If it has not, the auditor should evaluate the effect, if any, on the auditor's assessment of the risks of

material misstatement and ability to obtain sufficient appropriate audit evidence and should take appropriate action.

b. **Non-audit – other matters to be communicated to management or those charged with governance**
Matters to be communicated to management or those charged with governance, as appropriate, may include the following:
1) The accountant's responsibilities in the review engagement, as included in the engagement letter or other suitable form of written agreement.
2) Significant findings from the review, for example:
    ii. The accountant's views about significant qualitative aspects of the entity's accounting practices, including accounting policies, accounting estimates, and financial statement disclosures.
    iii. Significant findings from the performance of procedures, including situations when the accountant considered performance of additional procedures necessary in accordance with this section. The accountant may need to confirm that those charged with governance have the same understanding of the facts and circumstances relevant to specific transactions or events.
    iv. Matters arising that may lead to modification of the accountant's review report.

Significant difficulties, if any, encountered during the review, for example, unavailability of expected information, unexpected inability to obtain evidence that the accountant considers necessary for the review, or restrictions imposed on the accountant by management. In some circumstances, such difficulties may lead to the accountant's withdrawal from the engagement.

Multiple Choice

AUD 1-Q44

F. Communication with Component Auditors and Parties Other Than Management and Those Charged with Governance

> **Identify matters that should be communicated to component auditors in a group audit engagement.**

This section deals with communications between auditors in group audits. Specifically, communications from the group engagement team to a component auditor and vice-versa.

> *Hint*: The following terms are important to understand this representative task:
> - **Group engagement team** – Partners, including the group engagement partner, and staff who establish the overall group audit strategy, communicate with component auditors, perform work on the consolidation process, and evaluate the conclusions drawn from the audit evidence as the basis for forming an opinion on the group financial statements.
> - **Component** – An entity or business activity for which group or component management prepares financial information that is required by the applicable financial reporting framework to be included in the group financial statements.
> - **Component auditor** – An auditor who performs work on the financial information of a component that will be used as audit evidence for the group audit. A component auditor may be part of the group engagement partner's firm, a network firm of the group engagement partner's firm, or another firm.

These communications are impacted by the group engagement partner decision to assume responsibility for work of a component auditor. The following table summarizes the audit requirements for these communications:

	Group engagement team to component auditor	Component auditor to group engagement team
Assume responsibility for component auditor	AU-C 600.41 + .60	AU-C 600.42 + .61
Not assume responsibility for component auditor	AU-C 600.41	AU-C 600.42

a. **Communication from group engagement team to component auditor**

   1) Group Engagement Partner **Does NOT** Assume Responsibility for Work of the Component Auditor

   The group engagement team should communicate its requirements to a component auditor on a timely basis. The group engagement team's requirements often are communicated in a letter of instruction.

   This communication should include the following:
   i. A request that the component auditor, knowing the context in which the group engagement team will use the work of the component auditor, confirm that the component auditor will cooperate with the group engagement team.
   ii. The ethical requirements that are relevant to the group audit and, in particular, the independence requirements.
   iii. A list of related parties prepared by group management and any other related parties of which the group engagement team is aware. The group engagement team should request the component auditor to communicate on a timely basis related parties not previously identified by group management or the group engagement team. The group engagement team should identify such additional related parties to other component auditors.

iv. Identified significant risks of material misstatement of the group financial statements, due to fraud or error, that are relevant to the work of the component auditor.

2) Group Engagement Partner **Does** Assume Responsibility for Work of the Component Auditor
When the auditor of the group financial statements is assuming responsibility for the work of a component auditor, the required communications (see above):
   i. should set out the work to be performed and the form and content of the component auditor's communication with the group engagement team.
   ii. should include, in the case of an audit or review of the financial information of the component, component materiality (and the amount or amounts lower than the materiality for particular classes of transactions, account balances, or disclosures, if applicable) and the threshold above which misstatements cannot be regarded as clearly trivial to the group financial statements.

b. **Communication from component auditor to group engagement team**
3) Group Engagement Partner **Does NOT** Assume Responsibility for Work of the Component Auditor
The group engagement team should request a component auditor to communicate matters relevant to the group engagement team's conclusion, with regard to the group audit.

Such communication should include the following:
   i. Whether the component auditor has complied with ethical requirements relevant to the group audit, including independence and professional competence.
   ii. Identification of the financial information of the component on which the component auditor is reporting.
   iii. The component auditor's overall findings, conclusions, or opinion.

4) Group Engagement Partner **Does** Assume Responsibility for Work of the Component Auditor
When the auditor of the group financial statements is assuming responsibility for the work of a component auditor, the required communication requested from the component auditor (above) also should include the following:
   i. Whether the component auditor has complied with the group engagement team's requirements.
   ii. Information on instances of noncompliance with laws or regulations at the component or group level that could give rise to a material misstatement of the group financial statements.
   iii. Significant risks of material misstatement of the group financial statements, due to fraud or error, identified by the component auditor in the component and the component auditor's responses to such risks. The group engagement team should request the component auditor to communicate such significant risks on a timely basis.
   iv. A list of corrected and uncorrected misstatements of the financial information of the component (the list need not include misstatements that are below the threshold for clearly trivial misstatements communicated by the group engagement team).
   v. Indicators of possible management bias regarding accounting estimates and the application of accounting principles.
   vi. Description of any identified material weaknesses and significant deficiencies in internal control at the component level.
   vii. Other significant findings and issues that the component auditor communicated or expects to communicate to those charged with governance of the component, including fraud or suspected fraud involving component management, employees who have

significant roles in internal control at the component level, or others that resulted in a material misstatement of the financial information of the component.

viii. Any other matters that may be relevant to the group audit or that the component auditor wishes to draw to the attention of the group engagement team, including exceptions noted in the written representations that the component auditor requested from component management.

> **Identify matters that should be communicated to parties other than management and those charged with governance (e.g., communications required by law or regulation) for an audit or non-audit engagement.**

c. **Audit – communication with parties other than management and those charged with governance**
The auditor may become aware that the entity is subject to an audit requirement that is not encompassed in the terms of the engagement.

The communication to those charged with governance that an audit conducted in accordance with GAAS may not satisfy the relevant legal, regulatory, or contractual requirements may be necessary if, for example, an entity engages an auditor to perform an audit of its financial statements in accordance with GAAS and the auditor becomes aware that by law, regulation, or contractual agreement the entity also is required to have an audit performed in accordance with one or more of the following:
- Government Auditing Standards (GAGAS), also called Yellow Book
- OMB Circular A-133, Audits of States, Local Governments, and Non-Profit Organizations.
- Other compliance audit requirements, such as state or local laws or program-specific audits under federal audit guides.

1) Governmental Audits (GAGAS)
Per GAGAS 4.22: If auditors report separately (including separate reports bound in the same document) on internal control over financial reporting **and on compliance with provisions of laws, regulations, contracts, and grant agreements**, they should state in the auditors' report on the financial statements that they are issuing those additional reports. They should include a reference to the separate reports and also state that the reports on internal control over financial reporting and on compliance with provisions of laws, regulations, contracts, and grant agreements are an integral part of a GAGAS audit in considering the audited entity's internal control over financial reporting and compliance.

Per GAGAS 4.23: When performing GAGAS financial audits, auditors should communicate in the report on internal control over financial reporting and compliance, based upon the work performed, (1) significant deficiencies and material weaknesses in internal control; (2) instances of fraud and noncompliance with provisions of laws or regulations that have a material effect on the audit and any other instances that warrant the attention of those charged with governance; (3) noncompliance with provisions of contracts or grant agreements that has a material effect on the audit; and (4) abuse that has a material effect on the audit.

Per GAGAS 4.24: The AICPA requirements to communicate in writing significant deficiencies and material weaknesses identified during an audit form the basis for reporting significant deficiencies and material weaknesses in the GAGAS report on internal control over financial reporting when deficiencies are identified during the audit.

Multiple Choice

AUD 1-Q45 through AUD 1-Q46

G. A Firm's System of Quality Control, Including Quality Control at The Engagement Level

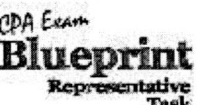

> Recognize a CPA firm's responsibilities for its accounting and auditing practice's system of quality control.

The objective of the firm is to establish and maintain a system of quality control to provide it with reasonable assurance that (QC 10.12):
- The firm and its personnel comply with professional standards and applicable legal and regulatory requirements, and
- Reports issued by the firm are appropriate in the circumstances.

a. **Elements of a system of quality control**
Per the AICPA quality control standards, the firm must establish and maintain a system of quality control. The system of quality control should include policies and procedures addressing each of the following elements:
   1) Leadership responsibilities for quality within the firm (the tone at the top)
   2) Relevant ethical requirements
   3) Acceptance and continuance of client relationships and specific engagements
   4) Human resources
   5) Engagement performance
   6) Monitoring

The firm should document its policies and procedures and communicate them to the firm's personnel. Although communication is enhanced if it is in writing, the communication of quality control policies and procedures is not required to be in writing.

   1) Leadership Responsibilities for Quality Within the Firm
   The firm should establish policies and procedures designed to promote an internal culture based on the recognition that quality is essential in performing engagements. Such policies and procedures should require the firm's leadership (managing partner or board of managing partners, CEO, or equivalent) to assume ultimate responsibility for the firm's system of quality control.

   2) Relevant Ethical Requirements
   The firm should establish policies and procedures designed to provide it with reasonable assurance that the firm and its personnel comply with relevant ethical requirements.

   The firm should establish policies and procedures designed to provide it with reasonable assurance that the firm; its personnel; and, when applicable, others subject to independence requirements (including network firm personnel) maintain independence when required by relevant ethical requirements. Such policies and procedures should enable the firm to
   - communicate its independence requirements to its personnel and, when applicable, others subject to them and
   - identify and evaluate circumstances and relationships that create threats to independence and to take appropriate action to eliminate those threats or reduce them to an acceptable level by applying safeguards or, if considered appropriate, to withdraw from the engagement when withdrawal is possible under applicable law or regulation.
   - At least annually, the firm should obtain **written confirmation of compliance with its policies and procedures on independence from all firm personnel** required to be independent by the requirements set forth in the "Independence Rule" (ET sec.

1.200.001) and related interpretations of the AICPA Code of Professional Conduct and the rules of state boards of accountancy and applicable regulatory agencies.

The firm should establish policies and procedures for all audit or attestation engagements for which regulatory or other authorities require the **rotation of personnel** after a specified period, in compliance with such requirements.

3) Acceptance and Continuance of Client Relationships and Specific Engagements
The firm should establish policies and procedures for the acceptance and continuance of client relationships and specific engagements, designed to provide the firm with reasonable assurance that it will undertake or continue relationships and engagements only when the firm
- is competent to perform the engagement and has the capabilities, including time and resources, to do so;
- can comply with legal and relevant ethical requirements; and
- has considered the integrity of the client and does not have information that would lead it to conclude that the client lacks integrity.

To minimize the risk of misunderstandings regarding the nature, scope, and limitations of the services to be performed, the firm should establish policies and procedures that provide for **obtaining an understanding with the client** regarding those services.

4) Human Resources
The firm should establish policies and procedures designed to provide it with reasonable assurance that it has sufficient personnel with the competence, capabilities, and commitment to ethical principles necessary to
- perform engagements in accordance with professional standards and applicable legal and regulatory requirements and
- enable the firm to issue reports that are appropriate in the circumstances.

The firm should establish policies and procedures to assign appropriate personnel with the necessary competence and capabilities to
- perform engagements in accordance with professional standards and applicable legal and regulatory requirements and
- enable the firm to issue reports that are appropriate in the circumstances.

5) Engagement Performance
The firm should establish policies and procedures designed to provide it with reasonable assurance that engagements are performed in accordance with professional standards and applicable legal and regulatory requirements and that the firm issues reports that are appropriate in the circumstances. Such policies and procedures should include the following:
- Matters relevant to promoting consistency in the quality of engagement performance
- Supervision responsibilities
- Review responsibilities

The firm should establish policies and procedures for addressing and resolving **differences of opinion** within the engagement team; with those consulted; and, when applicable, between the engagement partner and the engagement quality control reviewer. Such policies and procedures should enable a member of the engagement team to document that member's disagreement with the conclusions reached after appropriate consultation.

The firm should establish policies and procedures for engagement teams to complete the assembly of **final engagement files** on a timely basis after the engagement reports have been released.

The firm should establish policies and procedures for the **retention of engagement documentation** for a period sufficient to meet the needs of the firm, professional standards, laws, and regulations.

6) Monitoring
The firm should establish a monitoring process designed to provide it with reasonable assurance that the policies and procedures relating to the system of quality control are relevant, adequate, and operating effectively. This process should
- include an ongoing consideration and evaluation of the firm's system of quality control, including inspection or a periodic review of engagement documentation, reports, and clients' financial statements for a selection of completed engagements;
- require responsibility for the monitoring process to be assigned to a partner or partners or other persons with sufficient and appropriate experience and authority in the firm to assume that responsibility; and
- assign the performance of monitoring the firm's system of quality control to qualified individuals.

The firm should communicate to relevant engagement partners, and other appropriate personnel, deficiencies noted as a result of the monitoring process and recommendations for appropriate remedial action.

The firm should communicate, at least annually, the **results of the monitoring** of its system of quality control to engagement partners and other appropriate individuals within the firm, including the firm's leadership. This communication should be sufficient to enable the firm and these individuals to take prompt and appropriate action, when necessary, in accordance with their defined roles and responsibilities to provide a basis for them to rely on the firm's system of quality control. Information communicated should include the following:
- A description of the monitoring procedures performed
- The conclusions drawn from the monitoring procedures
- When relevant, a description of systemic, repetitive, or other significant deficiencies and of the actions taken to resolve or amend those deficiencies

The firm should establish policies and procedures designed to provide it with reasonable assurance that it deals appropriately with
- **complaints and allegations** that the work performed by the firm fails to comply with professional standards and applicable legal and regulatory requirements and
- **allegations of noncompliance** with the firm's system of quality control.

b. **Documentation of quality control**
   The firm should establish policies and procedures requiring appropriate documentation to provide evidence of the operation of each element of its system of quality control.

   The firm should establish policies and procedures that require retention of documentation for a period of time sufficient to permit those performing monitoring procedures and peer review of the firm to evaluate the firm's compliance with its system of quality control or for a longer period if required by law or regulation.

Apply quality control procedures on an audit or non-audit engagement.

The engagement partner should take responsibility for the overall quality on each audit engagement to which that partner is assigned. In fulfilling this responsibility, the engagement partner may delegate the performance of certain procedures to, and use the work of, other members of the engagement team and may rely upon the firm's system of quality control.

Within the context of the firm's system of quality control, engagement teams have a responsibility to implement quality control procedures that are applicable to the audit engagement and provide the firm with relevant information to enable the functioning of that part of the firm's system of quality control relating to **independence**.

The engagement partner should form a conclusion on **compliance with independence requirements** that apply to the audit engagement.

The objective of the auditor is to implement quality control procedures at the engagement level that provide the auditor with reasonable assurance that
- the audit complies with professional standards and applicable legal and regulatory requirements and
- the auditor's report issued is appropriate in the circumstances.

The engagement partner should take responsibility for the overall quality on each audit engagement to which that partner is assigned. In fulfilling this responsibility, the engagement partner may delegate the performance of certain procedures to, and use the work of, other members of the engagement team and may rely upon the firm's system of quality control.

The engagement partner should be satisfied that appropriate procedures regarding the **acceptance and continuance of client relationships** and audit engagements have been followed and should determine that conclusions reached in this regard are appropriate.

The engagement partner should be satisfied that the engagement team and any auditor's external specialists, collectively, have the **appropriate competence and capabilities** to
- perform the audit engagement in accordance with professional standards and applicable legal and regulatory requirements and
- enable an auditor's report that is appropriate in the circumstances to be issued.

On or before the date of the auditor's report, the engagement partner should, through a review of the audit documentation and discussion with the engagement team, be satisfied that **sufficient appropriate audit evidence has been obtained** to support the conclusions reached and for the auditor's report to be issued.

   1) Documentation
      The auditor should include in the audit documentation the following:

a) Issues identified with respect to compliance with relevant **ethical requirements** and how they were resolved
b) Conclusions on compliance with **independence requirements** that apply to the audit engagement and any relevant discussions with the firm that support these conclusions
c) Conclusions reached regarding the **acceptance and continuance of client relationships** and audit engagements
d) The nature and scope of, and conclusions resulting from, **consultations** undertaken during the course of the audit engagement

Multiple Choice

AUD 1-Q47 through AUD 1-Q50

Glossary: Ethics, Professional Responsibilities and General Principles

A

Acceptable level – level at which a reasonable and informed third party, who is aware of the relevant information, would be expected to conclude that a member's independence is not impaired

Accounting and auditing practice – A practice that performs engagements including audit, attestation, compilation, review, and any other services for which standards have been promulgated by the AICPA Auditing Standards Board (ASB) or the AICPA Accounting and Review Services Committee (ARSC)

Affiliate – an entity such as a subsidiary, partnership, or limited liability company [LLC]) that a financial statement attest client can control

Analytical procedures – evaluations of financial information through analysis of plausible relationships among both financial and nonfinancial data

Applicable financial reporting framework – the financial reporting framework adopted by management and, when appropriate, those charged with governance in the preparation and fair presentation of the financial statements, that is acceptable in view of the nature of the entity and the objective of the financial statements, or that is required by law or regulation

Attest client – a client that engages a member to perform an attest engagement or with respect to which a member performs an attest engagement

Attest engagement – an engagement that requires independence, as set forth in the AICPA Statements on Auditing Standards (SASs), Statements on Standards for Accounting and Review Services (SSARSs), and Statements on Standards for Attestation Engagements (SSAEs)

Attest engagement team – those individuals participating in the attest engagement, including those who perform concurring and engagement quality reviews

Audit documentation – the record of audit procedures performed, relevant audit evidence obtained, and conclusions the auditor reached (terms such as working papers or workpapers are also sometimes used)

Audit evidence – information used by the auditor in arriving at the conclusions on which the auditor's opinion is based

Audit file – one or more folders or other storage media, in physical or electronic form, containing the records that constitute the audit documentation for a specific engagement

Audit risk – the risk that the auditor may express an inappropriate audit opinion when the financial statements are materially misstated; audit risk is a function of the risks of material misstatement and detection risk

Auditor – the term used to refer to the person or persons conducting the audit, usually the engagement partner or other members of the engagement team, or, as applicable, the firm

B

Basic financial statements – financial statements excluding supplementary information and required supplementary information

Beneficially owned – describes a financial interest of which an individual or entity is not the record owner but has a right to some or all of the underlying benefits of ownership

C

Client – any person or entity, other than the member's employer, that engages a member or member's firm to perform professional services and, if different, the person or entity with respect to which professional services are performed

Close relative – a parent, sibling, or nondependent child

Comparative financial statements – a complete set of financial statements for one or more prior periods included for comparison with the financial statements of the current period

Component – an entity or business activity for which group or component management prepares financial information that is required by the applicable financial reporting framework to be included in the group financial statements

Component auditor – an auditor who performs work on the financial information of a component that will be used as audit evidence for the group audit. A component auditor may be part of the group engagement partner's firm, a network firm of the group engagement partner's firm, or another firm

Component management – management responsible for preparing the financial information of a component

Component materiality – the materiality for a component determined by the group engagement team for the purposes of the group audit

Confidential client information – any information obtained from the client that is not available to the public

Control risk – the risk that a misstatement that could occur in an assertion about a class of transaction, account balance, or disclosure and that could be material, either individually or when aggregated with other misstatements, will not be prevented, or detected and corrected, on a timely basis by the entity's internal control

Council – the AICPA Council

Covered member – an individual on the attest engagement team; an individual in a position to influence the attest engagement; or a partner, partner equivalent, or manager who provides more than 10 hours of non-attest services to the attest client within any fiscal year

D

Designated accounting standard-setter – a body designated by the Council of the AICPA to promulgate accounting principles generally accepted in the U.S.

Detection risk – the risk that the procedures performed by the auditor to reduce audit risk to an acceptably low level will not detect a misstatement that exists and that could be material, either individually or when aggregated with other misstatements

Direct financial interest – a financial interest that is owned directly by an individual or entity; or under the control of an individual or entity; or beneficially owned through an investment vehicle, estate, trust, or other intermediary when the beneficiary controls the intermediary or has the authority to supervise or participate in the intermediary's investment decisions

Documentation completion date – the date, no later than 60 days following the report release date, on which the auditor has assembled for retention a complete and final set of documentation in an audit file

E

Emphasis-of-matter paragraph – a paragraph included in the accountant's review report that is required by SSARSs, or is included at the accountant's discretion, and that refers to a matter appropriately presented or disclosed in the financial statements that, in the accountant's professional judgment, is of such importance that it is fundamental to the users' understanding of the financial statements

Engagement documentation – The record of the work performed, results obtained, and conclusions that the practitioner reached (also known as working papers or workpapers)

Engagement partner – the partner, or other person in the firm, who is responsible for the engagement and its performance and for the report that is issued on behalf of the firm and who, when required, has the appropriate authority from a professional, legal, or regulatory body

Engagement quality control review – a process designed to provide an objective evaluation, before the report is released, of the significant judgments the engagement team made and the conclusions it reached in formulating the report

Engagement quality control reviewer – a partner, other person in the firm, suitably qualified external person, outside of the engagement team, with sufficient and appropriate experience and authority to objectively evaluate the significant judgments that the engagement team made and the conclusions it reached in formulating the report

Engagement team – all partners and staff performing the engagement and any individuals engaged by the firm or a network firm who perform procedures on the engagement (excludes external specialists and client's internal audit function who provide direct assistance)

Error – mistakes in the financial statements, including arithmetical or clerical mistakes, and mistakes in the application of accounting principles, including inadequate disclosures

Experienced accountant – an individual (whether internal or external to the firm) who has practical review experience and a reasonable understanding of review processes; SSARSs and applicable legal and regulatory requirements; the business environment in which the entity operates; and review and financial reporting issues relevant to the entity's industry

Experienced auditor – an individual (whether internal or external to the firm) who has practical audit experience, and a reasonable understanding of audit processes; GAAS and applicable legal and regulatory requirements; the business environment in which the entity operates; and auditing and financial reporting issues relevant to the entity's industry

F

Financial interest – an ownership interest in an equity or a debt security issued by an entity, including rights and obligations to acquire such an interest and derivatives directly related to such interest

Financial reporting framework – a set of criteria used to determine measurement, recognition, presentation, and disclosure of all material items appearing in the financial statements (e.g., GAAP or IFRS)

Fair presentation framework – term used to refer to a financial reporting framework that requires compliance with the requirements of the framework and (a) acknowledges explicitly or implicitly that, to achieve fair presentation of the financial statements, it may be necessary for management to provide disclosures beyond those specifically required by the framework; or (b) acknowledges explicitly that it may be necessary for management to depart from a requirement of the framework to achieve fair presentation of the financial statements

Financial statement attest client – an entity whose financial statements are audited, reviewed, or compiled when the member's compilation report does not disclose a lack of independence

Financial statements – a structured representation of historical financial information, including related notes and disclosures, intended to communicate an entity's economic resources and obligations at a point in time or the changes therein for a period of time in accordance with a financial reporting framework

Firm – a form of organization permitted by law or regulation whose characteristics conform to resolutions of the Council of the AICPA and that is engaged in the practice of public accounting

Fraud – an intentional act that results in a misstatement in financial statements

G

Generally accepted accounting principles (GAAP) – agreed-upon rules and standards of financial reporting

Group – all the components whose financial information is included in the group financial statements; a group always has more than one component

Group audit – the audit of group financial statements

Group management – management responsible for the preparation and fair presentation of the group financial statements

Group-wide controls – controls designed, implemented, and maintained by group management over group financial reporting

H

Historical financial information – *i*nformation expressed in financial terms regarding a particular entity, derived primarily from that entity's accounting system, about economic events occurring in past time periods or about economic conditions or circumstances at points in time in the past.

I

Immediate family – a spouse, spousal equivalent, or dependent (regardless of whether the dependent is related).

Impaired – in connection with independence, to effectively extinguish independence (e.g., when a member's independence is impaired, the member is not independent)

Independence – state of mind that permits a member to perform an attest service without being affected by influences that compromise professional judgment, thereby allowing an individual to act with integrity and exercise objectivity and professional skepticism and avoidance of circumstances that would cause a reasonable and informed third party, who has knowledge of all relevant information, including the safeguards applied, to reasonably conclude that the integrity, objectivity, or professional skepticism of a firm or member of the attest engagement team is compromised

Indirect financial interest – a financial interest beneficially owned through an investment vehicle, an estate, a trust, or another intermediary, when the beneficiary neither controls the intermediary nor has the authority to supervise or participate in the intermediary's investment decisions

Inherent risk – the susceptibility of an assertion about a class of transaction, account balance, or disclosure to a misstatement that could be material, either individually or when aggregated with other misstatements, before consideration of any related controls

Inspection – a retrospective evaluation of the adequacy of the firm's quality control policies and procedures, its personnel's understanding of those policies and procedures, and the extent of the firm's compliance with them

Interpretation – pronouncements issued by the division of professional ethics to provide guidelines concerning the scope and application of the rules of conduct

J
Joint closely held investment – an investment in an entity or a property by the member and client (or the client's officers or directors or any owner who has the ability to exercise significant influence over the client) that enables them to control the entity or property

K
Key position – a position in which an individual has primary responsibility for significant accounting functions that support material components of the financial statements; primary responsibility for the preparation of the financial statements; or he ability to exercise influence over the contents of the financial statement (e.g., member of board of directors, CEO, CFO, COO, controller, director of internal audit, treasurer)

L
Lending institution – an entity that, as part of its normal business operations, makes loans

Loan – a contractual obligation to pay or right to receive money on demand or on a fixed or determinable date and includes a stated or implied rate of return to the lender (includes letter of credit, a line of credit, or a loan commitment; but not debt securities or leases).

M
Management – the person(s) with executive responsibility for the conduct of the entity's operations. For some entities, management includes some or all of those charged with governance; for example, executive members of a governance board or an owner-manager

Manager – a professional employee of the firm who has continuing responsibility for the planning and supervision of engagements for specified clients

Member – a member, associate member, affiliate member, or international associate of the AICPA

Member(s) in business – a member who is employed or engaged on a contractual or volunteer basis in a(n) executive, staff, governance, advisory, or administrative capacity in such areas as industry, the public sector, education, the not-for-profit sector, and regulatory or professional bodies (not a member engaged in public practice)

Misstatement – a difference between the amount, classification, presentation, or disclosure of a reported financial statement item what is required for the item to be presented fairly in accordance with the applicable financial reporting framework

Monitoring – a process comprising an ongoing consideration and evaluation of the firm's system of quality control

N
Network – a network is an association of entities that includes one or more firms that cooperate for the purpose of enhancing the firms' capabilities to provide professional services and share a brand name, common control, profits or costs, business strategy, professional resources, or quality control policies

Network firm – a firm or other entity that belongs to a network

Noncompliance – acts of omission or commission by the entity, either intentional or unintentional, which are contrary to the prevailing laws or regulations

Normal lending procedures, terms, and requirements – lending procedures, terms, and requirements that are reasonably comparable with those relating to loans of a similar character committed to other borrowers during the period in which the loan to the covered member is committed

O
Office – a reasonably distinct subgroup within a firm, whether constituted by formal organization or informal practice, in which personnel who make up the subgroup generally serve the same group of clients or work on the same categories of matters

Other-matter paragraph – a paragraph included in the accountant's review report that is required by SSARSs, or is included at the accountant's discretion, and that refers to a matter other than those presented or disclosed in the financial statements that, in the accountant's professional judgment, is relevant to users' understanding of the review, the accountant's responsibilities, or the accountant's review report

P
Partner – a proprietor, a shareholder, an equity or a non-equity partner, or any individual who assumes the risks and benefits of firm ownership

Partner equivalent – z professional employee who is not a partner of the firm but who either has the ultimate responsibility for the conduct of an attest engagement, including the authority to sign or affix the firm's name to an attest report or issue, or authorize others to issue, an attest report on behalf of the firm without partner approval

Period of the professional engagement – the period begins when a member either signs an initial engagement letter or begins to perform an attest engagement for a client, whichever is earlier; the period ends with the formal or informal notification of the termination of the professional relationship or by the issuance of a report, whichever is later

Personnel – partners and staff

Professional judgment – the application of relevant training, knowledge, and experience, within the context provided by auditing, accounting, and ethical standards, in making informed decisions about the courses of action that are appropriate in the circumstances of the audit engagement

Professional services – all services requiring accountancy or related skills that are performed by a member for a client, an employer, or on a volunteer basis

Professional skepticism – an attitude that includes a questioning mind, being alert to conditions that may indicate possible misstatement due to fraud or error, and a critical assessment of audit evidence

Public interest entities – all listed entities, including entities that are outside the United States whose shares, stock, or debt are quoted or listed on a recognized stock exchange or marketed under the regulations of a recognized stock exchange or other equivalent body

Public practice – performance of professional services for a client by a member or member's firm

Q

R

Reasonable assurance – a high, but not absolute, level of assurance.

Relevant ethical requirements – ethical requirements to which the firm and its personnel are subject, which consist of the AICPA Code of Professional Conduct together with rules of applicable state boards of accountancy and applicable regulatory agencies that are more restrictive

Report release date – the date the auditor grants the entity permission to use the auditor's report in connection with the financial statements

Required supplementary information – information that a designated accounting standards-setter requires to accompany an entity's basic financial statements

Review documentation – the record of review procedures performed, relevant review evidence obtained, and conclusions the accountant reached (terms such as working papers or workpapers are also sometimes used)

Review evidence – information used by the accountant to provide a reasonable basis for obtaining limited assurance.

Risk of material misstatement – the risk that the financial statements are materially misstated prior to the audit

S

Safeguards – actions or other measures that may eliminate a threat or reduce a threat to an acceptable level

Significant component – a component identified by the group engagement team (i) that is of individual financial significance to the group, or (ii) that, due to its specific nature or circumstances, is likely to include significant risks of material misstatement of the group financial statements

Source documents – the documents upon which evidence of an accounting transaction are initially recorded

Special purpose framework – A financial reporting framework other than GAAP that is one of the following bases of accounting: a. **Cash basis** – A basis of accounting that the entity uses to record cash receipts and disbursements and modifications of the cash basis having substantial support (for example, recording depreciation on fixed assets). b. **Tax basis** – A basis of accounting that the entity uses to file its tax return for the period covered by the financial statements. c. **Regulatory basis** – A basis of accounting that the entity uses to comply with the requirements or financial reporting provisions of a regulatory agency to whose jurisdiction the entity is subject (for example, a basis of accounting that insurance companies use pursuant to the accounting practices prescribed or permitted by a state insurance commission). d. **Contractual basis** – A basis of accounting that the entity uses to comply with an agreement between the entity and one or more third parties other than the accountant. e. **Other basis** – A basis of accounting that uses a definite set of logical, reasonable criteria that is applied to all material items appearing in financial statements. The cash-basis, tax-basis, regulatory-basis, and other-basis of accounting are commonly referred to as other comprehensive bases of accounting (OCBOA).

Specified parties – the intended users of the accountant's review report

Staff – professionals, other than partners, including any specialists that the firm employs

Subsequent events – events occurring between the date of the financial statements and the date of the accountant's review report

Subsequently discovered facts – facts that become known to the accountant after the date of the accountant's review report that, had they been known to the accountant at that date, may have caused the accountant to revise the accountant's review report

Suitably qualified external person – an individual outside the firm with the competence and capabilities to act as an engagement partner (for example, a partner of another firm)

Supplementary information – information presented outside the basic financial statements, excluding required supplementary information, that is not considered necessary for the financial statements to be fairly presented in accordance with the applicable financial reporting framework

T

Third-party service provider – an entity that the member does not control, individually or collectively with his or her firm or with members of his or her firm; an individual not employed by the member who assists the member in providing professional services to clients (for example, bookkeeping, tax return preparation, consulting, or attest services, including related clerical and data entry functions)

Those charged with governance – the person(s) or organization(s) (for example, a corporate trustee) with responsibility for overseeing the strategic direction of the entity and the obligations related to the accountability of the entity, including overseeing the financial reporting process

Threat(s) – in connection with independence, threats are relationships or circumstances that could impair independence

U

Updated report – a report issued by a continuing accountant that takes into consideration information that the accountant becomes aware of during the accountant's current engagement and that re-expresses the accountant's previous conclusions or, depending on the circumstances, expresses different conclusions on the financial statements of a prior period reviewed by the accountant as of the date of the accountant's current report

V

W

Written representation – a written statement by management provided to the accountant to confirm certain matters or to support other review evidence

X

Y

Z

Multiple Choice – Questions

AUD 1-Q1 A1358. What is the definition of fraud in an audit of financial statements?

A. An intentional act that results in a material misstatement in financial statements that are the subject of an audit.
B. The unintentional misapplication of accounting principles relating to amounts, classification, manner of presentation, or disclosure.
C. An intentional act that results in a material weakness in financial statements that are the subject of an audit.
D. Management's inability to design and implement programs and controls to prevent, deter, and detect material misstatements.

AUD 1-Q2 A1373. A CPA was engaged to audit the financial statements of a municipality that received federal financial assistance and that required a Single Audit for compliance with the terms of the financial assistance. Which of the following guidelines should the CPA consider?

	Generally Accepted Auditing Standards	Government Auditing Standards
A.	Yes	Yes
B.	Yes	No
C.	No	Yes
D.	No	No

AUD 1-Q3 A1356. Which of the following services provides the least assurance regarding the fairness of financial statements?

A. Review.
B. Audit.
C. Compilation.
D. Attestation.

AUD 1-Q4 A376. The concept of materiality would be least important to an auditor in determining the

A. Transactions that should be reviewed.
B. Need for disclosure of a particular fact or transaction.
C. Scope of the CPA's audit program relating to various accounts.
D. Effects of direct financial interest in the client upon the CPA's independence.

AUD 1-Q5 A180. A CPA purchased stock in a client corporation and placed it in a trust as an educational fund for the CPA's minor child. The trust securities are not material to the CPA's wealth but are material to the child's personal net worth. According to the AICPA Code of Professional Conduct, would this action impair the CPA's independence with the client?

A. No, because the CPA would not have a direct financial interest in the client.
B. Yes, because the stock would be a direct financial interest and materiality is a factor.
C. Yes, because the stock would be an indirect financial interest and materiality is not a factor.
D. Yes, because the stock would be a direct financial interest and materiality is not a factor.

AUD 1-Q6 A120. Under the ethical standards of the profession, which of the following is a "permitted loan" regardless of the date it was obtained?

A. Home mortgage loan.
B. Student loan.
C. Secured automobile loan.
D. Personal loan.

AUD 1-Q7 A153. A CPA audits the financial statements of a client. The CPA has also been asked to perform bookkeeping functions for the client. Under the AICPA Code of Professional Conduct, which of the following activities would impair the CPA's independence with respect to the client?

A. The CPA records transactions in accordance with classifications determined by management.
B. The CPA prepares financial statements from a trial balance provided by management.
C. The CPA posts adjusting journal entries prepared by management to the trial balance.
D. The CPA authorizes client transactions and reports them to management.

AUD 1-Q8 A88. Which of the following situations would not impair objectivity, integrity, or independence with respect to an audit client?

A. An auditor takes the client's audit committee to Las Vegas for the weekend.
B. An out-of-town client takes the audit engagement team out to dinner at a renowned local restaurant.
C. An auditor provides client management with box seats for the season at a major league baseball franchise.
D. A client takes the audit engagement team on a two-day ski trip after the audit team worked for two consecutive weekends.

AUD 1-Q9 A421. A CPA's retention of client's records as a means of enforcing payment of an overdue audit fee is an action that is

A. Not addressed by the AICPA Code of Professional Ethics.
B. Acceptable if sanctioned by state laws.
C. Prohibited under the AICPA rules of conduct.
D. A violation of generally accepted auditing standards.

AUD 1-Q10 A185. According to the AICPA Code of Professional Conduct, which of the following actions by a CPA most likely involves an act discreditable to the profession?

A. Refusing to provide the client with copies of the CPA's workpapers.
B. Auditing financial statements according to governmental auditing standards despite the client's preferences not to.
C. Accepting a commission from a non-attest function client.
D. Retaining client records after the client demands their return.

AUD 1-Q11 A124. According to the Code of Professional Conduct of the AICPA, for which type of service may a CPA receive a contingent fee?

A. Performing an audit of a financial statement.
B. Performing a review of a financial statement.
C. Performing an examination of prospective financial information.
D. Seeking a private letter ruling.

AUD 1-Q12 A135. In which of the following circumstances would a covered member's independence be impaired with respect to a nonissuer client?

A. The member is designated to serve as guardian of a friend's children if the need arises, and the friend's estate, which would be held in trust for the children, holds significant stock ownership in a client entity.
B. The member's spouse qualifies because of geographical residence to belong to a client's credit union, and all transactions with the credit union are conducted under normal operating practices.
C. The member owns municipal utility bonds issued by a client, and the bonds are not material to the member's wealth.
D. The member belongs to a client golf club that requires members to acquire a share of the club's debt securities.

AUD 1-Q13 A111. The Public Company Accounting Oversight Board was established by which of the following?

A. The Financial Accounting Standards Board.
B. The American Institute of Certified Public Accountants.
C. The Sarbanes-Oxley Act of 2002.
D. The International Accounting Standards Board.

AUD 1-Q14 A87. According to the Sarbanes-Oxley Act of 2002, which of the following non-audit services can be provided by a registered public accounting firm to the client contemporaneously with the audit when preapproval is granted by audit committee action?

A. Internal audit outsourcing services.
B. Tax services
C. Actuarial services related to the audit.
D. Advice on financial information system design.

AUD 1-Q15 A137. A cooling-off period of how many years is required before a member of an issuer's audit engagement team may begin working for the registrant in a key position?

A. One year.
B. Two years.
C. Three years.
D. Four years.

AUD 1-Q16 A165. An issuer may hire an employee of a registered public accounting firm who served on the audit engagement team within the previous year for which of the following positions?

A. Controller.
B. CFO.
C. CEO.
D. Staff accountant.

AUD 1-Q17 A449. Which of the following is not a requirement imposed by The SEC on public companies to strengthen auditor independence?

A. Engage auditors to report in accordance with the Foreign Corrupt Practices Act.
B. Issuers must report the nature of disagreements with the former auditors.
C. Issuers select auditors through audit committees.
D. Management acknowledges their responsibility for the fairness of the financial statements.

AUD 1-Q18 A115. According to the Sarbanes-Oxley Act of 2002, what is the maximum number of years an audit partner can perform audit services for an issuer before the auditor rotation is required?

A. 2 years.
B. 3 years.
C. 4 years.
D. 5 years

AUD 1-Q19 A66. An accountant can perform, with preapproval of the audit committee of the board of directors, which of the following non-audit services during the audit of an issuer?

A. Bookkeeping services
B. Human resource services.
C. Tax planning services.
D. Internal audit outsourcing services.

AUD 1-Q20 A189. According to the SEC, an auditor is not independent of its issuer audit client in which of the following situations?

A. The auditor's cousin has an insurance policy obtained from the issuer before it became an audit client.
B. The auditor has an automobile loan at standard terms from the audit client that is collateralized by the automobile.
C. The auditor has an investment in an entity that has the ability to exercise significant influence over the audit client.
D. The auditor's grandparent was in an accounting role at the audit client and ended employment before the period under audit began.

AUD 1-Q21 A91. According to the SEC, members of an issuer's audit committee may not

A. Establish procedures for employees to anonymously report fraud.
B. Be responsible for the compensation of any registered public accounting firm employed by the registrant to provide an audit report.
C. Accept any consulting, advisory, or other compensatory fee from the registrant for services other than as a member of the board.
D. Engage independent counsel as deemed necessary to carry out their duties.

AUD 1-Q22 A67. The controller of a small utility company has interviewed audit firms proposing to perform the annual audit of their employee benefit plan. According to the guidelines of the Department of Labor (DOL), the selected auditor must be

A. The firm that proposes the lowest fee for the work required.
B. Independent for purposes of examining financial information required to be filed annually with the DOL.
C. Included on the list of firms approved by the DOL.
D. From the same organization that performs the audit of the Company's financial statements

AUD 1-Q23 A293. Which of the following conditions most likely would pose the greatest risk in accepting a new audit engagement?

A. Staff will need to be rescheduled to cover this new client.
B. There will be a client-imposed scope limitation.
C. The firm will have to hire a specialist in one audit area.
D. The client's financial reporting system has been in place for 10 years.

AUD 1-Q24 A378. It is important for the CPA to consider the competence of the audit clients' employees because their competence bears directly and importantly upon the

A. Cost/benefit relationship of the system of internal control.
B. Achievement of the objectives of the system of internal control.
C. Comparison of recorded accountability with assets.
D. Timing of the tests to be performed.

AUD 1-Q25 A150. Before accepting an engagement to audit a new client, a CPA is required to obtain

A. An assessment of fraud risk factors likely to cause material misstatements.
B. An understanding of the prospective client's industry and business.
C. The prospective client's signature to a written engagement letter.
D. The prospective client's consent to make inquiries of the predecessor, if any.

AUD 1-Q26 A41. While auditing the financial statements of a nonpublic entity, a CPA was requested to change the audit engagement to a review engagement because of a scope limitation. If the CPA believes the client's request is reasonable, the CPA's review report should

  I. Refer to the scope limitation that caused the change.
  II. Describe the auditing procedures that have already been applied.

A. I only.
B. II only.
C. Both I and II.
D. Neither I nor II.

AUD 1-Q27 A245. An accountant agrees to the client's request to change an engagement from a review to a compilation of financial statements. The compilation report should include

A. No reference to the original engagement.
B. Reference to a departure from GAAS.
C. Scope limitations that may have resulted in the change of engagement.
D. Information about review procedures already performed.

AUD 1-Q28 A149. A CPA started to audit the financial statements of a nonissuer. After completing certain audit procedures, the client requested the CPA to change the engagement to a review because of a scope limitation. The CPA concludes that there is reasonable justification for the change. Under these circumstances, the CPA's review report should include a

A. Statement that a review is substantially less in scope than an audit.
B. Reference to the scope limitation that caused the changed engagement.
C. Description of the auditing procedures that were completed before the engagement was changed.
D. Reference to the CPA's justification for agreeing to change the engagement.

AUD 1-Q29 A138. A CPA is engaged to audit the financial statements of a nonissuer. After the audit begins, the client's management questions the extent of procedures and objects to the confirmation of certain contracts. The client asks the accountant to change the scope of the engagement from an audit to a review. Under these circumstances, the accountant should do each of the following, except

A. Issue an accountant's review report with a separate paragraph discussing the change in engagement scope.
B. Consider the additional audit effort and cost required to complete the audit.
C. Evaluate the possibility that financial statement information affected by the limitation on work to be performed may be incorrect or incomplete.
D. Consider the reason given for the client's request and assess whether the request is reasonable.

AUD 1-Q30 A62. The understanding with the client regarding a financial statement audit generally includes which of the following matters?

A. The expected opinion to be issued.
B. The responsibilities of the auditor.
C. The contingency fee structure.
D. The preliminary judgment about materiality.

AUD 1-Q31 A11. Which of the following factors most likely would cause a CPA to decline to accept a new audit engagement?

A. The CPA does **not** understand the entity's operations and industry.
B. Management acknowledges that the entity has had recurring operating losses.
C. The CPA is unable to review the predecessor auditor's working papers.
D. Management is unwilling to permit inquiry of its legal counsel.

AUD 1-Q32 A272. Which of the following statements most likely would be included in an engagement letter from an auditor to a client?

A. The CPA firm will provide absolute assurance about whether the financial statements are free of material misstatement.
B. The CPA firm is responsible for ensuring that the client complies with applicable laws.
C. The CPA firm will involve information technology specialists in the performance of the audit.
D. The CPA firm will adjust the financial statements to correct misstatements before issuing a report.

AUD 1-Q33 A369. The understanding between the client and the auditor as to the degree of responsibilities to be assumed by each are normally set forth in a (an)

A. Representation letter.
B. Engagement letter.
C. Management letter.
D. Comfort letter.

AUD 1-Q34 A82. Which of the following matters does an auditor usually include in the engagement letter?

A. Arrangements regarding fees and billing.
B. Analytical procedures that the auditor plans to perform.
C. Indications of negative cash flows from operating activities.
D. Identification of working capital deficiencies.

AUD 1-Q35 A10. An auditor's engagement letter most likely would include a statement that

A. Lists significant deficiencies discovered during the prior-year's audit.
B. Explains the analytical procedures that the auditor expects to apply.
C. Describes the auditor's responsibility to evaluate going-concern issues.
D. Limits the auditor's responsibility to detect errors and fraud.

AUD 1-Q36 A209. Which of the following circumstances would permit an independent auditor to accept an engagement after the close of the fiscal year?

A. Issuance of a disclaimer of opinion as a result of inability to conduct certain tests required by generally accepted auditing standards due to the timing of acceptance of the engagement.
B. Assessment of control risk below the maximum level.
C. Receipt of an assertion from the preceding auditor that the entity will be able to continue as a going concern.
D. Remedy of limitations resulting from accepting the engagement after the close of the end of the year, such as those relating to the existence of physical inventory.

AUD 1-Q37 A334. Which of the following statements is most accurate regarding sufficient and appropriate documentation?

A. Accounting estimates are not considered sufficient and appropriate documentation.
B. Sufficient and appropriate documentation should include evidence that the audit working papers have been reviewed.
C. If additional evidence is required to document significant findings or issues, the original evidence is not considered sufficient and appropriate and therefore should be deleted from the working papers.
D. Audit documentation is the property of the client, and sufficient and appropriate copies should be retained by the auditor for at least five years.

AUD 1-Q38 A1386. Which of the following statements is most accurate regarding audit documentation requirements?

A. The auditor should document findings that could result in a modification of the auditor's report.
B. If different audit procedures were performed due to a lack of responsiveness by the client, the lack of responsiveness should not be included in the working papers.
C. If an oral explanation serves as sufficient support for the work the auditor performed, the explanation should be documented in the working papers.
D. If the results of audit procedures indicate a need to revise the previous assessment of risk, the new assessment should be documented and the original assessment should be removed.

AUD 1-Q39 A1355. Which of the following statements is correct about actions taken after the documentation completion date?

A. An auditor must not make any amendments to audit documentation before the end of the specified retention period.
B. An auditor must not make any additions to audit documentation before the end of the specified retention period.
C. An auditor must not make any changes to audit documentation before the end of the specified retention period.
D. The auditor must not make any deletions to audit documentation before the end of the specified retention period.

AUD 1-Q40 A447. It would not be appropriate for the auditor to initiate discussion with the audit committee concerning

A. The extent to which the work of internal auditors will influence the scope of the audit.
B. Details of the procedures which the auditor intends to apply.
C. The extent to which change in the company's organization will influence the scope of the audit.
D. Details of potential problems which the auditor believes might cause a modified opinion.

AUD 1-Q41 A163. Which of the following is a correct statement regarding the nature and timing of communications between an accounting firm performing an initial audit of an issuer and the issuer's audit committee?

A. Prior to accepting the engagement, the firm must orally affirm its independence to the audit committee with all members present.
B. The firm must address all independence impairment issues on the date of the audit opinion.
C. Communications related to independence may occur in any form prior to issuance of the financial statements.
D. Prior to accepting the engagement, the firm should describe in writing all relationships that, as of the date of the communication, may reasonably be thought to bear on independence.

AUD 1-Q42 A113. Which of the following circumstances would be inappropriate for the auditor to communicate in writing to those charged with governance?

A. A material misstatement was noted by the auditor and corrected by management.
B. No significant deficiencies in internal control exist that would affect the financial statements.
C. The auditor is requesting representations regarding the financial statements from management.
D. Management has consulted with other accountants about accounting and auditing matters during the period under audit.

AUD 1-Q43 A31. Which of the following matters is an auditor required to communicate to an entity's audit committee?

A. Adjustments that were suggested by the auditor and recorded by management that have a significant effect on the entity's financial reporting process.
B. The auditor's consideration of risk factors in assessing the risk of material misstatement arising from the misappropriation of assets.
C. The results of the auditor's analytical procedures performed in the review stage of the engagement that indicate significant variances from expected amounts.
D. Changes in the auditor's preliminary judgment about materiality that were caused by projecting the results of statistical sampling for tests of transactions.

AUD 1-Q44 A1380. During an audit, an auditor discovers a fraudulent expense reimbursement for a low-level manager. The auditor determines that this transaction is inconsequential and several similar transactions would not be material to the financial statements in the aggregate. Which of the following statements best describes the auditor's required response to the discovery?

A. The auditor should fully investigate other transactions related to this manager to determine if fraud exists.
B. The auditor should bring the transaction to the attention of an appropriate level of management.
C. The auditor should report this finding to those charged with governance.
D. The auditor's responsibility is satisfied by documenting that the single transaction is inconsequential.

AUD 1-Q45 A12. An enterprise engaged a CPA to audit its financial statements in accordance with Government Auditing Standards (the Yellow Book) because of the provisions of government grant funding agreements. Under these circumstances, the CPA is required to report on the enterprise's internal controls either in the report on the financial statements or in

A. The report on the performance audit.
B. The notes to the financial statements.
C. A letter to the government funding agency.
D. A separate report.

AUD 1-Q46 A1384. An auditor determines that a client who received a federal grant fraudulently reported information to the federal government. The client's management refuses to acknowledge the fraud. Which of the following parties should the auditor contact first?

A. The state accountancy board.
B. The state attorney general's office.
C. The agency that provided the grant.
D. The recipients of the client's services.

AUD 1-Q47 A116. A CPA firm would best provide itself reasonable assurance of meeting its responsibility to offer professional services that conform with professional standards by

A. Establishing an understanding with each client concerning individual responsibilities in a signed engagement letter.
B. Assessing the risk that errors and fraud may cause the financial statements to contain material misstatements.
C. Developing specific audit objectives to support management's assertions that are embodied in the financial statements.
D. Maintaining a comprehensive system of quality control that is suitably designed in relation to its organizational structure.

AUD 1-Q48 A1121. A basic objective of a CPA firm is to provide professional services that conform with professional standards. Reasonable assurance of achieving this basic objective is provided through

A. A system of peer review.
B. Continuing professional education.
C. A system of quality control.
D. Compliance with generally accepted auditing standards.

AUD 1-Q49 A602. Within the context of quality control, the primary purpose of continuing professional education and training activities, is to enable a CPA firm to provide personnel within the firm with

A. Technical training that assures proficiency as an auditor.
B. Professional education that is required in order to perform with due professional care.
C. Knowledge required to fulfill assigned responsibilities and to satisfy applicable CPE requirements of the AICPA and regulatory agencies.
D. Knowledge required in order to perform a peer review.

AUD 1-Q50 A1042. In connection with the element of inspection, a CPA firm's system of quality control should ordinarily provide for the maintenance of

A. A file of minutes of staff meetings.
B. Updated personnel files.
C. Documentation to demonstrate compliance with its policies and procedures.
D. Documentation to demonstrate compliance with peer review directives.

Multiple Choice – Solutions

AUD 1-Q1 A1358. The correct answer choice is A. The definition of fraud is an intentional act resulting in a material misstatement in the financial statements.

Choice B is incorrect because it is an intentional, not an unintentional application of generally accepted accounting principles.

Choice C is incorrect because the result is a material misstatement, not a material weakness.

Choice D is incorrect because this is describing management's failure to design and implement internal controls to prevent and detect fraud, material misstatements, and material weakness.

AUD 1-Q2 A1373. The correct answer choice is A. Both generally accepted auditing standards and government auditing standards should be considered for the municipality.

Choice B is incorrect because it fails to consider government auditing standards.

Choice C is incorrect because it fails to consider generally accepted auditing standards.

Choice D is incorrect because it fails to consider both generally accepted auditing standards and government auditing standards.

AUD 1-Q3 A1356. The correct answer choice is C. Compilation of financial statements provides the least assurance. The order of assurance from most to least is audit, review, and compilation. Attestation services provide assurance in the order of examination, review, and agreed-upon procedures with an examination providing the greatest level of assurance.

Choices A, B, and D are incorrect because they all provide more assurance than a compilation.

AUD 1-Q4 A376. The correct answer is D. Per 1.240.010.2: If a covered member had or was committed to acquire any material indirect financial interest in an attest client during the period of the professional engagement, the self-interest threat to the covered member's compliance with the "Independence Rule" [1.200.001] would not be at an acceptable level and could not be reduced to an acceptable level by the application of safeguards. Accordingly, independence would be impaired. So, materiality is germane to indirect financial interests. However, per 1.240.010.1: If a covered member had or was committed to acquire any direct financial interest in an attest client during the period of the professional engagement, the self-interest threat to the covered member's compliance with the "Independence Rule" [1.200.001] would not be at an acceptable level and could not be reduced to an acceptable level by the application of safeguards. Accordingly, independence would be impaired. So, materiality in not germane to direct financial interests.

Answers A, B and C are incorrect because materiality would play a significant part in the professional decision-making process of all three of these choices.

AUD 1-Q5 A180. Choice D is correct. Per 1.240.010.1, If a covered member had or was committed to acquire any direct financial interest in an attest client during the period of the professional engagement, the self-interest threat to the covered member's compliance with the "Independence Rule" [1.200.001] would **not** be at an acceptable level and could not be reduced to an acceptable level by the application of safeguards.

Accordingly, independence would be impaired.

Per 1.245.020.2, when a covered member is a grantor of a trust, including a blind trust, the trust and its underlying investments are considered to be the covered member's direct financial interest if any of the following rights or responsibilities exist:
1. The covered member has the ability to amend or revoke the trust.
2. The covered member has authority to control the trust.
3. The covered member has ability to supervise or participate in the trust's investment decisions.
4. The underlying trust investments will ultimately revert to the covered member as the grantor of the trust.

However, the trust and the trust's underlying investments are not considered to be financial interests of a covered member if the covered member is the grantor of the trust and the covered member does not have any of the rights or responsibilities in items 1–4.

Choices A, B, and C are incorrect per the above explanation.

AUD 1-Q6 A120. Choice C is correct. According to the AICPA Code of Professional Conduct, Interpretation 1.260.020.4A., states that a fully secured automobile loan is permitted regardless of the date obtained and does not impair independence.

Choices A, B, and D are incorrect as these loans may impair independence rules/interpretations.

AUD 1-Q7 A153. Choice D is correct. According to the AICPA Code of Professional Conduct (1.295.120.3b), authorizing client transactions would impair a CPA's independence.
Choice A is incorrect because the CPA is using the instructions of management and not his own judgment.
Choice B is incorrect as this scenario does not impair independence as management prepared the trial balance.
Choice C is incorrect. Since management prepared the journal entries (and not the CPA), independence is not impaired.

AUD 1-Q8 A88. Choice B is correct.

Per 1.120.010, Threats to compliance with the "Integrity and Objectivity Rule" [1.100.001] would not be at an acceptable level and could not be reduced to an acceptable level by the application of safeguards and the member would be presumed to lack integrity in violation of the "Integrity and Objectivity Rule" in the following circumstances:
A. The member offers to a client or accepts gifts or entertainment from a client that violate the member's or client's policies or applicable laws, rules, and regulations; and
B. The member knows of the violation or demonstrates recklessness in not knowing.

A member should evaluate the significance of any threats to determine if they are at an acceptable level. Threats are at an acceptable level when gifts or entertainment are reasonable in the circumstances. The member should exercise judgment in determining whether gifts or entertainment would be considered reasonable in the circumstances. The following are examples of relevant facts and circumstances:
a. The nature of the gift or entertainment
b. The occasion giving rise to the gift or entertainment
c. The cost or value of the gift or entertainment
d. The nature, frequency, and value of other gifts and entertainment offered or accepted
e. Whether the entertainment was associated with the active conduct of business directly before, during, or after the entertainment
f. Whether other clients also participated in the entertainment
g. The individuals from the client and member's firm who participated in the entertainment

Threats to compliance with the "Integrity and Objectivity Rule" [1.100.001] would not be at an acceptable level and could not be reduced to an acceptable level through the application of safeguards if a member offers to a client or **accepts gifts or entertainment from a client that is not reasonable in the circumstances**. The member would be presumed to lack objectivity in violation of the "Integrity and Objectivity Rule" under these circumstances.

From the options listed, choice B appears to be the most reasonable and appears to be a small gesture given that the client is out-of-town.

Choice A is incorrect as a trip to Las Vegas is not reasonable in nature.

Choice C is incorrect as box seats at a baseball game are not reasonable in nature.

Choice D is incorrect as a ski trip is also not considered to be reasonable in nature.

AUD 1-Q9 A421. The correct answer is C. Per 1.400.200.3, "The member should return client-provided records in the member's custody or control to the client at the client's request." Per 1.400.200.11, "A member would be considered in violation of the "Acts Discreditable Rule" [1.400.001] if the member does not comply with the requirements of this interpretation."

Answer A is incorrect because it is addressed under Interpretation 1.400.200.

Answer B is incorrect because it is not acceptable under the professional standards.

Answer D is incorrect because this not specifically cited under GAAS.

AUD 1-Q10 A185. Choice D is correct. Per 1.400.200.3, "The member should return client-provided records in the member's custody or control to the client at the client's request." Per 1.400.200.11, "A member would be considered in violation of the "Acts Discreditable Rule" [1.400.001] if the member does not comply with the requirements of this interpretation."

Choices A, B, and C are incorrect per the above explanation.

AUD 1-Q11 A124. Choice D is correct. According to the AICPA Code of Professional Conduct, 1.510.010.4f., contingent fees are permitted when the client is seeking a private letter ruling as it is classified as a legal proceeding. A private letter ruling is an interpretation of a statute to a particular tax situation.

Choices A, B, and C are incorrect as these are prohibited contingent fee services by the AICPA.

AUD 1-Q12 A135. Choice C is correct. Ownership of the bonds is considered to be a direct financial interest and are not permitted according to the AICPA Independence rules.

Choice A is incorrect as the member is not a trustee.

Choice B is incorrect as independence is not impaired with a credit union membership.

Choice D is incorrect as a golf club membership does not impair independence.

AUD 1-Q13 A111. Choice C is correct. The Public Company Accounting Oversight Board was established by the Sarbanes Oxley Act of 2002. This board oversees the audits of public companies and other issuers in order to protect the interest of the users of financial statements.

Choices A, B, and D are incorrect per the above explanation.

AUD 1-Q14 A87. Choice B is correct. Tax services are permissible to an audit client when preapproved by the audit committee.

Choices A, C, and D are incorrect as these services are not permissible to audit clients and are prohibited by the Sarbanes-Oxley Act 2002.

AUD 1-Q15 A137. Choice A is correct. The Securities and Exchange Commission requires a cooling off period of one year before a member of the audit engagement team may begin working for a registrant in a key position.

Choices B, C, and D are incorrect per the explanation above.

AUD 1-Q16 A165. Choice D is correct. An employee of a public accounting firm who served on the engagement team may be employed as a staff accountant as this is not a Financial Reporting Oversight Role (FROR). A FROR is a role which a person is able to exercise influence over the financial statements or anyone who prepares them. Choices A, B, and C are incorrect as these positions are in a FROR and are subject to a one-year "cooling off" period. The "cooling off" period prohibits an employee of a public accounting firm from accepting a position in a FROR a year after providing audit services to that client.

AUD 1-Q17 A449. Answer A is correct because the Foreign Corrupt Practices Act represents an amendment to The Securities Exchange Act of 1934. It does NOT specify any requirements with respect to the engagement of independent CPAs.

Answer B is incorrect because it is a requirement of the SEC to strengthen auditor independence. The SEC's Form 8—K requires a registrant to submit written statements on any changes in auditors. The report must state whether there were any disagreements with the former auditor during the previous two-year period on any matter of accounting principle, disclosure, or audit scope or procedure, which could have caused the auditors to make reference in expressing their opinion on the subject matter of the disagreement, regardless of whether the disagreement was resolved to the auditor's satisfaction.

Answer C is incorrect because it is a requirement of the SEC to strengthen auditor independence. The SEC has adopted the requirement that the audit committee of a listed issuer will need to be directly responsible for the appointment, compensation, retention and oversight of the work of any registered public accounting firm engaged (including resolution of disagreements between management and the auditor regarding financial reporting) for the purpose of preparing or issuing an audit report or performing other audit, review or attest services for the issuer, and the independent auditor will have to report directly to the audit committee. These oversight responsibilities include the authority to retain the outside auditor, which includes the power not to retain (or to terminate) the outside auditor. In addition, in connection with these oversight responsibilities, the audit committee must have ultimate authority to approve all audit engagement fees and terms.

Answer D is incorrect because it is a requirement of the SEC to strengthen auditor independence. See Section 302 of Sarbanes-Oxley: The SEC shall, by rule, require, for each company filing quarterly and annual reports, **that the principal executive officer or officers and the principal financial officer or officers (or persons performing similar functions) certify in each report that**: (1) the signing officer has reviewed the report; (2) based on the officer's knowledge, the report does not contain any untrue statement of a material fact or omit to state a material fact necessary in order to make the statements made, in light of the circumstances under which such statements were made, not misleading; **(3) based on such officer's knowledge, the financial statements, and other financial information included in the report, fairly present in all material respects the financial condition and results of operations of the issuer as of, and for, the periods presented in the report**; (4) the signing officers: (A) are responsible for establishing and maintaining internal controls; (B) have designed such internal control to ensure that material information relating to the issuer and its consolidated subsidiaries is made known to such officers by others within those entities, particularly during the period in which the periodic reports are being prepared; (C) have evaluated the effectiveness of the issuer's internal controls as of a date within 90 days prior to the report; and (D) have presented in the report their conclusions about the effectiveness of their internal controls based on their evaluation as of that date. (5) the signing officers have disclosed to the issuer's auditors and the audit committee: (A) all significant deficiencies in the design or operation of internal controls which could adversely affect the issuer's ability to record, process, summarize, and report financial data and have identified for the issuer's auditors any material weaknesses in internal controls; and (B) any fraud, whether or not material, that involves mgt. or other employees who have a significant role in the issuer's internal controls. (6) the signing officers have indicated in the report whether or not there were significant changes in internal controls or in other factors that could significantly affect internal controls subsequent to the date of their evaluation, including any corrective actions with regard to significant deficiencies and material weaknesses.

AUD 1-Q18 A115. Choice D is correct. According to the Sarbanes-Oxley Act of 2002 (Section 203), the audit partner must rotate off the audit engagement after 5 consecutive years.

Choices A, B, and C are incorrect per the above rule.

AUD 1-Q19 A66. Choice C is correct. If tax planning services are preapproved by the audit committee, then this would be considered a permissible service for the entity (PCAOB Rule 3524).

Choices A, B, and D are incorrect as these services are prohibited by Sarbanes-Oxley and would impair the auditor's independence as the auditor is performing an internal function.

AUD 1-Q20 A189. Choice C is correct. If an auditor has the ability to exercise significant control over the client, this would impair independence.

Choice A is incorrect as a covered member does not apply to cousins and would not impair independence.

Choice B is incorrect as a fully collateralized automobile loan would not impair independence.

Choice D is incorrect as a covered member does not apply to grandparents and as such would not impair independence.

AUD 1-Q21 A91. Choice C is correct. Members of an issuer's audit committee may not accept any consulting, advisory, or other compensatory fee other than as a member of the board.

Choices A, B, and D are incorrect as these are activities that members of the audit committee are typically responsible for.

AUD 1-Q22 A67. Choice B is correct. Per the DOL guidelines, the auditor must be independent when reviewing financial information.

Choice A is incorrect as there is no requirement to use the firm with the lowest fee.

Choice C is incorrect because there is no list of approved firms.

Choice D is incorrect because there is no requirement that the auditor be from the same organization that performs the financial statement audit.

AUD 1-Q23 A293. Choice B is correct. A client imposed scope limitation indicates that the client may be hiding errors or fraud that could result in a material misstatement in the financial statements.

Choice A is incorrect as this is not an audit risk.

Choice C is incorrect as hiring a specialist would not increase (it would actually decrease) audit risk.

Choice D is incorrect as this would not indicate that there is audit risk if the system does not have any errors.

AUD 1-Q24 A378. The correct answer is B. Reasonable assurance that the objectives of accounting control are achieved depends on the competence and integrity of personnel... their contribution is to provide an environment conducive to accounting control rather than to provide assurance that it will be achieved.
Answer A is wrong because the cost/benefit relationship doesn't have anything to do with the competence of the client's personnel.

Answer C is wrong because comparison testing doesn't deal with internal control.

Answer D is wrong because the timing deals with substantive and analytical testing, not internal controls.

AUD 1-Q25 A150. Choice D is correct. Before a successor auditor is willing to accept a new audit client, the client must allow the successor auditor to make inquiries of the predecessor auditor. If the client is unwilling to grant permission, then the successor auditor must reevaluate the integrity of the client.

Choice A is incorrect as the fraud risk assessment is done during the planning phase of an audit.

Choice B is incorrect as this is done during the planning phase of the audit.

Choice C is incorrect. A signed engagement letter is obtained afterwards.

AUD 1-Q26 A41. Choice D is correct. If a client requests that the auditor change the type of engagement, an auditor must consider the reasonableness of the client request. A reasonable request for a change in engagement would be a change in the client's circumstance such that the client no longer needs an audit, or if there was a misunderstanding in the type of engagement that was to be performed. There is no requirement that the auditor must refer to the scope limitations or describe auditing procedures that have been applied.

As such, A, B, and C are incorrect. (see AU-C 210.14-17 and AR-C 90.86-89)

AUD 1-Q27 A245. The correct choice is A. If the accountant agrees to make the change, no reference should be made to the original engagement.

Choices B, C, and D are incorrect per the above explanation. Choice B is incorrect as the accountant would need to follow SSARS not GAAS.

AUD 1-Q28 A149. Choice A is correct. The auditor is required to include a statement that a review is substantially less in scope than an audit.

Choice B is incorrect. There is no requirement that the CPA include the scope limitation.

Choice C is incorrect as there is no requirement to include the procedures that were completed before the engagement was changed.

Choice D is incorrect as there is no requirement to include the justification for the change.

AUD 1-Q29 A138. The correct choice is A. If the type of engagement was changed, the accountant would not refer to the original engagement or a change in scope.

Choice B, C, and D are incorrect the accountant would perform the procedures before changing the engagement type.

AUD 1-Q30 A62. Choice B is correct. The agreement between an auditor and a client must include the responsibilities of an auditor, as well as the client responsibilities. This is done to ensure there is no misunderstanding on the timing of the audit as well as responsibility of work.

Choice A is incorrect as the type of opinion issued is based on the results of the auditor's procedures.

Choice C is incorrect as audits cannot be performed based on a contingent fee.

Choice D is incorrect as the auditor need not communicate the materiality assessment to the client.

AUD 1-Q31 A11. Choice D is correct. Management must permit auditors to inquire with the entity's legal counsel. Managements' unwillingness will cause a client-imposed scope limitation that will cause the auditor not to accept the engagement. Choice A is incorrect because the auditor may gain an understanding of the client's business prior to the start of the engagement. Choice B is incorrect because recurring operating losses alone do not affect the decision to accept a client (however it will affect the client's going concern). Choice C is incorrect because there are certain conditions that may not necessitate a review of prior year's work papers.

AUD 1-Q32 A272. Choice C is correct. The engagement letter would typically include items relating to the use of specialists.

Choice A is incorrect as a CPA does not provide absolute assurance – only reasonable assurance.

Choice B is incorrect as the client is responsible for ensuring compliance with applicable laws and regulations.

Choice D is incorrect as the client is responsible for making the adjustments in the financial statements. The CPA may recommend these adjustments but not actually make these adjustments.

AUD 1-Q33 A369. The correct answer is B. An "engagement letter" records the auditor's understandings with the client making clear the nature of the engagement and any limitations on the scope of the audit work.

Answer A is wrong because a "representation letter" is obtained by the auditor from management to confirm oral responses given by management to specific inquiries. Such letters reduce the possibility of misunderstandings concerning the matters that are the subject of the representations.

Answer C is wrong because the "management letter" is a formal report to the client in which the auditor sets forth deficiencies in internal control brought to light during the course of the auditor's study and evaluation of the system.

Answer D is wrong because a "comfort letter" is prepared for underwriters in conjunction with a public registration of securities.

AUD 1-Q34 A82. Choice A is correct. Billing and audit fees may be included in the client's engagement letter.

Choice B, C, and D are incorrect as these types of items are not included in the engagement letter.

AUD 1-Q35 A10. Choice D is correct. An audit contains reasonable assurance (not absolute assurance) that the financial statements are fairly stated. An auditor does not have full responsibility to detect fraud. Refer to AU-C 210.10 for further guidance. Choice A is incorrect as this is not discussed in the engagement letter but rather used in planning procedures. Choice B is incorrect as auditing procedures are not discussed with clients. Choice C is incorrect as going concern is not specifically addressed in the engagement letter.

AUD 1-Q36 A209. Choice D is correct. An auditor may accept an engagement after the close of the fiscal year if the auditor is able to address limitations that arise as a result and is able to perform procedures to gain assurance over the financial statement accounts.

Choice A is incorrect as it would not make sense for an auditor to accept an engagement if the result is to disclaim the financial statement accounts.

Choice B is incorrect as the assessment of control risk is not applicable.

Choice C is incorrect as the auditor would need to reassess going concern in the current year.

AUD 1-Q37 A334. Choice B is correct. Sufficient and appropriate documentation should include evidence that the audit working papers have been reviewed.

Choice A is incorrect as accounting estimates should be documented.

Choice C is incorrect as the original evidence should not be deleted.

Choice D is incorrect as audit documentation is considered to be the property of the auditor – not the client.

AUD 1-Q38 A1386. The correct answer choice is A. The auditor should document findings in their working papers that could result in a modified auditor's report.

Choice B is incorrect because the lack of responsiveness should be included in the working papers.

Choice C is incorrect because if an explanation is oral and is sufficient support then it is not required to be documented in the working papers.

Choice D is incorrect because the original assessment should not be removed after revising the assessment of risk.

AUD 1-Q39 A1355. The correct answer choice is D. After the documentation completion date; the auditor must not make any deletions until the specified retention period is met. The retention period for issuers is seven years.

Choice A is incorrect because the auditor may make amendments to the audit documentation but should date it and appropriately add a note as to the reason for the amendments.

Choice B is incorrect because the auditor may make additions but anything added must be dated and explain the reason for needing to add documentation.

Choice C is incorrect because the audit may make changes to the audit documentation, but again, it must be dated and include a reason for the change.

AUD 1-Q40 A447. The correct answer is B. It would be inappropriate for an auditor to discuss with the audit committee the "details" of the procedures which he intends to apply.

Answer A is incorrect because this is something that should be considered which will reduce both time and money.

Answer C is incorrect because this certainly may be discussed which again can potentially save time and money.

Answer D is incorrect because this is a requirement for the auditor to communicate the material misstatements that is causing the modified opinion to be issued.

AUD 1-Q41 A163. Choice D is correct. Prior to accepting an engagement, there must be written communication regarding independence.

Choice A is incorrect as the confirmation of independence cannot be oral – it must be written.

Choice B is incorrect as the communication regarding independence must take place before the date of the audit opinion.
Choice C is incorrect as the communication must be written.

AUD 1-Q42 A113. Choice B is correct. Although the auditor is required to communicate in writing significant deficiencies to management and the audit committee, the auditor should not communicate that no significant deficiencies have been noted.

Choice A is incorrect as this is an appropriate communication procedure to management.

Choice C is incorrect as these representations are communicated in writing.

Choice D is incorrect as these matters are communicated in writing.

AUD 1-Q43 A31. Choice A is correct. The auditor must communicate to the audit committee material corrected misstatements resulting from the audit. The auditor would also need to communicate material uncorrected misstatements.

Choices B, C, and D are incorrect because these are items that are part of the audit plan and are not typically communicated to management as they are based on the auditor's own internal risk assessment.

AUD 1-Q44 A1380. The correct answer choice is B because the auditor should bring the transactions to the attention of an appropriate level manager.

Choice A is incorrect because investigating other transactions is not required.

Choice C is incorrect because this shouldn't be reported to those charged with governance because the impact in the aggregate is not material to the financial statements.

Choice D is incorrect because the transactions should be reported to the appropriate level of management.

AUD 1-Q45 A12. Choice D is correct as the internal control report is required to be part of the financial statements or in a separate report.

Choices A and B are incorrect because according to Government Auditing Standards, the internal controls report is not included within the performance audit report or the notes to the financial statements.

Choice C is incorrect because there is no requirement to issue a letter to the government funding agency.

AUD 1-Q46 A1384. The correct answer choice is C because the agency that provided the grant would want to know when fraud exists first.

Choice A is incorrect because the state accountancy board is not a government agency.

Choice B is incorrect because the state attorney general's office didn't provide the grant.

Choice D is incorrect because the recipients of the client's services under the grant wouldn't be appropriate under these circumstances.

AUD 1-Q47 A116. The correct answer choice is D. A CPA firm that maintains a comprehensive system of quality control would provide reasonable assurance that their professional services conform to professional standards. Statements of Quality Control Standards (SQCS) are issued to provide guidance regarding quality control.

Choice A is incorrect because this would not be a firm-wide system of quality control.

Choice B and C are incorrect because they do not provide reasonable assurance that the firms professional services comply with professional standards.

AUD 1-Q48 A1121. The correct answer is C. The independent auditor is responsible for compliance with generally accepted auditing standards in an audit engagement. A firm of independent auditors also needs to comply with generally accepted auditing standards in conducting an audit practice. Thus, a firm should establish quality control policies and procedures to provide it with reasonable assurance of conforming to generally accepted auditing standards in its audit engagements. The nature and extent of a firm's quality control policies and procedures depend on factors such as its size, the degree of operating autonomy allowed its personnel and its practice offices, the nature of its practice, its organization, and appropriate cost-benefit considerations.

Generally accepted auditing standards relate to the conduct of individual audit engagements; quality control standards relate to the conduct of a firm's practice as a whole. Thus, generally accepted auditing standards and quality control policies and procedures that a firm adopts may both affect the conduct of individual audit engagements and the conduct of a firm's audit practice as a whole.

Answer A is incorrect because a peer review board checks the work of a select group of audit engagements, whereas a system of quality control relates to the firm as a whole.

Answer B is incorrect because continuing professional education is to keep CPA's active with their licensing requirements and to stay updated on changes.

Answer D is incorrect because compliance with GAAS relates to all auditors in public accounting.

AUD 1-Q49 A602. The correct answer is C. QC Section 10, *A Firm's System of Quality Control*, paragraph A20 states: "The continuing competence of the firm's personnel depends, to a significant extent, on an appropriate level of continuing professional development so that personnel maintain their knowledge and capabilities. Effective policies and procedures emphasize the need for all levels of firm personnel to participate in general and industry-specific continuing professional education (CPE) and other professional development activities that enable them to fulfill responsibilities assigned and to satisfy applicable CPE requirements of the AICPA and regulatory agencies."
Answer A is incorrect because this doesn't assure proficiency but only provides reasonable assurance.

Answer B is incorrect because this is not the primary purpose of quality control but is a generally accepted auditing standard.

Answer D is incorrect because a peer review is performed by a state review board and isn't the primary purpose of continuing professional education.

AUD 1-Q50 A1042. The correct answer is C. Per QC 10, A Firm's System of Quality Control, **Documentation of the System of Quality Control** (QC 10.62-64): "The firm should establish policies and procedures requiring appropriate documentation to provide evidence of the operation of each element of its system of quality control. (Ref: par. .A78–.A80). The firm should establish policies and procedures that require retention of documentation for a period of time sufficient to permit those performing monitoring procedures and peer review of the firm to evaluate the firm's compliance with its system of quality control or for a longer period if required by law or regulation. The firm should establish policies and procedures requiring documentation of complaints and allegations described in paragraph .60 and the responses to them."

Answer A is incorrect because a file of minutes of staff meetings is an internal document and not relevant to quality control.

Answer B is incorrect because it is an internal record of employees' information.

Answer D is incorrect because the documentation is not to demonstrate compliance with the peer review directives, but rather compliance with policies and procedures.

This page is intentionally left blank.

AUD 2 – Assessing Risk and Developing a Planned Response

A. Planning an Engagement   2A-1 – 2A-4
1. Developing an overall engagement strategy   1
2. Developing a detailed engagement plan   2

B. Understanding an Entity and Its Environment   2B-1 – 2B-6
1. External factors, including the applicable financial reporting framework   1
2. Internal factors, including nature of the entity, ownership and governance structures and risk strategy   3

C. Understand an Entity's Internal Control   2C-1 – 2C-15
1. Control environment and entity-level controls   2
2. Flow of transactions and design of internal controls   3
3. Implications of an entity using a service organization   4
4. Information Technology (IT) general and application controls   6
5. Limitations of controls and risk of management override   15

D. Assessing Risks Due to Fraud, Including Discussions Among the Engagement Team About the Risk of Material Misstatement Due to Fraud or Error   2D-1 – 2D-6

E. Identifying and Assessing the Risk of Material Misstatement, Whether Due to Error or Fraud, and Planning Further Procedures Responsive to Identified Risks   2E-1 – 2E-28
1. Impact of risks at the financial statement level   1
2. Impact of risks for each relevant assertion at the class of transaction, account balance and disclosure levels   4
3. Further procedures responsive to identified risks   28

F. Materiality   2F-1 – 2F-4
1. For the financial statements as a whole and performance materiality/tolerable misstatement   1

G. Planning for and Using the Work of Others, Including Group Audits, the Internal Audit Function and the Work of a Specialist   2G-1 – 2G-10

H. Specific Areas of Engagement Risk   2H-1 – 2H-6
1. An entity's compliance with laws and regulations, including possible illegal acts   1
2. Accounting estimates, including fair values   3
3. Related parties and related party transactions   4

Glossary: Assessing Risk and Developing a Planned Response   Glossary 2-1 – 2-5

Multiple Choice – Questions   MCQ 2-1 – 2-16

Multiple Choice – Solutions   MCQ 2-17 – 2-34

Assessing Risk and Developing a Planned Response

A. Planning an Engagement
1. Developing an overall engagement strategy

> Explain the purpose and significance of the overall engagement strategy for an audit or non-audit engagement.

> *Hint*: AU-C 300, *Planning an Audit* (AICPA) and AS 2101, *Audit Planning* (PCAOB) are almost identical.

a. The role and timing of planning
Planning an audit involves **establishing the overall audit strategy** for the engagement and **developing an audit plan**.

The nature and extent of planning activities will vary according to the size and complexity of the entity, the key engagement team members' previous experience with the entity, and changes in circumstances that occur during the audit engagement.

When developing the audit strategy and audit plan for issuers (see AS 2101.07, PCAOB) the auditor should evaluate whether the following matters are important to the company's financial statements and internal control over financial reporting and, if so, how they will affect the auditor's procedures:

1) Knowledge of the company's internal control over financial reporting obtained during other engagements performed by the auditor;
2) Matters affecting the industry in which the company operates, such as financial reporting practices, economic conditions, laws and regulations, and technological changes;
3) Matters relating to the company's business, including its organization, operating characteristics, and capital structure;
4) The extent of recent changes, if any, in the company, its operations, or its internal control over financial reporting;
5) The auditor's preliminary judgments about materiality, risk, and, in integrated audits, other factors relating to the determination of material weaknesses;
6) Control deficiencies previously communicated to the audit committee or management;
7) Legal or regulatory matters of which the company is aware;
8) The type and extent of available evidence related to the effectiveness of the company's internal control over financial reporting;
9) Preliminary judgments about the effectiveness of internal control over financial reporting;
10) Public information about the company relevant to the evaluation of the likelihood of material financial statement misstatements and the effectiveness of the company's internal control over financial reporting;
11) Knowledge about risks related to the company evaluated as part of the auditor's client acceptance and retention evaluation; and
12) The relative complexity of the company's operations.

Planning is not a discrete phase of an audit, but rather a continual and iterative process that often begins shortly after (or in connection with) the completion of the previous audit and continues until the completion of the current audit engagement. Planning, however, includes consideration of the timing of certain activities and audit procedures that need to be completed prior to the performance of further audit procedures. For example, planning includes the need to consider, prior to the auditor's identification and assessment of the risks of material misstatement, such matters as the following:

1) The analytical procedures to be applied as risk assessment procedures.
2) A general understanding of the legal and regulatory framework applicable to the entity and how the entity is complying with that framework.
3) The determination of materiality.
4) The involvement of specialists.
5) The performance of other risk assessment procedures.

b. Planning activities

The auditor should establish an **overall audit strategy** that sets the scope, timing, and direction of the audit and that guides the development of the audit plan.

In establishing the overall audit strategy, the auditor should consider:
- Industry
- Complexity
- Accounting principles
- Risk areas
- Major estimates

c. Documentation

The auditor should include in the audit documentation the following:
1) The overall audit strategy.
2) The audit plan.
3) Any significant changes made during the audit engagement to the overall audit strategy or the audit plan and the reasons for such changes.

2. Developing a detailed engagement plan

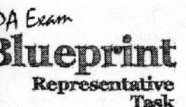

Prepare a detailed engagement plan for an audit or non-audit engagement starting with the prior-year engagement plan or with a template.

The auditor should develop an **audit plan** that includes a description of the following:
1) The nature and extent of planned risk assessment procedures, as determined under AU-C 315, *Understanding the Entity and Its Environment and Assessing the Risks of Material Misstatement*. See Topic 2B below.
2) The nature, timing, and extent of planned further audit procedures at the relevant assertion level, as determined under section 330, *Performing Audit Procedures in Response to Assessed Risks and Evaluating the Audit Evidence Obtained*. See Topic 2E.2 below.
3) Other planned audit procedures that are required to be carried out so that the engagement complies with generally accepted auditing standards.

The auditor should plan the nature, timing, and extent of direction and supervision of engagement team members and the review of their work.

> **Prepare supporting planning related materials (e.g., client assistance request listings, time budgets) for a detailed engagement plan starting with the prior-year engagement plan or with a template.**

a. Determining the Extent of Involvement of Professionals Possessing Specialized Skills
   The auditor should consider whether specialized skills are needed in performing the audit. If specialized skills are needed, the auditor should seek the assistance of a professional possessing such skills, who either may be on the auditor's staff or an outside professional. In such circumstances, the auditor should have sufficient knowledge to
   1) communicate the objectives of the other professional's work;
   2) evaluate whether the specified audit procedures will meet the auditor's objectives; and
   3) evaluate the results of the audit procedures applied as they relate to the nature, timing, and extent of further planned audit procedures.

   AU-C 620, *Using the Work of an Auditor's Specialist*, addresses the nonissuer auditor's use of the work of specialists in an audit. See review of <u>Topic 2G, Planning for And Using the Work of Others, Including Group Audits, The Internal Audit Function and The Work of a Specialist</u>.

   Direction of the engagement team involves informing the members of the engagement team of matters such as the following:
   a) Objectives
   b) Risks
   c) Client business
   d) Audit plan
   e) Problem areas

   Appropriate teamwork and training assist members of the engagement team to clearly understand the objectives of the assigned work. A brainstorming session is used for these matters.

   Supervision includes matters such as the following:
   a) Tracking the progress of the audit engagement
   b) Considering the competence and capabilities of individual members of the engagement team, including whether they have sufficient time to carry out their work, they understand their instructions, and the work is being carried out in accordance with the planned approach to the audit engagement
   c) Addressing significant findings or issues arising during the audit engagement, considering their significance, and modifying the planned approach appropriately
   d) Identifying matters for consultation or consideration by qualified engagement team members during the audit engagement

   1) Predecessor-successor communications
      Communicating with the predecessor auditor when there has been a change of auditors, in accordance with AU-C 210.

      If, due to unusual circumstances, such as pending, threatened, or potential litigation; disciplinary proceedings; or other unusual circumstances, the predecessor auditor decides not to respond fully to the inquiries, the predecessor auditor is expected to clearly state that the response is limited.

i. The communication with the predecessor auditor may be either written or oral.

ii. Matters subject to the auditor's inquiry of the predecessor auditor may include the following:
   a) Information that might bear on the integrity of management.
   b) Disagreements with management about accounting policies, auditing procedures, or other similarly significant matters.
   c) Communications to those charged with governance regarding fraud and noncompliance with laws or regulations by the entity.
   d) Communications to management and those charged with governance regarding significant deficiencies and material weaknesses in internal control.
   e) The predecessor auditor's understanding about the reasons for the change of auditors.

Multiple Choice

AUD 2-Q1 through AUD 2-Q2

Develop or modify a detailed engagement plan for an audit or non-audit engagement based on planning inputs and constraints.

The auditor should update and change the overall audit strategy and audit plan, as necessary, during the course of the audit.

The documentation of the overall audit strategy is a record of the key decisions considered necessary to properly plan the audit and communicate significant issues to the engagement team. For example, the auditor may summarize the overall audit strategy in the form of a memorandum that contains key decisions regarding the overall scope, timing, and conduct of the audit.

The documentation of the audit plan is a record of the planned nature, timing, and extent of risk assessment procedures, and further audit procedures, at the relevant assertion level in response to the assessed risks. It also serves as a record of the proper planning of the audit procedures that can be reviewed and approved prior to their performance. **The auditor may use standard audit programs** or audit completion checklists, tailored as needed to reflect the particular engagement circumstances.

A record of the significant changes to the overall audit strategy and the audit plan and resulting changes to the planned nature, timing, and extent of audit procedures, explain why the significant changes were made and why the overall strategy and audit plan were finally adopted for the audit. It also reflects the appropriate response to the significant changes occurring during the audit.

Multiple Choice

AUD 2-Q3

B. Understanding an Entity and Its Environment

Per AU-C 315.04, "The objective of the auditor is to identify and assess the risks of material misstatement, whether due to fraud or error, at the financial statement and relevant assertion levels, through understanding the entity and its environment, including the entity's internal control [reviewed in another section], thereby providing a basis for designing and implementing responses to the assessed risks of material misstatement." This objective is substantially equivalent to the objective stated in PCAOB AS 2110.3.

> *Hint*: The main sources of professional guidance that serve as the basis for this review are obtained from the following:
> AU-C 315, *Understanding the Entity and Its Environment and Assessing the Risks of Material Misstatement*, AICPA.
> AS 2110, *Identifying and Assessing Risks of Material Misstatement*, PCAOB.

The auditor's risk-based approach to auditing financial statements follows a four-step process:
1. Understand the Entity and Its Environment (including internal control)
2. Identify the Risks of Material Misstatement.
3. Assess the Risks of Material Misstatement.
4. Develop an Overall Response to the Risks of Material Misstatement.

> *Hint*: Step 1 is reviewed in this subsection (Topic B) and internal control related items are reviewed in a separate subsection (Blueprint Topic C). Steps 2, 3, and 4 are reviewed in Blueprint Topic E.

Obtaining an understanding of the entity and its environment (including internal control; reviewed in a separate section of the review material) is a continuous, dynamic process of gathering, updating, and analyzing information throughout the audit. The understanding of the entity establishes a frame of reference within which the auditor plans the audit and exercises professional judgment throughout the audit.

Understanding the entity and its environment is part of the risk-based framework used in performing audits. The auditor uses this framework for designing and performing further audit procedures. In using this risk-based framework the auditor should:
   a. Identify risks throughout the process of obtaining an understanding of the entity and its environment by considering the classes of transactions, account balances, and disclosures in the financial statements (more details are found in AU-C 315.A134-A135).
   b. Assess the identified risks and evaluate whether they relate more pervasively to the financial statements as whole and potentially affect many assertions.
   c. Relate the identified risks to what can go wrong at the relevant assertion level, taking into account the relevant controls that the auditor intends to test (more details are found in AU-C 315.A136-A138).
   d. Consider the likelihood of misstatement, including the possibility of multiple misstatements, and whether the potential misstatement is of a magnitude that could result in a material misstatement.
   e.
1. External factors, including the applicable financial reporting framework

> *Hint*: The author rearranged the representative tasks in this topic of the CPA exam blueprint for clarity.

> **Identify and document the relevant industry, regulatory and other external factors that impact an entity and/or the inherent risk of material misstatement, including the applicable financial reporting framework.**

The auditor should obtain an understanding of the following: Relevant industry, regulatory, and other external factors, including the applicable financial reporting framework.

a. Industry, regulatory, and other external factors
   1) *Industry factors*
      Relevant industry factors include industry conditions such as the competitive environment, supplier and customer relationships, and technological developments.

      Examples of matters the auditor may consider, include:
      i. the market and competition, including demand, capacity, and price competition.
      ii. cyclical or seasonal activity.
      iii. product technology relating to the entity's products.
      iv. energy supply and cost.

      The industry in which the entity operates may give rise to specific risks of material misstatement arising from the nature of the business or the degree of regulation. For example, long term contracts may involve significant estimates of revenues and expenses that give rise to risks of material misstatement. In such cases, it is important that the engagement team includes members with sufficient, relevant knowledge and experience.

   2) *Regulatory factors*
      Relevant regulatory factors include the regulatory environment. The regulatory environment encompasses, among other matters, the applicable financial reporting framework and the legal and political environment.

      Examples of matters the auditor may consider include the following:
      i. Accounting principles and industry-specific practices
      ii. Regulatory framework for a regulated industry
      iii. Laws and regulations that significantly affect the entity's operations, including direct supervisory activities
      iv. Taxation (corporate and other)
      v. Government policies currently affecting the conduct of the entity's business, such as monetary (including foreign exchange controls), fiscal, financial incentives (for example, government aid programs), and tariffs or trade restrictions policies
      vi. Environmental requirements affecting the industry and the entity's business

      AU-C 250, *Consideration of Laws and Regulations in an Audit of Financial Statements*, includes some specific requirements related to the legal and regulatory framework applicable to the entity and the industry or sector in which the entity operates.

   3) *Other external factors*
      Examples of other external factors affecting the entity that the auditor may consider, include the general economic conditions, interest rates and availability of financing, and inflation or currency revaluation.

b. Documentation

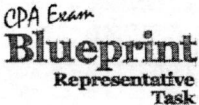

> Document the procedures that were performed to obtain an understanding of the relevant industry, regulatory and other external factors that impact an entity and/or the inherent risk of material misstatement, including the applicable financial reporting framework.

> Document the procedures that were performed to obtain an understanding of the relevant factors that define the nature of an entity, including the impact on the risk of material misstatement (e.g., its operations, ownership and governance structure, investment and financing plans, selection of accounting policies, and objectives and strategies).

The auditor should include in the audit documentation the following:
1) discussion among the engagement team, the significant decisions reached, how and when the discussion occurred, and the audit team members who participated;
2) key elements of the understanding obtained regarding each of the aspects of the entity and its environment and each of the internal control components, the sources of information from which the understanding was obtained, and the risk assessment procedures performed;
3) identified and assessed risks of material misstatement at the financial statement level and at the relevant assertion level; and
4) risks identified and related controls about which the auditor has obtained an understanding.

2. Internal factors, including nature of the entity, ownership and governance structures and risk strategy

> **Identify and document the relevant factors that define the nature of an entity, including the impact on the risk of material misstatement (e.g., its operations, ownership and governance structure, investment and financing plans, selection of accounting policies and objectives and strategies).**

a. Nature of the entity
The auditor should obtain an understanding of the following:
The **nature of the entity**, including
1) its operations;
2) its ownership and governance structures;
3) the types of investments that the entity is making and plans to make, including investments in entities formed to accomplish specific objectives; and
4) the way that the entity is structured and how it is financed,

to enable the auditor to understand the classes of transactions, account balances, and disclosures to be expected in the financial statements.

The **entity's selection and application of accounting policies**, including the reasons for changes thereto. The auditor should evaluate whether the entity's accounting policies are appropriate for its business and consistent with the applicable financial reporting framework and accounting policies used in the relevant industry.

The entity's **objectives and strategies** and those **related business risks** that may result in risks of material misstatement.

Examples of matters that the auditor may consider when obtaining an understanding of the nature of the entity include
1) *Business operations such as*
   i. the nature of revenue sources, products or services, and markets, including involvement in electronic commerce, such as Internet sales and marketing activities.
   ii. the conduct of operations (for example, stages and methods of production or activities exposed to environmental risks).
   iii. alliances, joint ventures, and outsourcing activities.
   iv. geographic dispersion and industry segmentation.
   v. the location of production facilities, warehouses, and offices and the location and quantities of inventories.
   vi. key customers and important suppliers of goods and services.
   vii. employment arrangements (including the existence of union contracts, pension and other postemployment benefits, stock option or incentive bonus arrangements, and government regulation related to employment matters).
   viii. research and development activities and expenditures.

ix. transactions with related parties.

2) *Investments and investment activities such as*
   i. planned or recently executed acquisitions or divestitures.
   ii. investments and dispositions of securities and loans.
   iii. capital investment activities.
   iv. investments in nonconsolidated entities, including partnerships, joint ventures, and investments in entities formed to accomplish specific objectives.

3) *Financing and financing activities such as*
   i. major subsidiaries and associated entities, including consolidated and nonconsolidated structures.
   ii. debt structure and related terms, including off balance sheet financing arrangements and leasing arrangements.
   iii. beneficial owners (local and foreign and their business reputation and experience) and related parties.
   iv. the use of derivative financial instruments.

4) *Financial reporting such as*
   i. accounting principles and industry-specific practices, including industry-specific significant categories (for example, loans and investments for banks or research and development for pharmaceuticals).
   ii. revenue recognition practices.
   iii. accounting for fair values.
   iv. foreign currency assets, liabilities, and transactions.
   v. accounting for unusual or complex transactions, including those in controversial or emerging areas (for example, accounting for stock-based compensation).

Hint: These factors offset inherent risk.

b. The Entity's Selection and Application of Accounting Policies
An understanding of the entity's selection and application of accounting policies may encompass such matters as
   1) the methods the entity uses to account for significant and unusual transactions.
   2) the effect of significant accounting policies in controversial or emerging areas for which a lack of authoritative guidance or consensus exists.
   3) significant changes in the entity's accounting policies and disclosures and the reasons for such changes.
   4) financial reporting standards, and laws and regulations that are new to the entity and when and how the entity will adopt such requirements.
   5) the financial reporting competencies of personnel involved in selecting and applying significant new or complex accounting standards.

c. Objectives and Strategies and Related Business Risks
The entity conducts its business in the context of industry, regulatory, and other internal and external factors.

To respond to these factors, the entity's management, or those charged with governance, define objectives, which are the overall plans for the entity. Strategies are the approaches by which management intends to achieve its objectives. The entity's objectives and strategies may change over time.

Business risk is broader than the risk of material misstatement of the financial statements, though it includes the latter.

Business risk may arise from change or complexity. A failure to recognize the need for change also may give rise to business risk. Business risk may arise, for example, from
1) the development of new products or services that may fail;
2) a market that, even if successfully developed, is inadequate to support a product or service; or
3) flaws in a product or service that may result in liabilities and reputational risk.

An understanding of the business risks facing the entity increases the likelihood of identifying risks of material misstatement. This is because most business risks will eventually have financial consequences and, therefore, an effect on the financial statements. However, the auditor does not have a responsibility to identify or assess all business risks because not all business risks give rise to risks of material misstatement.

Examples of matters that the auditor may consider when obtaining an understanding of the entity's objectives, strategies, and related business risks that may result in a risk of material misstatement of the financial statements include
1) industry developments (a potential related business risk might be, for example, that the entity does not have the personnel or expertise to deal with the changes in the industry).
2) new products and services (a potential related business risk might be, for example, product liability is increased).
3) expansion of the business (a potential related business risk might be, for example, that the demand has not been accurately estimated).
4) new accounting requirements (a potential related business risk might be, for example, incomplete or improper implementation or a cost increase).
5) regulatory requirements (a potential related business risk might be, for example, that legal exposure is increased).
6) current and prospective financing requirements (a potential related business risk might be, for example, financing is lost due to the entity's inability to meet requirements).
7) use of IT (a potential related business risk might be, for example, systems and processes are incompatible).
8) the effects of implementing a strategy, particularly any effects that will lead to new accounting requirements (a potential related business risk might be, for example, incomplete or improper implementation).

d. Measurement and Review of the Entity's Financial Performance
Management and others will measure and review those things they regard as important. Performance measures, whether external or internal, create pressures on the entity. These pressures, in turn, may motivate management or others to take action to improve the business performance or to misstate the financial statements.

Accordingly, an understanding of the entity's performance measures assists the auditor in considering whether pressures to achieve performance targets may result in management actions that increase the risks of material misstatement, including those due to fraud. AU-C 240 addresses the risks of fraud.

Examples of internally generated information used by management for measuring and reviewing financial performance, and which the auditor may consider, include
1) key performance indicators (financial and nonfinancial) and key ratios, trends, and operating statistics.

2) period-on-period financial performance analyses.
3) budgets; forecasts; variance analyses; segment information; and divisional, departmental, or other-level performance reports.
4) employee performance measures and incentive compensation policies.
5) comparisons of an entity's performance with that of competitors.

Internal measures may highlight unexpected results or trends requiring management to determine their cause and take corrective action (including, in some cases, the detection and correction of misstatements on a timely basis).

Performance measures also may indicate to the auditor that risks of misstatement of related financial statement information do exist. For example, performance measures may indicate that the entity has unusually rapid growth or profitability when compared with that of other entities in the same industry. Such information, particularly if combined with other factors, such as performance-based bonus or incentive remuneration, may indicate the potential risk of management bias in the preparation of the financial statements.

Multiple Choice

AUD 2-Q4 through AUD 2-Q5

C. **Understand an Entity's Internal Control**

Hint: The author rearranged the representative tasks in this topic of the CPA exam blueprint for clarity.

Hint: Quick reference summary for internal control:
1. Internal control
    a. Definition -- process effected by people to achieve entity's objectives
    b. Components-- environment, risk assessment, control activities, information and communication, monitoring
    c. Control activities -- [R I P S] Reviews, Information processing, physical controls, segregation of duties (authorization, recording, custody)
    d. Basic requirements -- Risk assessment procedures [document -- narrative, questionnaire, flowchart]
    e. Tests of controls
        - To test operating effectiveness of controls
        - Done ONLY if you wish to rely on controls
        - Includes -- Inquire Observe Inspect Reperform

2. Cycles
    Sales/Accounts Receivable/Cash Receipts
    - Sales order
    - Credit approval
    - Ship - bill of lading
    - Bill/Collect cash
    - Records - aging schedule, bad debts, sales returns

    Purchases/Accounts Payable/Cash Disbursements
    - Requisition
    - Purchase order
    - Receive goods
    - Approve for payment/Pay

    Personnel/Payroll
    - Authorization - personnel (human resource management)
    - Recording - payroll accounting
    - Custody - paycheck distribution

3. Control deficiencies -- communications
    - Required to the extent that they come to your attention
    - Must be written to management and those charged with governance
    - Show significant deficiencies and material weaknesses and potential effects on the financial statements
    - Not required to give recommendations
    - Cannot write that "no significant deficiencies found" but may write "no material weaknesses found"
    - Other communications to management about other deficiencies noted (other than significant deficiencies or material weaknesses) -- may be written or oral

4. Internal auditors
    - Competence
    - Objectivity - To whom do they answer in the client entity?

1. Control environment and entity-level controls

Exam Blueprint Representative Task

> Identify and document the significant components of an entity's control environment, including its entity-level controls.

> Perform and document the procedures to obtain an understanding of the significant components of an entity's control environment, including its entity-level controls.

> Identify and document the key controls within the flow of an entity's transactions relevant to an audit of an entity's financial statements, including an audit of an entity's internal controls.

The auditor should obtain an understanding of internal control relevant to the audit.

Although most controls relevant to the audit are likely to relate to financial reporting, not all controls that relate to financial reporting are relevant to the audit.

It is a matter of the auditor's professional judgment whether a control, individually or in combination with others, is relevant to the audit.

a. Nature and Extent of the Understanding of Relevant Controls
When obtaining an understanding of controls that are relevant to the audit, the auditor should evaluate the design of those controls and determine whether they have been implemented by performing procedures in addition to inquiry of the entity's personnel.

b. Components of Internal Control
   1) *Control environment*
      The auditor should obtain an understanding of the control environment.

      As part of obtaining this understanding, the auditor should evaluate whether
      i. management, with the oversight of those charged with governance, has created and maintained a culture of honesty and ethical behavior and
      ii. the strengths in the control environment elements collectively provide an appropriate foundation for the other components of internal control and whether those other components are not undermined by deficiencies in the control environment.

   2) *The entity's risk assessment process, if it exists*
      The auditor should obtain an understanding of whether the entity has a process for
      i. identifying business risks relevant to financial reporting objectives,
      ii. estimating the significance of the risks,
      iii. assessing the likelihood of their occurrence, and
      iv. deciding about actions to address those risks.

   3) *The information system, including the related business processes relevant to financial reporting and communication*
      The auditor should obtain an understanding of the information system, including the related business processes relevant to financial reporting.

   4) *Control activities relevant to the audit*
      The auditor should obtain an understanding of control activities relevant to the audit, which are those control activities the auditor judges to be necessary to understand, in order to assess the risks of material misstatement at the assertion level and design further audit procedures responsive to assessed risks.

An audit does not require an understanding of all the control activities related to each significant class of transactions, account balance, and disclosure in the financial statements or to every assertion relevant to them. However, the auditor should obtain an understanding of the process of reconciling detailed records to the general ledger for material account balances.

In understanding the entity's control activities, the auditor should obtain an understanding of how the entity has responded to risks arising from IT.

5) *Monitoring of controls*
The auditor should obtain an understanding of the major activities that the entity uses to monitor internal control over financial reporting, including those related to those control activities relevant to the audit, and how the entity initiates remedial actions to deficiencies in its controls.

If the entity has an internal audit function, the auditor should obtain an understanding of the nature of the internal audit function's responsibilities, how the internal audit function fits in the entity's organizational structure, and the activities performed, or to be performed.

The auditor should obtain an understanding of the sources of the information used in the entity's monitoring activities and the basis upon which management considers the information to be sufficiently reliable for the purpose.

2. Flow of transactions and design of internal controls

Perform a walkthrough and document the flow of transactions relevant to an audit of an entity's financial statements, including an audit of an entity's internal controls.

A **walkthrough** is a procedure in which the auditor follows a transaction from origination through the company's processes, including information systems, until it is reflected in the company's financial records, using the same documents and information technology that company personnel use.

Walkthrough procedures usually include a combination of inquiry, observation, inspection of relevant documents, and re-performance of controls.

In performing a walkthrough, at the points at which important processing procedures occur, the auditor questions the company's personnel about their understanding of what is required by the company's prescribed procedures and controls. These probing questions, combined with the other walkthrough procedures, allow the auditor to gain a sufficient understanding of the process and to be able to identify important points at which a necessary control is missing or not designed effectively. Additionally, probing questions that go beyond a narrow focus on the single transaction used as the basis for the walkthrough allow the auditor to gain an understanding of the different types of significant transactions handled by the process.

Perform tests of the design and implementation of internal controls relevant to an audit of an entity's financial statements, including an audit of an entity's internal controls.

Evaluate whether internal controls relevant to an audit of an entity's financial statements, including an audit of an entity's internal controls are effectively designed and placed in operation.

Testing the operating effectiveness of controls is different from obtaining an understanding of and evaluating the design and implementation of controls. However, the same types of audit procedures are used. The auditor may, therefore, decide it is efficient to test the operating effectiveness of controls at the same time the auditor is evaluating their design and determining that they have been implemented.

The auditor should **test the design effectiveness** of controls by determining whether the company's controls, if they are operated as prescribed by persons possessing the necessary authority and competence to perform the control effectively, satisfy the company's control objectives and can effectively prevent or detect errors or fraud that could result in material misstatements in the financial statements.

Procedures the auditor performs to test design effectiveness include a mix of inquiry of appropriate personnel, observation of the company's operations, and inspection of relevant documentation. **Walkthroughs** that include these procedures ordinarily are sufficient to evaluate design effectiveness.

Hint: Testing the design effectiveness of internal controls is one step on the path of testing the operating effectiveness of internal controls.

3. Implications of an entity using a service organization

Identify and document the purpose and significance of an entity's use of a service organization, including its impact on an audit of an entity's financial statements, including an audit of an entity's internal controls.

a. Purpose and significance of using a service organization
When obtaining an understanding of the user entity in accordance with AU-C 315, the user auditor should obtain an understanding of how the user entity uses the services of a service organization in the user entity's operations, including the following:
1) The nature of the services provided by the service organization and the significance of those services to the user entity, including their effect on the user entity's internal control.
2) The nature and materiality of the transactions processed or accounts or financial reporting processes affected by the service organization.
3) The degree of interaction between the activities of the service organization and those of the user entity.
4) The nature of the relationship between the user entity and the service organization, including the relevant contractual terms for the activities undertaken by the service organization.

When obtaining an understanding of internal control relevant to the audit in accordance with AU-C 315, the *user auditor* (an auditor who audits and reports on the financial statements of a user entity) should evaluate the design and implementation of relevant controls at the *user entity* (an entity that uses a service organization and whose financial statements are being audited) that relate to the services provided by the service organization, including those that are applied to the transactions processed by the service organization.

The user auditor should determine whether a sufficient understanding of the nature and significance of the services provided by the service organization, and their effect on the user entity's internal control relevant to the audit, has been obtained to provide a basis for the identification and assessment of risks of material misstatement.

> **Use a service organization report to determine the nature and extent of testing procedures to be performed in an audit of an entity's financial statements, including an audit of an entity's internal controls.**

    b. Using a type 1 or type 2 report to support the user auditor's understanding of the service organization
        1) Using Type 1 or Type 2 Reports
           A service organization may engage a service auditor to report on
               i. the description and design of its controls (**type 1 report**) or on
               ii. the description and design of its controls and their operating effectiveness (**type 2 report**).

           Type 1 or type 2 reports may be issued under Statement on Standards for Attestation Engagements No. 16, *Reporting on Controls at a Service Organization* (AT sec. 801), or under standards promulgated by an authorized or recognized standards-setting organization (for example, the International Auditing and Assurance Standards Board).

    c. Responding to the Assessed Risks of Material Misstatement
       In responding to assessed risks in accordance with AU-C 330, the user auditor should
       1) determine whether sufficient appropriate audit evidence concerning the relevant financial statement assertions is available from records held at the user entity and, if not,
       2) perform further audit procedures to obtain sufficient appropriate audit evidence or use another auditor to perform those procedures at the service organization on the user auditor's behalf.

4. Information Technology (IT) general and application controls

> *Hint*: Quick reference summary for auditing and IT [definitions, internal control, substantive tests]:
> 1. EDP department -- Control clerks, Operator, Programmer, Analyst, Librarian [C O P A L]
> 2. General and application controls
> 3. Batch vs. on-line real-time processing
> 4. Auditing around the computer (without using the computer)
> 5. Auditing through the computer
>   - Test data
>   - Integrated test facility
>   - Parallel simulation
>
> 6. Computers in auditing
>   - Spreadsheet
>   - Sampling
>   - Audit through computer - computer assisted audit techniques -- CAATS
>   - Manage engagement
>   - Word processing
>
> 7. Electronic evidence
>   - Electronic data interchange (EDI) may reduce or eliminate traditional paper trail
>   - Auditor may need more test of controls in these environments
>   - Auditor may need to do work at interim dates when electronic evidence exists at a certain point in time before this evidence may become non-retrievable (affect nature, timing, extent of tests)
>
> 8. IT Advantages
>   - Speed/accuracy
>   - Minimize redundancy
>   - Improve communications
>   - Remain competitive
>   - Facilitate additional analysis of data
>   - Backup/recovery
>
> 9. IT Disadvantages
>   - Cost
>   - Specialized personnel
>   - Backup/recovery
>   - Compatibility
>   - Loss of confidentiality
>   - Rely on others
>   - Audit trail
>   - Legal Issues
>
> 10. Internal control implications
>   - General vs application controls
>   - Access codes/passwords
>   - Backup/recovery
>   - Security over data
>   - Test for accurate processing of data
>   - Documentation

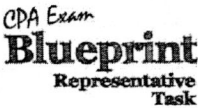

Identify and document an entity's key IT general and application controls, including their impact on the audit of an entity's financial statements, including an audit of an entity's internal controls.

a. IT general controls
General controls are relevant to an entire processing environment and all of the information systems and applications within it. General control objectives focus on the overall security and reliability of the system's operations and output.

Within an organization, systems often share a common set of policies and procedures defining objectives over logical access, program change management, system development, computer operations, backup and recovery, and physical access. Controls exist to achieve management's control objectives. A collection of controls, in combination with each other, aim to create an adequate internal control structure in accordance with Sarbanes-Oxley 404. The design and operating effectiveness of a control is evaluated to determine adequacy.

Logical access to programs and data	Program change management	Program development and SDLC	Computer operations and processing	Physical access to programs and data
Policy and procedure documentation User authentication and password policies Access administration • New user access authorization and provisioning • Access modification and revokation (job change or termination) • Privileged user appropriateness • Periodic user reviews	Policy and procedure documentation Change request and authorization Change testing Migration approval Implementation • Segregation of duties Emergency changes	Methodology for system development and acquisition • Planning • Analysis • Design and authorization • Development • Testing • Implementation • Verification Data migration	Data Transmission Incident and problem management Environmental controls Backup and recovery • Backup • Incident management • Contingency planning	Biometric devices Visitor logs

1) Logical access to programs and data controls
Logical access is the ability a user has to connect to a computer system. The primary control objective is to provide reasonable assurance that logical access to system resources (programs and data) is restricted to authorized individuals.

As a starting point to address this main objective, it is important for the organization to have policies over IT in place. Formal policies ensure all objectives are addressed consistently. Policy and procedure documentation communicates policy expectations to personnel. The design of most controls, not just logical access controls, can be evaluated by inspecting policies and procedure documentation.

In most computerized systems, authentication is required for access. Authentication is a way of verifying that a user has permission to access the system. A unique username and password is the most common approach for authentication. Sensitive information may dictate the need for two-factor authentication, or a combination of a password and another component (often a physical key, ID card, or biometric scan).

If a system uses passwords for authentication, the organization should establish rules for syntax and expiration. For example, management's password policy requires passwords that are: at least 8 characters in length; include alpha, numeric, and special characters; include upper and lower case letters; and expire after 90 days. Management has discretion as to what policies to adopt. Password policy variations are common in practice.

Once authenticated as a user, access within the processing environment is often restricted using roles, profiles, or permissions. Limitations are constructed based on job responsibilities and help systematically enforce segregation between duties.

Careful application of access administration controls is important to accomplish the primary logical access objective. When provisioning access to new users, procedures should be in place to guide how to properly request and approve access. Organizations need a rule-based authorization mechanism to provision access based on job function and prevent conflict in duty segregation. Equally, if not more important, access must be modified or revoked when a user's job function changes or employment is terminated. User accounts should be added, modified, and deleted in a timely manner.

Access management and control software supports access controls in large or complex organizations. Software can control user identification and passwords for multiple applications and may permit the use of single sign-on technology. Single sign-on allows the user to log-in once to gain access to all linked systems without additional prompts.

Privileged or super user (e.g., administrator in Windows, root in LINUX/UNIX, SAP_ALL in SAP, PeopleSoft Administrator in PeopleSoft, etc.) access appropriateness is a key internal control for system security. Inherently, this type of access is risky for the organization since access at this level could circumvent other system controls. Extreme care should be exercised to limit this level of access to a small, trustworthy group of individuals. Often, privileged access is granted only to a select few in the IT department such as system administrators and database administrators.

Management should perform a periodic (annually, semi-annually, or quarterly) review of user access rights to systems to verify rights are assigned appropriately based on job responsibilities. This review identifies any users with inappropriate access that might have been previously overlooked and corrects the oversight.

2) Program change management controls
   The main control objective for program change is that adequate controls ensure that changes to existing systems (or applications) are authorized, tested, approved, properly implemented, and documented. The controls put in place by an organization for program change mirror the system development lifecycle (SDLC) steps adopted by the organization.

   Policies and procedures over program change must be documented and adhered to by management. Within the procedure documentation, the method for initiating and requesting authorization for a change is outlined (e.g., submitting a change ticket). Typically, once a particular change has been requested, it must be authorized, tested, and approved prior to implementation. Each step must be completed sequentially unless it is an emergency change.

   In an organization with strong internal controls, an appropriate level of management will authorize every change to make certain it meets user requirements and does not exceed budgetary restrictions. Once authorization is granted, the change is made in the testing environment. A testing environment is established to determine potential issues that might result from the change in a relatively low risk environment rather than production, which would result in higher risk.

Formal testing is performed and sign-off is obtained from both users and information system personnel. Without sign-off, the implementation cannot proceed. Once obtained, sign-off constitutes migration approval and the change is now ready for implementation in the production environment. A change management administrator must perform the change migration or installation as dictated by proper segregation of duties. As such, the person who developed the change should not have access to implement it.

Occasionally, the system requires an emergency change which must be implemented immediately into production. The policy for emergency changes will likely differ from normal changes, either eliminating or expediting steps. For example, an email could suffice as appropriate documentation for the change request, rather than submitting a change ticket. Also, the change may bypass standard testing procedures assuming approval from a high-level manager is granted.

3) <u>Program development and system development lifecycle (SDLC) controls</u>
The general objective for program development and the system development lifecycle is that adequate controls are in place to ensure new systems (or applications) are authorized, tested, approved, properly implemented, and documented.

Controls over program development are not applicable to every organization during every audit (or attestation) period. Controls over the organization's adopted SDLC can only be evaluated for effectiveness when the organization has at least one instance of program development on which to judge. When the organization is only maintaining existing technology, these controls cannot be tested and controls over program change take precedence.

In periods when the organization does have new system development or acquisition projects, strict adherence to the adopted SDLC is necessary for an adequate internal control environment to exist. As with program change, each step of the SDLC corresponds to one or more internal controls. Since the SDLC can vary from organization to organization, the controls are also likely to vary.

An example of a control for the analysis stage of the SDLC is that management prepares appropriate system documentation. Appropriate, in this case, is defined by management. Often, appropriate documentation must include a discussion of scope and budget.

Once personnel clearly define and document the project in accordance management's documentation controls, the project must be approved by senior management. This senior-management approval, or project authorization, is a control that corresponds to the design/approval stage of the SDLC.

Organizations often address the remaining stages of a typical SDLC with a single control. This control ensures systems that are either developed or acquired are authorized, tested, and approved. Sign-off by an appropriate individual is typically required for each item. Finally, a review is performed post-implementation to verify processing accuracy.

Controls over data migration safeguard data as it is converted into different file formats and ensure the data is imported into the new system completely and accurately. Completeness and accuracy is determined by comparing and reviewing legacy data files. It is best practice to maintain legacy data files for reference during the entire conversion process.

4) Computer operations and processing controls
The primary objective for computer operations and processing is that adequate controls ensure system processing is authorized, scheduled, and deviations from scheduled processing are identified and resolved.

This control objective is mainly relevant to the batch processing, data interface and transmission, and backup and recovery. Controls provide reasonable assurance that processing (often referred to as job processing) is monitored appropriately and deviations are identified and resolved. Issues are addressed and resolved according to procedures over incident management. Instructions for incident management should be documented, reviewed periodically for changes, and approved by an appropriate individual.

Backup and recovery controls provide reasonable assurance that programs, files, and data are backed up periodically. A common backup rotation scheme is a grandfather-father-son scheme. The grandfather file is a monthly full backup that makes a copy of all data files to date. The father file is a weekly differential backup, copying only data that has changed since the last full backup. The son file is a daily incremental backup file, copying the transaction activity since the last incremental backup, not including any previous activity.

Contingency planning ensures processing continuity if adverse events occur to disrupt operations. Policies and the resulting internal controls increase awareness of procedures and mitigate risk. Adverse event scenarios should be evaluated based on likelihood and risk for data loss. Highly likely or exceedingly risky scenarios should take priority for training exercises and practice drills.

Environmental controls defend against conditions that might negatively impact computer hardware. Air conditioning should be adequate in terms of both temperature and humidity. Smoke detectors and the fire suppression systems should be inspected regularly for functionality. The axillary power supplies (e.g., uninterruptible power sources, standby generators) should be inspected for operability. The facility should be tidy and dust-free. Equipment should be elevated to protect against water damage. Controls ensure these expectations are met.

5) Physical access to programs and data
In regards to physical access, the main objective is to ensure controls are in place restrict access to facilities that house processing equipment and storage media to appropriate personnel. Care should be taken to restrict physical access to information systems, especially those relevant to financial reporting, to reduce the risk of unauthorized access, malicious or accidental damage, and other mishaps. Card readers and biometric devices may be used to ensure that physical access to computer facilities that house the financial applications and data (e.g. data centers) are restricted to appropriate personnel. Visitor logs, and the review of such logs, is used to document entry and exit of secure areas and identify unauthorized access.

b. IT application controls
Application controls are specific to a particular process or subsystem (e.g., accounts receivable) and relate to the use of IT to initiate, record (input), process, and report (output) data. The number and scope of controls are unique to the specific processing environment and align with management's polices.

Generally, application controls are either automated (programmed) or manual. When a control is performed manually, it is also called a user control.

1) Automated controls
   Automated controls are programmed to enforce organizational policies and procedures without user intervention. Due to their nature, controls of this type must be integrated into the design of the system and are not subject to breakdowns due to human failure. They are useful to help mitigate specific organizational risks ranging from fraud due unauthorized access to routine input errors.

   i. Application access controls
      An extension of general logical access controls, application access controls also secure access to and increase monitoring of specific processing operations and accounting tasks, such as posting adjusting journal entries. Within the general ledger application, for instance, the system is configured to require the review and approval of adjusting journal entries by a supervisor before being transferred to the general ledger. This control automatically prevents a user from posting the entry until proper approval is obtained. Additionally, the system is configured to restrict the level of access required to create adjusting journal entries in the general ledger system to appropriate personnel.

   ii. Input (validation) controls
       Programmed controls can significantly decrease the risk of input error and, by validating the data that a user inputs, it can increase data reliability. A small inaccuracy made while inputting data could lead to a much larger issue in the final financial statements. Input controls validate that the data is complete and accurate. If not, there are often warnings and error messages configured to alert users of inaccuracies and exceptions noted during data input. The user is unable to submit information without correcting the error.

       a) Preformatting forces the user to input data in a specific way, increasing consistency. A blank form is labeled to resemble a hardcopy document.
       b) Record counts keep track of the total of the number of records processed in a batch and can be used to identify incomplete data processing.
       c) A check digit, or checksum, confirms accuracy of data input manually by comparing the check digit to the sum or product of a predefined algorithm calculated using the other digits input by the user (e.g., 7 is the checksum for account number 1032017, 1+0+3+2+0+1=7).
       d) A field check, or allowed character check, restricts the type of information (e.g., numerical data only) the user inputs into a field.
       e) A validity check, similar to a field check, tests the input to ensure data is reasonable (valid) based on a set of programmed conditions (e.g., dates have a feasible day, month, and year).
       f) A null (missing) data check prevents the user from submitting a blank field that would result in incomplete records.
       g) Reasonableness tests, or limit checks, restrict values to within a certain upper and lower limit or range (e.g., billable hours per day < 12 hours)
       h) An edit check compares data to criteria, such as format, and rejects inappropriate data (e.g., a nine-digit social security number must use the XXX-XX-XXX format and only contain numbers).
       i) A hash total is a meaningless value that checks for completeness of the input (e.g., totaling the employees' identification numbers to ensure that all payroll records have been included in a payroll batch to be processed).
       j) A redundant data check, or duplicate check, prevents duplicate identifiers (e.g., product IDs) from being recorded in the system.

k) A logic check prevents illogical input based on predefined relationships (e.g., a customer has more than one order, but an order can only have one customer).

iii. Processing controls
Processing controls ensure data integrity exists throughout the manipulation and processing of the data by the computer. Data integrity includes accuracy, completeness, and consistency.

a) A control total is a meaningful value established prior to the processing of a batch transaction, confirming the processing was complete and accurate (e.g., total revenue).
b) A three-way match checks to make sure valid corresponding documents (e.g., invoice, purchase order, and receiving report) exist prior to generating a payment. A three-way match prevents erroneous or fraudulent cash disbursements and override would require creating a fictitious invoice, purchase order, and receiving report. Each document originates from a different source and requires a different level of system access to create. Plus, to prevent fictitious invoices, the system could require a valid customer number to be assigned to each invoice. The potential to override the control is low, especially without privileged user access, and requiring a valid customer number compensates for some of the risk if the three-way match control did not operate effectively. Controls build on one another to strengthen the internal control environment.

2) User (manual) controls
Manual controls require user execution of the control. Regardless of the advancement of automation technology, the review of system output continues to be an important manual control. The role of the user is to follow-up on exception reports and reconciliation reports. While a computer is able to identify inconsistencies, fixing the issue often requires user discretion on next steps.

i. Output controls
The user is often responsible to verify the output against source documents and control totals. The user is also responsible for determining if the output is reasonable, complete, and accurate using professional judgment. Audit trails and error listings are also reviewed by the user to identify issues and initiate follow-up procedures.

Internal controls are designed to be preventive, detective, or corrective. The timing and nature of the control allows it to be classified in one of the three categories.

3) Preventive controls
Preventive controls aim to deter the occurrence of errors and fraudulent activities and are designed to stop unauthorized acts before they happen. Security and access controls are typically classified as preventive. Examples consist of password policies to prevent unauthorized access and a proper request for access prior to when the access is provisioned. Physical access controls are also preventive since they deter intruders and protect an organization's data.

4) Detective controls
Detective controls help identify errors and fraud that have previously occurred within the organization when preventive controls fail to stop an undesirable act. Detective controls are in place to discover and communicate issues in a timely manner. Examples include reconciling that organization's account balances and the bank's balance reported on a bank statement, vouching an amount reported in the financial statements or other report to

corresponding source documents, and monitoring a variance between actual and budgeted amounts.

5) Corrective controls
Corrective controls correct errors and irregularities discovered after the fact. This type of control not only identifies an issue, but plays an active role in alleviating the issue and restoring functionality. An example of a corrective control is the removal of inappropriate user access following a user access review performed by managers.

Multiple Choice
AUD 2-Q6 through AUD 2-Q7

c. Testing control design and operational effectiveness

> Perform and document the tests of an entity's IT general and application controls, including controls relevant to the audit of an entity's financial statements, including an audit of an entity's internal controls.

As required by Section 404 of the Sarbanes-Oxley Act of 2002 (SOX 404), management must report on the company's internal control over financial reporting. Included in this report must be an assessment of the internal controls and statement regarding the framework used to determine operational effectiveness. Procedures must be sufficient to evaluate the design of the company's internal controls and to test for operating effectiveness.

1) Test of design (TOD)
The test of design evaluates if a control is suitably designed to prevent material misstatement or to detect it in a timely manner. The design is ineffective if implemented controls, in combination, do not meet the control objectives established by management or a key control is missing.

2) Test of operating effectiveness (TOE)
Operating effectiveness involves verifying if a control is operating as expected based on its design, without exceptions. An exception is an instance when the control was not performed, not performed consistently, or a criterion established by the control is not met.

The following chart outlines example risks and control considerations, control objectives, and controls.

Note: Be aware that this chart is not comprehensive and should not be memorized. Every organization is unique and will have a different set of internal controls. The controls below are for illustration only. Be prepared to identify internal controls for a given risk scenario.

Examples of IT General Controls (ITGCs) and Application Controls		
Risks and control considerations	Control objective	Controls
IT general controls		
Passwords do not meet policies for syntax and expiration. Users are added to the system prior to approval from a supervisor.	Controls provide reasonable assurance logical access to system programs and data is restricted to authorized personnel.	Passwords are configured to conform to organization policies for syntax and expiration. User access to the system is granted after approval from an appropriate supervisor. User access for terminated employees is removed from the system in a timely manner.

System access not removed timely after employee termination. Privileged user access not limited to appropriate personnel.		Privileged user access is authorized and limited to appropriate personnel.
System changes are not documented appropriately.

Unauthorized system changes are migrated to production.

Testing on program changes not completed prior to implementation. | Controls provide reasonable assurance changes to existing systems (or applications) are authorized, tested, approved, properly implemented, and documented. | Change requests are submitted and documented according to policy.

Changes are authorized, tested, and approved prior to implementation. |
New systems are installed prior to testing.	Controls provide reasonable assurance new systems are authorized, tested, approved, properly implemented, and documented.	System development projects require project authorization and senior-management approval.
Batch processing fails and no action to resolve is performed.	Controls provide reasonable assurance job processing is authorized, scheduled, and deviations from scheduled processing are identified and resolved.	Job processing issues are addressed and resolved according to procedures over incident management.
System failure causes unanticipated data loss and downtime.	Controls provide reasonable assurance programs, files, and data are backed up periodically.	A system backup is performed daily.
Malicious or accidental damage to computer equipment.	Controls provide reasonable assurance access to facilities that house processing equipment and storage media is restricted to appropriate personnel.	Card readers ensure physical access to computers is restricted to appropriate personnel only.
IT application controls		
Incomplete and inaccurate data processing is not identified.	Controls provide reasonable assurance batch processing transactions for critical financial data are	Batch processing reconciliations are performed daily and reviewed by a supervisor.

	accurate, with reconciliation activities to confirm accuracy.	
Inappropriate access to input adjusting entries. Unauthorized adjusting journal entries Inaccurate adjusting journal entries.	Controls provide reasonable assurance adjusting journal entries are approved and are complete and accurate.	Access to perform adjusting journal entries is restricted to appropriate personnel. Adjusting journal entries are reviewed and approved by an authorized individual and agree with supporting documentation.

5. Limitations of controls and risk of management override

Understand the limitations of internal controls and the potential impact on the risk of material misstatement of an entity's financial statements.

Controls over management override are important to effective ICFR for all entities and may be particularly important at smaller, less complex entities, because of the increased involvement of senior management in performing controls and in the period-end financial reporting process.

For smaller, less complex entities, the controls that address the risk of management override might be different from those at a larger entity. For example, a smaller, less complex entity might rely on more detailed oversight by those charged with governance that focuses on the risk of management override.

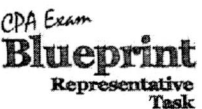

Identify and document the risks associated with management override of internal controls and the potential impact on the risk of material misstatement of an entity's financial statements.

Risks of material misstatement at the financial statement level refer to risks that relate pervasively to the financial statements as a whole and potentially affect many assertions.

Risks of this nature are not necessarily risks identifiable with specific assertions at the class of transactions, account balance, or disclosure level. Rather, they represent circumstances that may increase the risks of material misstatement at the assertion level (*for example, through management override of internal control*). Financial statement level risks may be especially relevant to the auditor's consideration of the risks of material misstatement arising from fraud.

Multiple Choice

AUD 2-Q8 through AUD 2-Q11

D. Assessing Risks Due to Fraud, Including Discussions Among the Engagement Team About the Risk of Material Misstatement Due to Fraud or Error

> *Hint:* Quick reference summary of fraud (material misstatement due to fraud):
> [Fraudulent financial reporting and misappropriation of assets]
> 1. Characteristics of fraud:
>   - incentive (pressure)
>   - opportunity
>   - rationalize (attitude)
> 2. Discussion among engagement personnel (brainstorming)
> 3. Identify risks that may lead to material misstatement due to fraud:
>   - interviews
>   - brainstorming
>   - fraud risk factors
>   - analytical procedures
>   - client acceptance/continuance
>   - entity's programs and controls
>   - revenue recognition/management estimates/inventory quantities
> 4. Respond to identified risks
>   - overall (personnel, predictability)
>   - specific (nature, timing, extent)
>   - test journal entries
>   - management override of controls
> 5. Communicate to management and audit committee (i.e., those charged with governance)
> 6. Document

Assess risks of material misstatement of an entity's financial statements due to fraud or error (e.g., during a brainstorming session), leveraging the combined knowledge and understanding of the engagement team.

> **Hint:** The main sources of professional guidance that serve as the basis for this review are obtained from:
> AU-C 240, *Consideration of Fraud in a Financial Statement Audit*, AICPA.
> AS 2401, *Consideration of Fraud in a Financial Statement Audit*, PCAOB.

This topic expands on how the requirements of *Understanding the Entity and Its Environment and Assessing the Risks of Material Misstatement* (AU-C 315) are to be applied regarding the **risks of material misstatement due to fraud**.

Per AU-C 240.15, "The objectives of the auditor are to:
1) identify and assess the risks of material misstatement of the financial statements due to fraud;
2) obtain sufficient appropriate audit evidence regarding the assessed risks of material misstatement due to fraud, through designing and implementing appropriate responses; and
3) respond appropriately to fraud or suspected fraud identified during the audit."

a. Characteristics of fraud
1) **Fraud is intentional** versus errors which are unintentional.

2) **Fraud** is an intentional act by one or more individuals among management, those charged with governance, employees, or third parties, involving the use of deception that results in a material misstatement in financial statements that are the subject of an audit.

3) Two types of intentional misstatements are relevant to the auditor—misstatements resulting from **fraudulent financial reporting** ("management fraud") and misstatements resulting from **misappropriation of assets** ("employee fraud").

4) Fraud, whether fraudulent financial reporting or misappropriation of assets, involves **incentive or pressure** to commit fraud, a **perceived opportunity** to do so, and some **rationalization** of the act (the Fraud Triangle).

5) **Fraud risk factors** include events or conditions that indicate an incentive or pressure to perpetrate fraud, provide an opportunity to commit fraud, or indicate attitudes or rationalizations to justify a fraudulent action.

6) Typically, management and employees engaged in fraud will take steps to **conceal the fraud** from auditors and others within and outside the entity.
   i. Fraud may be concealed through falsifying documentation --- an audit in accordance with GAAS rarely involves the authentication of such documentation.
   ii. Fraud also may be concealed through collusion among management, employees, or third parties.

b. Responsibility **for the Prevention and Detection of Fraud**
   1) **The Entity**
   The primary responsibility for the prevention and detection of fraud rests with both those charged with governance of the entity and management.

   2) **The Auditor**
   An auditor conducting an audit in accordance with GAAS is responsible for obtaining reasonable assurance that the financial statements, as a whole, are free from material misstatement, whether caused by fraud or error.
   i. Fraud is a broad legal concept and ***auditors do not make legal determinations of whether fraud has occurred***. Rather, the auditor's interest specifically relates to acts that result in a material misstatement of the financial statements.
   ii. Due to the inherent limitations of an audit, an unavoidable risk exists that ***some material misstatements of the financial statements may not be detected*** even though the audit is properly planned and performed in accordance with GAAS.
   iii. The risk of the auditor not detecting a material misstatement resulting from management fraud (e.g., fraudulent financial reporting) is greater than from employee fraud (e.g., misappropriation of assets) because management is frequently is a position to manipulate accounting records, present fraudulent financial information, or override control procedures designed to prevent similar frauds by other employees.
   Iv. When obtaining reasonable assurance, the auditor is responsible for
      a) Maintaining ***professional skepticism*** throughout the audit. Unless the auditor has reason to believe otherwise, the auditor may accept records and documents as genuine. If conditions identified during the audit cause the auditor to believe that a document may not be authentic, or that terms in a document have been altered and not disclosed to the auditor, the auditor should investigate further.
      b) Considering the potential for ***management override of controls***.
      c) Recognizing the fact that audit ***procedures that are effective in detecting error may not be effective for detecting fraud***.

c. Risk assessment procedures
Often, the fraud risk assessment is performed concurrently with the general risk assessment. The frameworks outlined in AU-C 315 and PCAOB AS 2110 apply to fraud risk assessment. This review section focuses on fraud-specific risk assessment procedures.

1) Conduct a Discussion Among Engagement Team Members
   The discussion should include an exchange of ideas (brainstorming) among the engagement team members about (AU-C 240.15):
   i. How and where the entity's financial statements might be susceptible to material misstatement due to fraud,
   ii. How management could perpetrate and conceal fraudulent financial reporting, and
   iii. How assets of the entity could be misappropriated.

2) Inquiries
   i. **Inquiries of Management** (AU-C 240.17-18)
      The auditor should make inquiries of management regarding:
      a) Management's *assessment of the risk* that the financial statements may be materially misstated due to fraud.
      b) Management's *process for identifying, responding to, and monitoring the risks of fraud* in the entity, including any specific risks of fraud that management has identified, or that have been brought to its attention, or classes or transactions, account balances, or disclosures for which a risk of fraud is likely to exist.
      c) Management's *communication, if any, to those charged with governance* regarding its processes for identifying and responding to the risks of fraud in the entity.
      d) Management's *communication, if any, to employees* regarding its views on business practices and ethical behavior.
      e) Whether management may have *knowledge of any actual, suspected, or alleged fraud*.

   ii. **Inquiries of Others Within the Entity** (AU-C 240.19-21)
       a) *Those Charged with Governance*
          The auditor should make inquiries to:
          - Understand how those charged with governance exercise oversight of management's processes for identifying and responding to the risks of fraud and the internal controls that management has established to mitigate these risks.
          - Determine their views about the risks of fraud and whether they have knowledge of any actual, suspected, or alleged fraud.

       b) *Internal Audit*
          The auditor should make inquiries to:
          - Obtain internal audit view about the risks of fraud.
          - Determine whether they have knowledge of any actual, suspected, or alleged fraud.
          - Determine whether they have performed any procedures to identify or detect fraud during the year.
          - Determine whether management has satisfactorily responded to any findings resulting from these procedures.

3) Analytical Procedures
   i. The auditor should evaluate whether unusual or unexpected relationships that have been identified, indicate risks of material misstatement due to fraud based on analytical procedures performed.
   ii. Analytical procedures should include procedures relating to revenue accounts.

d. Identification and Assessment of the Risks of Material Misstatement Due to Fraud
   1) The auditor should identify and assess the risks of material misstatement due to fraud at the financial statement level, and at the assertion level for classes of transactions, account balances and disclosures (like AU-C 315).

   2) The auditor's assessment should be ongoing throughout the audit (following the initial assessment).

   3) There is a presumption of fraud risk in revenue recognition and the audit should evaluate which types of revenue, revenue transactions, or assertions give rise to such risks.

   4) The auditor should treat assessed risk of material misstatement due to fraud as **significant risks**.
      i. To the extent not already done (related to AU-C 315), the auditor should obtain an understanding of the entity's related controls related to such risks (including the evaluation of whether such controls have been suitably designed and implemented to mitigate such fraud risks).

e. Responses to the Assessed Risk of Material Misstatements Due to Fraud
   1) **Overall Responses** (AU-C 240.28-30): The auditor should determine overall responses to address the risks of material misstatement due to fraud at the financial statement level (also discussed in AU-C 330).

      i. The auditor should design and perform further audit procedures whose nature, timing, and extent are responsive to the assessed risks of material misstatement due to fraud at the assertion level.
         a) Assign and supervise personnel taking into account their knowledge, skill, and ability.
         b) Evaluate whether the selection and application of accounting policies by the entity may be indicative of fraudulent financial reporting resulting from management's effort to manage earnings, or a bias that may create a material misstatement.
      ii. Incorporate an element of unpredictability in the selection of the nature, timing, and extent of audit procedures.

   2) **Response to Risks Related to Management Override of Controls** (AU-C 240.31-32): Management is in a position to manipulate accounting records and prepare fraudulent financial statements by overriding controls, that otherwise appear to be operating effectively --- and this risk is present in all entities.

      Even if specific risks of material misstatement, due to fraud, are not identified by the auditor, a possibility exists that management could override controls --- so**, the auditor should address the risk of management override of controls, apart from any conclusions regarding the existence of more specifically identifiable risks.**

This is done by designing and performing the following:
i. **Test the appropriateness of journal entries** recorded in the general ledger and other adjustments made in the preparation of the financial statements. These tests should include the following:
   a) Obtain an understanding of the entity's financial reporting process and controls over journal entries and other adjustments, including the suitability of design and implementation of such controls.
   b) Make inquiries of people involved in the financial reporting process about inappropriate or unusual activity relating to processing of journal entries or other adjustments.
   c) Consider fraud risk indicators, the nature and complexity of accounts, and entries processed outside the normal course of business.
   d) Select journal entries and other adjustments made at the end of a reporting period.
   e) Consider the need to test journal entries and other adjustments throughout the period.

ii. **Review accounting estimates for biases** and evaluate whether the circumstances producing the bias, represent a risk of material misstatement due to fraud.
   a) Perform a **retrospective review** of management judgments and assumptions related to significant accounting estimates reflected in the financial statements of the prior year.

iii. Evaluate whether **the business purpose** has significant unusual transactions, which could indicate that the transactions may have been entered into to engage in fraud. The auditor should evaluate whether:
   a) The form of the transaction is overly complex;
   b) The transaction involves unconsolidated related parties, including variable interest entities;
   c) The transaction involves related parties or relationships or transactions with related parties previously undisclosed to the auditor;
   d) The transaction involves other parties that do not appear to have the financial capability to support the transaction without assistance from the company, or any related party of the company;
   e) The transaction lacks commercial or economic substance, or is part of a larger series of connected, linked, or otherwise interdependent arrangements that lack commercial or economic substance individually or in the aggregate (e.g., the transaction is entered into shortly prior to period end and is unwound shortly after period end)
   f) The transaction occurs with a party that falls outside the definition of a related party (as defined by the accounting principles applicable to that company), with either party able to negotiate terms that may not be available for other, more clearly independent, parties on an arm's-length basis;
   g) The transaction enables the company to achieve certain financial targets;
   h) Management is placing more emphasis on the need for a particular accounting treatment than on the underlying economic substance of the transaction (e.g., accounting-motivated structured transaction); and
   i) Management has discussed the nature of, and accounting for, the transaction with the audit committee or another committee of the board of directors or the entire board.

f. Communications of Possible Fraud
   1) To Management
      If the auditor has identified fraud or has obtained information that indicates fraud may exist, the auditor should communicate these matters, on a timely basis, to the appropriate level of management in order to inform those with primary responsibility for the prevention and detection of fraud, of matters relevant to their responsibilities.

   2) To Those Charged with Governance
      If the auditor suspects fraud involving: (a) management; (b) employees who have significant roles in internal control; or, (c) others, when fraud results in a material misstatement in the financial statements, the auditor should communicate these matters to those charged with governance on a timely basis.

      If the auditor suspects fraud involving management, the auditor should communicate these suspicions to those charged with governance and discuss with them the nature, timing, and extent of audit procedures necessary to complete the audit.

      The auditor should communicate with those charged with governance any other matters related to fraud that are, in the auditor's professional judgment, relevant to their responsibilities.

   3) To Regulatory and Enforcement Authorities
      If the auditor has identified or suspects a fraud, the auditor should determine whether the auditor has a responsibility to report the occurrence or suspicion to a party outside the entity (i.e., regulatory or enforcement authorities).

g. Documentation
   The auditor should document the following:
   1. The discussion among engagement personnel in planning the audit regarding the susceptibility of the entity's financial statements to material misstatement due to fraud, including how and when the discussion occurred, the audit team members who participated, and the subject matter discussed.
   2. The procedures performed to obtain information necessary to identify and assess the fraud risks.
   3. The fraud risks that were identified at the financial statement and assertion levels, and the linkage of those risks to the auditor's response.
   4. If the auditor was able to identify, in a particular circumstance, improper revenue recognition as a fraud risk, and the reasons supporting the auditor's conclusion.
   5. The results of the procedures performed to address the assessed fraud risks, which include those procedures performed to further address the risk of management override of controls.
   6. Other conditions and analytical relationships that caused the auditor to believe that additional auditing procedures or other responses were required, and any further responses the auditor concluded were appropriate, to address such risks or other conditions.
   7. The nature of the communications about fraud made to management, those charged with governance, and others.

Multiple Choice

AUD 2-Q12 through AUD 2-Q20

E. **Identifying and Assessing the Risk of Material Misstatement, Whether Due to Error or Fraud, and Planning Further Procedures Responsive to Identified Risks**
   1. Impact of risks at the financial statement level

> **Identify and document the assessed impact of risks of material misstatement at the financial statement level, taking into account the effect of relevant controls.**

   a. Risk Assessment Procedures
   The auditor should perform **risk assessment procedures** to provide a basis for *the identification and assessment of risks of material misstatement* at the financial statement and relevant assertion levels. Risk assessment procedures include the following (see PCAOB AS 2110.5 and AU-C 315.27a, .07, .06b, .11, .06a and .06c):
   - Obtain an understanding of the entity and its environment (reviewed in Topic 2B).
   - Obtain an understanding of internal control over financial reporting (reviewed in Topic 2C).
   - Consider information from the client acceptance and retention evaluation, audit planning activities, past audits, and other engagements performed for the entity.
   - Perform analytical procedures.
   - Conduct a discussion among engagement team members regarding the risks of material misstatement.
   - Inquire of the audit committee, management, and others within the entity about the risks of material misstatement.
   - Observation and inspection.

   AU-C 315.05 notes, "Risk assessment procedures by themselves, however, do not provide sufficient appropriate audit evidence on which to base the audit opinion." In other words, the auditor must perform further audit procedures as a basis for the audit opinion.

   b. Consider Information from Other Areas
   The auditor should consider whether information obtained from other areas is relevant to identifying risks of material misstatements. These areas include the following:
   - Client acceptance and retention activities.
   - Audit planning activities.
   - Past audits (especially past misstatements and whether they were corrected on a timely basis).
   - Other engagements for the audit client.

   c. Perform Analytical Procedures
   Analytical procedures performed as risk assessment procedures may be used as follows (see AU-C 315.A14-17 and PCAOB AS 2110.46-48):
   - To identify aspects of the entity, of which the auditor was unaware, and may assist in assessing the risks of material misstatement in order to provide a basis for designing and implementing responses to the assessed risks.
   - Enhance the auditor's understanding of the client's business and the significant transactions and events that occurred since the prior audit.
   - Identify areas that might represent specific risks, including the existence of unusual transactions and events, and amounts, ratios, and trends that warrant investigation.

   Both financial and nonfinancial information may be used in the analytical procedures (e.g., sales and square footage to compute sales-per-square foot).

Analytical procedures that use data aggregated at a high level may provide only a broad initial indication about whether a material misstatement may exist. In such cases, other information that has been collected when identifying the risks of material misstatements should be considered.

Per PCAOB AS 2110.47, "In applying analytical procedures as risk assessment procedures, **the auditor should perform analytical procedures relating to revenue** with the objective of identifying unusual or unexpected relationships involving revenue accounts that might indicate a material misstatement, including material misstatement due to fraud."

d. Conduct a Discussion Among Engagement Team Members
The discussion among engagement team members, including the engagement partner, about the susceptibility of the entity's financial statements to material misstatements has the following objectives (see AU-C 315.A21-A23 and PCAOB AS 2110.49-51):
   1) More experienced engagement team members share their insights based on their knowledge of the entity.
   2) Exchange information about the business risks related to the entity and where the financial statements might be susceptible to material misstatements due to error or fraud.
   3) To gain a better understanding of the potential for material misstatements of the financial statements in specific areas assigned to engagement team members, and to understand how the results of the audit procedures they perform may affect other aspects of the audit, including the decisions about the nature, timing, and extent of further audit procedures.
   4) To share new information obtained throughout the audit that may affect the assessment of risks of material misstatement or the audit procedures performed to address these risks.

This discussion may be held concurrently with the discussion among the engagement team that is required by AU-C 240 (*Consideration of Fraud in a Financial Statement Audit*) to discuss the entity's financial statements to fraud.

The discussion may not include all members in a single discussion, nor is it necessary for all the members to be informed of all decisions reached in the discussion. **The engagement partner may discuss matters with key members of the engagement team while delegating discussion with other team members.**

e. Inquiries
   1) Inquiries of Management
      Much information about the entity is obtained from inquiries of management. The PCAOB emphasizes inquiries regarding fraud and fraud risks PCAOB AS 2110.58 reminds auditors:
      1. To determine when it is necessary to corroborate management's responses to inquiries and should take into account the fact that management is often in the best position to commit fraud.
      2. Should obtain evidence to **address inconsistencies in responses to inquiries**.

f. Observation and Inspection
Observation and inspection may support inquiries and may provide information about the entity and its environment. Examples include observation and inspection of (AU-C 315.A18):
   1) The entity's operations.
   2) Documents (such as business plans and strategies), records, and internal control manuals.
   3) Reports prepared by: management (e.g., quarterly management reports, interim financial statements); those charged with governance (e.g., minutes of board of director meetings); and, internal audit.
   4) The entity's premises and plant facilities.

g. Identifying and Assessing the Risks of Material Misstatements

> **Analyze identified risks to detect those that relate to an entity's financial statements as a whole (as contrasted to the relevant assertion level).**

The auditor should identify and assess the risks of material misstatement at the financial statement level and the assertion level (for classes of transactions, account balances, and disclosures). This process entails the following activities:

1) Identify risks of misstatement using information obtained from performing risk assessment procedures.

2) Evaluate whether the identified risks related **pervasively** to the financial statements as a whole and potentially affected many assertions. **Pervasive** effects on the financial statements are those that, in the auditor's professional judgment
    - are not confined to specific elements, accounts, or items of the financial statements;
    - are confined to a specific element, account, or item of the financial statements which represent or could represent a substantial portion of the financial statements; or
    - disclosures are fundamental to users' understanding of the financial statements.

3) Evaluate the types of potential misstatements that could result from the identified risks and the accounts, disclosures, and assertions that could be affected.

4) Assess the likelihood of misstatement (including multiple misstatements) and the magnitude of potential misstatement to assess the possibility that the risk could result in material misstatement to the financial statements (the auditor may take into account the planned degree of reliance on internal controls selected to test).

5) Identify significant accounts and disclosures and their relevant assertions.

6) An account or disclosure is a significant account or disclosure if there is a reasonable possibility that the account or disclosure could contain a misstatement that, individually or when aggregated with others, has a material effect on the financial statements (considering the risk of both overstatement and understatement). The determination of whether an account or disclosure is significant is based on inherent risk (without regard to the effect of controls).

7) Determine whether any of the identified and assessed risks of material misstatement are significant risks. Auditors should evaluate the following factors to determine which risks are significant risks:
    i. Whether the risk is a fraud risk (fraud risk is a significant risk).
    ii. Whether the risk is related to recent significant economic, accounting, or other developments.
    iii. The complexity of transactions.
    iv. Whether the risk involves significant transactions with related parties.
    v. The degree of complexity or judgment in the recognition or measurement of financial information related to the risk, especially those measurements involving a wide range of measurement uncertainty.
    vi. Whether the risk involves significant unusual transactions.

    The auditor will use these activities as a basis for designing and performing further audit procedures.

2. Impact of risks for each relevant assertion at the class of transaction, account balance and disclosure levels

> **Hint**: Quick reference summary
> 1. Evidence
>   a. Sufficient - quantity
>   b. Appropriate - quality
>   - observe
>   - external -- directly to auditor or held by client
>   - internal
>   - oral
>
> 2. Substantive tests
>   - Trace/vouch
>   - Reconcile
>   - Analytical procedures
>   - Confirm
>   - Examine

Identify and document risks and related controls at the relevant assertion level for significant classes of transactions, account balances and disclosures in an entity's financial statements.

a. A review of assertions
In representing that the financial statements are in accordance with the applicable financial reporting framework, management implicitly or explicitly makes assertions regarding the recognition, measurement, presentation, and disclosure of the various elements of financial statements and related disclosures.

Assertions used by the auditor to consider the different types of potential misstatements that may occur fall into the following three categories and may take the following forms:
   i. Assertions about **classes of transactions** and events for the period under audit, such as the following:
      a) *Occurrence*. Transactions and events that have been recorded have occurred and pertain to the entity.
      b) *Completeness*. All transactions and events that should have been recorded have been recorded.
      c) *Accuracy*. Amounts and other data relating to recorded transactions and events have been recorded appropriately.
      d) *Cutoff*. Transactions and events have been recorded in the correct accounting period.
      e) *Classification*. Transactions and events have been recorded in the proper accounts.
   ii. Assertions about **account balances** at the period-end, such as the following:
      a) *Existence*. Assets, liabilities, and equity interests exist.
      b) *Rights and obligations*. The entity holds or controls the rights to assets, and liabilities are the obligations of the entity.
      c) *Completeness*. All assets, liabilities, and equity interests that should have been recorded have been recorded.
      d) *Valuation and allocation*. Assets, liabilities, and equity interests are included in the financial statements at appropriate amounts, and any resulting valuation or allocation adjustments are appropriately recorded.

2E-4
Auditing and Attestation (AUD)
Copyright © 2018 Yaeger CPA Review. All rights reserved.

iii. Assertions about **presentation and disclosure**, such as the following:
   a) *Occurrence and rights and obligations.* Disclosed events, transactions, and other matters have occurred and pertain to the entity.
   b) *Completeness.* All disclosures that should have been included in the financial statements have been included.
   c) *Classification and understandability.* Financial information is appropriately presented and described, and disclosures are clearly expressed.
   d) *Accuracy and valuation.* Financial and other information is disclosed fairly and in appropriate amounts.

Relevant assertions are assertions that have a reasonable possibility of containing a misstatement or misstatements that would cause the financial statements to be materially misstated and, as such, are assertions that have a meaningful bearing on whether the account is fairly stated. Not all assertions pertaining to a particular account balance will always be relevant. For example, valuation may not be relevant to the cash account unless currency translation is involved; however, existence and completeness are always relevant. Similarly, valuation may not be relevant to the gross amount of the accounts receivable balance but is relevant to the related allowance accounts.

The auditor is required (by AU-C 315.26b) to use **relevant assertions** for classes of transactions, account balances, and disclosures in sufficient detail to form a basis for the assessment of risks of material misstatement and the design and performance of further audit procedures. The auditor also is required to use relevant assertions in assessing risks by relating the identified risks to what can go wrong at the relevant assertion, taking account of relevant controls that the auditor intends to test, and designing further audit procedures that are responsive to the assessed risks.

The auditor will consider how the identified risks may impact the relevant assertions which could result in a material misstatement to the financial statements.

Multiple Choice

AUD 2-Q21

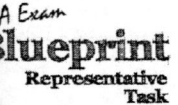

Analyze the potential impact of identified risks at the relevant assertion level for significant classes of transactions, account balances and disclosures in an entity's financial statements, taking account of the controls the auditor intends to test.

b. Develop a Response to Assessed Risks

> **Hint:** The main sources of professional guidance that serve as the basis for this review are obtained from the following:
> AU-C 330, *Performing Audit Procedures in Response to Assessed Risks and Evaluating the Audit Evidence Obtained*, AICPA.
> AS 2301, *The Auditor's Responses to the Risks of Material Misstatement*, PCAOB

This review section provides a "big picture" perspective regarding the auditor's response to assessed risks. A more "local" perspective (and many more details) is found in the review section entitled, **Perform Audit Procedures Responsive to Assessed Risks of Material Misstatement**.

The auditor has a responsibility to design and implement responses to the risks of material misstatement identified and assessed by the auditor. The auditor's objective is to obtain sufficient, appropriate audit evidence regarding the assessed risks of material misstatement, through designing and implementing appropriate responses to those risks.

The auditor's response has two prongs:
1) Design and implement **responses that have an overall effect** on how the audit is conducted (a "global perspective" response).
2) Design and implement responses involving the nature, timing, and extent of the audit procedures to be performed (a "local perspective" response).

> **Hint:** The key objective is that the auditor should provide a clear linkage between the auditor's further audit procedures and the risk assessment.

c. General Discussion of Audit Evidence
The audit procedures performed in response to the assessed risks of material misstatement are classified into two categories:
- **Substantive procedures** – Audit procedures designed to detect material misstatements at the assertion level. Substantive procedures comprise:
    - **Test of details** – Tests focused on the assertions within the classes of transactions, account balances, and disclosures.
    - **Substantive analytical procedures** – Analytical procedures focused on the assertions within the classes of transactions, account balances, and disclosures.
- **Test of controls** – An audit procedure to evaluate the operating effectiveness of controls in preventing, or detecting and correcting, material misstatements at the assertion level.

   1) Nature, Timing, and Extent
      i. **Nature**
         The nature of an audit procedure refers to its *purpose* (test of controls or substantive procedure) and its *type* (inspection, observation inquiry, confirmation, recalculation, re-performance, or analytical procedures). The nature of the audit procedure is most important in responding to the assessed risks.

         The auditor's assessed risks may affect both the types of audit procedures to perform and their combination (e.g., confirm the completeness of contract terms and inspect the contract document).

      ii. **Timing**
          Timing of an audit procedure refers to *when* it is performed or the *period* or data to which the audit evidence applies.

          The auditor may perform tests of controls or substantive procedures at an interim date or at the period-end. The higher the risk of material misstatement, the more likely it is that the auditor may decide it is more effective to perform substantive procedures nearer to or at the period-end.

      iii. **Extent**
           Extent of an audit procedure refers to the *quantity* to be performed (e.g., a sample size or the number of observations of a control activity).

           The extent of an audit procedure judged necessary is determined, after considering the materiality, assessed risk, and degree of assurance the auditor plans to obtain (assurance is 1 minus detection risk).

           In general, extent increases as the risks of material misstatement increases (see the audit risk model).

2) Selecting Items for Testing (Extent)
   Auditors may use the following methods for selecting items for testing:
   - select all items (100% examination),
   - select specific items, and
   - audit sampling.

   i. **100% Examination**
      100% examination is unlikely in the case of test of controls; however, it may be more common for tests of details.

      A 100% examination may be appropriate when
      a) the population is made of a small number of large value items,
      b) a significant risk exists, and other means do not provide sufficient appropriate audit evidence, or
      c) the repetitive nature of a calculation or other process performed automatically by an information system, makes 100% examination cost effective (use computer assisted audit techniques).

   ii. **Selecting Specific Items**
      The auditor may decide to select specific items from a population based on the auditor's understanding of the entity, the assessed risks of material misstatement, and the characteristics of the population being tested.

      This judgmental selection of specific items is subject to non-sampling risk (see AU-C 530).

      Specific items selected may include:
      - High value or key items (e.g., suspicious, unusual, risk prone, history of error, etc.).
      - All items over a certain amount (a quick way to test a large proportion of a population).
      - Items to obtain information (e.g., information about the nature of transactions).

      Selective testing does not constitute audit sampling. Consequently, the results of audit procedures applied to items selected this way, cannot be projected to the entire population. Furthermore, selective examination of specific items does not, by itself, provide sufficient appropriate audit evidence concerning the remainder of the population.

   iii. **Audit Sampling**
      Audit sampling is designed to enable conclusions to be drawn about an entire population on the basis of testing a sample drawn from the population. Audit sampling is discussed in the review of ***Audit Sampling*** (specifically, AU-C 530).

3) Evaluating the Sufficiency and Appropriateness of Audit Evidence
   Based on the audit procedures performed and the audit evidence obtained, the auditor should evaluate, before the conclusion of the audit, whether the assessments of the risks of material misstatement at the relevant assertion level remain appropriate.

The auditor should conclude whether sufficient appropriate audit evidence has been obtained, considering all relevant audit evidence, regardless of whether it appears to corroborate or contradict the assertions in the financial statements.

If the auditor has not obtained sufficient appropriate audit evidence about a relevant assertion, the auditor should attempt to obtain further audit evidence. If the auditor is unable to obtain sufficient appropriate audit evidence, the auditor should express a qualified opinion or disclaim an opinion on the financial statements (see AU-C 700 for more information on audit opinions).

4) Documentation
   The auditor should document:
   - the overall responses to address the assessed risks of material misstatement at the financial statement level and the nature, timing, and extent of the further audit procedures performed;
   - the linkage of those procedures with the assessed risks at the relevant assertion level; and
   - the results of the audit procedures, including the conclusions when such conclusions are not otherwise clear.

   If the auditor plans to use audit evidence about the operating effectiveness of controls obtained in previous audits, the auditor should include in the audit documentation, the conclusions reached about relying on such controls that were tested in a previous audit.

   The auditor should include in the audit documentation, the basis for any determination not to use external confirmation procedures for accounts receivable, when the account balance is material.

   The auditor's documentation should demonstrate that the financial statements agree or reconcile with the underlying accounting records.

> **Hint:** The main sources of professional guidance that serve as the basis for this review are obtained from the following:
> AU-C 330, *Performing Audit Procedures in Response to Assessed Risks and Evaluating the Audit Evidence Obtained*, AICPA
> AS 2201, *An Audit of Internal Control Over Financial Reporting That Is Integrated with An Audit of Financial Statements*, PCAOB.

   i. **Tests of Controls**
      The auditor should design and perform tests of controls to obtain sufficient appropriate audit evidence about the operating effectiveness of relevant controls if:
      a) the auditor intends to rely on the operating effectiveness of controls in determining the nature, timing, and extent of substantive procedures, or
      b) substantive procedures alone cannot provide sufficient appropriate audit evidence at the relevant assertion level (e.g., online sales that are exclusively done through the IT system).

      In designing and performing tests of controls, the auditor should obtain more persuasive audit evidence the greater the reliance the auditor places on the effectiveness of controls. In other words, a lower level of control risk requires more persuasive audit evidence.

Tests of internal controls are preformed to support the auditor's **reduced control risk assessment**. (Notwithstanding the tests of controls in an integrated audit related to public companies. See PCAOB's AS 2201.) Recall the **audit risk model** and use the model to recall the relationships between risk and audit procedures.

Audit Risk Model

$$AR = RMM \times DR$$
OR
$$AR = IR \times CR \times DR$$

Where:
AR = audit risk: The risk that the auditor expresses an inappropriate audit opinion when the financial statements are materially misstated.
RMM = risk of material misstatement: The risk that the financial statements are materially misstated prior to the audit. RMM consists of two components: RMM = IR × CR;
IR = inherent risk: The susceptibility of an assertion about a class of transaction, account balance, or disclosure, to a misstatement that could be material, either individually or when aggregated with other misstatements, before consideration of any related controls.
CR = control risk: The risk that a misstatement that could occur in an assertion about a class of transaction, account balance, or disclosure, and that could be material, either individually or when aggregated with other misstatements, will not be prevented, or detected and corrected, on a timely basis by the entity's internal control.
DR = detection risk: The risk that the procedures performed by the auditor to reduce audit risk to an acceptably low level will not detect a misstatement that exists and that could be material, either individually or when aggregated with other misstatements.

The auditor will only test controls (other than integrated audits) if he or she can reduce control risk. If the auditor can reduce control risk, this allows for a lower detection risk (for a given audit risk). The lower detection risk reduces substantive evidence requirements.

a) **Test of Controls: General Items**
   Test of controls. An audit procedure designed to evaluate the operating effectiveness of controls in preventing, or detecting and correcting, material misstatements at the assertion level.

   Tests of controls are performed only on those controls that the auditor has determined are suitably designed to prevent, or detect and correct, a material misstatement in a relevant assertion. If substantially different controls were used at different times during the period under audit, each is considered separately.

b) **Test of Controls: Design Effectiveness**
   Testing the operating effectiveness of controls is different from obtaining an understanding of and evaluating the design and implementation of controls. However, the same types of audit procedures are used. The auditor may, therefore, decide it is efficient to test the operating effectiveness of controls at the same time the auditor is evaluating their design and determining that they have been implemented.

The auditor should test the design effectiveness of controls by determining whether the company's controls, if they are operated as prescribed by persons possessing the necessary authority and competence to perform the control effectively, satisfy the company's control objectives and can effectively prevent or detect errors or fraud that could result in material misstatements in the financial statements.

Procedures the auditor performs to test design effectiveness, include a mix of inquiry of appropriate personnel, observation of the company's operations, and inspection of relevant documentation. **Walkthroughs** that include these procedures ordinarily are sufficient to evaluate design effectiveness.

NOTE: Testing the design effectiveness of internal controls is one step on the path of testing the operating effectiveness of internal controls.

c) **Test of Controls: Operating Effectiveness**
The auditor should design and perform tests of controls to obtain sufficient appropriate audit evidence about **the operating effectiveness** of relevant controls if:
1. the auditor intends to rely on the operating effectiveness of controls in determining the nature, timing, and extent of substantive procedures (i.e., reduce control risk to a lower level), or
2. substantive procedures alone cannot provide sufficient appropriate audit evidence at the relevant assertion level (e.g., online sales that are exclusively done through the IT system).

The auditor should test the operating effectiveness of a control by determining whether the control is operating as designed and whether the person performing the control possesses the necessary authority and competence to perform the control effectively.

In designing and performing tests of controls, the auditor should obtain more persuasive audit evidence, the greater the reliance the auditor places on the effectiveness of controls. In other words, a lower level of control risk requires more persuasive audit evidence.

If the auditor plans to rely on controls over a risk the auditor has determined to be a **significant risk**, the auditor should test the operating effectiveness of those controls in the current period.

Procedures the auditor performs to test operating effectiveness include a mix of inquiry of appropriate personnel, observation of the company's operations, inspection of relevant documentation, and re-performance of the control.

d) **Nature of Tests of Controls**
Inquiry alone is not sufficient to test the operating effectiveness of controls. Accordingly, other audit procedures are performed in combination with inquiry. In this regard, inquiry combined with inspection, recalculation, or re-performance may provide more assurance than inquiry and observation, because an observation is pertinent only at the point in time at which it is made. The following tests that the auditor might perform are presented in order of the evidence that they ordinarily would produce, from least to most:

inquiry, observation, inspection of relevant documentation, and re-performance of a control.

The nature of the particular control influences the type of audit procedure necessary to obtain audit evidence about whether the control was operating effectively. For example, if operating effectiveness is evidenced by documentation, the auditor may decide to inspect such documentation to obtain audit evidence about operating effectiveness. For other controls, however, documentation may not be available or relevant. For example, documentation of operation may not exist for some factors in the control environment, such as assignment of authority and responsibility, or for some types of control activities, such as control activities performed by a computer. In such circumstances, audit evidence about operating effectiveness may be obtained through inquiry in combination with other audit procedures, such as observation or the use of CAATs.

e) **Timing of Tests of Controls**
The auditor should test controls for the particular time or throughout the period for which the auditor intends to rely on those controls, subject to the following:
1. If the auditor obtains audit evidence about the operating effectiveness of controls during an *interim period*, the auditor should
   - obtain audit evidence about significant changes to those controls subsequent to the interim period and
   - determine the additional audit evidence to be obtained for the remaining period.
2. If the auditor plans to use *audit evidence from a previous audit* about the operating effectiveness of specific controls, the auditor should perform audit procedures to establish the continuing relevance of that information to the current audit. The auditor should obtain this evidence by performing inquiry, combined with observation or inspection, to confirm the understanding of those specific controls, and
   - *if there have been changes* that affect the continuing relevance of the audit evidence from the previous audit, the auditor should test the controls in the current audit and
   - *If there have been no changes*, the auditor should test the controls at least once every third year and should test some controls during each audit to avoid the possibility of testing all the controls on which the auditor tends to rely in a single audit period with no testing of controls in subsequent two audit periods.

Simply put, when the auditor performs interim testing (related to tests of controls or substantive procedures), the auditor should perform some audit procedures to "close the window" between the interim date and the period-end date. The objective here is to make sure that there is no time span where the auditor is totally in the dark regarding the client's financial transactions and/or processes.

f) **Extent of Tests of Controls**
When more persuasive audit evidence is needed regarding the effectiveness of a control, it may be appropriate to increase the extent of testing of the control.

In addition to the degree of reliance on controls, other matters the auditor may consider in determining the extent of tests of controls include the following:
1. The frequency of the performance of the control by the entity during the period.
2. The length of time during the audit period that the auditor is relying on the operating effectiveness of the control.
3. The expected rate of deviation from a control.
4. The relevance and reliability of the audit evidence to be obtained regarding the operating effectiveness of the control at the relevant assertion level.
5. The extent to which audit evidence is obtained from tests of other controls related to the relevant assertion.

However, the rate of expected deviation may indicate that obtaining audit evidence from the performance of tests of controls will not be sufficient to reduce the control risk at the relevant assertion level. If the rate of expected deviation is expected to be high, tests of controls for a particular assertion may not provide sufficient appropriate audit evidence.

g) **Deviations**
If deviations from controls, upon which the auditor intends to rely, are detected, the auditor should make specific inquiries to understand these matters and their potential consequences, and should determine whether:
1. the tests of controls that have been performed provide an appropriate basis for reliance on the controls, or
2. additional tests of controls are necessary, or
3. the potential risks of misstatement need to be addressed using substantive procedures (the auditor cannot reduce control risk).

The identification by the auditor of a material misstatement of the financial statements under audit, in circumstances that indicate that the misstatement would not have been detected by the entity's internal control, is an indicator of a **material weakness**.

The concept of effectiveness of the operation of controls recognizes that some deviations in the way controls are applied by the entity may occur. Deviations from prescribed controls may be caused by such factors as changes in key personnel, significant seasonal fluctuations in volume of transactions, and human error. The detected rate of deviation, in particular, in comparison with the expected rate, may indicate that the control cannot be relied on to reduce risk at the relevant assertion level to that assessed by the auditor.

ii. **Integrated audits**

> *Hint:* Generally, the concepts reviewed above in Test of Controls: Operating Effectiveness apply to integrated audits.

When an auditor is engaged to perform an audit of management's assessment of the effectiveness of **internal control over financial reporting** ("the audit of internal control over financial reporting") that is integrated with an audit of the financial statements.

Effective internal control over financial reporting provides reasonable assurance regarding the reliability of financial reporting and the preparation of financial statements for external purposes. If one or more **material weaknesses** exist, the company's internal control over financial reporting cannot be considered effective.

The auditor's objective in an audit of internal control over financial reporting, is to express an opinion on the effectiveness of the company's internal control over financial reporting. Because a company's internal control cannot be considered effective if one or more material weaknesses exist, to form a basis for expressing an opinion, the auditor must plan and perform the audit to obtain competent evidence that is sufficient to obtain reasonable assurance about whether material weaknesses exist as of the date specified in management's assessment. A material weakness in internal control over financial reporting may exist even when financial statements are not materially misstated.

The auditor should use the same suitable, recognized control framework to perform his or her audit of internal control over financial reporting as management uses for its annual evaluation of the effectiveness of the company's internal control over financial reporting. The COSO (The Committee of Sponsoring Organizations of the Treadway Commission) framework is the recognized framework.

The audit of internal control over financial reporting should be integrated with the audit of the financial statements. The objectives of the audits are not identical, however, and the auditor must plan and perform the work to achieve the objectives of both audits.

In an integrated audit of internal control over financial reporting and the financial statements, the auditor should design his or her testing of controls to accomplish the objectives of both audits simultaneously –
- To obtain sufficient evidence to support the auditor's opinion on internal control over financial reporting as of year-end, and
- To obtain sufficient evidence to support the auditor's control risk assessments for purposes of the audit of financial statements.

The auditor should use a **top-down approach** to the audit of internal control over financial reporting to select the controls to test. A top-down approach begins at the financial statement level and with the auditor's understanding of the overall risks to internal control over financial reporting. The auditor then focuses on entity-level controls and works down to significant accounts and disclosures and their relevant assertions. This approach directs the auditor's attention to accounts, disclosures, and assertions that present a reasonable possibility of material misstatement to the financial statements and related disclosures. The auditor then verifies his or her understanding of the risks in the company's processes, and selects for testing those controls that sufficiently address the assessed risk of misstatement to each relevant assertion.

The auditor must evaluate the severity of each control **deficiency** that comes to his or her attention to determine whether the deficiencies, individually or in combination, are **material weaknesses** as of the date of management's assessment. In planning and performing the audit, however, the auditor is not required to search for deficiencies that, individually or in combination, are less severe than a material weakness. The severity of a deficiency does not depend on whether a misstatement actually has occurred, but rather on whether there is a reasonable possibility that the company's controls will fail to prevent or detect a misstatement. The auditor should evaluate the effect of compensating controls when determining whether, a control deficiency or combination of deficiencies, is a material weakness. To have a mitigating effect, the compensating control should operate at a level of precision that would prevent or detect a misstatement that could be material.

The auditor must communicate, in writing, to management and the audit committee all material weaknesses identified during the audit. The written communication should be made prior to the issuance of the auditor's report on internal control over financial reporting. If the auditor concludes, that the oversight of the company's external financial reporting and internal control over financial reporting by the company's audit committee, is ineffective, the auditor must communicate that conclusion in writing to the board of directors. The auditor also should consider whether there are any deficiencies, or combinations of deficiencies, that have been identified during the audit that are **significant deficiencies** and must communicate such deficiencies, in writing, to the audit committee. The auditor also should communicate to management, in writing, all deficiencies in internal control over financial reporting (i.e., those deficiencies in internal control over financial reporting that are of a lesser magnitude than material weaknesses) identified during the audit and inform the audit committee when such a communication has been made.

> *Hint*: The CPA Exam often asks questions related to the control structure of an audit client. Make sure you have an understanding of the usual controls in each major transaction cycle.

iii. **Significant risks**
If the auditor plans to rely on controls over a risk the auditor has determined to be a **significant risk**, the auditor should test the operating effectiveness of those controls in the current period.

iv. **Deviations**
If deviations from controls upon which the audit intents to rely are detected, the auditor should make specific inquiries to understand these matters and their potential consequences and should determine whether --
  a) the tests of controls, that have been performed, provide an appropriate basis for reliance on the controls,
  b) additional tests of controls are necessary, or
  c) the potential risks of misstatement need to be addressed using substantive procedures (the auditor cannot reduce control risk).

Multiple Choice

AUD 2-Q22 through AUD 2-Q63

1) Substantive procedures
Irrespective of the assess risks of material misstatements, the auditor should design and perform substantive procedures for all relevant assertions related to each **material** class of transaction, account balance, and disclosure.

   i. **Nature of Substantive Procedures**
   Depending on the circumstances, the auditor may determine the following:
      a. Performing only substantive analytical procedures will be sufficient to reduce audit risk to an acceptably low level, such as, for example, when the auditor's assessment of risk is supported by audit evidence from tests of controls (a reduced level of control risk).
      b. Only tests of details are appropriate.
      c. A combination of substantive analytical procedures and tests of details are most responsive to the assessed risks.

ii. **Confirmations**
The auditor should use external confirmation procedures for accounts receivable (unless certain conditions are present; see AU-C 330.20).

iii. **Financial Statement Closing Process**
The auditor's substantive procedures should include audit procedures related to the financial statement closing process, such as:
- agreeing or reconciling the financial statements with the underlying accounting records and
- examining material journal entries and other adjustments made during the course of preparing the financial statements.

iv. **Significant Risks**
If the auditor has determined that an assessed risk of material misstatement at the relevant assertion level is a significant risk, the auditor should perform substantive procedures that are specifically responsive to that risk.

When the approach to a significant risk consists only of substantive procedures, those procedures should include tests of details.

v. **Timing of Substantive Procedures**
In most cases, audit evidence from a previous audit's substantive procedures provides little or no audit evidence for the current period.

If substantive procedures are performed at an interim date, the auditor should cover the remaining period by performing (a) substantive procedures, combined with tests of controls for the intervening period, or if the auditor determines that it is sufficient, (b) further substantive procedures only, that provide a reasonable basis for extending the audit conclusions from the interim date to the period-end.

If the auditor detects unexpected misstatements during the interim testing, the auditor should evaluate whether the related assessment of risk and the planned nature, timing, and extent of substantive procedures covering the remaining period, need to be modified. Such modification may include extending or repeating, at period-end, the procedures performed at the interim date.

Simply put, when the auditor performs interim testing (related to tests of controls or substantive procedures), the auditor should perform some audit procedures to "close the window" between the interim date and the period-end date. The objective here is to make sure that there is no time span where the auditor is totally in the dark regarding the client's financial transactions and/or processes.

vi. **Other Substantive Procedures – Auditing Financial Statement Items and Disclosures**
The following procedures are commonly used in audits of financial statements and have been used in CPA Exam questions.

> *Hint*: Unless stated elsewhere, the listings of typical substantive audit procedures contain a reference (at the end of the procedure) to the assertions that are tested as follows:
> PD = Presentation and Disclosure.
> EO = Existence or Occurrence.
> RO = Rights and Obligations.
> CC = Completeness and Cutoff.
> VAA = Valuation, Allocation and Accuracy.

a) **Cash**
Typical substantive audit procedures related to cash:
1. Count cash on hand at year-end to verify its existence (EO).
2. Send confirmation letters to financial institutions to verify existence of the amounts on deposit (EO).
3. Review bank statements to verify that book balances represent amounts to which the client has rights (RO).
4. Review year-end bank reconciliations to verify that cash has been properly stated as of year-end (CC).
5. Obtain a bank cutoff statement to verify whether the reconciling items on the year-end bank reconciliation have been properly reflected (CC).
6. Prepare a bank transfer schedule for the last week of the audit year and the first week of the following year to disclose misstatements of cash balances resulting from kiting (EO).
7. Review the cutoff of cash receipts and cash disbursements around year-end to verify that transactions affecting cash are recorded accurately and in the proper period (CC).
8. Perform analytical procedures to test the reasonableness of cash balances. Tests here may include comparisons to prior year cash balances. These procedures help verify the existence and completeness as well as the accuracy of cash transactions.
9. Test translation of any foreign currencies (VAA).
10. Inquire of management concerning compensating balance requirements and restrictions on cash. A compensating balance is an account with a bank in which a company has agreed to maintain a specified minimum amount; compensating balances are typically required under the terms of bank loan agreements. Such restrictions on cash, when material, should be disclosed in the financial statements (PD). Information about compensating balance requirements are included in the bank confirmation.
11. Foot summary schedules of cash and agree their total to the amount which will appear on the financial statements (VAA).
12. Reconcile summary schedules of cash to the general ledger (VAA).
13. Review disclosures for compliance with generally accepted accounting principles (PD).

> *Hint*: Make sure you understand the structure and use of a bank transfer schedule (to uncover kiting). Understand and be able to do a 2-column and 4-column (also called a proof of cash) bank reconciliation.

b) Accounts Receivable
Typical substantive audit procedures related to receivables:
1. Foot the accounts and notes receivable subsidiary ledgers to verify clerical accuracy (VAA).
2. Reconcile subsidiary ledgers to the general ledger control accounts to verify clerical accuracy (VAA).
3. Confirm accounts and notes receivable by direct communication with debtors to verify the existence and gross valuation of the accounts (EO).
4. Inspect notes on hand and confirm those not on hand by direct communication with holders. For notes receivable, the auditor will generally be able to inspect the actual note. This procedure is particularly important in situations in which the note is negotiable (i.e., salable) to third parties (EO).
5. Vouch receivables to supporting customer orders, sales orders, invoices, shipping documents, and credit memos to verify the existence of accounts, and occurrence and accuracy of sales transactions (EO).
6. Review the cutoff of sales and cash receipts around year-end to verify that transactions affecting accounts receivable are recorded in the proper period. A sale is properly recorded when title passes on the items being sold. Title passes for items sold FOB shipping point when the item is shipped from inventory; title passes for items sold FOB destination when the item is received by the purchaser. You should realize that a proper credit sales cutoff generally affects at least four components of the financial statements: accounts receivable, sales, cost of goods sold, and inventory. Cash receipts should be recorded when the check (or cash) is received from a customer (CC).
7. Inquire of management about pledging, or discounting of receivables to verify that appropriate disclosure is provided (PD).
8. Review loan agreements for pledging and factoring of receivables to verify that appropriate disclosure is provided (PD).
9. Inquire about factoring of receivables to verify that the client maintains rights to the accounts (RO).
10. Perform analytical procedures for accounts receivable, sales, notes receivable, and interest revenue. Typical ratios include: (a) the gross profit rate, (b) accounts receivable turnover, (c) the ratio of accounts receivable to credit sales, (d) the ratio of accounts written off to the ending accounts receivable, and (e) the ratio of interest revenue to notes receivable. These procedures typically provide evidence to support the existence, completeness, accuracy, and valuation assertions.
11. Age accounts receivable to test the adequacy of the allowance for doubtful accounts. An aging schedule is used to address the receivable valuation assertion. Such a schedule summarizes receivables by their age (e.g., 0–30 days since sale, 31–60 days since sale...). Estimates of the likely amount of bad debts in each age group are then made (typically based on historical experience) to estimate whether the amount in the allowance for doubtful accounts is adequate at year-end (VAA).
12. Discuss the adequacy of the allowance for doubtful accounts with management and the credit department and compare it to historical experience to verify valuation.
13. Consider changes in the economy or the company's customers that might affect the valuation of accounts receivable.
14. Examine cash receipts subsequent to year-end to test the adequacy of the allowance for doubtful accounts to determine appropriate valuation.

15. Review disclosures for compliance with generally accepted accounting principles (PD).

> *Hint*: Understand **lapping** (lapping is an embezzlement scheme in which cash collections from customers are stolen and the shortage is concealed by delaying the recording of subsequent cash receipts) and that its cause is usually due to a lack of segregation of duties in the cash function (where one person has responsibility for both recordkeeping and custody of cash).

c) **Inventory**

If inventory is material to the financial statements, the auditor should obtain sufficient appropriate audit evidence regarding the existence and condition of inventory by:
- attending physical inventory counting, unless impracticable, to:
    o evaluate management's instructions and procedures for recording and controlling the results of the entity's physical inventory counting, observe the performance of management's count procedures,
    o inspect the inventory (Inspecting inventory when attending physical inventory counting assists the auditor in ascertaining the existence of the inventory (though not necessarily its ownership) and in identifying obsolete, damaged, or aging inventory.), and
    o perform test counts (Performing test counts (for example, by tracing items selected from management's count records to the physical inventory and tracing items selected from the physical inventory to management's count records) provides audit evidence about the completeness and accuracy of those records.) and
- performing audit procedures over the entity's final inventory records to determine whether they accurately reflect actual inventory count results.

If inventory under the custody and control of a third party is material to the financial statements, the auditor should obtain sufficient, appropriate audit evidence regarding the existence and condition of that inventory by performing one or both of the following:
- Request confirmation from the third party regarding the quantities and condition of inventory held on behalf of the entity.
- Perform inspection or other audit procedures appropriate in the circumstances. (The higher the materiality of inventory, the more likely it is that the auditor will inspect the inventory.)

Typical substantive audit procedures related to inventory:
1. Observe the taking of the physical inventory and make test counts to verify the existence of inventory (and to a limited extent the ownership and valuation; see item 4.).
2. Perform test counts during the observation of the taking of the inventory and compare them to the client's counts and subsequently to the accumulated inventory to verify the accuracy of the count and its accumulation (CC).
3. Account for all inventory tags and count sheets to verify that inventory has been completely recorded (CC).

4. Examine inventory quality and condition to assess whether there may be evidence suggesting that it is in unsatisfactory condition (VAA); evidence about obsolescence.
5. Review cutoffs of sales, sales returns, purchases, and purchase returns around year-end to verify that transactions affecting inventory are recorded in the proper period. The objective is to include in inventory those items for which the client has legal title (CC).
6. Perform analytical procedures to test the reasonableness of inventory. Analytical procedures include calculation of gross profit margins by product, and inventory turnover rates. Analytical procedures are particularly effective at identifying obsolete inventory and, therefore, are useful in determining its proper valuation.
7. Review purchase and sales commitments to verify whether there may be a need to either accrue a loss and/ or provide disclosure. Generally, commitments are not disclosed in the financial statements unless uneconomic commitments result in a need to accrue significant losses (due to current price changes) (PD).
8. Test the inventory cost method to verify that it is in conformity with generally accepted accounting principles. Here the auditor will determine the method of pricing used and whether it is acceptable and consistent with the prior years (e.g., LIFO, FIFO) (VAA).
9. Test the pricing of inventory to verify that it is valued at the lower of cost or market and that inventory and cost of goods sold transactions are accurately recorded. As a general rule, inventories should not be carried in excess of their net realizable value. For wholesalers and retailers, the accuracy of pricing is determined by reference to vendor invoices. For manufacturers, it is determined by reference to vendor invoices, requisitions, and labor reports. In certain circumstances a specialist may be needed to assist in valuation of inventory (VAA).
10. Perform any necessary additional tests of inventory obsolescence to verify the valuation of inventory (VAA).
11. Inquire of management about pledging of inventory and verify the adequacy of disclosure.
12. Inquire of management as to the existence of consigned inventory to verify the adequacy of its disclosure. Know that inventory consigned out remains the property of the client until it is sold. Inventory consigned to the client should not be included in the physical count, since it belongs to the consignor (EO).
13. Confirm consigned inventory and inventory in warehouses. Some companies store inventory items in public warehouses. In such a situation, the auditor should confirm, in writing, with the custodian that the goods are being held. Additionally, if such holdings are significant, the auditor should apply one or more of the following procedures:
    - Review the client's control procedures relating to the warehouseman.
    - Obtain a CPA's report on the warehouseman's internal control.
    - Observe physical counts of the goods.
    - If warehouse receipts have been pledged as collateral, confirm with lenders details of the pledged receipts (EO).
14. Foot and extend summary inventory schedules to verify clerical accuracy (VAA).

15. Reconcile inventory summary schedules to the general ledger to verify clerical accuracy (VAA).
16. Review disclosures for compliance with generally accepted accounting principles (PD).

d) **Investment Securities**

For *valuations based on an investee's financial results* (excluding investments accounted for using the equity method of accounting), obtaining and reading the financial statements of the investee that have been audited by an auditor, whose report is satisfactory, may be sufficient for the purpose of obtaining sufficient appropriate audit evidence.

The method for determining *fair value* may be specified by the applicable financial reporting framework and may vary depending on the industry in which the entity operates or the nature of the entity. Quoted market prices for derivative instruments and securities, listed on national exchanges or over-the-counter markets, are available from sources such as financial publications, the exchanges, NASDAQ, or pricing services based on sources such as those. Quoted market prices obtained from those sources generally provide sufficient evidence of the fair value of the derivative instruments and securities.

Typical substantive audit procedures related to investment securities.
1. Inspect and count securities on hand and compare serial numbers with those shown on the records and, if appropriate, with prior year audit working papers. This procedure addresses the existence of the securities and provides evidence that no fraud involving "substitution" (e.g., unauthorized sale and subsequent repurchase) of securities has occurred during the year. When an auditor is unable to inspect and count securities held in a safe-deposit box at a bank until after the balance sheet date, a bank representative should be asked to confirm that there has been no access between the balance sheet date and the security count date (EO).
2. Vouch purchases and sales of securities during the year. This audit procedure will provide evidence relating to all financial statement assertions. Included here will be re-computation of gains and losses on security sales (EO).
3. Obtain confirmation of securities in the custody of others to verify their existence (EO).
4. Review the cutoff of cash receipts and disbursements around year-end to verify that transactions affecting investment securities transactions are recorded accurately and in the proper period (CC).
5. Review management's classification of securities held for investment (PD).
6. Determine the market value of securities classified as trading or available-for-sale at the date of the balance sheet (VAA).
7. Review audited financial statements of major investments to test whether they are properly valued at yearend. (VAA)
8. Test amortization of premiums and discounts to verify that investments are properly valued (VAA).
9. Perform analytical procedures to test the reasonableness of investment securities. A typical analytical procedure is to verify the relationship between interest and dividend income to the related securities. The auditor will also be able to re-compute the interest and dividend income if so desired.

10. Reconcile amounts of dividends received to published dividend records generally available from databases, maintained on the Internet, to verify the completeness and accuracy of dividend revenue (CC).
11. Inquire of management about pledging of investment securities and verify that appropriate disclosure is provided (PD).
12. Review loan agreements for pledging of investment securities and verify that appropriate disclosure is provided (PD).
13. Foot and extend summary investment security schedules to verify clerical accuracy (VAA).
14. Reconcile summary inventory schedules to the general ledger to verify clerical accuracy (VAA).
15. Review disclosures for compliance with generally accepted accounting principles (PD).

e) **Property, Plant and Equipment (PP&E)**
General approach to auditing PP&E: **New client**: The reasonableness of the entire account balance should be audited in detail. When a predecessor auditor exists, the successor will normally review the predecessor auditor's workpapers. **Continuing client**: The audit of PP&E consists largely of an analysis of the year's acquisitions and disposals (an input and output approach).

The relationship between PP&E and repairs and maintenance should be understood. A number of CPA questions address this area. A PP&E acquisition may improperly be recorded in the repair and maintenance expense account. Therefore, an analysis of repairs and maintenance may detect **understatements** of PP&E. Alternatively, an analysis of PP&E may disclose repairs and maintenance that have improperly been capitalized, thereby resulting in **overstatements** of PP&E. Expenditures that make the asset more productive or extend its useful life should be capitalized in the asset account (betterment) or as a debit to accumulated depreciation (life extension).

Typical substantive audit procedures related to PP&E:
1. Inspect major acquisitions of PP&E to verify their existence (EO).
2. Vouch additions and retirements to PP&E to verify their existence, accuracy, and the client's rights to them. Typically large PP&E transactions support will include original documents such as contracts, deeds, construction work orders, invoices, and authorization by the directors. This procedure will also help to identify transactions that should be expensed rather than capitalized (EO).
3. Review any leases for proper accounting to determine whether the related PP&E assets should be capitalized (EO).
4. Perform search for unrecorded retirements and for obsolete equipment (EO).
5. Review minutes of the board of directors (and shareholders) to verify that additions have been properly approved (RO).
6. Obtain or prepare an analysis of repairs and maintenance expense and vouch transactions to discover items that should have been capitalized (CC).
7. Inquire of management concerning any liens and restrictions on PP&E. PP&E may be pledged as security on a loan agreement. Such restrictions are disclosed in the notes to the financial statements (PD).
8. Review loan agreements for liens and restrictions on PP&E and verify that appropriate disclosure is provided (PD).

9. Perform analytical procedures to test the reasonableness (existence, completeness, and valuation) of PP&E. Typical analytical procedures involve a (a) comparison of total cost of PP&E divided by cost of goods sold, (b) comparison of repairs and maintenance on a monthly and annual basis, and (c) comparison of acquisitions and retirements for the current year with prior years.
10. Recalculate depreciation to establish proper valuation of PP&E. In addition, the existence of recurring losses on retired assets may indicate that depreciation charges are generally insufficient.
11. Consider any conditions that indicate that assets may be impaired to determine that the assets are properly valued. Indications of possible impairment include discontinuance of a business segment or type of product, excessive capacity, loss of major customers, etc. (VVA).
12. Foot PP&E summary schedules to verify clerical accuracy (VVA).
13. Reconcile summary PP&E schedules to the general ledger to verify clerical accuracy (VVA).
14. Review disclosures for compliance with generally accepted accounting principles (PD).

f) **Prepaid Assets**
Typical substantive audit procedures related to prepaid expenses:
1. Confirm deposits and insurance with third party to verify their existence and valuation.
2. Vouch additions to accounts (examine insurance policies and miscellaneous other support for deposit) to verify existence and accuracy.
3. Review the adequacy of insurance coverage (since a predominant prepaid is prepaid insurance) (PD).
4. Recalculate prepaid portions of prepaid assets to verify proper valuation.
5. Perform analytical procedures to test the reasonableness of prepaid assets. A primary procedure here is comparison with prior year balances and obtaining explanations for any significant changes (CC).
6. Foot prepaid summary schedules to verify accuracy.
7. Reconcile summary schedules to the general ledger to verify proper accuracy and valuation.
8. Review disclosures for compliance with generally accepted accounting principles (PD).

g) **Accounts Payable**
Sometimes accounts payable are confirmed with vendors. (Although confirmation is best suited to test the existence or occurrence assertion, and audit testing, related to accounts payable, is usually aimed at the completeness assertion – the auditor is concerned with understatement of accounts payable.) Accounts payable confirmations are most frequently used in circumstances involving (1) bad internal control, (2) bad financial position, and (3) situations when vendors do not send month-end statements. However, when an auditor has chosen to confirm payables despite the existence of vendor statements, the confirmation will generally request the vendor to send the month-end statement to the auditor. For this reason, the balance per the client's books is not included on such a confirmation (the auditor doesn't want to prompt the vendor).

A common audit test related to accounts payable is the **search for unrecorded liabilities**. The validity of this test comes from the following truism: Accounts payable get paid or the vendor will not do business with the audit client. So, any period-end accounts payable will be paid in the next period. So, we turn that around and get the following: At least some payments on accounts payable in the next period will be related to last period's accounts payable. The audit test takes next period (say, Jan. 20X1) payment on accounts payable and traces them back to the outstanding accounts payable at the prior period-end (say, Dec. 20X0). Some of the next period payments will related to accounts payable from the next period and the remainder will relate to accounts payable at the prior period-end. Auditors can use this procedure to determine if there were accounts payable at the prior period-end that should have been included in accounts payable, but were not included (incomplete; so the auditor is testing completeness).

Typical substantive audit procedures related to accounts payable (and accrued expenses).
1. Confirm accounts payable by direct correspondence with vendors. Confirmation of payables provides evidence relating to the occurrence, obligation, completeness, accuracy, and valuation assertions.
2. Inspect copies of notes and note agreements (EO).
3. Vouch balances payable to selected creditors by inspecting purchase orders, receiving reports, and invoices to verify existence, accuracy, valuation, and to a lesser extent, completeness.
4. Review the cutoff of purchases, purchase returns, and disbursements around year-end to verify that transactions are recorded in the proper period (CC).
5. Review purchase commitments to determine there is a need to either accrue a loss and/or provide disclosure (PD).
6. Inquire of management as to the completeness of payables.
7. Perform analytical procedures to test the reasonableness of payables. Examples include ratios such as, accounts payable divided by purchases, and accounts payable divided by total current liabilities (CC).
8. Perform search for unrecorded payables to determine whether liabilities have been completely recorded (CC). See earlier discussion.
9. Foot the subsidiary accounts payable ledger to test clerical accuracy (VAA).
10. Reconcile the subsidiary ledger to the general ledger control account to verify clerical accuracy (VAA).
11. Recalculate interest expense on any interest-bearing debt (VAA).
12. Recalculate year-end accrual for payroll. A typical procedure here is to allocate the total days in the payroll subsequent to year-end between the old and new years to determine whether the accrual is reasonable (VAA).
13. Recalculate other accrued liabilities. The approach for accruals is largely one of (1) testing computations made by the client in setting up the accrual, and (2) determining that the accruals have been treated consistently with the past. Examples of accounts requiring accrual include, property taxes, pension plans, vacation pay, service guarantees, commissions, utilities, and income taxes payable (VAA).
14. Review disclosures for compliance with generally accepted accounting principles (PD).

h) **Long-Term Debt**
Often, considerable analysis is performed on the ending balance of long-term debt. The low turnover of long-term debt makes is fairly easy to audit, which yields a cost-effective way to reduce audit risk. Confirmations are frequently

used; recall that when the debt is owed to banks, confirmation is obtained with the ***standard bank confirmation***. In addition, minutes of director and/or stockholder meetings will be reviewed to determine whether new borrowings have been properly authorized.

Typical substantive audit procedures related to long-term debt.

1. Confirm long-term debt with payees or appropriate third parties (including any applicable sinking fund transactions) (EO).
2. Obtain and inspect copies of debt agreements to verify whether provisions have been met and disclosed (EO).
3. Review bank confirmations for any indication of unrecorded debt (CC).
4. Trace receipt of funds (and payments) to the bank account and to the cash receipts journal to verify that the funds were properly received (or disbursed) by the company (EO).
5. Review the cutoff of cash receipts and disbursements around year-end to verify that transactions affecting debt are recorded in the proper period (CC).
6. Review minutes of board of directors' and/or shareholders' meetings to verify that transactions have been properly authorized and, if necessary, that an opinion of an attorney has been obtained regarding the legality of the debt (RO).
7. Inquire of management as to the completeness of debt.
8. Inquire of management concerning pledging of assets related to debt (PD).
9. Review debt agreements for details on pledged assets and for events that may result in default on the loan (PD).
10. Perform analytical procedures to verify the overall reasonableness of long-term debt and interest expense (CC).
11. Foot summary schedules of long-term debt to test clerical accuracy (VAA).
12. Reconcile summary schedules of long-term debt to the general ledger to verify clerical accuracy (VAA).
13. Vouch entries in long-term debt accounts to test existence, obligation, and accuracy of debt.
14. Recalculate interest expense and accrued interest payable to determine accuracy of the amounts.
15. Review disclosures for compliance with generally accepted accounting principles (PD).

i) **Equity**
Auditors will perform procedures to verify the number of shares authorized, issued, and outstanding of **capital stock**. Generally, auditors will confirm directly with the registrar and stock transfer agent.

Retained earnings is fairly easy to audit. Net income will be audited through the audit procedures used on revenues and expenses. Dividends will be audited though examination of authorization (by the board). The nature of any prior period adjustments is examined to determine whether they meet the criteria for an adjustment to retained earnings. Recall that this type of adjustment typically is a correction of prior years' income.

Typical substantive audit procedures related to owners' equity.
1. Confirm stocks authorized, issued, and outstanding with the independent registrar and stock transfer agent (if applicable) (EO).

2. For a corporation that acts as its own stock registrar and transfer agent, reconcile the stock certificate book to transactions recorded in the general ledger (EO).
3. Inspect treasury stock certificates to verify that transactions have been completely recorded and that client has control of certificates (CC).
4. Vouch transactions and trace receipt of funds (and payment) to the bank account and to the cash receipts journal to verify that the funds were properly received (or disbursed) by the company (EO).
5. Review minutes of the board of directors' and/or shareholders' meetings to verify that stock transactions and dividends have been properly authorized (RO).
6. Review Articles of Incorporation, bylaws, and minutes for provisions relating to stock options, and dividends restriction (PD).
7. Inquire of the client's legal counsel to obtain information concerning any unresolved legal issues (RO).
8. Review the Articles of Incorporation and bylaws for the propriety of equity transactions (RO).
9. Perform analytical procedures to test the reasonableness of dividends (CC).
10. Agree amounts that will appear on the financial statements to the general ledger (VAA).
11. Vouch dividend payments to verify that amounts have been paid (VAA).
12. Vouch all entries affecting retained earnings (VAA).
13. Recalculate treasury stock transactions (VAA).
14. Review disclosures for compliance with generally accepted accounting principles (PD).

j) **Revenues**

Basic audit approach: Most revenue items are verified through the audit of the related asset accounts. Note the asset-revenue linkage in the following table:

Balance Sheet Account	Linked Revenues
Accounts receivable	Sales
Notes receivable	Interest income
Investments	Interest, Dividends, Gains on sales
Property, Plant & Equipment	Rent, Gains on sales

Hint: The key to auditing revenue is to understand revenue recognition criteria which is reviewed in the FAR material.

Circumstances that are related to potential fraudulent revenues include the following:

1. **Bill and hold transactions.** Transactions in which a customer agrees to purchase goods but the seller retains physical possession until the customer requests shipment to designated locations. Because delivery has not yet occurred, such transactions do not ordinarily qualify for recognition. The primary requirements to qualify for revenue recognition are as follows: that the buyer make an absolute commitment to purchase; has assumed the risks and rewards of the product: and is unable to accept delivery because of some compelling reason. **Bill and hold transactions initiated by the seller are never legitimate.**

2. **Side agreements.** Agreements used to alter the terms and conditions of recorded sales transactions, often to convince customers to accept delivery of goods and services. Side agreements are frequently hidden from the board of directors and may create obligations that relieve the customer of the risks and rewards of ownership. Accordingly, side agreement terms *may* preclude revenue recognition.

3. **Channel stuffing (trade loading).** A marketing practice that suppliers sometimes use to boost sales, by inducing distributors to buy substantially more inventory than they can promptly resell. Inducements may range from deep discounts on the inventory to threats of losing the distributorship if inventory is not purchased. Channel stuffing may result in the need to increase the level of anticipated sales returns.

4. **Related-party transactions.** A variety of potential misstatements may occur due to transactions with related parties. For example, sales of the same inventory back and forth among affiliated companies may "freshen" receivables (boomerang sales).

Substantive procedure approach for revenues not verified in the audit of balance sheet accounts.
- Perform analytical procedures related to revenue accounts.
- Obtain or prepare analyses of selected revenue accounts.
- Vouch selected transactions and determine that they represent proper revenue for the period.

k) **Expenses**

Basic audit approach: Most expense items are verified through the audit of the related asset or liability accounts. Note the asset/liability-revenue linkage in the following table:

Balance Sheet Account	Linked Expenses
Accounts receivable	Bad debt expense
Inventories	Purchased, Cost of goods sold, Payroll
Property, Plant & Equipment	Depreciation, Repairs and maintenance, Insurances
Accrued liabilities	Commissions, Fees, Warranty expense, Utilities
Long-term debt	Interest expense

Substantive procedure approach for expenses not verified in the audit of balance sheet accounts.
- Perform analytical procedures related to expense accounts.
- Obtain or prepare analyses of selected expense accounts.
- Vouch selected transactions.

Hint: Be familiar with the following other audit evidence terms:

Examine	A reasonably detailed study of a document or record to determine specific facts about it.
Scan	A less detailed examination of a document or record to determine whether there is something unusual warranting further investigation.
Read	An examination of written information to determine facts pertinent to the audit.
Compute	A calculation done by the auditor independent of the client. **Re-compute**: When the auditor tests a client computation by performing it again.
Foot	Addition of a column of numbers to determine whether the total is the same as the client's.
Count	A determination of assets on hand at a given time. This term should be associated with the type of evidence defined as physical examination.
Vouch	The use of documents to verify recorded transactions or amounts.
Trace	An instruction normally associated with documentation or re-performance. The instruction should state what the auditor is tracing and where it is being traced from and to. Often, an audit procedure that includes the term *trace* will also include a second instruction, such as *compare* or *recalculate*.
Compare	A comparison of information in two different locations. The instructions should state which information is being compared in as much detail as practical.

Hint: One can view the auditor's selection of audit procedures as a process that balances the selected audit procedures against the assessed risks of material misstatement. Simply put, higher assessed risks will require more types of audit procedures (nature), more extensive audit evidence (extent), and a focus on the time period from which to obtain the audit evidence (timing).

It's helpful to visualize the auditor's evidence selection process as balancing a scale. On one side of the scale is the assessed risks of material misstatements. On the other side of the scale is the audit evidence requirements needed to balance the scale. The audit evidence portion of the scale can be represented by the following audit evidence matrix:

	TOC	SAP	STOD
Prior Year		N/a	N/a
Interim Period			
Period-End			

Where:
TOC = Test of controls
SAP = Substantive analytical procedures
STOD = Substantive test of details.

The auditor "weights" each cell of the audit evidence matrix using his or her professional judgment such that the audit evidence matrix portion of the scale "weighs" the same as the assessed risks of material misstatements side of the scale.

Multiple Choice

AUD 2-Q64 through AUD 2-Q95

3. Further procedures responsive to identified risks

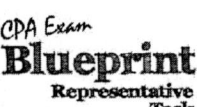

Develop planned audit procedures that are responsive to identified risks of material misstatement due to fraud or error at the relevant assertion level for significant classes of transactions and account balances.

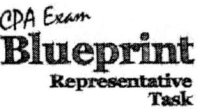

Analyze the risk of material misstatement, including the potential impact of individual and cumulative misstatements, to provide a basis for developing planned audit procedures.

    a. Risks for Which Substantive Procedures Alone Do Not Provide Sufficient Appropriate Audit Evidence
For some risks, the auditor may judge that it is not possible or practicable to obtain sufficient appropriate audit evidence only from substantive procedures. These risks may relate to highly automated processing with little or no manual intervention (e.g., internet sales). In such cases, the entity's controls over such risks are relevant to the audit, and the auditor should obtain an understanding of them.

    b. Revision of Risk Assessment
The auditor's assessment of the risk of material misstatement at the assertion level may change during the course of the audit as additional audit evidence is obtained. If this evidence (or new information) is inconsistent with the original risk assessment, the auditor should revise the risk assessment and modify the further planned audit procedures accordingly.

    c. Documentation
The auditor should include in the audit documentation the
1) Discussion among the engagement team including the significant decisions reached, how and when the discussion occurred, and the audit team members who participated;
2) Key elements of the understanding obtained regarding each of the aspects of the entity and its environment and each of the internal control components, the sources of information, and the risk assessment procedures performed;
3) Identified and assessed risks of material misstatement at the financial statement level and at the relevant assertion level; and
4) Risks identified and related controls about which the auditor has obtained an understanding.

F. Materiality

> *Hint*: The author rearranged the representative tasks in this topic of the CPA exam blueprint for clarity.

1. For the financial statements as a whole and performance materiality/tolerable misstatement

> **Understand materiality as it relates to the financial statements as a whole.**

> **Understand the use of performance materiality and tolerable misstatement in an audit of an issuer or nonissuer.**

> *Hint*: The main sources of professional guidance that serve as the basis for this review are obtained from the following:
> AU-C 320, *Materiality in Planning and Performing an Audit*, AICPA.
> AS 2105, *Consideration of Materiality in Planning and Performing an Audit*, PCAOB.

a. **Materiality** is the amount of **misstatements**, including omissions, that individually or in the aggregate, could reasonably be expected to influence the economic decisions of users made on the basis of the financial statements (AU-C 320.02). An auditor should apply the concept of materiality appropriately in planning and performing an audit of financial statements (AU-C 320.08 and PCAOB AS No. 2105.3).

b. Materiality Types
Auditors should be alert while planning and performing audit procedures for misstatements that could be material due to **quantitative or qualitative** factors. In other words, auditors consider not only the **size (quantitative)** but also the **nature (qualitative factors)** of uncorrected misstatements, and the particular *circumstances of their occurrence*, when evaluating their effect on the financial statements (AU-C 320.06).

Circumstances that may affect the evaluation of misstatements include the following (see AU-C 450.A23 for more examples): The misstatement --
  1. affects compliance with regulatory requirements;
  2. affects compliance with debt covenants or other contractual requirements;
  3. has the effect of increasing management compensation;
  4. changes a loss into income or vice versa; and,
  5. increases the sensitivity of the circumstances surrounding the misstatement (e.g., the implications of misstatements involving fraud).

Simply stated, auditors look at misstatements and ask themselves what are the non-obvious implications of the misstatement. For example, if you uncover a small quantitative (quantitatively immaterial) fraud, this could be a red flag signal regarding the caliber of management and their propensity to commit other frauds, so this misstatement may, in fact, be qualitatively material.

c. Materiality Amounts
Auditors set and work with three related materiality amounts.

  1) **Materiality** refers to an amount related to the financial statements as a whole. One can think of this as a "global" or "big picture" view of materiality.

  2) **Performance materiality** (AU-C 320.0) is set less than materiality for the financial statements as a whole, and is set to reduce to an appropriately low level, the probability that the aggregate of uncorrected and undetected misstatements exceeds materiality for the financial statements as a

whole. If applicable, performance materiality also refers to the amount or amounts set by the auditor at less than the materiality level for classes of transactions, account balances, or disclosures. One can think of this as a more "local" view of materiality. In other words, the auditor divides the materiality (global) and allocates some of the materiality to specific audit areas (e.g., an account balance; local). However, the determination of performance materiality is not a simple mechanical calculation and involves the exercise of professional judgment (AU-C 320.A14). This audit process reduces the likelihood that, the aggregated uncorrected and undetected misstatements at the local levels, does not exceed materiality (for the financial statements as a whole).

3) **Tolerable misstatement** (see AU-C 530, Audit Sampling) is a monetary amount set by the auditor in respect of which the auditor seeks to obtain an appropriate level of assurance that the monetary amount set by the auditor is not exceeded by the actual misstatement in the population (AU-C 530.05). **Tolerable misstatement is the application of performance materiality to a particular sampling procedure** (AU-C 530.A6). Tolerable misstatement may be the same or less than performance materiality. One can think of tolerable misstatement as even more "local" than performance materiality (although they may be identical in certain settings).

The general relationship between these three materiality amounts is shown below.

Materiality > Performance Materiality ≥ Tolerable Misstatement

The following relationship exemplifies these materiality concepts.

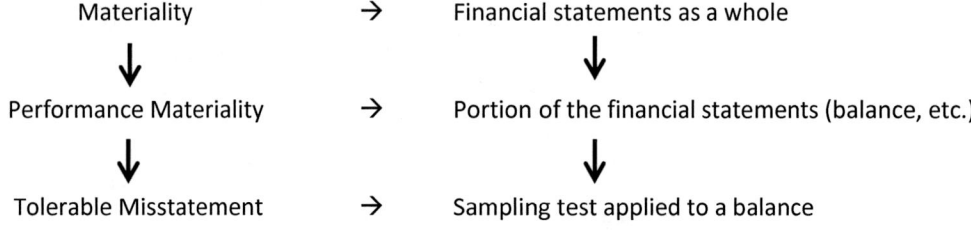

a. **Determining Materiality**

Calculate materiality for an entity's financial statements as a whole.

Calculate the materiality level (or levels) to be applied to classes of transactions, account balances and disclosures in an audit of an issuer or nonissuer.

Calculate performance materiality or tolerable misstatement for the purposes of assessing the risk of material misstatement and determining the nature, timing and extent of further audit procedures in an audit of an issuer or nonissuer.

The auditor's determination of materiality is a *matter of professional judgment* and is affected by the auditor's perception of the financial information needs of the users of the financial statements (AU-C 320.04).

A percentage is often applied to a chosen benchmark as a starting point in determining materiality for the financial statements as a whole. Factors that may affect the identification of a benchmark include the following (AU-C 320.A5):
1) the element of the financial statements;
2) whether users of the particular entity's financial statements tend to focus on certain items;

3) the nature of the entity and the industry and economic environment in which the entity operates;
4) the entity's ownership structure and how it is financed; and
5) the relative volatility of the benchmark.

Benchmarks are often obtained from (AU-C 320.A14):
1) prior periods' financial statements;
2) period-to-date financial statements,
3) budgets or forecasts for the current period, adjusted for significant changes in the circumstances of the entity; and relevant changes of conditions in the industry or economic environment in which the entity operates.

Examples of benchmarks include (AU-C 320.A6):
- profit before taxes,
- total revenue,
- gross profit,
- total expenses,
- total equity, or
- net assets.

PCAOB AS2105.6 notes that, "To determine the nature, timing, and extent of audit procedures, the materiality level for the financial statements as a whole **needs to be expressed as a specified amount**."

b. **Use of Materiality**
The concept of materiality is applied by the auditor (AU-C 320.05)
1) in both planning and performing the audit;
2) in evaluating the effect of identified misstatements on the audit and the effect of **uncorrected misstatements**, if any, on the financial statements, and
3) in forming the opinion in the auditor's report.

The auditor's materiality judgments provide a basis for (AU-C 320.06):
1) determining the nature and extent of risk assessment procedures;
2) identifying and assessing the risks of material misstatements; and
3) determining the nature, timing, and extent of further audit procedures.

c. **Revising materiality**
The auditor should revise materiality for the financial statements as a whole (and, if applicable, performance materiality and tolerable misstatement) if the auditor becomes aware of information during the audit that would have caused the auditor to set a different materiality initially (AU-C 320.12). This information could include (AU-C 320.A16):
1) a change in circumstances that occurred during the audit,
2) new information, or
3) a change in the auditor's understanding of the entity and its operations as a result of performing further audit procedures.

PCAOB AS 2105.12 notes that, "If the auditor's reevaluation [of materiality] results in a lower amount for the materiality level or levels or tolerable misstatement than initially established by the auditor, the auditor should (1) evaluate the effect, if any, of the lower amount or amounts on his or her risk assessments and audit procedures and (2) modify the nature, timing, and extent of audit procedures as necessary to obtain sufficient appropriate audit evidence."

d. **Documenting materiality**
The auditor should include the following amounts and factors considered in their determination of materiality in the audit documentation (AU-C 320.14):
1) Materiality for the financial statements as a whole.
2) The materiality level or levels for particular classes of transactions, account balances, or disclosures.
3) Performance materiality.
4) Any revisions of materiality as the audit progressed.

Multiple Choice

AUD 2-Q96

G. Planning for and Using the Work of Others, Including Group Audits, the Internal Audit Function and the Work of a Specialist

Hint: The author rearranged the representative tasks in this section of the CPA exam blueprint for clarity.

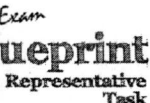

Identify the factors to consider in determining the extent to which an engagement team can use the work of the internal audit function in an audit or non-audit engagement.

The external auditor may be able to use the work of the internal audit function in obtaining audit evidence in a constructive and complementary manner depending on
1) the level of competency of the internal audit function,
2) whether the internal audit function's organizational status and relevant policies and procedures adequately support the objectivity of the internal auditors, and
3) whether the internal audit function applies a systematic and disciplined approach, including quality control.

a. Evaluating the Internal Audit Function
The external auditor should determine whether the work of the internal audit function can be used in obtaining audit evidence by evaluating the following:
1) the extent to which the internal audit function's organizational status and relevant policies and procedures support the objectivity of the internal auditors;
2) the level of competence of the internal audit function; and
3) the application by the internal audit function of a systematic and disciplined approach, including quality control.

The external auditor should not use the work of the internal audit function in obtaining audit evidence if the external auditor determines that
1) the function's organizational status and relevant policies and procedures do not adequately support the objectivity of internal auditors;
2) the function lacks sufficient competence; or
3) the function does not apply a systematic and disciplined approach, including quality control.

b. Determining the nature and extent of work of the internal audit function that can be used in obtaining audit evidence

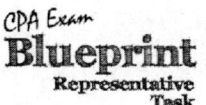

Determine the nature and scope of the work of the internal audit function that can be used in an audit or non-audit engagement.

As a basis for determining the areas and the extent to which the work of the internal audit function can be used, the external auditor should consider the nature, timing, and extent of the work that has been performed, or is planned to be performed, by the internal audit function and its relevance to the external auditor's overall audit strategy and audit plan.

The external auditor should make all significant judgments in the audit engagement, including when using the work of the internal audit function in obtaining audit evidence.

To prevent undue use of the internal audit function in obtaining audit evidence, **the external auditor should plan to use less of the work of the function and perform more of the work directly:**
1) The ***more judgment*** is involved in ...
   i. planning and performing relevant audit procedures or
   ii. evaluating the audit evidence obtained;

2) the *higher the assessed risk of material misstatement* at the assertion level, with special consideration given to significant risks;
3) the less the internal audit function's organizational status and relevant policies and procedures adequately support the objectivity of the internal auditors; and
4) the lower the level of competence of the internal audit function.

c. **Using internal audit work as audit evidence**
If the external auditor plans to use the work of the internal audit function in obtaining audit evidence, the external auditor should discuss the planned use of the work with the function as a basis for coordinating their respective activities.

In determining the nature and extent of work that may be assigned to internal auditors providing direct assistance, and the nature, timing, and extent of direction, supervision, and review that is appropriate in the circumstances, the external auditor should consider
1) the external auditor's evaluation of the existence and significance of threats to the internal auditors' objectivity, the effectiveness of the safeguards applied to reduce or eliminate the threats, and the level of competence of the internal auditors who will be providing such assistance;
2) the assessed risk of material misstatement; and
3) the amount of judgment involved in ...
    i. planning and performing relevant audit procedures and
    ii. evaluating the audit evidence obtained.

d. **Documentation**
If the external auditor uses the work of the internal audit function in obtaining audit evidence, the external auditor should include the following in the audit documentation:
1) The results of the evaluation of ...
    i. the function's organizational status and relevant policies and procedures to adequately support the objectivity of the internal auditors;
    ii. the level of competence of the function; and
    iii. the application by the function of a systematic and disciplined approach, including quality control
2) The nature and extent of the work used (including the period covered by, and the results of, such work) and the basis for that decision
3) The audit procedures performed by the external auditor to evaluate the adequacy of the work used, including the procedures performed by the external auditor to re-perform some of the body of work of the internal audit function in obtaining audit evidence

If the external auditor uses, either the work of the internal audit function in obtaining audit evidence, or internal auditors to provide direct assistance, or both, external auditor still has sole responsibility for the audit opinion expressed.

e. **Non-audit engagements**
Generally, the use of internal auditors in non-audit engagements follows the requirements of AU-C 610.

Multiple Choice

AUD 2-Q97 through AUD 2-Q104

f. Management's specialist

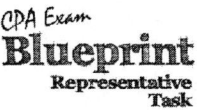

> **Identify the factors to consider in determining the extent to which an engagement team should use the work of a specialist in an audit or non-audit engagement.**

> **Perform procedures to utilize the work of a specialist to obtain evidence in an audit or non-audit engagement.**

The preparation of an entity's financial statements may require expertise in a field other than accounting or auditing, such as, actuarial calculations, valuations, or engineering data.

The entity uses a management's specialist in these fields to obtain the needed expertise to prepare the financial statements. Failure to do so, when such expertise is necessary, increases the risks of material misstatement and may be a significant deficiency or material weakness.

If information to be used as audit evidence has been prepared using the work of a management's specialist, the auditor should, to the extent necessary, taking into account the significance of that specialist's work for the auditor's purposes,
- evaluate the competence, capabilities, and objectivity of that specialist;
- obtain an understanding of the work of that specialist; and
- evaluate the appropriateness of that specialist's work as audit evidence for the relevant assertion.

1) The Competence, Capabilities, and Objectivity of a Management's Specialist
    Competence relates to the nature and level of expertise of the management's specialist.

    Capability relates to the ability of the management's specialist to exercise that competence in the circumstances.

    Factors that influence capability may include, for example, geographic location and the availability of time and resources.

    Objectivity relates to the possible effects that bias, conflict of interest, or the influence of others may have on the professional or business judgment of the management's specialist.

    The competence, capabilities, and objectivity of a management's specialist, and any controls within the entity over that specialist's work, are important factors with regard to the reliability of any information produced by a management's specialist.

    Information regarding the competence, capabilities, and objectivity of a management's specialist may come from a variety of sources, such as the following:
    - Personal experience with previous work of that specialist.
    - Discussions with that specialist.
    - Discussions with others who are familiar with that specialist's work.
    - Knowledge of that specialist's qualifications, membership in a professional body or industry association, license to practice, or other forms of external recognition.
    - Published papers or books written by that specialist.
    - An auditor's specialist, if any, that assists the auditor in obtaining sufficient appropriate audit evidence with respect to information produced by the management's specialist.

Matters relevant to evaluating the competence, capabilities, and objectivity of a management's specialist include whether that specialist's work is subject to technical performance standards or other professional or industry requirements, for example, ethical standards and other membership requirements of a professional body or industry association, accreditation standards of a licensing body, or requirements imposed by law or regulation.

A broad range of circumstances may threaten objectivity, for example, self-interest threats, advocacy threats, familiarity threats, self-review threats, and intimidation threats. Interests and relationships creating threats may include the following:
- Financial interests.
- Business and personal relationships.
- Provision of other services.

2) An understanding of the work of the management's specialist includes an understanding of the relevant field of expertise. An understanding of the relevant field of expertise may be obtained in conjunction with the auditor's determination of whether the auditor has the expertise to evaluate the work of the management's specialist, or whether the auditor needs an auditor's specialist for this purpose.

Aspects of the field of the management's specialist relevant to the auditor's understanding may include
- whether that specialist's field has areas of specialty within it that are relevant to the audit.
- whether any professional or other standards and regulatory or legal requirements apply.
- what assumptions and methods are used by the management's specialist and whether they are generally accepted within that specialist's field and appropriate for financial reporting purposes.
- the nature of internal and external data or information the management's specialist uses.

3) Considerations when evaluating the appropriateness of the work of the management's specialist, as audit evidence for the relevant assertion may include
   i. the relevance and reasonableness of that specialist's findings or conclusions, their consistency with other audit evidence, and whether they have been appropriately reflected in the financial statements;
   ii. if that specialist's work involves use of significant assumptions and methods, the relevance and reasonableness of those assumptions and methods; and
   iii. if that specialist's work involves significant use of source data, the relevance, completeness, and accuracy of that source data.

4) Reference to the Specialist in the Auditor's Report
Per AS 1210, *Using the Work of a Specialist* (PCAOB): Except as discussed below, the auditor should not refer to the work or findings of the specialist. Such a reference might be misunderstood to be a qualification of the auditor's opinion or a division of responsibility, neither of which is intended. Further, there may be an inference that the auditor, making such reference, performed a more thorough audit than an auditor who does not make such reference.

The auditor may, as a result of the report or findings of the specialist, decide to add explanatory language to his or her standard report or depart from an unqualified opinion.

Reference to and identification of the specialist may be made in the auditor's report if the auditor believes such reference will facilitate an understanding of the reason for the explanatory paragraph or the departure from the unqualified opinion.

g. Auditor's specialist
If expertise in a field other than accounting or auditing is necessary to obtain sufficient appropriate audit evidence, the auditor should determine whether to use the work of an auditor's specialist.

1) The auditor should evaluate whether the auditor's specialist has the necessary competence, capabilities, and objectivity for the auditor's purposes.

   In the case of an auditor's external specialist, the evaluation of objectivity should include inquiry regarding interests and relationships that may create a threat to the objectivity of the auditor's specialist.

2) The auditor should obtain a sufficient understanding of the field of expertise of the auditor's specialist to enable the auditor to
   - determine the nature, scope, and objectives of the work of the auditor's specialist for the auditor's purposes and
   - evaluate the adequacy of that work for the auditor's purposes.

3) The auditor should evaluate the adequacy of the work of the auditor's specialist for the auditor's purposes, including
   i. the relevance and reasonableness of the findings and conclusions of the auditor's specialist and their consistency with other audit evidence.
   ii. If the work of the auditor's specialist involves the use of significant assumptions and methods,
      a) obtaining an understanding of those assumptions and methods and
      b) evaluating the relevance and reasonableness of those assumptions and methods in the circumstances, giving consideration to the rationale and support provided by the specialist, and in relation to the auditor's other findings and conclusions.
   iii. If the work of the auditor's specialist involves the use of source data that is significant to the work of the auditor's specialist, the relevance, completeness, and accuracy of that source data.

   If the auditor determines that the work of the auditor's specialist is not adequate for the auditor's purposes, the auditor should
   - agree with the auditor's specialist on the nature and extent of further work to be performed by the auditor's specialist or
   - perform additional audit procedures appropriate to the circumstances.

4) Audit Report
   The auditor should not refer to the work of an auditor's specialist in an auditor's report containing an unmodified opinion.

   If the auditor makes reference to the work of an auditor's external specialist in the auditor's report, because such reference is relevant to an understanding of a modification to the auditor's opinion, the auditor should indicate in the auditor's report that such reference **does not** reduce the auditor's responsibility for that opinion.

Multiple Choice

AUD 2-Q105 through AUD 2-Q109

h. Component auditor

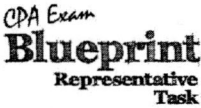

> Identify the factors to consider in determining the extent to which an auditor can use the work of a component auditor in a group audit.

> Determine the nature and scope of the work of a component auditor, including the identification of significant components that can be used in a group audit.

1) Gaining an understanding of the environment regarding the use of component auditors
   The group engagement team should obtain an understanding of the group, its components, and their environments that is sufficient to identify components that are likely to be significant components.

   In a new engagement, the group engagement team's understanding of the group, its components, and their environments may be obtained from the following:
   i. Information provided by group management
   ii. Communication with group management
   iii. When applicable, communication with the previous group engagement team, component management, or component auditors

   The group engagement team's understanding may include matters such as the following:
   i. The group structure, including both the legal and organizational structure (that is, how the group financial reporting system is organized).
   ii. Components' business activities that are significant to the group, including the industry and regulatory, economic, and political environments in which those activities take place.
   iii. The use of service organizations, including shared service centers.
   iv. A description of group-wide controls.
   v. The complexity of the consolidation process.
   vi. Whether component auditors, that are not from the group engagement partner's firm or network, will perform work on the financial information of any of the components and group management's rationale for engaging more than one auditor, if applicable.
   vii. Whether the group engagement team…
      - will have unrestricted access to those charged with governance of the group, group management, those charged with governance of the component, component management, component information, and the component auditors (including relevant audit documentation sought by the group engagement team) and
      - will be able to perform necessary work on the financial information of the components.

2) Decision to use component auditors
   Regardless of whether reference will be made in the auditor's report on the group financial statements to the audit of a component auditor, the group engagement team should obtain an understanding of the following:
   i. Whether a component auditor understands and will comply with the ethical requirements that are relevant to the group audit and, in particular, is independent.
   ii. A component auditor's professional competence.
   iii. The extent, if any, to which the group engagement team will be able to be involved in the work of the component auditor.

iv. Whether the group engagement team will be able to obtain information affecting the consolidation process from a component auditor.
v. Whether a component auditor operates in a regulatory environment that actively oversees auditors.

Factors that may affect the group engagement partner's decisions whether to use the work of a component auditor to provide audit evidence for the group audit, and whether to make reference to the audit of a component auditor in the auditor's report on the group financial statements include the following:
- Differences in the financial reporting framework applied in preparing the financial statements of the component and that applied in preparing the group financial statements.
- Whether the audit of the financial statements of the component will be completed in time to meet the group reporting timetable.
- Differences in the auditing and other standards applied by the component auditor and those applied in the audit of the group financial statements.
- Whether it is impracticable for the group engagement team to be involved in the work of a component auditor.

It will not be necessary to obtain an understanding of the auditors of those components for which the group engagement team plans to perform analytical procedures at group level only.

The nature, timing, and extent of the group engagement team's procedures to obtain an understanding of a component auditor are affected by factors, such as previous experience with, or knowledge of, the component auditor and the degree to which the group engagement team and the component auditor are subject to common policies and procedures, such as the following:
i. Whether the group engagement team and a component auditor share the following:
   - Common policies and procedures for performing the work (for example, audit methodologies).
   - Common quality control policies and procedures.
   - Common monitoring policies and procedures.

ii. The consistency or similarity of the following:
   - Laws and regulations or legal system.
   - Professional oversight, discipline, and external quality assurance.
   - Education and training.
   - Professional organizations and standards.
   - Language and culture.

3) Communications between group engagement team and component auditor
The group engagement team should communicate its requirements to a component auditor on a timely basis. This communication should include the following:
   i. A request that the component auditor, knowing the context in which the group engagement team will use the work of the component auditor, confirm that the component auditor will cooperate with the group engagement team.
   ii. The ethical requirements that are relevant to the group audit and, in particular, the independence requirements.
   iii. A list of related parties prepared by group management and any other related parties of which the group engagement team is aware. The group engagement team should request the component auditor to communicate on a timely basis to related parties not

previously identified by group management or the group engagement team. The group engagement team should identify such additional related parties to other component auditors.

    iv. Identified significant risks of material misstatement of the group financial statements, due to fraud or error, that are relevant to the work of the component auditor.

The group engagement team should request a component auditor to communicate matters relevant to the group engagement team's conclusion, with regard to the group audit. Such communication should include the following:
- Whether the component auditor has complied with ethical requirements relevant to the group audit, including independence and professional competence.
- Identification of the financial information of the component on which the component auditor is reporting.
- The component auditor's overall findings, conclusions, or opinion.

The group engagement team should evaluate a component auditor's communication.

The group engagement team should discuss significant findings and issues arising from that evaluation with the component auditor, component management, or group management, as appropriate.

4) Sufficiency and appropriateness of audit evidence
The auditor is required to obtain sufficient appropriate audit evidence on which to base the audit opinion.

The group engagement team should evaluate whether sufficient appropriate audit evidence, on which to base the group audit opinion, has been obtained from the audit procedures performed on the consolidation process, and the work performed by the group engagement team and the component auditors on the financial information of the components.

The group engagement partner should evaluate the effect on the group audit opinion of any uncorrected misstatements (either identified by the group engagement team or communicated by component auditors) and any instances in which there has been an inability to obtain sufficient appropriate audit evidence.

5) Audit reports
When the auditor of the group financial statements is assuming responsibility for the work performed by a component auditor, the group engagement team is required, by the provisions of this section, to be involved in the work of the component auditor.

In some circumstances, the group engagement partner may conclude that it will not be possible, due to restrictions imposed by group management, for the group engagement team to obtain sufficient appropriate audit evidence through the group engagement team's work or use of the work of component auditors, and the possible effect of this inability, will result in a disclaimer of opinion on the group financial statements. In such circumstances, the auditor of the group financial statements should do the following:
a. in the case of a new engagement, not accept the engagement, or, in the case of a continuing engagement, withdraw from the engagement when withdrawal is possible under applicable law or regulation, or
b. when the entity is required by law or regulation to have an audit, having performed the audit of the group financial statements to the extent possible, disclaim an opinion on the group financial statements.

Having gained an understanding of each component auditor, the group engagement partner should decide whether to make reference to a component auditor in the auditor's report on the group financial statements.

Reference to the audit of a component auditor in the auditor's report on the group financial statements should not be made unless:
i. the group engagement partner has determined that the component auditor has performed an audit of the financial statements of the component in accordance with the relevant requirements of GAAS, and
ii. the component auditor has issued an auditor's report that is not restricted as to use.

If the component's financial statements are prepared using a different financial reporting framework from that used for the group financial statements, **reference to the audit of a component auditor, in the auditor's report on the group financial statements, should not be made unless**
i. the measurement, recognition, presentation, and disclosure criteria that are applicable to all material items in the component's financial statements under the financial reporting framework used by the component, are similar to the criteria that are applicable to all material items in the group's financial statements under the financial reporting framework used by the group, and
ii. the group engagement team has obtained sufficient appropriate audit evidence for purposes of evaluating the appropriateness of the adjustments to convert the component's financial statements to the financial reporting framework used by the group without the need to assume responsibility for, and, thus, be involved in, the work of the component auditor. (Ref: par. .A54–.A57)

When the group engagement partner decides to make reference to the audit of a component auditor in the auditor's report on the group financial statements, the report on the group financial statements should clearly indicate the following:
i. that the component was not audited by the auditor of the group financial statements but was audited by the component auditor.
ii. the magnitude of the portion of the financial statements audited by the component auditor.
iii. when the component's financial statements are prepared using a different financial reporting framework from that used for the group financial statements, the auditor of the group financial statements is taking responsibility for evaluating the appropriateness of the adjustments to convert the component's financial statements to the financial reporting framework used by the group.
iv. when the component auditor's report on the component's financial statements does not state that the audit of the component's financial statements was performed in accordance with GAAS or the standards promulgated by the PCAOB, but, the group engagement partner has determined that the component auditor performed additional audit procedures in order to meet the relevant requirements of GAAS. Therefore, the set of auditing standards used by the component auditor, plus the additional audit procedures were performed by the component auditor to meet the relevant requirements of GAAS.

If the group engagement partner decides to **name a component auditor in the auditor's report** on the group financial statements
- the component auditor's express permission should be obtained.

- the component auditor's report should be presented together with that of the auditor's report on the group financial statements.

If the opinion of a component auditor is modified, or that report includes an emphasis-of-matter or other-matter paragraph, the auditor of the group financial statements should determine the effect that this may have on the auditor's report on the group financial statements. When deemed appropriate, the auditor of the group financial statements should either, modify the opinion on the group financial statements, or include an emphasis-of-matter paragraph or an other-matter paragraph, in the auditor's report on the group financial statements.

If the group engagement partner decides to assume responsibility for work of a component auditor, no reference should be made to the component auditor in the auditor's report on the group financial statements.

H. Specific Areas of Engagement Risk

1. An entity's compliance with laws and regulations, including possible illegal acts

   a. **Illegal Acts**

   Illegal acts are violations of laws or governmental regulations. These are acts attributable to the entity whose financial statements are under audit, or acts by management and employees acting on behalf of the entity. Personal misconduct by the entity's personnel, unrelated to their business activities, is not covered herein.

   Whether an act is, in fact, illegal is a determination that is normally beyond the auditor's professional competence. Auditors know financial statement and auditing stuff. However, auditors may recognize some illegal acts. The determination as to whether a particular act is illegal would generally be based on the advice of an informed expert qualified to practice law and may have to await final determination by a court of law.

   Illegal acts vary considerably in their relation to the financial statements. Generally, the further removed an illegal act is from the events and transactions ordinarily reflected in financial statements, the less likely the auditor is to become aware of the act or to recognize its possible illegality.

   1) **Direct Effect**

   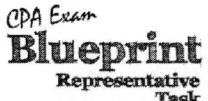

   > Understand the accountant's responsibilities with respect to laws and regulations that have a direct effect on the determination of material amounts or disclosures in an entity's financial statements for an audit or non-audit engagement.

   The auditor considers laws and regulations that are generally recognized by auditors to have a **direct and material effect** on the determination of financial statement amounts. For example: tax laws affect accruals and expense for the period; laws and regulations may affect the amount of revenue accrued under a government contract; etc.

   The auditor considers violations of laws and regulations from the perspective of their impact on the financial statement amounts, rather than from the perspective of legality *per se*.

   2) **Indirect Effect**

   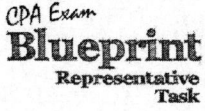

   > Understand the accountant's responsibilities with respect to laws and regulations that are fundamental to an entity's business but do not have a direct effect on the entity's financial statements in an audit or non-audit engagement.

   Entities may be affected by many other laws and regulations, including those related to securities trading, occupational safety and health, food and drug administration, environmental protection, equal employment, and price-fixing or other antitrust violations.

   Generally, these laws and regulations relate more to an entity's operating aspects, than to its financial and accounting aspects, and their **financial statement effect is indirect**.

   The auditor ordinarily doesn't have sufficient basis for recognizing possible violations of indirect effect of laws and regulations. The indirect effect is normally the result of the need to disclose a contingent liability, because of the allegation or determination of illegality.

   Even when violations of such laws and regulations can have consequences material to the financial statements, the auditor may not become aware of the existence of the illegal act unless he is informed by the client, or there is evidence of a governmental agency investigation or enforcement proceeding in the records, documents, or other information normally inspected in an audit of the financial statements.

Perform tests of compliance with laws and regulations that have a direct effect on material amounts or disclosures in an entity's financial statements in an audit or non-audit engagement.

The auditor's responsibility to detect and report misstatements resulting from illegal acts having a **direct and material effect** on the determination of financial statement amounts is the same as that for misstatements caused by error or fraud.

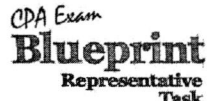

Perform tests of compliance with laws and regulations that are fundamental to an entity's business, but do not have a direct effect on the entity's financial statements for an audit or non-audit engagement.

For indirect effect of illegal acts, the auditor should
  i. Inquire of management and, when appropriate, those charged with governance, about whether the entity is in compliance with such laws and regulations
  ii. Inspect correspondence, if any, with the relevant licensing or regulatory authorities.

Auditor's should obtain written representations from management concerning the absence of violations or possible violations of laws or regulations, whose effects should be considered for disclosure in the financial statements or as a basis for recording a loss contingency.

b. Audit procedures related to illegal acts
If the auditor becomes aware of a known or suspected illegal act, the auditor should obtain an understanding of the nature of the act and the circumstances in which it has occurred, and further information, to evaluate the possible effect on the financial statements.

If the auditor suspects an illegal act may exist, the auditor should discuss the matter with management (at a level above those involved with the suspected noncompliance, if possible) and, when appropriate, those charged with governance. If management or, as appropriate, those charged with governance, do not provide sufficient information that supports that the entity is in compliance with laws and regulations and, in the auditor's professional judgment, the effect of the suspected noncompliance (illegal act) may be material to the financial statements, the auditor should consider the need to obtain legal advice.

If sufficient information about suspected noncompliance cannot be obtained, the auditor should evaluate the effect of the lack of sufficient appropriate audit evidence on the auditor's opinion

The auditor should evaluate the implications of noncompliance in relation to other aspects of the audit, including the auditor's risk assessment and the reliability of written representations, and take appropriate action.

c. Reporting illegal acts
If the auditor suspects that management, or those charged with governance, are involved in noncompliance (illegal acts), the auditor should communicate the matter to the next higher level of authority at the entity, if it exists. When no higher authority exists, or if the auditor believes that the communication may not be acted upon or is unsure about the person to whom to report, the auditor should consider the need to obtain legal advice.

If the auditor concludes that the noncompliance has a material effect on the financial statements, and it has not been adequately reflected in the financial statements, the auditor should, in accordance with AU-C 705, *Modifications to the Opinion in the Independent Auditor's Report*, express a qualified or adverse opinion on the financial statements.

If the auditor is precluded by management, or those charged with governance, from obtaining sufficient appropriate audit evidence to evaluate whether noncompliance that may be material to the financial statements has, or is likely to have, occurred, the auditor should express a qualified opinion or disclaim an opinion on the financial statements on the basis of a limitation on the scope of the audit, in accordance with AU-C 705.

If the auditor is unable to determine whether noncompliance has occurred because of limitations imposed by the circumstances, rather than by management or those charged with governance, the auditor should evaluate the effect on the auditor's opinion, in accordance with AU-C 705.

Multiple Choice

AUD 2-Q110 through AUD 2-Q112

2. Accounting estimates, including fair values

   > *Hint:* Quick reference summary for fair value:
   > - Review and test management's process
   > - Independently develop an estimate
   > - Review subsequent events

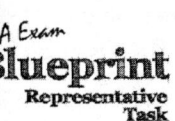

   > **Recognize the potential impact of significant accounting estimates on the risk of material misstatement, including the indicators of management bias.**

   a. Accounting estimates (including fair value measurements)
      When performing risk assessment procedures and related activities to obtain an understanding of the entity and its environment, the auditor should obtain an understanding of the following in order to provide a basis for the identification and assessment of risks of material misstatement for accounting estimates:
      - Accounting requirements related to estimates, including disclosures (applicable financial reporting framework).
      - How management identifies those transactions, events, and conditions that may give rise to the need for accounting estimates to be recognized or disclosed in the financial statements. In obtaining this understanding, the auditor should make inquiries of management about changes in circumstances that may give rise to new, or the need to revise existing, accounting estimates.
      - How management makes the accounting estimates and the data on which they are based, including
        i. the method(s), including, when applicable, the model, used in making the accounting estimate;
        ii. relevant controls over the estimation process;
        iii. whether management has used a specialist;
        iv. the assumptions underlying the accounting estimates;
        v. whether there has been, or ought to have been, a change from the prior period in the method(s) or assumption(s) for making the accounting estimates and, if so, why; and
        vi. whether and, if so, how management has assessed the effect of estimation uncertainty.

1) Retrospective review of estimates
   The auditor should review the outcome of accounting estimates included in the prior period financial statements or, when applicable, their subsequent re-estimation for the purpose of the current period. The nature and extent of the auditor's review takes account of the nature of the accounting estimates and whether the information obtained from the review would be relevant to identifying and assessing risks of material misstatement of accounting estimates made in the current period financial statements. However, the review is not intended to call into question the auditor's professional judgments made in the prior periods that were based on information available at the time.

   The auditor should determine
   i. whether management has appropriately applied the requirements of the applicable financial reporting framework relevant to the accounting estimate and
   ii. whether the methods for making the accounting estimates are appropriate and have been applied consistently, and whether changes from the prior period, if any, in accounting estimates or the method for making them, are appropriate in the circumstances.

3. Related parties and related party transactions

> **Perform procedures to identify related party relationships and transactions for an audit or non-audit engagement, including consideration of significant unusual transactions and transactions with executive officers.**

> **Analyze the potential impact of related party relationships and transactions on the risk of material misstatement for an audit or non-audit engagement, including consideration of significant unusual transactions and transactions with executive officers.**

a. Related party transactions
   A related party is defined by the FASB ASC (U.S. GAAP) glossary and includes affiliates of the entity, parties accounted for using the equity method by the investing entity, trusts for the benefit of employees (e.g., pensions), principal owners of the entity and immediate families, management of the entity and members of their immediate families, other parties with control or can significantly influence the management or operating policies

   The auditor has a responsibility to perform audit procedures to identify, assess, and respond to the risks of material misstatement arising from the entity's failure to appropriately account for, or disclose, related party relationships, transactions, or balances.

   In addition, an understanding, of the entity's related party relationships and transactions, is relevant to the auditor's evaluation of whether one or more fraud risk factors are present, as required by AU-C 240, because fraud may be more easily committed through related parties.

   Owing to the inherent limitations of an audit, an unavoidable risk exists that some material misstatements of the financial statements may not be detected, even though the audit is properly planned and performed in accordance with generally accepted auditing standards (GAAS). In the context of related parties, the potential effects of inherent limitations on the auditor's ability to detect material misstatements are greater because of reasons such as the following:
   - Management may be unaware of the existence of all related party relationships and transactions.
   - Related party relationships may present a greater opportunity for collusion, concealment, or manipulation by management.

The objectives of the auditor are to obtain an understanding of related party relationships and transactions, sufficient to be able
1) to recognize fraud risk factors, if any, arising from related party relationships and transactions that are relevant to the identification and assessment of the risks of material misstatement due to fraud.
2) conclude, based on the audit evidence obtained, whether the financial statements, insofar as they are affected by those relationships and transactions, achieve fair presentation.
3) obtain sufficient appropriate audit evidence about whether related party relationships and transactions have been appropriately identified, accounted for, and disclosed in the financial statements.

As part of the risk assessment procedures (see AU-C 240 and AU-C 315), the auditor should gain an understanding of the entity's related party relationships and transactions.

Generally, the auditor will inquire of management regarding
- the identity of related parties;
- the nature of the relationships with the related parties; and,
- the type and purpose of transactions with the related parties.

Audit procedures the auditor should perform regarding related parties include the following:
1) The auditor should remain alert when inspecting records or documents, for arrangements or other information, that may indicate the existence of related party relationships or transactions that management has not previously identified or disclosed to the auditor.
2) If the auditor identifies significant transactions outside the entity's normal course of business, when performing audit procedures, the auditor should inquire of management about the following:
   i. The nature of these transactions.
   ii. Whether related parties could be involved.
3) In addition to inquiry, the auditor should
   i. Evaluate the business rationale (or lack thereof) of the transactions, to determine if they were entered into to engage in fraudulent financial reporting;
   ii. Evaluate whether the terms of the transactions are consistent with management's explanations;
   iii. Evaluate whether the transactions have been appropriately accounted for and disclosed; and
   iv. Obtain audit evidence that the transactions have been appropriately authorized and approved.
   v. Share with the other members of the engagement team the identity of the entity's related parties and other relevant information obtained about the related parties.

If the auditor identifies related parties, or significant related party transactions, that management has not previously identified or disclosed to the auditor, the auditor should
1) promptly communicate the relevant information to the other members of the engagement team.
2) request management to identify all transactions with the newly identified related parties for the auditor's further evaluation.
3) inquire why the entity's controls over related party relationships and transactions failed to enable the identification or disclosure of the related party relationships or transactions.
4) perform appropriate substantive audit procedures relating to such newly identified related parties or significant related party transactions.

5) reconsider the risk that other related parties or significant related party transactions may exist that management has not previously identified or disclosed to the auditor, and perform additional audit procedures as necessary.
6) evaluate the implications for the audit if the nondisclosure by management appears intentional (and, therefore, indicative of a risk of material misstatement due to fraud).

If management has made an assertion in the financial statements to the effect that a related party transaction was conducted on terms equivalent to those prevailing in an arm's length transaction, the auditor should obtain sufficient appropriate audit evidence about the assertion.

Unless all of those charged with governance are involved in managing the entity, the auditor should communicate with those charged with governance, significant findings and issues arising during the audit in connection with the entity's related parties.

The auditor should include in the audit documentation the names of the identified related parties and the nature of the related party relationships.

Multiple Choice

AUD 2-Q113 through AUD 2-Q116

Glossary: Assessing Risk and Developing a Planned Response

A

Analytical procedures – evaluations of financial information through analysis of plausible relationships among both financial and nonfinancial data

Appropriateness (of audit evidence) – the measure of the quality of audit evidence (that is, its relevance and reliability in providing support for the conclusions on which the auditor's opinion is based)

Assertions – representations by management, explicit or otherwise, that are embodied in the financial statements as used by the auditor to consider the different types of potential misstatements that may occur

Audit documentation – the record of audit procedures performed, relevant audit evidence obtained, and conclusions the auditor reached (terms such as *working papers* or *workpapers* are also sometimes used)

Audit evidence – information used by the auditor in arriving at the conclusions on which the auditor's opinion is based. Audit evidence includes both information contained in the accounting records underlying the financial statements and other information. *Sufficiency of audit evidence* is the measure of the quantity of audit evidence. The quantity of the audit evidence needed is affected by the auditor's assessment of the risks of material misstatement and also by the quality of such audit evidence. *Appropriateness of audit evidence* is the measure of the quality of audit evidence; that is, its relevance and its reliability in providing support for the conclusions on which the auditor's opinion is based.

Audit risk – the risk that the auditor expresses an inappropriate audit opinion when the financial statements are materially misstated

Audit sampling (sampling) – the selection and evaluation of less than 100 percent of the population of audit relevance such that the auditor expects the items selected (the sample) to be representative of the population and, thus, likely to provide a reasonable basis for conclusions about the population

Auditor's specialist – an individual or organization possessing expertise in a field other than accounting or auditing, whose work in that field is used by the auditor to assist the auditor in obtaining sufficient appropriate audit evidence; an auditor's specialist may be either an auditor's internal specialist (who is a partner or staff, including temporary staff, of the auditor's firm or a network firm) or an auditor's external specialist

B

Business risk – a risk resulting from significant conditions, events, circumstances, actions, or inactions that could adversely affect an entity's ability to achieve its objectives and execute its strategies or from the setting of inappropriate objectives and strategies

C

Complementary user entity controls – controls that management of the service organization assumes, in the design of its service, will be implemented by user entities, and which, if necessary to achieve the control objectives stated in management's description of the service organization's system, are identified as such in that description

Control risk – the risk that a misstatement that could occur in an assertion about a class of transaction, account balance, or disclosure and that could be material, either individually or when aggregated with other misstatements, will not be prevented, or detected and corrected, on a timely basis by the entity's internal control

D

Deficiency – a deficiency in internal control over financial reporting exists, when the design or operation of a control does not allow management or employees, in the normal course of performing their assigned functions, to prevent or detect misstatements on a timely basis. A deficiency in *design* exists when (a) a control necessary to meet the control objective is missing or (b) an existing control is not properly designed so that, even if the control operates as designed, the control objective would not be met. A deficiency in *operation* exists when a properly designed control does not operate as designed, or when the person performing the control does not possess the necessary authority or competence to perform the control effectively.

Detection risk – the risk that the procedures performed by the auditor to reduce audit risk to an acceptably low level, will not detect a misstatement that exists and that could be material, either individually or when aggregated with other misstatements

E
Engagement partner – the partner or other person in the firm who is responsible for the audit engagement and its performance and for the auditor's report that is issued on behalf of the firm and who, when required, has the appropriate authority from a professional, legal, or regulatory body
Engagement quality control review – a process designed to provide an objective evaluation, before the report is released, of the significant judgments the engagement team made and the conclusions it reached in formulating the auditor's report
Engagement quality control reviewer – a partner, another person in the firm, a suitably qualified external person, or a team made up of such individuals, none of whom is part of the engagement team, with sufficient and appropriate experience and authority to objectively evaluate the significant judgments that the engagement team made and the conclusions it reached in formulating the auditor's report
Engagement team – all partners and staff performing the engagement and any individuals engaged by the firm, or a network firm, who perform audit procedures on the engagement; excludes an auditor's external specialist engaged by the firm or a network firm and individuals within the client's internal audit function who provide direct assistance
Expertise – skills, knowledge, and experience in a particular field
Extent of an audit procedure – refers to the quantity of audit procedures to be performed (for example, a sample size or the number of observations of a control activity); also see nature of an audit procedure and timing of an audit procedure
F
Firm – a form of organization permitted by law or regulation whose characteristics conform to resolutions of the Council of the AICPA and that is engaged in public practice
Fraud – an intentional act by one or more individuals among management, those charged with governance, employees, or third parties, involving the use of deception that results in a misstatement in financial statements that are the subject of an audit
Fraud risk factors — Events or conditions that indicate an incentive or pressure to perpetrate fraud, provide an opportunity to commit fraud, or indicate attitudes or rationalizations to justify a fraudulent action
G
H
I
Inherent risk – the susceptibility of an assertion about a class of transaction, account balance, or disclosure to a misstatement that could be material, either individually or when aggregated with other misstatements, before consideration of any related controls
Internal control – a process effected by those charged with governance, management, and other personnel that is designed to provide reasonable assurance about the achievement of the entity's objectives with regard to the reliability of financial reporting, effectiveness and efficiency of operations, and compliance with applicable laws and regulations
J
K
L
M
Management's specialist – an individual or organization possessing expertise in a field other than accounting or auditing, whose work in that field is used by the entity to assist the entity in preparing the financial statements.
Material weakness – a material weakness is a deficiency, or a combination of deficiencies, in internal control over financial reporting, such that there is a reasonable possibility that a material misstatement of the company's annual or interim financial statements will not be prevented or detected on a timely basis
Materiality – the amount of misstatements, including omissions, that individually or in the aggregate, could reasonably be expected to influence the economic decisions of users made on the basis of the financial statements
Misstatement – a difference between the amounts, classification, presentation, or disclosure of a reported financial statement item and the amount, classification, presentation, or disclosure that is required for the item to be presented fairly, in accordance with the applicable financial reporting framework; misstatements can arise from fraud or error

Monitoring – a process comprising an ongoing consideration and evaluation of the firm's system of quality control, including inspection or a periodic review of engagement documentation, reports, and clients' financial statements, for a selection of completed engagements, designed to provide the firm with reasonable assurance that its system of quality control is designed appropriately and operating effectively

N

Nature of an audit procedure – refers to the purpose (test of controls or substantive procedure) and type (inspection, observation, inquiry, confirmation, recalculation, re-performance, or analytical procedure) of an audit procedure; also see extent of an audit procedure and timing of an audit procedure

Network – an association of entities

Network firm – a firm or other entity that belongs to a network

Non-sampling risk – the risk that the auditor reaches an erroneous conclusion for any reason not related to sampling risk

O

P

Partner – any individual with authority to bind the firm with respect to the performance of a professional services engagement; partner may include an employee with this authority who has not assumed the risks and benefits of ownership (title varies by firm)

Performance materiality – the amount or amounts set by the auditor, at less than materiality for the financial statements as a whole, and is set to reduce to an appropriately low level the probability that the aggregate of uncorrected and undetected misstatements exceeds materiality for the financial statements as a whole; performance materiality is to be distinguished from tolerable misstatement.

Personnel – partners and staff

Pervasive – a term used in the context of misstatements, to describe the effects on the financial statements of misstatements, or the possible effects on the financial statements of misstatements, if any, that are undetected due to an inability to obtain sufficient appropriate audit evidence

Population – the entire set of data from which a sample is selected and about which the auditor wishes to draw conclusions

Preconditions for an audit – the use by management of an acceptable financial reporting framework in the preparation and fair presentation of the financial statements and the agreement of management and, when appropriate, those charged with governance, to the premise on which an audit is conducted

Professional judgment – the application of relevant training, knowledge, and experience, within the context provided by auditing, accounting, and ethical standards, in making informed decisions about the courses of action that are appropriate in the circumstances of the audit engagement

Professional skepticism – an attitude that includes a questioning mind, being alert to conditions that may indicate possible misstatement due to fraud or error, and a critical assessment of audit evidence.

Professional standards – standards promulgated by the AICPA Auditing Standards Board or the AICPA Accounting and Review Services Committee, or other standards-setting bodies that set auditing and attest standards applicable to the engagement being performed and relevant ethical requirements

Q

R

Recurring audit – an audit engagement for an existing audit client for whom the auditor performed the preceding audit

Related party – a party defined as a related party in the FASB ASC (U.S. GAAP); includes affiliates of the entity, parties accounted for using the equity method by the investing entity, trusts for the benefit of employees (e.g., pensions), principal owners of the entity and immediate families, management of the entity and members of their immediate families, other parties with control or can significantly influence the management or operating policies

Relevant assertion – a financial statement assertion that has a reasonable possibility of containing a misstatement or misstatements that would cause the financial statements to be materially misstated

Relevant ethical requirements – ethical requirements to which the engagement team and engagement quality control reviewer are subject

Representative sample – evaluation of the sample will result in conclusions that, subject to the limitations of sampling risk, are similar to those that would be drawn if the same procedures were applied to the entire population

Risk assessment procedures – the audit procedures performed to obtain an understanding of the entity and its environment, including the entity's internal control, to identify and assess the risks of material misstatement, whether due to fraud or error, at the financial statement and relevant assertion levels

Risk of material misstatement – the risk that the financial statements are materially misstated prior to the audit including inherent risk and control risk

S

Service auditor – a practitioner who reports on controls at a service organization

Service organization – an organization or segment of an organization that provides services to user entities that are relevant to those user entities' internal control over financial reporting

Service organization's system – the policies and procedures designed, implemented, and documented by management of the service organization to provide user entities with the services covered by the service auditor's report

Significant accounts and disclosures – an account or disclosure with a reasonable possibility it could contain a misstatement that, individually or when aggregated with others, has a material effect on the financial statements (considering the risk of both overstatement and understatement); significance is based on inherent risk (without regard to the effect of controls)

Significant deficiency – a significant deficiency is a deficiency, or a combination of deficiencies, in internal control over financial reporting that is less severe than a material weakness, yet important enough to merit attention by those responsible for oversight of the company's financial reporting

Significant risk – an identified and assessed risk of material misstatement that, in the auditor's professional judgment, requires special audit consideration

Staff – professionals, other than partners, including any specialists that the firm employs

Subservice organization – a service organization used by another service organization to perform some of the services provided to user entities that are relevant to those user entities' internal control over financial reporting

Substantive procedure – an audit procedure designed to detect material misstatements at the assertion level. Substantive procedures comprise: (a) test of details (classes of transactions, account balances, and disclosures); and, (b) substantive analytical procedures

Sufficiency (of audit evidence) – the measure of the quantity of audit evidence, affected by the auditor's assessment of the risks of material misstatement and quality of evidence

Suitably qualified external person – an individual outside the firm with the competence and capabilities to act as an engagement partner (e.g., a partner of another firm)

T

Test of controls – an audit procedure designed to evaluate the operating effectiveness of controls in preventing, or detecting and correcting, material misstatements at the assertion level

Those charged with governance – the person(s) or organization(s) (e.g., a corporate trustee) with responsibility for overseeing the strategic direction of the entity and the obligations related to the accountability of the entity, overseeing the financial reporting process; may include management personnel (e.g., owner-managers)

Timing of an audit procedure – refers to when an audit procedure is performed or the period or date to which the audit evidence applies; also see extent of an audit procedure and nature of an audit procedure

Tolerable misstatement – a monetary amount set by the auditor in respect of which the auditor seeks to obtain an appropriate level of assurance that the monetary amount set by the auditor is not exceeded by the actual misstatement in the population; tolerable misstatement is also the application of performance materiality to a particular sampling procedure

U

Uncorrected misstatements – misstatements that the auditor has accumulated during the audit and that have not been corrected

User auditor – an auditor who audits and reports on the financial statements of a user entity

User entity – an entity that uses a service organization and whose financial statements are being audited

V

W

Walkthrough – a procedure in which the auditor follows a transaction from origination through the company's processes, including information systems, until it is reflected in the company's financial records, using the same documents and information technology that company personnel use; walkthrough procedures usually include a combination of inquiry, observation, inspection of relevant documents, and re-performance of controls

X

Y

Z

This page is intentionally left blank.

Multiple Choice – Questions

AUD 2-Q1 A247. A successor auditor's inquiries of the predecessor auditor should include questions regarding

A. The predecessor's evaluation of audit risk and judgment about materiality.
B. Subsequent events that occurred since the predecessor's audit report was issued.
C. The predecessor's understanding as to the reasons for the change in auditors.
D. The predecessor's knowledge of accounting matters of continuing significance.

AUD 2-Q2 A102. Which of the following would a successor auditor ask the predecessor auditor to provide after accepting an audit engagement?

A. Disagreements between the predecessor auditor and management as to significant accounting policies and principles.
B. The predecessor auditor's understanding of the reasons for the change of auditors.
C. Facts known to the predecessor auditor that might bear on the integrity of management.
D. Matters that may facilitate the evaluation of financial reporting consistency between the current and prior years.

AUD 2-Q3 A352. Those procedures specifically outlined in an audit program are primarily designed to

A. Gather evidence.
B. Detect errors or fraud.
C. Test internal control.
D. Protect the auditor in the event of litigation.

AUD 2-Q4 A40. Which of the following procedures would a CPA most likely perform in the planning stage of a financial statement audit?

A. Obtain representations from management regarding the availability of all financial records.
B. Communicate with the audit committee concerning the prior year's audit adjustments.
C. Make inquiries of the client's attorney regarding pending and threatened litigation and assessments.
D. Compare recorded financial information with anticipated results from budgets and forecasts.

AUD 2-Q5 A118. Which of the following procedures would a CPA most likely perform in the planning phase of a financial statement audit?

A. Make inquiries of the client's lawyer concerning pending litigation.
B. Perform cutoff tests of cash receipts and disbursements.
C. Compare financial information with nonfinancial operating data.
D. Recalculate the prior year's accruals and deferrals.

AUD 2-Q6 A391. After a preliminary phase of the review of a client's computer controls, an auditor may decide not to perform control tests related to the control procedures within the computer portion of the client's internal control system. Which of the following would not be a valid reason for choosing to omit control tests?

A. The controls appear adequate.
B. The controls duplicate operative controls existing elsewhere in the system.
C. There appear to be major weaknesses that would preclude reliance on the stated procedure.
D. The time and dollar costs of testing exceed the time and dollar savings in substantive testing if the controls tests show the controls to be operative.

AUD 2-Q7 A408. The auditor's preliminary understanding of the client's EDP system is primarily obtained by

A. Inspection.
B. Observation.
C. Inquiry.
D. Evaluation.

AUD 2-Q8 A204. Which of the following is an inherent limitation of internal controls?

A. Judgmental sampling.
B. Collusion.
C. Segregation of duties.
D. Employee peer review.

AUD 2-Q9 A275. Which of the following represents an inherent limitation of internal controls?

A. Bank reconciliations are not performed on a timely basis.
B. The CEO can request a check with no purchase order.
C. Customer credit checks are not performed.
D. Shipping documents are not matched to sales invoices.

AUD 2-Q10 A322. An auditor is concerned about a policy of management override as a limitation of internal control. Which of the following tests would best assess the validity of the auditor's concern?

A. Matching purchase orders to accounts payable.
B. Verifying that approved spending limits are not exceeded.
C. Tracing sales orders to the revenue account.
D. Reviewing minutes of board meetings.

AUD 2-Q11 A170. Which of the following statements is correct regarding internal control?

A. A well-designed internal control environment ensures the achievement of an entity's business objectives.
B. An inherent limitation to internal control is the fact that controls can be circumvented by management override.
C. A well-designed and operated internal control environment should detect collusion perpetrated by two people.
D. Internal control is a necessary business function and should be designed and operated to detect all errors and fraud.

AUD 2-Q12 A85. What is the primary objective of the fraud brainstorming session?

A. Determine audit risk and materiality.
B. Identify whether analytical procedures should be applied to the revenue accounts.
C. Assess the potential for material misstatement due to fraud.
D. Determine whether the planned procedures in the audit program will satisfy the general audit objectives.

AUD 2-Q13 A86. While performing an audit of the financial statements of a company for the year ended December 31, year 1, the auditor notes that the company's sales increased substantially in December, year 1, with a corresponding decrease in January, year 2. In assessing the risk of fraudulent financial reporting or misappropriation of assets, what should be the auditor's initial indication about the potential for fraud in sales revenue?

A. There is a broad indication of misappropriation of assets.
B. There is an indication of theft of the entity's assets.
C. There is an indication of embezzling receipts.
D. There is a broad indication of financial reporting fraud.

AUD 2-Q14 A43. Which of the following characteristics most likely would heighten an auditor's concern about the risk of material misstatement arising from fraudulent financial reporting?

A. There is a lack of interest by management in maintaining an earnings trend.
B. Computer hardware is usually sold at a loss before being fully depreciated.
C. Management had frequent disputes with the auditor on accounting matters.
D. Monthly bank reconciliations usually include several large checks outstanding.

AUD 2-Q15 A229. Which of the following situations represents a risk factor that relates to misstatements arising from misappropriation of assets?

A. A high turnover of senior management.
B. A lack of independent checks.
C. A strained relationship between management and the predecessor auditor.
D. An inability to generate cash flow from operations.

AUD 2-Q16 A248. Which of the following most likely would cause an auditor to consider whether a client's financial statements contain material misstatements?

A. Management did not disclose to the auditor that it consulted with other accountants about significant accounting matters.
B. The chief financial officer will not sign the management representation letter until the last day of the auditor's field work.
C. Audit trails of computer-generated transactions exist only for a short time.
D. The results of an analytical procedure disclose unexpected differences.

AUD 2-Q17 A257. Which of the following situations most likely could lead to an embezzlement scheme?

A. The accounts receivable bookkeeper receives a list of payments prepared by the cashier and personally makes entries in the customers' accounts receivable subsidiary ledger.
B. Each vendor invoice is matched with the related purchase order and receiving report by the vouchers payable bookkeeper who personally approves the voucher for payment.
C. Access to blank checks and signature plates is restricted to the cash disbursements bookkeeper who personally reconciles the monthly bank statement.
D. Vouchers and supporting documentation are examined and then canceled by the treasurer who personally mails the checks to vendors.

AUD 2-Q18 A309. When performing a substantive test of a random sample of cash disbursements, an auditor is supplied with a photocopy of vendor invoices supporting the disbursements for one particular vendor rather than the original invoices. The auditor is told that the vendor's original invoices have been misplaced. What should the auditor do in response to this situation?

A. Increase randomly the number of items in the substantive test to increase the reliance that may be placed on the overall test.
B. Reevaluate the risk of fraud, and design alternate tests for the related transactions.
C. Increase testing by agreeing more of the payments to this particular vendor to the photocopies of its invoices.
D. Count the missing original documents as misstatements, and project the total amount of the error based on the size of the population and the dollar amount of the errors.

AUD 2-Q19 A159. Prior to, or in conjunction with, the information-gathering procedures for an audit, audit team members should discuss the potential for material misstatement due to fraud. Which of the following best characterizes the mind-set that the audit team should maintain during this discussion?

A. Presumptive.
B. Judgmental.
C. Criticizing.
D. Questioning.

AUD 2-Q20 A57. Which of the following situations most likely represents the highest risk of a misstatement arising from misappropriations of assets?

A. A large number of bearer bonds on hand.
B. A large number of inventory items with low sales prices.
C. A large number of transactions processed in a short period of time.
D. A large number of fixed assets with easily identifiable serial numbers.

AUD 2-Q21 A104. Which of the following is a management assertion regarding the category account balances at the period end?

A. Transactions and events that have been recorded have occurred and pertain to the entity.
B. Transactions and events have been recorded in the proper accounts.
C. The entity holds or controls the rights to assets, and liabilities are obligations of the entity.
D. Amounts and other data related to transactions and events have been recorded appropriately.

AUD 2-Q22 A79. When the operating effectiveness of a control is not evidenced by written documentation, an auditor should obtain evidence about the control's effectiveness by

A. Mailing confirmations.
B. Inquiry and other procedures such as observation
C. Analytical procedures
D. Recalculating the balance in related accounts

AUD 2-Q23 A80. An auditor is evaluating a client's internal controls. Which of the following situations would be the most difficult internal control issue for an auditor to detect?

A. The accounting staff neglects the control, due to increased transactions to be processed.
B. The technology department writes a program that does not properly implement the control, due to a lack of understanding.
C. Two employees, who work in different departments, are circumventing an internal control.
D. Someone erroneously disables edit checks in a software program designed to identify control exceptions.

AUD 2-Q24 A81. Inherent risk and control risk differ from detection risk in which of the following ways?

A. Inherent risk and control risk are calculated by the client.
B. Inherent risk and control risk exist independently of the audit.
C. Inherent risk and control risk are controlled by the auditor.
D. Inherent risk and control risk exist as a result of the auditor's judgment about materiality.

AUD 2-Q25 A29. The ultimate purpose of assessing control risk is to contribute to the auditor's evaluation of the risk that

A. Specific internal control activities are not operating as designed.
B. The collective effect of the control environment may not achieve the control objective
C. Tests of controls may fail to identify activities relevant to assertions.
D. Material misstatements may exist in the financial statements.

AUD 2-Q26 A30. After making inquiries about credit granting policies, an auditor selects a sample of sales transactions and examines evidence of credit approval. This test of controls most likely supports management's financial statement assertion(s) of

	Rights and obligations	Valuation or allocation
A.	Yes	Yes
B.	Yes	No
C.	No	Yes
D.	No	No

AUD 2-Q27 A1. After testing a client's internal control activities, an auditor discovers a number of deficiencies in the internal controls. Under these circumstances the auditor most likely would

A. Issue a disclaimer of opinion about the internal controls as part of the auditor's report.
B. Increase the assessment of control risk and increase the extent of substantive tests.
C. Issue a modified opinion of this finding as part of the auditor's report.
D. Withdraw from the audit because the internal controls are ineffective.

AUD 2-Q28 A2. Which of the following procedures would be most effective in reducing audit risk?

A. Discussion with responsible individuals.
B. Examination of evidence.
C. Inquiries of senior management.
D. Analytical procedures.

AUD 2-Q29 A3. After testing a client's internal control activities, an auditor discovers a number of significant deficiencies in the operation of a client's internal controls. Under these circumstances the auditor most likely would

A. Issue a disclaimer of opinion about the internal controls as part of the auditor's report.
B. Increase the assessed level of control risk and increase the extent of substantive tests.
C. Issue a qualified opinion of this finding as part of the auditor's report.
D. Withdraw from the audit because the internal controls are ineffective.

AUD 2-Q30 A4. Which of the following is an inherent limitation in internal control?

A. Incompatible duties.
B. Lack of segregation of duties.
C. Faulty human judgment.
D. Lack of an audit committee.

AUD 2-Q31 A20. As a result of tests of controls, an auditor assesses control risk too high. This incorrect assessment most likely occurred because

A. Control risk based on the auditor's sample is less than the true operating effectiveness of the client's control activity.
B. The auditor believes that the control activity relates to the client's assertions when, in fact, it does not.
C. The auditor believes that the control activity will reduce the extent of substantive testing when, in fact, it will not.
D. Control risk based on the auditor's sample is greater than the true operating effectiveness of the client's control activity.

AUD 2-Q32 A222. An audit client failed to maintain copies of its procedures manuals and organizational flowcharts. What should the auditor do in an audit of financial statements?

A. Issue a modified opinion on the basis of a scope limitation.
B. Document the auditor's understanding of internal controls.
C. Assess control risk at the maximum level.
D. Restrict the auditor's responsibility to assess the effectiveness of controls in the audit engagement letter.

AUD 2-Q33 A195. Which of the following best represents a key control for ensuring sales are properly authorized when assessing control risks for sales?

A. The separation of duties between the billing department and the cash receipts approval department.
B. The use of an approved price list to determine unit selling price.
C. Copies of approved sales orders sent to the shipping, billing, and accounting departments.
D. Sales orders are sent to the credit department for approval.

AUD 2-Q34 A199. A client maintains a large data center where access is limited to authorized employees. How may an auditor best determine the effectiveness of this control activity?

A. Inspect the policy manual establishing this control activity.
B. Ask the chief technology officer about known problems.
C. Observe whether the data center is monitored.
D. Obtain a list of current data center employees.

AUD 2-Q35 A200. Detection risk differs from both control risk and inherent risk in that detection risk

A. Exists independently of the financial statement audit.
B. Can be changed at the auditor's discretion.
C. Arises from risk factors relating to fraud.
D. Should be assessed in nonquantitative terms.

AUD 2-Q36 A201. To provide assurance that each voucher is submitted and paid only once, an auditor most likely would examine a sample of paid vouchers and determine whether each voucher is

A. Stamped "paid" by the check signer.
B. Returned to the vouchers payable department.
C. Supported by a vendor's invoice and purchase order.
D. Prenumbered and accounted for.

AUD 2-Q37 A271. In a financial statement audit, inherent risk is evaluated to help an auditor assess which of the following?

A. The internal audit department's objectivity in reporting to the audit committee a material misstatement of a financial statement assertion.
B. The risk that the internal control system will not detect a material misstatement of a financial statement assertion.
C. The risk that the audit procedures implemented will not detect a material misstatement of a financial statement assertion.
D. The susceptibility of a financial statement assertion to a material misstatement assuming there are no related controls.

AUD 2-Q38 A284. Which of the following factors is most relevant when an auditor considers the client's organizational structure in the context of control risk?

A. Management's attitude toward information processing and accounting departments.
B. The organization's recruiting and hiring practices.
C. Physical proximity of the accounting function to upper management.
D. The suitability of the client's lines of reporting.

AUD 2-Q39 A321. Which of the following activities performed by a department supervisor most likely would help in the prevention or detection of a payroll fraud?

A. Distributing paychecks directly to department employees.
B. Setting the pay rate for departmental employees.
C. Hiring employees and authorizing them to be added to payroll.
D. Approving a summary of hours each employee worked during the pay period.

AUD 2-Q40 A323. When an auditor plans to rely on controls that have changed since they were last tested, which of the following courses of action would be most appropriate?

A. Test the operating effectiveness of such controls in the current audit.
B. Document that reliance and proceed with the original audit strategy.
C. Inquire of management as to the effectiveness of the controls.
D. Report the reliance in the report on internal controls.

AUD 2-Q41 A324. In which of the following circumstances would an auditor expect to find that an entity implemented automated controls to reduce risks of misstatement?

A. When errors are difficult to predict.
B. When misstatements are difficult to define.
C. When large, unusual, or nonrecurring transactions require judgment.
D. When transactions are high-volume and recurring.

AUD 2-Q42 A297. Which of the following factors is most likely to affect the extent of the documentation of the auditor's understanding of a client's system of internal controls?

A. The industry and the business and regulatory environments in which the client operates.
B. The degree to which information technology is used in the accounting function.
C. The relationship between management, the board of directors, and external stakeholders.
D. The degree to which the auditor intends to use internal audit personnel to perform substantive tests.

AUD 2-Q43 A299. Which of the following procedures is considered a test of controls?

A. An auditor reviews the entity's check register for unrecorded liabilities.
B. An auditor evaluates whether a general journal entry was recorded at the proper amount.
C. An auditor interviews and observes appropriate personnel to determine segregation of duties.
D. An auditor reviews the audit workpapers to ensure proper sign-off.

AUD 2-Q44 A182. Which of the following should an auditor do when control risk is assessed at the maximum level?

A. Perform fewer substantive tests of details.
B. Perform more tests of controls.
C. Document the assessment.
D. Document the control structure more extensively.

AUD 2-Q45 A157. Which of the following is a definition of control risk?

A. The risk that a material misstatement will not be prevented or detected on a timely basis by the client's internal controls.
B. The risk that the auditor will not detect a material misstatement.
C. The risk that the auditor's assessment of internal controls will be at less than the maximum level.
D. The susceptibility of material misstatement assuming there are no related internal control, policies, or procedures.

AUD 2-Q46 A158. Which of the following is not a component of internal control?

A. Control environment.
B. Control activities.
C. Inherent risk.
D. Monitoring

AUD 2-Q47 A160. Each of the following types of controls is considered to be an entity-level control, except those
A. Relating to the control environment.
B. Pertaining to the company's risk assessment process.
C. Regarding the company's annual stockholder meeting.
D. Addressing policies over significant risk management practices.

AUD 2-Q48 A128. A company employs three accounts payable clerks and one treasurer. Their responsibilities are as follows:

Employee	Responsibility
Clerk 1	Reviews vendor invoices for proper signature approval.
Clerk 2	Enters vendor invoices into the accounting system and verifies payment terms.
Clerk 3	Posts entered vendor invoices to the accounts payable ledger for payment and mails checks.
Treasurer	Reviews the vendor invoices and signs each check.

Which of the following would indicate a weakness in the company's internal control?

A. Clerk 1 opens all of the incoming mail.
B. Clerk 2 reconciles the accounts payable ledger with the general ledger monthly.
C. Clerk 3 mails the checks and remittances after they have been signed.
D. The treasurer uses a stamp for signing checks.

AUD 2-Q49 A52. Obtaining an understanding of an internal control involves evaluating the design of the control and determining whether the control has been

A. Authorized.
B. Implemented
C. Tested.
D. Reperformed.

AUD 2-Q50 A56. Which of the following is the best way to compensate for the lack of adequate segregation of duties in a small organization?
A. Disclosing lack of segregation of duties to the external auditors during the annual review.
B. Replacing personnel every three or four years.
C. Requiring accountants to pass a yearly background check.
D. Allowing for greater management oversight of incompatible activities.

AUD 2-Q51 A107. Which of the following matters relating to an entity's operations would an auditor most likely consider as an inherent risk factor in planning an audit?

A. The entity's fiscal year ends on June 30.
B. The entity enters into derivative transactions as hedges.
C. The entity's financial statements are generated at an outside service center.
D. The entity's financial data are available only in computer-readable form.

AUD 2-Q52 A108. Which of the following is a factor in the control environment?

A. Segregation of duties.
B. Information processing.
C. Performance reviews.
D. Management's philosophy and operating style.

AUD 2-Q53 A110. Providing more supervision during an audit of a nonissuer in response to assessed risks of material misstatement at the financial statement level is an example of

A. A substantive response.
B. Further audit procedures.
C. Tests of controls.
D. An overall response.

AUD 2-Q54 A345. Proper segregation of duties calls for separation of the

A. Authorization, approval, and execution functions.
B. Authorization, execution, and payment functions.
C. Receiving, shipping, and custodial functions.
D. Authorization, recording, and custodial functions.

AUD 2-Q55 A370. The auditor's review of the client's system of internal control is documented in order to substantiate
A. Conformity of the accounting records with generally accepted accounting principles.
B. Representation as to adherence to requirements of management.
C. Representation as to compliance with generally accepted auditing standards.
D. The fairness of the financial statement presentation.

AUD 2-Q56 A374. How does the extent of substantive tests required to constitute sufficient appropriate audit evidence vary with the auditor's reliance on internal control?

A. Randomly.
B. Disproportionately.
C. Directly.
D. Inversely.

AUD 2-Q57 A384. Which of the following audit tests would be regarded as a "test of controls?"
A. Tests of the specific items making up the balance given in a general ledger account.
B. Tests of the inventory pricing to vendors' invoices.
C. Tests of the signatures on cancelled checks to board of directors' authorizations.
D. Tests of the additions to property, plant, and equipment by physical inspections.

AUD 2-Q58 A387. Which of the following is essential to determine whether the necessary internal control procedures were prescribed and are being followed?

A. Developing questionnaires and checklists.
B. Studying and evaluating administrative control policies.
C. Reviewing the system and testing controls.
D. Observing employee functions and making inquiries.

AUD 2-Q59 A388. In general, a material internal control weakness may be defined as a condition in which material errors or fraud would ordinarily not be detected within a timely period by
A. An auditor during the normal study and evaluation of the system of internal control.
B. A controller when reconciling accounts in the general ledger.
C. Employees in the normal course of performing their assigned functions.
D. The chief financial officer when reviewing interim financial statements.

AUD 2-Q60 A399. Which of the following would be least likely to be included in an auditor's tests of controls?

A. Inspection.
B. Observation.
C. Inquiry.
D. Confirmation.

AUD 2-Q61 A405. Tests of controls are concerned primarily with each of the following questions except

A. How were the procedures performed?
B. Why were the procedures performed?
C. Were the necessary procedures performed?
D. By whom were the procedures performed?

AUD 2-Q62 A438. An auditor evaluates the existing system of internal control in order to

A. Determine the extent of control tests which must be performed.
B. Determine the extent of substantive tests which must be performed.
C. Ascertain whether fraud is probable.
D. Ascertain whether any employees have incompatible functions.

AUD 2-Q63 A443. In the audit of ledger accounts, what is appropriate test of procedures?
A. Equipment.
B. Bonds payable
C. Bank charges.
D. Sales.

AUD 2-Q64 A72. Which of the following explanations most likely would satisfy an auditor who questions management about significant debits to accumulated depreciation accounts in the current year?

A. Prior years' depreciation expenses were erroneously understated.
B. Current year's depreciation expense was erroneously understated.
C. The estimated remaining useful lives of plant assets were revised upward.
D. Plant assets were retired during the current year.

AUD 2-Q65 A25. In which of the following circumstances is substantive testing of accounts receivable before the balance sheet date most appropriate?

A. The client has a new sales incentive program in place.
B. Internal controls during the remaining period are effective.
C. There is a high turnover of senior management.
D. It is a first engagement of a new client.

AUD 2-Q66 A39. Before applying principal substantive tests to an entity's accounts receivable at an interim date, an auditor should

A. Consider the likelihood of assessing the risk of incorrect rejection too low.
B. Project sampling risk at the maximum for tests covering the remaining period.
C. Ascertain that accounts receivable are immaterial to the financial statements.
D. Assess the difficulty in controlling the incremental audit risk.

AUD 2-Q67 A219. An auditor is determining if internal control relative to the revenue cycle of a wholesaling entity is operating effectively in minimizing the failure to prepare sales invoices. The auditor most likely would select a sample of transactions from the population represented by the

A. Cash receipts file.
B. Shipping document file.
C. Customer order file.
D. Sales invoice file.

AUD 2-Q68 A221. Which of the following procedures would an auditor most likely perform prior to the balance sheet date?

A. Review subsequent events.
B. Perform search for unrecorded liabilities.
C. Send inquiry letter to client's legal counsel.
D. Review detail and test significant travel and entertainment expenses.

AUD 2-Q69 A276. An auditor's tests of controls for completeness for the revenue cycle usually include determining whether
A. Each receivable is collected subsequent to the year end.
B. An invoice is prepared for each shipping document.
C. Each invoice is supported by a customer purchase order.
D. Each credit memo is properly approved.

AUD 2-Q70 A246. Which of the following describes a weakness in accounts payable procedures?

A. The accounts payable clerk files invoices and supporting documentation after payment.
B. The accounts payable clerk manually verifies arithmetic on the vendor invoice.
C. The accounts payable system compares the receiving report to the vendor invoice.
D. The accounts payable manager issues purchase orders.

AUD 2-Q71 A255. Which of the following could be difficult to determine because electronic evidence may not be retrievable after a specific period?

A. The acceptance level of detection risk.
B. The timing of control and substantive tests.
C. Whether to adopt substantive or reliance test strategies.
D. The assessed level of inherent risk.

AUD 2-Q72 A316. How does Office of Management and Budget Circular A-133, Audits of States, Local Governments, and Non-Profit Organizations, define a sub recipient?

A. As a nonfederal entity that provides a federal award to another entity to carry out a federal program.
B. As an individual who receives and expends federal awards received from a pass-through entity.
C. As a dealer, distributor, merchant, or other seller providing goods or services that are required for the conduct of a federal program.
D. As a nonfederal entity that expends federal awards received from another entity to carry out a federal program.

AUD 2-Q73 A325. Which of the following explanations best describes why an auditor may decide to reduce tests of details for a particular audit objective?

A. The audit is being performed soon after the balance sheet date.
B. Audit staff are experienced in performing the planned procedures.
C. Analytical procedures have revealed no unusual or unexpected results.
D. There were many transactions posted to the account during the period.

AUD 2-Q74 A296. Which of the following payroll control activities would most effectively ensure that payment is made only for work performed?

A. Require all employees to record arrival and departure by using the time clock.
B. Have a payroll clerk recalculate all time cards.
C. Require all employees to sign their time cards.
D. Require employees to have their direct supervisors approve their time cards.

AUD 2-Q75 A125. Which of the following controls should prevent an invoice for the purchase of merchandise from being paid twice?

A. The check signer accounts for the numerical sequence of receiving reports used in support of each payment.
B. An individual independent of cash operations prepares a bank reconciliation.
C. The check signer reviews and cancels the voucher packets.
D. Two check signers are required for all checks over a specified amount.

AUD 2-Q76 A132. Which of the following statements best describes why an auditor would use only substantive procedures to evaluate specific relevant assertions and risks?

A. The relevant internal control components are not well documented.
B. The internal auditor already has tested the relevant controls and found them effective.
C. Testing the operating effectiveness of the relevant controls would not be efficient.
D. The cost of substantive procedures will exceed the cost of testing the relevant controls.

AUD 2-Q77 A133. Which of the following courses of action is the most appropriate if an auditor concludes that there is a high risk of material misstatement?

A. Use smaller, rather than larger, sample sizes.
B. Perform substantive tests as of an interim date.
C. Select more effective substantive tests.
D. Increase of tests of controls.

AUD 2-Q78 A64. A government internal audit function is presumed to be free from organizational independence impairments for reporting internally when the head of the organization

A. Is not accountable to those charged with governance.
B. Performs auditing procedures that are consistent with generally accepted accounting principles.
C. Is a line-manager of the unit under audit.
D. Is removed from political pressures to conduct audits objectively, without fear of political reprisal.

AUD 2-Q79 A105. While performing interim audit procedures of accounts receivable, numerous unexpected errors are found resulting in a change of risk assessment. Which of the following audit responses would be most appropriate?

A. Move detailed analytical procedures from year end to interim.
B. Increase the dollar threshold of vouching customer invoices.
C. Send negative accounts receivable confirmations instead of positive accounts receivable confirmations.
D. Use more experienced audit team members to perform year-end testing.

AUD 2-Q80 A106. Which of the following types of risk increases when an auditor performs substantive analytical audit procedures for financial statement accounts at an interim date?

A. Inherent.
B. Control.
C. Detection.
D. Sampling

AUD 2-Q81 A342. During the first part of the current fiscal year, the client company began dealing with certain customers on a consignment basis. Which of the following auditing procedures is least likely to bring this new fact to the auditor's attention?

A. Tracing of shipping documents to the sales journal.
B. Test of cash receipts transactions.
C. Confirmation of accounts receivable.
D. Observation of physical inventory.

AUD 2-Q82 A350. In the audit of a medium sized manufacturing company, which one of the following areas would be expected to require the least amount of audit time?

A. Owners' equity.
B. Revenue.
C. Assets.
D. Liabilities.

AUD 2-Q83 A354. Jackson, the purchasing agent of Judd Hardware Wholesalers, has a relative who owns a retail hardware store. Jackson arranged for hardware to be delivered by manufacturers to the retail store on a C.O.D. basis thereby enabling his relative to buy at Judd's wholesale price. Jackson was probably able to accomplish this because of Judd's poor internal control over

A. Purchase orders.
B. Purchase requisitions.
C. Cash receipts.
D. Perpetual inventory records.

AUD 2-Q84 A360. The physical count of inventory of a retailer was higher than shown by perpetual records. Which of the following could explain the difference?

A. Inventory items had been counted but the tags placed on the items had not been taken off the items and added to the inventory accumulation sheets.
B. Credit memos for several items returned by customers had not been prepared.
C. No journal entry had been made on the retailer's books for several items returned to its suppliers.
D. An item purchased "FOB shipping point" had not arrived and had not been reflected in the perpetual records.

AUD 2-Q85 A371. The auditor is concerned with establishing that dividends are paid to stockholders of the client corporation owning stock as of the

A. Issue date.
B. Declaration date.
C. Record date.
D. Payment date.

AUD 2-Q86 A393. Propex Corporation uses a voucher register and does not record invoices in a subsidiary ledger. Propex will probably benefit most from the additional cost of maintaining an accounts payable subsidiary ledger if

A. There are usually invoices in an unmatched invoice file.
B. Vendors' requests for confirmation of receivables often go unanswered for several months until paid invoices can be reviewed.
C. Partial payments to vendors are continuously made in the ordinary course of business.
D. It is difficult to reconcile vendors' monthly statements.

AUD 2-Q87 A414. The auditor is most likely to verify accrued commissions payable in conjunction with the

A. Sales cutoff review.
B. Verification of contingent liabilities.
C. Review of post balance sheet date disbursements.
D. Audit of trade accounts payable.

AUD 2-Q88 A425. The sequence of steps in gathering evidence as the basis of the auditor's opinion is:

A. Substantive tests, internal control review and control tests.
B. Internal control review, substantive tests, and control tests.
C. Internal control review, control tests and substantive tests.
D. Control tests, internal control review and substantive tests.

AUD 2-Q89 A428. Which of the following procedures is least likely to be performed before the balance sheet date?

A. Observation of inventory.
B. Review of internal control over cash disbursements.
C. Search for unrecorded liabilities.
D. Confirmation of receivables.

AUD 2-Q90 A429. With respect to an internal control measure that will assure accountability for fixed asset retirements, management should implement a system that includes

A. Continuous analysis of miscellaneous revenue to locate any cash proceeds from sale of plant assets.
B. Periodic inquiry of plant executives by internal auditors as to whether any plant assets have been retired.
C. Continuous utilization of serially numbered retirement work orders.
D. Periodic observation of plant assets by the internal auditors.

AUD 2-Q91 A430. An auditor would be most likely to learn of slow-moving inventory through

A. Inquiry of sales personnel.
B. Inquiry of stores personnel.
C. Physical observation of inventory.
D. Review of perpetual inventory records.

AUD 2-Q92 A434. Which of the following is a primary function of the purchasing department?

A. Authorizing the acquisition of goods.
B. Ensuring the acquisition of goods of a specified quality.
C. Verifying the propriety of goods acquired.
D. Reducing expenditures for goods acquired.

AUD 2-Q93 A446. Which of the following procedures would best detect the theft of valuable items from an inventory that consists of hundreds of different items selling for $1 to $10 and a few items selling for hundreds of dollars?

A. Maintain a perpetual inventory of only the most valuable items with frequent periodic verification of the validity of the perpetual inventory record.
B. Have an independent CPA firm prepare an internal control report on the effectiveness of the administrative and accounting controls over inventory.
C. Have separate warehouse space for the more valuable items with sequentially numbered tags.
D. Require an authorized officer's signature on all requisitions for the more valuable items.

AUD 2-Q94 A451. In determining the adequacy of the allowance for uncollectible accounts, the least reliance should be placed upon which of the following?

A. The credit manager's opinion.
B. An aging schedule of past due accounts.
C. Collection experience of the client's collection agency.
D. Ratios calculated showing the past relationship of the valuation allowance to net credit sales.

AUD 2-Q95 A452. When title to merchandise in transit has passed to the audit client, the auditor engaged in the performance of a purchase cutoff will encounter the greatest difficulty in gaining assurance with respect to the

A. Quantity.
B. Quality.
C. Price.
D. Terms.

AUD 2-Q96 A19. Which of the following statements is correct concerning materiality in a financial statement audit?

A. Analytical procedures performed during an audit's final review stage usually decrease materiality levels.
B. If the materiality amount used in evaluating audit findings increases from the amount used in planning, the auditor should apply additional substantive tests.
C. The auditor's materiality judgments generally involve quantitative, but not qualitative, considerations.
D. Materiality levels are generally considered in terms of the smallest aggregate level of misstatement that could be considered material to any one of the financial statements.

AUD 2-Q97 A76. Which of the following factors should an external auditor obtain updated information about when assessing an internal auditor's competence?

A. Determining who the internal auditor reports to.
B. The educational level and professional experiences of the internal auditor.
C. Whether policies prohibit the internal auditor from auditing areas where relatives are employed.
D. Whether the board of directors, audit committee, or owner-manager oversees employment decisions related to the internal auditor.

AUD 2-Q98 A223. Which of the following factors most likely would assist an independent auditor in assessing the objectivity of the internal auditor?

A. The organizational status of the director of internal audit.
B. The professional certifications of the internal audit staff.
C. The consistency of the internal audit reports with the results of work performed.
D. The appropriateness of internal audit conclusions in the circumstances.

AUD 2-Q99 A197. In assessing the competence of internal auditors, an independent CPA most likely would obtain information about the

A. Influence of management on the scope of the internal auditors' duties.
B. Policies limiting internal auditors from communicating with the audit committee.
C. Quality of the internal auditors' working paper documentation.
D. Entity's ability to continue as a going concern for a reasonable period of time.

AUD 2-Q100 A280. When assessing the competence of the internal auditors, an independent CPA should obtain information about the
A. Organizational level to which the internal auditors report.
B. Quality of the internal auditors' working paper documentation.
C. Policies prohibiting internal auditors from auditing sensitive matters.
D. Internal auditors' preliminary assessed level of control risk.

AUD 2-Q101 A172. When assessing internal auditors' objectivity, an independent auditor should

A. Consider the policies that prohibit the internal auditors from auditing areas where they were recently assigned.
B. Review the internal auditors' reports to determine that their conclusions are consistent with the work performed.
C. Verify that the internal auditors' assessment of control risk is comparable to the independent auditor's assessment.
D. Evaluate the quality of the internal auditors' working paper documentation and their recent audit recommendations.

AUD 2-Q102 A173. During a financial statement audit an internal auditor may provide direct assistance to the independent CPA in performing

	Tests of controls	Substantive tests
A.	Yes	Yes
B.	Yes	No
C.	No	Yes
D.	No	No

AUD 2-Q103 A183, The company being audited has an internal auditor that is both competent and objective. The independent auditor wants to assign tasks for the internal auditor to perform. Under these circumstances, the independent auditor may

A. Allow the internal auditor to perform tests of internal controls.
B. Allow the internal auditor to audit a major subsidiary of the company.
C. Not assign any task to the internal auditor because of the internal auditor's lack of independence.
D. Allow the internal auditor to perform analytical procedures, but not be involved with any tests of details.

AUD 2-Q104 A422. Which of the following best describes how the detailed audit program of the CPA who is engaged to audit the financial statements of a large publicly held company compares with the audit client's comprehensive internal audit program?

A. The comprehensive internal audit program is more detailed and covers areas that would normally not be examined by the CPA.
B. The comprehensive internal audit program is more detailed although it covers less areas than would normally be covered by the CPA.
C. The comprehensive internal audit program is substantially identical to the audit program used by the CPA because both review substantially the same areas.
D. The comprehensive internal audit program is less detailed and covers fewer areas than would normally be reviewed by the CPA.

AUD 2-Q105 A38. An auditor intends to use the work of an actuary who has a relationship with the client. Under these circumstances, the auditor

A. Is required to disclose the contractual relationship in the auditor's report.
B. Should assess the risk that the actuary's objectivity might be impaired.
C. Is not permitted to rely on the actuary because of a lack of independence
D. Should communicate this matter to the audit committee as a material weakness.

AUD 2-Q106 A192. Evidence concerning the proper segregation of duties for receiving and depositing cash receipts ordinarily is obtained by

A. Completing an internal control questionnaire that describes the control activities.
B. Observing the employees who are performing the control activities.
C. Performing substantive tests to verify the details of the bank balance.
D. Preparing a flow chart of the duties performed and the entity's available personnel.

AUD 2-Q107 A285. An auditor who uses the work of a specialist may refer to the specialist in the auditor's report if the

A. Auditor believes that the specialist's findings are reasonable in the circumstances.
B. Specialist's findings support the related assertions in the financial statements.
C. Auditor modifies the report because of the difference between the client's and the specialist's valuations of an asset.
D. Specialist's findings provide the auditor with greater assurance of reliability about management's representations.

AUD 2-Q108 A253. Which of the following statements is correct concerning an auditor's use of the work of an actuary in assessing a client's pension obligations?

A. The auditor is required to understand the objectives and scope of the actuary's work.
B. The reasonableness of the actuary's assumptions is strictly the auditor's responsibility.
C. The client is required to consent to the auditor's use of the actuary's work.
D. If the actuary has a relationship with the client, the auditor may not use the actuary's work.

AUD 2-Q109 A403. When outside firms of non-accountants specializing in the taking of physical inventories are used to count, list, price, and subsequently compute the total dollar amount of inventory on hand at the date of the physical count, the auditor will ordinarily

A. Consider the report of the outside inventory-taking firm to be an acceptable substitute procedure to the observation of physical inventories.
B. Make or observe some physical counts of the inventory, recompute certain inventory calculations and test certain inventory transactions.
C. Not reduce the extent of work on the physical count of inventory.
D. Consider the reduced audit effort with respect to the physical count of inventory as a scope limitation.

AUD 2-Q110 A45. Which of the following statements is correct regarding the auditor's consideration of the possibility of indirect illegal acts by clients?

A. The auditor has a responsibility to detect illegal acts that have a material and direct effect on the financial statements
B. The auditor's training, experience, and understanding of the client should be used to provide a basis for the determination as to whether illegal acts have occurred
C. If specific information concerning an illegal act comes to the auditor's attention, the auditor should apply audit procedures specifically directed to ascertaining whether an illegal act has occurred.
D. If an illegal act has occurred, the auditor should express a qualified opinion or an adverse opinion on the financial statements taken as a whole.

AUD 2-Q111 A319. During the audit of a new client, the auditor determined that management had given illegal bribes to municipal officials during the year under audit and for several prior years. The auditor notified the client's board of directors, but the board decided to take no action because the amounts involved were immaterial to the financial statements. Under these circumstances, the auditor should

A. Add an explanatory paragraph emphasizing that certain matters, while not affecting the unmodified opinion, require disclosure.
B. Report the illegal bribes to the municipal official at least one level above those persons who received the bribes.
C. Consider withdrawing from the audit engagement and disassociating from future relationships with the client.
D. Issue an "except for" modified opinion or an adverse opinion with a separate paragraph that explains the circumstances.

AUD 2-Q112 A294. Which of the following information that comes to an auditor's attention most likely would raise a question about the occurrence of illegal acts?

A. The exchange of property for similar property in a nonmonetary transaction.
B. The discovery of unexplained payments made to government employees.
C. The presence of several difficult-to-audit transactions affecting expense accounts.
D. The failure to develop adequate procedures that detect unauthorized purchases.

AUD 2-Q113 A261. Which of the following events least likely would indicate the existence of related party transactions?

A. Making a loan with no scheduled date for the funds to be repaid.
B. Maintaining compensating balance arrangements for the benefit of principal stockholders.
C. Borrowing funds at an interest rate significantly below prevailing market rates.
D. Writing off obsolete inventory to net realizable value just before year end.

AUD 2-Q114 A295. Which of the following steps should an auditor perform first to determine the existence of related parties?

A. Examine invoices, contracts, and purchasing orders.
B. Request a list of related parties from management.
C. Review the company's business structure.
D. Review proxy and other materials filed with the SEC.

AUD 2-Q115 A50. In auditing related party transactions, an auditor ordinarily places primary emphasis on

A. The probability that related party transactions will recur.
B. Confirming the existence of the related parties.
C. Verifying the valuation of the related party transactions.
D. The adequacy of the disclosure of the related party transactions.

AUD 2-Q116 A418. For a reporting entity that has participated in related party transactions that are material, disclosure in the financial statements should include

A. The nature of the relationship and the terms and manner of settlement.
B. Details of the transactions within major classifications.
C. A statement to the effect that a transaction was consummated on terms no less favorable than those that would have been obtained if the transaction had been with an unrelated party.
D. A reference to deficiencies in the entity's system of internal accounting control.

Multiple Choice – Solutions

AUD 2-Q1 A247. Choice C is correct. The successor auditor should inquire as to the predecessor's understanding of the change in auditors and determine if it is similar to the client's reasoning. This may reveal integrity about the client.

Choices A, B, and D are incorrect as these are not required questions that a successor auditor should make.

AUD 2-Q2 A102. Choice D is correct. Inquiries regarding matters that can assist with the financial reporting consistency is something that the successor auditor should inquire from the predecessor auditor.
Choices A, B, and C are incorrect as these items are discussed prior to accepting the audit engagement.

AUD 2-Q3 A352. The correct answer is A. Auditing procedures are the means by which the auditor performs his audit in accordance with GAAS. The auditor's primary purpose is not to detect errors or fraud (answer B), or to prevent litigation (answer D). Rather, it is to gather sufficient appropriate audit evidence to enable him to express an opinion on the financial statements taken as a whole. Answer C is the testing of internal controls which is wrong because the procedures outlined in audit programs are not primarily designed to test internal controls; rather, they are designed to gather evidence.

AUD 2-Q4 A40. Choice D is correct. Comparing actual results with forecasted results and budgets is a procedure that an auditor would perform during the planning phase of the audit.

Choice A is incorrect as management representations are typically obtained during the audit completion phase.

Choice B is incorrect as this is something that would be done during the prior year.

Choice C is incorrect as legal inquiries are done as part of substantive audit testing.

AUD 2-Q5 A118. Choice C is correct. This is an analytical procedure that is performed in the planning phase of an audit.

Choices A, B, and D are incorrect as these are procedures that are performed during the year-end fieldwork. These procedures are not typically performed during the planning phase.

AUD 2-Q6 A391. The correct answer is A. The fact that the controls appear adequate is not a sufficient enough reason for reliance on the controls. Before an auditor can rely upon a control procedure to reduce control risk, tests of the control must be performed.

Answer B is incorrect because when the controls duplicate operative controls existing elsewhere in the system, the auditor does not need to test both.

Answer C is incorrect because when weak controls are not going to be relied upon, control testing may be omitted.

Answer D is incorrect because tests of the controls can be omitted if the cost of tests of controls is greater than the savings from reduced substantive testing resulting from the reliance upon the controls.

AUD 2-Q7 A408. The correct answer is C. An auditor's understanding of a client's system of internal control whether manual, mechanical, or electronic, is primarily but not exclusively obtained by inquiry. The first step taken by an auditor would be to inquire of management about the EDP system. The auditor would then perform other procedures, such as, inspection, observation, and evaluation.

AUD 2-Q8 A204. Choice B is correct. Collusion, human error, and management overrides are examples of inherent limitations of internal controls.

Choices A, C, and D are incorrect as these are not examples of inherent limitations of internal controls.

AUD 2-Q9 A275. Choice B is correct. An inherent limitation in internal control is one where management can override existing controls that are in place. In this situation, management has the ability to override existing controls.

Choices A, C, and D are incorrect as these are examples of a Company failing to institute proper controls.

AUD 2-Q10 A322. Choice B is correct. If spending limits are exceeded, then this might indicate that management is overriding internal controls.
Choice A, C, and D are incorrect as these procedures would not indicate if management is overriding controls or not.

AUD 2-Q11 A170. Choice B is correct as since management designs and implements controls, there is always the risk that management can override controls.

Choice A is incorrect. A control environment alone cannot ensure that the entity's business objectives will be met. Also, "ensure" is too strong as an auditor cannot ensure that an entity's business objectives will be met.
Choice C is incorrect. Even with a well designed internal control structure, collusion may not be detected.

Choice D is incorrect as internal controls cannot detect all errors and fraud.

AUD 2-Q12 A85. Choice C is correct. The purpose of a fraud brainstorming session is to assess the likelihood of fraud.

Choice A is incorrect as this is mainly discussed in the planning phase after internal control testing has been completed and assessing the level of detection risk.

Choice B is incorrect as this is done during the planning phase of the audit and not the primary objective during the fraud brainstorming session.

Choice D is incorrect as this is not the primary focus in a fraud brainstorming session.

AUD 2-Q13 A86. Choice D is correct. This is an indication of financial reporting fraud as the Company's sales revenue appear to be misstated based on the changing sales trend.

Choice A is incorrect because there is no evidence that an employee or management has misappropriated assets.

Choice B is incorrect as there is no indication that there has been theft of an entity's assets.

Choice C is incorrect as there is no indication of embezzlement.

AUD 2-Q14 A43. Choice C is correct. Frequent disputes between the auditor and management would indicate that the auditor disagrees with the way that management is preparing the financial statements. As such, there is a greater risk that the financial statements are materially misstated.

Choice A is incorrect because it would be riskier if management was preoccupied with the earnings trend.

Choice B is incorrect because selling computer hardware before the asset is fully depreciated would not indicate that there is risk of material misstatement.

Choice D is incorrect, as it is common for a client to have several large checks outstanding since this depends on the time when the checks are cashed.

AUD 2-Q15 A229. Choice B is correct. A lack of independent checks is a risk factor that relates to misstatements from misappropriation of assets.

Choice A is incorrect as a high turnover of senior management would not result in misstatements arising from a misappropriation of assets.

Choice C is incorrect as this would not be a cause for misstatements resulting from misappropriation of assets.

Choice D is incorrect as an inability to generate cash flows from operations would not necessarily result in a misstatement arising from a misappropriation of assets.

Note: Choices A, C and D are risk factors related to fraudulent financial reporting.

AUD 2-Q16 A248. Choice D is correct. If the results of analytical procedures indicate that there are unexpected differences, this may indicate that there is a material misstatement in the financials.

Choice A is incorrect as this would not indicate that there are material misstatements in the financial statements.

Choice B is incorrect as the management representation letter is typically signed on the last day of fieldwork.

Choice C is incorrect as this would indicate a control weakness but not heighten the auditor's concern about whether material misstatements exist in the financial statements.

AUD 2-Q17 A257. Choice C is correct. Access to blank checks and signature plates is restricted to the cash disbursement bookkeeper who reconciles the bank statements can lead to an embezzlement scheme. Someone who is in charge of cash receipts or cash disbursements should not perform the bank reconciliation.

Choices A, B, and D are incorrect as these are appropriate segregated functions.

AUD 2-Q18 A309. Choice B is correct. In this situation, the auditor should reevaluate the risk of fraud and design alternate tests for the related transactions.

Choice A, C, and D are incorrect as choice B would be the most accurate response.

AUD 2-Q19 A159. Choice D is correct. During the audit, an auditor should maintain an attitude of professional skepticism: An attitude that includes a questioning mind, being alert to conditions that may indicate possible misstatement due to fraud or error, and a critical assessment of audit evidence.

Choice A, B, and C are incorrect as these do not show that an auditor is maintaining professional skepticism.

AUD 2-Q20 A57. Choice A is correct. Bearer bonds represent a risk to an organization because they are unregistered bonds that can be sold by anyone. As such, these bonds are easy to misappropriate and can be easily converted into cash.

Choice B is incorrect because having a large amount of inventory on hand would not necessarily mean that it would be subject to misappropriation. It would depend on if there were proper controls over safeguarding the inventory. Further, inventory that has a low sales price would not usually be subject to misappropriation – it would normally be inventory that has a high sales price.

Choice C is incorrect because posting a large number of transactions in a short period does not necessarily mean that there is a high risk of asset misappropriation.

Choice D is incorrect, as having fixed assets with serial numbers would actually decrease the risk of asset misappropriation since the assets are easily traceable.

AUD 2-Q21 A104. Choice C is correct. Rights and obligations represent the account balance assertion that the entity has the rights to the assets, liabilities, and obligations of the entity.

Choice A, B, and D are incorrect because these assertions deal with the category transaction classes.

AUD 2-Q22 A79. Choice B is correct. Inquiry and observation are procedures used to test the operating effectiveness of internal controls.

Choices A, C, and D are incorrect as these are substantive procedures and are not used during controls testing. Substantive procedures are used to provide assurance on the dollar value of a particular account balance and are not used to test control effectiveness.

AUD 2-Q23 A80. Choice C is correct because it is the most difficult to detect internal control issues when two employees are circumventing internal controls (collusion) as it would be easier for the employees to cover up each other.

Choice A is incorrect because even if the employee neglects the control, it can be detected when the auditor performs controls testing procedures.

Choice B is incorrect as this would be uncovered when the auditor performs tests of internal controls.

Choice D is incorrect as this would be detected when the auditor performs controls testing.

AUD 2-Q24 A81. Choice B is correct. Inherent and control risks exist independently of the audit and the auditor cannot change these risks --- the auditor assesses these risks.

Choice A is incorrect as the client does not calculate these risks – the auditor assesses these risks.

Choice C is incorrect as these risks are not controlled by the auditor. The auditor can only control detection risk.

Choice D is incorrect as inherent and control risk are not based on the auditor's judgment about materiality.

AUD 2-Q25 A29. Choice D is correct. Ultimately, auditors are concerned with the risk of undetected material misstatements in the financial statements. Assessing control risk will help the auditor gauge the extent of substantive testing that needs to be performed.

Choice A is incorrect because determining whether material misstatements exist in the financial statements is more of a concern for auditors.

Choice B is incorrect because this is not the auditor's ultimate goal when assessing control risks.

Choice C is incorrect because identification of activities is usually done when understanding the client's internal control structure via reading a narrative.

AUD 2-Q26 A30. Choice C is correct. If a sales transaction does not contain proper credit approval, this would cause concern as to whether sales and related receivables are properly valued because there is no guarantee that the receivable will be received by the customer (as their credit standing is unknown). Testing for credit approval would not test for rights and obligations as credit approval would not indicate that the Company has a legal right to the receivable (this would be evidenced by a sales agreement or a signed sales order form).

AUD 2-Q27 A1. The correct answer is B. When an auditor cannot rely on an entity's internal controls due to deficiencies in the internal control structure, the auditor assesses control risk at the maximum and increases the extent of substantive testing to reduce audit risk to a desirable level.

Answers A and C are incorrect as an increase in control risk does not result in a disclaimer or a modification of opinion.

Answer D is incorrect because an increase in control risk does not necessitate an auditor withdrawing from an engagement as an auditor may increase the amount of substantive testing to be gain comfort over the financial statements.

AUD 2-Q28 A2. The correct answer is B. In order to reduce audit risk in order to express an opinion, an auditor has to gather and examine evidence.

Answer A is incorrect because a discussion with responsible individuals would not lessen the amount of audit risk by the same amount as an auditor examining evidence.

Answer C is incorrect because inquiries of senior management is a procedure done be an auditor, in order to become aware and familiar to the client's business and operations. It does not lessen the amount of audit risk by the same amount as an auditor examining evidence.

Answer D is incorrect because analytical procedures are a type of evidence along with tests of controls and substantive tests of details. So, answer D is contained in answer B which makes answer B the best answer.

AUD 2-Q29 A3. Choice B is correct. When an auditor cannot rely on an entity's internal controls due to deficiencies in the internal control structure, the auditor assesses control risk at the maximum and increases the extent of substantive testing to reduce audit risk to a desirable level. In other words, CR goes up (so RMM goes up) so DR must go down which means increase the extent of substantive testing.

Choice A and C are incorrect as an increase in control risk does not result in a disclaimer or a qualification of opinion C.

Choice D is incorrect because an increase in control risk does not necessitate an auditor withdrawing from an engagement as an auditor may increase the amount of substantive testing to be gain comfort over the financial statements.

AUD 2-Q30 A4. Choice C is correct. Even the best internal controls can fail when they rely on human judgment.

Choices A and B are incorrect as incompatible duties and a lack of segregation of duties can be resolved by changing the duties of individuals responsible for certain controls.

Choice D is incorrect as a lack of an audit committee can be created by the Company or its Board of directors. Human judgment is the only item that cannot be rectified.

AUD 2-Q31 A20. Choice D is correct. An auditor will assess control risk too high when the deviation rate of the auditor's sample is greater than the true deviation rate if the auditor had tested the entire population. This is known as sampling risk.

Choice A is incorrect because a sample which has a low deviation rate will assess the control risk too low because the auditor's sample has a lower deviation rate than if the auditor had tested the entire population.

Choice B is incorrect because testing the incorrect assertion will not cause control risk to increase.

Choice C is incorrect because if the auditor believed that the control will reduce substantive testing, then the control risk will be assessed lower – not higher.

AUD 2-Q32 A222. Choice B is correct. The auditor would document the understanding of internal controls.

Choice A is incorrect as this would not warrant a modified opinion.

Choice C is incorrect as this would not warrant assessing control risk at the highest level as an auditor may still be able to gain comfort on internal controls.

Choice D is incorrect as an auditor may not restrict the users of this report in this situation.

AUD 2-Q33 A195. Choice D is correct. Ensuring that sales orders are sent to the credit department for approval would test for proper authorization.

Choice A is incorrect as this would ensure that there is proper segregation of duties.

Choice B is incorrect as this would ensure that items are sold at an approved price.

Choice C is incorrect as this would ensure that approved sales orders are sent to the proper departments.

AUD 2-Q34 A199. Choice C is correct. A direct observation by an independent auditor provides the most reliable support over the effectiveness of the control.

Choice A is incorrect as inspecting the policy manual would not providence evidence about the operating effectiveness of the control activity.

Choice B is incorrect as direct observation would provide more reliable evidence.

Choice D is incorrect as this procedure would not provide evidence about the operating effectiveness.

AUD 2-Q35 A200. Choice B is correct. Detection risk is the only risk that can be changed upon discretion of the auditor. Control risk and audit risk exist independent of the auditor.

Choice A is incorrect as detection risk is not independent of the financial statement audit.

Choice C is incorrect as detection risk does not arise as a result of fraud.

Choice D is incorrect as detection risk can be assessed in quantitative terms.

AUD 2-Q36 A201. Choice A is correct. Stamping "paid" by the check signer would ensure that the voucher is submitted and paid only once.

Choice B is incorrect as this procedure would not ensure that the voucher is paid once.

Choice C is incorrect as this procedure would only ensure that there is adequate support for payment.

Choice D is incorrect as prenumbering does not ensure that vouchers are paid once. All these risks can be assessed in quantitative or nonquantitative terms.

AUD 2-Q37 A271. Choice D is correct. Inherent risk is the susceptibility of a financial statement assertion to a material misstatement assuming that there are no related controls.
Choice A is incorrect as the internal auditor's objectivity does not play a part in inherent risk.
Choice B is incorrect as this is control risk.
Choice C is incorrect as this is detection risk.

AUD 2-Q38 A284. Choice D is correct. The suitability of the client's lines of reporting is a relevant factor when an auditor considers the client's organizational structure in the context of control risk. This is one of the COSO components of internal control.

Choice A is incorrect as management's attitude is not the most relevant factor.

Choice B is incorrect as the organization's recruiting and hiring policies are not relevant when considering the client's organizational structure.

Choice C is incorrect as the physical proximity is not relevant when considering the organizational structure.

AUD 2-Q39 A321. Choice D is correct. Approving a summary of hours each employee worked during the pay period would assist in the prevention and detection of fraud.

Choices A, B, and C are incorrect as these procedures would not assist in the prevention or detection of fraud.

AUD 2-Q40 A323. Choice A is correct. When an auditor plans to rely on controls, the auditor must test the operating effectiveness of such controls.

Choice B is incorrect as the auditor would still need to test the operating effectiveness of the controls.

Choice C is incorrect as A is a better procedure for testing the operating effectiveness.

Choice D is incorrect as the auditor does not include this in the report.

AUD 2-Q41 A324. Choice D is correct. Automated controls are more effective when transactions are high-volume and recurring.

Choices A, B, and C are incorrect as manual controls are more appropriate in these circumstances.

AUD 2-Q42 A297. Choice B is correct. If the client's internal system of internal controls is complex, the documentation will also be more (i.e. more flowcharts, diagrams, and narratives) complex/detailed.

Choice A is incorrect as would not affect the extent of documentation.

Choice C is incorrect as the upper management relationship would not impact the extent of documentation.

Choice D is incorrect as the use of internal auditors to perform substantive tests would not impact the extent of documenting the understanding of internal controls.

AUD 2-Q43 A299. Choice C is correct. Interviewing and direct observation are both examples of controls testing.

Choices A and B are incorrect as these are examples of substantive tests.

Choice D is incorrect as this is a procedure performed by the auditor during the audit completion.

AUD 2-Q44 A182. Choice C is correct. An auditor should document the fact that control risk is assessed the maximum level and the reasons for the assessment.

Choice A is incorrect as control risk assessed at the maximum level would cause an auditor to perform more – not less, substantive tests of details.

Choice B is incorrect as the auditor may have already performed tests of controls in order to assess control risk.

Choice D is incorrect as the auditor would have already documented the control structure prior to assessing the control risk.

AUD 2-Q45 A157. Choice A is correct. Control risk is defined as the risk that a material misstatement will not be detected on a timely basis due to the entity's internal controls.

Choice B is incorrect as this is the definition of detection risk.

Choice C is incorrect as there is not a valid risk in auditing.

Choice D is incorrect as this is the definition of inherent risk.

AUD 2-Q46 A158. Choice C is correct. Inherent risk is not one of the components of internal control. The five components of internal control (COSO) are
Communication and Information
Risk Assessment
Control Environment
Control Activities
Monitoring

Choices A, B, and D are incorrect as these are all internal control components.

AUD 2-Q47 A160. Choice C is correct. Entity-level controls are controls that relate to the control environment and risk assessment and the overall organization. Controls over the annual stockholder meeting are not entity-wide as it relates to a particular process.

Choices A, B, and D are incorrect as these are controls that relate to the entity's control environment and risk assessment.

AUD 2-Q48 A128. Choice C is correct. If the same person posts the invoices and mails the checks then this would indicate incompatible duties. To have a proper segregation of duties, the person who posts invoices should not mail the checks. The check signer should be the one who mails the checks. Recall that there should be separation between authorization, physical handling, and recording.

Choice A is incorrect because there are no incompatible duties.

Choice B is incorrect as there are no incompatible duties.

Choice D is incorrect as using a stamp to sign a check is not an internal control weakness as long as there is no one else who has access to the stamp.

AUD 2-Q49 A52. Choice B is correct. When an auditor obtains an understanding of a Company's internal control structure, the auditor seeks to determine whether the control is implemented and in place.

Choice A is incorrect because determining as to whether an item is properly authorized occurs when the control is tested.

Choice C is incorrect since the auditor tests the effectiveness of internal controls after the auditor obtains an understanding of the control and determines whether the control has been implemented.

Choice D is incorrect, as an auditor reperforms control activities when testing internal controls – not when obtaining an understanding of the controls.

AUD 2-Q50 A56. Choice D is correct. In a small organization, the most effective way to compensate for the lack of segregation of duties is to have greater management oversight of incompatible functions.

Choice A is incorrect, because disclosing the lack of segregation would not be effective since there is no preventative measure.

Choice B is incorrect, as replacing employees would not eliminate the risk involved.

Choice C is incorrect because background checks do not assist in reducing the risk of having a lack of segregation of duties.

AUD 2-Q51 A107. Choice B is correct. Derivative transactions entered into as hedges are an inherent risk factor as these transactions are subject to complex calculations and estimates by management.

Choice A is incorrect as the fiscal year end does not affect the inherent risk of the entity.

Choice C is incorrect as generating financial statements in an outside service center would not affect inherent risk. However, it would affect the control risk as the auditor would need to rely on the controls of the outside service center.

Choice D is incorrect as evidence only being in electronic form would affect the control risk - not the inherent risk.

AUD 2-Q52 A108. Choice D is correct. The control environment sets the tone of an organization. The control environment is known as the "tone at the top" and defines the corporate culture. As such, it consists of managements operating style and philosophy.

Choice A is incorrect as segregation of duties is a factor of control activities – not the control environment.

Choice B is incorrect as information processing is a factor of information and communication – not the control environment.

Choice C is incorrect as performance reviews is a factor of control activities – not the control environment.

AUD 2-Q53 A110. Choice D is correct. Providing more supervision during an audit (such as more senior level audit team members) is an example of an overall response to an increase in the risk of material misstatement.

Choice A is incorrect this is not an appropriate response.

Choice B is incorrect as in this case, the auditor is not performing additional tests of detail.

Choice C is incorrect as the auditor is not performing additional tests of controls.

AUD 2-Q54 A345. The correct answer is D. There are four general types of segregation of duties for the prevention of errors and fraud:
1. Separation of operational responsibility from record keeping responsibility.
2. Separation of the custody of assets from accounting (record keeping).
3. Separation of the authorization of transactions from custody of related assets.
4. Separation of duties within the accounting function.

AUD 2-Q55 A370. The correct answer is C. Documentation of the work performed is organized in the audit workpapers, which provides important support for the auditor's opinion, including his representation as to compliance with GAAS.

Answer A is wrong because conformity with accounting records doesn't deal with internal controls.

Answer B is wrong because the adherence to management's requirements is a not a representation reported on in an audit of internal controls.

Answer D is wrong because it deals with a traditional audit and is not internal control related.

AUD 2-Q56 A374. The correct answer is D. The extent of substantive tests required to constitute sufficient appropriate audit evidence should vary inversely with the auditor's reliance on internal control. The combination of the auditor's reliance on internal control and on his other auditing procedures should provide a reasonable basis for his opinion in all cases, although the portion of reliance derived from the respective sources may properly vary between cases. This is a conceptual application of the audit risk model: CR goes up; DR goes down; extent of substantive tests go up and CR goes down; DR goes up; extent of substantive tests go down.

Answers A and B can be eliminated from the get go because that relationship is not random and isn't measured disproportionately.

Answer C is wrong because the relationship is inverse (opposite), not direct.

AUD 2-Q57 A384. The correct answer is C. Tests of controls test the operation of controls. When we test for authorized signatures on cancelled checks we are obtaining reasonable assurance that a specific control is functioning.

Answers A, B and D are incorrect because they fall into the area of substantive testing. Tests of balances are substantive tests of details of financial statement amounts. They provide the auditor with direct evidence of the balances in accounting records and related data presented in financial statements.

AUD 2 Q58 A387. The correct answer is C. Developing questionnaires and checklists A and observing employee functions D and making inquiries are primarily methods of obtaining an understanding of the client's system of internal control as it should be operating. We must still ascertain that the systems, as we understand them, are being followed. The purpose of tests of controls is to provide reasonable assurance that the accounting control procedures are being applied as prescribed.

AUD 2-Q59 A388. The correct answer is C. The auditor's evaluation of accounting control with reference to each significant class of transactions and related assets should be a conclusion as to whether the prescribed procedures and compliance therewith are satisfactory for his purpose. The procedures and compliance should be considered satisfactory if the auditor's review and tests disclose no condition he believes to be a material weakness for this purpose. In this context, a material weakness means a condition in which the auditor believes the prescribed procedures or the degree of compliance with them does not provide reasonable assurance that errors or fraud in amounts that would be material in the financial statements being audited would be prevented or detected within a timely period by employees in the normal course of performing their assigned functions.

Answer A is wrong because management, not the auditor, should evaluate their internal control.

Answer B is wrong because controller is not likely to identify internal control weaknesses when reconciling accounts. The internal control weaknesses would likely be identified when reviewing processes and procedures.

Answer D is wrong because it says interim financial statements which are unaudited. The hope is that the CFO would identify and catch errors in the annual report for instance.

AUD 2-Q60 A399. The correct answer is D. Confirmations are a substantive test.

Answer A is incorrect because inspection is a necessary test to validate controls.

Answer B is incorrect because observation is often used in testing controls especially with the observing of segregation of duties and for when no audit trail exists.

Answer C is incorrect because interviewing different personnel and making inquiries is often used in tests of controls; especially in the understanding phase.

AUD 2-Q61 A405. The correct answer is B. Answers A, C and D are all questions that test of controls are concerned with and are incorrect. Accounting control requires not only that certain procedures be performed but that they be performed properly and independently. Tests of controls, therefore, are concerned primarily with these questions: Were the necessary procedures performed, how were they performed, and by whom were they performed?

AUD 2-Q62 A438. The correct answer is B. There is to be a proper study and evaluation of the existing internal control as a basis for reliance and for the determination of the resultant extent of the tests to which auditing procedures are to be restricted. The "resultant extent of tests" refer to substantive tests.

Answer A is incorrect because control tests are a part of the study and evaluation of internal controls not the extent of substantive testing.

Answers C and D are incorrect because ascertaining fraud or employees with incompatible functions are conclusions the auditor reaches as a result of his evaluation of the system of internal control. Based on these conclusions and others, the auditor determines the nature, timing, and extent of substantive procedures.

AUD 2-Q63 A443. The correct answer is D. Tests of "procedures" would be particularly appropriate when reviewing sales transactions. Tests of procedures include those tests generally related to a review of the client's system of internal control, particularly compliance tests.

Answer A and B are incorrect because they are balance sheet accounts that are usually tested with substantive tests; not "procedures."

Answer C is incorrect because bank charges are tested through the review of bank statements.

AUD 2-Q64 A72. Choice D is correct. The journal entry to retire an asset is the following:

	Dr.	Cr.
Accumulated Depreciation	XX	
Plant Asset		XX

If an entity had numerous asset retirements during the year, then there would be a significant amount of debits to accumulated depreciation.

Choice A is incorrect because if depreciation expense was understated in the previous year, the following journal entry would be made:

	Dr.	Cr.
Retained Earnings	XX	
Accumulated Depreciation		XX

Therefore, there would be a credit to accumulated depreciation.

Choice B is incorrect. If depreciation expense is understated, then there would be a lesser amount credited to accumulated depreciation – not a debit.

Choice C is incorrect because since a change in useful life is a prospective change, then the future credits to accumulated depreciation would be less. There would be no current year debit to accumulated depreciation.

AUD 2-Q65 A25. Choice B is correct. If an auditor determines that the client's internal control structure is effective, then the overall control risk is assessed as low, which means the auditor can place more reliance on the client's internal controls. As such, it is more likely that an auditor will perform substantive testing at an interim date. However, even if an auditor performs substantive testing at an interim date, year-end substantive testing will still need to be performed.

Choice A is incorrect because a new sales incentive program may increase overall audit risk and an auditor may choose to perform substantive testing after the balance sheet date.
Choice C is incorrect because a high turnover in management is more of an audit risk factor that would cause the auditor to perform more substantive testing at year-end and less at an interim date.
Choice D is incorrect because during new engagements, the auditor will likely perform more tests after the balance sheet date as the overall audit risk is greater with new client engagements.

AUD 2-Q66 A39. Choice D is correct. An auditor may perform testing at an interim date but must also take into account performing procedures after the balance sheet date. As such, the auditor will need to determine if interim procedures are cost-effective.

Choice A is incorrect because the risk of incorrect rejection is not affected by the timing of audit procedures.

Choice B is incorrect because sampling risk is not projected higher for testing during the remaining period.

Choice C is incorrect because an auditor would still need to gain comfort over the accounts receivable balance at year-end and would still need to perform substantive testing in the remaining period.

AUD 2-Q67 A219. Choice B is correct. Shipping documents provide evidence as to whether a sale has occurred (sales are shipped; so if the auditor is worried about a failure to prepare a sales invoice (completeness assertion), she or he would trace a sample of shipments back to their respective invoices).

Choice A is incorrect because examining the cash receipts file would not provide support as to whether the entity prepares sales invoices.

Choice C is incorrect as examining the customer order file would not provide evidence as to whether the entity prepares sales invoices.

Choice D is incorrect because a sales invoice file would include only prepared invoices rather than ones not prepared.

AUD 2-Q68 A221. Choice D is correct. Prior to the balance sheet date, the auditor may choose to test significant travel and entertainment expenses. Keep in mind that the auditor may need to update testing after the balance sheet date.

Choices A, B, and C are incorrect as these are performed after the balance sheet date.
Note: The explanation for the incorrect answer is more about what is not done prior to the balance sheet date.

AUD 2-Q69 A276. Choice B is correct. An auditor tests for the completeness of sales by ensuring that an invoice is prepared for each shipping document.

Choice A is incorrect as this tests for the existence and valuation of sales.

Choice C is incorrect as this tests for the existence of sales.

Choice D is incorrect as this tests for the accuracy of receivables – not for completeness.

AUD 2-Q70 A246. Choice D is correct. Purchase orders should be issued by the purchasing department – not the accounts payable department. This is would be an instance of incompatible duties. Choices A, B, and C are incorrect as these would indicate correct procedures that should be performed by the accounts payable department.

AUD 2-Q71 A255. Choice B is correct as the timing of control and substantive tests may need to be altered depending on evidence availability.

Choice A is incorrect as this is based on the assessed level of material misstatement.

Choice C is incorrect as this is not dependent on the length of time electronic evidence is available.

Choice D is incorrect as this risk is assessed independent of the audit.

AUD 2-Q72 A316. Choice D is correct. A nonfederal entity that expands federal rewards received from another entity to carry out a federal program is a subrecipient.

Choices A and B are incorrect as these are classified as a recipient.

Choice C is incorrect as this would be classified as a vendor.

AUD 2-Q73 A325. Choice C is correct. If the results of analytical procedures show that there are no unusual or unexpected results, then the auditor may decide to reduce tests of details. Recall the audit risk model: DR (detect risk) can be decomposed into AP × TD (AP is the risk that analytical procedures will not detect a material misstatement and TD is the risk that substantive tests of details will not detect a material misstatement (often represented by the acceptable risk of incorrect acceptance in sampling). If analytical procedures are effective and do not indicate any material misstatement, the auditor can lower TD which results in a reduced level of substantive tests of details.

Choice A and B are incorrect as these have nothing to do with the decision of whether to reduce the tests of details.

Choice D is incorrect as many transactions would actually increase the tests of details.

AUD 2-Q74 A296. Choice D is correct. Requiring employees to have their direct supervisors approve their time cards would be the most effective method for ensuring that payment is made for work performed.

Choice A is incorrect as choice D would be a more effective method.

Choice B is incorrect as this would only ensure the accuracy of the payment.

Choice C is incorrect as requiring employees to sign their time cards would not ensure that payment is made for work performed.

AUD 2-Q75 A125. Choice C is correct. Ensuring that the check signer reviews and cancels the voucher packets acknowledging that the payment has been made would prevent an invoice being paid twice.

Choice A is incorrect as this would only ensure that the item paid for has been received.

Choice B is incorrect as this would not ensure that merchandise is paid twice- it would only ensure that bank reconciliations are prepared by an independent individual.

Choice D is incorrect as this would not ensure that the check is paid twice – it would only ensure that the check is properly authorized.

AUD 2-Q76 A132. Choice C is correct. If testing the controls would be inefficient, then the auditor would perform substantive testing.

Choice A is incorrect. If the internal control component are not well documented, the auditor would still need to perform tests of controls and gain and understanding of the Company's internal controls.

Choice B is incorrect as the external auditor cannot completely rely on the result of the internal auditor. The auditor would still need to perform his own testing to gain assurance over the financial statements.

Choice D is incorrect. In this case, the auditor would perform both controls testing and substantive procedures.

AUD 2-Q77 A133. Choice C is correct. If there is a higher risk of material misstatement, the auditor will perform more effective substantive tests. The auditor must modify the nature, timing, or extent of testing. This choice related to nature.

Choice A is incorrect as smaller sample sizes would be used if there was a low risk of material misstatement. This choice is on the wrong side of extent.

Choice B is incorrect as the auditor would perform more tests at year-end. This choice is on the wrong side of timing.

Choice D is incorrect as the auditor would most likely increase substantive tests.

AUD 2-Q78 A64. Choice D is correct because an internal auditor is independent when he/she is removed from any government political pressures and is free to conduct audits objectively.

Choice A is incorrect because internal auditors are responsible to those charged with governance.

Choice B is incorrect because the procedures should be consistent with Generally Accepted Governmental Auditing Standards (GAGAS).

Choice C is incorrect because serving under the manager under the audit may impair independence.

AUD 2-Q79 A105. Choice D is correct. An increase in errors would lead to an increase in inherent risk. The increase in inherent risk requires the auditor to change the nature, timing, and extent of audit testing. As such, there is more testwork (extent) that is performed at year-end (timing) rather than at an interim date. Using more experienced audit team members (nature) would also provide a greater level of assurance.

Choice A is incorrect because performing more procedures at an interim date would provide less assurance and is not an appropriate response to an increase in audit risk.

Choice B is incorrect because an increase in audit risk would cause a decrease in the dollar threshold of vouching invoices.

Choice C is incorrect as positive account receivable confirmations provide more assurance than negative confirmations. When audit risk increases, auditors would more likely send out positive confirmations. Remember, positive confirmations require the recipient to send a response stating whether the amount stated on the confirmation is correct or incorrect. Negative confirmations only require a response if the amount stated on the confirmation is incorrect.

AUD 2-Q80 A106. Choice C is correct. Detection risk increases when the auditor performs more tests at an interim date as opposed to at year-end. Detection risk will decrease when more procedures are performed at year-end. Detection risk is affected by the nature, timing, and extent of audit procedures.

Choice A and B are incorrect as inherent risk and control risk exist independently of the audit and cannot be changed based on the auditors' audit procedures. Auditors assess IR and CR.

Choice D is incorrect as sampling risk is the risk that the sample that the auditor selects and tests from is not representative of the entire population and would lead to a different conclusion had the auditor tested the entire account balance.

AUD 2-Q81 A342. The correct answer is D. Consignment is a special marketing arrangement whereby the consignor ships goods to the consignee, but the consignor retains legal title and risk of loss for the goods until sold by the consignee. The consignee will remit the proceeds (less commission and expenses) to the consignor on a periodic basis as the goods are sold. So the inventory is NOT on the client's premises.

Answer A is wrong because the tracing of shipping documents to the sales journal will show that merchandise shipped is not being recorded as a sale (i.e., shipment on consignment basis). This will be shipments that are NOT recorded as sales (which is correct since the sale is not recorded until the consignee sells the consigned items).

Answer B is wrong because we may be able to detect consignment sales in reviewing cash receipt transactions.

Answer C is wrong because if we come across numerous small periodic payments for an individual customer, rather than one or two large payments, then consignment accounts may be recognizable.

Consignment sales should come to light in reviewing confirmation exceptions. Deposits in transit would be a common type of exception due to consignment sales. Although consignment sales could also come to the attention of the auditor through observation of the physical inventory, the question asks for the "least" likely audit procedure of the four. The observation of the physical inventory on hand would not likely bring inventory at the consignee's place of business to the auditor's attention.

AUD 2-Q82 A350. The correct answer is A. Since the firm is medium-sized, it is assumed that there are not that many transactions affecting owners' equity (e.g., dividends, splits, options, warrants) Consequently, the audit of assets, liabilities, revenues and expenses would probably cover a good part of the owners' equity accounts as well making answers B, C and D wrong.

AUD 2-Q83 A354. The correct answer is A. The purchase order is a formal written offer to buy, giving specific descriptions of goods, quantity, terms required, shipping specifications, etc. The purchase order is the only documentation of the four choices which is sent to the vendor. If not properly controlled, including numerical control and proper authorization, the purchase order could be used by Jackson for the benefit of third parties.

AUD 2-Q84 A360. The correct answer is B. Only answer B represents a situation which could explain the difference. The items returned were included in the physical count, but not captured in the perpetual records through a credit memo.

Answer A is incorrect and represents a situation in which the inventory count could be less than the perpetual records. The counts did not make it to the accumulation sheet which would understate the count.

Answer C is incorrect and would yield a count less than the perpetual records. The inventory was returned and not included in the count, but the perpetual records were not reduced for the returns.

Answer D is incorrect and represents a situation which would increase both the physical count of inventory and perpetual records and would, therefore, have no effect on the difference.

AUD 2-Q85 A371. The correct answer is C. The auditor is concerned with establishing that dividends are paid to stockholders of the client corporation owning stock as of the record date.
Answer A and D, are wrong because the issue (payment) date is when a stock dividend is issued and cash is paid out.

Answer B is wrong because the declaration date is the date when the board of directors authorized the payment of the dividend.

AUD 2-Q86 A393. The correct answer is C. A subsidiary ledger represents such a detailed record and would prevent overpayments.

Answer A is wrong because even if an accounts payable subsidiary ledger is maintained, there will still be a file of unmatched invoices.

Answer B is wrong because answering vendor confirmation requests on a more timely basis may be a good business practice, but would not create any immediate or direct benefit.

Answer D is wrong because although it represents a benefit of establishing a subsidiary ledger, we would probably benefit most by maintaining detailed records of partial payments.

AUD 2-Q87 A414. The correct answer is A. If the commission is based on the total volume of sales or some other objective measure, the auditor should verify the computation of the accrual by applying the prescribed rate to the amount used as a base. If sales are used as the base a proper cutoff would be critical to a proper commission accrual.

Answer B is wrong because contingent liabilities have nothing to do with the sales commission process.

Answer C is wrong because disbursements post balance sheet would be tracked via bank statements and does not speak to verifying the accuracy of the year-end accrual.

Answer D is wrong because trade accounts payable do not deal with the sales commission process.

AUD 2-Q88 A425. The correct answer is C. The auditor performs a proper study and evaluation of the existing internal control to determine the nature, timing, and extent of substantive procedures. So logically, substantive tests come after a proper study and evaluation of internal control. Internal control review and control tests are both part of the auditor's study and evaluation of internal control. The purpose of control tests is to provide reasonable assurance that the accounting control procedures are being applied as prescribed. Note: private companies do not require control testing. The auditor determines if the controls will be tested. The amount of substantive testing increases when the auditor does not test the clients controls.

Answer A is incorrect because substantive tests are the last step.

Answer B is incorrect because control tests would not be performed prior to substantive testing.

Answer D is incorrect because internal control reviews should happen before control tests can be done.

AUD 2-Q89 A428. The correct answer is C. Although a variety of unrecorded liabilities may be discovered during the course of an audit, the most common and important tests for the search of unrecorded liabilities include a review of:

1. Unpaid vouchers entered in the voucher register subsequent to the balance sheet date.
2. Invoices received by the client after the balance sheet date.
3. Unmatched invoices and unbilled items such as for merchandise received but not billed for as of the balance sheet date.
4. Review of subsequent to year-end cash disbursements and relate these payments back to vendor invoices to see if any should be recorded at year-end.

All 4 of these procedures are done at or after year-end (not before).

Answer A is incorrect because observation of inventory should be performed as close to possible to the balance sheet date or an interim date.

Answer B is incorrect because the review of internal control should be performed during the entire period under review (which includes time periods before year-end).

Answer D is incorrect because confirmation of receivables can be done at the balance sheet date or at an interim date.

AUD 2-Q90 A429. The correct answer is C. The most important control over the disposal of fixed assets is the existence of a formal system to inform management of the sale, trade-in, abandonment, or theft of assets. The continuous utilization of serially numbered retirement work orders will achieve this objective.

Answer A is incorrect because not all dispositions result in cash proceeds.

Answer B is incorrect because the periodic observation of plant assets will reveal errors on a periodic basis only.

Answer D is incorrect because the periodic observations will reveal only periodic errors.

AUD 2-Q91 A430. The correct answer is D. The auditor must watch for products which have been dropped from the client's line of merchandise or are beginning to move slowly. Careful review of perpetual inventory records will usually reveal such instances. In addition, during the course of inventory taking the auditor should examine such slow-moving items and determine if the client has identified them as obsolete (if appropriate).

Answers A and B are incorrect because inquiry of sales and store personnel will not reveal slow-moving inventory.

Answer C is incorrect because physical observation will not show slow-moving inventory.

AUD 2-Q92 A434. The correct answer is B. It is common for companies to establish purchasing departments to ensure an adequate quality of goods and services at a minimum price. For good internal control, the purchasing department should not be responsible for the authorization or receipt of goods. The department charged with authorization to purchase goods should have as its primary objective the reduction of expenditures for goods acquired.

Answer A is incorrect because authorization should not be done by the purchasing department. Authorization should be done by the management function within the receiving department, usually the highest ranking member of the department.

Answer C is incorrect because the verifying of the propriety of goods should be done by the receiving department since they are first to see the goods after they have been shipped.

Answer D is incorrect because it is important to reduce costs but not the primary function of the purchasing department.

AUD 2-Q93 A446. The correct answer is A. Perpetual inventory records constitute a most important part of an internal control system for inventory. Such records discourage inventory theft and waste, since storekeepers and other employees are aware of the accountability over goods established by the continuous record of goods received, issued, and on hand. The record however, must be periodically verified through the physical counting of goods.

Answer B is incorrect because it deals with internal controls which involve compliance testing, not auditing procedures.

Answer C is incorrect because though it is a good idea, it can be circumvented.

Answer D is incorrect because though it is a good control to have it wouldn't detect theft of lower cost items.

AUD 2-Q94 A451. The correct answer is A. In interviewing the credit manager (inquiry), the auditor's purpose is to obtain any evidence in his possession in order for the auditor to make a judgment, but not to rely on the credit manager's opinion. "Auditing through conversation" is NOT sufficient.

Answer B is incorrect because this is the starting point for a review of the collectability.

Answer C is incorrect because this is a procedure that the auditor would do to obtain an understanding of the collection policies.

Answer D is incorrect because analytical procedures may be used.

AUD 2-Q95 A452. The correct answer is B. The auditor will have difficulty in gaining assurance as to the quality of goods. If at all possible, goods should be inspected on a test basis when received.

A distinction must be made between purchases made on FOB destination basis and those made on FOB shipping point basis. For FOB destination purchases, only inventory received prior to the balance sheet date should be included in inventory and accounts payable at year-end. For FOB shipping point purchases, inventory and related accounts payable must be recorded in the current period if shipment occurred before the balance sheet date.

Answers A, C and D are incorrect because the auditor will gain assurance with respect to quantity, price and terms directly from vendors' invoices.

AUD 2-Q96 A19. Choice D is correct. Materiality levels are considered in terms of the smallest misstatement that could affect the client's financial statements.

Choice A is incorrect because analytical procedures do not have an effect on materiality levels.

Choice B is incorrect because an increase in the materiality levels usually leads to a decrease in substantive testing.

Choice C is incorrect because materiality levels include both quantitative and qualitative considerations.

AUD 2-Q97 A76. Choice B is correct. Assessing the education level of an auditor would determine the level of competence of an internal auditor.

Choice A is incorrect as assessing the reporting structure does not provide any information on the level of competence of the internal auditor. This assesses the objectivity of the auditor.

Choice C is incorrect as this may impair the objectivity of the internal auditor – but will not affect the competence of the internal auditor.

Choice D is incorrect as this would not affect the competence of the internal auditor.

AUD 2-Q98 A223. Choice A is correct as the objectivity is assessed by the organizational status of the director.

Choice B is incorrect as this would assess the competence of the internal auditor.

Choice C is incorrect as this would not assess the objectivity of the internal auditor.

Choice D is incorrect as this would not assess the objectivity of the internal auditor.

AUD 2-Q99 A197. Choice C is correct. Assessing the quality of the internal auditor's working paper documentation would assist an independent CPA in determining the competence of an internal auditor.

Choice A, B, and D are incorrect as these procedures would not assist the independent auditor to gain assurance over the internal auditor's competency.

AUD 2-Q100 A280. Choice B is correct. When assessing the competence of internal auditors, the CPA should obtain information about the quality of internal auditors' working paper documentation.

Choices A, and C are incorrect as these would not provide information as to the competence level of internal auditors.

Choice D is incorrect as this is the job of an external auditor, not an internal auditor.

AUD 2-Q101 A172. Choice A is correct. An auditor would assess objectivity by determining that the internal auditors cannot audit areas in which they recently posted.

Choices B, C, and D are incorrect as these do not address objectivity.

AUD 2-Q102 A173. Choice A is correct. An internal auditor may assist the external auditor in performing both tests of controls and substantive tests. The independent auditor must address the objectivity and competency of the internal auditor.

Choices B, C, and D are incorrect per the above explanation.

AUD 2-Q103 A183. Choice A is correct. During an audit, an internal auditor may assist an external auditor with tests of controls as well as substantive testing.

Choice B is incorrect as an internal auditor may not solely audit a major subsidiary. The internal auditor may assist with testwork but the external auditor will need to supervise the work.

Choice C is incorrect; the question states that the internal auditor is objective.

Choice D is incorrect as the internal auditor may assist the independent auditor with tests of details and/or internal controls testing.

AUD 2-Q104 A422. The correct answer is A. The objective of internal auditing is to assist all members of management in the effective discharge of their responsibilities, by furnishing them with analyses, appraisals, recommendations, and pertinent comments concerning the activities reviewed. The internal auditor is concerned with any phase of business activity wherein he or she can be of service to management. This involves going beyond the accounting and financial records to obtain a full understanding of the operations under review.

Answer B is incorrect because an internal audit covers more areas.

Answer C is incorrect because they are not similar.

Answer D is incorrect because an internal audit program is more detailed.

The internal auditor is primarily concerned with evaluation, compliance, and verification. Verification of financial statements would include work similar to that of independent public accountants; the internal auditor is directly concerned with the detection and prevention of fraud. The internal auditor's areas of audit work certainly cover numerous areas beyond that reviewed by the CPA.

AUD 2-Q105 A38. Choice B is correct. According to AU-C 620, an auditor may use the work of a management specialist (an actuary is considered a specialist) even if the specialist is related to the client. If the specialist has a relationship with the client, the auditor will need to assess the specialist's independence and objectivity as the auditor will be relying on the specialist's work.

Choice A is incorrect because AU-C 620 does not require that the auditor disclose this information.

Choice C is incorrect because the auditor may use a specialist that has a relationship with the client as long as the specialist is objective and the auditor may rely on the specialist's work.

Choice D is incorrect as a specialist having a relationship with a client is not considered to be a material weakness.

AUD 2-Q106 A192. Choice B is correct. Observing employees who are performing control activities is the best way to ensure proper segregation of duties.

Choices A, C, and D are incorrect as these procedures would not provide evidence regarding segregation of duties.

AUD 2-Q107 A285. Choice C is correct. The auditor may refer to the specialist if the difference between the client's and specialist's asset valuation caused the auditor to modify the report.

Choices A, B, and D are incorrect as in these cases, the auditor would not refer to the work of the specialist.

AUD 2-Q108 A253. Choice A is correct. The auditor is required to understand the objective and the scope of the actuary's work.

Choice B is incorrect as this is the responsibility of the actuary.

Choice C is incorrect as there is no such requirement.

Choice D is incorrect. The auditor may still use the actuary's work but must evaluate the actuary's objectivity.

AUD 2-Q109 A403. The correct answer is B. The fact that the inventory is counted by an outside inventory firm of non-accountants is not, by itself, a satisfactory substitute for the auditor's own observation or taking of some physical counts. The auditor's concern, in this respect, is to satisfy himself as to the effectiveness of the counting procedures used.

In view of the above, the auditor "would examine the outside firms' programs, observe its procedures and controls, make or observe some physical counts of inventory, recompute calculations of the submitted inventory on a test basis and apply appropriate tests to the intervening transactions. The independent auditor ordinarily may reduce the extent of his work on the physical count of inventory because of the work of an outside inventory firm, but any restriction on the auditor's judgment concerning the extent of his contact with the inventory would be a scope restriction."

Answer A is incorrect because subordinating judgment would not follow GAAS standards of fieldwork.

Answer C is incorrect because it will reduce the extent of work.

Answer D is incorrect because there should still be sufficient effort so as to not make the extent of the auditor's judgment about the physical inventory count lead to a scope limitation

AUD 2-Q110 A45. Choice C is correct. For illegal acts that have an indirect effect on the financial statements, an auditor has the responsibility to apply specific audit procedures if information regarding illegal acts comes to the auditor's attention.

Choice A is incorrect, as this only applies to illegal acts that have a direct effect on the financial statements.

Choice B is incorrect because the auditor's training is in accounting – not in detecting illegal acts.

Choice D is incorrect because a qualified or an adverse opinion is only given if an auditor does not have comfort that the financial statements are free of material misstatement.

AUD 2-Q111 A319. Choice C is correct. The auditor may consider withdrawing from the engagement if the client does not take any action.

Choice A is incorrect as the auditor should consider withdrawing from the engagement.

Choice B is incorrect as the auditor does not have the authority to do so.

Choice D is incorrect as a modified or adverse opinion would not be appropriate in these cases

AUD 2-Q112 A294. Choice B is correct. The discovery of unexplained payments made to government employees may indicate an occurrence of illegal acts (bribe).

Choice A is incorrect as the exchange of property is not indicative of an illegal act.

Choice C is incorrect as this may not be indicative of an illegal act if it is normal and customary in a client's business.

Choice D is incorrect as this is indicative of a control weakness.

AUD 2-Q113 A261. Choice D is correct. Writing off obsolete inventory to net realizable value before year end would not indicate existence of related party transactions.

Choice A is incorrect as this type of loan differs from market terms and as such may indicate a related party transaction.

Choice B is incorrect as this type of arrangement may indicate a related party transaction.

Choice C is incorrect as borrowing funds at a significantly low interest rate may indicate a related party transaction.

AUD 2-Q114 A295. Choice B is correct. In order to determine the existence of related parties, the auditor should first request a list of related parties from management.

Choice A is incorrect as it would be beneficial if the auditor first performed choice B to be aware of any parties were related.

Choice C is incorrect as this is unlikely to provide information about the existence of related parties.

Choice D is incorrect as it would be beneficial if the auditor first inquired with management.

AUD 2-Q115 A50. Choice D is correct. When auditing related party transactions, it is the responsibility of the auditor to determine whether the transactions are properly disclosed.

Choice A is incorrect, as it is not the responsibility of the auditor to determine the likelihood of related party transactions.

Choice B is incorrect, as it is more important to the auditor to determine whether a related party transaction occurred, as opposed to whether a related party exists.

Choice C is incorrect, as it is not usually possible for an auditor to determine the valuation of a related party transaction. (See AU-C 550 and AS 2410).

AUD 2-Q116 A418. The correct answer is A. Disclosure in the financial statements for a reporting entity that has participated in related party transactions should include:
1. The nature of the relationship.
2. A description of the transactions for the period reported on, including amounts, if any, and any such other information as deemed necessary to an understanding of the effects on the financial statements.
3. The dollar volume of transactions and the effects of any change in the method of establishing terms from that used in the preceding period.
4. Amounts due from or to related parties and, if not otherwise apparent, the terms and manner of settlement.

Answer choice A covers items 1 and 4 above.

Answer B is incorrect because the details of transactions within major classifications may not be required if the auditor feels it's not required.

Answer C is incorrect because this is not a required statement.

Answer D is incorrect because internal controls have nothing to do with related party transactions.

AUD 3 – Performing Further Procedures and Obtaining Evidence

A. Understanding Sufficient and Appropriate Evidence	3A-1 – 3A-5
B. Sampling Techniques	3B-1 – 3B-11
C. Performing Specific Procedures to Obtain Evidence	3C-1 – 3C-14
1. Analytical procedures	1
2. External confirmations	7
3. Inquiry of management and others	11
4. Observation and inspection	12
5. Recalculation and reperformance	13
6. All other procedures	13
D. Specific Matters That Require Special Consideration	3D-1 – 3D-18
1. Opening balances	1
2. Investments in securities and derivative instruments	3
3. Inventory and inventory held by others	6
4. Litigation, claims and assessments	8
5. An entity's ability to continue as a going concern	11
6. Accounting estimates, including fair value estimates	16
E. Misstatements and Internal Control Deficiencies	3E-1 – 3E-4
F. Written Representations	3F-1 – 3F-5
G. Subsequent Events and Subsequently Discovered Facts	3G-1 – 3G-7
Glossary: Performing Further Procedures and Obtaining Evidence	Glossary 3-1 – 3-3
Multiple Choice – Questions	MCQ 3-1 –16
Multiple Choice – Solutions	MCQ 3-17 – 3-33

Performing Further Procedures and Obtaining Evidence

A. Understanding Sufficient and Appropriate Evidence

> *Hint*: The main sources of professional guidance that serve as the basis for this review are obtained from the following:
> AU-C 500, *Audit Evidence*, AICPA.
> AS 1105, *Audit Evidence*, PCAOB
> AR-C 70, *Preparation of Financial Statements*, AICPA
> AR-C 80, *Compilation Engagements*, AICPA
> AR-C 90, *Review of Financial Statements*, AICPA

> Conclude on the sufficiency and appropriateness of evidence obtained during the audit engagement for an issuer or nonissuer.

Audit evidence is **all the information used by the auditor in arriving at the conclusions on which the audit opinion is based** and includes the information contained in the *accounting records* underlying the financial statements and other information.

However, because *accounting records* alone do not provide sufficient appropriate audit evidence, on which to base an audit opinion on the financial statements, *the auditor should obtain other audit evidence*.

Auditors are not expected to examine all information that may exist.

a. Sufficient appropriate audit evidence
The auditor should consider the sufficiency and appropriateness of audit evidence to be obtained when assessing risks and designing further audit procedures.

Sufficiency is the measure of the *quantity* of audit evidence. The quantity of audit evidence needed is affected by the risk of misstatement (the greater the risk, the more audit evidence is likely to be required) and also by the quality of such audit evidence (the higher the quality, the less the audit evidence that may be required).

Multiple Choice

> AUD 3-Q1

Appropriateness is the measure of the *quality* of audit evidence, that is, its *relevance* and its *reliability* in providing support for, or detecting misstatements in, the classes of transactions, account balances, and disclosures and related assertions.

Relevance means that evidence obtained speaks to the validity of the assertion being examined. A given set of audit procedures may provide audit evidence that is relevant to certain assertions but not to others. For example, inspection of records and documents related to the collection of receivables after the period end may provide audit evidence regarding both existence and valuation, although not necessarily the appropriateness of period-end cutoffs.

The auditor often obtains audit evidence from different sources, or of a different nature, that is relevant to the same assertion. For example, the auditor may analyze the aging of accounts receivable and the subsequent collection of receivables to obtain audit evidence relating to the valuation of the allowance for doubtful accounts; age speaks to net realizable value (NRV); subsequent collection surely speaks to NRV.

> **Hint:** Make sure your audit evidence relates to the assertion being tested.

Obtaining audit evidence relating to a particular assertion, for example, the physical existence of inventory, is not a substitute for obtaining audit evidence regarding another assertion, for example, rights and obligations.

The **reliability** of audit evidence is influenced by its source and by its nature, and is dependent on the individual circumstances under which it is obtained.

Generalizations about the reliability of various kinds of audit evidence can be made; however, such generalizations are subject to important exceptions.

Even when audit evidence is obtained from sources external to the entity, circumstances may exist that could affect the reliability of the information obtained. For example, audit evidence obtained from an independent external source may not be reliable if the source is not knowledgeable.

While recognizing that exceptions may exist, the following 5 generalizations about the reliability of audit evidence are useful:
1) Audit evidence is more reliable when it is obtained from knowledgeable independent sources outside the entity.
2) Audit evidence that is generated internally is more reliable when the related controls imposed by the entity are effective.
3) Audit evidence obtained directly by the auditor (for example, observation of the application of a control) is more reliable than audit evidence obtained indirectly or by inference (for example, inquiry about the application of a control).
4) Audit evidence is more reliable when it exists in documentary form, whether paper, electronic, or other medium (for example, a contemporaneously written record of a meeting is more reliable than a subsequent oral representation of the matters discussed).
5) Audit evidence provided by original documents is more reliable than audit evidence provided by photocopies, facsimiles or documents that have been filmed, digitized, or otherwise transformed into electronic form.

Multiple Choice

> AUD 3-Q2 through AUD 3-Q3

The auditor should consider the reliability of the information to be used as audit evidence, for example, photocopies; facsimiles; or filmed, digitized, or other electronic documents, including consideration of controls over their preparation and maintenance where relevant. **However, an audit rarely involves the authentication of documentation, nor is the auditor trained as or expected to be an expert in such authentication.**

1) Information produced by the entity
   When information produced by the entity is used by the auditor to perform further audit procedures, the auditor should obtain audit evidence about the accuracy and completeness of the information.

   Example: When auditing revenue by applying standard prices to records of sales volume, the auditor should consider the accuracy of the price information and the completeness and accuracy of the sales volume data.

Obtaining audit evidence about the completeness and accuracy of the information produced by the entity's information system, may be performed concurrently with the actual audit procedure. In other situations, the auditor may have obtained audit evidence of the accuracy and completeness of such information by testing controls over the production and maintenance of the information.

However, in some situations the auditor may determine that additional audit procedures are needed. For example, these additional procedures may include using computer-assisted audit techniques (CAATs) to recalculate the information.

> **Hint:** Somewhere in the audit process the auditor must have an "anchor:" A "hard" piece of evidence that can be used to make good inferences. Without an anchor, you have GIGO (Garbage In, Garbage Out).

2) Triangulation (inconsistency in audit evidence)
Obtaining audit evidence from different sources, or of a different nature, may indicate that an individual item of audit evidence is not reliable. For example, when audit evidence obtained from one source **is inconsistent** with that obtained from another, the auditor should determine what additional audit procedures are necessary to *resolve the inconsistency*.

b. Audit procedures
Auditors use the following 8 audit procedures:

1) **Inspection of records or documents**
Inspection consists of **examining records or documents**, whether internal or external, in paper form, electronic form, or other media.

Inspection of records and documents provides audit evidence of varying degrees of reliability, depending on their nature and source and, in the case of internal records and documents, on the effectiveness of the controls over their production.

Some documents represent direct audit evidence of the existence of an asset, for example, a document constituting a financial instrument such as a stock or bond. Inspection of such documents may not necessarily provide audit evidence about ownership or value.
In addition, inspecting an executed contract may provide audit evidence relevant to the entity's application of accounting principles, such as revenue recognition.

2) **Inspection of tangible assets**
Inspection of tangible assets consists of **physical examination of the assets**.

Inspection of tangible assets may provide appropriate audit evidence with respect to their existence, but not necessarily about the entity's rights and obligations or the valuation of the assets.

Inspection of individual inventory items ordinarily accompanies the observation of inventory counting.

For example, when observing an inventory count, the auditor may inspect individual inventory items (such as opening containers included in the inventory count to ensure that they are not empty) to verify their existence.

3) **Observation**
   Observation consists of looking at a process or procedure being performed by others. Examples include observation of the counting of inventories by the entity's personnel and observation of the performance of control activities.

   Observation provides audit evidence about the performance of a process or procedure, but is limited to the point in time at which the observation takes place and by the fact that the act of being observed may affect how the process or procedure is performed.

4) **Inquiry**
   Inquiry consists of **seeking information of knowledgeable persons**, both financial and nonfinancial, inside or outside the entity.

   Inquiry is an audit procedure that is used extensively throughout the audit and often is complementary to performing other audit procedures.

   Inquiries may range from formal written inquiries to informal oral inquiries.

   Evaluating responses to inquiries is an integral part of the inquiry process. The auditor should resolve any significant inconsistencies in the information obtained.

   The auditor should perform audit procedures in addition to the use of inquiry to obtain sufficient appropriate audit evidence.

   Inquiry alone ordinarily does not provide sufficient appropriate audit evidence to detect a material misstatement at the relevant assertion level. Moreover, inquiry alone is not sufficient to test the operating effectiveness of controls.

5) **Confirmation**
   Confirmation, which is a specific type of inquiry, is the process of obtaining a representation of information or of an existing condition directly from a third party. For example, the auditor may seek direct confirmation of receivables by communication with debtors.

   Confirmations are frequently used in relation to account balances and their components but need not be restricted to these items.

6) **Recalculation**
   Recalculation consists of checking the mathematical accuracy of documents or records.

   Recalculation can be performed through the use of information technology; for example, by obtaining an electronic file from the entity and using CAATs to check the accuracy of the summarization of the file.

7) **Re-performance**
   Re-performance is the **auditor's independent execution of procedures or controls** that were originally performed as part of the entity's internal control, either manually or through the use of CAATs; for example, re-performing the aging of accounts receivable.

8) **Analytical Procedures**
Analytical procedures consist of evaluations of financial information made by a study of plausible relationships among both financial and nonfinancial data.

Analytical procedures also encompass the investigation of identified fluctuations and relationships that are inconsistent with other relevant information or deviate significantly from predicted amounts.

> *Hint*: Memory tip -- I, I, O, I, C, R, R, AP
> **I-R** = Inspect Records/Documents
> **I-TA** = Inspect Tangible Assets
> **O** = Observation
> **I** = Inquiry
> **C** = Confirmation
> **Recalc** = Recalculation
> **Re-perf** = Reperformance
> **AP** = Analytical Procedures

c. Sufficiency and appropriateness of evidence

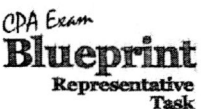

> Conclude on the sufficiency and appropriateness of evidence obtained during a non-audit engagement based on the objectives and reporting requirements of the engagement.

1) Preparation of financial statements (not a compilation or a review) (AR-C 70)
Per AR-70.04: An engagement to prepare financial statements does not require the accountant to verify the accuracy or completeness of the information provided by management, or otherwise gather evidence to express an opinion or a conclusion, on the financial statements or otherwise report on the financial statements.

2) Compilation engagements (AR-C 80)
Per AR-80.02: Because a compilation engagement is not an assurance engagement, a compilation engagement does not require the accountant to verify the accuracy or completeness of the information provided by management, or otherwise gather evidence to express an opinion or a conclusion on the financial statements.

3) Review of financial statements (AR-C 90)
AR-C 90.17: The accountant should design and perform **analytical procedures** and **make inquiries** and **perform other procedures**, as appropriate, to obtain limited assurance as a basis for reporting whether the accountant is aware of any material modifications that should be made to the financial statements in order for the statements to be in accordance with the applicable financial reporting framework based on the accountant's
  i. understanding of the industry,
  ii. knowledge of the entity, and
  iii. awareness of the risk that the accountant may unknowingly fail to modify, the accountant's review report on financial statements, that are materially misstated.

AR-C 90.26: The accountant should obtain evidence that the financial statements agree or reconcile with the accounting records.
AR-C 90.31: The accountant should evaluate whether sufficient appropriate review evidence has been obtained from the procedures performed and, if not, the accountant should perform other procedures judged by the accountant to be necessary in the circumstances, to be able to form a conclusion on the financial statements.

B. Sampling Techniques

> *Hint:* Quick reference summary of audit sampling:
>
> 1. Terminology
>   - Risk of assessing control risk too low -- overreliance
>   - Risk of assessing control risk too high -- under reliance
>   - Incorrect acceptance
>   - Incorrect rejection
>   - Error, exception, deviation
>
> 2. Attribute sampling -- sample size factors
>   - Tolerable rate -- inverse
>   - Expected population error rate -- direct
>   - Risk of assessing control risk too low -- inverse (compliment of confidence level)
>   Formula: **sample error rate + allowance for sampling risk < tolerable error rate**
>
> 3. Variables sampling -- sample size factors
>   - Confidence level (reliability) - direct
>   - Precision - direct
>   - Variability within the population - direct
>   - Tolerable misstatement - inverse
>
> 4. Sampling plans
>   - Determine objective of test
>   - Define population and deviation
>   - Determine sample size
>   - Select sampling technique
>   - Perform sampling plan
>   - Evaluate results/Document

> *Hint:* The main sources of professional guidance that serve as the basis for this review are obtained from the following:
> AU-C 530, *Audit Sampling*, AICPA.
> AICPA Audit Guide, *Audit Sampling*.
> AS 2315, *Audit Sampling*, PCAOB.

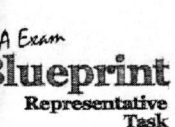

Understand the purpose and application of sampling techniques in an audit or non-audit engagement.

Audit sampling (sampling) is the selection and evaluation of less than 100 percent of the population of audit relevance such that the auditor expects the items selected (the sample) to be ***representative of the population*** and, thus, likely to provide a reasonable basis for conclusions about the population. The objective of the auditor, when using audit sampling, is to provide a reasonable basis for the auditor to draw conclusions about the population from which the sample is selected.

The examination of fewer than 100 percent of the items comprising an account balance or class of transactions is ***not*** audit sampling (e.g., an auditor may examine only a few transactions from an account balance or class of transactions to (*a*) gain an understanding of the nature of an entity's operations or (*b*) clarify the auditor's understanding of the entity's internal control).

Audit sampling requires specific actions, so the auditor can quantify (mathematically) sampling risk and project to the population. These actions are reviewed below.

The categories (statistical versus non-statistical) differ in that statistical sampling uses mathematical rules to quantify sampling risk. Non-statistical sampling does not quantify sampling risk and conclusions are reached about populations on a judgmental basis – so this is often termed ***judgmental sampling***. Typical non-statistical sampling methods include the following:

a. **Directed (Judgmental) Sampling**
   Used when the attributes of the population items determine whether or not an item is selected for testing. This method is used when the auditor wants to target the investigation. Selection is based on some judgmental criteria established by the auditor.

   Common attributes include:
   - Dollar magnitude (i.e., pick the biggest dollar amount)
   - Date of items
   - Parties to the items (certain employees, certain customers, certain vendors, etc.)
   - Items most likely to contain errors

b. **Block Sampling**
   The auditor tests blocks of items but the selection of the blocks is random. A block is a short run of sequential items in a population. Auditor must determine how many blocks to examine. Starting point for each block is random. Ordinarily, it is acceptable to use block samples only if a reasonable number of blocks are used (too few blocks could yield a non-representative sample). Block sampling can supplement other samples when there is a high likelihood of misstatement for a known period.

c. **Haphazard Sampling**
   The auditor uses a mentally generated random selection process (sort of a "throwing darts at a list of transactions" approach).

   The problem with this method is that it is rarely random --- auditors can, unknowingly, inject bias into their selection process.

   The decision whether to use a statistical or non-statistical sampling approach is a matter for the auditor's professional judgment. However, the amount of items examined in a non-statistical sample should be the same as the sample size in a statistical sample (auditors cannot use non-statistical sampling to justify examining a lesser amount of evidence). It is equally acceptable, under professional standards, for auditors to use either statistical or non-statistical sampling methods.

   Audit sampling is used for both test of controls (attributes sampling) and for tests of details of transactions and substantive tests of balances (variables sampling).

d. **Primary sampling methods**
   1) **Attributes Sampling**
      Attributes sampling is used in tests of controls. It's a sampling method that tests the occurrence of an "attribute." Typically, the attribute of interest to auditors is "deviations from a prescribed control procedure." If the projected upper deviation rate exceeds the auditor's tolerable deviation rate, the control is deemed ineffective (and the auditor will need to expand his/her substantive tests of details).

Multiple Choice

AUD 3-Q4 through AUD 3-Q6

2) **Substantive Tests of Details**
   Monetary unit sampling (MUS), also called dollar unit sampling, is often used in substantive tests of details. (Classical variables sampling is also used; see the discussion below.) MUS is a method that uses attributes sampling theory to express a conclusion in dollar amounts rather than as a rate of occurrence.

   MUS has many similarities to attributes sampling and non-statistical sampling --- including the 14 steps (discussed below). However, MUS does have some differences, including the following:
   i. **The Definition of the *Sampling Unit* is an Individual Dollar**
      Each individual dollar that composes an account balance is the sampling unit for MUS. Since dollars are the sampling unit, MUS automatically emphasizes larger physical units in a balance.

      A physical unit is a free-standing unit within an account --- like a customer balance in accounts receivable. However, the customer balance contains many sampling units (individual dollars).

   ii. **The Population Size is the Recorded Dollar Population**
       Example: Accounts receivable balance of $5,789,500 --- so the population has the size of 5,789,500 (5,789,500 individual dollars).

Multiple Choice

AUD 3-Q7

e. **Audit risk model and sampling**
   Like other areas of an audit, the audit risk model is used to help the auditor visualize and control risk components. The audit risk model is expanded to account for risk related to sampling. Recall the form of the audit risk model.

   Audit Risk Model. AR = RMM × DR (or, IR × CR × DR); where

   AR = audit risk: The risk that the auditor expresses an inappropriate audit opinion when the financial statements are materially misstated.

   RMM = risk of material misstatement: The risk that the financial statements are materially misstated prior to the audit. RMM consists of two components: RMM = IR × CR;
   where;
   IR = inherent risk: The susceptibility of an assertion about a class of transaction, account balance, or disclosure to a misstatement, that could be material, either individually or when aggregated with other misstatements, before consideration of any related controls.
   CR = control risk: The risk that a misstatement that could occur in an assertion about a class of transaction, account balance, or disclosure, and that could be material, either individually or when aggregated with other misstatements, will not be prevented, or detected and corrected, on a timely basis by the entity's internal control.

   DR = detection risk: The risk that the procedures performed by the auditor to reduce audit risk to an acceptably low level will not detect a misstatement that exists, and that could be material, either individually or when aggregated with other misstatements.

When using audit sampling, the auditor decomposes DR into two sub-risks: **DR = AP × TD**; where **AP** = Analytical procedures risk (and other relevant substantive tests): The risk, analytical procedures, (and other relevant substantive tests) will not detect a material misstatement that exists.

TD = Test of details, allowable **risk of incorrect acceptance** for this substantive test: The risk that the audit sample will not detect a material misstatement that exists.

f. **Non-sampling and Sampling Risk**

Two things can cause a sample to be non-representative: **Non-sampling Error** and **Sampling Error**. The risk of these occurring are termed **Non-sampling Risk** and **Sampling Risk**, respectively. Both of these risks can be ***controlled***.

1) **Non-sampling risk** includes all aspects of audit risk that are not due to sampling. It is controlled by adequate planning and supervision of audit work and proper adherence to quality control standards. The following are examples of non-sampling risk:
   i. The failure to select appropriate audit procedures
   ii. The failure to recognize misstatements in documents examined
   iii. Misinterpreting the results of audit tests

2) **Sampling risk** is the risk that the auditor's conclusion, based on a sample, might be different from the conclusion that would be reached if the test were applied in the same way to the entire population.
   i. Tests of controls sampling risks include the **risk of assessing control risk too high** and the **risk of assessing control risk too low**.
   ii. Substantive test sampling risks include **the risk of incorrect rejection** and the **risk of incorrect acceptance**.

Risk of assessing control risk too high (alpha risk, type I error) is the risk that the assessed level of control risk based on the sample is greater than the true operating effectiveness of the control structure policy or procedure. ***This risk relates to audit efficiency***. If the auditor assesses control risk too high, substantive tests will consequently be expanded beyond the necessary level, leading to audit inefficiency. (Under reliance on internal control)

Risk of assessing control risk too low (beta risk, type II error) is the risk that the assessed level of control risk based on the sample is less than the true operating effectiveness of the control structure policy or procedure. ***This risk relates to audit effectiveness***. If the auditor assesses control risk too low, substantive tests will not be expanded to the necessary level to ensure an effective audit. Because, taking such action may result in materially misstated financial statements. Controlling this risk is generally considered of greater audit concern than controlling the risk of assessing control risk too high. (Over reliance on internal control)

Risk of incorrect rejection (alpha risk, type I error) is the risk that the sample supports the conclusion that the recorded account balance is materially misstated when it is not materially misstated. Like the risk of assessing control risk too high, ***this risk relates to audit efficiency***. If the sample results incorrectly indicate that an account balance is materially misstated, the performance of additional audit procedures will generally lead to the correct conclusion.

Risk of incorrect acceptance (beta risk, type II error) is the risk that the sample supports the conclusion that the recorded account balance is not materially misstated when it is materially misstated. Like the risk of assessing control risk too low, ***this risk relates to audit effectiveness***. If the sample results indicate that an account balance is not misstated, when it is misstated, the auditor will not perform additional procedures and the financial statements may include such misstatements.

Sampling risk and auditor decisions are summarized in following tables.

g. **Attributes Sampling (test of control)**

The Test of Controls Sample Indicates:	TRUE OPERATING EFFECTIVENESS OF THE CONTROL IS	
	Adequate for Planned Assessed Level of Control Risk (controls are working)	Inadequate for Planned Assessed Level of Control Risk (controls not working)
Extent of operating effectiveness is adequate (controls are working)	Correct Decision	Incorrect Decision: Risk of Assessing Control Risk Too Low (lack of audit effectiveness)
Extent of operating effectiveness is inadequate (controls not working)	Incorrect Decision: Risk of Assessing Control Risk Too High (lack of audit efficiency)	Correct Decision

h. **Sampling in Substantive Tests of details**

The Substantive Test Sample Indicates:	THE POPULATION ACTUALLY IS	
	Not Materially Misstated	Materially Misstated
The population is not materially misstated	Correct Decision	Incorrect Decision: Risk of Incorrect Acceptance (lack of audit effectiveness)
The population is materially misstated	Incorrect Decision: Risk of Incorrect Rejection (lack of audit efficiency)	Correct Decision

Multiple Choice

AUD 3-Q8 through AUD 3-Q9

i. **The sampling process**

Audit sampling follows a 3-step process (with 14 sub-steps):

Step 1: Plan the sample → **Step 2:** Select the sample and perform the audit tests → **Step 3:** Evaluate the results

Step 1: Plan the sample (to control non-sampling risk).
1) State the objectives of the audit test (e.g., test a control, test a balance, etc.).
2) Decide whether audit sampling applies.
3) Control testing: Define attributes and exception conditions. Substantive tests of details: Define a misstatement.
4) Define the population.
5) Define the sampling unit.

6) Control testing: Specify the tolerable exception rate. Substantive tests of details: Specify tolerable misstatement.
7) Control testing: Specify acceptable risk of assessing control risk too low. Substantive tests of details: Specify acceptable risk of incorrect acceptance.
8) Control testing: Estimate the population exception rate. Substantive tests of details: Estimate the misstatements in the population.
9) Determine the initial sample size.

Step 2: Select the sample and perform the audit tests.
10) Select the sample.
11) Perform the audit procedures.

Step 3: Evaluate the results.
12) Generalize from the sample to the population.
13) Control testing: Analyze exceptions. Substantive tests of details: Analyze the misstatements.
14) Decide the acceptability of the population.

j. **Sample size**

The auditor should determine a **sample size** sufficient to reduce sampling risk to an acceptably low level.

The level of sampling risk that the auditor is willing to accept affects the sample size required. The lower the risk the auditor is willing to accept, the greater the sample size necessary.

The sample size can be determined by the application of a statistically based formula or through the exercise of professional judgment. Various factors typically influence determination of sample size:

1) For tests of controls, consider the following:
   i. The tolerable rate of deviation of the population to be tested.
   ii. The auditor's determination of the tolerable deviation rate is a function of both, the planned assessed level of control risk, and the degree of assurance desired by the sample. A low assessed level of control risk and a high degree of assurance from the sample yields a low tolerable rate.
   iii. The expected rate of deviation of the population to be tested, (an estimate of the deviation rate in the entire population). If the expected population deviation rate exceeds the tolerable rate, tests of controls (attribute sampling) will not be performed -- and control risk will not be reduced.
   iv. The desired level of assurance (**complement of risk of overreliance**) that the tolerable rate of deviation is not exceeded by the actual rate of deviation in the population; the auditor may decide the desired level of assurance based on the extent to which the auditor's risk assessment takes into account relevant controls
   v. The number of sampling units in the population, if the population is very small

2) For substantive tests of details, consider the following:
   i. The auditor's desired level of assurance (**complement of risk of incorrect acceptance**) that tolerable misstatement is not exceeded by actual misstatement in the population. The auditor may decide the desired level of assurance based on the following:
      - The auditor's assessment of the risk of material misstatement.
      - The assurance obtained from other substantive procedures directed at the same assertion.
      - Tolerable misstatement.
      - Expected misstatement for the population.

- Stratification of the population when performed.
- For some sampling methods, the number of sampling units in each stratum.

Multiple Choice
AUD 3-Q10 through AUD 3-Q11

The auditor uses the above factors to determine the sample size, using computer software or a sample size table (see the AICPA Audit Guide, *Audit Sampling*).

The above factors have the following impact on sample size.

Attributes Sampling (Tests of Controls)	
Increases in:	Effect on Sample Size
Risk of assessing control risk too low	Decrease
Tolerable rate	Decrease
Expected population deviation rate	Increase
Population	Increase

Sampling in Substantive Tests of Details	
Increases in:	Effect on Sample Size
Risk of incorrect acceptance	Decrease
Risk of incorrect rejection	Decrease
Tolerable misstatement	Decrease
Expected misstatement	Increase
Population	Increase
Variance (standard deviation)	Increase

Hint: Sample size computation can be complicated. A brief example is illustrated below.

Multiple Choice
AUD 3-Q12 through AUD 3-Q15

k. **Sample size formula method – no misstatements expected**
Auditors use "Confidence (Reliability) Factors" to compute a sample size.

Note the following table:

Confidence (Reliability) Factors		
Risk of Incorrect Acceptance (%)	Confidence of Sample (%)	Confidence Factor (CF)
37%	63%	1
14%	86%	2
5%	95%	3

For example, if the auditor assesses the tolerable misstatement (TM) as $15,000, expected misstatement at zero, and the risk of incorrect acceptance as 5%, the sampling interval is calculated to be $5,000 (TM ÷ CF; $15,000 ÷ 3 = $5,000). If the recorded amount of the population is $500,000, the sample size is 100 ($500,000 ÷ $5,000).

l. **Sample size formula method – some misstatements expected**
The method is the same as above, but the confidence factor is obtained from a more complex table of factors. The auditor must compute the ratio of Expected Misstatement (EM) to Tolerable Misstatement and use that in the confidence factor table (see the AICPA Audit Guide, *Audit Sampling* for details).

Using the above example, if the auditor expects $3,000 of misstatement in the population. The ratio of EM/TM is $3,000 ÷ $15,000 = 0.20. Using the table (not shown), the confidence factor (with 5% risk of incorrect acceptance) is 4.63. The sampling interval is calculated to be $3,240 (TM ÷ CF; $15,000 ÷ 4.63 = $3,240). If the recorded amount of the population is $500,000, the sample size is (rounded up to next integer) 155 ($500,000 ÷ $3,240 = 154.3).

m. **Sample selection**
The auditor should select items for the sample in such a way that the auditor can reasonably expect the sample to be **representative** of the relevant population and likely to provide the auditor with a reasonable basis for conclusions about the population.

Audit sampling involves selection techniques that are probabilistic (random) in nature. Random selection techniques include the following:
1) Simple random (each item in the population has an equal chance of being selected for the sample).
   i. Use a random number generator (software).
2) Systematic random.
   i. Compute the selection (sample) interval: Population ÷ sample size (if using sample size tables).
   ii. Select a random starting point between 1 and the selection interval.
   iii. Now select every j^{th} item from that point (where j=selection interval).
3) Probability weighted, including monetary unit (dollars are the sampling units); also called probability proportionate to sample size (PPS).
   i. PPS is suited to testing for overstatement errors. (It is not suited to testing for zero and understated balances since these items will not be available for sample selection.)

Multiple Choice

AUD 3-Q16 through AUD 3-Q17

When statistical sampling is used, the sample **must** be a probabilistic one and appropriate statistical evaluation methods must be used with the sample results to make the sampling risk computations. It is **never acceptable** to evaluate a non-probabilistic sample as if it were a statistical sample.

n. **Audit procedures**
The auditor should investigate the nature and cause of any deviations or misstatements identified and evaluate their possible effect on the purpose of the audit procedure and on other areas of the audit.

In analyzing the deviations and misstatements identified, the auditor may observe that many have a common feature (for example, type of transaction, location, product line, or period of time). In such circumstances, the auditor may decide to identify all items in the population that possess the common feature and extend audit procedures to those items. In addition, such deviations or misstatements may be intentional and may indicate the possibility of fraud.

o. **Classical variables sampling**
   Classical variables sampling (CVS) models use normal distribution theory to evaluate selected characteristics of a population on the basis of a sample of the items constituting the population.

   Much of what you learned in an undergraduate statistics class is used in classical variables sampling. The same steps described earlier apply to CVS.

   The main methods of CVS include the following:
   1) **Mean-per-unit estimation** is a classical variables sampling technique that projects the sample average to the total population by multiplying the sample average by the number of items in the population.
      i. Determine audit values for each sample item.
      ii. Calculate the average audit amount.
      iii. Multiply this average audit amount times the number of units in the population to obtain the estimated population value.
   2) **Difference estimation** is a classical variables sampling technique that uses the average difference between audited amounts and individual recorded amounts, to estimate the total audited amount of a population and an allowance for sampling risk.
      i. Determine audit values for each sample item.
      ii. Calculate the difference between the audit value and book value for each sample item.
      iii. Calculate the average difference.
      iv. Determine the estimated population value by multiplying the average difference by the total population units, and adding or subtracting this value from the recorded book value.
   3) **Ratio estimation** is a classical variables sampling technique that uses the ratio of audited amounts, to recorded amounts in the sample, to estimate the total dollar amount of the population and an allowance for sampling risk.
      i. Determine audit values for each sample item.
      ii. Calculate the ratio between the sum of sample audit values and sample book values.
      iii. Determine the estimated population value by multiplying the total population book value times this ratio.
   4) **The regression approach** is similar to the difference and ratio approaches. This approach has the effect of using both the average ratio and the average difference in calculating an estimate of the total amount for the population.
   5) **Difference and ratio estimation** are used as alternatives to mean-per-unit estimation. The auditor should use these approaches when applicable because they require a smaller sample size (i.e., they are more efficient than mean-per-unit estimation).
      i. One factor in the calculation of sample size, for classical variables sampling models, is the estimated standard deviation. If the standard deviation of differences or ratios is smaller than the standard deviation of audit values, these two methods will produce a smaller sample size.
      ii. Difference estimation will be used if the differences between sample audit values and book values are a relatively constant dollar amount, regardless of account size.
      iii. Ratio estimation will be used if the differences are a constant percentage of book values.
      iv. In order to use either difference or ratio estimation, the following constraints must be met:
         a) The individual book values must be known and must sum to the total book value.
         b) There must be more than a few differences (twenty is often suggested as a minimum) between audit and book values.

- v. These two methods will usually be more efficient than mean-per-unit estimation when stratification of the population is not possible.
6) **Stratification** separates a population into relatively homogeneous groups to reduce the sample size by minimizing the effect of variation of items (i.e., the standard deviation) in the population.
    - i. Although stratification may be applied with any of the classical methods, it is most frequently used with the mean-per-unit estimation method.
    - ii. Know that the primary objective of stratification is to decrease the effect of variance in the total population and thereby reduce sample size.

Multiple Choice
AUD 3-Q18 through AUD 3-Q21

Hint: AS 2315 (PCAOB) is substantially the same as AU-C 530 (AICPA).

- p. U.S. auditing standards versus international standards on auditing
    1) AU-C 530 versus ISA 530

    ISA 530 (paragraph 8) states that, "The auditor shall select items for the sample in such a way that each sampling unit in the population has a chance of selection." AU-C 530 (paragraph 8) states that, "The auditor should select items for the sample in such a way that the auditor can reasonably expect the sample to be representative of the relevant population and likely to provide the auditor with a reasonable basis for conclusions about the population." The ASB worded AU-C a little differently because they thought the ISA was too imprecise.

    ISA 530 allows auditors to consider, in extremely rare circumstances, misstatements or deviations as anomalies. The ASB does not allow auditors to treat any misstatements or deviations as anomalies and states (AU-C APP B, ISA 530, *Audit Sampling*, Compared to Section 530, *Audit Sampling*),"The ASB believes that the deletion from section 530 of the option to consider a misstatement as an anomaly will enhance audit quality because misstatements identified by the auditor during audit sampling will be treated in the same manner as any other misstatement identified by the auditor and, thus, will prevent the misuse of anomalies."

> Use sampling techniques to extrapolate the characteristics of a population from a sample of items tested.

q. **Projecting and evaluating the results**
   The auditor should **project the results of audit sampling** to the population.

   The auditor should evaluate the results of the audit sample, including sampling risk, and whether the use of audit sampling has provided a reasonable basis for conclusions about the population that has been tested.

   For *attribute sampling* (testing of internal controls), CPA Exam questions tend to focus on the computed upper deviation rate and the implications for the auditor's assessment of control risk (and the impact on substantive testing). The evaluation of an attribute sample is a 2-step process.

   Step 1: Calculate the computed upper deviation rate (CUDR):

   CUDR = Sample Deviation Rate + Allowance for Sampling Risk

   Where:
   Sample Deviation Rate = Number of deviations in the sample ÷ sample size,
   Allowance for Sampling Risk = 1 – Confidence Level (alternatively, it may be given in the problem).

   Step 2: Compare the CUDR to the Tolerable Rate of Deviation (TRD).

   If **CUDR < TRD**, the sampling results support the planned reduction in control risk.
   If **CUDR > TRD**, the sampling results do not support the planned reduction in control risk and the auditor will need to increase substantive testing.

   For *probability proportional to size sampling*, CPA exam questions tend to focus on projected misstatement (using MUS). Two situations tend to occur.

   Situation 1: The recorded amount is less than the sampling interval.
   In Situation 1, the projected misstatement is computed as follows: Taint × Sampling Interval; where, Taint = selected account misstatement ÷ recorded account balance (i.e., it's the misstatement in the account stated as a percentage).
   Situation 2: The recorded amount is greater than the sampling interval.
   In Situation 2, the projected misstatement equals the actual misstatement.

   > *Hint*: Projecting and evaluating the results of audit sampling is complicated (especially related to probability proportional to size sampling) and beyond the scope of the CPA exam.

C. Performing Specific Procedures to Obtain Evidence
   1. Analytical procedures

> **Hint:** Quick reference summary of analytical procedures:
>
> **What?** Does the number make sense? Includes comparisons, ratios, budgets, nonfinancial data
> **When?** Required for planning and overall review. May be used during the audit as a substantive test.
> **Why?** Usually very efficient (more than effective)

> **Hint**: The main sources of professional guidance that serve as the basis for this review are obtained from the following:
> AU-C 520, *Analytical Procedures*, AICPA.
> AU-C 315, *Understanding the Entity and Its Environment and Assessing the Risks of Material Misstatement*, AICPA.
> AS 2305, *Substantive Analytical Procedures*, PCAOB.
> AS 2810, *Evaluating Audit Results*, PCAOB.
> AS 2110, *Identifying and Assessing Risks of Material Misstatement*, PCAOB.

> **Hint**: The use of analytical procedures in audit or non-audit engagements is substantially the same as regards professional requirements.

Analytical procedures are evaluations of financial information through analysis of plausible relationships among both financial and nonfinancial data. Analytical procedures also encompass such investigation, as is necessary, of identified fluctuations or relationships that are inconsistent with other relevant information, or that differ from expected values by a significant amount.

Analytical procedures include the consideration of comparisons of the entity's financial information with:
- comparable information for prior periods.
- anticipated results of the entity, such as budgets or forecasts, or expectations of the auditor, such as an estimation of depreciation.
- similar industry information, such as a comparison of the entity's ratio of sales to accounts receivable and gross margin percentages, with industry averages or other entities of comparable size in the same industry.

Analytical procedures also include consideration of relationships, for example
  1) among elements of financial information, such as gross margin percentages, that would be expected to conform to a predictable pattern based on recent history of the entity and industry.
  2) between financial information and relevant nonfinancial information, such as payroll costs to number of employees.

Various methods may be used to perform analytical procedures. These methods range from performing simple comparisons to performing complex analyses using advanced statistical techniques. Analytical procedures may be applied to consolidated financial statements, components, and individual elements of information.

Multiple Choice

AUD 3-Q22 through AUD 3-Q23

Scanning is a type of analytical procedure involving the auditor's exercise of professional judgment to review accounting data, to identify significant or unusual items to test.

A basic premise underlying the application of analytical procedures is that plausible relationships among data, may reasonably be expected to exist and continue, in the absence of known conditions to the contrary. The reasons that make relationships plausible are an important consideration, because data sometimes appears to be related when it is not, which may lead the auditor to erroneous conclusions. In addition, the presence of an unexpected relationship may provide important evidence when appropriately scrutinized.

If analytical procedures identify fluctuations or relationships that are inconsistent with other relevant information, or that differ from expected values by a significant amount, the auditor should investigate such differences by, inquiring of management and obtaining audit evidence relevant to management's responses, and performing other audit procedures as necessary in the circumstances.

Multiple Choice

AUD 3-Q24

Determine the suitability of substantive analytical procedures to provide evidence to support an identified assertion.

The suitability of a particular analytical procedure will depend upon the auditor's assessment of how effective it will be in detecting a misstatement that, individually or when aggregated with other misstatements, may cause the financial statements to be materially misstated.

The expected effectiveness and efficiency of a substantive analytical procedure in addressing risks of material misstatement depends on, among other things, (*a*) the nature of the assertion, (*b*) the plausibility and predictability of the relationship, (*c*) the availability and reliability of the data used to develop the expectation, and (*d*) the precision of the expectation.

a. **Nature of the assertion**
   The determination of the suitability of particular substantive analytical procedures is influenced by the nature of the assertion and the auditor's assessment of the risk of material misstatement. For example, if controls over payroll processing are deficient, the auditor may need to perform more extensive tests of details for assertions related to compensation.

b. **Plausibility and predictability of the relationship**
   When more persuasive audit evidence is desired from substantive analytical procedures, more predictable relationships are necessary to develop the expectation. Relationships in a stable environment are usually more predictable than relationships in a dynamic or unstable environment. Relationships involving income statement accounts tend to be more predictable than relationships involving only balance sheet accounts, because income statement accounts represent transactions over a period of time, whereas balance sheet accounts represent amounts as of a point in time. Relationships involving transactions subject to management discretion may be less predictable. For example, management may elect to incur maintenance expense rather than replace plant and equipment, or they may delay advertising expenditures.

Multiple Choice

AUD 3-Q25 through AUD 3-Q26

Substantive analytical procedures are generally more effective for large volumes of transactions that tend to be predictable over time. The application of planned analytical procedures is based on the expectation that relationships among data exist and continue in the absence of known conditions to the contrary. Particular conditions that can cause variations in these relationships include, for example, specific unusual transactions or events, accounting changes, business changes, random fluctuations, or misstatements.

In some cases, even an unsophisticated predictive model may be effective as an analytical procedure. For example,
1) When an entity has a known number of employees, at fixed rates of pay throughout the period, it may be possible for the auditor to use this data to estimate the total payroll costs for the period with a high degree of accuracy, thereby providing audit evidence for a significant item in the financial statements and reducing the need to perform tests of details on the payroll.
2) The use of widely recognized trade ratios (such as profit margins for different types of retail entities) can often be used effectively in substantive analytical procedures to provide evidence to support the reasonableness of recorded amounts.

> **Develop an expectation of recorded amounts or ratios when performing analytical procedures in an audit or non-audit engagement and determine whether the expectation is sufficiently precise to identify a misstatement in the entity's financial statements or disclosures.**

c. **Availability of the data used to develop the expectation**
Data may or may not be readily available to develop expectations for some assertions. For example, the auditor may consider whether financial information, such as budgets or forecasts, and nonfinancial information, such as the number of units produced or sold, is available to design substantive analytical procedures.

d. **Precision of the expectation**
In evaluating whether the expectation is sufficiently precise, when performing a substantive analytical procedure, it is appropriate for the auditor to take into account whether substantive analytical procedures are the only substantive procedures planned to address a particular risk of misstatement at the relevant assertion level, or whether the risk will be addressed through a combination of substantive analytical procedures and tests of details.
1) A *less* precise expectation may be appropriate, when evidence obtained from performing the substantive analytical procedure will be combined with audit evidence from performing tests of details.
2) A *more* precise expectation, however, is necessary when the substantive analytical procedure is the only procedure planned to address a particular risk of misstatement for a relevant assertion.

As expectations become more precise, the range of expected differences becomes narrower, and accordingly, the likelihood increases that significant differences from the expectations are due to misstatements.

When expectations are developed at a more detailed level, it is more likely that the analytical procedure will more effectively address the assessed risk of misstatement to which it is directed.
1) Monthly amounts may be more effective than annual amounts, and comparisons by location or line of business, usually are more effective than companywide comparisons.
2) The appropriate level of detail may be influenced by the nature of the entity, its size, and its complexity.

3) The risk that material misstatements may be obscured by offsetting factors increases as an entity's operations become more complex and diversified. Disaggregation of the information helps reduce this risk.

Multiple Choice

AUD 3-Q27 through AUD 3-Q28

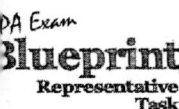

Perform analytical procedures during engagement planning for an audit or non-audit engagement.

AU-C 315.06b notes that risk assessment procedures should include analytical procedures (often referred to as planning analytical procedures).

Analytical procedures performed as risk assessment procedures, may identify aspects of the entity of which the auditor was unaware, and may assist in assessing the risks of material misstatement in order to provide a basis for designing and implementing responses to the assessed risks.

Analytical procedures performed as risk assessment procedures may, include both financial and nonfinancial information (for example, the relationship between sales and square footage of selling space or volume of goods sold).

Analytical procedures may enhance the auditor's understanding of the client's business and the significant transactions and events that have occurred since the prior audit, and also may help to identify the existence of unusual transactions or events and amounts, ratios, and trends that might indicate matters that have audit implications.

Unusual or unexpected relationships that are identified **may assist the auditor in identifying risks of material misstatement, especially risks of material misstatement due to fraud.**

Per AS 2110.47 (for issuers): In applying analytical procedures as risk assessment procedures, the **auditor should perform analytical procedures relating to revenue** with the objective of identifying unusual or unexpected relationships involving revenue accounts that might indicate a material misstatement, including material misstatement due to fraud.

Multiple Choice

AUD 3-Q29 through AUD 3-Q34

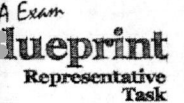

Perform analytical procedures near the end of an audit engagement that assist the auditor when forming an overall conclusion about whether the financial statements are consistent with the auditor's understanding of the entity.

Per AS 2810.05-.08 (AU-C 530 is similar in the requirements): In the overall review, the auditor should read the financial statements and disclosures and perform analytical procedures to evaluate the auditor's conclusions formed regarding significant accounts and disclosures and assist in forming an opinion on whether the financial statements, as a whole, are free of material misstatement.

As part of the overall review, the auditor should evaluate whether:
1) The evidence gathered in response to unusual or unexpected transactions, events, amounts, or relationships previously identified during the audit is sufficient; and
2) Unusual or unexpected transactions, events, amounts, or relationships indicate risks of material misstatement that were not identified previously, including, **in particular, fraud risks.**

> *Hint*: If the auditor discovers a previously unidentified risk of material misstatement or concludes that the evidence gathered is not adequate, he or she should modify his or her audit procedures, or perform additional procedures as necessary in accordance with AS 2810.36 and/or AU-C 330.07b (feedback on the risk assessment; reassess the risk; modify (e.g., extend) audit procedures in response to risk assessment).

The nature and extent of the analytical procedures performed during the overall review may be similar to the analytical procedures performed as risk assessment procedures. The auditor should perform analytical procedures relating to revenue through the end of the reporting period (for issuers; AS 2810.07).

The auditor should obtain corroboration for management's explanations regarding significant unusual or unexpected transactions, events, amounts, or relationships. If management's responses to the auditor's inquiries appear to be implausible, inconsistent with other audit evidence, imprecise, or not at a sufficient level of detail to be useful, the auditor should perform procedures to address the matter.

Multiple Choice
AUD 3-Q35 through AUD 3-Q38

e. **Reliability of data**

> Evaluate the reliability of data from which an expectation of recorded amounts or ratios is developed when performing analytical procedures in an audit or non-audit engagement.

1) Nonissuers
   Per AU-C 520.A17: The reliability of data is influenced by its source and nature and is dependent on the circumstances under which it is obtained. Accordingly, the following are relevant when determining whether data is reliable for purposes of designing substantive analytical procedures:
   i. The source of the information available. For example, information may be more reliable when it is obtained from independent sources outside the entity.
   ii. The comparability of the information available. For example, broad industry data may need to be supplemented to be comparable to that of an entity that produces and sells specialized products.
   iii. The nature and relevance of the information available. For example, whether budgets have been established, as results to be expected, rather than as goals to be achieved.
   iv. Controls over the preparation of the information that are designed to ensure its completeness, accuracy, and validity. For example, controls over the preparation, review, and maintenance of budgets.

Multiple Choice
AUD 3-Q39

2) Issuers
   Per AS 2305.16 (PCOB): Before using the results obtained from substantive analytical procedures, the auditor **should**, either test the design and operating effectiveness of controls over financial information used in the substantive analytical procedures, or perform other procedures to support the completeness and accuracy of the underlying information. The auditor obtains assurance from analytical procedures based upon the consistency of the recorded amounts with expectations developed from data derived from other sources. The reliability of the data used to develop the expectations should be appropriate for the desired level of assurance from the analytical procedure. The auditor should assess the reliability of the data, by considering the source of the data, and the conditions under which it was gathered, as well as other knowledge the auditor may have about the data. The following

factors influence the auditor's consideration of the reliability of data for purposes of achieving audit objectives:
  i. Whether the data was obtained from independent sources outside the entity or from sources within the entity
  ii. Whether sources within the entity were independent of those who are responsible for the amount being audited
  iii. Whether the data was developed under a reliable system with adequate controls
  iv. Whether the data was subjected to audit testing in the current or prior year
  v. Whether the expectations were developed using data from a variety of sources

f. Significance of the differences

> **Evaluate the significance of the differences of recorded amounts from expected values when performing analytical procedures in an audit or non-audit engagement.**

The expectation should be precise enough to provide the desired level of assurance that differences that may be potential material misstatements, individually or when aggregated with other misstatements, would be identified for the auditor to investigate. As expectations become more precise, the range of expected differences becomes narrower and, accordingly, the likelihood increases that significant differences from the expectations are due to misstatements. The precision of the expectation depends on, among other things, the auditor's identification and consideration of factors that significantly affect the amount being audited and the level of detail of data used to develop the expectation.

The auditor's determination of the amount of difference from the expectation that can be accepted without further investigation, is influenced by materiality, and the desired level of assurance, while taking into account the possibility that a misstatement, individually or when aggregated with other misstatements, may cause the financial statements to be materially misstated. AU-C 330 requires the auditor to obtain more persuasive audit evidence, the higher the auditor's assessment of risk. Accordingly, as the assessed risk increases, the amount of difference considered acceptable without further investigation decreases in order to achieve the desired level of persuasive evidence.

Readers should review popular ratio analyses used as analytical procedures.
Typical ratios include: (a) the gross profit rate, (b) accounts receivable turnover, (c) the ratio of accounts receivable to credit sales, (d) the ratio of accounts written off to the ending accounts receivable, (e) the ratio of interest revenue to notes receivable, (f) debt/equity, (g) inventory turnover, (h) profit margin and (i) return on assets

Multiple Choice

AUD 3-Q40 through AUD 3-Q41

2. External confirmations

> *Hint:* The main sources of professional guidance that serve as the basis for this review are obtained from the following:
> AU-C 505, *External Confirmations*, AICPA.
> AS 2310, *The Confirmation Process*, PCAOB.

Prepare external confirmation requests to obtain relevant and reliable evidence in an audit engagement of an issuer or nonissuer, including considerations when using electronic confirmations.

Confirmation is the process of obtaining and evaluating a direct communication (paper or electronic) from a third party, in response to a request for information about a particular item affecting financial statement assertions.

Confirmation is a form of audit evidence where, the auditor COMMUNICATES DIRECTLY with a THIRD PARTY (outside the entity).

Confirmations tend to be reliable, because it is audit evidence obtained from an outside independent third party.

a. **External confirmation process**
When using external confirmation procedures, the auditor should maintain control over external confirmation requests, including
1) Determine the information to be confirmed or requested;
2) Select the appropriate confirming party;
3) Design the confirmation requests, including determining that requests are properly directed to the appropriate confirming party and provide for being responded to directly to the auditor; and
4) Send the requests, including follow-up requests, when applicable, to the confirming party.
5) Evaluate the information, or lack thereof, provided by the third party about the audit objectives, including the reliability of that information.

The confirmation process is essentially the same for nonissuers and issuers.

The auditor is required to consider whether external confirmation procedures are to be performed as substantive audit procedures, and is required to use external confirmation procedures for accounts receivable *unless*
- the overall account balance is immaterial,
- external confirmation procedures would be ineffective, or
- the auditor's assessed level of risk of material misstatement, at the relevant assertion level, is low, and the other planned substantive procedures address the assessed risk.

Determining the information to be confirmed is dependent on the management assertion(s) to be tested. For example, if the auditor wants to test the existence of cash, he or she will send a standard bank confirmation to the client's bank(s). Also, selecting the appropriate confirming party is a function of the information being confirmed. For example, banks have people that respond to standard bank confirmations from auditors and these people will handle the response.

Multiple Choice

AUD 3-Q42 through AUD 3-Q45

There are two types of confirmation requests: the **positive form** and the **negative form**.

1) **Positive Form**
   Some positive forms request the respondent to indicate whether he or she agrees with the information stated on the request. Other positive forms, referred to as **blank forms**, do not state the amount (or other information) on the confirmation request, but requests the recipient to fill in the balance or furnish other information.

   There is a risk that recipients of a positive form of confirmation request with the information to be confirmed contained on it (not a blank form) may sign and return the confirmation without verifying that the information is correct --- blank forms may be used as one way to mitigate this risk. Thus,
   i. The use of blank form confirmation requests may provide a greater degree of assurance about the information confirmed.
   ii. However, blank forms might result in lower response rates because additional effort may be required of the recipients; consequently, the auditor may have to perform more follow-up or more alternative procedures.

   Including a list of items or invoices being confirmed (not a blank form) may improve the response rate for confirmations.

   Positive forms provide audit evidence only when responses are received from the recipients; nonresponses do not provide audit evidence about the financial statement assertions being addressed.

Multiple Choice

AUD 3-Q46 through AUD 3-Q48

2) **Negative Form**
   The negative form requests the **recipient to respond only if he or she disagrees with the information stated on the request.**

   Negative confirmations provide less persuasive audit evidence than positive confirmations. However, negative confirmation requests may be used to reduce audit risk to an acceptable level when
   - the combined assessed level of inherent and control risk is low,
   - a large number of small balances is involved,
   - a very low exception rate is expected, and
   - the auditor has no reason to believe that the recipients of the requests are unlikely to give them consideration.

   For example, in the examination of demand deposit (checking) accounts in a financial institution, it may be appropriate for an auditor to include negative confirmation requests with the customers' regular statements, when the combined assessed level of inherent and control risk is low, and the auditor has no reason to believe that the recipients will not consider the requests.

   The auditor should consider performing other substantive procedures to supplement the use of negative confirmations.

   Negative confirmation requests may generate responses indicating misstatements, and are more likely to do so if the auditor sends a large number of negative confirmation requests and such misstatements are widespread. The auditor should investigate relevant information provided on negative confirmations that have been returned to the auditor to determine the effect such information may have on the audit. If the auditor's investigation of responses to negative confirmation requests indicates a pattern of misstatements, the auditor should reconsider his or her combined assessed level of inherent and control risk and consider the effect on planned audit procedures.

Multiple Choice

AUD 3-Q49

Use external confirmations to obtain relevant and reliable evidence in an audit engagement of an issuer or nonissuer, including considerations when using electronic confirmations.

During the performance of confirmation procedures, the **auditor should maintain control over the confirmation requests and responses.** Maintaining control means establishing direct communication between the intended recipient and the auditor, to minimize the possibility that the results will be biased, because of interception and alteration of the confirmation requests or responses. The auditor should use a process that will prevent the audit client from interfering with the confirmation process and mislead the auditor.

Oral confirmations should be documented in the workpapers.

The auditor's consideration of the **reliability of the information obtained through the confirmation** process to be used as audit evidence, includes consideration of the **risks** that
- the information obtained may not be from an authentic source,
- a respondent may not be knowledgeable about the information to be confirmed, and
- the integrity of the information may have been compromised.

Responses received electronically (for example, by fax or e-mail) involve risks relating to reliability because proof of origin or identity of the confirming party may be difficult to establish, and alterations may be difficult to detect. The auditor may determine that it is appropriate to address such risks by utilizing a system or process that validates the respondent or by directly contacting the purported sender (for example, by telephone) to validate the identity of the sender of the response and to validate that the information received by the auditor corresponds to what was transmitted by the sender. In addition, the auditor should consider requesting the purported sender to mail the original confirmation directly to the auditor.

Multiple Choice

AUD 3-Q50

> Analyze external confirmation responses in the audit of an issuer or nonissuer to determine the need for follow-up or further investigation.

1) Management refuses external confirmations
   A refusal by management to allow the auditor to perform external confirmation procedures is a limitation on the audit evidence the auditor seeks to obtain; therefore, the auditor is required to inquire about the reasons for the limitation.

   A common reason offered by management is the existence of a legal dispute or ongoing negotiation with the intended confirming party, the resolution of which may be affected by an untimely confirmation request.

   The auditor is required to seek audit evidence about the validity and reasonableness of the reasons for management's refusal, because of the risk that management may be attempting to deny the auditor access to audit evidence that may reveal fraud or error.

2) Nonresponses to confirmations
   When the auditor has not received replies to positive confirmation requests, he or she should **apply alternative procedures** to the nonresponses to obtain the evidence necessary to reduce audit risk to an acceptably low level.

   Examples: In the examination of accounts receivable, alternative procedures may include examination of subsequent cash receipts (including matching such receipts with the actual items being paid), shipping documents, or other client documentation to provide evidence for the existence assertion.

   In the examination of accounts payable, alternative procedures may include examination of subsequent cash disbursements, correspondence from third parties, or other records to provide evidence for the completeness assertion.

3) Evaluating the results of confirmation procedures
   After performing any alternative procedures, the auditor should evaluate the combined evidence provided by the confirmations and the alternative procedures to determine whether sufficient evidence has been obtained about all the applicable financial statement assertions. In performing that evaluation, the auditor should consider
   i. the reliability of the confirmations and alternative procedures;
   ii. the nature of any exceptions, including the implications, both quantitative and qualitative, of those exceptions;
   iii. the evidence provided by other procedures; and
   iv. whether additional evidence is needed.

   If the combined evidence provided by the confirmations, alternative procedures, and other procedures is not sufficient, the auditor should request additional confirmations or extend other tests, such as tests of details or analytical procedures.

Multiple Choice

AUD 3-Q51 through AUD 3-Q52

3. Inquiry of management and others

> *Hint*: The main sources of professional guidance that serve as the basis for this review are obtained from the following:
> AU-C 500.A23-A26, *Audit Evidence* (AICPA).
>
> Written representations covered by AU-C 580, *Written Representations* (AICPA) and AS 2805, *Management Representations* (PCAOB) are addressed elsewhere in the review.

> **Inquire of management and others to gather evidence and document the results in an audit or non-audit engagement.**

Inquiry consists of seeking information of knowledgeable persons, both financial and nonfinancial, within the entity or outside the entity. Inquiry is used extensively throughout the audit, in addition to other audit procedures.

Inquiries may range from formal written inquiries to informal oral inquiries. Evaluating responses to inquiries is an integral part of the inquiry process.

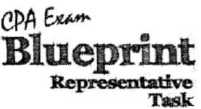

> **Analyze responses obtained during structured or informal interviews with management and others and ask relevant and effective follow-up questions during the interview in an audit or non-audit engagement.**

Responses to inquiries may provide the auditor with information not previously possessed, or with corroborative audit evidence. Alternatively, responses might provide information that differs significantly from other information that the auditor has obtained (for example, information regarding the possibility of management override of controls). In some cases, responses to inquiries provide a basis for the auditor to modify or perform additional audit procedures.

Although corroboration of evidence obtained through inquiry is often of particular importance, in the case of inquiries about management intent, the information available to support management's intent may be limited. In these cases, understanding management's past history of carrying out its stated intentions, management's stated reasons for choosing a particular course of action, and management's ability to pursue a specific course of action, may provide relevant information to corroborate the evidence obtained through inquiry.

Regarding some matters, the auditor may consider it necessary to obtain written representations from management and, when appropriate, those charged with governance to confirm responses to oral inquiries.

4. Observation and inspection

> *Hint:* The main sources of professional guidance that serve as the basis for this review are obtained from the following:
> AU-C 500.A17 and A14-A16, *Audit Evidence* (AICPA).

Perform tests of operating effectiveness of internal controls, including the analysis of exceptions to identify deficiencies in an audit of financial statements or an audit of internal control.

a. Observation
Observation consists of looking at a process or procedure being performed by others (for example, the auditor's observation of inventory counting by the entity's personnel or the performance of control activities).

Observation provides audit evidence about the performance of a process or procedure but is **limited to the point in time at which the observation takes place** and by the fact that the act of being observed may affect how the process or procedure is performed.

b. Inspection
Inspection involves examining records or documents, whether internal or external, in paper form, electronic form, or other media or a physical examination of an asset. Inspection is used in test of controls and substantive tests of details.

Evaluate evidence through the use of observation and inspection procedures in an audit or non-audit engagement.

Inspection of records and documents provides audit evidence of varying degrees of reliability, depending on their nature and source and, in the case of internal records and documents, the effectiveness of the controls over their production. An example of inspection used as a test of controls is inspection of records for evidence of authorization.

1) Inspection and Management Assertions
Some documents represent direct audit evidence of the existence of an asset (for example, a document constituting a financial instrument, such as a stock or bond). Inspection of such documents may not necessarily provide audit evidence about ownership or value. In addition, inspecting an executed contract may provide audit evidence relevant to the entity's application of accounting policies, such as revenue recognition.

Inspection of tangible assets may provide reliable audit evidence with respect to their existence, but not necessarily about the entity's rights and obligations, or the valuation of the assets. Inspection of individual inventory items may accompany the observation of inventory counting. For example, when observing an inventory count, the auditor may inspect individual inventory items (such as opening containers included in the inventory count to determine whether they are full or empty) to verify their existence.

5. Recalculation and reperformance

   Hint: The main sources of professional guidance that serve as the basis for this review are obtained from the following:
   AU-C 500.A19-A20, *Audit Evidence* (AICPA).

   Use recalculation and reperformance to obtain evidence in an audit or non-audit engagement.

   a. Recalculation
   Recalculation consists of checking the mathematical accuracy of documents or records. Recalculation may be performed manually or electronically. Recalculation is used often in auditing.

   b. Reperformance
   Reperformance involves the independent execution of procedures or controls that were originally performed as part of the entity's internal control.

6. All other procedures

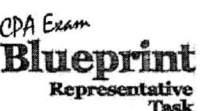

   Identify other procedures in addition to those set out in professional standards, as necessary, to achieve the audit objectives in an audit of an issuer or a nonissuer.

   Auditors use many procedures to achieve their audit objectives. Generally, the procedure(s) used is a function of verifying the management reported information against the external criteria -- e.g., the client's information in the financial statements are in conformity with GAAP. Therefore, the procedure depends on the financial statement item being examined.

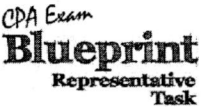

   Perform other procedures in addition to those set out in professional standards, as necessary, to achieve the audit objectives in an audit of an issuer or nonissuer.

   Performing procedures is linked to management assertions. Auditors often report to "direction of testing" when linking how to perform a procedure and management assertions.

   Generally, if the auditor is concerned with existence, he or she would test from a client listing of items (e.g., listing of equipment) to the actual item (e.g., equipment out on the factory floor). The auditor is concerned that items listed by the client and included in assets on the balance sheet (e.g., equipment) do exist and tracing these items to their actual physical location will verify their existence. If the items actually exist, every item on the listing will be in a physical location.

   Generally, if the auditor is concerned with completeness, he or she would test from the actual item back to the listing. The auditor is concerned that items listed by the client and included in the assets on the balance sheet (e.g., equipment) are missing some items, and tracing actual physical items from their location back to the listing, will test for completeness (items omitted from the list, but actually do exist, the auditor is unable to trace them back to the listing.)

Multiple Choice

AUD 3-Q53

Hint: The multiple-choice questions (MCQs) associated with this review section, illustrate the variety of questions that may be asked related to the numerous other procedures an auditor may perform during an audit engagement.

a. Consideration of omitted procedures after the report release date
   1) Introduction and Scope
   AU-C 585 addresses the auditor's responsibilities when, *subsequent to the report release date*, the auditor becomes aware that one or more auditing procedures that the auditor considered necessary in the circumstances existing at the time of the audit were omitted from the audit of the financial statements.

   (AU-C 560, *Subsequent Events and Subsequently Discovered Facts*, is applicable when a fact becomes known to the auditor after the report release date that, had it been known to the auditor at that date, may have caused the auditor to revise the auditor's report.)

   2) Objectives
   The objectives of the auditor are to
      i. assess the effect of omitted procedures of which the auditor becomes aware on the auditor's present ability to support the previously expressed opinion on the financial statements, and
      ii. respond appropriately.

   3) Requirements
   The auditor should assess the effect of the omitted procedure on the auditor's present ability to support the previously expressed opinion on the financial statements.

   If the auditor concludes that an omitted procedure, of which the auditor has become aware, impairs the auditor's present ability to support a previously expressed opinion on the financial statements, and the auditor believes that there are users currently relying, or likely to rely, on the previously released report, **the auditor should promptly perform the omitted procedure, or alternative procedures**, to determine whether there is a satisfactory basis for the auditor's previously expressed opinion.

   The auditor should include in the audit documentation the procedures performed.

   When, as a result of the subsequent performance of an omitted procedure or alternative procedures, the auditor becomes aware of facts regarding the financial statements that existed at the report release date that, had they been known to the auditor at that date, may have caused the auditor to revise the auditor's report, the auditor should apply the provisions of AU-C 560 (see Topic 3G).

Multiple Choice

AUD 3-Q54 through AUD 3-Q58

D. **Specific Matters That Require Special Consideration**
   1. Opening balances

   > **Hint:** The main sources of professional guidance that serve as the basis for this review are obtained from the following:
   > AU-C 510, *Opening Balances – Initial Audit Engagements, Including Reaudit Engagements* (AICPA)

   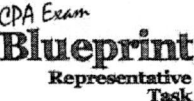

   > **Test whether prior-period closing balances have been correctly brought forward to the current period or restated in the audit of an issuer or nonissuer, including investigation of differences.**

   In addition to financial statement amounts, opening balances include matters requiring disclosure that existed at the beginning of the period, such as contingencies and commitments.

   a. Auditor objective
      The objective of the auditor, in conducting an initial audit engagement, including a reaudit engagement, is to obtain sufficient appropriate audit evidence regarding opening balances about whether
      - opening balances contain **misstatements** that materially affect the current period's financial statements and
      - appropriate accounting policies reflected in the opening balances have been **consistently applied** in the current period's financial statements, or changes, thereto, are appropriately accounted for and adequately presented and disclosed in accordance with the applicable financial reporting framework.

      1) Opening balance requirements
         The auditor should obtain sufficient appropriate audit evidence about whether the **opening balances contain misstatements** that materially affect the current period's financial statements by
         i. determining whether the prior period's closing balances have been correctly brought forward to the current period or, when appropriate, have been restated;
         ii. determining whether the opening balances reflect the application of appropriate accounting policies; and
         iii. evaluating whether audit procedures performed in the current period provide evidence relevant to the opening balances and performing one or both of the following:
             a) When the prior year financial statements were audited, reviewing the predecessor auditor's audit documentation to obtain evidence regarding the opening balances
             b) Performing specific audit procedures to obtain evidence regarding the opening balances

         If the auditor obtains audit evidence that the opening balances contain misstatements that could materially affect the current period's financial statements, the auditor should perform such additional audit procedures as are appropriate in the circumstances to determine the effect on the current period's financial statements. If the auditor concludes that such misstatements exist in the current period's financial statements, the auditor should communicate the misstatements to the appropriate level of management and those charged with governance, in accordance with AU-C 260, *The Auditor's Communication with Those Charged with Governance*.

         The auditor should obtain sufficient appropriate audit evidence about whether the accounting policies reflected in the opening balances have been **consistently applied** in the current period's financial statements and whether changes in the accounting policies have been appropriately accounted for, and adequately presented and disclosed in accordance with the applicable financial reporting framework.

2) Consistency of accounting policies
    If the auditor concludes that
    i. the current period's accounting policies are not consistently applied regarding opening balances, in accordance with the applicable financial reporting framework, or
    ii. a change in accounting policies is not appropriately accounted for, or adequately presented or disclosed, in accordance with the applicable financial reporting framework, the auditor should express a *qualified* opinion or an *adverse* opinion, as appropriate, in accordance with AU-C 705.

2. Investments in securities and derivative instruments

> *Hint*: The main sources of professional guidance that serve as the basis for this review are obtained from the following:
> AU-C 501.04-10, *Audit Evidence – Specific Considerations for Selected Items* (AICPA).
>
> The PCAOB's standard (AS 2503: *Auditing Derivative Instruments, Hedging Activities, and Investments in Securities*) is more detailed than the AICPA's standard, AU-C 501.04-.10.

CPA Exam Blueprint Representative Task

> **Identify the considerations relating to the measurement and disclosure of the fair value of investments in securities and derivative instruments in an audit of an issuer or nonissuer.**

> **Test management's assumptions, conclusions and adjustments related to the valuation of investments in securities and derivative instruments in an audit of an issuer or nonissuer.**

The requirements for issuers and nonissuers are substantially equivalent.

a. Audit procedures
  1) Securities
     When investments in securities are valued, based on an investee's financial results, excluding investments accounted for using the equity method of accounting, the auditor should obtain sufficient appropriate audit evidence in support of the investee's financial results, as follows:
     i. Obtain and read available financial statements of the investee and the accompanying audit report, if any, including determining whether the report of the other auditor is satisfactory for this purpose.
     ii. If the investee's financial statements are not audited, or if the audit report on such financial statements is not satisfactory to the auditor, apply, or request that the investor entity arrange with the investee, to have another auditor apply appropriate auditing procedures to such financial statements, considering the materiality of the investment in relation to the financial statements of the investor entity.
     iii. If the carrying amount of the investment reflects factors that are not recognized in the investee's financial statements, or fair values of assets that are materially different from the investee's carrying amounts, obtain sufficient appropriate audit evidence in support of such amounts.
     iv. If the difference between the financial statement period of the entity and the investee has, or could have, a material effect on the entity's financial statements, determine whether the entity's management has properly considered the lack of comparability and determine the effect, if any, on the auditor's report

  2) Timing issues
     With respect to subsequent events and transactions of the investee, occurring after the date of the investee's financial statements but before the date of the auditor's report, the auditor should obtain and read available interim financial statements of the investee, and make appropriate inquiries of management of the investor, to identify such events and transactions that may be material to the investor's financial statements, and that may need to be recognized or disclosed in the investor's financial statements.

  3) Reporting
     If the auditor is not able to obtain sufficient appropriate audit evidence because of an inability to perform one or more of these procedures, the auditor should determine the

effect on the auditor's opinion, in accordance with AU-C 705, *Modifications to the Opinion in the Independent Auditor's Report*.

4) Investments in derivative instruments and securities measured or disclosed at fair value
   With respect to investments in derivative instruments, and securities measured or disclosed at fair value, the auditor should
   i. determine whether the applicable financial reporting framework specifies the method to be used to determine the fair value of the entity's derivative instruments and investments in securities and
   ii. evaluate whether the determination of fair value is consistent with the specified valuation method.

5) Values from broker-dealers
   If **estimates of fair value of derivative instruments or securities are obtained from broker-dealers or other third-party sources,** based on valuation models, the auditor should understand the method used by the broker-dealer or other third-party source in developing the estimate, and consider the applicability of AU-C 500, *Audit Evidence*.

   i. <u>Quoted prices</u>
      For certain derivative instruments and securities, quoted market prices may be obtained from broker-dealers, who are market makers in or through the National Quotation Bureau. However, using such a price quote to test valuation assertions may require special knowledge to understand the circumstances in which the quote was developed. For example, quotations published by the National Quotation Bureau may not be based on recent trades and may be only an indication of interest and not an actual price for which a counterparty will purchase or sell the underlying derivative instrument or security.

   ii. <u>Valuation models</u>
      If quoted market prices are not available for the derivative instrument or security, estimates of fair value frequently may be obtained from broker-dealers or other third-party sources, based on proprietary valuation models, or from the entity, based on internally or externally developed valuation models, (for example, the Black-Scholes option pricing model). Understanding the method used by the broker-dealer, or other third-party source, in developing the estimate may include, for example, understanding whether a pricing model or cash flow projection was used. The auditor also may determine that it is necessary to obtain estimates from more than one pricing source.

      For example, this may be appropriate if either of the following occurs:
      - The pricing source has a relationship with an entity that might impair its objectivity, such as an affiliate or a counterparty involved in selling or structuring the product.
      - The valuation is based on assumptions that are highly subjective or particularly sensitive to changes in the underlying circumstances.

6) Values from the client entity
   If derivative instruments or securities are **valued by the entity using a valuation model**, the auditor should obtain sufficient appropriate audit evidence supporting management's assertions about fair value determined using the model.

   Examples of valuation models include the present value of expected future cash flows, option-pricing models, matrix pricing, option-adjusted spread models, and fundamental analysis.

7) Impairment losses
   The auditor should
   i. evaluate management's conclusion (including the relevance of the information considered) about the need to recognize an impairment loss for a decline in a security's fair value below its cost or carrying amount and
   ii. obtain sufficient appropriate audit evidence supporting the amount of any impairment adjustment recorded, including evaluating whether the requirements of the applicable financial reporting framework have been complied with.

   Regardless of the valuation method used, the applicable financial reporting framework might require recognizing, in earnings or other comprehensive income, an impairment loss for a decline in fair value that is other than temporary. Determinations of whether losses are other than temporary, may involve estimating the outcome of future events and making judgments in determining whether factors exist that indicate that an impairment loss has been incurred at the end of the reporting period. These judgments are based on subjective as well as objective factors, including knowledge and experience about past and current events and assumptions about future events.

   The following are examples of such factors:
   i. Fair value is significantly below cost or carrying value and
      a) the decline is attributable to adverse conditions specifically related to the security or specific conditions in an industry or a geographic area.
      b) the decline has existed for an extended period of time.
      c) for an equity security, management has the intent to sell the security or it is more likely than not that it will be required to sell the security before recovery.
      d) for a debt security, management has the intent to sell the security or it is more likely than not it will be required to sell the security before the security's anticipated recovery of its amortized cost basis (for example, if the entity's cash, or working capital requirements, or contractual or regulatory obligations, indicate that the debt security will be required to be sold before the forecasted recovery occurs).
   ii. The security has been downgraded by a rating agency.
   iii. The financial condition of the issuer has deteriorated.
   iv. Dividends have been reduced or eliminated or scheduled interest payments have not been made.
   v. The entity recorded losses from the security subsequent to the end of the reporting period.
   Evaluating the relevance of the information considered may include obtaining evidence about the above factors that tend to corroborate or conflict with management's conclusions.

8) Unrealized appreciation or depreciation
   The auditor should obtain sufficient appropriate audit evidence about the amount of unrealized appreciation, or depreciation in the fair value of a derivative that is recognized or that is disclosed, because of the ineffectiveness of a hedge, including evaluating whether the requirements of the applicable financial reporting framework have been complied with.

Multiple Choice

AUD 3-Q59 through AUD 3-Q60

3. Inventory and inventory held by others

> **Hint**: The main sources of professional guidance that serve as the basis for this review are obtained from the following:
> AU-C 501.11-15, *Audit Evidence – Specific Considerations for Selected Items* (AICPA).

If inventory is material to the financial statements, the auditor should obtain sufficient appropriate audit evidence regarding the existence and condition of inventory
- by attending physical inventory counting, unless it is impracticable to
    - evaluate management's instructions and procedures for recording and controlling the results of the entity's physical inventory counting,
    - observe the performance of management's count procedures,
    - inspect the inventory, and
    - perform test counts and
- by performing audit procedures over the entity's final inventory records to determine whether they accurately reflect actual inventory count results.

If physical inventory counting is conducted at a date other than the date of the financial statements, the auditor should perform audit procedures to obtain audit evidence about whether changes in inventory between the count date and the date of the financial statements are recorded properly (referred to as the roll-forward period).

If the auditor is unable to attend physical inventory counting due to unforeseen circumstances, the auditor should make or observe some physical counts on an alternative date and perform audit procedures on intervening transactions.

If attendance at physical inventory counting is impracticable, the auditor should perform alternative audit procedures to obtain sufficient appropriate audit evidence regarding the existence and condition of inventory.

If inventory under the custody and control of a third party is material to the financial statements, the auditor should obtain sufficient appropriate audit evidence regarding the existence and condition of that inventory by performing one or both of the following:
- Request confirmation from the third party regarding the quantities and condition of inventory held on behalf of the entity.
- Perform inspection or other audit procedures appropriate in the circumstances.

Analyze management's instructions and procedures for recording and controlling the results of an entity's physical inventory counting in an audit of an issuer or nonissuer.

a. Evaluate management's instructions and procedures
Matters relevant in evaluating management's instructions and procedures for recording and controlling the physical inventory counting include, for example, the following:
- The application of appropriate control activities (for example, the collection of used physical inventory *count records, accounting for unused physical inventory count records, and count and recount* procedures).
- The accurate identification of the stage of completion of work in progress; slow moving, obsolete, or damaged items; and inventory owned by a third party (for example, on consignment).
- The procedures used to estimate physical quantities, when applicable, such as may be needed in estimating the physical quantity of a coal pile.
- Control over the movement of inventory between areas and the shipping and receipt of inventory before and after the cutoff date.

Observe the performance of inventory counting procedures, inspect the inventory and perform test counts to verify the ending inventory quantities in an audit of an issuer or nonissuer.

b. Observe the Performance of Management's Count Procedures
Observing the performance of management's count procedures (for example, those relating to control over the movement of inventory before, during, and after the count) assists the auditor in obtaining audit evidence that management's instructions and count procedures are designed and implemented adequately. In addition, the auditor may obtain copies of cutoff information, such as details of the movement of inventory, to assist the auditor in performing audit procedures over the accounting for such movements at a later date.

1) Inspect the inventory
Inspecting inventory when attending physical inventory counting assists the auditor in ascertaining the existence of the inventory (though not necessarily its ownership) and in identifying obsolete, damaged, or aging inventory.

2) Perform test counts
Performing test counts (for example, by tracing items selected from management's count records to the physical inventory and tracing items selected from the physical inventory to management's count records) provides audit evidence about the completeness and accuracy of those records.

In addition to recording the auditor's test counts, obtaining copies of management's completed physical inventory count records assists the auditor in performing subsequent audit procedures to determine whether the entity's final inventory records accurately reflect actual inventory count results.

3) Use of management's specialists
Management may engage specialists who have expertise in the taking of physical inventories to count, list, price, and subsequently compute the total dollar amount of inventory on hand at the date of the physical count. For example, entities such as retail stores, hospitals, and automobile dealers may use specialists in this manner.

Multiple Choice

AUD 3-Q61 through AUD 3-Q66

4. Litigation, claims and assessments

> **Hint:** The main sources of professional guidance that serve as the basis for this review are obtained from the following:
> AU-C 501.16-24, *Audit Evidence – Specific Considerations for Selected Items* (AICPA).

> **Perform appropriate audit procedures, such as inquiring of management and others, reviewing minutes and sending external confirmations, to detect the existence of litigation, claims and assessments in an audit of an issuer or nonissuer.**

The requirements for issuers and nonissuers are substantially equivalent.

a. Audit procedures
Management is the primary source of information about events or conditions considered in the financial accounting for, and reporting of, litigation, claims, and assessments, because these matters are within the direct knowledge and, often, control of management.

The auditor's procedures with respect to litigation, claims, and assessments include the following:
1) Making inquiries of management, which may include a discussion about the policies and procedures adopted for identifying, evaluating, and accounting for litigation, claims, and assessments involving the entity that may give rise to a risk of material misstatement
2) Obtaining written representations from management, in accordance with AU-C 580, *Written Representations*, that all known actual or possible litigation, claims, and assessments, whose effects should be considered when preparing the financial statements, have been disclosed to the auditor and accounted for and disclosed in accordance with the applicable financial reporting framework

The auditor should design and perform audit procedures **to identify** litigation, claims, and assessments involving the entity that may give rise to a risk of material misstatement, including:
- inquiring of management and, when applicable, others within the entity, including in-house legal counsel;
- obtaining from management a description and evaluation of litigation, claims, and assessments that existed at the date of the financial statements being reported on, and during the period from the date of the financial statements to the date the information is furnished, including an identification of those matters referred to legal counsel;
- reviewing minutes of meetings of those charged with governance; documents obtained from management concerning litigation, claims, and assessments; and correspondence between the entity and its external legal counsel; and
- reviewing legal expense accounts and invoices from external legal counsel.

For actual or potential litigation, claims, and assessments identified, the auditor should **obtain audit evidence** relevant to the following factors:
- The period in which the underlying cause for legal action occurred
- The degree of probability of an unfavorable outcome
- The amount or range of potential loss

1) Communication with the entity's legal counsel
    i. <u>External Counsel</u>
       Unless the audit procedures required to identify litigation, claims, and assessments indicate that no actual or potential litigation, claims, or assessments that may give rise to a risk of material misstatement exist, the auditor should seek direct communication with the entity's external legal counsel. The auditor should do so through a letter of inquiry, prepared by management, and sent by the auditor requesting the entity's external legal counsel to communicate directly with the auditor.

    ii. <u>In-house Counsel</u>
        In addition to the direct communications with the entity's external legal counsel, the auditor should, in cases where the entity's in-house legal counsel has the responsibility for the entity's litigation, claims, and assessments, seek direct communication with the entity's in-house legal counsel through a letter of inquiry similar to the letter sent to external legal counsel. Audit evidence obtained from in-house legal counsel in this manner is not, however, a substitute for the auditor seeking direct communication with the entity's external legal counsel.

    iii. <u>Letter of Inquiry</u>
         The auditor should request management to authorize the entity's legal counsel to discuss applicable matters with the auditor. The auditor should request, through letter(s) of inquiry, the entity's legal counsel to inform the auditor of any litigation, claims, and assessments, that the counsel is aware of, together with an assessment of the outcome of the litigation, claims, and assessments, and an estimate of the financial implications, including costs involved.

         The auditor should document the basis for any determination not to seek direct communication with the entity's legal counsel.

         The auditor should modify the opinion in the auditor's report, if:
         - the entity's legal counsel refuses to respond appropriately to the letter of inquiry and the auditor is unable to obtain sufficient appropriate audit evidence by performing alternative audit procedures or
         - management refuses to give the auditor permission to communicate or meet with the entity's external legal counsel.

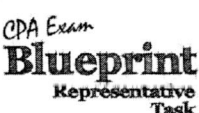
CPA Exam
Blueprint
Representative Task

Analyze management's estimate of the liability associated with litigation, claims and assessments in an audit of an issuer or nonissuer.

The client's legal counsel may communicate to the auditor his view that an unfavorable outcome is 'probable' or 'remote;' however, the legal counsel is not required to use those terms in communicating the evaluation to the auditor. The auditor may find other wording sufficiently clear, as long as the terms can be used to classify the outcome of the uncertainty under one of the three probability classifications established in FASB ASC 450.

Hint: Recall the three probability classifications used in FASB ASC 450:

Probable: The future event or events are **likely** to occur.
Reasonably Possible: The chance of the future event or events occurring is more that remote but less than likely.
Remote: The chance of the future event or events occurring is **slight**.

Management's actions related to contingent losses should conform to FASB ASC 450 and the auditor will assess the accuracy of management's accounting for contingent losses. Generally, the accounting for contingent losses is as follows:

1) The loss is probable and can be reasonably estimated: Accrue the loss contingency.
2) The loss is reasonably possible: Disclose the loss contingency. Disclosure includes: (i) The nature of the contingency and (ii) An estimate of the possible loss or range of loss, or a statement that such an estimate cannot be made.
3) The loss cannot be reasonably estimated: Disclose the loss contingency.
4) The loss is remote: Do nothing.

Multiple Choice

AUD 3-Q67 through AUD 3-Q76

5. An entity's ability to continue as a going concern

> *Hint*: The main sources of professional guidance that serve as the basis for this review are obtained from the following:
> AU-C 570, *The Auditor's Consideration of an Entity's Ability to Continue as a Going Concern* (AICPA).
> AS 2415, *Consideration of an Entity's Ability to Continue as a Going Concern* (PCAOB).

> *Hint:* SAS 132, *The Auditor's Consideration of an Entity's Ability to Continue as a Going Concern*, is eligible for testing starting in Q1 2018, superseding SAS 126. The changes include:
> - Auditors are required to separately evaluate (1) the appropriateness of management's determination of the entity's going concern and (2) whether substantial doubt about an entity's ability to continue as a going concern for a reasonable period of time exists, based on the audit evidence obtained.
> - If the entity relies on financial support by third parties or the entity's owner-manager, the auditor is required either obtain a letter from management about the third-party commitment or confirm directly with the supporting party.
> - The auditor is now required to ask management about conditions or events beyond the period of management's evaluation that may have an effect on the entity's ability to continue as a going concern. Note that management must make their evaluation first, before the auditor's inquiry.

> **Identify the factors that could cause substantial doubt about an entity's ability to continue as a going concern for a reasonable period of time in an audit of an issuer or nonissuer.**

> **Perform procedures related to the assessment of management's evaluation and conclusion regarding an entity's ability to continue as a going concern in an audit of an issuer or nonissuer.**

The requirements for issuers and nonissuers are substantially equivalent.

Continuation of an entity as a going concern is assumed in financial reporting in the absence of significant information to the contrary. Ordinarily, information that significantly contradicts the going concern assumption relates to the entity's inability to continue to meet its obligations as they become due without substantial disposition of assets, outside the ordinary course of business, restructuring of debt, externally forced revisions of its operations, or similar actions.

a. Auditor responsibility and objectives
The auditor's responsibility is to evaluate whether there is substantial doubt about the entity's ability to continue as a going concern for a reasonable period of time. The auditor's evaluation is based on the auditor's knowledge of relevant conditions or events that exist at, or have occurred prior to, the date of the auditor's report. Information about such conditions or events is obtained from the application of audit procedures planned and performed to achieve audit objectives that are related to management's assertions embodied in the financial statements being audited, as described in AU-C 315, *Understanding the Entity and Its Environment and Assessing the Risks of Material Misstatement*.

The objectives of the auditor are to:
- evaluate and conclude, based on the audit evidence obtained, whether there is substantial doubt about the entity's ability to continue as a going concern for a reasonable period of time;
- assess the possible financial statement effects, including the adequacy of disclosure regarding uncertainties about the entity's ability to continue as a going concern for a reasonable period of time; and
- determine the implications for the auditor's report.

1) **Identifying conditions or events that indicate substantial doubt could exist**
   The auditor should consider whether the results of the procedures performed during the course of the audit identify conditions or events that, when considered in the aggregate, indicate there could be substantial doubt about the entity's ability to continue as a going concern for a reasonable period of time (one year from the date the financial statements are issued).

   Per AS 2415.06: In performing audit procedures, the auditor may identify information about certain conditions or events that, when considered in the aggregate, indicate there could be substantial doubt about the entity's ability to continue as a going concern for a reasonable period of time. The significance of such conditions and events will depend on the circumstances, and some may have significance only when viewed in conjunction with others. The following are examples of such conditions and events:
   - *Negative trends*—for example, recurring operating losses, working capital deficiencies, negative cash flows from operating activities, adverse key financial ratios
   - *Other indications of possible financial difficulties*—for example, default on loan or similar agreements, arrearages in dividends, denial of usual trade credit from suppliers, restructuring of debt, noncompliance with statutory capital requirements, need to seek new sources or methods of financing or to dispose of substantial assets
   - *Internal matters*—for example, work stoppages or other labor difficulties, substantial dependence on the success of a particular project, uneconomic long-term commitments, need to significantly revise operations
   - *External matters that have occurred*—for example, legal proceedings, legislation, or similar matters that might jeopardize an entity's ability to operate; loss of a key franchise, license, or patent; loss of a principal customer or supplier; uninsured or underinsured catastrophe such as a drought, earthquake, or flood

   The auditor should consider the need to obtain additional information about such conditions or events, as well as the appropriate audit evidence to support information that mitigates the auditor's doubt.

2) **Consideration of management's plans when the auditor believes there is substantial doubt**
   If, after considering the identified conditions or events in the aggregate, the auditor believes there is substantial doubt about the entity's ability to continue as a going concern for a reasonable period of time, the auditor should obtain information about management's plans that are intended to mitigate the adverse effects of such conditions or events. The auditor should
   i. assess whether it is likely that the adverse effects would be mitigated by management's plans for a reasonable period of time;

   ii. identify those elements of management's plans that are particularly significant to overcoming the adverse effects of the conditions or events and plan, and **perform procedures to obtain audit evidence** about them, including, when applicable, considering the adequacy of support regarding the ability to obtain additional financing or the planned disposal of assets; and

iii. assess whether it is likely that such plans can be effectively implemented.
Management's plans may include the following:
- a) Plans to dispose of assets.
- b) Plans to borrow money or restructure debt.
- c) Plans to delay expenditures.
- d) Plans to increase ownership equity.

When prospective financial information is particularly significant to management's plans, the auditor should request management to provide that information and should consider the adequacy of support for significant assumptions underlying that information. The auditor should give particular attention to assumptions that are
- material to the prospective financial information.
- especially sensitive or susceptible to change.
- inconsistent with historical trends.

The auditor's consideration should be based on knowledge of the entity, its business, and its management, and should include (*a*) reading the prospective financial information and the underlying assumptions and (*b*) comparing prospective financial information from prior periods with actual results, and comparing prospective information for the current period with results achieved to date. If the auditor becomes aware of factors, the effects of which are not reflected in such prospective financial information, the auditor should discuss those factors with management and, if necessary, request revision of the prospective financial information.

3) **Consideration of financial statement effects**
   i. <u>Substantial Doubt Continues</u>
   When, after considering management's plans, the auditor concludes there is substantial doubt about the entity's ability to continue as a going concern for a reasonable period of time, the auditor should consider the possible effects on the financial statements and the **adequacy of the related disclosure**.

   ii. <u>Substantial Doubt is Alleviated</u>
   When the auditor concludes, primarily because of the auditor's consideration of management's plans, that substantial doubt about the entity's ability to continue as a going concern for a reasonable period of time has been alleviated, the auditor should consider the need for, and evaluate the adequacy of, disclosure of the principal conditions or events that initially caused the auditor to believe there was substantial doubt. The auditor's consideration of disclosure should include the possible effects of such conditions or events, and any mitigating factors, including management's plans.

4) **Written representations**
   If the auditor believes, before consideration of management's plans, there is substantial doubt about the entity's ability to continue as a going concern for a reasonable period of time, the auditor should obtain written representations from management
   i. regarding its plans, that are intended to mitigate the adverse effects of conditions or events, that indicate there is substantial doubt about the entity's ability to continue as a going concern for a reasonable period of time, and the likelihood that those plans can be effectively implemented, and
   ii. that the financial statements disclose all the matters of which management is aware that are relevant to the entity's ability to continue as a going concern, including principal conditions or events and management's plans.

5) **Consideration of the effects on the auditor's report**
If, after considering identified conditions or events and management's plans, the auditor concludes that substantial doubt about the entity's ability to continue as a going concern for a reasonable period of time remains, the auditor should **include an emphasis-of-matter paragraph** in the auditor's report to reflect that conclusion.

The auditor's conclusion about the entity's ability to continue as a going concern should be expressed through the use of the phrase "substantial doubt about its (the entity's) ability to continue as a going concern" or similar wording, that includes the terms *substantial doubt* and *going concern*. In a going-concern emphasis-of-matter paragraph, the auditor should not use conditional language in expressing a conclusion concerning the existence of substantial doubt about the entity's ability to continue as a going concern.

If the auditor concludes that the entity's disclosures with respect to the entity's ability to continue as a going concern for a reasonable period of time are inadequate, the auditor should modify the opinion.

Nothing in this section precludes an auditor from disclaiming an opinion in cases involving uncertainties. When the auditor disclaims an opinion, the report should not include the going-concern emphasis-of-matter paragraph described above but, rather, describe the substantive reasons for the auditor's disclaimer of opinion in the auditor's report. The auditor should consider the adequacy of disclosure of the uncertainties and their possible effects on the financial statements even when disclaiming an opinion.

6) **Comparative financial statement presentations**
If substantial doubt about the entity's ability to continue as a going concern for a reasonable period of time existed at the date of prior period financial statements that are presented on a comparative basis, and that doubt has been removed in the current period, the going-concern emphasis-of-matter paragraph included in the auditor's report on the financial statements of the prior period should not be repeated.

7) **Eliminating a going-concern emphasis-of-matter paragraph from a reissued report**
The auditor may be requested to reissue an auditor's report and eliminate a going-concern emphasis-of-matter paragraph contained therein. Although an auditor has no obligation to reissue the report, if the auditor decides to reissue the report, the auditor should reassess the going-concern status of the entity by
  i. performing audit procedures related to the event or transaction that prompted the request to reissue the report without the going-concern emphasis-of-matter paragraph.
  ii. performing the procedures listed in AU-C 560, *Subsequent Events and Subsequently Discovered Facts*, at or near the date of reissuance.
  iii. considering the conditions or events that indicated substantial doubt, management's plans, and written representations based on the conditions or circumstances at the date of reissuance.
  iv. considering the implications for the auditor's report in accordance with AU-C 560.

8) **Documentation**
If the auditor believes, before consideration of management's plans, there is substantial doubt about the ability of the entity to continue as a going concern for a reasonable period of time, the auditor should document the following:
  i. The conditions or events that led the auditor to believe that there is substantial doubt about the entity's ability to continue as a going concern for a reasonable period of time.

ii. The elements of management's plans that the auditor considered to be particularly significant to overcoming the adverse effects of the conditions or events.

iii. The audit procedures performed to evaluate the significant elements of management's plans and evidence obtained.

iv. The auditor's conclusion as to whether substantial doubt about the entity's ability to continue as a going concern for a reasonable period of time remains or is alleviated. If substantial doubt remains, the auditor also should document the possible effects of the conditions or events on the financial statements and the adequacy of the related disclosures. If substantial doubt is alleviated, the auditor also should document the auditor's conclusion as to the need for, and, if applicable, the adequacy of, disclosure of the principal conditions or events that initially caused the auditor to believe there was substantial doubt.

v. The auditor's conclusion with respect to the effects on the auditor's report.

Multiple Choice

AUD 3-Q77 through AUD 3-Q84

6. Accounting estimates, including fair value estimates

> *Hint*: The main sources of professional guidance that serve as the basis for this review are obtained from the following:
> AU-C 540, *Auditing Accounting Estimates, Including Fair Value Accounting Estimates, and Related Disclosures* (AICPA).
> AS 2501, *Auditing Accounting Estimates* (PCAOB).
> AS 2502, *Auditing Fair Value Measurements and Disclosures* (PCAOB).

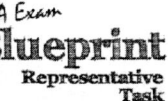

Perform procedures to analyze an entity's calculations and detailed support for significant accounting estimates in an audit of an issuer or nonissuer, including consideration of information that contradicts assumptions made by management.

Evaluate the reasonableness of significant accounting estimates in an audit of an issuer or nonissuer.

The auditor's objective, when evaluating accounting estimates, is to obtain sufficient appropriate audit evidence to provide reasonable assurance that
- All accounting estimates that could be material to the financial statements have been developed.
- Those accounting estimates are reasonable in the circumstances.
- The accounting estimates are presented in conformity with applicable accounting principles and are properly disclosed.

a. Evaluating reasonableness of estimates
   In evaluating the reasonableness of an estimate, the auditor normally concentrates on key factors and assumptions that are
   1) Significant to the accounting estimate.
   2) Sensitive to variations.
   3) Deviations from historical patterns.
   4) Subjective and susceptible to misstatement and bias.

   The auditor normally should consider the historical experience of the entity in making past estimates as well as the auditor's experience in the industry. However, changes in facts, circumstances, or entity's procedures may cause factors, different from those considered in the past, to become significant to the accounting estimate.

   In evaluating reasonableness, the auditor should obtain an understanding of how management developed the estimate. Based on that understanding, the auditor should use one, or a combination of the following approaches:
   - Review and test the process used by management to develop the estimate.
   - Develop an independent expectation of the estimate to corroborate the reasonableness of management's estimate.
   - Review subsequent events or transactions occurring prior to the date of the auditor's report.

b. Evaluating the reasonableness of fair value measurements
   The auditor's testing of fair value measurements and disclosures follow the same basic process that is used to test estimates. The following information applies to issuers.

   Because of the wide range of possible fair value measurements, from relatively simple to complex, and the varying levels of risk of material misstatement associated with the process for determining fair values, the auditor's planned audit procedures can vary significantly in nature, timing, and extent. For example, substantive tests of the fair value measurements may involve (*a*) testing management's significant assumptions, the valuation model, and the underlying data, (*b*) developing independent fair value estimates for corroborative purposes, or (*c*) reviewing subsequent events and transactions.

Some fair value measurements are inherently more complex than others. This complexity arises, either because of the nature of the item being measured at fair value, or because of the valuation method used to determine fair value. For example, in the absence of quoted prices in an active market, an estimate of a security's fair value may be based on valuation methods such as the discounted cash flow method or the transactions method. Complex fair value measurements normally are characterized by greater uncertainty regarding the reliability of the measurement process. This greater uncertainty may be a result of:
- The length of the forecast period
- The number of significant and complex assumptions associated with the process
- A higher degree of subjectivity associated with the assumptions and factors used in the process
- A higher degree of uncertainty associated with the future occurrence or outcome of events underlying the assumptions used
- Lack of objective data when highly subjective factors are used

The auditor uses both, the understanding of management's process for determining fair value measurements, and his or her assessment of the risk of material misstatement, to determine the nature, timing, and extent of the audit procedures.

1) **Testing management's significant assumptions, the valuation model, and the underlying data**
   The auditor's understanding of the reliability of the process used by management, to determine fair value, is an important element in support of the resulting amounts, and therefore affects the nature, timing, and extent of audit procedures. When testing the entity's fair value measurements and disclosures, the auditor evaluates whether:
   i. Management's assumptions are reasonable and reflect, and are not inconsistent with, market information.
   ii. The fair value measurement was determined using an appropriate model, if applicable.
   iii. Management used relevant information that was reasonably available at the time.

   Estimation methods and assumptions, and the auditor's consideration and comparison of fair value measurements determined in prior periods, if any, to results obtained in the current period, may provide evidence of the reliability of management's processes. However, the auditor also considers whether variances from the prior-period fair value measurements result from changes in market or economic circumstances.

   Where applicable, the auditor should evaluate whether the significant assumptions used by management, in measuring fair value, taken individually and as a whole, provide a reasonable basis for the fair value measurements and disclosures in the entity's financial statements.

   The auditor should test the data used to develop the fair value measurements and disclosures, and evaluate whether the fair value measurements have been properly determined from such data and management's assumptions. Specifically, the auditor evaluates whether the data on which the fair value measurements are based, including the data used in the work of a specialist, is accurate, complete, and relevant; and whether fair value measurements have been properly determined using such data and management's assumptions. The auditor's tests also may include, for example, procedures such as verifying the source of the data, mathematical recomputation of inputs, and reviewing of information for internal consistency, including whether such information is consistent with management's intent and ability to carry out specific courses of action.

2) **Developing independent fair value estimates for corroborative purposes**
   The auditor may make an independent estimate of fair value (for example, by using an auditor-developed model) to corroborate the entity's fair value measurement.

   When developing an independent estimate using management's assumptions, the auditor evaluates those assumptions for reasonableness.

   Instead of using management's assumptions, the auditor may develop his or her own assumptions, to make a comparison with management's fair value measurements. In that situation, the auditor, nevertheless, understands management's assumptions. The auditor uses that understanding to ensure that his or her independent estimate takes into consideration all significant variables, and to evaluate any significant difference from management's estimate.

   The auditor also should test the data used to develop the fair value measurements and disclosures.

3) **Reviewing subsequent events and transactions**
   Events and transactions that occur after the balance sheet date but before the date of the auditor's report (for example, a sale of an investment shortly after the balance sheet date), may provide audit evidence regarding management's fair value measurements as of the balance sheet date.

   Some subsequent events or transactions may reflect changes in circumstances occurring after the balance sheet date and thus do not constitute appropriate evidence of the fair value measurement at the balance sheet date. For example, the prices of actively traded marketable securities that change after the balance sheet date. When using a subsequent event or transaction to substantiate a fair value measurement, the auditor considers only those events or transactions that reflect circumstances existing at the balance-sheet date.

Multiple Choice

AUD 3-Q85 through AUD 3-Q86

E. Misstatements and Internal Control Deficiencies

> *Hint*: The main sources of professional guidance that serve as the basis for this review are obtained from the following:
> AU-C 265, *Communicating Internal Control Related Matters Identified in an Audit* (AICPA).
> AU-C 450, *Evaluation of Misstatements Identified During the Audit* (AICPA).
> AS 2201, *An Audit of Internal Control Over Financial Reporting That Is Integrated with An Audit of Financial Statements* (PCAOB).
> AS 2810, *Evaluating Audit Results* (PCAOB).

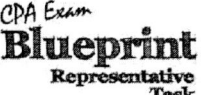

Prepare a summary of corrected and uncorrected misstatements.

The auditor should accumulate misstatements identified during the audit, other than those that are **clearly trivial**.

> *Hint*: "Clearly trivial" is not another expression for "not material." Matters that are clearly trivial will be of a smaller order of magnitude than the materiality level established in accordance with AU-C 320, *Materiality in Planning and Performing an Audit* (AICPA) and AS 2105, *Consideration of Materiality in Planning and Performing an Audit* (PCAOB), and will be inconsequential, whether taken individually or in aggregate and whether judged by any criteria of size, nature, or circumstances. **When there is any uncertainty about whether one or more items are clearly trivial, the matter is not considered trivial.**

The auditor may designate an amount below which misstatements are clearly trivial and do not need to be accumulated. In such cases, the amount should be set so that any misstatements below that amount would not be material to the financial statements, individually or in combination with other misstatements, considering the possibility of undetected misstatement.

The auditor's accumulation of misstatements should include the auditor's best estimate of the total misstatement in the accounts and disclosures that he or she has tested, and not just the amount of misstatements specifically identified (*factual misstatements;* also *known misstatements*). This includes misstatements related to accounting estimates (*judgmental misstatements*) and *projected misstatements* from substantive procedures that involve audit sampling, as determined in accordance with AU-C 530, *Audit Sampling* (AICPA) and AS 2315, *Audit Sampling* (PCAOB).

Multiple Choice

AUD 3-Q87

a. Misstatements relating to accounting estimates
   If the auditor concludes that the amount of an accounting estimate included in the financial statements is unreasonable, or was not determined in conformity with the relevant requirements of the applicable financial reporting framework, he or she should treat the difference, between that estimate and a reasonable estimate determined in conformity with the applicable accounting principles, as a misstatement. If a range of reasonable estimates is supported by sufficient appropriate audit evidence and the recorded estimate is outside of the range of reasonable estimates, the auditor should treat the difference between the recorded accounting estimate and the closest reasonable estimate as a misstatement.

> *Hint*: If an accounting estimate is determined in conformity with the relevant requirements of the applicable financial reporting framework, and the amount of the estimate is reasonable, a difference between an estimated amount best supported by the audit evidence and the recorded amount of the accounting estimate, ordinarily would not be considered to be a misstatement.

Determine the effect of uncorrected misstatements on an entity's financial statements in an audit or non-audit engagement.

b. **Considerations as the audit progresses**
   The auditor should determine whether the overall audit strategy and audit plan need to be modified if:
   1) The nature of accumulated misstatements and the circumstances of their occurrence indicate that other misstatements might exist that, in combination with accumulated misstatements, could be material; or
   2) The aggregate of misstatements accumulated during the audit approaches the materiality level or levels used in planning and performing the audit.

   > *Hint*: When the aggregate of accumulated misstatements approaches the materiality level, or levels used in planning and performing the audit, there likely will be greater than an appropriately low level of risk, and that possible undetected misstatements, when combined with the aggregate of misstatements accumulated during the audit that remain uncorrected, could be material to the financial statements. If the auditor's assessment of this risk is unacceptably high, he or she should perform additional audit procedures, or determine that management has adjusted the financial statements so that the risk that the financial statements are materially misstated has been reduced to an appropriately low level.
   >
   > Recall that auditing is a feedback oriented process. If the auditor encounters errors, he or she must feedback that information and potentially modify the audit plan from that point forward. For example, suppose the auditor has a planned detection risk of 4% based on an audit risk of 2%, and an assessed inherent risk of 50%, and assessed control risk of 100% (the auditor plans on using substantive test of details only). During the audit work, the auditor uncovers a significant number of misstatements in the account --- actually enough misstatements to realize that the inherent risk should have been assessed at 90%. The revised inherent risk would yield a revised planned detection risk of 2.22% --- which is much lower than the original 4% and will require a significant increase in extent and enhanced nature in the going-forward audit procedures.

   The auditor should communicate accumulated misstatements to management on a timely basis to provide management with an opportunity to correct them.

   If management has examined an account or a disclosure in response to misstatements detected by the auditor and has made corrections to the account or disclosure, the auditor should evaluate management's work to determine whether the corrections have been recorded properly and whether uncorrected misstatements remain.

c. **Evaluation of the effect of uncorrected misstatements**
   The auditor should evaluate whether uncorrected misstatements are material, individually or in combination with other misstatements. In making this evaluation, the auditor should evaluate the misstatements in relation to the specific accounts and disclosures involved and to the financial statements as a whole, taking into account relevant quantitative and qualitative factors.

   The auditor's evaluation of uncorrected misstatements should include evaluation of the effects of uncorrected misstatements detected in prior years, and misstatements detected in the current year that relate to prior years.

   The auditor cannot assume that an instance of error or fraud is an isolated occurrence. Therefore, the auditor should evaluate the nature and effects of the individual misstatements accumulated during the audit on the assessed risks of material misstatement. This evaluation is important in determining whether the risk assessments remain appropriate (recall the above discussion about auditing as a feedback oriented process).

Multiple Choice

AUD 3-Q88 through AUD 3-Q89

d. **Evaluating whether misstatements might be indicative of fraud**
The auditor should evaluate whether identified misstatements might be indicative of fraud and, in turn, how they affect the auditor's evaluation of materiality and the related audit responses.

If the auditor believes that a misstatement is or might be intentional, and if the effect on the financial statements could be material or cannot be readily determined, the auditor should perform procedures to obtain additional audit evidence to determine whether fraud has occurred or is likely to have occurred and, if so, its effect on the financial statements and the auditor's report thereon.

For misstatements that the auditor believes are or might be intentional, the auditor should evaluate the implications on the integrity of management or employees and the possible effect on other aspects of the audit. If the misstatement involves higher-level management, it might be indicative of a more pervasive problem, such as an issue with the integrity of management, even if the amount of the misstatement is small. In such circumstances, the auditor should reevaluate the assessment of fraud risk and the effect of that assessment on (a) the nature, timing, and extent of the necessary tests of accounts or disclosures and (b) the assessment of the effectiveness of controls. The auditor also should evaluate whether the circumstances or conditions indicate possible collusion involving employees, management, or external parties and, if so, the effect of the collusion on the reliability of evidence obtained.

If the auditor becomes aware of information indicating that fraud or another illegal act has occurred or might have occurred, he or she also must determine his or her responsibilities under professional standards.

e. **Effect of misstatements on assessment of internal control**

Determine the effect of identified misstatements on the assessment of internal control over financial reporting in an audit of an issuer or nonissuer.

See AS 2201, An Audit of Internal Control Over Financial Reporting That Is Integrated with An Audit of Financial Statements (PCOAB) and AU-C 265, Communicating Internal Control Related Matters Identified in an Audit (AICPA).

The auditor should determine whether, on the basis of the audit work performed, the auditor has identified one or more deficiencies in internal control.

If the auditor has identified one or more deficiencies in internal control, the auditor should evaluate each deficiency to determine, on the basis of the audit work performed, whether, individually or in combination, they constitute significant deficiencies or material weaknesses.

If the auditor determines that a deficiency, or a combination of deficiencies, in internal control is not a material weakness, the auditor should consider whether prudent officials, having knowledge of the same facts and circumstances, would likely reach the same conclusion.

f. **Significance of internal control deficiencies on risk of material misstatement**

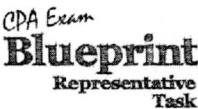

> Evaluate the significance of internal control deficiencies on the risk of material misstatement of financial statements in an audit of an issuer or nonissuer.

The auditor must evaluate the severity of each control **deficiency** that comes to his or her attention to determine whether the deficiencies, individually or in combination, are material weaknesses.

The severity of a deficiency depends on:
1) Whether there is a reasonable possibility that the company's controls will fail to prevent or detect a misstatement of an account balance or disclosure; and
2) The magnitude of the potential misstatement resulting from the deficiency or deficiencies.

Risk factors affect whether there is a reasonable possibility that a deficiency, or a combination of deficiencies, will result in a misstatement of an account balance or disclosure. The factors include, but are not limited to, the following:
- The nature of the financial statement accounts, disclosures, and assertions involved;
- The susceptibility of the related asset or liability to loss or fraud;
- The subjectivity, complexity, or extent of judgment required to determine the amount involved;
- The interaction or relationship of the control with other controls, including whether they are interdependent or redundant;
- The interaction of the deficiencies; and
- The possible future consequences of the deficiency.

Factors that affect the magnitude of the misstatement that might result from a deficiency or deficiencies in controls include, but are not limited to, the following:
- The financial statement amounts or total of transactions exposed to the deficiency; and
- The volume of activity in the account balance or class of transactions exposed to the deficiency that has occurred in the current period or that is expected in future periods.

The auditor should evaluate the effect of compensating controls when determining whether a control deficiency or combination of deficiencies is a material weakness. To have a mitigating effect, the compensating control should operate at a level of precision that would prevent or detect a misstatement that could be material.

Multiple Choice

AUD 3-Q90

F. **Written Representations**

> *Hint:* The main sources of professional guidance that serve as the basis for this review are obtained from the following:
> AU-C 590, *Written Representations* (AICPA).
> AS 2805, *Management Representations* (PCAOB).
> AR-C 90, *Review of Financial Statements* (AICPA).

a. **Identify written representations**

> Identify the written representations that should be obtained from management or those charged with governance in an audit or non-audit engagement.

1) **Audit engagements**
   The auditor should request written representations from management with appropriate responsibilities for the financial statements and knowledge of the matters concerned.

   During an audit, management makes many representations to the auditor, both oral and written, in response to specific inquiries or through the financial statements. Such representations from management are part of the evidential matter the independent auditor obtains, but they are not a substitute for the application of those auditing procedures necessary to afford a reasonable basis for an opinion regarding the financial statements under audit.

   Written representations from management ordinarily confirm representations explicitly or implicitly given to the auditor, indicate and document the continuing appropriateness of such representations, and reduce the possibility of misunderstanding concerning the matters that are the subject of the representations.

   Written representations from management should be obtained for all financial statements and periods covered by the auditor's report. For example, if comparative financial statements are reported on, the written representations obtained at the completion of the most recent audit should address all periods being reported on.

   The specific written representations obtained by the auditor will depend on the circumstances of the engagement and the nature and basis of presentation of the financial statements.

   The auditor should provide a copy of the representation letter to the audit committee if management has not already provided the representation letter to the audit committee.

2) **Non-audit engagements (reviews; AR-C 90)**
   Written representations are necessary information that the accountant requires in connection with a review of the entity's financial statements. Accordingly, similar to responses to inquiries, written representations are review evidence.

   Written representations are an important source of review evidence. If management modifies or does not provide the requested written representations, it may alert the accountant to the possibility that one or more significant issues may exist. Further, a request for written, rather than oral, representations, in many cases, may prompt management to consider such matters more rigorously, thereby enhancing the quality of the representations.

The accountant should request written representations from members of management who have appropriate responsibilities for the financial statements and knowledge of the matters concerned.

b. **Prepare written representations**

> Assist in the preparation of required written representations that should be obtained from management or those charged with governance in an audit or non-audit engagement.

1) **Audit engagements**
   Specific representations should relate to the following matters:

   Financial Statements
   a) Management's acknowledgment of its responsibility for the fair presentation in the financial statements of financial position, results of operations, and cash flows in conformity with generally accepted accounting principles.
   b) Management's belief that the financial statements are fairly presented in conformity with generally accepted accounting principles.

   Completeness of Information
   c) Availability of all financial records and related data, including the names of all related parties and all relationships and transactions with related parties.
   d) Completeness and availability of all minutes of meetings of stockholders, directors, and committees of directors.
   e) Communications from regulatory agencies concerning noncompliance with or deficiencies in financial reporting practices.
   f) Absence of (1) unrecorded transactions and (2) side agreements or other arrangements (either written or oral) undisclosed to the auditor.

   Recognition, Measurement, and Disclosure
   g) Management's belief that the effects of any uncorrected financial statement misstatements aggregated by the auditor during the current engagement and pertaining to the latest period presented are immaterial, both individually and in the aggregate, to the financial statements taken as a whole. (A summary of such items should be included in or attached to the letter.)
   h) Management's acknowledgment of its responsibility for the design and implementation of programs and controls to prevent and detect fraud.
   i) Knowledge of fraud or suspected fraud, affecting the entity involving (1) management, (2) employees who have significant roles in internal control, or (3) others where the fraud could have a material effect on the financial statements.
   j) Knowledge of any allegations of fraud or suspected fraud, affecting the entity received in communications from employees, former employees, analysts, regulators, short sellers, or others.
   k) Plans or intentions that may affect the carrying value or classification of assets or liabilities.
   l) Information concerning related party transactions and amounts receivable from or payable to related parties, including support for any assertion that a transaction with a related party was conducted on terms equivalent to those prevailing in an arm's-length transaction. See FASB Statement No. 57, Related Party Disclosures [FASB ASC 850-10-50-1], which gives the requirements for related party disclosures.

m) Guarantees, whether written or oral, under which the entity is contingently liable.
n) Significant estimates and material concentrations known to management that are required to be disclosed in accordance with the AICPA's Statement of Position 94-6, Disclosure of Certain Significant Risks and Uncertainties.
o) Violations or possible violations of laws or regulations whose effects should be considered for disclosure in the financial statements or as a basis for recording a loss contingency.
p) Un-asserted claims or assessments that the entity's lawyer has advised are probable of assertion and must be disclosed in accordance with Financial Accounting Standards Board (FASB) Statement No. 5, Accounting for Contingencies [ASC 450].
q) Other liabilities, and gain or loss contingencies, that are required to be accrued or disclosed by FASB Statement No. 5 [ASC 450].
r) Satisfactory title to assets, liens or encumbrances on assets, and assets pledged as collateral.
s) Compliance with aspects of contractual agreements that may affect the financial statements.

Subsequent Events
t) Information concerning subsequent events.

Multiple Choice

AUD 3-Q91 through AUD 3-Q92

i. **The representation letter**
The written representations should be addressed to the auditor.

The date of the written representations should be as of the date of the auditor's report on the financial statements.

The written representations should be for all financial statements and period(s) referred to in the auditor's report.

The letter should be signed by those members of management with overall responsibility for financial and operating matters, who the auditor believes are responsible for and knowledgeable about, directly or through others in the organization, the matters covered by the representations. Such members of management normally include the *chief executive officer* and *chief financial officer* or others with equivalent positions in the entity.

Multiple Choice

AUD 3-Q93

ii. **Doubt about the reliability of written representations and requested written representations not provided**
If the auditor has concerns about the competence, integrity, ethical values, or diligence of management or about management's commitment to, or enforcement of, these, the auditor should determine the effect that such concerns may have on the reliability of representations (oral or written) and audit evidence in general.

In particular, if written representations are inconsistent with other audit evidence, the auditor should perform audit procedures to attempt to resolve the matter. If the matter remains unresolved, the auditor should reconsider the assessment of the competence, integrity, ethical values, or diligence of management or of management's commitment to, or enforcement of, these and should determine the effect that this may have on the reliability of representations (oral or written) and audit evidence in general.

If the auditor concludes that the written representations are not reliable, the auditor should take appropriate action, including determining the possible effect on the opinion in the auditor's report in accordance with section 705, *Modifications to the Opinion in the Independent Auditor's Report*.

The auditor should **disclaim an opinion** on the financial statements in accordance with section 705 or withdraw from the engagement if
   a) the auditor concludes that sufficient doubt exists about the integrity of management such that the written representations are not reliable or
   b) management does not provide the required written representations (scope restriction).

If management does not provide one or more of the requested written representations, the auditor should
   a) discuss the matter with management;
   b) reevaluate the integrity of management and evaluate the effect that this may have on the reliability of representations (oral or written) and audit evidence in general; and
   c) take appropriate actions, including determining the possible effect on the opinion in the auditor's report in accordance with section 705.

2) **Non-audit engagements (reviews; AR-C 90)**
For all financial statements presented and all periods covered by the **review**, the accountant should request management to provide written representations that are dated as of the date of the accountant's review report stating that:
   i. management has fulfilled its responsibility for the preparation and fair presentation of the financial statements in accordance with the applicable financial reporting framework, as set out in the terms of the engagement.
   ii. management acknowledges its responsibility for designing, implementing, and maintaining internal control relevant to the preparation and fair presentation of financial statements, including its responsibility to prevent and detect fraud.
   iii. management has provided the accountant with all relevant information and access, as agreed upon in the terms of the engagement.
   iv. management has responded fully and truthfully to all of the accountant's inquiries
   v. all transactions have been recorded and are reflected in the financial statements.
   vi. management has disclosed to the accountant its knowledge of fraud or suspected fraud affecting the entity involving management, employees who have significant roles in internal control, or others, when the fraud could have a material effect on the financial statements.
   vii. management has disclosed to the accountant its knowledge of any allegations of fraud or suspected fraud affecting the entity's financial statements communicated by employees, former employees, regulators, or others.
   viii. management has disclosed to the accountant all known instances of noncompliance or suspected noncompliance with laws and regulations whose effects should be considered when preparing financial statements.
   ix. whether management believes that the effects of uncorrected misstatements are immaterial, individually and in the aggregate, to the financial statements as a whole. A

summary of such items should be included in, or attached to, the written representation.

x. management has disclosed to the accountant all known actual or possible litigation and claims whose effects should be considered when preparing the financial statements, and it has appropriately accounted for and disclosed such litigation and claims in accordance with the applicable financial reporting framework.

xi. whether management believes that significant assumptions used by it in making accounting estimates are reasonable.

xii. management has disclosed to the accountant the identity of the entity's related parties and all of the related party relationships and transactions of which it is aware, and it has appropriately accounted for and disclosed such relationships and transactions.

xiii. all events occurring subsequent to the date of the financial statements, and for which the applicable financial reporting framework requires adjustment or disclosure, have been adjusted or disclosed.

If, in addition to the representations required above, the accountant determines that it is necessary to obtain one or more written representations to support other review evidence relevant to the financial statements, the accountant should request such other written representations.

The written representations should be in the form of a representation letter addressed to the accountant.

Because the accountant is concerned with events occurring up to the date of the accountant's review report that may require adjustment to, or disclosure in, the financial statements, the written representations are dated as of the date of the accountant's review report on the financial statements.

When the accountant is unable to perform the inquiry, analytical procedures, and other review procedures the accountant considers necessary to obtain limited assurance as a basis for reporting, whether the accountant is aware of any material modifications that should be made to the financial statements in order for the statements to be in accordance with the applicable financial reporting framework, or management does not provide the accountant with a representation letter, the review will be incomplete. A review that is incomplete does not provide an adequate basis for issuing a review report.

If, in relation to the written representations required above
- management does not provide the written representations, or
- the accountant concludes that there is cause to doubt management's integrity such that the written representations provided are not reliable, then the accountant should discuss the matter with management and those charged with governance, as appropriate. If management does not provide the required representations or the accountant continues to doubt management's integrity, such that the written representations provided may not be reliable, the accountant should withdraw from the engagement.

Multiple Choice

AUD 3-Q94 through AUD 3-Q96

G. Subsequent Events and Subsequently Discovered Facts

> *Hint:* Quick reference summary of subsequent discovery of facts:
> 1. Subsequent discovery of facts
>   - Would it have affected report?
>   - Is it addressed with other procedures?
>   - Can you get client's permission to do work?
>   - Are statements misstated?
>   - Encourage client to recall statements and adjust and reissue.
>   - If client refuses, you notify all known users of financial statements that they cannot rely on your report.

> *Hint:* The main sources of professional guidance that serve as the basis for this review are obtained from the following:
> AU-C 560, *Subsequent Events and Subsequently Discovered Facts* (AICPA).
> AS 2801, *Subsequent Events* (PCAOB).
> AS 2905: *Subsequent Discovery of Facts Existing at the Date of the Auditor's Report* (PCAOB).
> AR-C 80, *Compilation Engagements* (AICPA).
> AR-C 90, *Review of Financial Statements* (AICPA).

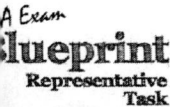

> **Perform procedures to identify subsequent events that could affect an entity's financial statements or the auditor's report, including 1) events that occur between the date of the financial statements and the date of the auditor's report and 2) facts that become known to the auditor after the date of the auditor's report in an audit of an issuer or nonissuer.**

a. **Subsequent events**

An independent auditor's report ordinarily is issued in connection with historical financial statements that purport to present financial position at a stated date and results of operations and cash flows for a period ended on that date.

However, events or transactions sometimes occur subsequent to the balance-sheet date, but prior to the issuance of the financial statements and auditor's report, and have a material effect on the financial statements and therefore require adjustment or disclosure in the statements. These occurrences hereinafter are referred to as "**subsequent events**."

The figure below illustrates the time line related to subsequent events.

Period Covered by Subsequent Events Review

Client's Ending Balance Sheet Date		Audit Report Date		Date Client Issues Financial Statements (F/S)
	Period to which Review for Subsequent Events Applies		Period for Processing the F/S	

There are two types of subsequent events:
1. Those that require financial statement adjustment.
2. Those that do not require financial statement adjustment.

The **first type** (often referred as Type I subsequent events by auditors) consists of those events that provide additional evidence with respect to conditions that existed at the date of the balance sheet and affect the estimates inherent in the process of preparing financial statements.

- All information that becomes available prior to the issuance of the financial statements should be used by management in its evaluation of the conditions on which the estimates were based.
- **The financial statements should be adjusted** for any changes in estimates resulting from the use of such evidence.
- Identifying events that require adjustment of the financial statements under the criteria stated above calls for the exercise of judgment and knowledge of the facts and circumstances.

- For example:
    a) A loss on an uncollectible trade account receivable, as a result of a customer's deteriorating financial condition leading to bankruptcy subsequent to the balance sheet date, would be indicative of conditions existing at the balance sheet date, thereby calling for adjustment of the financial statements before their issuance.
    b) On the other hand, a similar loss resulting from a customer's major casualty such as a fire or flood subsequent to the balance sheet date, would *not* be indicative of conditions existing at the balance sheet date and adjustment of the financial statements would *not* be appropriate (this is an example of the second type of subsequent event).

The **second type** (often referred as Type II subsequent events by auditors) consists of those events that provide evidence, with respect to conditions, that did not exist at the date of the balance sheet being reported on but arose subsequent to that date.

- **These events should not result in adjustment** of the financial statements.
- Some of these events, however, may be of such a nature that disclosure of them is required to keep the financial statements from being misleading. (Disclosed through an emphasis-of-matter paragraph; see AU-C 706.A2.)
- Examples of events of the second type that require disclosure to the financial statements (but should not result in adjustment) are:
    a) Sale of a bond or capital stock issue.
    b) Purchase of a business.
    c) Settlement of litigation when the event giving rise to the claim took place subsequent to the balance sheet date.
    d) Loss of plant or inventories as a result of fire or flood.
    e) Losses on receivables resulting from conditions (such as a customer's major casualty) arising subsequent to the balance sheet date.

Multiple Choice

AUD 3-Q97 through AUD 3-Q98

1) **Audit procedures**
   There is a period after the balance sheet date with which the auditor must be concerned in completing various phases of his audit.

   This period is known as the "subsequent period" and is considered to extend to the date of the auditor's report.

   Its duration will depend upon the practical requirements of each audit and may vary from a relatively short period to one of several months.

Certain specific procedures are applied to transactions occurring after the balance sheet date such as
- the examination of data to assure that proper cutoffs have been made and
- the examination of data which provide information to aid the auditor in his evaluation of the assets and liabilities as of the balance sheet date.

In addition, the independent auditor should perform other auditing procedures with respect to the period after the balance sheet date, for the purpose of ascertaining the occurrence of subsequent events that may require adjustment or disclosure essential to a fair presentation of the financial statements in conformity with GAAP.

These procedures should be performed at or near the completion of the field work.

The auditor should:
i. Read the latest available interim financial statements; compare them with the financial statements being reported upon; and make any other comparisons considered appropriate in the circumstances. The auditor should inquire of management having responsibility for financial and accounting matters, as to whether the interim statements have been prepared on the same basis as that used for the statements under audit.
ii. Inquire of and discuss with officers and other executives having responsibility for financial and accounting matters (limited where appropriate to major locations) as to:
   a) Whether any substantial contingent liabilities or commitments existed at the date of the balance sheet being reported on or at the date of inquiry.
   b) Whether there was any significant change in the capital stock, long-term debt, or working capital to the date of inquiry.
   c) The current status of items, in the financial statements being reported on, that were accounted for on the basis of tentative, preliminary, or inconclusive data.
   d) (iv)Whether any unusual adjustments had been made during the period from the balance sheet date to the date of inquiry.
iii. Read the available minutes of meetings of stockholders, directors, and appropriate committees; as to meetings for which minutes are not available, inquire about matters dealt with at such meetings.
iv. Inquire of client's legal counsel concerning litigation, claims, and assessments.
v. Obtain a letter of representations, dated as of the date of the auditor's report, as to whether any events occurred subsequent to the date of the financial statements being reported on, that in the officer's opinion would require adjustment or disclosure in these statements.
vi. Make such additional inquiries or perform such procedures as he or she considers necessary and appropriate to dispose of questions that arise in carrying out the foregoing procedures, inquiries, and discussions.

Multiple Choice

AUD 3-Q99 through AUD 3-Q100

2) **Reissued financial statements**
When financial statements are reissued, for example, in reports filed with the Securities and Exchange Commission or other regulatory agencies, events that require disclosure in the reissued financial statements, to keep them from being misleading, may have occurred subsequent to the original issuance of the financial statements.

Events occurring between the time of original issuance and reissuance of financial statements should not result in adjustment of the financial statements unless the adjustment meets the criteria for the correction of an error or the criteria for prior period adjustments set forth in FASB ASC 250 (*Accounting Changes and Error Corrections*).

Occasionally, a subsequent event of the second type has such a material impact on the entity that the auditor may wish to include in his report an explanatory paragraph directing the reader's attention to the event and its effects. (See AU-C 706.A2.)

Multiple Choice

AUD 3-Q101

b. **Subsequent discovery of facts**

When the auditor becomes aware of information which relates to financial statements previously reported on by him, but which was not known to him at the date of his report, and which is of such a nature and from such a source that he would have investigated it had it come to his attention during the course of his audit, he should, as soon as practicable, undertake to determine whether the information is reliable and whether the facts existed at the date of his report. In this connection, the auditor should discuss the matter with his client at whatever management levels he deems appropriate, including the board of directors, and request cooperation in whatever investigation may be necessary.

When the subsequently discovered information is found both to be reliable and to have existed at the date of the auditor's report, the auditor should take action if the nature and effect of the matter are such that

- his report would have been affected if the information had been known to him at the date of his report and had not been reflected in the financial statements and
- he believes there are persons currently relying, or likely to rely, on the financial statements who would attach importance to the information (consideration should be given, among other things, to the time elapsed since the financial statements were issued).

Multiple Choice

AUD 3-Q102 through AUD 3-Q106

1) **Client refuses to disclose subsequently discovered facts**

The steps that can appropriately be taken will depend upon the degree of certainty of the auditor's knowledge that there are persons who are currently relying, or who will rely, on the financial statements and the auditor's report, and who would attach importance to the information, and the auditor's ability, as a practical matter, to communicate with them.

Unless the auditor's attorney recommends a different course of action, the auditor should take the following steps to the extent applicable:

  i. Notification to the client that the auditor's report must no longer be associated with the financial statements.
  ii. Notification to regulatory agencies having jurisdiction over the client that the auditor's report should no longer be relied upon.
  iii. Notification to each person known to the auditor to be relying on the financial statements, that his report should no longer be relied upon. In many instances, it will not be practicable for the auditor to give appropriate individual notification to stockholders or investors at large, whose identities ordinarily are unknown to him; notification to a regulatory agency having jurisdiction over the client will usually be the only practicable way for the auditor to provide appropriate disclosure. Such notification should be accompanied by a request that the agency take whatever steps it may deem appropriate to accomplish the necessary disclosure. The Securities and Exchange

Commission and the stock exchanges are appropriate agencies for this purpose as to corporations within their jurisdictions.

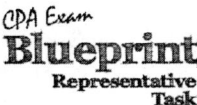

Perform procedures to identify subsequent events that could affect an entity's financial statements or the accountant's report, including 1) events that occur between the date of the financial statements and the date of the report and 2) facts that become known to the accountant after the date of the report in a non-audit engagement.

Determine whether identified subsequent events are appropriately reflected in an entity's financial statements and disclosures in an audit or non-audit engagement.

1) **Compilation engagements (AR-C 80)**
   When, during the performance of the compilation engagement, evidence or information that subsequent events that require adjustment of, or disclosure in, the financial statements comes to the accountant's attention, the accountant should propose the appropriate revisions to management.

   In the course of performing a compilation engagement on the client's financial statements, the accountant may become aware of a departure from the applicable financial reporting framework (including inadequate disclosure) that is material to the financial statements. Such departure includes, subsequent events that are not adequately accounted for or disclosed in the financial statements.

   If the financial statements are not revised, or the departure is not disclosed in the notes to the financial statements, the accountant should modify the compilation report to disclose the departure. The departure would be disclosed in a separate paragraph of the report, including disclosure of the effects of the departure on the financial statements if such effects have been determined by management or are readily known to the accountant as the result of the accountant's procedures. The accountant is not required to determine the effects of a departure if management has not done so or such effects are not readily known to the accountant as a result of the accountant's procedures. However, in such circumstances, the accountant is required to state in the report that such determination has not been made by management.

2) **Review of financial statements (AR-C 90)**
   i. **Subsequent events in a review engagement**
   When evidence or information that subsequent events that require adjustment of, or disclosure in, the financial statements comes to an accountant's attention during a review engagement, the accountant should request that management consider whether each such event is appropriately reflected in the financial statements in accordance with the applicable financial reporting framework.

   ii. **Subsequently discovered facts in a review engagement**
   a) <u>Before Report Release Date</u>
   The accountant is not required to perform any review procedures regarding the financial statements after the date of the accountant's review report. However, if a subsequently discovered fact becomes known to the accountant before the report release date, the accountant should
   - discuss the matter with management and, when appropriate, those charged with governance and

- determine whether the financial statements need revision and, if so, inquire how management intends to address the matter in the financial statements.

If management revises the financial statements, the accountant should perform the review procedures necessary in the circumstances on the revision. The accountant also should either
- date the accountant's review report as of a later date or
- include an additional date in the accountant's review report on the revised financial statements that is limited to the revision (that is, dual-date the accountant's review report for that revision), thereby indicating that the accountant's review procedures subsequent to the original date of the accountant's review report are limited solely to the revision of the financial statements described in the relevant note to the financial statements.

If management does not revise the financial statements in circumstances when the accountant believes they need to be revised, the accountant should modify the accountant's review report, as appropriate.

b) <u>After Report Release Date</u>
If a subsequently discovered fact becomes known to the accountant after the report release date, the accountant should
- discuss the matter with management and, when appropriate, those charged with governance and
- determine whether the financial statements need revision and, if so, inquire how management intends to address the matter in the financial statements.

If management does not revise the financial statements in circumstances when the accountant believes they need to be revised, then
- if the ***reviewed financial statements have not been made available to third parties***, the accountant should notify management and those charged with governance, unless all of those charged with governance are involved in managing the entity, *not* to make the reviewed financial statements available to third parties before the necessary revisions have been made and a new accountant's review report on the revised financial statements has been provided. If the reviewed financial statements are, nevertheless, subsequently made available to third parties without the necessary revisions, the accountant should assess whether the steps taken by management are timely and appropriate to ensure that anyone in receipt of those financial statements is informed of the situation, including that the reviewed financial statements are not to be used.

- if the *reviewed financial statements have been made available to third parties*, the accountant should assess whether the steps taken by management are timely and appropriate to ensure that anyone in receipt of the reviewed financial statements is informed of the situation, including that the reviewed financial statements are not to be used. If management does not take the necessary steps, the accountant should notify management and those charged with governance (unless all of those charged with governance are involved in managing the entity) that the accountant will seek to prevent future use of the accountant's review report. If, despite such notification, management or those charged with governance do not take the necessary steps, the accountant should take appropriate action to seek to prevent use of the accountant's review report. The accountant's course of action depends upon the accountant's legal and ethical rights and obligations. Consequently, the accountant may consider it appropriate to seek legal advice.

Hint: SAS 133, *Auditor involvement with Exempt Offering Documents*, is eligible for testing starting in Q1 2018. The standard addresses securities exempt from registration under the Securities Act of 1933, such as:
- municipal securities
- franchise offerings
- crowdfunding
- short-term commercial paper (maturity of nine months or less)

If the auditor prepares an auditor's report on financial statements that included in an exempt offering document and assist with other activities (e.g., read a draft of the offering or participates in a due diligence discussion), he or she is now required to perform subsequent event procedures.

If revisions are required in the offering due to subsequent events and management doesn't make adjustments, the auditor should not agree with the inclusion of their report with the offering.

This page is intentionally left blank.

Copyright © 2018 Yaeger CPA Review. All rights reserved.

Glossary: Performing Further Procedures and Obtaining Evidence

A

Accounting estimate – an approximation of a monetary amount in the absence of a precise means of measurement

Analytical procedures – evaluations of financial information through analysis of plausible relationships among both financial and nonfinancial data

Attributes sampling – a sampling plan enabling the auditors to estimate the deviation rate in a population

Audit sampling (sampling) – the selection of less than 100% of the population of audit relevance, and the evaluation of that sample, such that the auditor expects the items selected (the sample) to be representative of the population, and thus likely to provide a reasonable basis for conclusions about the population

Auditor's point estimate or auditor's range – the amount or range of amounts, respectively, derived from audit evidence for use in evaluating the recorded or disclosed amount(s)

B

C

D

Date of the auditor's report – the date that the auditor dates the report on the financial statements

Date of the financial statements – the date of the end of the latest period covered by the financial statements

Deficiency in internal control – a deficiency in internal control exists when the design or operation of a control does not allow management or employees, in the normal course of performing their assigned functions, to prevent, or detect and correct, misstatements on a timely basis

Deviation rate – a defined rate of departure from prescribed controls. Also referred to as occurrence rate or exception rate

Difference estimation – a classical variables sampling plan that uses the difference between the audited (correct) values and the book values of items in a sample to calculate the estimated total audited value of the population.

Discovery sampling – a procedure for determining the sample size required to have a stipulated probability of observing at least one occurrence, when the expected population deviation rate is at a designated level

E

Estimation uncertainty – the susceptibility of an accounting estimate and related disclosures to an inherent lack of precision in its measurement

Exception – a response that indicates a difference between information requested to be confirmed, or contained in the entity's records, and information provided by the confirming party

External confirmation – audit evidence obtained as a direct written response to the auditor from a third party (the confirming party), either in paper form or by electronic or other medium (e.g., through the auditor's direct access to information held by a third party)

F

G

H

I

Initial audit engagement – an engagement in which either (a) the financial statements for the prior period were not audited, or (b) the financial statements for the prior period were audited by a predecessor auditor.

J

K

L

M

Management bias – a lack of neutrality, by management, in the preparation and fair presentation of information

Management's point estimate – the amount selected by management for recognition or disclosure in the financial statements as an accounting estimate

Material weakness – a deficiency, or a combination of deficiencies, in internal control, such that there is a reasonable possibility that a material misstatement of the entity's financial statements will not be prevented, or detected and corrected, on a timely basis

Mean-per-unit estimation – a classical variables sampling plan enabling auditors to estimate the average dollar value of items in a population by determining the average value of items in a sample

Misstatement – a difference between the amount, classification, presentation, or disclosure of a reported financial statement item, and the amount, classification, presentation, or disclosure that is required for the item to be in accordance with the applicable financial reporting framework

N

Negative confirmation request – a request that the confirming party respond directly to the auditor *only if* the confirming party disagrees with the information provided in the request

Nonresponse – a failure of the confirming party to respond, or fully respond, to a positive confirmation request or a confirmation request returned undelivered

Non-sampling risk – the risk that the auditor reaches an erroneous conclusion for any reason not related to sampling risk (e.g., use of inappropriate audit procedures, misinterpretation of audit evidence, failure to recognize a misstatement or deviation)

O

Opening balances – those account balances that exist at the beginning of the period, based upon the closing balances of the prior period and reflect the effects of transactions and events of prior periods and accounting policies applied in the prior period

Outcome of an accounting estimate – the actual monetary amount that results from the resolution of the underlying transaction(s), event(s), or condition(s) addressed by the accounting estimate

P

Performance materiality – the amount (or amounts) set by the auditor at less than materiality for the financial statements as a whole, to reduce, to an appropriately low level, the probability that the aggregate of uncorrected and undetected misstatements exceeds materiality for the financial statements as a whole

Population – the entire set of data from which a sample is selected and about which the auditor wishes to draw conclusions

Positive confirmation request – a request that the confirming party respond directly to the auditor, by providing the requested information or indicating whether the confirming party agrees or disagrees with the information in the request

Predecessor auditor – the auditor from a different audit firm who has reported on the most recent audited financial statements, or was engaged to perform, but did not complete, an audit of the financial statements

Probability-proportional-to-size (PPS) sampling – a variables sampling procedure that uses attributes theory to express a conclusion in monetary (dollar) amounts

Projected misstatements – the auditor's best estimate of misstatements in populations, involving the projection of misstatements identified in audit samples, to the entire population from which the samples were drawn

Q

R

Ratio estimation – a classical variables sampling plan enabling auditors to use the ratio of audited (correct) values to book values of items in a sample, to calculate the estimated total audited value of the population

Reasonable period of time – a period of time not to exceed one year beyond the date of the financial statements being audited

Re-audit – an initial audit engagement to audit financial statements that have been previously audited by a predecessor auditor

Risk of assessing control risk too high – the risk that the assessed level of control risk, based on the sample, is greater than the true operating effectiveness of the control; that is, the auditor concludes that the system operates *less* effectively than it actually does

Risk of assessing control risk too low – this risk is the possibility that the assessed level of control risk, based on the sample, is less than the true operating effectiveness of the controls; that is, the auditor concludes that the system operates *more* effectively than it actually does.

Risk of incorrect acceptance – the risk that sample results indicate that a population is not materially misstated when, in fact, it is materially misstated

Risk of incorrect rejection – the risk that sample results indicate that a population is materially misstated when, in fact, it is not

S

Sampling risk – the risk that the auditor's conclusion based on a sample may be different from the conclusion if the entire population was subjected to the same audit procedure

Sampling unit – the individual items constituting a population; the sampling units might be physical items (for example, checks listed on deposit slips, credit entries on bank statements, sales invoices, or accounts receivable) or monetary units

Significant deficiency – a deficiency, or a combination of deficiencies, in internal control that is less severe than a material weakness yet important enough to merit attention by those charged with governance

Statistical sampling – audit sampling that uses the laws of probability for selecting and evaluating a sample from a population for the purpose of reaching a conclusion about the population

Stratification – division of the population into groups

Subsequent events – events occurring between the date of the financial statements and the date of the auditor's report

Subsequently discovered facts – facts that become known to the auditor after the date of the auditor's report that, had they been known to the auditor at that date, may have caused the auditor to revise the auditor's report

T

Tolerable misstatement – a monetary amount set by the auditor, in respect of which, the auditor seeks to obtain an appropriate level of assurance that the monetary amount set by the auditor is not exceeded by the actual misstatement in the population

Tolerable rate of deviation – a rate of deviation from prescribed internal control procedures set by the auditor, in respect of which, the auditor seeks to obtain an appropriate level of assurance that the rate of deviation, set by the auditor, is not exceeded by the actual rate of deviation in the population

U

Uncorrected misstatements – misstatements that the auditor has accumulated during the audit and that have not been corrected

V

Variables sampling – sampling plans designed to estimate a numerical measurement of a population, such as dollar value

W

Written representation – a written statement by management provided to the auditor to confirm certain matters or to support other audit evidence. Written representations in this context do not include financial statements, the assertions therein, or supporting books and records

X

Y

Z

This page is intentionally left blank.

Multiple Choice – Questions

AUD 3-Q1 A21. At the conclusion of an audit, an auditor is reviewing the evidence gathered in support of the financial statements. With regard to the valuation of inventory, the auditor concludes that the evidence obtained is not sufficient to support management's representations. Which of the following actions is the auditor most likely to take?

A. Consult with the audit committee and issue a disclaimer of opinion.
B. Consult with the audit committee and issue a qualified opinion.
C. Obtain additional evidence regarding the valuation of inventory.
D. Obtain a statement from management supporting their inventory valuation.

AUD 3-Q2 A70. Which of the following types of audit evidence provides the least assurance of reliability?

A. Receivable confirmations received from the client's customers.
B. Pre-numbered receiving reports completed by the client's employees.
C. Prior months' bank statements obtained from the client.
D. Municipal property tax bills prepared in the client's name.

AUD 3-Q3 A268. Which of the following terms identifies a requirement for audit evidence?

A. Appropriate.
B. Adequate.
C. Reasonable.
D. Disconfirming.

AUD 3-Q4 A32. For which of the following audit tests would a CPA most likely use attribute sampling?

A. Identifying entries posted to incorrect accounts.
B. Estimating the amount in an expense account.
C. Evaluating the reasonableness of depreciation expense.
D. Selecting receivables for confirmation of account balances.

AUD 3-Q5 A123. For which of the following audit tests would an auditor most likely use attribute sampling?

A. Inspecting purchase orders for proper approval by supervisors.
B. Making an independent estimate of recorded payroll expense.
C. Determining that all payables are recorded at year end.
D. Selecting accounts receivable for confirmation of account balances.

AUD 3-Q6 A453. A CPA auditing inventory may appropriately apply sampling for attributes in order to estimate the

A. Average price of inventory items.
B. Percentage of slow-moving inventory items.
C. Dollar value of inventory.
D. Physical quantity of inventory items.

AUD 3-Q7 A437. Jones, CPA, believes the industry-wide occurrence rate of client billing errors is 3% and has established a maximum acceptable occurrence rate of 5%. In the review of client invoices Jones should use

A. Discovery sampling.
B. Attribute sampling.
C. Stratified sampling.
D. Variables sampling.

AUD 3-Q8 A184. An auditor discovers that an account balance believed not to be materially misstated based on an audit sample was materially misstated based on the total population of the account balance. This is an example of which of the following sampling types of risks?

A. Incorrect rejection.
B. Incorrect acceptance.
C. Assessing control risk too low.
D. Assessing control risk too high.

AUD 3-Q9 A109. Which of the following statements about audit sampling risks is correct for a nonissuer?

A. Non-sampling risk arises from the possibility that, when a substantive test is restricted to a sample, conclusions might be different than if the auditor had tested each item in the population
B. Non-sampling risk can arise because an auditor failed to recognize misstatements.
C. Sampling risk is derived from the uncertainty in applying audit procedures to specific risks.
D. Sampling risk includes the possibility of selecting audit procedures that are not appropriate to achieve the specific objective.

AUD 3-Q10 A215. Which of the following would be a consideration in planning an auditor's sample for a test of controls?

A. Preliminary judgments about materiality levels.
B. The auditor's allowable risk of assessing control risk is too high.
C. The level of detection risk for the account.
D. The auditor's allowable risk of assessing control risk is too low.

AUD 3-Q11 A266. As a result of sampling procedures applied as tests of controls, an auditor incorrectly assesses control risk higher than appropriate. The most likely explanation for this situation is that

A. The deviation rate in the auditor's sample is less than the tolerable rate, but the deviation rate in the population exceeds the tolerable rate.
B. The deviation rate in the auditor's sample exceeds the tolerable rate, but the deviation rate in the population is less than the tolerable rate.
C. The deviation rates of both the auditor's sample and the population exceed the tolerable rate.
D. The deviation rates of both the auditor's sample and the population are less than the tolerable rate.

AUD 3-Q12 A287. In attribute sampling, a 25% change in which of the following factors will have the smallest effect on the size of the sample?

A. Tolerable rate of deviation.
B. Number of items in the population.
C. Degree of assurance desired.
D. Planned assessed level of control risk.

AUD 3-Q13 A169. Which of the following statements is ordinarily correct about the sample size in statistical sampling when testing controls?

A. The expected population deviation rate has little effect on determining the sample size.
B. As the population size doubles, the sample size should also double.
C. As the tolerable deviation rate increases, the sample size should also increase.
D. The population size has little effect on the sample size.

AUD 3-Q14 A140. Which of the following statements is generally correct about the sample size in statistical sampling when testing internal controls?

A. As the population size doubles, the sample size should increase by about 67%.
B. The sample size is inversely proportional to the expected error rate.
C. There is no relationship between the tolerable error rate and the sample size.
D. The population size has little or no effect on the sample size.

AUD 3-Q15 A415. When using a statistical sampling plan, the auditor would probably require a smaller sample if the

A. Population increases.
B. Desired precision interval narrows.
C. Desired reliability decreases.
D. Expected error occurrence rate increases.

AUD 3-Q16 A279. Which of the following is the primary objective of probability proportional to sample size (PPS)?

A. To identify overstatement errors.
B. To increase the proportion of smaller-value items in the sample.
C. To identify items where controls were not properly applied.
D. To identify zero and negative balances.

AUD 3-Q17 A343. If certain forms are not consecutively numbered

A. Selection of a random sample probably is not possible.
B. Systematic sampling may be appropriate.
C. Stratified sampling should be used.
D. Random number tables cannot be used.

AUD 3-Q18 A380. The major reason that the difference and ratio estimation methods would be expected to produce audit efficiency is that the

A. Number of members of the populations of differences or ratios is smaller than the number of members of the population of book values.
B. Beta risk may be completely ignored.
C. Calculations required in using difference or ratio estimation are less arduous and fewer than those required when using direct estimation.
D. Variability of the populations of differences or ratios is less than that of the populations of book values or audited values.

AUD 3-Q19 A435. Use of the ratio estimation sampling technique to estimated dollar amounts is inappropriate when

A. The total book value is known and corresponds to the sum of all the individual book values.
B. A book value for each sample item is unknown.
C. There are some observed differences between audited values and book values.
D. The audited values are nearly proportional to the book values.

AUD 3-Q20 A1344. As a result of control testing, a CPA has decided to reduce control risk. What is the impact on substantive testing sample size if all other factors remain constant?

A. The sample size would be irrelevant.
B. The sample size would be higher.
C. The sample size would be lower.
D. The sample size would be unaffected.

AUD 3-Q21 A1378. In a test of purchase orders, the auditor selected a random sample of 60 items out of a population of 1,200 purchase orders. The auditor discovered $4,000 in overstatement in the sample. The company's materiality is $65,000. The tolerable misstatement for purchases is $50,000. What should the auditor do next?

A. Pass on the exceptions.
B. Propose an adjustment to purchases.
C. Consider expanding the size of the sample.
D. Project the detected error to the entire population.

AUD 3-Q22 A48. Which of the following would *not* be considered an analytical procedure?

A. Converting dollar amounts of income statement account balances to percentages of net sales for comparison with industry averages.
B. Developing the current year's expected net sales based on the sales trend of similar entities within the same industry.
C. Projecting a deviation rate by comparing the results of a statistical sample with the actual population characteristics.
D. Estimating the current year's expected expenses based on the prior year's expenses and the current year's budget.

AUD 3-Q23 A97. Which of the following would be considered an analytical procedure?

A. Testing purchasing, shipping, and receiving cutoff activities.
B. Comparing inventory balances to recent sales activities.
C. Projecting the deviation rate of a statistical sample to the population.
D. Reconciling physical counts to perpetual records and general ledger balances.

AUD 3-Q24 A444. Which of the following analytical procedures should be applied to the income statement?

A. Select sales and expense items and trace amounts to related supporting documents.
B. Ascertain that the net income amount in the statement of cash flows agrees with the net income amount in the income statement.
C. Obtain from the proper client representatives, the beginning and ending inventory amounts that were used to determine cost of sales.
D. Compare the actual revenues and expenses with the corresponding figures of the previous year and investigate significant differences.

AUD 3-Q25 A224. Auditors try to identify predictable relationships when applying analytical procedures. Relationships involving transactions from which of the following accounts most likely would yield the highest level of evidence?

A. Interest expense.
B. Allowance for doubtful accounts.
C. Accounts receivable.
D. Accounts payable.

AUD 3-Q26 A318. Analytical procedures are most appropriate when testing which of the following types of transactions?

A. Payroll and benefit liabilities.
B. Acquisitions and disposals of fixed assets.
C. Operating expense transactions.
D. Long-term debt transactions.

AUD 3-Q27 A270. An auditor's decision whether to apply analytical procedures as substantive tests usually is determined by the

A. Availability of documentary evidence that should be verified.
B. Extent of accounting estimates used in preparing the financial statements.
C. Precision and reliability of the data used to develop expectations.
D. Number of transactions recorded just before and just after the year end.

AUD 3-Q28 A333. When applying analytical procedures during an audit, which of the following is the best approach for developing expectations?

A. Considering unaudited account balances and ratios to calculate what adjusted balances should be.
B. Identifying reasonable explanations for unexpected differences before talking to client management.
C. Considering the pattern of several unusual changes without trying to explain what caused them.
D. Comparing client data with client-determined expected results to reduce detailed tests of account balances.

AUD 3-Q29 A24. Which of the following is an analytical procedure that an auditor most likely would perform when planning an audit?

A. Confirming bank balances with the financial institutions.
B. Scanning accounts receivable for amounts over credit limits.
C. Re-calculating inventory extensions of physical inventory counts.
D. Comparing the current-year account balances for conformity with predictable patterns.

AUD 3-Q30 A269. When performing analytical procedures in the planning stage, the auditor most likely would develop expectations by reviewing which of the following sources of information?

A. Unaudited information from internal quarterly reports.
B. Various account assertions in the planning memorandum.
C. Comments in the prior-year's management letter.
D. The control risk assessment relating to specific financial assertions.

AUD 3-Q31 A282. Analytical procedures used in the planning phase of an audit should focus on

A. Documenting the risk factors relating to the susceptibility of assets to misappropriation.
B. Identifying the internal control activities that could reduce the assessed level of control risk.
C. Discovering uncorrected misstatements that should be communicated to the audit committee.
D. Enhancing the auditor's understanding of the transactions and events that have occurred since the last audit.

AUD 3-Q32 A252. Which of the following is an analytical procedure that an auditor most likely would perform when planning an audit?

A. Confirming a sample of accounts payable.
B. Scanning payroll files for terminated employees.
C. Comparing current-year balances to budgeted balances.
D. Recalculating interest expense based on notes payable balances.

AUD 3-Q33 A168. Which of the following statements is correct concerning analytical procedures used in planning an audit engagement?

A. They often replace the tests of controls that are performed to assess control risk.
B. They usually use financial and nonfinancial data aggregated at a high level.
C. They usually involve the comparison of assertions developed by management to ratios calculated by an auditor.
D. They are often used to develop an auditor's preliminary judgment about control risk.

AUD 3-Q34 A181. Which of the following analytical procedures most likely would be used during the planning stage of an audit?

A. Comparing current-year to prior-year sales volumes.
B. Reading the financial statements and notes and considering the adequacy of evidence.
C. Comparing the current-year ratio of aggregate salaries paid to the number of employees to the prior-year's ratio.
D. Reading the letter from the client's attorney and considering the threat of litigation.

AUD 3-Q35 A286. Which of the following ratios would an engagement partner most likely consider in the overall review stage of an audit?

A. Total liabilities/net sales.
B. Accounts receivable/inventory.
C. Cost of goods sold/average inventory.
D. Current assets/quick assets.

AUD 3-Q36 A335. If not already performed during the overall review stage of the audit, the auditor should perform analytical procedures relating to which of the following transaction cycles?

A. Payroll.
B. Revenue.
C. Purchasing.
D. Inventory.

AUD 3-Q37 A142. A primary objective of analytical procedures used in the final review stage of an audit is to

A. Identify account balances that represent specific risks relevant to the audit.
B. Gather evidence from tests of details to corroborate financial statement assertions.
C. Detect fraud that may cause the financial statements to be misstated.
D. Assist the auditor in evaluating the overall financial statement presentation.

AUD 3-Q38 A152. Which of the following activities is an analytical procedure an auditor would perform in the final overall review stage of an audit to ensure that the financial statements are free from material misstatement?

A. Reading the minutes of the board of directors' meetings for the year under audit.
B. Obtaining a letter concerning potential liabilities from the client's attorney.
C. Comparing the current year's financial statements with those of the prior year.
D. Ensuring that a representation letter signed by management is in the file.

AUD 3-Q39 A15. Which of the following factors would most likely influence an auditor's consideration of the reliability of data when performing analytical procedures?

A. Whether the data were developed in a computerized or a manual accounting system.
B. Whether the data were prepared on the cash basis or in conformity with GAAP
C. Whether the data were developed under a system with adequate controls.
D. Whether the data were processed in an online system or a batch entry system

AUD 3-Q40 A214. For the fiscal year ending December 31, previous year and the current year, Justin Co. has net sales of $1,000,000 and $2,000,000; average gross receivables of $100,000 and $300,000; and allowance for uncollectible accounts receivable of $30,000 and $50,000, respectively. If the accounts receivable turnover and the ratio of allowance for uncollectible accounts receivable to gross accounts receivable are calculated, which of the following best represents the conclusions to be drawn? (Use year-end balances)

A. Accounts receivable turnovers are 10.0 and 6.6 and the ratios of uncollectible accounts receivable to gross accounts receivable are 0.30 and 0.16, respectively. Examine allowance for possible overstatement of the allowance.
B. Accounts receivable turnovers are 10.0 and 6.6 and the ratios of uncollectible accounts receivable to gross accounts receivable are 0.30 and 0.16, respectively. Examine allowance for possible understatement of the allowance.
C. Accounts receivable turnovers are 14.3 and 8.0 and the ratios of uncollectible accounts receivable to gross accounts receivable is 0.42 and 0.20, respectively. Examine allowance for possible overstatement of the allowance.
D. Accounts receivable turnovers are 14.3 and 8.0 and the ratios of uncollectible accounts receivable to gross accounts receivable are 0.42 and 0.20, respectively. Examine allowance for possible understatement of the allowance.

AUD 3-Q41 A301. An auditor's analytical procedures indicate a lower than expected return on an equity method investment. This situation most likely could have been caused by

A. An error in recording amortization of the excess of the investor's cost over the investment's underlying book value.
B. The investee's decision to reduce cash dividends declared per share of its common stock.
C. An error in recording the unrealized gain from an increase in the fair value of available-for sale securities in the income account for trading securities.
D. A substantial fluctuation in the price of the investee's common stock on a national stock exchange.

AUD 3-Q42 A1353. Which of the following procedures is performed first for unreturned positive confirmations of accounts receivable?

A. Comparing current sales with budgeted sales.
B. Sending second requests for confirmation of accounts receivable.
C. Performing subsequent procedures.
D. Asking the client to obtain additional correspondence from the customers.

AUD 3-Q43 A58. An auditor is required to confirm accounts receivable if the accounts receivable balances are

A. Older than the prior year.
B. Material to the financial statements.
C. Smaller than expected.
D. Subject to valuation estimates.

AUD 3-Q44 A121. In confirming a client's accounts receivable in prior years, an auditor discovered many differences between recorded account balances and confirmation replies. These differences were resolved and were not misstatements. In defining the sampling unit for the current year's audit, the auditor most likely would choose

A. Customers with credit balances.
B. Small account balances.
C. Individual overdue balances.
D. Individual invoices.

AUD 3-Q45 A59. Under which of the following circumstances should an auditor consider confirming the terms of a large complex sale?

A. When the assessed level of control risk over the sale is low.
B. When the assessed level of detection risk over the sale is high.
C. When the combined assessed level of inherent and control risk over the sale is moderate.
D. When the combined assessed level of inherent and control risk over the sale is high.

AUD 3-Q46 A33. Which of the following strategies most likely could improve the response rate of the confirmations of accounts receivable?

A. Restrict the selection of accounts to be confirmed to those customers with large balances.
B. Include a list of items or invoices that constitute the customers' account balances.
C. Explain to customers that discrepancies will be investigated by an independent third party.
D. Ask customers to respond to the confirmation requests directly to the auditor by fax.

AUD 3-Q47 A244. The blank form of accounts receivable confirmations may be less efficient than the positive form because

A. Shipping documents need to be inspected.
B. Recipients may sign the forms without proper investigation.
C. More nonresponses to the requests are likely to occur.
D. Subsequent cash receipts need to be verified.

AUD 3-Q48 A147. When an auditor decides to confirm accounts receivable balances rather than individual invoices, it most likely would be beneficial to include with the confirmations

A. Copies of the client's shipping documents that support the account balances.
B. List of the items that the customer typically purchases
C. Client-prepared statements of account that show the details of the account balances.
D. Copies of the customers' purchase orders that support the account balances.

AUD 3-Q49 A366. Johnson is engaged in the audit of a utility which supplies power to a residential community. All accounts receivable balances are small and internal control is effective. Customers are billed bi-monthly. In order to determine the validity of the accounts receivable balances at the balance sheet date, Johnson would most likely

A. Examine evidence of subsequent cash receipts instead of sending confirmation requests.
B. Send positive confirmation requests.
C. Send negative confirmation requests.
D. Use statistical sampling instead of sending confirmation requests.

AUD 3-Q50 A326. During the confirmation of accounts receivable, an auditor receives a confirmation via the client's fax machine. Which of the following actions should an auditor take?

A. Not accept the confirmation and select another customer's balance to confirm.
B. Not accept the confirmation and treat it as an exception.
C. Accept the confirmation and file it in the working papers.
D. Accept the confirmation but verify the source and content through a telephone call to the respondent.

AUD 3-Q51 A389. Auditor confirmation of accounts payable balances at the balance sheet date may be unnecessary because

A. This is a duplication of cutoff tests.
B. Accounts payable balances at the balance sheet date may not be paid before the audit is completed.
C. Correspondence with the audit client's attorney will reveal all legal action by vendors for nonpayment.
D. There is likely to be other reliable external evidence available to support the balances.

AUD 3-Q52 A424. An auditor would be least likely to use confirmations in connection with the audit of

A. Inventories.
B. Long-term debt.
C. Property, plant, and equipment.
D. Stockholders' equity.

AUD 3-Q53 A1396. An auditor will most likely use computer-assisted audit techniques, rather than manual techniques, when it is necessary to

A. Examine all data in an accounts payable file.
B. Review approval of dividends.
C. Verify unrecorded legal liabilities.
D. Assess compliance with policies and procedures related to information security.

AUD 3-Q54 A71. An auditor is considering whether the omission of the confirmation of investments impairs the auditor's ability to support a previously expressed unmodified opinion. The auditor need not perform this omitted procedure if

A. The results of alternative procedures that were performed compensate for the omission.
B. The auditor's assessed level of detection risk is low.
C. The omission is documented in a communication with the audit committee.
D. No individual investment is material to the financial statements taken as a whole.

AUD 3-Q55 A74. Subsequent to issuing a report on audited financial statements, a CPA discovers that the accounts receivable confirmation process omitted a number of accounts that are material, in the aggregate. Which of the following actions should the CPA take immediately?

A. Bring the matter to the attention of the board of directors or audit committee.
B. Withdraw the auditor's report from those persons currently relying on it.
C. Perform alternative procedures to verify account balances.
D. Discuss the potential financial statement adjustments with client management.

AUD 3-Q56 A190. On March 1, Green, CPA, expressed an unmodified opinion on the financial statements of Ajax Co. On July 1, Green's internal inspection program discovered that engagement personnel failed to observe Ajax's physical inventory. Green believes that this omission impairs Green's ability to support the unmodified opinion. If Ajax's creditors are currently relying on Green's opinion, Green should first

A. Request Ajax's management to communicate to its creditors that Green's opinion should not be relied on.
B. Reissue Green's auditor's report with an emphasis of matter paragraph describing the departure from GAAS.
C. Undertake to apply the alternative procedures that would provide a satisfactory basis for Green's opinion.
D. Advise Ajax's board of directors to disclose this development in its next interim report.

AUD 3-Q57 A155. After an audit report is issued, an auditor discovers that an important audit procedure was not performed. Which of the following procedures would an auditor take first?

A. Determine if alternative procedures were performed to compensate for the omitted procedure.
B. Let the current report stand and correct material errors on the next audit report.
C. Immediately notify known users of the omitted audit procedure.
D. Require that the client notify financial statements users of the omitted procedures.

AUD 3-Q58 A1374. The client asked the auditor to audit financial statements covering the current year. The auditor did not observe at the prior year's physical inventory. Which of the following actions would the auditor most likely take?

A. Withdraw from the engagement and provide no assurance on the current year's financial statements.
B. Rely on management's representation that the prior year's balances are correct.
C. Audit the financial statements and express an opinion with a scope limitation.
D. Audit the prior year inventory using alternative substantive procedures.

AUD 3-Q59 A35. In establishing the existence and ownership of long-term investments in the form of publicly-traded stock, an auditor most likely would inspect the securities or

A. Correspond with the investee company to verify the number of shares owned.
B. Confirm the number of shares owned that are held by an independent custodian.
C. Apply analytical procedures to the dividend income and investments accounts.
D. Inspect the cash receipts journal for amounts that could represent the sale of securities.

AUD 3-Q60 A432. Which of the following is not one of the auditor's primary objectives in an audit of marketable securities?

A. To determine whether securities are authentic.
B. To determine whether securities are the property of the client.
C. To determine whether securities actually exist.
D. To determine whether securities are properly classified on the balance sheet.

AUD 3-Q61 A42. To obtain assurance that all inventory items in a client's inventory listing are valid, an auditor most likely would trace

A. Inventory tags noted during the auditor's observation to items listed in receiving reports and vendors' invoices.
B. Items listed in receiving reports and vendors' invoices to the inventory listing.
C. Inventory tags noted during the auditor's observation to items in the inventory listing.
D. Items in the inventory listing to inventory tags and the auditor's recorded count sheets.

AUD 3-Q62 A23. The auditor's inventory observation test counts are traced to the client's inventory listing to test for which of the following financial statement assertions?

A. Completeness.
B. Rights and obligations.
C. Valuation or allocation.
D. Presentation and disclosure.

AUD 3-Q63 A262. As part of the process of observing a client's physical inventories, an auditor should be alert to

A. The inclusion of any obsolete or damaged goods.
B. Any change in the method of pricing from prior years.
C. The existence of outstanding purchase commitments.
D. The verification of inventory values assigned to goods in process.

AUD 3-Q64 A302. Under which of the following conditions may an auditor's observation procedure for inventory, be performed during or after the end of the period under audit?

A. When the client maintains periodic inventory records.
B. When the auditor finds minimal variations in client records and test counts in prior periods.
C. When total inventory has not varied more than 5% in the last five years.
D. When well-kept perpetual inventory records are checked by the client periodically by comparisons with physical counts.

AUD 3-Q65 A178. A portion of a client's inventory is in public warehouses. Evidence of the existence of this merchandise can most efficiently be acquired through which of the following methods?

A. Analytical procedures.
B. Confirmation.
C. Calculation.
D. Inquiry.

AUD 3-Q66 A353. An auditor will usually trace the details of the test counts made during the observation of the physical inventory to the final inventory schedule. This audit procedure is undertaken to provide evidence that items physically present and observed by the auditor at the time of the physical inventory count are

A. Owned by the client.
B. Not obsolete.
C. Physically present at the time of the preparation of the final inventory schedule.
D. Included in the final inventory schedule.

AUD 3-Q67 A226. Which of the following procedures would an auditor most likely perform regarding litigation?

A. Confirm directly with the clerk of the court that the client's litigation is properly disclosed.
B. Discuss with management its policies and procedures for identifying and evaluating litigation.
C. Inspect the legal documents in the client's lawyer's possession regarding pending litigation.
D. Confirm the details of pending litigation with the client's adversaries' legal representatives.

AUD 3-Q68 A234. A client is a defendant in a patent infringement lawsuit by a major competitor. Which of the following items would least likely be included in the attorney's response to the auditor's letter of inquiry?

A. A description of potential litigation in other matters or related to an unfavorable verdict in the patent infringement lawsuit.
B. A discussion of case progress and the strategy currently in place by client management to resolve the lawsuit.
C. An evaluation of the probability of loss and a statement of the amount or range of loss if an unfavorable outcome is reasonably possible.
D. An evaluation of the ability of the client to continue as a going concern if the verdict is unfavorable and maximum damages are awarded.

AUD 3-Q69 A198. Which of the following procedures would an auditor most likely perform to assist in the evaluation of loss contingencies?

A. Checking arithmetic accuracy of the accounting records.
B. Performing appropriate analytical procedures.
C. Obtaining a letter of audit inquiry from the client's lawyer.
D. Reading the financial statements, including footnotes.

AUD 3-Q70 A203. An auditor requests a client to send letters of audit inquiry to attorneys who have been consulted concerning litigation, claims, and assessments. The primary reason for this request is to obtain

A. The attorneys' assurance that litigation, claims, and assessments that are probable of assertion are properly accounted for.
B. Corroboration of the information furnished by management concerning litigation, claims, and assessments.
C. A description of litigation, claims, and assessments that have a reasonable possibility of unfavorable outcomes.
D. The opinion of an expert whether any loss contingencies are reasonably possible, probable, or remote.

AUD 3-Q71 A278. Which of the following procedures most likely would assist an auditor to identify litigation, claims, and assessments?

A. Inspect checks included with the client's cutoff bank statement.
B. Obtain a letter of representations from the client's underwriter of securities.
C. Apply ratio analysis on the current-year's liability accounts.
D. Read the file of correspondence from taxing authorities.

AUD 3-Q72 A304. What is an auditor's primary method to corroborate information on litigation, claims, and assessments?

A. Examining legal invoices sent by the client's attorney.
B. Verifying attorney-client privilege through interviews.
C. Reviewing the response from the client's lawyer to a letter of audit inquiry.
D. Reviewing the written representation letter obtained from management.

AUD 3-Q73 A174. In auditing contingent liabilities, which of the following procedures would an auditor most likely perform?

A. Confirm the details of outstanding purchase orders.
B. Apply analytical procedures to accounts payable.
C. Read the minutes of the board of directors' meetings.
D. Perform tests of controls on the cash disbursement activities.

AUD 3-Q74 A144. Which of the following statements extracted from a client's lawyer's letter concerning litigation, claims, and assessments most likely would cause the auditor to request clarification?

A. "We believe that the possible liability to the company is nominal in amount."
B. "We believe that the action can be settled for less than the damages claimed."
C. "We believe that the plaintiff's case against the company is without merit."
D. "We believe that the company will be able to defend this action successfully."

AUD 3-Q75 A349. A CPA has received an attorney's letter in which no significant disagreements with the client's assessments of contingent liabilities were noted. The resignation of the client's lawyer shortly after receipt of the letter should alert the auditor that

A. Undisclosed un-asserted claims may have arisen.
B. The attorney was unable to form a conclusion with respect to the significance of litigation, claims and assessments.
C. The auditor must begin a completely new procedures over contingent liabilities.
D. An adverse opinion will be necessary.

AUD 3-Q76 A416. Auditors often request that the audit client send a letter of inquiry to those attorneys who have been consulted with respect to litigations, claims, or assessments. The primary reason for this request is to provide the auditor with

A. An estimate of the dollar amount of the probable loss.
B. An expert opinion as to whether a loss is possible, probable, or remote.
C. Information concerning the progress of cases to date.
D. Corroborative evidential matter.

AUD 3-Q77 A206. An auditor believes that there is substantial doubt about an entity's ability to continue as a going concern for a reasonable period of time. In evaluating the entity's plans for dealing with the adverse effects of future conditions and events, the auditor most likely would consider, as a mitigating factor, the entity's plans to

A. Extend the due dates of existing loans.
B. Operate at increased levels of production.
C. Accelerate expenditures for research and development projects.
D. Issue stock options to key executives.

AUD 3-Q78 A243. A CPA firm is completing the fieldwork for an audit of Swenson Co. for the current year ended December 31. The manager in charge of the audit is performing the final steps in the evidence accumulation phase of the audit and notes that there have been several changes in Swenson during the year under audit. Which of the following items would indicate there could be substantial doubt about Swenson's ability to continue as a going concern for a reasonable period of time?

A. Cash infusion by a venture capital firm.
B. Recurring working capital shortages.
C. A lack of significant contracts with new customers.
D. Term debt refinanced with a new bank.

AUD 3-Q79 A175. An auditor believes there is substantial doubt about an entity's ability to continue as a going concern for a reasonable period of time. In evaluating the entity's plans for dealing with the adverse effects of future conditions and events, the auditor most likely would consider, as a mitigating factor, the entity's plans to

A. Purchase production facilities currently being leased from a third party.
B. Postpone expenditures to upgrade its information technology system.
C. Pay cash dividends that are in arrears to the preferred stockholders.
D. Increase the useful lives of plant assets for depreciation purposes.

AUD 3-Q80 A176. An auditor concludes that there is substantial doubt about an issuer entity's ability to continue as a going concern for a reasonable period of time. The entity's financial statements adequately disclose its financial difficulties. Under these circumstances, the auditor's report is required to include an explanatory paragraph that specifically uses the phrase(s)

	"Except for the effects of such adjustments"	"Possible discontinuance of the entity's operations"
A.	Yes	Yes
B.	Yes	No
C.	No	Yes
D.	No	No

AUD 3-Q81 A143. Which of the following conditions or events most likely would cause an auditor to have substantial doubt about an entity's ability to continue as a going concern?

A. Significant related party transactions are pervasive.
B. Usual trade credit from suppliers is denied.
C. Arrearages in preferred stock dividends are paid.
D. Restrictions on the disposal of principal assets are present.

AUD 3-Q82 A145. After considering management's plans, an auditor concludes that there is substantial doubt about a client's ability to continue as a going concern for a reasonable period of time. The auditor's responsibility includes

A. Issuing an adverse opinion
B. Indicating to the client's audit committee whether management's plans for dealing with the adverse effects of the financial difficulties can be effectively implemented.
C. Considering the adequacy of disclosure about the client's possible inability to continue as a going concern.
D. Issuing a qualified opinion.

AUD 3-Q83 A47. Which of the following audit procedures most likely would assist an auditor in identifying conditions and events that may indicate there could be substantial doubt about an entity's ability to continue as a going concern?

A. Confirmation of accounts receivable from principal customers.
B. Reconciliation of interest expense with debt outstanding.
C. Confirmation of bank balances.
D. Review of compliance with terms of debt agreements.

AUD 3-Q84 A54. An auditor should consider which of the following when evaluating the ability of a company to continue as a going concern?

A. Audit fees.
B. Future assurance services.
C. Management's plans for disposal of assets.
D. Issuance of new preferred stock.

AUD 3-Q85 A232. In evaluating the reasonableness of an entity's accounting estimates, an auditor most likely concentrates on key factors and assumptions that are

A. Stable and not sensitive to variation.
B. Objective and not susceptible to bias.
C. Deviations from historical patterns.
D. Similar to industry guidelines.

AUD 3-Q86 A249. Which of the following statements is correct regarding accounting estimates?

A. The auditor's objective is to evaluate whether accounting estimates are reasonable in the circumstances.
B. Accounting estimates should be used when data concerning past events can be accumulated in a timely, cost-effective manner.
C. An important accounting estimate is management's listing of accounts receivable greater than 90 days past due.
D. Accounting estimates should not be used when the outcome of future events related to the estimated item is unknown.

AUD 3-Q87 A65. Each of the following is a type of known misstatement, except

A. An inaccuracy in processing data
B. The misapplication of accounting principles.
C. Differences between management and the auditor's judgment regarding estimates
D. A difference between the classification of a reported financial statement element and the classification according to generally accepted accounting principles.

AUD 3-Q88 A233. A client decides not to make an auditor's proposed adjustments that collectively are not material and wants the auditor to issue the report based on the unadjusted numbers. Which of the following statements is correct regarding the financial statement presentation?

A. The financial statements are free from material misstatement, and no disclosure is required in the notes to the financial statements.
B. The financial statements do not conform with generally accepted accounting principles (GAAP).
C. The financial statements contain unadjusted misstatements that should result in a modified opinion.
D. The financial statements are free from material misstatement, but disclosure of the proposed adjustments is required in the notes to the financial statements.

AUD 3-Q89 A310. An auditor finds several errors in the financial statements that the client prefers not to correct. The auditor determines that the errors are not material in the aggregate. Which of the following actions by the auditor is most appropriate?

A. Document the errors in the summary of uncorrected errors, and document the conclusion that the errors do not cause the financial statements to be misstated.
B. Document the conclusion that the errors do not cause the financial statements to be misstated, but do not summarize uncorrected errors in the working papers.
C. Summarize the uncorrected errors in the working papers, but do not document whether the errors cause the financial statements to be misstated.
D. Do not summarize the uncorrected errors in the working papers, and do not document a conclusion about whether the uncorrected errors cause the financial statements to be misstated.

AUD 3-Q90 A260. Which of the following actions should the auditor take in response to discovering a deviation from the prescribed control procedure?

A. Make inquiries to understand the potential consequence of the deviation.
B. Assume that the deviation is an isolated occurrence without audit significance.
C. Report the matter to the next higher level of authority within the entity.
D. Decrease the sample size of tests of controls.

AUD 3-Q91 A265. In obtaining written representations from management, materiality limits ordinarily would apply to representations related to

A. Amounts concerning related party transactions.
B. Fraud involving members of management.
C. The availability of financial records.
D. The completeness of minutes of directors' meetings.

AUD 3-Q92 A60. For which of the following matters is a management representation letter required to contain specific representations?

A. Length of a material contract with a new customer.
B. Information concerning fraud by the CFO.
C. Reason for a significant increase in revenue over the prior year.
D. The competency and objectivity of the internal audit department.

AUD 3-Q93 A305. Which of the following management roles would typically be acknowledged in a management representation letter?

A. Management has the responsibility for the design of controls to detect fraud.
B. Management communicates its views on ethical behavior to its employees.
C. Management's knowledge of fraud is communicated to the audit committee.
D. Management's compensation is contingent upon operating results.

AUD 3-Q94 A161. Which of the following statements would not normally be included in a management representation letter for a review of interim financial information?

A. To the best of our knowledge and belief, no events have occurred subsequent to the balance sheet and through the date of this letter that would require adjustment to or disclosure in the interim financial information.
B. We acknowledge our responsibility for the design and implementation of programs and controls to prevent and detect fraud.
C. We understand that a review consists principally of performing analytical procedures and making inquiries about the interim financial information.
D. We have made available to you all financial records and related data.

AUD 3-Q95 A1347. Which of the following statements would an auditor most likely require management to indicate in a written representation letter obtained for an audit?

A. Management acknowledges its responsibilities for the design and implementation of programs and controls to detect fraud.
B. Management plans to expand into international operations during the next few years.
C. Management believes the financial statements are accurately stated in accordance with generally accepted auditing standards (GAAS).
D. Management believes the company is the premier company in its industry regarding service to customers.

AUD 3-Q96 A1348. An auditor is reporting on comparative financial statements for three years. Which of the following statements is correct regarding written representations from management?

A. The representation letter needs to address the prior year's financial statements not covered in the report.
B. The representation letter needs to address only the most current year covered in the report.
C. The representation letter needs to address only the two most recent years covered in the report.
D. The representation letter needs to address all of the years being covered in the report.

AUD 3-Q97 A237. Which of the following items would most likely require an adjustment to the financial statements for the year ended December 31, year 1?

A. Uninsured loss of inventories purchased in year 1 as a result of a flood in year 2.
B. Settlement of litigation in year 2 over an event that occurred in year 2.
C. Loss on an uncollectible trade receivable recorded in year 1 from a customer that declared bankruptcy in year 2.
D. Proceeds from a capital stock issuance in year 2 which was being approved by the board of directors in year 1.

AUD 3-Q98 A329. An auditor should be aware of subsequent events that provide evidence concerning conditions that did not exist at year end but arose after year end. These events may be important to the auditor because they may

A. Require adjustments to the financial statements as of the year end.
B. Have been recorded based on preliminary accounting estimates.
C. Require disclosure to keep the financial statements from being misleading.
D. Have been recorded based on year-end tests for asset obsolescence.

AUD 3-Q99 A239. Which of the following procedures would an auditor most likely perform in obtaining evidence about subsequent events?

A. Examine changes in the quoted market prices of investments purchased since the year end.
B. Compare the latest available interim financial information with the financial statements being reported upon.
C. Apply analytical procedures to the details of the balance sheet accounts that were tested at interim dates.
D. Inquire about payroll checks that were recorded before the year end but cashed after the year end.

AUD 3-Q100 A146. Which of the following procedures would an auditor most likely perform to obtain evidence about the occurrence of subsequent events?

A. Determine whether inventory ordered before the year end was included in the physical count.
B. Inquire about payroll checks that were recorded before year end but cashed after year end.
C. Investigate changes in capital stock recorded after year end.
D. Review tax returns prepared by management after year end.

AUD 3-Q101 A411. Under which of the following circumstances may audited financial statements contain a note disclosing a subsequent event which is labeled unaudited?

A. When the subsequent event does not require adjustment of the financial statements.
B. When the event occurs after the completion of fieldwork and before issuance of the auditor's report.
C. When audit procedures with respect to the subsequent event were not performed by the auditor.
D. When the event occurs between the date of the auditor's original report and the date of the reissuance of the report.

AUD 3-Q102 A263. After issuing an auditor's report, an auditor has no obligation to make continuing inquiries concerning audited financial statements unless

A. Information about a material transaction that occurred just after the auditor's report was issued is deemed to be reliable.
B. A final resolution is made of a contingent liability that had been disclosed in the financial statements.
C. Information that existed at the report date and may affect the report comes to the auditor's attention.
D. An event occurs just after the auditor's report was issued that affects the entity's ability to continue as a going concern.

AUD 3-Q103 A177. After issuing an auditor's report, an auditor becomes aware of facts that existed at the report date that would have affected the report had the auditor known of the facts at the time. What is the *first thing* the auditor should do?

A. Notify each member of the board of directors that the auditor's report may not be associated with the financial statements from this point forward.
B. Issue revised financial statements and auditor's report describing the reason for the revision in a note to the financial statements.
C. Determine whether there are persons currently relying on, or likely to rely on, the financial statements and whether those persons would attach importance to the information.
D. Notify regulatory agencies having jurisdiction over the client that the auditor's report should not be relied upon from this point forward.

AUD 3-Q104 A1368. Before issuing an unmodified report on a compliance audit, an auditor becomes aware of an instance of material noncompliance occurring after the period covered by the audit. The least appropriate response by the auditor would be to

A. Discuss the matter with management and, if appropriate, those charged with governance.
B. Issue a modified compliance report describing the subsequent noncompliance.
C. Determine whether the noncompliance relates to conditions that existed as of period end or arose subsequent to the reporting period.
D. Modify the standard compliance report to include a paragraph describing the nature of the subsequent noncompliance.

AUD 3-Q105 A1370. Which of the following events that occurred after a client's calendar-year end, but before the audit report date, would require disclosure in the notes to the financial statements, but no adjustment in the financial statements?

A. New convertible bonds are issued to expand the company's product line.
B. A loss is reported on uncollectible accounts of an acknowledged distressed customer.
C. A fixed asset used in operations is sold at a substantial profit.
D. Negotiations have resulted in compensation adjustments for union employees retroactive to the fourth quarter.

AUD 3-Q106 A1379. Which of the following factors should an auditor consider most important upon subsequent discovery of facts that existed at the date of the audit report and would have affected the report?

A. The cost-to-benefit ratio of performing additional procedures to better determine the impact of the newly discovered facts.
B. The potential impact on financial statements and associated audit reports for the previous five years.
C. The client's willingness to pay additional fees for the additional procedures to be performed.
D. The client's willingness to issue revised financial statements or other disclosures to persons known to be relying on the financial statement.

Multiple Choice – Solutions

AUD 3-Q1 A21. Choice C is correct. If an auditor concludes that additional information is needed to substantiate the balance in inventory, then additional substantive procedures must be performed to compensate.

Choices A and B are incorrect. An auditor may still perform additional auditing procedures to prevent issuing a qualified opinion or a disclaimer.

Choice D is incorrect because a statement from management would not compensate for the lack of evidence obtained.

AUD 3-Q2 A70. Choice B is correct. Pre-numbered receiving reports are considered to be internal evidence – evidence that is sourced from the client itself. This type of evidence (internal) is considered to be the least reliable (versus external).

Choices A, C, and D are all forms of external evidence and are sourced from third-parties. External evidence is considered more reliable than internal evidence.

AUD 3-Q3 A268. Choice A is correct. Audit evidence should be sufficient and appropriate.

Choice B is incorrect as this is not the relevant term.

Choice C is incorrect as this is the level of required assurance.

Choice D is incorrect as this is not the relevant term.

AUD 3-Q4 A32. Choice A is correct. Attribute sampling is used when performing tests of controls and serves the purpose of testing for a particular attribute. An attribute is defined as a qualitative characteristic that a unit of a population possesses or does not possess. As such, an auditor is testing to determine whether the attribute of the correct posting exists.

Choice B is incorrect, as estimating the amount in an expense account is a substantive test and requires variable sampling.

Choice C is incorrect because evaluating the reasonableness of depreciation expense is a substantive test and requires the use of variable sampling.

Choice D is incorrect because selecting receivables for confirmation involves a variable sampling approach.

AUD 3-Q5 A123. Choice A is correct. Attribute sampling is used by auditors to test whether internal controls are operating effectively. In this scenario, the auditor is testing whether purchase orders are properly approved (the proper approval is the attribute) by supervisors.

Choice B, C, and D are incorrect as these are all substantive tests rather than control tests and an auditor would likely use variables sampling or PPS sampling – not attribute sampling.

AUD 3-Q6 A453. The correct answer is B. Attribute sampling is a statistical method used to estimate the proportion of items in a population containing a specific characteristic or attribute of interest. This proportion is called the occurrence rate and is the ratio of the items containing the specific attribute to the total number of population items. Attribute sampling is commonly used in performing tests of compliance. Attribute sampling would be used to estimate the percentage of slow-moving items, based on whatever criteria the auditor establishes in defining "slow-moving."

Choice A is incorrect because the average price of inventory items is used for estimation sampling which uses the average items value for estimating the value of the population.

Choice C is incorrect because dollar value inventory is not a type of sampling.

Choice D is incorrect because the physical quantity of inventory items represents the population size and is required information when using any sampling method.

AUD 3-Q7 A437. The correct answer is B. Since Jones is interested in determining the rate of occurrence of errors, he should use attribute sampling.

Choice A is incorrect because discovery sampling deals with the probability of discovering at least one error.

Choice C is incorrect because stratified sampling deals with elements of the total population being divided into 2 or more sub parts.

Choice D is incorrect because variables sampling is used for substantive testing (e.g., test of balances).

DISCOVERY sampling: For some audit procedures, the auditor expects to find no exceptions, but, if even one exception is found, it is sufficient to require extensive follow-up. Discovery sampling deals with the probability of discovering at least one error.

ATTRIBUTE sampling: This is a statistical method used to estimate the proportion of items in a population containing a characteristic (attribute) of interest. Auditors are usually interested in the occurrences of errors.

STRATIFIED sampling: This is a sampling method in which all elements of the total population are divided into two or more sub-populations. Each sub-population is then independently tested and statistically measured.

VARIABLES sampling: The objective of this type of sampling is to measure the dollar value of an account or some similar total. Variable sampling is used primarily for substantive tests (tests of balances).

AUD 3-Q8 A184. Choice B is correct. The risk of incorrect acceptance occurs when the auditor accepts the account balance and concludes that it is not materially misstated when in fact it is materially misstated.

Choice A is incorrect as incorrect rejection would occur when the auditor concludes that the balance is materially misstated when in fact it is not.

Choices C and D are incorrect as they refer to controls testing – not dollar amounts.

AUD 3-Q9 A109. Choice B is correct. Non-sampling risk can be affected by performing inadequate or inappropriate audit procedures that can cause the auditor to fail to recognize material misstatements.

Choice A is incorrect as this is the definition of sampling risk.

Choice C is incorrect as this is the definition of audit risk, not sampling risk.

Choice D is incorrect as this is the definition of non-sampling risk – not sampling risk.

AUD 3-Q10 A215. Choice D is correct. The auditor's allowable risk of assessing control risk too low has an indirect relation to the sample size when performing test of controls. For example, if there is a high level of acceptable control risk, the sample size will be lower.

Choice A is incorrect as materiality levels do not have an effect on controls testing.

Choice B is incorrect as this does not have an effect on the sample size.

Choice C is incorrect as the level of detection risk for an account does not have an effect on the sample size of controls testing.

AUD 3-Q11 A266. Choice B is correct. Assessing control risk too high is the result of the computed upper deviation rate in the auditor's sample exceeding the tolerable rate but the actual deviation rate is less than the tolerable rate.

Choice A is incorrect as this would result in the auditor assessing control risk too low.

Choice C is incorrect as there would be no sampling error in this case.

Choice D is incorrect as there would be no sampling error in this case.

AUD 3-Q12 A287. Choice B is correct. When there is a large population, population size will not have an effect on the sample size.

Choice A, C, and D are incorrect because these items have an effect on the sample size.

AUD 3-Q13 A169. Choice D is correct. When performing statistical sampling, the population size has little effect on the sample size.

Choice A is incorrect as the expected population deviation rate has a direct effect on the sample size.

Choice B is incorrect as the sample size will not necessarily double.

Choice C is incorrect because the sample size will decrease.

AUD 3-Q14 A140. Choice D is correct. When performing statistical sampling on internal controls, the population size has little or no effect on the sample size.

Choice A is incorrect. This would not cause an increase of 67% in the sample size.

Choice B is incorrect as the sample size is directly proportional to the expected error rate.

Choice C is incorrect as there is an inverse relationship between the tolerable error rate and the sample size.

AUD 3-Q15 A415. When planning a statistical test, the required sample size will be determined after consideration of the following factors:
1. Population size;
2. Expected error rate;
3. Specified precision;
4. Specified confidence level (reliability).

The population size is normally given. The expected error rate would be estimated from prior experience or from information gained from preliminary audit procedures. The specified precision is the difference between the expected error rate and the upper error limit that would be acceptable. The confidence level is the likelihood that a correct decision has been made. The following generalizations can be made assuming all other variables are constant:
  i. The greater the population size, the greater the sample size.
  ii. The greater the expected error rate, the greater the sample size.
  iii. The tighter the specified precision, the greater the sample size.
  iv. The greater the specified confidence level, the greater the sample size.

The correct answer is C. When the desired reliability decreases (specified confidence level) the required sample size will be smaller.

Answer choices A, B, and D all would require larger sample sizes.

AUD 3-Q16 A279. Choice A is correct. The primary objective of probability PPS is to identify overstatement errors.

Choice B is incorrect because PPS requires a larger sample size.

Choice C is incorrect because the purpose of PPS sampling is to estimate the dollar value of error in a population.

Choice D is incorrect as PPS sampling does not identify zero and negative balances.

AUD 3-Q17 A343. The correct answer is B. Random number tables can be used if the auditor establishes correspondence between the digits in the table and the population. The auditor can renumber the population to obtain correspondence. The systematic sampling technique has the advantage of enabling the auditor to obtain a sample from a population of unnumbered documents. If the documents are unnumbered, there is no necessity to number them, as required under the random table selection technique. The auditor may just count off the sampling interval to select the documents.

Choices A and D are wrong because random sampling/random number tables are sampling selection techniques and are possible.

Choice C is wrong because stratification is merely a technique of dividing a population into homogeneous sub-groups (groups with similar characteristics). Once the population is stratified, a sampling selection technique would still be applied (i.e., random number table, systematic, cluster).

AUD 3-Q18 A380. The correct answer is D. Estimation sampling for variables; estimate the average item value as the basis for estimating the total value of the population. Ratio and difference estimation represent alternatives to estimation sampling for variables. In ratio estimation, the auditors use a sample to estimate the ratio of the audited value of the population to its book value. In difference estimation, the auditors use a sample to estimate the average difference between the audited value and book value of items in a population. The ratio or differences in audited and book values of population items form a ratio or difference population. A ratio or difference population generally has a smaller standard deviation (less variability) than does the population of item dollar values in other sampling methods. As a result, a smaller sample size is required.

The keyword is "major reason", answers A, B and C are possible but not the major reason for audit efficiency, which makes them incorrect.

AUD 3-Q19 A435. The correct answer is B. These are the four conditions are necessary in order to use ratio estimation:
1. Each population item must have a book value.
2. The total population book value must correspond to the sum of the item book values.
3. An audited value must be ascertained for each sample item.
4. Differences between audited and book values must not be too rare.

In ratio estimation, the number of differences is a dominant factor in determining the sample size required to achieve given levels of reliability and precision, with the size of the sample varying inversely with the frequency of the differences.

The ratio estimation method is based on the relationship between the total audited value of the sample items and the total book value of these same items. Use of this method is inappropriate where a book value for each sample item is unknown.

Choice A is incorrect because this is information you would need to know when using ratio estimation sampling.

Choice C is incorrect because there are observed differences which would mean it's not rare.

Choice D is incorrect because having proportional audited and book values would mean that each population item has a book value.

AUD 3-Q20 A1344. The correct answer choice is C. Sample size has a direct relationship, so, if control risk is lower, then the sample size can be smaller. Control risk is the risk that your internal controls will not prevent misstatements.

Choice A is incorrect because sample size directly correlates with the level of risk and is therefore relevant.

Choice B is incorrect because you wouldn't need a larger sample when control risk is reduced.

Choice D is incorrect because sample size directly correlates with the level of risk and does have an effect.

AUD 3-Q21 A1378. The correct answer choice is D. The auditor should project the detected error to the entire population.

Choice A is incorrect because the auditor should not pass on the exceptions at this stage.

Choice B is incorrect because proposing an adjustment to purchases is not the proper action to do next.

Choice C is incorrect because there is no need to expand the sample size.

AUD 3-Q22 A48. Choice C is correct. Analytical procedures are used to evaluate financial information through possible relationships between financial and nonfinancial data. If there is a variation between the auditor's anticipated amount and actual amount, the auditor may investigate any significant variances. Choice C is not an analytical procedure because it does not compare financial and nonfinancial data – instead it is actually a statistical sampling method.

Choice A is incorrect because comparison of information to industry averages is a common analytical procedure.

Choice B is incorrect, as trend analysis is also considered to be a common analytical procedure.

Choice D is incorrect since comparing results to the prior year, as well as prior year's budget, is a common analytical procedure.

AUD 3-Q23 A97. Choice B is correct. Analytical procedures help define relationships between financial and nonfinancial data. Comparing inventory balances to sales transactions will help an auditor understand if the ending inventory balances appear reasonable.

Choice A is incorrect as this is a test of detail procedure.

Choice C is incorrect as this is an extrapolation of a statistical sampling procedure in order to evaluate sample results.

Choice D is incorrect as this is a test of detail procedure.

AUD 3-Q24 A444. The correct answer is D. The comparison of the financial information with information for a comparable prior period represents "analytical procedures."

Choice A is incorrect because it is an audit procedure known as "vouching."

Choice B is incorrect because it is an audit procedure called "cross referencing."

Choice C is incorrect because it is an audit procedure called "inquiry."

AUD 3-Q25 A224. Choice A is correct. Relationships among income statement accounts are more predictable than balance sheet accounts.

Choices B, C, and D are incorrect as these are all balance sheet accounts.

AUD 3-Q26 A318. Choice C is correct. Analytical procedures are most appropriate when testing income statement accounts.

Choices A, B, and D are incorrect as these are all balance sheet accounts.

AUD 3-Q27 A270. Choice C is correct. The decision whether to apply analytical procedures during substantive tests is determined by the precision and reliability of the data to develop expectations.

Choice A is incorrect as this is a substantive procedure.

Choices B and D are incorrect as these are not factors that are used when considering whether to apply analytical procedures.

AUD 3-Q28 A333. Choice B is correct. When developing analytical procedures, it is best to develop reasonable explanations for unexpected differences before talking to client management.

Choice A is incorrect as unaudited account balances are not reliable.

Choice C is incorrect as choice B would be a more effective procedure.

Choice D is incorrect as since the evidence is obtained from the client, it is not as reliable.

AUD 3-Q29 A24. Choice D is correct. When planning the audit, analytical procedures consist of the auditor reviewing the financial statements at a high level in order to obtain a better understanding of the client.

Choice A is incorrect because this is a substantive procedure.

Choice B is incorrect because scanning is typically a substantive audit procedure.

Choice C is incorrect because recalculating inventory extensions is also a substantive procedure that provides assurance over account balances. Choices A, B and C would be done after planning.

AUD 3-Q30 A269. Choice A is correct. When performing analytical procedures in the planning stage, the auditor would use unaudited information from internal quarterly reports.

Choices, B, C, and D are incorrect as these would not be proper sources of information when performing analytical procedures.

AUD 3-Q31 A282. Choice D is correct. Analytical procedures in the planning phase of an audit are used to enhance the auditor's understanding of the transactions and events that have occurred since the last audit.

Choice A is incorrect as the documentation of risk factors is not related to the performance of analytical procedures.

Choice B is incorrect as the identification of internal control activities is not related to the performance of analytical procedures.

Choice C is incorrect as discovering uncorrected misstatements occurs when analytical procedures are performed in conjunction with substantive testing.

AUD 3-Q32 A252. Choice C is correct. An auditor would most likely compare current-year balances to budgeted balances as a planning procedure.

Choices A, B, and D are incorrect as these are substantive tests performed during year-end testing.

AUD 3-Q33 A168. Choice B is correct. Analytical procedures performed during the planning phase of an audit usually use financial and nonfinancial data aggregated at a high level.

Choice A is incorrect as analytical procedures do not replace tests of controls. Note that analytical procedures are a substantive test.

Choice C is incorrect as analytical procedures do not involve the comparison of management assertions to auditor ratios.

Choice D is incorrect as analytical procedures do not assist an auditor in developing control risk.

AUD 3-Q34 A181. Choice A is correct. Comparing current-year to prior year sales volumes is an analytical procedure that is typically done in the planning stage of the audit.
Choice B and D are incorrect as these are not considered to be analytical procedures.

Choice C is incorrect as this procedure would not be done in the planning phase – it would likely be done in conjunction with substantive audit procedures.

AUD 3-Q35 A286. Choice C is correct. Cost of goods sold/average inventory is the inventory turnover ratio and helps the auditor assess the entity's performance.

Choice A is incorrect as it would not be useful to perform this calculation as it would not indicate anything about the entity's performance. It would make more sense to divide sales revenue by total assets.

Choice B is incorrect as it would not be useful to perform this calculation. It would make more sense to divide sales revenue by accounts receivable.

Choice D is incorrect as performing this calculation would not provide any useful information regarding the entity's performance.

AUD 3-Q36 A335. Choice B is correct. The auditor should perform analytical procedures on the revenue cycle as this is usually the most risky transaction cycle.

Choices A, C, and D are incorrect per the above explanation.

AUD 3-Q37 A142. Choice D is correct. The objective of performing analytical procedures in the final audit stage is to assess the reasonableness of the overall financial statements.

Choice A is incorrect as this is the purpose of performing analytical procedures during the planning stage of the audit.

Choice B is incorrect as this is the purpose of performing analytical procedures in conjunction with substantive audit procedures.

Choice C is incorrect as fraud assessment is not performed in the final review stage.

AUD 3-Q38 A152. Choice C is correct. Comparing the current year's financial statements to the previous years is final analytical procedures performed at the end of the audit. Final overall review procedures tend to be "big picture" procedures.

Choice A is incorrect as reading the board of directors' meeting minutes is not considered an analytical procedure.

Choice B is incorrect as this is not considered an analytical procedure.

Choice D is incorrect as this would not be considered an analytical procedure.

AUD 3-Q39 A15. Choice C is correct. When an entity has strong and effective internal controls, the auditor can rely on these controls.

Choice A is incorrect because the reliability of data is not affected by the type of accounting system a client uses as some clients use computerized or manual or a mix of both.

Choice B is incorrect as the basis of accounting does not affect the reliability of data and choice D is incorrect as the data processing system does not affect the reliability of data.

AUD 3-Q40 A214. Choice B is correct. Accounts receivable turnover is calculated as:

Accounts receivable turnover
= Net sales / Total Receivables
December 31, Previous year
= 1,000,000 / 100,000 = 10
December 31, Current year
= 2,000,000 / 300,000 = 6.7

Uncollectible accounts receivable ratio:
Uncollectible accounts receivable/Total receivables
December 31, Previous year = 30,000 / 100,000 = .3
December 31, Current year = 50,000 / 300,000 = .16

It appears that there is an understatement in the allowance account due to the fact that accounts receivable tripled whereas the allowance account decreased as a percentage of receivables.

Choices A, C, and D are incorrect per the above explanation.

AUD 3-Q41 A301. Choice A is correct. Under the equity method of accounting, the amortization of the excess of the investor's cost over the book value reduces the investor's income. This could lower the return on investment.

Choice B is incorrect. Dividends are reduced from the investment itself.

Choice C is incorrect. An error should have no impact on the calculated return on an equity method investment.

Choice D is incorrect. A substantial fluctuation in the price of the investee's common stock on a national stock exchange would have no impact as equity method investments are usually not reported at fair value.

AUD 3-Q42 A1353. The correct answer choice is B. Sending a second request for confirming accounts receivables is a normal procedure if the initial request doesn't prompt a response from the customer.

Choice A is incorrect because that is an analytical procedure typically used during the planning phase to determine potential accounts to look at further during substantive testing.

Choice C is incorrect because an auditor wouldn't perform subsequent procedures until later in the audit, after assessing both control risk and detection risk.

Choice D is incorrect because the confirmation should be performed by the auditor, not the client.

AUD 3-Q43 A58. Choice B is correct. The use of confirmations are required if the accounts receivable balance is material to the financial statements (AU-C 505)

Choice A is incorrect, as the aging of the receivable may affect its collectability but is not a requirement when determining whether to confirm the receivable.

Choice C is incorrect, as there is no requirement to send confirmations if the balance in accounts receivable is not material (see AU-C 505)

Choice D is incorrect because valuation estimates (bad debts) are linked to the age of the receivable and determines whether the receivable should be written off.

AUD 3-Q44 A121. Choice D is correct. The auditor would more than likely choose individual invoices in order to receive accurate responses based on an individual order. The differences in prior years were probably timing differences --- not misstatements, but can be time consuming to reconcile.

Choice A is incorrect as an auditor would not likely choose customers with credit balances.

Choice B is incorrect as the discrepancies in prior years would not cause the auditor to choose small account balances to test.

Choice C is incorrect as this would not be the auditor's primary focus.

AUD 3-Q45 A59. Choice D is correct. An auditor would consider confirming the terms of a sale if the risk of material misstatement (RMM) are high (recall RMM = IR × CR). If both inherent risk and control risk are high, then the detection risk must be reduced by the auditor, who would need to perform more procedures. One such procedure may include confirming the terms of a sale.

Choice A is incorrect because when the assessed level of control risk is low, then the overall RMM is low as well and there is a less likelihood that the auditor would confirm the terms of a large complex sale.

Choice B is incorrect because if detection risk is high, the RMM is low and it is less likely that the auditor would confirm the terms of a large complex sale.

Choice C is incorrect, as an auditor is more likely to perform additional auditing procedures when the inherent and control risk are high.

AUD 3-Q46 A33. Choice B is correct. Including details on the confirmation that make it easier for the responder to return the confirmation (such as amount owed) is likely to increase the response rate.

Choice A is incorrect because only including customers with large receivables is not likely to increase the response rate.

Choice C is incorrect as the customer may choose to agree with the confirmation amount listed to avoid an investigation.

Choice D is incorrect because faxed responses are less desirable by an auditor since the auditor will need to verify the source of the fax. Usually, faxed responses are a last-minute resort and are used when audit deadlines are looming.

AUD 3-Q47 A244. Choice C is correct. More nonresponses are likely to occur as greater effort is required for a response.

Choice A is incorrect as shipping documents are not required to be inspected when using the blank form.

Choice B is incorrect as blank forms do not include the account balance so recipients cannot simply sign off.

Choice D is incorrect as this is not a consequence of using the blank form.

AUD 3-Q48 A147. Choice C is correct. It would be helpful for the auditor to include a statement prepared by the client of how the accounts receivable balance is computed.

Choice A is incorrect as it would not be helpful to include shipping documents as this would not be useful to customers.

Choice B is incorrect as it would not be helpful to include this in the confirmation.

Choice D is incorrect as it would be more helpful to include individual purchase orders when the auditor confirms individual invoices.

AUD 3-Q49 A366. The correct answer is C. Direct communication with debtors is generally considered to be the most essential and conclusive step in the verification of accounts receivable. The positive confirmation calls for a reply in every case and the negative confirmation calls for a reply only in such cases where the debtor disagrees with the indicated balance due.

The negative form is useful particularly when internal control surrounding accounts receivable is considered to be effective, when a large number of small balances are involved, and when the auditor has no reason to believe the persons receiving the requests are unlikely to give them consideration.

Choice A is wrong because the examination of subsequent cash receipts is an added auditing procedure, but not a substitute for sending confirmation requests.

Choice B is wrong because positive confirmation isn't preferred for many small receivables when the company has effective internal controls.

Choice D is wrong because while statistical sampling may help to determine which accounts will be confirmed, it is not a substitute for the actual confirmation. Statistical sampling and confirmation of not incompatible.

AUD 3-Q50 A326. Choice D is correct. If the auditor receives a faxed confirmation, the auditor should accept the confirmation and verify the source and content through a telephone call.

Choices A, B, and C are incorrect due to the explanation above.

AUD 3-Q51 A389. The correct answer is D. The auditor will find in the client's possession externally created evidence such as vendors' invoices and statements which substantiate accounts payable. The auditor may find it unnecessary to confirm accounts payable for the reason that the accounts payable balance will be paid before the audit is completed, rather than that it not having been paid, as described in choice B, which is why that choice is incorrect.

Choice A is wrong because though it may be duplicating the cutoff tests, it is a choice in the structure of the audit.

Choice C is wrong because corresponding with the client's attorney should happen as part of the complete audit to support evidential matter.

AUD 3-Q52 A424. The correct answer is C. One would be "least" likely to use confirmations in connection with property, plant, and equipment.

Choices A, B and D would all use confirmations as shown below:
Choice A is incorrect because confirmations are frequently used to determine quantities held by others (e.g., consignment sales and inventory held in warehouses).

Choice B is incorrect because confirmations are used to determine amounts, due dates and interest rates for long-term debt.

Choice D is incorrect because confirmations are used to determine the number of shares of capital stock outstanding by a trustee or transfer agent.

AUD 3-Q53 A1396. The correct answer choice is A Examining an entire accounts payable file would be very time consuming but the computer-assisted audit techniques (CAAT) would save a significant amount of time and allow for 100% sampling.

Choice B is incorrect because the approval of dividends is done by reviewing the board minutes where the approval took place, so there would be no need for CAAT.

Choice C is incorrect because verifying unrecorded legal liabilities would not need CAAT but rather inquiry of the client's attorney.

Choice D is incorrect because this relates to internal controls and not transactions.

AUD 3-Q54 A71. Choice A is correct. If alternative procedures compensate for the omitted procedure, then the auditor need not perform the omitted procedure.

Choice B is incorrect because even if the auditor's assessed level of the detection risk is low, that would not be sufficient to compensate for an omitted procedure. The auditor would still need some sort of comfort to compensate for the lack of procedures performed. Remember, the auditor must plan and perform the audit to ensure that detection risk is low.

Choice C is incorrect because communicating an item to the audit committee does not compensate for the omitted procedure. The auditor would still need some sort of comfort to compensate for the lack of procedures performed.

Choice D is incorrect because even if no individual investment was material to the financial statements, the auditor would need to consider the total amount of investments and its materiality to the financial statements taken as a whole.

AUD 3-Q55 A74. Choice C is correct. When an auditor omits a procedure, the first step needed to be done is to perform alternative procedures that can compensate for the omitted procedure.
Choice A is incorrect as bringing the matter to the attention of the board is not necessarily needed unless the auditor was unable to compensate for the omitted procedures.

Choice B is incorrect. The auditor would first need to perform alternative procedures to compensate for the omitted procedures. The auditor would only withdraw from the engagement if the client did not make any material adjustments.

Choice D incorrect. This step would be done after the auditor performed alternative procedures and determined that an adjustment would need to be made.

AUD 3-Q56 A190. Choice C is correct. If there is an omitted procedure in a previously issued audit report, the first step is to apply alternative procedures to see whether the alternative procedures compensate for the omitted procedures.

Choices A, B, and D are incorrect as this is not the first step that an auditor would take after discovering omitted procedures.

AUD 3-Q57 A155. Choice A is correct. If an auditor discovers that there were omitted procedures, the first step is to determine if the auditor had performed alternative procedures to compensate for and support the omitted procedure. If so, then there is no further steps necessary.
Choices B is incorrect as it is not advisable that the auditor correct material errors in the next audit report.

Choice C is incorrect as there is no need to notify users if there are alternative procedures that compensate for the omitted procedure.

Choice D is incorrect as there is no need for this if there are alternative procedures that compensate for the omitted procedure.

AUD 3-Q58 A1374. The correct answer choice is D. The auditor would use alternative substantive procedures to validate last year's inventory.

Choice A is incorrect because withdrawing from the engagement wouldn't be appropriate under these circumstances.

Choice B is incorrect because some substantive work around the inventory must be performed, the auditor cannot rely on management representations alone.

Choice C is incorrect because this is not a scope limitation because alternative procedures may be performed.

AUD 3-Q59 A35. Choice B is correct. As part of the auditor's substantive testing procedures, an auditor will need to verify the securities held by a third party to gain comfort that the securities exist.

Choice A is incorrect because an investee company would not provide the auditor assurance over the number of shares owned.

Choice C is incorrect because analytical procedures would not provide the auditor comfort over the existence assertion.

Choice D is incorrect because inspecting the cash receipts journal would not provide comfort over whether the securities exist or not.

AUD 3-Q60 A432. The correct answer is A. In the audit of investments in securities the auditor attempts to determine that adequate internal controls exist with respect to the acquisition, holding, and disposition of such securities. Other objectives include determining that the securities actually exist, are the property of the client, are valued in accordance with generally accepted accounting principles, and are properly classified on the balance sheet. In addition to these objectives, the auditor's testing is intended to ascertain that all revenue arising from such investments has been promptly collected and properly recorded.

An auditor is not a detective or investigator and is not expected to determine whether or not the physical securities are authentic.

Choices B, C and D are all primary objectives relating to marketable securities.

AUD 3-Q61 A42. Choice D is correct. In this scenario, the auditor's purpose is to determine whether the inventory listing is accurate. The auditor begins with the inventory listing and traces back to the count sheets and inventory tags to confirm that the inventory exists.

Choice A is incorrect because this test would provide assurance that the inventory items purchased were properly approved.

Choice B is incorrect because this test would provide assurance that items purchased were received. This is a difficult test to perform because the inventory item may have been sold by the time the auditor conducts the test.

Choice C is incorrect because this test would provide assurance that the inventory listing is complete. The auditor is not seeking to gain comfort over the completeness assertion in this scenario, but wants to gain comfort as to whether the inventory exists.

AUD 3-Q62 A23. Choice A is correct because tracing from the client's physical inventory to the general ledger gives the auditor the assurance that all inventory is accounted for.

Choice B is incorrect because this test does not test for rights or obligations.

Choice C is incorrect because an auditor is not examining the value of inventory.

Choice D is incorrect because an auditor is not examining the notes to the financial statements to review proper presentation and disclosure.

AUD 3-Q63 A262. Choice A is correct. After observing the inventory count, the auditor should be alert to any inclusion of obsolete or damaged goods.

Choices B, C, and D are incorrect as these cannot be determined after merely observing the inventory count.

AUD 3-Q64 A302. Choice D is correct. When the client maintains well-kept inventory records with comparisons with physical counts, this would allow for observation during or after the period.

Choice A is incorrect. Periodic inventory levels are only updated on a date when the physical inventory is taken.

Choice B is incorrect as the auditor may not rely on the results of substantive procedure tests performed in the prior year.

Choice C is incorrect as this would not affect the auditor's procedures.

AUD 3-Q65 A178. Choice B is correct. Evidence of existence can best be confirmed by inventory confirmations to verify the amount held in the public warehouse.

Choices A, C, and D are incorrect as these procedures do not test for existence.

AUD 3-Q66 A353. The correct answer is D. This is a test of completeness.

Choice A is not correct because the fact that the inventory is physically present and observed does NOT give the auditor assurance as to ownership or realization. Separate audit procedures must be performed to ascertain legal ownership or the existence of slow moving or obsolete inventories. If goods were shipped FOB shipping point, they may have been included in the final inventory schedule when prepared, but not physically present.

Choice B is not correct because the tracing does not speak to obsolescence.

Choice C is not correct. Of course, they were physically present, the auditor had counted them as part of their test counts.

AUD 3-Q67 A226. Choice B is correct. An auditor would typically discuss with management its policies and procedures for identifying litigation.

Choice A is incorrect as an auditor would not typically confirm with the clerk of the court.

Choice C is incorrect as the auditor would not inspect legal documents in the client's lawyer's possession regarding pending litigation.

Choice D is incorrect as the auditor would not confirm the details of pending litigation with the client's adversaries' legal representatives.

AUD 3-Q68 A234. Choice D is correct. Legal counsel does not have the expertise to evaluate whether an entity may continue as a going concern. Only an auditor would have the ability to evaluate this.

Choices A, B, and C are incorrect as these are items that are included in the attorney's response.

AUD 3-Q69 A198. Choice C is correct. Obtaining a letter of audit inquiry from the client's lawyer would most likely assist the auditor in the evaluation of a loss contingency.

Choices A, B, and D are incorrect as these procedures would not provide information regarding loss contingencies.

AUD 3-Q70 A203. Choice B is correct. An external auditor requests a client to send audit inquiry letters to corroborate information furnished by management.

Choice A is incorrect as the attorney is not an expert cannot provide assurance but rather provides his/her opinion on the loss and the degree of an unfavorable outcome

Choice C is incorrect as this is not the primary reason for issuing the request.

Choice D is incorrect as these are accounting terms – not legal terms.

AUD 3-Q71 A278. Choice D is correct. Reading files of correspondence from the taxing authorities would give the auditor insight as to whether there are any unrecorded liabilities.

Choices A, B, and C are incorrect as these procedures would not assist the auditor in identifying litigations, claims and assessments.

AUD 3-Q72 A304. Choice C is correct. The author's primary method to corroborate information on litigation, claims, and assessments is to review the responses from the client's lawyer to a letter of audit inquiry.

Choice A is incorrect as this would provide assurance over the amount of legal expense that the client recorded.

Choice B is incorrect as this would not provide corroborating information.

Choice D is incorrect as this would not provide assurance over litigation, claims, and assessments,

AUD 3-Q73 A174. Choice C is correct. When auditing contingent liabilities, an auditor would examine the board of directors' meeting minutes to determine whether any discussion about contingent liabilities has taken place.

Choices A, B, and D are incorrect as these procedures would not test for contingent liabilities.

AUD 3-Q74 A144. Choice B is correct. The lawyer's response is vague and the auditor would need to seek clarification on the amount that the client is responsible for as the response indicates a potential liability for the client.

Choice A is incorrect as the lawyer is indicating that the potential impact to the client is nominal, which would indicate that there is no need to have an accrual.

Choices C and D are incorrect because the lawyer's letter indicates it is not probable that the client will have a liability. As such, no disclosure is required.

AUD 3-Q75 A349. The correct answer is A. In some circumstances, a lawyer may be required by his Code of Professional Responsibility to resign his engagement if his advice concerning financial accounting and reporting litigation, claims and assessments is disregarded by the client. When the auditor is aware that a client has changed lawyers or that a lawyer engaged by the client has resigned, the auditor should consider the need for inquiries concerning the reasons the lawyer is no longer associated with the client.

The resignation of a lawyer by itself does not require an adverse opinion, nor would the auditor have to re-examine all evidence already gathered in his review of contingent liabilities. However, such a resignation may represent a disagreement between an attorney and his client with regard to possible un-asserted claims which the attorney deems necessary to be disclosed.

Choice B is incorrect because the attorney stated in their letter that there were no significant disagreements with the client's assessment of contingent liabilities.

Choice C and D are incorrect because the auditor need only consider additional inquiries and not complete new procedures over contingent liabilities.

AUD 3-Q76 A416. The correct answer is D. A letter of audit inquiry to the client's lawyer is the auditor's primary means of obtaining corroboration of the information furnished by management concerning litigations, claims, and assessments. However, evidential matter obtained from inside counsel is not a substitute for information outside counsel refuses to furnish.

Choice A is incorrect because the amount of a probable loss is part of the evidence obtained.

Choice B is incorrect because again this would be part of the desired evidence that the auditor is trying to obtain. Furthermore, these are accounting terms.

Choice C is incorrect because information concerning the progress of cases is what the auditor is trying to obtain and is not the primary reason.

AUD 3-Q77 A206. Choice A is correct. Plans to delay expenditures and extend the due date of loan payments may mitigate a going concern problem.

Choices B, C, and D are incorrect as these situations would not indicate any adverse effects in the Company's business.

AUD 3-Q78 A243. Choice B is correct as recurring working capital shortages could indicate a going concern problem.

Choice A is incorrect this would indicate that an entity would more than likely continue in the foreseeable future due to new investors.

Choice C is incorrect as an entity does not always need new customers each year as long as the entity had a good customer base.

Choice D is incorrect as this would not indicate a going concern problem.

AUD 3-Q79 A175. Choice B is correct. If an entity postpones expenditures to upgrade its information technology system, this may mitigate a going concern problem.

Choice A, C, and D are incorrect as these are not negative going concern indicators.

AUD 3-Q80 A176. Choice D is correct. When an auditor concludes that there is substantial doubt about an entity's ability to continue as a going concern, an auditor must include the terms "substantial doubt" and "going concern." The phrases above need not be included.

Choices A, B, and C are incorrect per the above explanation

AUD 3-Q81 A143. Choice B is correct. If a supplier denies usual trade credit, this may indicate substantial doubt about an entity's ability to continue as a going concern as an entity may not be able to meet amounts due to suppliers.

Choice A is incorrect as the existence of related party transactions is not a negative going concern indicator.

Choice C is incorrect as payment of arrearages preferred stock dividends is not a negative going concern indicator.

Choice D is incorrect as Company restrictions on the disposal of assets is not a going concern indicator.

AUD 3-Q82 A145. Choice C is correct. When there is substantial doubt about an entity's ability to continue as a going concern, the auditor must assess the adequacy of the Company's disclosure.

Choice A and D are incorrect because there is no need to issue a qualified or adverse opinion unless the going concern is not disclosed.

Choice B is incorrect as there is no such requirement.

AUD 3-Q83 A47. Choice D is correct. Going concern refers to an entity's ability to be in business one year from the balance sheet date. Violation of debt agreements may cause the loan to be due immediately.

Choice A is incorrect as confirmation of accounts receivable would indicate if accounts receivable are valid and exist at the balance sheet date.

Choice B is incorrect as this procedure assesses the reasonableness of interest expense.

Choice C is incorrect as confirmation of bank balances would test to see if cash is stated fairly at the balance sheet date.

AUD 3-Q84 A54. Choice C is correct. If management plans to dispose of assets in the near future, this may indicate that there is a doubt as to whether the entity can function as a going concern.

Choice A is incorrect, as audit fees do not have an effect on the entity's ability to survive one year from the balance sheet date.

Choice B is incorrect, as future assurance services do not have an effect on the entity's ability to continue in the future.

Choice D is incorrect because issuing new stock would not create doubt about an entity's ability to continue as a going concern. Refer to AU-C 570 for further information regarding going concern indicators.

AUD 3-Q85 A232. Choice C is correct. When evaluating accounting estimates, an auditor would most likely concentrate on key factors that deviate from historical patterns.

Choice A is incorrect as assumptions may be subject to variations depending on the type of assumption or financial statement account.

Choice B is incorrect as the auditor would most likely be concerned with assumptions that *are* susceptible to bias and are subjective.

Choice D is incorrect as the auditor would focus attention to accounting estimates that are *not* similar to industry guidelines.

AUD 3-Q86 A249. Choice A is correct. The auditor's purpose is to evaluate whether accounting estimates are reasonable in nature.

Choice B is incorrect as estimates are used when data cannot be accumulated in a timely manner.

Choice C is incorrect as this listing comes right from the clients records and is not an estimate.

Choice D is incorrect as accounting estimates are used in these types of situations.

AUD 3-Q87 A65. Choice C is correct. A known misstatement is a *specific* type of misstatement that is *identified* during the audit. An auditor's *estimate* would not considered to be known because it is not specific. This would be considered a likely misstatement.

Choices A, B, and D are incorrect because these are known misstatements that have been specifically identified during the audit based on the auditor's procedures.

AUD 3-Q88 A233. Choice A is correct. There would be no disclosure required if the effect of not including the proposed adjustments is immaterial.

Choice B is incorrect as this would be the case of the proposed adjustments not included are material.

Choice C is incorrect as a modified opinion would not be issued unless the proposed adjustments were material.

Choice D is incorrect as there is no requirement to disclose this.

AUD 3-Q89 A310. Choice A is correct. The auditor must document the errors in the summary of undetected errors, and document the conclusion that the errors do not cause the financial statements to be misstated.

Choices B, C, and D are incorrect as A is the most appropriate response.

AUD 3-Q90 A260. Choice A is correct. When discovering a deviation, the auditor should make inquiries to understand the potential consequence of the deviation.

Choice B is incorrect as this is not an assumption that the auditor should make.

Choice C is incorrect as there is no requirement that the auditor report this to the next higher level of authority.

Choice D is incorrect as the auditor would not decrease the sample size due to a deviation.

AUD 3-Q91 A265. Choice A is correct. In obtaining written representations from management, materiality limits would apply to representations related to related party transactions. (Just as GAAP only applies to material amounts or transactions; so immaterial related party transactions do not require disclosure per FASB Statement No. 57, *Related Party Disclosures* [FASB ASC 850-10-50-1]).

Choice B is incorrect as these are significant no matter what level.

Choices C and D are incorrect as materiality levels do not apply to these items.

AUD 3-Q92 A60. Choice B is correct. The purpose of a management representation letter is for management to declare that the information provided to the auditor is fair and accurate and there are no material omissions. If the CFO committed fraud, this information would affect the information the auditor received and as such, needs to be included in the management representation letter.

Choice A is incorrect, as the management representation letter is not an appropriate place to disclose this information.

Choice C and D are incorrect, as this information is documented in the auditor's working papers and not the management representation letter.

AUD 3-Q93 A305. Choice A is correct. This would typically be included in a management representation letter.

Choice B and C are incorrect as these items would typically be stated in internal controls document.

Choice D is incorrect as this is stated in an employee agreement.

AUD 3-Q94 A161. Choice C is correct. This statement indicates the auditor's understanding of the engagement and would be included in the engagement letter. A management representation letter ensures that management has accountability for the information provided to the accountant.

Choices A, B, and D are incorrect as these are all representations that management would make.

AUD 3-Q95 A1347. The correct answer choice is A. It is required of issuer management to take responsibilities surrounding the design and implementation of programs and controls to detect fraud and attest to it in a management representation letter.

Choice B is incorrect because this would be a forward-looking statement regarding expanding operations and would not be required in a management representation letter.

Choice C is incorrect because stating that the statements (or more precisely, the audit procedures) are in accordance with GAAS is not required of management to state in a management representation letter. This would be a statement in the audit report.

Choice D is incorrect because this would be management's opinion and is not a required statement in the management representation letter.

AUD 3-Q96 A1348. The correct answer choice is D. The management representation letter should address the financial statements across all years presented.

Choice A is incorrect because the management representation letter should cover all years presented, not just the prior year.

Choice B is incorrect because both the prior year should be presented as well as the current year must be addressed.

Choice C is incorrect because when three years of financials are presented, the earliest year must be included.

AUD 3-Q97 A237. Choice C is correct. The loss would be recorded in year 1 since the situation existed at the December 31 year 1 balance sheet date.

Choice A is incorrect as this would only affect year 2.

Choice B is incorrect as this would only affect year 2.

Choice D is incorrect as there is no effect in year 1.

AUD 3-Q98 A329. Choice C is correct. Events that did not exist at year end but arose after year end may require disclosure in the financial statements.

Choice A is incorrect as the event did not exist at year-end.

Choice B is incorrect as they are not based on accounting estimates.

Choice D is incorrect as this test would not need to be performed.

AUD 3-Q99 A239. Choice B is correct. When performing subsequent events procedures, an accountant will compare the latest available internal financial information with the financial statements being reported upon.

Choice A is incorrect as this would not provide information about subsequent events.

Choice C is incorrect as this would be a procedure to update year-end testing.

Choice D is incorrect as this would not provide details about any subsequent events.

AUD 3-Q100 A146. Choice C is correct. This is an example of a subsequent event that may require disclosure in the financial statements.

Choice A is incorrect as this is not considered to be a subsequent event.

Choice B is incorrect as this is not considered to be a subsequent event.

Choice D is incorrect as auditors are not required to review tax returns as part of subsequent event procedures.

AUD 3-Q101 A411. The correct answer is D. Two types of subsequent events require evaluation by the auditor: those that have a direct effect on the financial statements and require adjustment and those that have no direct effect on the financial statements but a footnote are advisable. With respect to subsequent events requiring disclosure only, if an event.... occurs between the date of the independent auditor's original report and the date of the reissuance of such report, and if the event comes to the attention of the independent auditor, the event may be disclosed in a separate note to the financial statements captioned somewhat as follows:

Event (Unaudited) Subsequent to the date of the Report of the Independent Auditor

Choice A is incorrect because if there is no required adjustment of the financial statements then there is no required note.

Choice B is incorrect because the audit report hasn't been issued yet so there is no need to provide a note but possibly leave a disclosure.

Choice C is incorrect because the subsequent event would occur after the auditor's report has been issued so there is no need to provide a note

AUD 3-Q102 A263. Choice C is correct. An auditor has no obligation to make continuing queries unless information that existed at the report date may affect the report and comes to the auditor's attention.

Choices A, B, and D are incorrect as the auditor has no obligation to make continuing inquiries for these events.

AUD 3-Q103 A177. Choice C is correct. If an auditor becomes aware of material information that may have affected the report, the auditor would _first_ need to determine who the individuals are that are relying on the information and _then_ take appropriate action.

Choice A, B, and D are incorrect as these are steps that are done after determining whether there are users that rely on such omitted information.

AUD 3-Q104 A1368. The correct answer choice is B. Issuing a modified compliance report is the least appropriate because the material noncompliance occurred after the period covered by the audit.

Choice A is incorrect because discussing with management and those charged with governance wouldn't be the least appropriate.

Choice C is incorrect because the existence of the conditions of noncompliance should be determined before the completion of the compliance audit and wouldn't be the least appropriate.

Choice D is incorrect because modifying the standard compliance report wouldn't be the least appropriate under these circumstances.

AUD 3-Q105 A1370. The correct answer choice is A. The issuing of convertible bonds wouldn't impact the books until future periods but is significant enough to notify the information users of the financial statements of the future plans.

Choice B is incorrect because this would require an adjustment to allowance for doubtful accounts.

Choice C is incorrect because this would not require an adjustment in the income statement or disclosure.

Choice D is incorrect because this would require an adjustment to the payroll expense account on the income statement and a disclosure.

AUD 3-Q106 A1379. The correct answer choice is D. The client's willingness to revise financial statements and provide other disclosures to information users is the most important thing that the auditor should consider.

Choices A and C are incorrect because the cost-to-benefit ratio is important but not the most important and the same is true relating to whether the client is willing to pay additional fees.

Choice B is incorrect because you wouldn't go back 5 years.

This page is intentionally left blank.

AUD 4 – Forming Conclusions and Reporting

A. Reports on Auditing Engagements — 4A-3 – 4A-47
1. Forming an audit opinion, including modification of an auditor's opinion — 3
2. Form and content of an audit report, including the use of emphasis-of-matter and other-matter (explanatory) paragraphs — 7
3. Audit of internal control integrated with an audit of financial statements — 34

B. Reports on Attestation Engagements — 4B-1 – 4B-31
1. General standards for attestation reports — 1
2. Agreed-upon procedures reports — 19
3. Reporting on controls at a service organization — 24

C. Accounting and Review Service Engagements — 4C-1 – 4C-18
1. Preparation engagements [AR-C 70] — 2
2. Compilation reports [AR-C 80] — 4
3. Review reports [AR-C 90] — 8

D. Reporting on Compliance — 4D-1 – 4D-17

E. Other Reporting Considerations — 4E-1 – 4E-40
1. Comparative statements and consistency between periods — 1
2. Other information in documents with audited statements — 4
3. Review of interim financial information — 6
4. Supplementary information — 16
5. Single statements — 20
6. Special-purpose and other country frameworks — 23
7. Letter for underwriters and filings with the SEC — 27
8. Alerts that restrict the use of written communication — 35
9. Additional requirements under Government Accountability Office Government Audit Standards — 37

Glossary: Forming Conclusions and Reporting — Glossary 4-1 – 4-5

Multiple Choice – Questions — MCQ 4-1 – 4-17

Multiple Choice – Solutions — MCQ 4-18 – 4-32

Forming Conclusions and Reporting

Hint: Quick reference summary for forming conclusions and reporting:

Audit reports (You must know when they're issued and how they're worded.)
1. Qualified -- "except for"
   Major GAAP departure (Material)
   Major scope limitation (Material)
2. Disclaimer -- no opinion
   Very major scope limitation (Pervasive)
3. Adverse - "not present fairly"
   Very major GAAP departure (Pervasive)
4. Emphasis of Matter (opinion still unmodified)
   Going concern -- substantial doubt
   Inconsistency
   Others at auditor's discretion
5. Other Matter
   Restrict distribution, if applicable

Headings for audit reports (subtitles) of nonissuers

Unmodified	Qualified	Adverse	Disclaimer
Report on F/S	Report on F/S	Report on F/S	Report on F/S
Mgt's Respon	Mgt's Respon	Mgt's Respon	Mgt's Respon
Auditors Resp	Auditors Resp	Auditors Resp	Auditors Resp
------	Basis for Q Op	Basis for A Op	Basis for D Op
Opinion	**Qualified Opin**	**Adverse Opin**	**Disclaimer of Opin**
Emphasis of Matter	Emphasis of Matter	Emphasis of Matter	Emphasis of Matter
Other Matter	Other Matter	Other Matter	Other Matter

Report on other legal & regulatory requirements

General parts of a report:
1. Title (for audits, reviews, and agreed-upon procedures)
2. Address
3. Service type
4. What we worked on
5. Date of #4 (what we worked on)
6. Responsibilities of parties
7. Professional standards followed
8. Description of procedures - general
9. Conclusion
10. Inherent Limitations - if any
11. Restrict distributions - if applicable
12. Sign and date

Special purpose frameworks
1. Types
   a. Cash basis
   b. Tax basis
   c. Regulatory basis
   d. Contractual basis
2. Description
   a. Use different names for financial statements (not GAAP names) / Disclosures

Special considerations
1. Specific elements, accounts, or items of a financial statement **OR** a single financial statement (general purpose or special purpose framework)
2. Incomplete presentation of a financial statement (but following GAAP)
    a. Include emphasis-of-matter paragraph in the audit report

Negative assurance
1. Review
2. Comfort letter
3. Compliance with contract as part of audit

Restrict distribution
1. Control deficiencies --------------------/ BY-
2. Auditor communications --------------------/ PRODUCT
3. Compliance with contract as part of audit --------------------/ REPORT
4. Agreed-upon procedures
5. Regulatory basis
6. Contractual basis

Government auditing standards (Yellow Book)
1. Must follow all of GAAS and issue report on financial statements
2. Must issue written report on internal controls
3. Must issue written report on compliance with laws and regulations
4. Must issue additional reports for A-I 33 audits

Attestations
1. Report on a subject matter or an assertion about the subject matter that is the responsibility of another party.
2. Used for anything other than historical financial statement(s) taken as a whole (may be nonfinancial data)
3. Levels -- examination, review, agreed-upon procedures (AUP)
4. AUP -- CPA, client, and third party agree on procedures to be used. Third party must assume responsibility for sufficiency of procedures. Report on findings based on specific procedures performed on subject matter.
5. Forecasts and projections
    a. Forecast - based on conditions expected to exist
    b. Projection - hypothetical assumptions
    c. General use - used by anyone (not projections)
    d. Limited use - users deal directly with preparer
    e. Accounting services - examination, compilation, AUP
    f. "May differ from actual"
    g. "No responsibility to update"

A. Reports on Auditing Engagements
1. Forming an audit opinion, including modification of an auditor's opinion

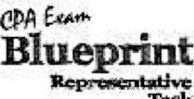

> **Identify the factors that an auditor should consider when forming an opinion on an entity's financial statements.**

> **Identify the type of opinion that an auditor should render on the audit of an issuer or nonissuer's financial statements, including unmodified (or unqualified), qualified, adverse or disclaimer of opinion.**

> **Hint**: Be sure to clearly identify when the CPA Exam is asking about an issuer (PCAOB standards apply) or a nonissuer (AICPA standards apply). This distinction determines what report template to use.

Reports are essential to audit and other assurance engagements because they communicate the auditor's findings. Users of financial statements rely on the auditor's report to provide assurance on the company's financial statements.

The following **conditions must be met** in order to issue a standard (unmodified/unqualified) audit report:
1) The financial statements **present fairly, in all material respects, the financial position, results of operations, and cash flows of the entity**.
2) **All required financial statements** were evaluated during audit (including balance sheet, income statement, statement of retained earnings, and statement of cash flows).
3) The auditor accumulated **sufficient evidence** to make his or her opinion.
4) Statements are in conformity with **GAAP**, with adequate disclosures included in the footnotes and other parts of the financial statements.
5) **No explanatory language is required** because there are no circumstances requiring the addition of explanatory language to the report.

If **any** of the conditions are **NOT met**, one of the other types of audit reports must be issued.

The other types of reports are:
- Unqualified with explanatory paragraph or modified wording
- Qualified – except for the effects of the matter(s) to which the qualification relates, the financial statements present fairly, in all material respects, the financial position, results of operations, and cash flows of the entity in conformity with generally accepted accounting principles
- Adverse – financial statements do not present fairly the financial position, results of operations, or cash flows of the entity in conformity with generally accepted accounting principles.
- Disclaimer – auditor does not express an opinion on the financial statements

a. **Standard report for an integrated audit of financial statements and internal control over financial reporting for issuers (PCAOB)**

> **Hint**: When performing an integrated audit of financial statements and internal control over financial reporting, the auditor may choose to issue a combined report or separate reports on the company's financial statements and on internal control over financial reporting.

The auditor's standard (unmodified) report includes:
- expresses the auditor's opinion [opinion]
- identifies the basis for the auditor's opinion which describes the nature of an audit, addresses the financial statements audited, and outlines both the responsibilities of management and the auditor [basis for opinion]

b. **Unmodified opinions for nonissuers (AICPA)**
Similar to issuers, the auditor for a nonissuer (private company) should express an unmodified opinion when the auditor concludes that the financial statements are presented fairly, in all material respects, in accordance with the applicable financial reporting framework. The report will include a statement about the nature of the audit, management and auditor responsibilities in the audit, and an opinion. Modifications to the report are required if either the financial statements are materially misstated or there is insufficient evidence to determine the statements are free from misstatement.

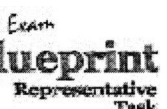

> **Identify the factors that an auditor should consider when it is necessary to modify the audit opinion on an issuer or nonissuer's financial statements, including when the financial statements are materially misstated and when the auditor is unable to obtain sufficient appropriate audit evidence.**

c. **Departures from the standard report for issuers (PCAOB)**
The auditor must understand the circumstances when a standard report is inappropriate and the type of opinion issued under the circumstances.

Discussed below, this chart summarizes the important concepts when departing from a standard report:

Conditions that require a departure from a standard report	1. Scope limitation • Imposed by client • Caused by circumstances 2. GAAP issue
Types of opinions other than unmodified/unqualified	• Qualified • Adverse • Disclaimer of Opinion
Degrees of materiality	• Material but NOT pervasive • Material AND pervasive

1) **Conditions that require a departure from a standard report**
   i. **The scope of the audit has been restricted (scope limitation)**
      When the auditor has not accumulated sufficient appropriate audit evidence to conclude whether the financial statements are stated in accordance with GAAP, a scope restriction exists.

      There are two major causes of scope restrictions:
      a) Restrictions **imposed by the client**
         Auditors are often concerned when their scope is restricted by the client – they are concerned about the possibility that management is trying to prevent the discovery of misstated information (e.g., hide fraud). The auditor must analyze the signaling value of client-imposed scope restrictions.

         > *Example:* Management refuses to permit the auditor to confirm material receivables or to physically examine inventory.

      b) Restrictions **caused by circumstances**
         Auditors should watch for client-imposed scope restrictions made to look like scope restrictions caused by circumstances.

         > *Example*: The engagement is not agreed on until after year-end and it's not possible to observe inventories, confirm receivables, or perform other important procedures at the balance sheet date (because the auditor is not there).

ii. **The financial statements have not been prepared in accordance with GAAP (GAAP departure)**
This includes departures from adequate footnote disclosures. This would also include omitted a required financial statement (e.g., the statement of cash flows).

If the scope of the audit has been restricted or a GAAP departure is present, and it is material, an opinion other than an unqualified opinion must be issued.

2) **Types of opinions**
The three types of opinions under these conditions are outlined below.

   i. **Qualified Opinion**
   This report can result from:
   - A limitation of scope or
   - Failure to follow GAAP (applicable financial reporting framework).

   A qualified opinion report can only be used when the auditor concludes that the overall financial statements are fairly stated.

   When an auditor issues a qualified opinion, she or he must use the term *except for* in the opinion paragraph.
   It is unacceptable to use the term "except for" with any other type of audit opinion.

   ii. **Adverse Opinion**
   Issued only when the auditor believes that the overall financial statements are so materially misleading that they do not present fairly the financial position, results of operations, and cash flows in conformity with GAAP (applicable financial reporting framework).

   The adverse opinion report can arise only when **the auditor has knowledge, after an adequate investigation, of the absence of conformity with GAAP** (applicable financial reporting framework).

   This condition is uncommon and thus the adverse opinion is rarely used; however, it is part of the body of knowledge.

   iii. **Disclaimer of Opinion**
   Issued when **the auditor has been unable to satisfy him or herself that the overall financial statements are fairly presented**.

   A disclaimer may arise because of a **severe limitation on the scope of the audit.**

   The disclaimer is distinguished from an adverse opinion in that the **disclaimer can arise only from a lack of knowledge by the auditor** (versus the adverse opinion where the auditor must have knowledge that the financial statements are not fairly stated).

3) **Materiality**
   Both disclaimers and adverse opinions are used only **when the condition is highly material**.

   The following table summarizes the interaction between materiality and the form of opinion:

Reason for Modification	Material but NOT Pervasive*	Material and Pervasive**
GAAP issue	Qualified opinion	Adverse opinion
Scope restriction	Qualified opinion	Disclaimer of opinion

   The following table explains the levels of materiality:

Materiality Level	Significance in Terms of Users' Perspective
Immaterial	Users' decisions unlikely to be affected by the amount.
*Material (but not pervasive)	Decisions affected of users who are specifically interested in the misstated account. Overall financial statements are fair.
**Highly Material (pervasive)	Most or all decisions affected by misstatement. Overall financial statements are unfair.

d. **Modified opinions for nonissuers (AICPA)**
   The discussion for issuers under the heading **DEPARTURES FROM THE STANDARD REPORT** is generally applicable to nonissuers. There are only a few editorial differences with the formatting of the report – the concepts are the same. The issuer's standard report is referred to as an *unmodified opinion* by nonissuers.

Multiple Choice

AUD 4-Q1 through AUD 4-Q14

2. Form and content of an audit report, including the use of emphasis-of-matter and other-matter (explanatory) paragraphs

> Identify the appropriate form and content of an auditor's report for an audit of an issuer or nonissuer's financial statements, including the appropriate use of emphasis-of-matter and other-matter (i.e., explanatory) paragraphs.

a. **Explanatory language added to the auditor's standard report for issuers (PCAOB)**
Certain circumstances, while not affecting the auditor's unqualified opinion, may require explanatory language or increased emphasis. The language may be included in one of the following:
- Introductory paragraph
- Critical audit matters (CAMs)*
- Emphasis-of-matter paragraphs (emphasis paragraphs)
- Explanatory language or paragraphs

*[A detailed discussion of CAMs is not included in this text. CAMs are not eligible for testing until Q3 2019.]

> *Hint:* **Eligible for testing starting in Q3 2018**, PCAOB Release 2017-001, *Auditor's Report on an Audit of Financial Statements when the Auditor Expresses an Unqualified Opinion and Related Amendments to PCAOB Standards*, makes changes to the auditor's report, including:
> - The auditor's tenure is disclosed (i.e., first year the auditor began serving consecutively as the company's auditor is disclosed).
> - New language is included. Reports must now add the phrase "whether due to error **or fraud**" in a description of the auditor's responsibility under PCAOB to get "reasonable assurance about whether the financial statements are free of material misstatements." The prior standard did not require the auditor's report to contain the phrase whether due to error or fraud.
> - Reports must include section headers/titles (e.g., "Opinion on the Financial Statements").
> - **The opinion section is now required to be first, followed by a "Basis for the Opinion" section.**
> - It would include a statement that the auditor must be **independent**.
> - Communication of critical audit matters (CAMs)*
>
> *Everything testable in Q3 2018 except "critical audit matter section" and all matters related to CAMs **will be eligible for testing in Q3 2019**.
>
> | Unqualified | Qualified | Adverse | Disclaimer |
> |---|---|---|---|
> | **Opinion** | **Qualified Opin** | **Adverse Opin** | **Disclaimer of Opin** |
> | Basis for Op | Basis for Q Op | Basis for A Op | Basis for D Op |
> | Report on F/S | Report on F/S | Report on F/S | Report on F/S |
> | Mgt's Respon | Mgt's Respon | Mgt's Respon | Mgt's Respon |
> | Auditors Resp | Auditors Resp | Auditors Resp | Auditors Resp |
> | [Emphasis of Matter]* | [Emphasis of Matter]* | [Emphasis of Matter]* | [Emphasis of Matter]* |
> | [Explanatory Matter]* | [Explanatory Matter]* | [Explanatory Matter]* | [Explanatory Matter]* |
>
> *[If applicable. Location of added language or paragraph varies by subject matter.]

> *Hint*: Critical audit matters (CAMs) are defined as a matter that was communicated or required to be communicated to the audit committee and that: (1) relates to accounts or disclosures that are material to the financial statements and (2) involved especially challenging, subjective, or complex auditor judgment.

Matter-of-emphasis and explanatory paragraphs do *not* impact the opinion expressed by the auditor over the financial statements. An unqualified opinion remains unqualified.

In any report on financial statements, the auditor may emphasize a matter regarding the financial statements. However, phrases such as "with the foregoing [following] explanation" should *not* be used in the opinion paragraph if a matter-of-emphasis paragraph is included in the auditor's report.

These matter-of-emphasis paragraphs are never required; they may be added solely at the auditor's discretion. Situations that would be appropriately discussed in a matter-of-emphasis paragraph include:
- Significant transactions (i.e., transactions with related parties)
- Unusually important subsequent events (e.g., hurricane or other catastrophe that has significant effect on the company's financial position)
- Accounting matters affecting the comparability of the financial statements with those of the preceding period (excludes change in accounting principles)
- Significant litigation or regulatory actions and future outcome uncertainties
- Relationships with other entities within business enterprise (e.g., entity is a component or subsidiary not requiring consolidation).

Situations that would **require** an explanatory paragraph include:
- Substantial doubt about the entity's ability to continue as a going concern.
- The auditor's opinion is based in part on the report of another auditor.
- Material change between periods in accounting principles or in the method of their application.
- Changes in reporting entity.
- A material misstatement in previously issued financial statements has been corrected.
- Management is required to report on the company's internal controls over financial reporting but such report is not required to be audited.
- Certain circumstances relating to reports on comparative financial statements exist.
- Selected quarterly financial data required by SEC Regulation S-K has been omitted or has not been reviewed.
- Supplementary information required by the Financial Accounting Standards Board (FASB), the Governmental Accounting Standards Board (GASB), or the Federal Accounting Standards Advisory Board (FASAB) has been omitted, the presentation of such information departs materially from FASB, GASB, or FASAB guidelines, the auditor is unable to complete prescribed procedures with respect to such information, or the auditor is unable to remove substantial doubts about whether the supplementary information conforms to FASB, GASB, or FASAB guidelines.
- Change in an investee year end that has a material effect on financial statements.
- Other information in a document containing audited financial statements is materially inconsistent with information appearing in the financial statements.

> *Hint*: Recently added is required explanatory language concerning situations when management is required to report on internal controls over financial reporting without auditor evaluation and reporting.
>
> *The company is not required to have, nor were we engaged to perform, and audit of internal control over financial reporting. As a part of our audits we are required to obtain an understanding of internal control over financial reporting but not for the purpose of expressing an opinion on the effectiveness of the Company's internal control over financial reporting. Accordingly, we express no such opinion.*

Some of the most often encountered situations that require explanatory language being added to the auditor's standard report for an issuer are reviewed below.

Circumstance	Explanation	Modification
Going concern issue	If, after considering identified conditions and events and management's plans, the auditor concludes that substantial doubt about the entity's ability to continue as a going concern for a reasonable period of time remains, the audit report should include an explanatory paragraph (following the opinion paragraph) to reflect that conclusion.	Add explanatory paragraph **Example:** The auditor's conclusion about the entity's ability to continue as a going concern should be expressed through the use of the phrase "*substantial doubt about its (the entity's) ability to continue as a going concern*" [or similar wording that includes the terms *substantial doubt* and *going concern*].
Opinion based in part on report of another auditor (e.g., predecessor auditor)	When the auditor decides to make reference to the report of another auditor as a basis for his or her opinion, he or she should disclose this fact in the opinion paragraph. The opinion should refer to the report of the other auditor. These references indicate division of responsibility for performance of the audit. If the financial statements of the **prior period were audited by a predecessor auditor, and the predecessor's report on the prior period is not reissued**, in addition to expressing an opinion on the current period's financial statements, the auditor should add explanatory language: • That the financial statements of the prior period were audited by a predecessor auditor • The type of opinion expressed by the predecessor auditor and, if the opinion was modified, the reasons therefore • The nature of an emphasis-of-matter paragraph or other-matter paragraph included in the predecessor auditor's report, if any • The date of that report. When current period financial statements are **audited and presented in comparative form** with compiled or reviewed financial statements for the prior period, and the report on the prior period is not reissued, the auditor should include explanatory language in the current period auditor's report that includes the following: • The service performed in the prior period • The date of the report on that service • A description of any material modifications noted in that report • A statement that the service was less in scope than an audit and does not provide the basis for an opinion. If the **prior period financial statements were not audited, reviewed, or compiled, the financial statements** should be clearly marked to indicate their status, and the auditor's report should include explanatory language to indicate that the auditor has not audited, reviewed, or compiled the prior period financial statements and that the auditor assumes no responsibility for them.	Disclose in introductory paragraph (opinion paragraph) Add explanatory paragraph **Example:** *We did not audit the financial statements of B Company, a wholly-owned subsidiary, which statements reflect total assets of $_____ and $_____ as of December 31, 20X2 and 20X1, respectively, and total revenues of $_____ and $_____ for the years then ended. Those statements were audited by other auditors whose report has been furnished to us, and our opinion, insofar as it relates to the amounts included for B Company, is based solely on the report of the other auditors.*

Change in Accounting Principle with a material effect	As discussed in AS 2820, *Evaluating Consistency of Financial Statements*, the auditor should evaluate a change in accounting principle to determine whether:<ul><li>the newly adopted accounting principle is a generally accepted accounting principle,</li><li>the method of accounting for the effect of the change is in conformity with generally accepted accounting principles,</li><li>the disclosures related to the accounting change are adequate, and</li><li>the company has justified that the alternative accounting principle is preferable.</li></ul>If the auditor concludes that the criteria for a change in accounting principle (noted above) are not met, the auditor should consider the matter to be a departure from generally accepted accounting principles and, if the effect of the change in accounting principle is material, issue a qualified or adverse opinion. A change in accounting principle that has a material effect on the financial statements should be recognized in the auditor's report on the audited financial statements through the addition of an explanatory paragraph. If the auditor concludes that the criteria above have been met, the explanatory paragraph in the auditor's report should include identification of the nature of the change and a reference to the note disclosure describing the change.	**Add explanatory paragraph** **Example** – the adoption of a new accounting pronouncement: *As discussed in Note X to the financial statements, the company has changed its method of accounting for [describe accounting method change] in [year(s) of financial statements that reflect the accounting method change] due to the adoption of [name of accounting pronouncement].* **Example** – change in accounting principle not due to adoption of a new accounting pronouncement: *As discussed in Note X to the financial statements, the company has elected to change its method of accounting for [describe accounting method change] in [year(s) of financial statements that reflect the accounting method change].* The explanatory paragraph relating to a change in accounting principle should be included in reports on financial statements in the year of the change and in subsequent years until the new accounting principle is applied in all periods presented. If the accounting change is accounted for by retrospective application to the financial statements of all prior periods presented, the additional paragraph is needed only in the year of the change.
Prior material misstatement corrected	Correction of a material misstatement in previously issued financial statements should be recognized in the auditor's report through the addition of an explanatory paragraph. The explanatory paragraph should include:<ul><li>a statement that the previously issued financial statements have been restated for the correction of a misstatement in the respective period and</li><li>a reference to the company's disclosure of the correction of the misstatement.</li></ul>	**Add explanatory paragraph** **Example:** *As discussed in Note X to the financial statements, the 20X2 financial statements have been restated to correct a misstatement.* The paragraph need not be repeated in subsequent years.

Multiple Choice

AUD 4-Q15

b. **Emphasis-of-matter and other-matter paragraphs in the auditor's report for nonissuers (AICPA)**
Sometimes the auditor includes additional communications in the auditor's report when the auditor considers it necessary to
- draw users' attention to a matter or matters presented or disclosed in the financial statements that are of such importance that they are fundamental to users' understanding of the financial statements (*emphasis-of-matter paragraph*) or
- draw users' attention to any matter or matters other than those presented or disclosed in the financial statements that are relevant to users' understanding of the audit, the auditor's responsibilities, or the auditor's report (*other-matter paragraph*).

If the auditor expects to include an emphasis-of-matter or other-matter paragraph in the auditor's report, the auditor should communicate with those charged with governance regarding this expectation and the proposed wording of this paragraph.

1) **Emphasis-of-matter paragraph (nonissuer)**

> **Hint:** An emphasis-of-matter paragraph is used to emphasize something that is presented or disclosed in the financial statements.

When the auditor includes an emphasis-of-matter paragraph in the auditor's report, the auditor should
- include it immediately after the opinion paragraph in the auditor's report,
- use the heading "**Emphasis of Matter**" or other appropriate heading,
- include in the paragraph a clear reference to the matter being emphasized and to where relevant disclosures that fully describe the matter can be found in the financial statements, and
- indicate that the auditor's opinion is not modified with respect to the matter emphasized.

i. **Required Inclusion of an Emphasis-of-Matter Paragraph**
The following paragraphs in other AU-C sections **require the auditor to include an emphasis-of-matter paragraph in the auditor's report** in certain circumstances.

a) *Subsequent Events and Subsequently Discovered Facts* (AU-C 560)
If there are subsequently discovered facts that became known to the auditor after the report release date and if management revises the financial statements (consistent with the subsequent facts) and if the auditor's opinion on the revised financial statements differs from the opinion the auditor previously expressed, disclose the following matters in an emphasis-of-matter or other-matter paragraph:
- The date of the auditor's previous report.
- The type of opinion previously expressed.
- The substantive reasons for the different opinion.
- That the auditor's opinion on the revised financial statements is different from the auditor's previous opinion.

b) *The Auditor's Consideration of an Entity's Ability to Continue as a Going Concern* (AU-C 570)
If, after considering identified conditions or events and management's plans, the auditor concludes that substantial doubt about the entity's ability to continue as a going concern for a reasonable period of time remains, the

auditor should include an emphasis-of-matter paragraph in the auditor's report to reflect that conclusion.

The auditor's conclusion about the entity's ability to continue as a going concern should be expressed through the use of the phrase *"substantial doubt about its (the entity's) ability to continue as a going concern"* or similar wording that includes the terms **substantial doubt** and **going concern**. This is referred to as a going-concern emphasis-of-matter paragraph.

c) ***Consistency of Financial Statements* (AU-C 708)**
If the auditor concludes that the **entity's change in accounting principle** was proper (see AU-C 708.07) and the change in accounting principle has a material effect on the financial statements, the auditor should include an emphasis-of-matter paragraph in the auditor's report that describes that change in accounting principle and provides a reference to the entity's disclosure. (This also applies to a change in accounting estimate that is inseparable from the effect of a related change in accounting principle.)

When a **change in the reporting entity** results in financial statements that, in effect, are those of a different reporting entity, the auditor should include an emphasis-of-matter paragraph in the auditor's report that describes the change in the reporting entity and provides a reference to the entity's disclosure, unless the change in reporting entity results from a transaction or event.

If an entity's financial statements contain an **investment accounted for by the equity method**, the auditor's evaluation of consistency should include consideration of the investee. If the investee makes a change in accounting principle that is material to the investing entity's financial statements, the auditor should include an emphasis-of-matter paragraph in the auditor's report to describe the change in accounting principle.

The auditor should include an emphasis-of-matter paragraph in the auditor's report when there are **adjustments to correct a material misstatement in previously issued financial statements**. The auditor should include this type of emphasis-of-matter paragraph in the auditor's report when the related financial statements are restated to correct the prior material misstatement. The paragraph need not be repeated in subsequent periods.

The emphasis-of-matter paragraph should include
- a statement that the previously issued financial statements have been restated for the correction of a material misstatement in the respective period and
- a reference to the entity's disclosure of the correction of the material misstatement.

d) ***Special Considerations—Audits of Financial Statements Prepared in Accordance with Special Purpose Frameworks* (AU-C 800)**
The auditor's report on special purpose financial statements (but not regulatory basis financial statements with general use) should include an emphasis-of-matter paragraph, under an appropriate heading, that
- indicates that the financial statements are prepared in accordance with the applicable special purpose framework,

- refers to the note to the financial statements that describes that framework, and
- states that the special purpose framework is a basis of accounting other than GAAP.

In addition to the required emphasis-of-matter paragraphs listed above, the following are examples of circumstances when the auditor *may consider it necessary to include an emphasis-of-matter paragraph*:
- An uncertainty relating to the future outcome of unusually important litigation or regulatory action.
- A major catastrophe that has had, or continues to have, a significant effect on the entity's financial position.
- Significant transactions with related parties.
- Unusually important subsequent events.

2) **Other-matter paragraph (nonissuer)**

> *Hint*: Used to communicate a matter that is not presented or disclosed in the financial statements.

If the auditor considers it necessary to communicate a matter other than those that are presented or disclosed in the financial statements that, in the auditor's professional judgment, is relevant to users' understanding of the audit, the auditor's responsibilities, or the auditor's report, the auditor should:
- do so in a paragraph in the auditor's report with the heading "**Other Matter**" or other appropriate heading.
- should include this paragraph immediately after the opinion paragraph and any emphasis-of-matter paragraph or elsewhere in the auditor's report if the content of the other-matter paragraph is relevant to the "Other Reporting Responsibilities" section.

i. **Required Inclusion of an Other-Matter Paragraph**
The following paragraphs in other AU-C sections **require the auditor to include an other-matter paragraph in the auditor's report** in certain circumstances.

a) *Subsequent Events and Subsequently Discovered Facts* **(AU-C 560)**
If there are subsequently discovered facts that became known to the auditor after the report release date (see AU-C 560) and if management revises the financial statements (consistent with the subsequent facts) and if the auditor's opinion on the revised financial statements differs from the opinion the auditor previously expressed, disclose the following matters in an emphasis-of-matter or other-matter paragraph:
- The date of the auditor's previous report.
- The type of opinion previously expressed.
- The substantive reasons for the different opinion.
- That the auditor's opinion on the revised financial statements is different from the auditor's previous opinion.

b) ***Forming an Opinion and Reporting on Financial Statements* (AU-C 700)**
If the financial statements of the prior period were audited by a predecessor auditor, and the predecessor auditor's report on the prior period's financial statements is not reissued, in addition to expressing an opinion on the current period's financial statements, the auditor should state the following in an other matter paragraph:
- That the financial statements of the prior period were audited by a predecessor auditor
- The type of opinion expressed by the predecessor auditor and, if the opinion was modified, the reasons therefore
- The nature of an emphasis-of-matter paragraph or other-matter paragraph included in the predecessor auditor's report, if any
- The date of that report.

When current period financial statements are audited and presented in comparative form with compiled or reviewed financial statements for the prior period, and the report on the prior period is not reissued, the auditor should

include an other-matter paragraph in the current period auditor's report that includes the following:
- The service performed in the prior period
- The date of the report on that service
- A description of any material modifications noted in that report
- A statement that the service was less in scope than an audit and does not provide the basis for the expression of an opinion on the financial statements.

If the prior period financial statements were not audited, reviewed, or compiled, the financial statements should be clearly marked to indicate their status, and the auditor's report should include an other-matter paragraph to indicate that the auditor has not audited, reviewed, or compiled the prior period financial statements and that the auditor assumes no responsibility for them.

c) ***Other Information in Documents Containing Audited Financial Statements* (AU-C 720)**
When the auditor identifies a material inconsistency prior to the report release date that requires revision of the other information and management refuses to make the revision, the auditor should communicate this matter to those charged with governance and
- **include in the auditor's report an other-matter paragraph describing the material inconsistency.**
- withhold the auditor's report; or
- when withdrawal is possible under applicable law or regulation, withdraw from the engagement.

d) ***Supplementary Information in Relation to the Financial Statements as a Whole* (AU-C 725)**
When the entity presents the supplementary information with the financial statements, the auditor should report on the supplementary information in either (*a*) an other matter paragraph or (*b*) in a separate report on the supplementary information.

e) ***Required Supplementary Information* (AU-C 730)**
The auditor should include an other-matter paragraph in the auditor's report on the financial statements to refer to the required supplementary information.

f) ***Special Considerations—Audits of Financial Statements Prepared in Accordance with Special Purpose Frameworks* (AU-C 800)**
Except for the general use regulatory basis financial statements, the auditor's report on special purpose financial statements should include an other-matter paragraph, under an appropriate heading, that restricts the use of the auditor's report when the special purpose financial statements are prepared in accordance with
- a contractual basis of accounting,
- a regulatory basis of accounting, or
- an other-basis of accounting

g) ***Reporting on Compliance with Aspects of Contractual Agreements or Regulatory Requirements in Connection with Audited Financial Statements* (AU-C 806)**
When a report on compliance is included in the auditor's report on the financial statements, the auditor's report should include an other-matter paragraph that includes a reference to the specific covenants or paragraphs of the contractual agreement or regulatory requirement, insofar as they relate to accounting matters.

A summary of explanatory information for nonissuers:

Circumstance	Modification	
	Matter-of-emphasis paragraph	Other-matter paragraph
Subsequent events/subsequently discovered facts	✓ (if referring to a matter presented or disclosed in financial statements)	✓ (if referring to a matter **not** presented or disclosed in financial statements)
Going concern issue	✓	
Change in accounting principle with a material effect	✓	
Change in reporting entity	✓	
Prior material misstatement corrected	✓	
Special purpose frameworks	✓	
Opinion based in part on report of another auditor (e.g., predecessor auditor)		✓
Reporting on compliance or regulatory requirements		✓
Supplementary information		✓

c. **Example reports**

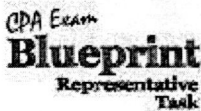

Prepare a draft auditor's report starting with a report example (e.g., an illustrative audit report from professional standards) for an audit of an issuer or nonissuer.

The following illustrative audit reports for an issuer and nonissuer are shown below.

1) **Issuer (PCOAB) audit reports**
   Standard Unqualified Report – Single Year
   Standard Unqualified Report – Comparative
   Scope Restriction Qualification
   GAAP Violation Qualification
   Inadequate Disclosure Qualification
   Omitted Statement of Cash Flows Qualification
   Change in Accounting Principle without Reasonable Justification Qualification
   Adverse Opinion
   Disclaimer of Opinion

   Note: These reports have been updated to comply with PCAOB 2017-001, eligible for testing after July 1, 2018.

2) **Nonissuer (AICPA) opinions**
   Unmodified Opinion – Single Year
   Unmodified Opinion – Comparative
   Scope Restriction Qualification
   GAAP Violation Qualification
   Inadequate Disclosure Qualification
   Adverse Opinion
   Disclaimer of Opinion

Standard Unqualified Report – Single Year (Issuer)

[Eligible for testing Q3 2018; updated per PCAOB 2017-001.]

<u>Report of Independent Registered Public Accounting Firm</u>
To the shareholders and the board of directors of X Company, ⟵ Addressee

Opinion on the Financial Statements

Opinion Section:
We have audited the accompanying balance sheet of X Company (the "Company") as of December 31, 20X2, the related statements of operations, stockholders' equity, and cash flows, for the period ended December 31, 20X2, and the related notes [and schedules] (collectively referred to as the "financial statements"). In our opinion, the financial statements present fairly, in all material respects, the financial position of the Company as of [at] December 31, 20X2 and the results of its operations and its cash flows for the period ended December 31, 20X2, in conformity with [the applicable financial reporting framework].

Basis for Opinion

Basis for Opinion Section:
These financial statements are the responsibility of the Company's management. Our responsibility is to express an opinion on the Company's financial statements based on our audits. We are a public accounting firm registered with the Public Company Accounting Oversight Board (United States) ("PCAOB") and are required to be independent with respect to the Company in accordance with the U.S. federal securities laws and the applicable rules and regulations of the Securities and Exchange Commission and the PCAOB. We conducted our audits in accordance with the standards of the PCAOB. Those standards require that we plan and perform the audit to obtain reasonable assurance about whether the financial statements are free of material misstatement, **whether due to error or fraud.** Our audits included performing procedures to assess the risks of material misstatement of the financial statements, whether due to error or fraud, and performing procedures that respond to those risks. Such procedures included examining, on a test basis, evidence regarding the amounts and disclosures in the financial statements. Our audits also included evaluating the accounting principles used and significant estimates made by management, as well as evaluating the overall presentation of the financial statements. We believe that our audits provide a reasonable basis for our opinion. ⟵ Explanatory language [if applicable]

Critical Audit Matters [if applicable]
The critical audit matters communicated below are matters arising from the current period audit that were communicated or required to be communicated to the audit committee and that: (1) relate to accounts or disclosures that are material to the financial statements and (2) involved our especially challenging, subjective, or complex judgments. Critical audit matters do not alter in any way our opinion on the financial statements, taken as a whole, and we do not provide separate opinions on the critical audit matters or on the accounts or disclosures to which they relate.
[Include critical audit matters] ⟵ Critical Audit Matters, when effective

[Signature]
We have served as the Company's auditor since [year]. ⟵ Auditor Tenure

[City and State or Country]
[Date

Standard Unqualified Report – Comparative (Issuer)

[Eligible for testing Q3 2018; updated per PCAOB 2017-001.]

<u>Report of Independent Registered Public Accounting Firm</u>
To the shareholders and the board of directors of X Company,

Opinion on the Financial Statements
We have audited the accompanying balance sheets of X Company (the "Company") as of December 31, 20X2 and 20X1, the related statements of operations, stockholders' equity, and cash flows, for each of the three years in the period ended December 31, 20X2, and the related notes [and schedules] (collectively referred to as the "financial statements"). In our opinion, the financial statements present fairly, in all material respects, the financial position of the Company as of [at] December 31, 20X2 and 20X1, and the results of its operations and its cash flows for each of the three years in the period ended December 31, 20X2, in conformity with [the applicable financial reporting framework].

Basis for Opinion
These financial statements are the responsibility of the Company's management. Our responsibility is to express an opinion on the Company's financial statements based on our audits. We are a public accounting firm registered with the Public Company Accounting Oversight Board (United States) ("PCAOB") and are required to be independent with respect to the Company in accordance with the U.S. federal securities laws and the applicable rules and regulations of the Securities and Exchange Commission and the PCAOB. We conducted our audits in accordance with the standards of the PCAOB. Those standards require that we plan and perform the audit to obtain reasonable assurance about whether the financial statements are free of material misstatement, **whether due to error or fraud.** Our audits included performing procedures to assess the risks of material misstatement of the financial statements, whether due to error or fraud, and performing procedures that respond to those risks. Such procedures included examining, on a test basis, evidence regarding the amounts and disclosures in the financial statements. Our audits also included evaluating the accounting principles used and significant estimates made by management, as well as evaluating the overall presentation of the financial statements. We believe that our audits provide a reasonable basis for our opinion.

Critical Audit Matters [if applicable]
The critical audit matters communicated below are matters arising from the current period audit that were communicated or required to be communicated to the audit committee and that: (1) relate to accounts or disclosures that are material to the financial statements and (2) involved our especially challenging, subjective, or complex judgments. Critical audit matters do not alter in any way our opinion on the financial statements, taken as a whole, and we do not provide separate opinions on the critical audit matters or on the accounts or disclosures to which they relate.
[Include critical audit matters]

[Signature]
We have served as the Company's auditor since [year].

[City and State or Country]
[Date

Scope Restriction Qualification (Issuer)

[Eligible for testing Q3 2018; updated per PCAOB 2017-001.]

<u>Report of Independent Registered Public Accounting Firm</u>
To the shareholders and the board of directors of X Company,

Opinion on the Financial Statements
We have audited the accompanying balance sheets of X Company as of December 31, 20X2 and 20X1, and the related statements of income, retained earnings, and cash flows for each of the years then ended, and the related notes [and schedules] (collectively referred to as the "financial statements"). In our opinion, except for the effects of the adjustments, if any, as might have been determined to be necessary had we been able to examine evidence regarding the foreign affiliate investments and earnings, as described below, the financial statements present fairly, in all material respects, the financial position of the Company as of December 31, 20X2 and 20X1, and the results of its operation and its cash flows for the years then ended in conformity with accounting principles generally accepted in the United States of America.

We were unable to obtain audited financial statements supporting the Company's investment in a foreign affiliate stated at $_____ and $_____ at December 31, 20X2 and 20X1, respectively, or its equity in earnings of that affiliate of $_____ and $_____, which is included in net income for the years then ended as described in Note X to the financial statements; nor were we able to satisfy ourselves as to the carrying value of the investment in the foreign affiliate or the equity in its earnings by other auditing procedures. ← **Scope Restriction**

Basis for Opinion
These financial statements are the responsibility of the Company's management. Our responsibility is to express an opinion on the Company's financial statements based on our audits. We are a public accounting firm registered with the Public Company Accounting Oversight Board (United States) ("PCAOB") and are required to be independent with respect to the Company in accordance with the U.S. federal securities laws and the applicable rules and regulations of the Securities and Exchange Commission and the PCAOB. Except as discussed above, we conducted our audits in accordance with the standards of the PCAOB. Those standards require that we plan and perform the audit to obtain reasonable assurance about whether the financial statements are free of material misstatement, **whether due to error or fraud.** Our audits included performing procedures to assess the risks of material misstatement of the financial statements, whether due to error or fraud, and performing procedures that respond to those risks. Such procedures included examining, on a test basis, evidence regarding the amounts and disclosures in the financial statements. Our audits also included evaluating the accounting principles used and significant estimates made by management, as well as evaluating the overall presentation of the financial statements. We believe that our audits provide a reasonable basis for our opinion.

Critical Audit Matters [if applicable]
[Include critical audit matters]

[Signature]
We have served as the Company's auditor since [year].

[City and State or Country]
[Date]

Hint: Explanatory paragraph [scope restriction] is after the opinion paragraph following the adoption of PCAOB 2017-001.

GAAP Violation Qualification (Issuer)

[Eligible for testing Q3 2018; updated per PCAOB 2017-001.]

<u>Report of Independent Registered Public Accounting Firm</u>

To the shareholders and the board of directors of X Company,

Opinion on the Financial Statements
We have audited the accompanying balance sheets of X Company as of December 31, 20X2 and 20X1, and the related statements of income, retained earnings, and cash flows for each of the years then ended, and the related notes [and schedules] (collectively referred to as the "financial statements"). In our opinion, except for the effects of not capitalizing certain lease agreements, as described below, the financial statements present fairly, in all material respects, the financial position of the Company as of December 31, 20X2 and 20X1, and the results of its operations and its cash flows for the years then ended in conformity with accounting principles generally accepted in the United States of America. ←------ Qualified opinion

The Company has excluded, from property and debt in the accompanying balance sheets, certain lease obligations that, in our opinion, should be capitalized in order to conform with accounting principles generally accepted in the United States of America. If these lease obligations were capitalized, property would be increased by $_____ and $_____, long-term debt by $_____ and $_____, and retained earnings by $_____ and $_____ as of December 31, 20X2 and 20X1, respectively. Additionally, net income would be increased (decreased) by $_____ and $_____ and earnings per share would be increased (decreased) by $_____ and $_____, respectively, for the years then ended.

As more fully described in Note X to the financial statements, the Company has excluded certain lease obligations from property and debt in the accompanying balance sheets. In our opinion, accounting principles generally accepted in the United States of America require that such obligations be included in the balance sheets. [Used if the GAAP violation is discussed in the notes to the financial statements.]

Basis for Opinion
These financial statements are the responsibility of the Company's management. Our responsibility is to express an opinion on the Company's financial statements based on our audits. We are a public accounting firm registered with the Public Company Accounting Oversight Board (United States) ("PCAOB") and are required to be independent with respect to the Company in accordance with the U.S. federal securities laws and the applicable rules and regulations of the Securities and Exchange Commission and the PCAOB. Except as discussed above, we conducted our audits in accordance with the standards of the PCAOB. Those standards require that we plan and perform the audit to obtain reasonable assurance about whether the financial statements are free of material misstatement, **whether due to error or fraud.** Our audits included performing procedures to assess the risks of material misstatement of the financial statements, whether due to error or fraud, and performing procedures that respond to those risks. Such procedures included examining, on a test basis, evidence regarding the amounts and disclosures in the financial statements. Our audits also included evaluating the accounting principles used and significant estimates made by management, as well as evaluating the overall presentation of the financial statements. We believe that our audits provide a reasonable basis for our opinion.

Critical Audit Matters [if applicable]
[Include critical audit matters]

[*Signature*]
We have served as the Company's auditor since [year].

[*City and State or Country*]
[*Date*]

Inadequate Disclosure Qualification (Issuer)

[Eligible for testing Q3 2018; updated per PCAOB 2017-001.]

<u>Report of Independent Registered Public Accounting Firm</u>

To the shareholders and the board of directors of X Company,

Opinion on the Financial Statements
We have audited the accompanying balance sheets of X Company as of December 31, 20X2 and 20X1, and the related statements of income, retained earnings, and cash flows for each of the years then ended, and the related notes [and schedules] (collectively referred to as the "financial statements"). In our opinion, except for the omission of the information discussed in the following paragraph, the financial statements present fairly, in all material respects, the financial position of the Company as of December 31, 20X2 and 20X1, and the results of its operations and its cash flows for the years then ended in conformity with accounting principles generally accepted in the United States of America.

← Qualified opinion

The Company's financial statements do not disclose [*describe the nature of the omitted disclosures*]. In our opinion, disclosure of this information is required by accounting principles generally accepted in the United States of America.

Basis for Opinion
These financial statements are the responsibility of the Company's management. Our responsibility is to express an opinion on the Company's financial statements based on our audits. We are a public accounting firm registered with the Public Company Accounting Oversight Board (United States) ("PCAOB") and are required to be independent with respect to the Company in accordance with the U.S. federal securities laws and the applicable rules and regulations of the Securities and Exchange Commission and the PCAOB. Except as discussed above, we conducted our audits in accordance with the standards of the PCAOB. Those standards require that we plan and perform the audit to obtain reasonable assurance about whether the financial statements are free of material misstatement**, whether due to error or fraud.** Our audits included performing procedures to assess the risks of material misstatement of the financial statements, whether due to error or fraud, and performing procedures that respond to those risks. Such procedures included examining, on a test basis, evidence regarding the amounts and disclosures in the financial statements. Our audits also included evaluating the accounting principles used and significant estimates made by management, as well as evaluating the overall presentation of the financial statements. We believe that our audits provide a reasonable basis for our opinion.

Critical Audit Matters [if applicable]
[Include critical audit <u>matters</u>]

[Signature]
We have served as the Company's auditor since [year].

[City and State or Country]
[Date]

Omitted Statement of Cash Flows Qualification (Issuer)

[Eligible for testing Q3 2018; updated per PCAOB 2017-001.]

<u>Report of Independent Registered Public Accounting Firm</u>

To the shareholders and the board of directors of X Company,

Opinion on the Financial Statements
We have audited the accompanying balance sheets of X Company as of December 31, 20X2 and 20X1, and the related statements of income and retained earnings for each of the years then ended, and the related notes [and schedules] (collectively referred to as the "financial statements". In our opinion, except that the omission of a statement of cash flows results in an incomplete presentation as explained in the following paragraph, the financial statements present fairly, in all material respects, the financial position of the Company as of December 31, 20X2 and 20X1, and the results of its operations for the years then ended in conformity with accounting principles generally accepted in the United States of America.

The Company declined to present a statement of cash flows for the years ended December 31, 20X2 and 20X1. Presentation of such statement summarizing the Company's operating, investing, and financing activities is required by accounting principles generally accepted in the United States of America.

Basis for Opinion
These financial statements are the responsibility of the Company's management. Our responsibility is to express an opinion on the Company's financial statements based on our audits. We are a public accounting firm registered with the Public Company Accounting Oversight Board (United States) ("PCAOB") and are required to be independent with respect to the Company in accordance with the U.S. federal securities laws and the applicable rules and regulations of the Securities and Exchange Commission and the PCAOB. Except as discussed above, we conducted our audits in accordance with the standards of the PCAOB. Those standards require that we plan and perform the audit to obtain reasonable assurance about whether the financial statements are free of material misstatement, **whether due to error or fraud.** Our audits included performing procedures to assess the risks of material misstatement of the financial statements, whether due to error or fraud, and performing procedures that respond to those risks. Such procedures included examining, on a test basis, evidence regarding the amounts and disclosures in the financial statements. Our audits also included evaluating the accounting principles used and significant estimates made by management, as well as evaluating the overall presentation of the financial statements. We believe that our audits provide a reasonable basis for our opinion.

Critical Audit Matters [if applicable]
[Include critical audit matters]

[Signature]
We have served as the Company's auditor since [year].

[City and State or Country]
[Date]

Change in Accounting Principle Without Reasonable Justification Qualification (Issuer)

[Eligible for testing Q3 2018; updated per PCAOB 2017-001.]

<u>Report of Independent Registered Public Accounting Firm</u>

To the shareholders and the board of directors of X Company,

Opinion on the Financial Statements
We have audited the accompanying balance sheets of X Company as of December 31, 20X2 and 20X1, and the related statements of income, retained earnings, and cash flows for each of the years then ended, and the related notes [and schedules] (collectively referred to as the "financial statements"). In our opinion, except for the change in accounting principle discussed in the following paragraph, the financial statements present fairly, in all material respects, the financial position of the Company as of December 31, 20X2 and 20X1, and the results of its operations and its cash flows for the years then ended in conformity with accounting principles generally accepted in the United States of America.

As disclosed in Note X to the financial statements, the Company adopted, in 20X2, the first-in, first-out method of accounting for its inventories, whereas it previously used the last-in, first-out method. Although use of the first-in, first-out method is in conformity with accounting principles generally accepted in the United States of America, in our opinion the Company has not provided reasonable justification that this accounting principle is preferable as required by those principles.

Basis for Opinion
These financial statements are the responsibility of the Company's management. Our responsibility is to express an opinion on the Company's financial statements based on our audits. We are a public accounting firm registered with the Public Company Accounting Oversight Board (United States) ("PCAOB") and are required to be independent with respect to the Company in accordance with the U.S. federal securities laws and the applicable rules and regulations of the Securities and Exchange Commission and the PCAOB. Except as discussed above, we conducted our audits in accordance with the standards of the PCAOB. Those standards require that we plan and perform the audit to obtain reasonable assurance about whether the financial statements are free of material misstatement, **whether due to error or fraud.** Our audits included performing procedures to assess the risks of material misstatement of the financial statements, whether due to error or fraud, and performing procedures that respond to those risks. Such procedures included examining, on a test basis, evidence regarding the amounts and disclosures in the financial statements. Our audits also included evaluating the accounting principles used and significant estimates made by management, as well as evaluating the overall presentation of the financial statements. We believe that our audits provide a reasonable basis for our opinion.

Critical Audit Matters [if applicable]
[Include critical audit matters]

[*Signature*]
We have served as the Company's auditor since [year].

[*City and State or Country*]
[*Date*]

Adverse Opinion (Issuer)

[Eligible for testing Q3 2018; updated per PCAOB 2017-001.]

<u>Report of Independent Registered Public Accounting Firm</u>

To the shareholders and the board of directors of X Company, → Adverse opinion

Opinion on the Financial Statements
We have audited the accompanying balance sheets of X Company as of December 31, 20X2 and 20X1, and the related statements of income, retained earnings, and cash flows for each of the years then ended, and the related notes [and schedules] (collectively referred to as the "financial statements"). In our opinion, because of the effects of the matters discussed in the following paragraphs, the financial statements do **not** present fairly, in conformity with accounting principles generally accepted in the United States of America, the financial position of the Company as of December 31, 20X2 and 20X1, or the results of its operations or its cash flows for the years then ended.

As discussed in Note X to the financial statements, the Company carries its property, plant and equipment accounts at appraisal values, and provides depreciation on the basis of such values. Further, the Company does not provide for income taxes with respect to differences between financial income and taxable income arising because of the use, for income tax purposes, of the installment method of reporting gross profit from certain types of sales. Accounting principles generally accepted in the United States of America require that property, plant and equipment be stated at an amount not in excess of cost, reduced by depreciation based on such amount, and that deferred income taxes be provided.

Because of the departures from accounting principles generally accepted in the United States of America identified above, as of December 31, 20X2 and 20X1, inventories have been increased $_____ and $_____ by inclusion in manufacturing overhead of depreciation in excess of that based on cost; property, plant and equipment, less accumulated depreciation, is carried at $_____ and $_____ in excess of an amount based on the cost to the Company; and deferred income taxes of $_____ and $_____ have not been recorded; resulting in an increase of $_____ and $_____ in retained earnings and in appraisal surplus of $_____ and $_____, respectively. For the years ended December 31, 20X2 and 20X1, cost of goods sold has been increased $_____ and $_____, respectively, because of the effects of the depreciation accounting referred to above and deferred income taxes of $_____ and $_____ have not been provided, resulting in an increase in net income of $_____ and $_____, respectively.

Basis for Opinion
These financial statements are the responsibility of the Company's management. Our responsibility is to express an opinion on the Company's financial statements based on our audits. We are a public accounting firm registered with the Public Company Accounting Oversight Board (United States) ("PCAOB") and are required to be independent with respect to the Company in accordance with the U.S. federal securities laws and the applicable rules and regulations of the Securities and Exchange Commission and the PCAOB. Except as discussed above, we conducted our audits in accordance with the standards of the PCAOB. Those standards require that we plan and perform the audit to obtain reasonable assurance about whether the financial statements are free of material misstatement, **whether due to error or fraud.** Our audits included performing procedures to assess the risks of material misstatement of the financial statements, whether due to error or fraud, and performing procedures that respond to those risks. Such procedures included examining, on a test basis, evidence regarding the amounts and disclosures in the financial statements. Our audits also included evaluating the accounting principles used and significant estimates made by management, as well as evaluating the overall presentation of the financial statements. We believe that our audits provide a reasonable basis for our opinion.

Critical Audit Matters [if applicable]
[Include critical audit matters]

[*Signature*]
We have served as the Company's auditor since [year].

[*City and State or Country*]
[*Date*]

Disclaimer of Opinion (Issuer)

[Eligible for testing Q3 2018; updated per PCAOB 2017-001.]

<u>Report of Independent Registered Public Accounting Firm</u>

To the shareholders and the board of directors of X Company,   ← Disclaimer opinion

Disclaimer of Opinion on the Financial Statements
We were engaged to audit the accompanying balance sheets of X Company as of December 31, 20X2 and 20X1, and the related statements of [titles of the financial statements, e.g., income, comprehensive income, stockholders' equity, and cash flows], and the related notes [and schedules] (collectively referred to as the "financial statements"). As described in the following paragraph, because the Company did not take physical inventories and we were not able to apply other auditing procedures to satisfy ourselves as to inventory quantities and the cost of property and equipment, we were not able to obtain sufficient appropriate audit evidence to provide a basis for an audit opinion on the financial statements, and we do not express, an opinion on these financial statements.

The Company did not make a count of its physical inventory in 20X2 or 20X1, stated in the accompanying financial statements at $_____ as of December 31, 20X2, and at $_____ as of December 31, 20X1. Further, evidence supporting the cost of property and equipment acquired prior to December 31, 20X1, is no longer available. The Company's records do not permit the application of other auditing procedures to inventories or property and equipment.

Basis for Disclaimer of Opinion
These financial statements are the responsibility of the Company's management. We are a public accounting firm registered with the Public Company Accounting Oversight Board (United States) ("PCAOB") and are required to be independent with respect to the Company in accordance with the U.S. federal securities laws and the applicable rules and regulations of the Securities and Exchange Commission and the PCAOB.

[*Signature*]
We have served as the Company's auditor since [year].

[*City and State or Country*]
[*Date*]

Unmodified Opinion – Single Year (Nonissuer)

Independent Auditor's Report

[*Appropriate Addressee*]

[*Entity Name*]

Report on the Financial Statements

We have audited the accompanying financial statements of ABC Company, which comprise the balance sheet as of December 31, 20X1, and the related statements of income, changes in stockholders' equity, and cash flows for the year then ended, and the related notes to the financial statements.

Management's Responsibility for the Financial Statements

Management is responsible for the preparation and fair presentation of these financial statements in accordance with accounting principles generally accepted in the United States of America; this includes the design, implementation, and maintenance of internal control relevant to the preparation and fair presentation of financial statements that are free from material misstatement, whether due to fraud or error.

Auditor's Responsibility

Our responsibility is to express an opinion on these financial statements based on our audit. We conducted our audit in accordance with auditing standards generally accepted in the United States of America. Those standards require that we plan and perform the audit to obtain reasonable assurance about whether the financial statements are free from material misstatement.

An audit involves performing procedures to obtain audit evidence about the amounts and disclosures in the financial statements. The procedures selected depend on the auditor's judgment, including the assessment of the risks of material misstatement of the financial statements, whether due to fraud or error. In making those risk assessments, the auditor considers internal control relevant to the entity's preparation and fair presentation of the financial statements in order to design audit procedures that are appropriate in the circumstances, but not for the purpose of expressing an opinion on the effectiveness of the entity's internal control. Accordingly, we express no such opinion. An audit also includes evaluating the appropriateness of accounting policies used and the reasonableness of significant accounting estimates made by management, as well as evaluating the overall presentation of the financial statements.

We believe that the audit evidence we have obtained is sufficient and appropriate to provide a basis for our audit opinion.

Opinion

In our opinion, the financial statements referred to above present fairly, in all material respects, the financial position of ABC Company as of December 31, 20X1, and the results of its operations and its cash flows for the year then ended in accordance with accounting principles generally accepted in the United States of America.

Report on Other Legal and Regulatory Requirements

[*Form and content of this section of the auditor's report will vary depending on the nature of the auditor's other reporting responsibilities.*]

[*Auditor's signature*]

[*Auditor's city and state*]

[*Date of the auditor's report*]

Unmodified Opinion – Comparative (Nonissuer)

Independent Auditor's Report

[*Appropriate Addressee*]

[*Entity Name*]

Report on the Financial Statements

We have audited the accompanying consolidated financial statements of ABC Company and its subsidiaries, which comprise the consolidated balance sheets as of December 31, 20X1 and 20X0, and the related consolidated statements of income, changes in stockholders' equity, and cash flows for the years then ended, and the related notes to the financial statements.

Management's Responsibility for the Financial Statements

Management is responsible for the preparation and fair presentation of these consolidated financial statements in accordance with accounting principles generally accepted in the United States of America; this includes the design, implementation, and maintenance of internal control relevant to the preparation and fair presentation of consolidated financial statements that are free from material misstatement, whether due to fraud or error.

Auditor's Responsibility

Our responsibility is to express an opinion on these consolidated financial statements based on our audits. We conducted our audits in accordance with auditing standards generally accepted in the United States of America. Those standards require that we plan and perform the audit to obtain reasonable assurance about whether the consolidated financial statements are free from material misstatement.

An audit involves performing procedures to obtain audit evidence about the amounts and disclosures in the consolidated financial statements. The procedures selected depend on the auditor's judgment, including the assessment of the risks of material misstatement of the consolidated financial statements, whether due to fraud or error. In making those risk assessments, the auditor considers internal control relevant to the entity's preparation and fair presentation of the consolidated financial statements in order to design audit procedures that are appropriate in the circumstances, but not for the purpose of expressing an opinion on the effectiveness of the entity's internal control. Accordingly, we express no such opinion. An audit also includes evaluating the appropriateness of accounting policies used and the reasonableness of significant accounting estimates made by management, as well as evaluating the overall presentation of the consolidated financial statements.

We believe that the audit evidence we have obtained is sufficient and appropriate to provide a basis for our audit opinion.

Opinion

In our opinion, the consolidated financial statements referred to above present fairly, in all material respects, the financial position of ABC Company and its subsidiaries as of December 31, 20X1 and 20X0, and the results of their operations and their cash flows for the years then ended in accordance with accounting principles generally accepted in the United States of America.

Report on Other Legal and Regulatory Requirements

[*Form and content of this section of the auditor's report will vary depending on the nature of the auditor's other reporting responsibilities.*]

[*Auditor's signature*]

[*Auditor's city and state*]

[*Date of the auditor's report*]

Scope Restriction Qualification (Nonissuer)

Independent Auditor's Report

[*Appropriate Addressee*]

[*Entity Name*]

Report on the Financial Statements

We have audited the accompanying financial statements of ABC Company, which comprise the balance sheet as of December 31, 20X1, and the related statements of income, changes in stockholders' equity, and cash flows for the year then ended, and the related notes to the financial statements.

Management's Responsibility for the Financial Statements

Management is responsible for the preparation and fair presentation of these financial statements in accordance with accounting principles generally accepted in the United States of America; this includes the design, implementation, and maintenance of internal control relevant to the preparation and fair presentation of financial statements that are free from material misstatement, whether due to fraud or error.

Auditor's Responsibility

Our responsibility is to express an opinion on these financial statements based on our audit. We conducted our audit in accordance with auditing standards generally accepted in the United States of America. Those standards require that we plan and perform the audit to obtain reasonable assurance about whether the financial statements are free from material misstatement.

An audit involves performing procedures to obtain audit evidence about the amounts and disclosures in the financial statements. The procedures selected depend on the auditor's judgment, including the assessment of the risks of material misstatement of the financial statements, whether due to fraud or error. In making those risk assessments, the auditor considers internal control relevant to the entity's preparation and fair presentation of the financial statements in order to design audit procedures that are appropriate in the circumstances, but not for the purpose of expressing an opinion on the effectiveness of the entity's internal control. Accordingly, we express no such opinion. An audit also includes evaluating the appropriateness of accounting policies used and the reasonableness of significant accounting estimates made by management, as well as evaluating the overall presentation of the financial statements.

We believe that the audit evidence we have obtained is sufficient and appropriate to provide a basis for our qualified audit opinion.

Basis for Qualified Opinion

ABC Company's investment in XYZ Company, a foreign affiliate acquired during the year and accounted for under the equity method, is carried at $XXX on the balance sheet at December 31, 20X1, and ABC Company's share of XYZ Company's net income of $XXX is included in ABC Company's net income for the year then ended. We were unable to obtain sufficient appropriate audit evidence about the carrying amount of ABC Company's investment in XYZ Company as of December 31, 20X1 and ABC Company's share of XYZ Company's net income for the year then ended because we were denied access to the financial information, management, and the auditors of XYZ Company. Consequently, we were unable to determine whether any adjustments to these amounts were necessary.

Qualified Opinion

In our opinion, except for the possible effects of the matter described in the Basis for Qualified Opinion paragraph, the financial statements referred to above present fairly, in all material respects, the financial position of ABC Company as of December 31, 20X1, and the results of its operations and its cash flows for the year then ended in accordance with accounting principles generally accepted in the United States of America.

Report on Other Legal and Regulatory Requirements

[*Form and content of this section of the auditor's report will vary depending on the nature of the auditor's other reporting responsibilities.*]

[*Auditor's signature*]

[*Auditor's city and state*]

GAAP Violation Qualification (Nonissuer)

Independent Auditor's Report

[*Appropriate Addressee*]

[*Entity Name*]

Report on the Financial Statements

We have audited the accompanying financial statements of ABC Company, which comprise the balance sheets as of December 31, 20X1 and 20X0, and the related statements of income, changes in stockholders' equity, and cash flows for the years then ended, and the related notes to the financial statements.

Management's Responsibility for the Financial Statements

Management is responsible for the preparation and fair presentation of these financial statements in accordance with accounting principles generally accepted in the United States of America; this includes the design, implementation, and maintenance of internal control relevant to the preparation and fair presentation of financial statements that are free from material misstatement, whether due to fraud or error.

Auditor's Responsibility

Our responsibility is to express an opinion on these financial statements based on our audits. We conducted our audits in accordance with auditing standards generally accepted in the United States of America. Those standards require that we plan and perform the audit to obtain reasonable assurance about whether the financial statements are free from material misstatement.

An audit involves performing procedures to obtain audit evidence about the amounts and disclosures in the financial statements. The procedures selected depend on the auditor's judgment, including the assessment of the risks of material misstatement of the financial statements, whether due to fraud or error. In making those risk assessments, the auditor considers internal control relevant to the entity's preparation and fair presentation of the financial statements in order to design audit procedures that are appropriate in the circumstances, but not for the purpose of expressing an opinion on the effectiveness of the entity's internal control. Accordingly, we express no such opinion. An audit also includes evaluating the appropriateness of accounting policies used and the reasonableness of significant accounting estimates made by management, as well as evaluating the overall presentation of the financial statements.

We believe that the audit evidence we have obtained is sufficient and appropriate to provide a basis for our qualified audit opinion.

Basis for Qualified Opinion

The Company has stated inventories at cost in the accompanying balance sheets. Accounting principles generally accepted in the United States of America require inventories to be stated at the lower of cost or market. If the Company stated inventories at the lower of cost or market, a write down of $XXX and $XXX would have been required as of December 31, 20X1 and 20X0, respectively. Accordingly, cost of sales would have been increased by $XXX and $XXX, and net income, income taxes, and stockholders' equity would have been reduced by $XXX, $XXX, and $XXX, and $XXX, $XXX, and $XXX, as of and for the years ended December 31, 20X1 and 20X0, respectively.

Qualified Opinion

In our opinion, except for the effects of the matter described in the Basis for Qualified Opinion paragraph, the financial statements referred to above present fairly, in all material respects, the financial position of ABC Company as of December 31, 20X1 and 20X0, and the results of its operations and its cash flows for the years then ended in accordance with accounting principles generally accepted in the United States of America.

Report on Other Legal and Regulatory Requirements

[*Form and content of this section of the auditor's report will vary depending on the nature of the auditor's other reporting responsibilities.*]

[*Auditor's signature*]

[*Auditor's city and state*]

[*Date of the auditor's report*]

Inadequate Disclosure Qualification (Nonissuer)

Independent Auditor's Report

[*Appropriate Addressee*]

[*Entity Name*]

Report on the Financial Statements

We have audited the accompanying financial statements of ABC Company, which comprise the balance sheets as of December 31, 20X1 and 20X0, and the related statements of income, changes in stockholders' equity, and cash flows for the years then ended, and the related notes to the financial statements.

Management's Responsibility for the Financial Statements

Management is responsible for the preparation and fair presentation of these financial statements in accordance with accounting principles generally accepted in the United States of America; this includes the design, implementation, and maintenance of internal control relevant to the preparation and fair presentation of financial statements that are free from material misstatement, whether due to fraud or error.

Auditor's Responsibility

Our responsibility is to express an opinion on these financial statements based on our audits. We conducted our audits in accordance with auditing standards generally accepted in the United States of America. Those standards require that we plan and perform the audit to obtain reasonable assurance about whether the financial statements are free from material misstatement.

An audit involves performing procedures to obtain audit evidence about the amounts and disclosures in the financial statements. The procedures selected depend on the auditor's judgment, including the assessment of the risks of material misstatement of the financial statements, whether due to fraud or error. In making those risk assessments, the auditor considers internal control relevant to the entity's preparation and fair presentation of the financial statements in order to design audit procedures that are appropriate in the circumstances, but not for the purpose of expressing an opinion on the effectiveness of the entity's internal control. Accordingly, we express no such opinion. An audit also includes evaluating the appropriateness of accounting policies used and the reasonableness of significant accounting estimates made by management, as well as evaluating the overall presentation of the financial statements.

We believe that the audit evidence we have obtained is sufficient and appropriate to provide a basis for our qualified audit opinion.

Basis for Qualified Opinion

The Company's financial statements do not disclose [*describe the nature of the omitted information that is not practicable to present in the auditor's report*]. In our opinion, disclosure of this information is required by accounting principles generally accepted in the United States of America.

Qualified Opinion

In our opinion, except for the omission of the information described in the Basis for Qualified Opinion paragraph, the financial statements referred to above present fairly, in all material respects, the financial position of ABC Company as of December 31, 20X1 and 20X0, and the results of its operations and its cash flows for the years then ended in accordance with accounting principles generally accepted in the United States of America.

Report on Other Legal and Regulatory Requirements

[*Form and content of this section of the auditor's report will vary depending on the nature of the auditor's other reporting responsibilities.*]

[*Auditor's signature*]

[*Auditor's city and state*]

[*Date of the auditor's report*]

Adverse Opinion (Nonissuer)

Independent Auditor's Report

[*Appropriate Addressee*]

[*Entity Name*]

Report on the Consolidated Financial Statements

We have audited the accompanying consolidated financial statements of ABC Company and its subsidiaries, which comprise the consolidated balance sheet as of December 31, 20X1, and the related consolidated statements of income, changes in stockholders' equity, and cash flows for the year then ended, and the related notes to the financial statements.

Management's Responsibility for the Financial Statements

Management is responsible for the preparation and fair presentation of these consolidated financial statements in accordance with accounting principles generally accepted in the United States of America; this includes the design, implementation, and maintenance of internal control relevant to the preparation and fair presentation of consolidated financial statements that are free from material misstatement, whether due to fraud or error.

Auditor's Responsibility

Our responsibility is to express an opinion on these consolidated financial statements based on our audit. We conducted our audit in accordance with auditing standards generally accepted in the United States of America. Those standards require that we plan and perform the audit to obtain reasonable assurance about whether the consolidated financial statements are free from material misstatement.

An audit involves performing procedures to obtain audit evidence about the amounts and disclosures in the consolidated financial statements. The procedures selected depend on the auditor's judgment, including the assessment of the risks of material misstatement of the consolidated financial statements, whether due to fraud or error. In making those risk assessments, the auditor considers internal control relevant to the entity's preparation and fair presentation of the consolidated financial statements in order to design audit procedures that are appropriate in the circumstances, but not for the purpose of expressing an opinion on the effectiveness of the entity's internal control. Accordingly, we express no such opinion. An audit also includes evaluating the appropriateness of accounting policies used and the reasonableness of significant accounting estimates made by management, as well as evaluating the overall presentation of the consolidated financial statements.

We believe that the audit evidence we have obtained is sufficient and appropriate to provide a basis for our adverse audit opinion.

Basis for Adverse Opinion

As described in Note X, the Company has not consolidated the financial statements of subsidiary XYZ Company that it acquired during 20X1 because it has not yet been able to ascertain the fair values of certain of the subsidiary's material assets and liabilities at the acquisition date. This investment is therefore accounted for on a cost basis by the Company. Under accounting principles generally accepted in the United States of America, the subsidiary should have been consolidated because it is controlled by the Company. Had XYZ Company been consolidated, many elements in the accompanying consolidated financial statements would have been materially affected. The effects on the consolidated financial statements of the failure to consolidate have not been determined.

Adverse Opinion

In our opinion, because of the significance of the matter discussed in the Basis for Adverse Opinion paragraph, the consolidated financial statements referred to above do not present fairly the financial position of ABC Company and its subsidiaries as of December 31, 20X1, or the results of their operations or their cash flows for the year then ended in accordance with accounting principles generally accepted in the United States of America.

Report on Other Legal and Regulatory Requirements

[*Form and content of this section of the auditor's report will vary depending on the nature of the auditor's other reporting responsibilities.*]

[*Auditor's signature*]
[*Auditor's city and state*]
[*Date of the auditor's report*]

Disclaimer of Opinion (Nonissuer)

Independent Auditor's Report

[*Appropriate Addressee*]

[*Entity Name*]

Report on the Financial Statements

We were engaged to audit the accompanying financial statements of ABC Company, which comprise the balance sheet as of December 31, 20X1, and the related statements of income, changes in stockholders' equity, and cash flows for the year then ended, and the related notes to the financial statements.

Management's Responsibility for the Financial Statements

Management is responsible for the preparation and fair presentation of these financial statements in accordance with accounting principles generally accepted in the United States of America; this includes the design, implementation, and maintenance of internal control relevant to the preparation and fair presentation of financial statements that are free from material misstatement, whether due to fraud or error.

Auditor's Responsibility

Our responsibility is to express an opinion on these financial statements based on conducting the audit in accordance with auditing standards generally accepted in the United States of America. Because of the matters described in the Basis for Disclaimer of Opinion paragraph, however, we were not able to obtain sufficient appropriate audit evidence to provide a basis for an audit opinion.

Basis for Disclaimer of Opinion

We were not engaged as auditors of the Company until after December 31, 20X1, and, therefore, did not observe the counting of physical inventories at the beginning or end of the year. We were unable to satisfy ourselves by other auditing procedures concerning the inventory held at December 31, 20X1, which is stated in the balance sheet at $XXX. In addition, the introduction of a new computerized accounts receivable system in September 20X1 resulted in numerous misstatements in accounts receivable. As of the date of our audit report, management was still in the process of rectifying the system deficiencies and correcting the misstatements. We were unable to confirm or verify by alternative means accounts receivable included in the balance sheet at a total amount of $XXX at December 31, 20X1. As a result of these matters, we were unable to determine whether any adjustments might have been found necessary in respect of recorded or unrecorded inventories and accounts receivable, and the elements making up the statements of income, changes in stockholders' equity, and cash flows.

Disclaimer of Opinion

Because of the significance of the matters described in the Basis for Disclaimer of Opinion paragraph, we have not been able to obtain sufficient appropriate audit evidence to provide a basis for an audit opinion. Accordingly, we do not express an opinion on these financial statements.

Report on Other Legal and Regulatory Requirements

[*Form and content of this section of the auditor's report will vary depending on the nature of the auditor's other reporting responsibilities.*]

[*Auditor's signature*]

[*Auditor's city and state*]

[*Date of the auditor's report*]

Multiple Choice

AUD 4-Q16 through AUD 4-Q16

3. Audit of internal control integrated with an audit of financial statements

> *Hint*: The professional standards related to audits of internal control over financial reporting that is integrated with an audit of the financial statements are very similar (and in many cases, exactly the same) for issuers (AS 2201) and nonissuers (AU-C 940).

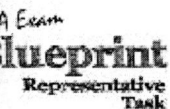

> **Identify the factors that an auditor should consider when forming an opinion on the effectiveness of internal control in an audit of internal control.**

Effective internal control over financial reporting provides reasonable assurance regarding the reliability of financial reporting and the preparation of financial statements for external purposes.
If one or more **material weaknesses** exist, the company's internal control over financial reporting cannot be considered effective.

The auditor's objective in an audit of internal control over financial reporting is to express an opinion on the effectiveness of the company's internal control over financial reporting. Because a company's internal control cannot be considered effective if one or more material weaknesses exist, to form a basis for expressing an opinion, the auditor must **plan and perform the audit to obtain appropriate evidence that is sufficient to obtain reasonable assurance about whether material weaknesses exist as of the date specified in management's assessment**. A material weakness in internal control over financial reporting may exist even when financial statements are not materially misstated.

a. Integrating the audits
The audit of internal control over financial reporting should be integrated with the audit of the financial statements.

The objectives of the audits are not identical, however, and the auditor must plan and perform the work to achieve the objectives of both audits.

In an integrated audit of internal control over financial reporting and the financial statements, the auditor should design his or her testing of controls to accomplish the objectives of both audits simultaneously. The auditor must obtain sufficient evidence to support both:
   a) the auditor's opinion on internal control over financial reporting as of year-end, and
   b) the auditor's control risk assessments for purposes of the audit of financial statements.

Obtaining sufficient evidence to support assessing control risk as "low" for purposes of the financial statement audit ordinarily allows the auditor to reduce the amount of audit work that otherwise would have been necessary to form an opinion on the financial statements.

b. Role of risk assessment
Risk assessment underlies the entire audit process, including
- the determination of significant accounts and disclosures and relevant assertions,
- the selection of controls to test, and
- the determination of the evidence necessary for a given control.

c. Addressing the risk of fraud
When planning and performing the audit of internal control over financial reporting, the auditor should take into account the results of his or her fraud risk assessment.

As part of identifying and testing entity-level controls and selecting other controls to test, the auditor should evaluate whether the company's controls sufficiently address identified risks of material misstatement due to fraud, and controls intended to address the risk of management override of other controls. Controls that might address these risks include –

1) Controls over significant transactions that are outside the normal course of business for the company or that otherwise appear to be unusual due to their timing, size, or nature ("significant unusual transactions"), particularly those that result in late or unusual journal entries;
2) Controls over journal entries and adjustments made in the period-end financial reporting process;
3) Controls over related party transactions;
4) Controls related to significant management estimates; and
5) Controls that mitigate incentives for, and pressures on, management to falsify or inappropriately manage financial results.

If the auditor identifies deficiencies in controls designed to prevent or detect fraud during the audit of internal control over financial reporting, the auditor should take into account those deficiencies when developing his or her response to risks of material misstatement during the financial statement audit.

d. Using a top-down approach
The auditor should use a top-down approach to the audit of internal control over financial reporting to select the controls to test.

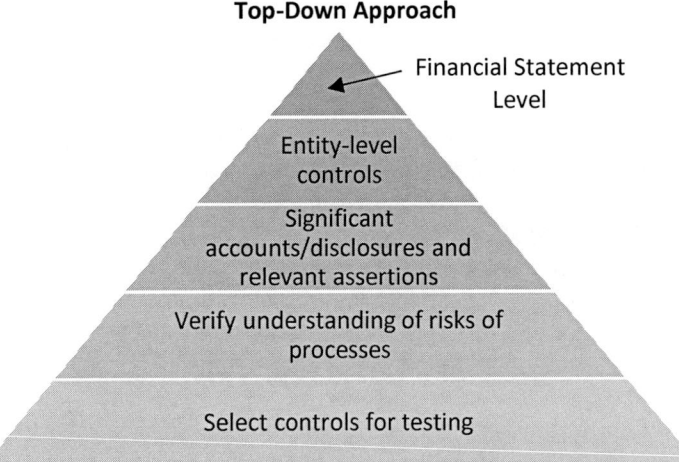

1) A top-down approach begins at the **financial statement level** and with the auditor's understanding of the **overall risks to internal control over financial reporting**.

2) The auditor then focuses on **entity-level controls**

   Identifying Entity-Level Controls
   Entity-level controls include:
   - Controls related to the control environment;
   - Controls over management override;
   - The company's risk assessment process;
   - Centralized processing and controls, including shared service environments;
   - Controls to monitor results of operations;
   - Controls to monitor other controls, including activities of the internal audit function, the audit committee, and self-assessment programs;

- Controls over the period-end financial reporting process; and
- Policies that address significant business control and risk management practices.

3) The auditor then works down to **significant accounts and disclosures and their relevant assertions**.

<u>Identifying significant accounts and disclosures and their relevant assertions</u>
The auditor should identify significant accounts and disclosures and their relevant assertions. Relevant assertions are those financial statement assertions that have a reasonable possibility of containing a misstatement that would cause the financial statements to be materially misstated. The financial statement assertions include:
- Existence or occurrence
- Completeness
- Valuation or allocation
- Rights and obligations
- Presentation and disclosure

Hint: The auditor may base his or her work on assertions that differ from those used by the PCAOB if the auditor has selected and tested controls over the pertinent risks in each significant account and disclosure that have a reasonable possibility of containing misstatements that would cause the financial statements to be materially misstated. (This statement is made since the AICPA's management assertions are structured a little differently.)

4) The auditor then **verifies his or her understanding of the risks** in the company's processes.

The risk factors that the auditor should evaluate in the identification of significant accounts and disclosures and their relevant assertions are the same in the audit of internal control over financial reporting as in the audit of the financial statements; accordingly, significant accounts and disclosures and their relevant assertions are the same for both audits. The auditor also should understand how IT affects the company's flow of transactions.

Hint: The identification of risks and controls within IT is not a separate evaluation. Instead, it is an integral part of the top-down approach used to identify significant accounts and disclosures and their relevant assertions, and the controls to test, as well as to assess risk and allocate audit effort as described by AS 2201.

How does the auditor verify his or her understanding? Performing walkthroughs is frequently the most effective way of achieving the objectives just described. In performing a walkthrough, the auditor follows a transaction from origination through the company's processes, including information systems, until it is reflected in the company's financial records, using the same documents and information technology that company personnel use. Walkthrough procedures usually include a combination of inquiry, observation, inspection of relevant documentation, and re-performance of controls.

5) The auditor then **selects for testing** those controls that sufficiently address the assessed risk of misstatement to each relevant assertion.

e. Selecting controls to test
The auditor should test controls that are important to the auditor's conclusion about whether the company's controls sufficiently address the assessed risk of misstatement to each relevant assertion.

f. Testing controls
   1) Testing Design Effectiveness
      The auditor should test the design effectiveness of controls by determining whether the company's controls **are operated as prescribed** by persons possessing the necessary authority and competence to perform the control effectively, satisfy the company's control objectives and can effectively prevent or detect errors or fraud that could result in material misstatements in the financial statements.

      Procedures the auditor performs to test design effectiveness include a mix of inquiry of appropriate personnel, observation of the company's operations, and inspection of relevant documentation.

      Walkthroughs that include these procedures ordinarily are sufficient to evaluate design effectiveness.

   2) Testing Operating Effectiveness
      The auditor should test the operating effectiveness of a control by **determining whether the control is operating as designed** and whether the person performing the control possesses the necessary authority and competence to perform the control effectively.

      Procedures the auditor performs to test operating effectiveness include a mix of inquiry of appropriate personnel, observation of the company's operations, inspection of relevant documentation, and re-performance of the control.

   3) Relationship of Risk to the Evidence to be obtained
      For each control selected for testing, the evidence necessary to persuade the auditor that the control is effective depends upon the risk associated with the control. The risk associated with a control consists of the risk that the control might not be effective and, if not effective, the risk that a material weakness would result.

      When the auditor identifies deviations from the company's controls, he or she should determine the effect of the deviations on his or her assessment of the risk associated with the control being tested and the evidence to be obtained, as well as on the operating effectiveness of the control.

      The evidence provided by the auditor's tests of the effectiveness of controls depends upon the mix of the *nature, timing, and extent* of the auditor's procedures.

      d) *Roll-Forward Procedures*
         When the auditor reports on the effectiveness of controls as of a specific date and obtains evidence about the operating effectiveness of controls at an interim date, he or she should determine what additional evidence concerning the operation of the controls for the remaining period is necessary.

         The additional evidence that is necessary to update the results of testing from an interim date to the company's year-end depends on the following factors -
         - The specific control tested prior to the as-of date, including the risks associated with the control and the nature of the control, and the results of those tests;
         - The sufficiency of the evidence obtained at an interim date;
         - The length of the remaining period; and

- The possibility that there have been any significant changes in internal control over financial reporting subsequent to the interim date.

g. Special considerations for subsequent years' audits
In subsequent years' audits, the auditor should incorporate knowledge obtained during past audits he or she performed of the company's internal control over financial reporting into the decision-making process for determining the nature, timing, and extent of testing necessary.

h. Evaluating identified deficiencies
The auditor must *evaluate the severity of each control deficiency* that comes to his or her attention to determine whether the deficiencies, individually or in combination, are **material weaknesses** as of the date of management's assessment.

The severity of a deficiency depends on
- Whether there is a reasonable possibility that the company's controls will fail to prevent or detect a misstatement of an account balance or disclosure; and
- The magnitude of the potential misstatement resulting from the deficiency or deficiencies.

The severity of a deficiency does not depend on whether a misstatement actually has occurred but rather on whether there is a reasonable possibility that the company's controls will fail to prevent or detect a misstatement.

> *Hint*: The evaluation of whether a control deficiency presents a reasonable possibility of misstatement can be made without quantifying the probability of occurrence as a specific percentage or range.

> *Hint*: Multiple control deficiencies that affect the same financial statement account balance or disclosure increase the likelihood of misstatement and may, in combination, constitute a material weakness, even though such deficiencies may individually be less severe. Therefore, the auditor should determine whether individual control deficiencies that affect the same significant account or disclosure, relevant assertion, or component of internal control collectively result in a material weakness.

The auditor should evaluate the effect of **compensating controls** when determining whether a control deficiency or combination of deficiencies is a material weakness. To have a mitigating effect, the compensating control should operate at a level of precision that would prevent or detect a misstatement that could be material.

1) Indicators of Material Weaknesses
Indicators of material weaknesses in internal control over financial reporting include
   i. Identification of fraud, whether or not material, on the part of senior management;
   ii. Restatement of previously issued financial statements to reflect the correction of a material misstatement;
   iii. Identification by the auditor of a material misstatement of financial statements in the current period in circumstances that indicate that the misstatement would not have been detected by the company's internal control over financial reporting; and
   iv. Ineffective oversight of the company's external financial reporting and internal control over financial reporting by the company's audit committee.

When evaluating the severity of a deficiency, or combination of deficiencies, the auditor also should determine the level of detail and degree of assurance that would ***satisfy prudent officials in the conduct of their own affairs*** that they have reasonable assurance that transactions are recorded as necessary to permit the preparation of financial statements in conformity with generally accepted accounting principles. If the auditor determines that a deficiency, or combination of deficiencies, might prevent prudent officials in the conduct of their own affairs from concluding that they have reasonable assurance that transactions are recorded as necessary to permit the preparation of financial statements in conformity with generally accepted accounting principles, then the auditor should treat the deficiency, or combination of deficiencies, as an indicator of a material weakness.

i. Forming an opinion
The auditor should form an opinion on the effectiveness of internal control over financial reporting by evaluating evidence obtained from all sources, including the auditor's testing of controls, misstatements detected during the financial statement audit, and any identified control deficiencies.

After forming an opinion on the effectiveness of the company's internal control over financial reporting, the auditor should evaluate the presentation of the elements that management is required, under the SEC's rules, to present in its annual report on internal control over financial reporting.

If the auditor determines that any required elements of management's annual report on internal control over financial reporting are incomplete or improperly presented, the auditor should:
- modify his or her report to include an explanatory paragraph describing the reasons for this determination and
- If the auditor determines that the required disclosure about a material weakness is not fairly presented in all material respects, the auditor should issue an adverse opinion.

The auditor may form an opinion on the effectiveness of internal control over financial reporting only when there have been no restrictions on the scope of the auditor's work. A scope limitation requires the auditor to disclaim an opinion or withdraw from the engagement.

j. Obtaining written representations
In an audit of internal control over financial reporting, the auditor should obtain written representations from management:
1) Acknowledging management's responsibility for establishing and maintaining effective internal control over financial reporting;
2) Stating that management has performed an evaluation and made an assessment of the effectiveness of the company's internal control over financial reporting and specifying the control criteria;
3) Stating that management did not use the auditor's procedures performed during the audits of internal control over financial reporting or the financial statements as part of the basis for management's assessment of the effectiveness of internal control over financial reporting;
4) Stating management's conclusion, as set forth in its assessment, about the effectiveness of the company's internal control over financial reporting based on the control criteria as of a specified date;
5) Stating that management has disclosed to the auditor all deficiencies in the design or operation of internal control over financial reporting identified as part of management's evaluation, including separately disclosing to the auditor all such deficiencies that it believes to be significant deficiencies or material weaknesses in internal control over financial reporting;
6) Describing any fraud resulting in a material misstatement to the company's financial statements and any other fraud that does not result in a material misstatement to the company's financial statements, but involves senior management or management or other

employees who have a significant role in the company's internal control over financial reporting;

7) Stating whether control deficiencies identified and communicated to the audit committee during previous engagements have been resolved, and specifically identifying any that have not; and

8) Stating whether there were, subsequent to the date being reported on, any changes in internal control over financial reporting or other factors that might significantly affect internal control over financial reporting, including any corrective actions taken by management with regard to significant deficiencies and material weaknesses.

The failure to obtain written representations from management, including management's refusal to furnish them, constitutes a limitation on the scope of the audit. When the scope of the audit is limited, the auditor should either withdraw from the engagement or disclaim an opinion. Further, the auditor should evaluate the effects of management's refusal on his or her ability to rely on other representations, including those obtained in the audit of the company's financial statements.

k. Communicating certain matters
The auditor must communicate, in writing, to management and the audit committee all material weaknesses identified during the audit.

The written communication should be made prior to the issuance of the auditor's report on internal control over financial reporting.

If the auditor concludes that the oversight of the company's external financial reporting and internal control over financial reporting by the company's audit committee is ineffective, the auditor must communicate that conclusion in writing to the board of directors.

The auditor also should consider whether there are any deficiencies, or combinations of deficiencies, that have been identified during the audit that are significant deficiencies and must communicate such deficiencies, in writing, to the audit committee. This communication should be made in a timely manner and prior to the issuance of the auditor's report on internal control over financial reporting.

The auditor also should communicate to management, in writing, all deficiencies in internal control over financial reporting (*i.e.*, those deficiencies in internal control over financial reporting that are of a lesser magnitude than material weaknesses) identified during the audit, and inform the audit committee when such a communication has been made. The auditor should communicate this information to the audit committee in a timely manner and prior to the issuance of the auditor's report on internal control over financial reporting. When making this communication, it is not necessary for the auditor to repeat information about such deficiencies that has been included in previously issued written communications, whether those communications were made by the auditor, internal auditors, or others within the organization.

1) **Material Weaknesses**
If there are deficiencies that, individually or in combination, result in one or more material weaknesses, the auditor must express an adverse opinion on the company's internal control over financial reporting, unless there is a restriction on the scope of the engagement.

When expressing an adverse opinion on internal control over financial reporting because of a material weakness, the auditor's report must include:
- The definition of a **material weakness**. A **material weakness** is a deficiency, or a combination of deficiencies, in internal control over financial reporting, such that there is a reasonable possibility that a material misstatement of the company's

annual or interim financial statements will not be prevented or detected on a timely basis.
- A statement that a material weakness has been identified and an identification of the material weakness described in management's assessment.

The auditor should determine the effect his or her adverse opinion on internal control has on his or her opinion on the financial statements.

Identify the appropriate form and content of a report on the audit of internal control, including report modifications and the use of separate or combined reports for the audit of an entity's financial statements and the examination of internal control.

l. Separate or combined reports
    The auditor may choose to issue a combined report (*i.e.*, one report containing both an opinion on the financial statements and an opinion on internal control over financial reporting) or separate reports on the company's financial statements and on internal control over financial reporting.

m. Report modifications
    The auditor should modify his or her report if any of the following conditions exist.
    - Elements of management's annual report on internal control are incomplete or improperly presented,
    - There is a restriction on the scope of the engagement,
    - The auditor decides to refer to the report of other auditors as the basis, in part, for the auditor's own report,
    - There is other information contained in management's annual report on internal control over financial reporting, or
    - Management's annual certification pursuant to Section 302 of the Sarbanes-Oxley Act is misstated.

    1) **Elements of Management's Annual Report on Internal Control Over Financial Reporting Are Incomplete or Improperly Presented**
       If the auditor determines that elements of management's annual report on internal control over financial reporting are incomplete or improperly presented, the auditor should modify his or her report to include an explanatory paragraph describing the reasons for this determination. If the auditor determines that the required disclosure about a material weakness is not fairly presented in all material respects, the auditor should follow the direction of the guidance for expressing an adverse opinion because of material weakness of internal control.

    2) **Scope Limitations**
       The auditor can express an opinion on the company's internal control over financial reporting only if the auditor has been able to apply the procedures necessary in the circumstances. If there are restrictions on the scope of the engagement, the auditor should withdraw from the engagement or disclaim an opinion. A disclaimer of opinion states that the auditor does not express an opinion on the effectiveness of internal control over financial reporting.

       When disclaiming an opinion because of a scope limitation, the auditor should state that the scope of the audit was not sufficient to warrant the expression of an opinion and, in a separate paragraph or paragraphs, the substantive reasons for the disclaimer. The auditor should not identify the procedures that were performed nor include the statements describing the characteristics of an audit of internal control over financial reporting; to do so might overshadow the disclaimer.

When the auditor plans to disclaim an opinion and the limited procedures performed by the auditor caused the auditor to conclude that a material weakness exists, the auditor's report also should include:
- The definition of a material weakness.
- A description of any material weaknesses identified in the company's internal control over financial reporting. This description should provide the users of the audit report with specific information about the nature of any material weakness and its actual and potential effect on the presentation of the company's financial statements issued during the existence of the weakness.

The auditor may issue a report disclaiming an opinion on internal control over financial reporting as soon as the auditor concludes that a scope limitation will prevent the auditor from obtaining the reasonable assurance necessary to express an opinion. The auditor is not required to perform any additional work prior to issuing a disclaimer when the auditor concludes that he or she will not be able to obtain sufficient evidence to express an opinion.

If the auditor concludes that he or she cannot express an opinion because there has been a limitation on the scope of the audit, the auditor should communicate, in writing, to management and the audit committee that the audit of internal control over financial reporting cannot be satisfactorily completed.

3) **Opinions Based, in Part, on the Report of Another Auditor**
When another auditor has audited the financial statements and internal control over financial reporting of one or more subsidiaries, divisions, branches, or components of the company, the auditor should determine whether he or she may serve as the principal auditor and use the work and reports of another auditor as a basis, in part, for his or her opinion.

If the auditor decides it is appropriate to serve as the principal auditor of the financial statements, then that auditor also should be the principal auditor of the company's internal control over financial reporting. When serving as the principal auditor of internal control over financial reporting, the auditor should decide whether to make reference in the report on internal control over financial reporting to the audit of internal control over financial reporting performed by the other auditor.

When the auditor decides to make reference to the report of the other auditor as a basis, in part, for his or her opinion on the company's internal control over financial reporting, the auditor should refer to the report of the other auditor when describing the scope of the audit and when expressing the opinion.

4) **Management's Annual Report on Internal Control over Financial Reporting Containing Additional Information**
Management's annual report on internal control over financial reporting may contain information in addition to the elements that are required by SEC rules and subject to the auditor's evaluation.

> *Hint*: As a reminder, management's report on internal control over financial reporting is required to include the following:
> 1. A statement of management's responsibility for establishing and maintaining adequate internal control over financial reporting for the company;
> 2. A statement identifying the framework used by management to conduct the required assessment of the effectiveness of the company's internal control over financial reporting;
> 3. An assessment of the effectiveness of the company's internal control over financial reporting as of the end of the company's most recent fiscal year, including an explicit statement as to whether that internal control over financial reporting is effective; and
> 4. A statement that the registered public accounting firm that audited the financial statements included in the annual report, has issued an attestation report on management's assessment of the company's internal control over financial reporting.

If management's annual report on internal control over financial reporting could reasonably be viewed by users of the report as including such additional information, the auditor should disclaim an opinion on the information.

If the auditor believes that management's additional information contains a material misstatement of fact, he or she should discuss the matter with management. If, after discussing the matter with management, the auditor concludes that a material misstatement of fact remains, the auditor should notify management and the audit committee, in writing, of the auditor's views concerning the information. AS 2405, *Illegal Acts by Clients* and Section 10A of the Securities Exchange Act of 1934 may also require the auditor to take additional action.

> *Hint*: If management makes the types of disclosures required by SEC rules and subject to the auditor's evaluation outside its annual report on internal control over financial reporting, and includes them elsewhere within its annual report on the company's financial statements, the auditor would not need to disclaim an opinion. However, in that situation, the auditor's responsibilities are the same as those described in this paragraph if the auditor believes that the additional information contains a material misstatement of fact.

5) **Management's Annual Certification Pursuant to Section 302 of the Sarbanes-Oxley Act is Misstated**
If matters come to the auditor's attention as a result of the audit of internal control over financial reporting that lead him or her to believe that modifications to the disclosures about changes in internal control over financial reporting (addressing changes in internal control over financial reporting occurring during the fourth quarter) are necessary for the annual certifications to be accurate and to comply with the requirements of Section 302 of the Sarbanes-Oxley Act and Securities Exchange Act Rule 13a-14(a) or 15d-14(a), whichever applies, the auditor should follow the communication responsibilities as described in AS 4105, *Reviews of Interim Financial Information*, for any interim period. However, if management and the audit committee do not respond appropriately, in addition to the responsibilities described in AS 4105, the auditor should modify his or her report on the audit of internal control over financial reporting to include an explanatory paragraph describing the reasons the auditor believes management's disclosures should be modified.

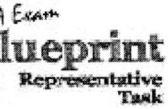

> **Prepare a draft report for an audit of internal control integrated with the audit of an entity's financial statements, starting with a report example (e.g., an illustrative report from professional standards).**

n. Combined report – Issuer (PCAOB)
    The following **example of a combined report,** expressing an unqualified opinion on financial statements and an unqualified opinion on internal control over financial reporting, illustrates the report elements described in this review (above).

Report of Independent Registered Public Accounting Firm

To the shareholders and the board of directors of W Company,

Opinions on the Financial Statements and Internal Control over Financial Reporting
We have audited the accompanying balance sheets of W Company (the "Company") as of December 31, 20X8 and 20X7, and the related statements of [titles of financial statements, e.g., income, comprehensive income, stockholders' equity, and cash flows] for each of the years in the three-year period ended December 31, 20X8, and the related notes [and schedules] (collectively referred to as the "financial statements"). *We also have audited the Company's internal control over financial reporting as of December 31, 20X8, based on [Identify control criteria, for example, "criteria established in Internal Control - Integrated Framework (20XX) issued by the Committee of Sponsoring Organizations of the Treadway Commission (COSO)."]*

In our opinion, the financial statements referred to above present fairly, in all material respects, the financial position of the Company as of December 31, 20X8 and 20X7, and the results of its operations and its cash flows for each of the years in the three-year period ended December 31, 20X8 in conformity with accounting principles generally accepted in the United States of America. Also, in our opinion, W Company maintained, in all material respects, effective internal control over financial reporting as of December 31, 20X8, based on [Identify control criteria, for example, "criteria established in Internal Control - Integrated Framework; (20XX) issued by (COSO).

Basis for Opinion
The Company's management is responsible for these financial statements, for maintaining effective internal control over financial reporting, and for its assessment of the effectiveness of internal control over financial reporting, included in the accompanying [title of management's report]. Our responsibility is to express an opinion on the Company's financial statements and an opinion on the Company's internal control over financial reporting based on our audits. We are a public accounting firm registered with the Public Company Accounting Oversight Board (United States) ("PCAOB") and are required to be independent with respect to the Company in accordance with the U.S. federal securities laws and the applicable rules and regulations of the Securities and Exchange Commission and the PCAOB.

We conducted our audits in accordance with the standards of the PCAOB. Those standards require that we plan and perform the audits to obtain reasonable assurance about whether the financial statements are free of material misstatement, whether due to error or fraud, and whether effective internal control over financial reporting was maintained in all material respects.

Our audits of the financial statements included performing procedures to assess the risks of material misstatement of the financial statements, whether due to error or fraud, and performing procedures that respond to those risks. Such procedures included examining, on a test basis, evidence regarding the amounts and disclosures in the financial statements. Our audits also included evaluating the accounting principles used and significant estimates made by management, as well as evaluating the overall presentation of financial statements. Our audit of internal control over financial reporting included obtaining an understanding of internal control over financial reporting, assessing the risk that a material weakness exists, and testing and evaluating the design and operating effectiveness of internal control based on the assessed risk. Our audits also included performing such other procedures as we considered necessary in the circumstances. We believe that our audits provide a reasonable basis for our opinions.

Definition and Limitation of Internal Control Over Financial Reporting
A company's internal control over financial reporting is a process designed to provide reasonable assurance regarding the reliability of financial reporting and the preparation of financial statements for external purposes in accordance with generally accepted accounting principles. A company's internal control over financial reporting includes those policies and procedures that (1) pertain to the maintenance of records that, in reasonable detail, accurately and fairly reflect the transactions and dispositions of the assets of the company; (2) provide reasonable assurance that transactions are recorded as necessary to permit preparation of financial statements in accordance with generally accepted accounting principles, and that receipts and expenditures of the company are being made only in accordance with authorizations of management and directors of the company; and (3) provide reasonable assurance regarding prevention or timely detection of unauthorized acquisition, use, or disposition of the company's assets that could have a material effect on the financial statements.

Because of its inherent limitations, internal control over financial reporting may not prevent or detect misstatements. Also, projections of any evaluation of effectiveness to future periods are subject to the risk that controls may become inadequate because of changes in conditions, or that the degree of compliance with the policies or procedures may deteriorate.

Critical Audit Matters [if applicable]
[Include critical audit matters]

[Signature]
We have served as the Company's auditor since [year].
[City and State or Country]
[Date]

1) Issue a Separate Report on Internal Control over Financial Reporting
    i. <u>Impact on Auditor's Report on Financial Statements</u>
       If the auditor chooses to issue a separate report on internal control over financial reporting, he or she should add the following paragraph (immediately following the opinion paragraph) to the auditor's report on the financial statements

       We also have audited, in accordance with the standards of the Public Company Accounting Oversight Board (United States), W Company's internal control over financial reporting as of December 31, 20X8, based on [identify control criteria] and our report dated [date of report, which should be the same as the date of the report on the financial statements] expressed [include nature of opinion].

    ii. <u>Impact on Auditor's Report on Internal Control over Financial Reporting</u>
        The auditor also should add the following paragraph to the report on internal control over financial reporting (immediately following the opinion paragraph)

        We also have audited, in accordance with the standards of the Public Company Accounting Oversight Board (United States), the [identify financial statements] of W Company and our report dated [date of report, which should be the same as the date of the report on the effectiveness of internal control over financial reporting] expressed [include nature of opinion].

Multiple Choice

AUD 4-Q17

o. Combined Report – Nonissuer (AICPA)

<u>**Independent Auditor's Report**</u>

[Appropriate Addressee]

[Entity Name]

Report on the Financial Statements and Internal Control

We have audited the accompanying financial statements of ABC Company, which comprise the balance sheet as of December 31, 20XX, and the related statements of income, changes in stockholders' equity, and cash flows for the year then ended, and the related notes to the financial statements. We also have audited ABC Company's internal control over financial reporting as of December 31, 20XX, based on [identify criteria – Generally, COSO in the U.S.A.].

Management's Responsibility for the Financial Statements and Internal Control over Financial Reporting

Management is responsible for the preparation and fair presentation of these financial statements in accordance with accounting principles generally accepted in the United States of America; this includes the design, implementation, and maintenance of effective internal control over financial reporting relevant to the preparation and fair presentation of financial statements that are free from material misstatement, whether due to fraud or error. Management is also responsible for its assessment about the effectiveness of internal control over financial reporting, included in the accompanying [title of management's report].

Auditor's Responsibility

Our responsibility is to express an opinion on these financial statements and an opinion on the entity's internal control over financial reporting based on our audits. We conducted our audits in accordance with auditing standards generally accepted in the United States of America. Those standards require that we plan and perform the audits to obtain reasonable assurance about whether the financial statements are free from material misstatement and whether effective internal control over financial reporting was maintained in all material respects.

An audit of financial statements involves performing procedures to obtain audit evidence about the amounts and disclosures in the financial statements. The procedures selected depend on the auditor's judgment, including the assessment of the risks of material misstatement of the financial statements, whether due to fraud or error. In making those risk assessments, the auditor considers internal control relevant to the entity's preparation and fair presentation of the financial statements in order to design audit procedures that are appropriate in the circumstances. An audit of financial statements also includes evaluating the appropriateness of accounting policies used and the reasonableness of significant accounting estimates made by management, as well as evaluating the overall presentation of the financial statements.

An audit of internal control over financial reporting involves performing procedures to obtain evidence about whether a material weakness exists. The procedures selected depend on the auditor's judgment, including the assessment of the risk that a material weakness exists. An audit of internal control over financial reporting also involves obtaining an understanding of internal control over financial reporting and testing and evaluating the design and operating effectiveness of internal control over financial reporting based on the assessed risk.

We believe that the audit evidence we have obtained is sufficient and appropriate to provide a basis for our audit opinions.

Definition and Inherent Limitations of Internal Control over Financial Reporting

An entity's internal control over financial reporting is a process effected by those charged with governance, management, and other personnel, designed to provide reasonable assurance regarding the preparation of reliable financial statements in accordance with accounting principles generally accepted in the United States of America. An entity's internal control over financial reporting includes those policies and procedures that (1) pertain to the maintenance of records that, in reasonable detail, accurately and fairly reflect the transactions and dispositions of the assets of the entity; (2) provide reasonable assurance that transactions are recorded as necessary to permit preparation of financial statements in accordance with accounting principles generally accepted in the United States of America, and that receipts and expenditures of the entity are being made only in accordance with authorizations of management and those charged with governance; and (3) provide reasonable assurance regarding prevention, or timely detection and correction of unauthorized acquisition, use, or disposition of the entity's assets that could have a material effect on the financial statements.

Because of its inherent limitations, internal control over financial reporting may not prevent, or detect and correct, misstatements. Also, projections of any assessment of effectiveness to future periods are subject to the risk that controls may become inadequate because of changes in conditions, or that the degree of compliance with the policies or procedures may deteriorate.

Opinions

In our opinion, the financial statements referred to above present fairly, in all material respects, the financial position of ABC Company as of December 31, 20XX, and the results of its operations and its cash flows for the year then ended in accordance with accounting principles generally accepted in the United States of America. Also, in our opinion, ABC Company maintained, in all material respects, effective internal control over financial reporting as of December 31, 20XX, based on [identify criteria].

Report on Other Legal and Regulatory Requirements

[Form and content of this section of the auditor's report will vary depending on the nature of the auditor's other reporting responsibilities.]

[Auditor's signature]
[Auditor's city and state]
[Date of the auditor's report]

B. Reports on Attestation Engagements
1. General standards for attestation reports

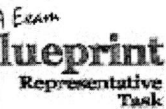

> **Identify the factors that a practitioner should consider when issuing an examination or review report for an attestation engagement.**

> **Hint:** *SSAE 18, Attestation Standards: Clarification and Recodification,* redrafted attestation standards as per a recent clarity project and also aligns them to international attestation standards. **SSAE 18 is eligible for testing in 2018.**
>
> Remember that attestation standards involve examination, review, and agreed-upon procedures.

Attestation engagements are engagements, except for those services discussed below*, in which a certified public accountant in public practice (practitioner) is engaged to issue or does issue an examination, a review, or an agreed-upon procedures report on subject matter, or an assertion about the subject matter that is the responsibility of another party.

Attestation standards (SSAEs) provide guidance and establish a broad framework for a variety of attest services increasingly demanded of the accounting profession. The standards and related interpretive commentary are designed to provide professional guidelines that will enhance both consistency and quality in the performance of such services.

For years, attest services generally were limited to expressing a positive opinion on historical financial statements on the basis of an audit in accordance with generally accepted auditing standards (GAAS). However, certified public accountants increasingly have been requested to provide, and have been providing, assurance on representations other than historical financial statements, and in forms other than the positive opinion. In responding to these needs, certified public accountants have been able to generally apply the basic concepts underlying GAAS to these attest services. As the range of attest services has grown, however, it has become increasingly difficult to do so.

As the need for other attestation services increases, attestation standards (SSAEs) and related interpretive commentary have provided a general framework for and set reasonable boundaries around the attest function. The standards and commentary:
- provide useful and necessary guidance to certified public accountants engaged to perform new and evolving attest services and
- guide AICPA standard-setting bodies in establishing, if deemed necessary, interpretive standards for such services.

*Professional services provided by practitioners that are not covered by SSAEs include the following:
- Services performed in accordance with Statements on Auditing Standards (SASs) (i.e., audits of financial statements).
- Services performed in accordance with Statements on Standards for Accounting and Review Services (SSARSs) (i.e., prepared, compiled and reviewed financial statements).
- Services performed in accordance with the Statement on Standards for Consulting Services (SSCS), such as engagements in which the practitioner's role is solely to assist the client (for example, acting as the company accountant in preparing information other than financial statements), or engagements in which a practitioner is engaged to testify as an expert witness in accounting, auditing, taxation, or other matters, given certain stipulated facts.
- Engagements in which the practitioner is engaged to advocate a client's position—for example, tax matters being reviewed by the Internal Revenue Service.
- Tax engagements in which a practitioner is engaged to prepare tax returns or provide tax advice.

a. Definition of an attestation engagement
   1) Definitions and Underlying Concepts
      i. **Requirements**
         SSAEs use two categories of professional requirements, identified by specific terms, to describe the degree of responsibility they impose on practitioners, as follows:
         - *Unconditional requirements* – the practitioner is required to comply. SSAEs use the words *must* or *is required* to indicate an unconditional requirement.
         - *Presumptively mandatory requirements* – *generally required,* however, in rare circumstances, the practitioner may depart from a presumptively mandatory requirement, provided the practitioner documents his or her justification for the departure and how the alternative procedures performed in the circumstances were sufficient to achieve the objectives of the presumptively mandatory requirement. SSAEs use the word *should* to indicate a presumptively mandatory requirement.

         A practitioner may report on a written assertion or may report directly on the subject matter.

      ii. **Subject matter**
         The subject matter of an attest engagement may take many forms, including the following:
         a) Historical or prospective performance or condition (for example, historical or prospective financial information, performance measurements, and backlog data)
         b) Physical characteristics (for example, narrative descriptions, square footage of facilities)
         c) Historical events (for example, the price of a market basket of goods on a certain date)
         d) Analyses (for example, break-even analyses)
         e) Systems and processes (for example, internal control)
         f) Behavior (for example, corporate governance, compliance with laws and regulations, and human resource practices)

         The subject matter may be as of a point in time or for a period of time.

      iii. **Assertion**
         An assertion is any declaration or set of declarations about whether the subject matter is based on or in conformity with the criteria selected.

         A written assertion may be presented to a practitioner in a number of ways, such as in a narrative description, within a schedule, or as part of a representation letter appropriately identifying what is being presented and the point in time or period of time covered.

         When a written assertion has *not* been obtained, a practitioner may still report on the subject matter; however, the form of the report will vary depending on the circumstances and its use should be restricted.

      iv. **Responsible party**
         The *responsible party* is defined as the person or persons, either as individuals or representatives of the entity, responsible for the subject matter.

If the nature of the subject matter is such that no such party exists, a party who has a reasonable basis for making a written assertion about the subject matter may provide such an assertion (and is referred to as the *responsible party*).

The practitioner may be engaged to gather information to enable the responsible party to evaluate the subject matter in connection with providing a written assertion.

Regardless of the procedures performed by the practitioner, the responsible party must accept responsibility for its assertion and the subject matter and must not base its assertion solely on the practitioner's procedures.

Because the practitioner's role in an attest engagement is that of an *attester*, the practitioner should not take on the role of the responsible party in an attest engagement. Therefore, the need to clearly identify a responsible party is a prerequisite for an attest engagement.

A practitioner may accept an engagement to perform an examination, a review or an agreed-upon procedures engagement on subject matter, or an assertion related thereto, provided that one of the following conditions is met:
- The party wishing to engage the practitioner is responsible for the subject matter, or has a reasonable basis for providing a written assertion about the subject matter, if the nature of the subject matter is such that a responsible party does not otherwise exist.
- The party wishing to engage the practitioner is not responsible for the subject matter but is able to provide the practitioner, or have a third party who is responsible for the subject matter, provide the practitioner with evidence of the third party's responsibility for the subject matter.

The practitioner should obtain written acknowledgment or other evidence of the responsible party's responsibility for the subject matter, or the written assertion, as it relates to the objective of the engagement. The responsible party can acknowledge that responsibility in a number of ways, for example, in an engagement letter, a representation letter, or the presentation of the subject matter, including the notes thereto, or the written assertion. If the practitioner is not able to directly obtain written acknowledgment, the practitioner should obtain other evidence of the responsible party's responsibility for the subject matter (for example, by reference to legislation, a regulation, or a contract).

b. **Attestation standards: a framework for understanding attestation engagements**
   The attestation standards provide a convenient framework for understanding the requirements related to an attestation engagement. The attestation standards are used to review the components of an attestation engagement.

   1) General standards
      i. The practitioner must have adequate technical training and proficiency to perform in the attestation engagement.
      ii. The practitioner must have adequate knowledge of the subject matter which can be obtained through formal or continuing education and/or practical experience.

iii. The practitioner must have reason to believe that the subject matter is capable of evaluation against criteria that are suitable and available to users.

Suitable criteria must have each of the following attributes:

Objectivity	*Measurability*
Criteria should be free from bias	Criteria should permit reasonably consistent measurements, qualitative or quantitative, of subject matter.
Completeness	*Relevance*
Criteria should be sufficiently complete so that those relevant factors that would alter a conclusion about subject matter are not omitted.	Criteria should be relevant to the subject matter.

Generally considered suitable	Criteria that are established or developed by groups composed of experts, that follow due process procedures, including exposure of the proposed criteria for public comment
Evaluate suitability based on attributes	Criteria established or developed by the client, the responsible party, industry associations, or other groups that do not follow due process procedures or do not as clearly represent the public interest

Availability:
The criteria should be available to users in one or more of the following ways:
- Available publicly
- Available to all users through inclusion in a clear manner in the presentation of the subject matter or in the assertion
- Available to all users through inclusion in a clear manner in the practitioner's report
- Well understood by most users, although not formally available (for example, "The distance between points A and B is twenty feet;" the criterion of distance measured in feet is considered to be well understood)
- Available only to specified parties; for example, terms of a contract or criteria issued by an industry association that are available only to those in the industry

If criteria are only available to specified parties, the practitioner's report should be restricted to those parties who have access to the criteria.

iv. The practitioner must maintain independence in mental attitude in all matters relating to the engagement.
v. The practitioner must exercise due professional care in the planning and performance of the engagement and the preparation of the report.

2) Standards of Fieldwork
   i. The practitioner must:
      - adequately plan the work
      - properly supervise any assistants
      - obtain sufficient evidence to provide a reasonable basis for the conclusion that is expressed in the report

   a) Planning
      Planning an attest engagement involves developing an overall strategy for the expected conduct and scope of the engagement.

      To develop such a strategy, practitioners need to have sufficient knowledge to enable them to understand adequately the events, transactions, and practices that, in their judgment, have a significant effect on the subject matter or the assertion.

      Factors to be considered by the practitioner in planning an attest engagement include the following:
      - The criteria to be used.
      - Preliminary judgments about attestation risk* and materiality for attest purposes.
      - The nature of the subject matter or the items within the assertion that are likely to require revision or adjustment.
      - Conditions that may require extension or modification of attest procedures.
      - The nature of the report expected to be issued.

      ***Attestation risk** is the risk that the practitioner may unknowingly fail to appropriately modify his or her attest report on the subject matter, or an assertion that is materially misstated. It consists of (*a*) the risk (consisting of *inherent risk* and *control risk*) that the subject matter or assertion contains deviations or misstatements that could be material and (*b*) the risk that the practitioner will not detect such deviations or misstatements (*detection risk*).

      The nature, extent, and timing of planning will vary with the nature and complexity of the subject matter or the assertion and the practitioner's prior experience with management. As part of the planning process, the practitioner should consider the nature, extent, and timing of the work to be performed to accomplish the objectives of the attest engagement. Nevertheless, as the attest engagement progresses, changed conditions may make it necessary to modify planned procedures.

      The practitioner should **establish an understanding with the client** regarding the services to be performed for each engagement. The following points should be considered:
      - Such an understanding reduces the risk that either the practitioner or the client may misinterpret the needs or expectations of the other party.
      - The understanding should include the objectives of the engagement, management's responsibilities, the practitioner's responsibilities, and limitations of the engagement.
      - The practitioner should document the understanding in the working papers, preferably through a written communication with the client.

- If the practitioner believes an understanding with the client has not been established, he or she should decline to accept or perform the engagement.

b) <u>Supervision</u>
Supervision involves directing the efforts of assistants who participate in accomplishing the objectives of the attest engagement and determining whether those objectives were accomplished.

Elements of supervision include instructing assistants, staying informed of significant problems encountered, reviewing the work performed, and dealing with differences of opinion among personnel.

The extent of supervision appropriate in a given instance depends on many factors, including the nature and complexity of the subject matter and the qualifications of the persons performing the work.

The work performed by each assistant should be reviewed to determine whether it was adequately performed and to evaluate whether the results are consistent with the conclusion to be presented in the practitioner's report.

c) <u>Obtaining evidence</u>
Selecting and applying procedures that will accumulate evidence that is sufficient, in the circumstances, to provide a reasonable basis for the level of assurance to be expressed in the attest report. This requires the careful exercise of professional judgment.

The practitioner should consider the following when establishing a proper combination of procedures:
  i. Evidence obtained from independent sources outside an entity, provides greater assurance about the subject matter or the assertion than evidence secured solely from within the entity.
  ii. Information obtained from the independent attester's direct personal knowledge (such as through physical examination, observation, computation, operating tests, or inspection) is more persuasive than information obtained indirectly.
  iii. The more effective the controls over the subject matter are, the more assurance they provide about the subject matter or the assertion.

Types of attest engagements	
Examination	High level of assurance
Review	Moderate level of assurance

For an examination, the practitioner's objective is to **accumulate sufficient evidence to restrict attestation risk to a level that is, in the practitioner's professional judgment, appropriately low for the high level of assurance that may be imparted by his or her report.** In such an engagement, a practitioner should select from all available procedures to restrict attestation risk to an appropriately low level.

For a review the objective is to **accumulate sufficient evidence to restrict attestation risk to a moderate level.** To accomplish this, the types of procedures performed generally are limited to inquiries and analytical procedures

As part of the attestation procedures, the practitioner considers the written assertion ordinarily provided by the responsible party. If a written assertion cannot be obtained from the responsible party, the practitioner should consider the effects on his or her ability to obtain sufficient evidence to form a conclusion about the subject matter. When the practitioner's client is the responsible party, a failure to obtain a written assertion should result in the practitioner concluding that a scope limitation exists. When the practitioner's client is not the responsible party and a written assertion is not provided, the practitioner may be able to conclude that he or she has sufficient evidence to form a conclusion about the subject matter.

3) Representation Letter
During an attest engagement, the responsible party makes many representations to the practitioner, both oral and written, in response to specific inquiries or through the presentation of subject matter or an assertion. Such representations from the responsible party are part of the evidential matter the practitioner obtains.

Written representations from the responsible party ordinarily confirm representations explicitly or implicitly given to the practitioner, indicate and document the continuing appropriateness of such representations, and reduce the possibility of misunderstanding concerning the matters that are the subject of the representations.

In an **examination or a review engagement**, a practitioner should consider obtaining a *representation letter from the responsible party*. When **the client is not the responsible party**, the practitioner should consider *obtaining a letter of written representations from the client as part of the attest engagement*. Examples of matters that might appear in such a representation letter include the following:
- A statement acknowledging responsibility for the subject matter and, when applicable, the assertion.
- A statement acknowledging responsibility for selecting the criteria, where applicable.
- A statement acknowledging responsibility for determining that such criteria are appropriate for its purposes, where the responsible party is the client.
- The assertion about the subject matter based on the criteria selected.
- A statement that all known matters contradicting the assertion and any communication from regulatory agencies affecting the subject matter or the assertion have been disclosed to the practitioner.
- Availability of all records relevant to the subject matter.
- A statement that any known events subsequent to the period (or point in time) of the subject matter being reported on, that would have a material effect on the subject matter (or, if applicable, the assertion) have been disclosed to the practitioner.
- Other matters as the practitioner deems appropriate.

4) Refusal to Furnish a Representation Letter
If the responsible party or the client refuses to furnish all written representations that the practitioner deems necessary, the practitioner should consider the effects of such a refusal on his or her ability to issue a conclusion about the subject matter.

If the practitioner believes that the representation letter is necessary to obtain sufficient evidence to issue a report, the responsible party's refusal, or the client's refusal, to furnish such evidence in the form of written representations constitutes a **limitation on the scope of an examination sufficient to preclude an unqualified opinion,** and is ordinarily sufficient to cause the practitioner to disclaim an opinion or withdraw from an examination engagement.

5) Standards of Reporting
    i. ***The practitioner must identify the subject matter or the assertion being reported on and state the character of the engagement in the report.***
    The practitioner who accepts an attest engagement should issue a report on the subject matter or the assertion or withdraw from the attest engagement. If the practitioner is reporting on the assertion, the assertion should be bound with, or accompany, the practitioner's report or the assertion should be clearly stated in the practitioner's report.

    The statement of the character of an attest engagement includes the following two elements:
    - a description of the nature and scope of the work performed and
    - a reference to the professional standards governing the engagement.

    The terms *examination* and *review* should be used to describe engagements to provide, respectively, a high level and a moderate level of assurance. The reference to professional standards should be accomplished by referring to "attestation standards established by the American Institute of Certified Public Accountants."

    ii. ***The practitioner must state the practitioner's conclusion about the subject matter or the assertion in relation to the criteria against which the subject matter was evaluated.***
    However, if conditions exist that, individually or in combination, result in one or more material misstatements or deviations from the criteria, the practitioner should modify the report and, to most effectively communicate with the reader of the report, should ordinarily express his or her conclusion directly on the subject matter, not on the assertion.

    The practitioner should consider the concept of materiality in applying this standard. The practitioner should consider both qualitative and quantitative aspects of omissions and misstatements.

    The term *general use* applies to attest reports that are not restricted to specified parties. General-use attest reports should be limited to two levels of assurance: one based on a restriction of attestation risk, to an appropriately low level (an *examination*) and the other based on a restriction of attestation risk to a moderate level (a *review*). In an engagement to achieve a high level of assurance (an *examination*), the practitioner's conclusion should be expressed in the form of an opinion. When attestation risk has been restricted only to a moderate level (a *review*), the conclusion should be expressed in the form of negative assurance.

Type of engagement	Level of assurance	Conclusion format
Examination	High assurance	Opinion
Review	Moderate assurance	Negative assurance

    iii. ***The practitioner must state all of the practitioner's significant reservations about the engagement, the subject matter, and, if applicable, the assertion related thereto in the report.***

a) Reservations about the Engagement
Reservations about the engagement refers to any unresolved problem that the practitioner had in complying with these attestation standards, interpretive standards, or the specific procedures agreed to by the specified parties.

The practitioner should not express an unqualified conclusion unless the engagement has been conducted in accordance with the attestation standards. Such standards will not have been complied with if the practitioner has been unable to apply all the procedures that he or she considers necessary in the circumstances.

Restrictions on the scope of an engagement, whether imposed by the client or by such other circumstances, as the timing of the work or the inability to obtain sufficient evidence, may require the practitioner to qualify the assurance provided, to disclaim any assurance, or to withdraw from the engagement.

The practitioner's decision to provide a qualified opinion, to disclaim an opinion, or to withdraw, because of a scope limitation in an examination engagement, depends on an assessment of the effect of the omitted procedure(s) on his or her ability to express assurance.
- This assessment will be affected by the nature and magnitude of the potential effects of the matters in question, and by their significance to the subject matter or the assertion.
- If the potential effects are pervasive to the subject matter or the assertion, a disclaimer or withdrawal is more likely to be appropriate.
- When restrictions that significantly limit the scope of the engagement are imposed by the client or the responsible party, the practitioner generally should disclaim an opinion or withdraw from the engagement.

The reasons for a qualification or disclaimer should be described in the practitioner's report.

In a **review engagement**, when the practitioner is unable to perform the inquiry and analytical or other procedures he or she considers necessary to achieve the limited assurance contemplated by a review, or when the client is the responsible party and does not provide the practitioner with a written assertion, the review will be incomplete. A review that is incomplete is not an adequate basis for issuing a review report and, accordingly, the practitioner should withdraw from the engagement.

b) Reservations about the Subject Matter
Reservations about the subject matter or the assertion refers to any unresolved reservation about the assertion or about the conformity of the subject matter with the criteria, including the adequacy of the disclosure of material matters.

They can result in either a qualified or an adverse opinion, depending on the materiality of the departure from the criteria against which the subject matter or the assertion was evaluated, or a modified conclusion in a review engagement.

Reservations about the subject matter or the assertion may relate to the measurement, form, arrangement, content, or underlying judgments and assumptions applicable to the subject matter or the assertion and its appended notes, including, for example, the terminology used, the amount of detail given, the classification of items, and the bases of amounts set forth.

The practitioner considers whether a particular reservation should affect the report given the circumstances and facts of which he or she is aware at the time.

Type of engagement	Type of restriction	Opinion
Examination	Scope restriction	Qualified, disclaimer or withdrawal
Review	Scope restriction	Withdraw
Examination	Subject matter	Qualified or adverse
Review	Subject matter	Modified

iv. *The practitioner must state in the report that the report is intended solely for the information and use of the specified parties under the following circumstances:*
- *When the criteria used to evaluate the subject matter are determined by the practitioner to be appropriate only for a limited number of parties who either participated in their establishment or can be presumed to have an adequate understanding of the criteria*
- *When the criteria used to evaluate the subject matter are available only to specified parties*
- *When reporting on subject matter and a written assertion has not been provided by the responsible party*
- *When the report is on an attestation engagement to apply agreed-upon procedures to the subject matter.*

A restricted-use report should alert readers to the restriction on the use of the report by indicating that the report is not intended to be and should not be used by anyone other than the specified parties.

> *Example*:
> *This report is intended solely for the information and use of [the specified parties] and is not intended to be and should not be used by anyone other than these specified parties.*

Multiple Choice

AUD 4-Q18

c. Examination reports

> **Prepare a draft examination or review report for an attestation engagement starting with a report example (e.g., an illustrative report from professional standards).**

When expressing an opinion, the practitioner should clearly state whether, in his or her opinion,
- the subject matter is based on (or in conformity with) the criteria in all material respects or
- the assertion is presented (or fairly stated), in all material respects, based on the criteria.

Reports expressing an opinion may be qualified or modified for some aspect of the subject matter, the assertion or the engagement.

However, if conditions exist that, individually or in combination, result in one or more material misstatements or deviations from the criteria, the practitioner should modify the report and, to most effectively communicate with the reader of the report, should ordinarily express his or her conclusion directly on the subject matter, not on the assertion.

In addition, such reports may emphasize certain matters relating to the attest engagement, the subject matter, or the assertion.

1) **Examination Report on Subject Matter**
   The practitioner's examination report on subject matter should include the following:
   - A title that includes the word *independent*
   - An identification of the subject matter and the responsible party
   - A statement that the subject matter is the responsibility of the responsible party
   - A statement that the practitioner's responsibility is to express an opinion on the subject matter based on his or her examination
   - A statement that the examination was conducted in accordance with attestation standards established by the American Institute of Certified Public Accountants, and, accordingly, included procedures that the practitioner considered necessary in the circumstances
   - A statement that the practitioner believes the examination provides a reasonable basis for his or her opinion
   - The practitioner's opinion on whether the subject matter is based on (or in conformity with) the criteria in all material respects
   - A statement restricting the use of the report to specified parties under the following circumstances:
     a) When the criteria used to evaluate the subject matter are determined by the practitioner to be appropriate only for a limited number of parties who either participated in their establishment or can be presumed to have an adequate understanding of the criteria
     b) When the criteria used to evaluate the subject matter are available only to the specified parties
     c) When a written assertion has not been provided by the responsible party (The practitioner should also include a statement to that effect in the introductory paragraph of the report.)
   - The manual or printed signature of the practitioner's firm
   - The date of the examination report

i. Example of Examination Report on Subject Matter
   General Use Report
   This is a standard examination report on subject matter for **general use**. This report pertains to subject matter for which suitable criteria exist and are available to all users through inclusion in a clear manner in the presentation of the subject matter. A written assertion has been obtained from the responsible party.

   Independent Accountant's Report

   [Appropriate Addressee]

   We have examined [identify the subject matter, for example, the accompanying schedule of investment returns of XYZ Company for the year ended December 31, 20XX]. XYZ Company's management is responsible for [identify the subject matter, for example, presenting the schedule of investment returns] in accordance with (or based on) [identify the criteria, for example, the ABC criteria set forth in Note 1]. Our responsibility is to express an opinion on [identify the subject matter, for example, the schedule of investment returns] based on our examination.

   Our examination was conducted in accordance with attestation standards established by the American Institute of Certified Public Accountants. Those standards require that we plan and perform the examination to obtain reasonable assurance about whether [identify the subject matter, for example, the schedule of investment returns] is in accordance with (or based on) the criteria, in all material respects. An examination involves performing procedures to obtain evidence about [identify the subject matter, for example, the schedule of investment returns]. The nature, timing, and extent of the procedures selected depend on our judgment, including an assessment of the risks of material misstatement of [identify the subject matter, for example, the schedule of investment returns], whether due to fraud or error. We believe that the evidence we obtained is sufficient and appropriate to provide a reasonable basis for our opinion.

   [Include a description of significant inherent limitations, if any, associated with the measurement or evaluation of the subject matter against the criteria.]

   [Additional paragraph(s) may be added to emphasize certain matters relating to the attestation engagement or the subject matter.]

   In our opinion, [identify the subject matter, for example, the schedule of investment returns of XYZ Company for the year ended December 31, 20XX or the schedule of investment returns referred to above], is presented in accordance with (or based on) [identify the criteria, for example, the ABC criteria set forth in Note 1], in all material respects.

   [Practitioner's signature]
   [Practitioner's city and state]
   [Date of practitioner's report]

Restricted Use Report

This is an examination report on subject matter. Although suitable criteria exist, use of the **report is restricted** because the criteria are available only to specified parties. A written assertion has been obtained from the responsible party.

Independent Accountant's Report

[Appropriate Addressee]

We have examined [identify the subject matter, for example, the number of widgets sold by XYZ Company to ABC Company (or tons of coal mined by XYZ Company... or gallons of gas sold in the United States by XYZ Company to ABC Company) during the year ended December 31, 20XX,] to determine whether it has been calculated in accordance with (or based on) [identify the criteria, for example, the agreement dated (date) between ABC Company and XYZ Company, as further described in Note 1]. XYZ Company's management is responsible for [identify the subject matter, for example, calculating the number of widgets sold]. Our responsibility is to express an opinion on [identify the subject matter, for example, the number of widgets sold by XYZ Company to ABC Company (or tons of coal mined by XYZ Company... or gallons of gas sold in the United States by XYZ Company to ABC Company) during the year ended December 31, 20XX,] based on our examination.

Our examination was conducted in accordance with attestation standards established by the American Institute of Certified Public Accountants. Those standards require that we plan and perform the examination to obtain reasonable assurance about whether [identify the subject matter, for example, the number of widgets sold, tons of coal mined, or gallons of gas sold] is in accordance with (or based on) the criteria, in all material respects. An examination involves performing procedures to obtain evidence about [identify the subject matter, for example, the number of widgets sold, tons of coal mined, or gallons of gas sold]. The nature, timing, and extent of the procedures selected depend on our judgment, including an assessment of the risks of material misstatement of [identify the subject matter, for example, the number of widgets sold by XYZ Company to ABC Company (or tons of coal mined by XYZ Company, or gallons of gas sold in the United States by XYZ Company to ABC Company], whether due to fraud or error. We believe that the evidence we obtained is sufficient and appropriate to provide a reasonable basis for our opinion.

[Include a description of significant inherent limitations, if any, associated with the measurement or evaluation of the subject matter against the criteria.]

[Additional paragraph(s) may be added to emphasize certain matters relating to the attestation engagement or the subject matter.]

In our opinion, [identify the subject matter, for example, the number of widgets sold by XYZ Company to ABC Company (or tons of coal mined by XYZ Company, or gallons of gas sold in the United States by XYZ Company to ABC Company) during the year ended December 31, 20XX,] has been calculated in accordance with (or based on) [identify the criteria, for example, the agreement dated (date) between ABC Company and XYZ Company, as further described in Note 1], in all material respects.

This report is intended solely for the information and use of [identify the specified parties, for example, ABC Company and XYZ Company], and is not intended to be and should not be used by anyone other than the specified parties.

[Practitioner's signature]
[Practitioner's city and state]
[Date of practitioner's report

2) **Examination Report on an Assertion**
    The practitioner's examination report on an assertion should include the following:
    a) A title that includes the word *independent*
    b) An identification of the assertion and the responsible party (When the assertion does not accompany the practitioner's report, the first paragraph of the report should also contain a statement of the assertion.)
    c) A statement that the assertion is the responsibility of the responsible party
    d) A statement that the practitioner's responsibility is to express an opinion on the assertion based on his or her examination
    e) A statement that the examination was conducted in accordance with attestation standards established by the American Institute of Certified Public Accountants, and, accordingly, included procedures that the practitioner considered necessary in the circumstances
    f) A statement that the practitioner believes the examination provides a reasonable basis for his or her opinion
    g) The practitioner's opinion on whether the assertion is presented (or fairly stated), in all material respects, based on the criteria
    h) A statement restricting the use of the report to specified parties under the following circumstances:
        o When the criteria used to evaluate the subject matter are determined by the practitioner to be appropriate only for a limited number of parties who either participated in their establishment or can be presumed to have an adequate understanding of the criteria
        o When the criteria used to evaluate the subject matter are available only to the specified parties
    i) The manual or printed signature of the practitioner's firm
    j) The date of the examination report

   i. Example of Examination Report on An Assertion
   General Use Report
   This report is a standard examination report on an assertion for **general use**. The report pertains to subject matter for which suitable criteria exist and are available to all users through inclusion in a clear manner in the presentation of the subject matter. A written assertion has been obtained from the responsible party.

   Independent Accountant's Report

   [Appropriate Addressee]

   We have examined management of XYZ Company's assertion that [identify the assertion, including the subject matter and the criteria, for example, the accompanying schedule of investment returns of XYZ Company for the year ended December 31, 20XX, is presented in accordance with [or based on] the ABC criteria set forth in Note 1]. XYZ Company's management is responsible for its assertion. Our responsibility is to express an opinion on management's assertion based on our examination.

   Our examination was conducted in accordance with attestation standards established by the American Institute of Certified Public Accountants. Those standards require that we plan and perform the examination to obtain reasonable assurance about whether management's assertion is fairly stated, in all material respects. An examination involves performing procedures to obtain evidence about management's assertion. The nature, timing, and extent of the procedures selected depend on our judgment, including an assessment of the risks of material misstatement of management's assertion, whether due to fraud or error. We believe that the evidence we obtained is sufficient and appropriate to provide a reasonable basis for our opinion.

[Include a description of significant inherent limitations, if any, associated with the easurement or evaluation of the subject matter against the criteria.]

[Additional paragraph(s) may be added to emphasize certain matters relating to the attestation engagement or the subject matter.]

In our opinion, management's assertion that [identify the assertion, including the subject matter and the criteria, for example, the accompanying schedule of investment returns of XYZ Company for the year ended December 31, 20XX, is presented in accordance with [or based on] the ABC criteria set forth in Note 1] is fairly stated, in all material respects.

[Practitioner's signature]
[Practitioner's city and state]
[Date of practitioner's report]

d. Review reports
In a review report, the practitioner's conclusion should state whether any information came to the practitioner's attention on the basis of the work performed that indicates that
- the subject matter is not based on (or in conformity with) the criteria or
- the assertion is not presented (or fairly stated) in all material respects based on the criteria.

1) **Review Report on Subject Matter**
The practitioner's review report on subject matter should include the following:
- A title that includes the word *independent*
- An identification of the subject matter and the responsible party
- A statement that the subject matter is the responsibility of the responsible party
- A statement that the review was conducted in accordance with attestation standards established by the American Institute of Certified Public Accountants
- A statement that a review is substantially less in scope than an examination, the objective of which is an expression of opinion on the subject matter, and accordingly, no such opinion is expressed
- A statement about whether the practitioner is aware of any material modifications that should be made to the subject matter in order for it to be based on (or in conformity with), in all material respects, the criteria, other than those modifications, if any, indicated in his or her report
- A statement restricting the use of the report to specified parties under the following circumstances:
    a) When the criteria used to evaluate the subject matter are determined by the practitioner to be appropriate only for a limited number of parties who either participated in their establishment or can be presumed to have an adequate understanding of the criteria
    b) When the criteria used to evaluate the subject matter are available only to the specified parties
    c) When a written assertion has not been provided by the responsible party and the responsible party is not the client (The practitioner should also include a statement to that effect in the introductory paragraph of the report.)
- The manual or printed signature of the practitioner's firm
- The date of the review report

i. Example of Review Report on Subject Matter
General Use Report
This is a standard review report on subject matter for general use. The report pertains to subject matter for which suitable criteria exist and are available to all users through inclusion in a clear manner in the presentation of the subject matter. A written assertion has been obtained from the responsible party.

Independent Accountant's Review Report

[Appropriate Addressee]

We have reviewed [identify the subject matter, for example, the accompanying schedule of investment returns of XYZ Company for the year ended December 31, 20XX]. XYZ Company's management is responsible for [identify the subject matter, for example, presenting the schedule of investment returns] in accordance with (or based on) [identify the criteria, for example, the ABC criteria set forth in Note 1]. Our responsibility is to express a conclusion on [identify the subject matter, for example, the schedule of investment returns] based on our review.

Our review was conducted in accordance with attestation standards established by the American Institute of Certified Public Accountants. Those standards require that we plan and perform the review to obtain limited assurance about whether any material modifications should be made to [identify the subject matter, for example, the schedule of investment returns] in order for it to be in accordance with (or based on) the criteria. A review is substantially less in scope than an examination, the objective of which is to obtain reasonable assurance about whether [identify the subject matter, for example, the schedule of investment returns] is in accordance with (or based on) the criteria, in all material respects, in order to express an opinion. Accordingly, we do not express such an opinion. We believe that our review provides a reasonable basis for our conclusion.

[Include a description of significant inherent limitations, if any, associated with the measurement or evaluation of the subject matter against the criteria.]

[Additional paragraph(s) may be added to emphasize certain matters relating to the attestation engagement or the subject matter.]

Based on our review, we are not aware of any material modifications that should be made to [identify the subject matter, for example, the accompanying schedule of investment returns of XYZ Company for the year ended December 31, 20XX], in order for it be in accordance with (or based on) [identify the criteria, for example, the ABC criteria set forth in Note 1].

[Practitioner's signature]
[Practitioner's city and state]
[Date of practitioner's report]

2) **Review Report on An Assertion**
   The practitioner's review report on an assertion should include the following:
   - A title that includes the word *independent*
   - An identification of the assertion and the responsible party (When the assertion does not accompany the practitioner's report, the first paragraph of the report should also contain a statement of the assertion.)
   - A statement that the assertion is the responsibility of the responsible party
   - A statement that the review was conducted in accordance with attestation standards established by the American Institute of Certified Public Accountants
   - A statement that a review is substantially less in scope than an examination, the objective of which is an expression of opinion on the assertion, and accordingly, no such opinion is expressed
   - A statement about whether the practitioner is aware of any material modifications that should be made to the assertion in order for it to be presented (or fairly stated), in all material respects, based on (or in conformity with) the criteria, other than those modifications, if any, indicated in his or her report
   - A statement restricting the use of the report to specified parties under the following circumstances:
     a) When the criteria used to evaluate the subject matter are determined by the practitioner to be appropriate only for a limited number of parties who either participated in their establishment or can be presumed to have an adequate understanding of the criteria
     b) When the criteria used to evaluate the subject matter are available only to the specified parties
   - The manual or printed signature of the practitioner's firm
   - The date of the review report

i. Example of Review Report on an Assertion
   Restricted Use Report
   This is a review report on an assertion. Although suitable criteria exist for the subject matter, the report is restricted as to use since the criteria are available only to specified parties. A written assertion has been obtained from the responsible party.

   Independent Accountant's Review Report

   [Appropriate Addressee]

   We have reviewed management of XYZ Company's assertion that [identify the assertion, including the subject matter and the criteria, for example, the accompanying schedule of investment returns of XYZ Company for the year ended December 31, 20XX, is presented in accordance with (or based on) the ABC criteria set forth in Note 1]. XYZ Company's management is responsible for its assertion. Our responsibility is to express a conclusion on management's assertion based on our review.

   Our review was conducted in accordance with attestation standards established by the American Institute of Certified Public Accountants. Those standards require that we plan and perform the review to obtain limited assurance about whether any material modifications should be made to management's assertion in order for it to be fairly stated. A review is substantially less in scope than an examination, the objective of which is to obtain reasonable assurance about whether management's assertion is fairly stated, in all material respects, in order to express an opinion. Accordingly, we do not express such an opinion. We believe that our review provides a reasonable basis for our conclusion. [Include a description of significant inherent limitations, if any, associated with the measurement or evaluation of the subject matter against the criteria.] [Additional paragraph(s) may be added to emphasize certain matters relating to the attestation engagement or the subject matter.] Based on our review, we are not aware of any material modifications that should be made to management of XYZ Company's assertion in order for it to be fairly stated.

   This report is intended solely for the information and use of [identify the specified parties, for example, ABC Company and XYZ Company], and is not intended to be, and should not be, used by anyone other than the specified parties.

   [Practitioner's signature]
   [Practitioner's city and state]
   [Date of practitioner's report]

2. Agreed-upon procedures reports

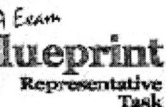

> **Identify the factors that a practitioner should consider when issuing an agreed-upon procedures report for an attestation engagement.**

> *Hint*: The main sources of professional guidance that serve as the basis for this review are obtained from the following:
> AT Section 201, *Agreed-Upon Procedures Engagements*

   a. Agreed-upon procedures engagements
An agreed-upon procedures engagement is one in which a practitioner is engaged by a client to issue a report of findings based on specific procedures performed on subject matter. This type of attestation engagement would consider the following factors:
- The services of a practitioner are obtained for purposes of independence.
- The client and practitioner agree on the procedures to be performed.
- The client takes responsibility for the sufficiency of the procedures for their purposes. Ordinarily the practitioner should communicate directly with and obtain affirmative acknowledgment from each of the specified parties.
- The report on such engagement is restricted to the specified parties.
- Standards for attestation engagements should be followed by the practitioner.
- A written assertion is generally not required.
- The practitioner should obtain evidential matter from applying the agreed-upon procedures to provide a reasonable basis for the finding or findings expressed in his or her report, **but need not perform additional procedures outside the scope of the engagement** to gather additional evidential matter.

> *Hint*: The practitioner should not report on an engagement when specified parties do not agree upon the procedures performed or to be performed and do not take responsibility for the sufficiency of the procedures for their purposes.

      1) Subject Matter and Related Assertions
The subject matter of an agreed-upon procedures engagement may take many different forms and may be at a point in time or covering a period of time. The criteria against which the specific subject matter needs to be measured may be stated within the procedures referred to in the practitioner's report.

An assertion is any declaration or set of declarations about whether the subject matter is based on or in conformity with the criteria selected. A written assertion is generally not required in an agreed-upon procedures engagement unless specifically required by another attest standard (for example, AT Section 601.11, *Compliance Attestation*).

      2) Procedures to Be Performed
Examples of appropriate procedures include the following:
- Execution of a sampling application after agreeing on relevant parameters.
- Inspection of specified documents evidencing certain types of transactions or detailed attributes thereof.
- Confirmation of specific information with third parties.
- Comparison of documents, schedules, or analyses with certain specified attributes.
- Performance of specific procedures on work performed by others.
- Performance of mathematical computations.

Examples of inappropriate procedures include the following:
- Mere reading of the work performed by others solely to describe their findings.
- Evaluating the competency or objectivity of another party.
- Obtaining an understanding about a particular subject.
- Interpreting documents outside the scope of the practitioner's professional expertise.

3) Involvement of a Specialist
The practitioner's education and experience enable him or her to be knowledgeable about business matters in general, but he or she is not expected to have the expertise of a person trained for or qualified to engage in the practice of another profession or occupation.

In certain circumstances, it may be appropriate to involve a specialist to assist the practitioner in the performance of one or more procedures. The following are examples:
- An attorney might provide assistance concerning the interpretation of legal terminology involving laws, regulations, rules, contracts, or grants.
- A medical specialist might provide assistance in understanding the characteristics of diagnosis codes documented in patient medical records.
- An environmental engineer might provide assistance in interpreting environmental remedial action regulatory directives that may affect the agreed-upon procedures applied to an environmental liabilities account in a financial statement.
- A geologist might provide assistance in distinguishing between varying physical characteristics of a generic minerals group related to information to which the agreed-upon procedures are applied.

The practitioner and the specified parties should explicitly agree to the involvement of the specialist in assisting a practitioner in the performance of an agreed-upon procedures engagement. This agreement may be reached when obtaining agreement on the procedures performed or to be performed and acknowledgment of responsibility for the sufficiency of the procedures. The practitioner's report should describe the nature of the assistance provided by the specialist.

b. Findings
A practitioner should present the results of applying agreed-upon procedures to specific subject matter in the form of findings.

The practitioner should not provide negative assurance about whether the subject matter or the assertion is fairly stated based on the criteria. For example, the practitioner should not include a statement in his or her report that "nothing came to my attention that caused me to believe that the [*identify subject matter*] is not presented based on [or the assertion is not fairly stated based on] [*identify criteria*]."

The practitioner should report all findings from application of the agreed-upon procedures.

The concept of materiality does not apply to findings to be reported in an agreed-upon procedures engagement unless the definition of materiality is agreed to by the specified parties. Any agreed-upon materiality limits should be described in the practitioner's report.

The practitioner should avoid vague or ambiguous language in reporting findings.

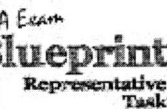

Prepare a draft agreed-upon procedures report for an attestation engagement starting with a report example (e.g., an illustrative report from professional standards).

c. Reporting

The practitioner's report on agreed-upon procedures should be in the form of procedures and findings. The practitioner's report should contain the following elements:

- A title that includes the word *independent*.
- Identification of the specified parties.
- Identification of the subject matter (or the written assertion related thereto) and the character of the engagement.
- Identification of the responsible party.
- A statement that the subject matter is the responsibility of the responsible party.
- A statement that the procedures performed were those agreed to by the specified parties identified in the report.
- A statement that the agreed-upon procedures engagement was conducted in accordance with attestation standards established by the AICPA.
- A statement that the sufficiency of the procedures is solely the responsibility of the specified parties and a disclaimer of responsibility for the sufficiency of those procedures.
- A list of the procedures performed (or reference thereto) and related findings.
- Where applicable, a description of any agreed-upon materiality limits.
- A statement that the practitioner was not engaged to and did not conduct an examination of the subject matter, the objective of which would be the expression of an opinion, a disclaimer of opinion on the subject matter, and a statement that if the practitioner had performed additional procedures, other matters might have come to his or her attention that would have been reported.
- A statement of restrictions on the use of the report because it is intended to be used solely by the specified parties.
- Where applicable, reservations or restrictions concerning procedures or findings.
- For an agreed-upon procedures engagement on prospective financial information, all items required for reports on the results of applying agreed-upon procedures.
- Where applicable, a description of the nature of the assistance provided by a specialist.
- The manual or printed signature of the practitioner's firm.
- The date of the report.

Hint: The practitioner should **not** provide negative assurance.

1) Example of report on agreed-upon procedures
   The following is an illustration of an agreed-upon procedures report.

   Independent Accountant's Report on Applying
   Agreed-Upon Procedures

   [Appropriate Addressee]

   We have performed the procedures enumerated below, which were agreed to by [identify the specified party(ies), for example, the audit committees and managements of ABC Inc. and XYZ Fund], on [identify the subject matter, for example, the accompanying Statement of Investment Performance Statistics of XYZ Fund for the year ended December 31, 20X1]. XYZ Fund's management is responsible for [identify the subject matter, for example, the Statement of Investment Performance Statistics for the year ended December 31, 20X1]. The sufficiency of these procedures is solely the responsibility of the parties specified in this report. Consequently, we make no representation regarding the sufficiency of the procedures enumerated below either for the purpose for which this report has been requested or for any other purpose.

   [Include paragraphs to enumerate procedures and findings.]

   This agreed-upon procedures engagement was conducted in accordance with attestation standards established by the American Institute of Certified Public Accountants. We were not engaged to and did not conduct an examination or review, the objective of which would be the expression of an opinion or conclusion, respectively, on [identify the subject matter, for example, the accompanying Statement of Investment Performance Statistics of XYZ Fund for the year ended December 31, 20X1]. Accordingly, we do not express such an opinion or conclusion. Had we performed additional procedures, other matters might have come to our attention that would have been reported to you.

   [Additional paragraph(s) may be added to describe other matters.]

   This report is intended solely for the information and use of [identify the specified party(ies), for example, the audit committees and managements of ABC Inc. and XYZ Fund], and is not intended to be, and should not be, used by anyone other than the specified parties.

   [Practitioner's signature]
   [Practitioner's city and state]
   [Date of practitioner's report]

2) Explanatory Language
   The practitioner also may include explanatory language about matters such as the following:
   - Disclosure of stipulated facts, assumptions, or interpretations (including the source thereof) used in the application of agreed-upon procedures.
   - Description of the condition of records, controls, or data to which the procedures were applied.
   - Explanation that the practitioner has no responsibility to update his or her report.
   - Explanation of sampling risk.

3) Dating of Report
   The date of completion of the agreed-upon procedures should be used as the date of the practitioner's report.

4) Restrictions on the Performance of Procedures
   When circumstances impose restrictions on the performance of the agreed-upon procedures, the practitioner should attempt to obtain agreement from the specified parties for modification of the agreed-upon procedures. When such agreement cannot be obtained (for example, when the agreed-upon procedures are published by a regulatory agency that

will not modify the procedures), the practitioner should describe any restrictions on the performance of procedures in his or her report or withdraw from the engagement.

5) Adding Specified Parties (Nonparticipant Parties)
Subsequent to the completion of the agreed-upon procedures engagement, a practitioner may be requested to consider the addition of another party as a specified party (*a nonparticipant party*). The practitioner may agree to add a nonparticipant party as a specified party, based on consideration of such factors as the identity of the nonparticipant party and the intended use of the report.

If the practitioner does agree to add the nonparticipant party, he or she should obtain affirmative acknowledgment, normally in writing, from the nonparticipant party agreeing to the procedures performed and of its taking responsibility for the sufficiency of the procedures.

d. Written representations
A practitioner may find a representation letter to be a useful and practical means of obtaining representations from the responsible party.

Multiple Choice

AUD 4-Q19

3. **Reporting on controls at a service organization**
   Reports on controls at a service organization are often referred to as a Type 1 or Type 2 report.

   A **Type 1 report** is one that contains management's description of internal controls and the suitability of the design of the controls. A Type 1 report includes:
   - Management's description of the service organization's system.
   - A written assertion by management of the service organization about whether, in all material respects, and based on suitable criteria,
     a) management's description of the service organization's system fairly presents the service organization's system that was designed and implemented **as of a specified date.**
     b) the controls related to the control objectives stated in management's description of the service organization's system were suitably designed to achieve those control objectives **as of the specified date.**
   - A service auditor's report that expresses an opinion on the matters listed above.

   A **Type 2 report** is one that contains management's description of internal controls and the suitability of the design *and operating effectiveness* of the controls. A Type 2 report includes:
   - Management's description of the service organization's system.
   - A written assertion by management of the service organization about whether, in all material respects, and based on suitable criteria,
     a) management's description of the service organization's system fairly presents the service organization's system that was designed and implemented throughout the specified period.
     b) the controls related to the control objectives stated in management's description of the service organization's system were suitably designed **throughout the specified period to achieve those control objectives.**
     c) the controls related to the control objectives stated in management's description of the service organization's system operated effectively **throughout the specified period to achieve those control objectives.**
   - A service auditor's report that expresses an opinion on the matters listed above and includes a description of the tests of controls and the results thereof.

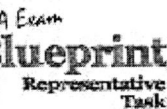

> **Identify the factors that a service auditor should consider when reporting on the examination of controls at a service organization.**

The objectives of the service auditor are to:
- obtain reasonable assurance about whether, in all material respects, based on suitable criteria, that:
  a) management's description of the service organization's system fairly presents the system that was designed and implemented throughout the specified period (or in the case of a type 1 report, as of a specified date).
  b) the controls related to the control objectives stated in management's description of the service organization's system were suitably designed throughout the specified period (or in the case of a type 1 report, as of a specified date).
  c) when included in the scope of the engagement, the controls operated effectively to provide reasonable assurance that the control objectives stated in management's description of the service organization's system were achieved throughout the specified period.
- report on the matters above in accordance with the service auditor's findings.

If management refuses to provide a written assertion, it represents a scope limitation and consequently, the service auditor should withdraw from the engagement. If law or regulation does not allow the service auditor to withdraw from the engagement, the service auditor should disclaim an opinion. If management will not provide the service auditor with a written assertion, the service auditor should not circumvent the requirement to obtain an assertion by performing a service auditor's engagement under AT 101, *Attest Engagements*.

a. Assessing the suitability of the criteria
   As required by the third general standard of the attestation standards, the service auditor should assess whether management has used suitable criteria
   - in preparing its description of the service organization's system;
   - in evaluating whether controls were suitably designed to achieve the control objectives stated in the description; and
   - in the case of a type 2 report, in evaluating whether controls operated effectively throughout the specified period to achieve the control objectives stated in the description of the service organization's system.

b. Materiality
   When planning and performing the engagement, the service auditor should evaluate materiality with respect to the fair presentation of management's description of the service organization's system; the suitability of the design of controls to achieve the related control objectives stated in the description and; in the case of a type 2 report, the operating effectiveness of the controls to achieve the related control objectives stated in the description.

   Materiality with respect to the **fair presentation of management's description of the service organization's system and with respect to the design of controls** primarily includes the consideration of qualitative factors; for example, whether:
   - management's description of the service organization's system includes the significant aspects of the processing of significant transactions.
   - management's description of the service organization's system omits or distorts relevant information.

- the controls have the ability, as designed, to provide reasonable assurance that the control objectives stated in management's description of the service organization's system would be achieved.

Materiality with respect to the **operating effectiveness of controls,** includes the consideration of both quantitative and qualitative factors; for example, the tolerable rate and observed rate of deviation (a quantitative matter) and the nature and cause of any observed deviations (a qualitative matter).

c. Obtaining an understanding of the service organization's system
The service auditor should obtain an understanding of the service organization's system, including controls that are included in the scope of the engagement.

d. Evidence
   1) Obtaining Evidence Regarding Management's Description of the Service Organization's System
   The service auditor should obtain and read management's description of the service organization's system and should evaluate whether those aspects of the description that are included in the scope of the engagement are presented fairly, including whether
      i. the control objectives stated in management's description of the service organization's system are reasonable in the circumstances.
      ii. controls identified in management's description of the service organization's system were implemented.
      iii. complementary user entity controls, if any, are adequately described.
      iv. services performed by a subservice organization, if any, are adequately described, including whether the inclusive method or the carve-out method has been used in relation to them.

   The service auditor should determine through inquiries made in combination with other procedures whether the service organization's system has been implemented. Such other procedures should include observation and inspection of records and other documentation of the manner in which the service organization's system operates and controls are applied.

   2) Obtaining Evidence Regarding the Design of Controls
   The service auditor should determine which of the controls at the service organization are necessary to achieve the control objectives stated in management's description of the service organization's system and should assess whether those controls were suitably designed to achieve the control objectives by
      - identifying the risks that threaten the achievement of the control objectives stated in management's description of the service organization's system, and
      - evaluating the linkage of the controls identified in management's description of the service organization's system with those risks.

   3) Obtaining Evidence Regarding the Operating Effectiveness of Controls
      i. Assessing Operating Effectiveness
      When designing and performing tests of controls, the service auditor should:
         - perform other procedures in combination with inquiry, to obtain evidence about the following:
            a) How the control was applied.
            b) The consistency with which the control was applied.
            c) By whom or by what means the control was applied.

- determine whether the controls to be tested depend on other controls, and if so, whether it is necessary to obtain evidence supporting the operating effectiveness of those other controls.
- determine an effective method for selecting the items to be tested to meet the objectives of the procedure.

e. Opinions
   1) Modified Opinions
   The service auditor's **opinion should be modified** and the service auditor's report should contain a clear description of all the reasons for the modification, if the service auditor concludes that
   - management's description of the service organization's system is not fairly presented, in all material respects;
   - the controls are not suitably designed to provide reasonable assurance that the control objectives stated in management's description of the service organization's system would be achieved if the controls operated as described;
   - in the case of a type 2 report, the controls did not operate effectively throughout the specified period to achieve the related control objectives stated in management's description of the service organization's system; or
   - the service auditor is unable to obtain sufficient appropriate evidence

   If the service auditor plans to **disclaim an opinion** because of the inability to obtain sufficient appropriate evidence, and, based on the limited procedures performed, has concluded
   - certain aspects of management's description of the service organization's system are not fairly presented, in all material respects;
   - certain controls were not suitably designed to provide reasonable assurance that the control objectives stated in management's description of the service organization's system would be achieved if the controls operated as described; or
   - in the case of a type 2 report, certain controls did not operate effectively throughout the specified period to achieve the related control objectives stated in management's description of the service organization's system,
   - then, the service auditor should identify these findings in his or her report.

   If the service auditor plans to disclaim an opinion, the service auditor should not identify the procedures that were performed nor include statements describing the characteristics of a service auditor's engagement in the service auditor's report; to do so might overshadow the disclaimer.

Multiple Choice

AUD 4-Q20

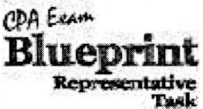

> Prepare a draft report for an engagement to report on the examination of controls at a service organization, starting with a report example (e.g., an illustrative report from professional standards).

f. Example – Type 1 Service Auditor's Report

Independent Service Auditor's Report on XYZ Service Organization's Description of Its [type or name of] System and the Suitability of the Design of Controls

To: XYZ Service Organization

*We have examined XYZ Service Organization's description of its [type or name of] system entitled, "XYZ Service Organization's Description of Its [type or name of] System," for processing user entities' transactions [or identification of the function performed by the system] **as of [date]** (description) and the suitability of the design of the controls included in the description to achieve the related control objectives stated in the description, based on the criteria identified in "XYZ Service Organization's Assertion" (assertion). The controls and control objectives included in the description are those that management of XYZ Service Organization believes are likely to be relevant to user entities' internal control over financial reporting, and the description does not include those aspects of the [type or name of] system that are not likely to be relevant to user entities' internal control over financial reporting.*

[A statement such as the following is added to the service auditor's report when information that is not covered by the report is included in the description of the service organization's system.]

The information included in [section number where the other information is presented], "Other Information Provided by XYZ Service Organization," is presented by management of XYZ Service Organization to provide additional information and is not a part of XYZ Service Organization's description of its [name or type of] system made available to user entities as of [date]. Information about XYZ Service Organization's [describe the nature of the information, for example, business continuity planning, privacy practices, and so on] has not been subjected to the procedures applied in the examination of the description of the [name or type of] system and of the suitability of the design of controls to achieve the related control objectives stated in the description of the [name or type of] system.

[A statement such as the following is added to the report when the service organization uses a subservice organization, the carve-out method is used to present the subservice organization, and complementary subservice organization controls are required to meet the control objectives.]

XYZ Service Organization uses a subservice organization to [identify the function or service provided by the subservice organization]. The description includes only the control objectives and related controls of XYZ Service Organization and excludes the control objectives and related controls of the subservice organization. The description also indicates that certain control objectives specified by XYZ Service Organization can be achieved only if complementary subservice organization controls assumed in the design of XYZ Service Organization's controls are suitably designed and operating effectively, along with the related controls at XYZ Service Organization. Our examination did not extend to controls of the subservice organization, and we have not evaluated the design or operating effectiveness of such complementary subservice organization controls.

[A statement such as the following is added to the assertion when complementary user entity controls are required to meet the control objectives.]

The description indicates that certain control objectives specified in the description can be achieved only if complementary user entity controls assumed in the design of XYZ Service Organization's controls are suitably designed and operating effectively, along with related controls at the service organization. Our examination did not extend to such complementary user entity controls, and we have not evaluated the suitability of the design or operating effectiveness of such complementary user entity controls.

Service Organization's Responsibilities
In [section number where assertion is presented], XYZ Service Organization has provided an assertion about the fairness of the presentation of the description and suitability of the design of the controls to achieve the related control objectives stated in the description. XYZ Service Organization is responsible for preparing the description and its assertion, including the completeness, accuracy, and method of presentation of the description and assertion, providing the services covered by the description, specifying the control objectives and stating them in the description, identifying the risks that threaten the achievement of the control objectives, selecting the criteria stated in the assertion, and designing, implementing, and documenting controls that are suitably designed and operating effectively to achieve the related control objectives stated in the description.

Service Auditor's Responsibilities
Our responsibility is to express an opinion on the fairness of the presentation of the description and on the suitability of the design of the controls to achieve the related control objectives stated in the description, based on our examination. Our examination was conducted in accordance with attestation standards established by the American Institute of Certified Public Accountants. Those standards require that we plan and perform the examination to obtain reasonable assurance about whether, in all material respects, based on the criteria in management's assertion, the description is fairly presented and the controls were suitably designed to achieve the related control objectives stated in the description as of [date]. We believe that the evidence we obtained is sufficient and appropriate to provide a reasonable basis for our opinion.

An examination of a description of a service organization's system and the suitability of the design of controls involves
- *performing procedures to obtain evidence about the fairness of the presentation of the description and the suitability of the design of the controls to achieve the related control objectives stated in the description, based on the criteria in management's assertion.*
- *assessing the risks that the description is not fairly presented and that the controls were not suitably designed to achieve the related control objectives stated in the description.*
- *evaluating the overall presentation of the description, suitability of the control objectives stated in the description, and suitability of the criteria specified by the service organization in its assertion.*

Inherent Limitations
The description is prepared to meet the common needs of a broad range of user entities and their auditors who audit and report on user entities' financial statements and may not, therefore, include every aspect of the system that each individual user entity may consider important in its own particular environment. Because of their nature, controls at a service organization may not prevent, or detect and correct, all misstatements in processing or reporting transactions [or identification of the function performed by the system]. Also, the projection to the future of any evaluation of the fairness of the presentation of the description, or conclusions about the suitability of the design of the controls to achieve the related control objectives, is subject to the risk that controls at a service organization may become ineffective.

Other Matter
We did not perform any procedures regarding the operating effectiveness of controls stated in the description and, accordingly, do not express an opinion thereon.

Opinion
In our opinion, in all material respects, based on the criteria described in XYZ Service Organization's assertion
  a. *the description fairly presents the [type or name of] system that was designed and implemented as of [date].*
  b. *the controls related to the control objectives stated in the description were suitably designed to provide reasonable assurance that the control objectives would be achieved if the controls operated effectively as of [date] and subservice organizations and user entities applied the complementary controls assumed in the design of XYZ Service Organization's controls as of [date].*

Restricted Use
This report is intended solely for the information and use of management of XYZ Service Organization, user entities of XYZ Service Organization's [type or name of] system as of [date], and their auditors who audit and report on such user entities' financial statements or internal control over financial reporting and have a sufficient understanding to consider it, along with other information, including information about controls implemented by

user entities themselves, when assessing the risks of material misstatements of user entities' financial statements. This report is not intended to be, and should not be, used by anyone other than the specified parties.

[Service auditor's signature]
[Service auditor's city and state]
[Date of the service auditor's report]

g. **Example** – Type 2 Service Auditor's Report

Independent Service Auditor's Report on XYZ Service Organization's Description of Its [type or name of] System and the Suitability of the Design and Operating Effectiveness of Controls

To: XYZ Service Organization

Scope
We have examined XYZ Service Organization's description of its [type or name of] system entitled "XYZ Service Organization's Description of Its [type or name of] System" for processing user entities' transactions [or identification of the function performed by the system] **throughout the period [date] to [date]** (description) and the suitability of the design and operating effectiveness of the controls included in the description to achieve the related control objectives stated in the description, based on the criteria identified in "XYZ Service Organization's Assertion" (assertion). The controls and control objectives included in the description are those that management of XYZ Service Organization believes are likely to be relevant to user entities' internal control over financial reporting, and the description does not include those aspects of the [type or name of] system that are not likely to be relevant to user entities' internal control over financial reporting.

[…Same as Type 1…]

The information included in [section number where the other information is presented], "Other Information Provided by XYZ Service Organization" is presented by management of XYZ Service Organization to provide additional information and is not a part of XYZ Service Organization's description of its [name or type of] system made available to user entities **during the period [date] to [date]**. Information about XYZ Service Organization's [describe the nature of the information, for example, business continuity planning, privacy practices, and so on] has not been subjected to the procedures applied in the examination of the description of the [name or type of] system and of the suitability of the design and operating effectiveness of controls to achieve the related control objectives stated in the description of the [name or type of] system.

[…Same as Type 1…]

Service Organization's Responsibilities
In [section number where the assertion is presented], XYZ Service Organization has provided an assertion about the fairness of the presentation of the description and suitability of the design **and operating effectiveness** of the controls to achieve the related control objectives stated in the description. XYZ Service Organization is responsible for preparing the description and assertion, including the completeness, accuracy, and method of presentation of the description and assertion, providing the services covered by the description, specifying the control objectives and stating them in the description, identifying the risks that threaten the achievement of the control objectives, selecting the criteria stated in the assertion, and designing, implementing, and documenting controls that are suitably designed and operating effectively to achieve the related control objectives stated in the description.

Service Auditor's Responsibilities
Our responsibility is to express an opinion on the fairness of the presentation of the description and on the suitability of the design **and operating effectiveness** of the controls to achieve the related control objectives stated in the description, based on our examination.

Our examination was conducted in accordance with attestation standards established by the American Institute of Certified Public Accountants. Those standards require that we plan and perform the examination to obtain reasonable assurance about whether, in all material respects, based on the criteria in management's assertion, the description is fairly presented and the controls were suitably designed and operating effectively to achieve the related control objectives stated in the description **throughout the period [date] to [date]**. We believe that the evidence we obtained is sufficient and appropriate to provide a reasonable basis for our opinion.

An examination of a description of a service organization's system and the suitability of the design **and operating effectiveness** of controls involves
- performing procedures to obtain evidence about the fairness of the presentation of the description and the suitability of the design and operating effectiveness of the controls to achieve the related control objectives stated in the description, based on the criteria in management's assertion.
- assessing the risks that the description is not fairly presented and that the controls were not suitably designed or operating effectively to achieve the related control objectives stated in the description.
- testing the operating effectiveness of those controls that management considers necessary to provide reasonable assurance that the related control objectives stated in the description were achieved.
- evaluating the overall presentation of the description, suitability of the control objectives stated in the description, and suitability of the criteria specified by the service organization in its assertion.

Inherent Limitations
The description is prepared to meet the common needs of a broad range of user entities and their auditors who audit and report on user entities' financial statements and may not, therefore, include every aspect of the system that each individual user entity may consider important in its own particular environment. Because of their nature, controls at a service organization may not prevent, or detect and correct, all misstatements in processing or reporting transactions [or identification of the function performed by the system]. Also, the projection to the future of any evaluation of the fairness of the presentation of the description, or conclusions about the suitability of the design or operating effectiveness of the controls to achieve the related control objectives, is subject to the risk that controls at a service organization may become ineffective.

Description of Tests of Controls
The specific controls tested and the nature, timing, and results of those tests are listed in [section number where the description of tests of controls is presented].

Opinion
In our opinion, in all material respects, based on the criteria described in XYZ Service Organization's assertion:
  a. the description fairly presents the [type or name of] system that was designed and implemented throughout the period [date] to [date].
  b. the controls related to the control objectives stated in the description were suitably designed to provide reasonable assurance that the control objectives would be achieved if the controls operated effectively throughout the period [date] to [date] and subservice organizations and user entities applied the complementary controls assumed in the design of XYZ Service Organization's controls throughout the period [date] to [date].
  c. the controls operated effectively to provide reasonable assurance that the control objectives stated in the description were achieved throughout the period [date] to [date] if complementary subservice organization and user entity controls assumed in the design of XYZ Service organization's controls operated effectively throughout the period [date] to [date].

Restricted Use
This report, including the description of tests of controls and results thereof in [section number where the description of tests of controls is presented], is intended solely for the information and use of management of XYZ Service Organization, user entities of XYZ Service Organization's [type or name of] system during some or all of the period [date] to [date], and their auditors who audit and report on such user entities' financial statements or internal control over financial reporting and have a sufficient understanding to consider it, along with other information, including information about controls implemented by user entities themselves, when assessing the risks of material misstatement of user entities' financial statements. This report is not intended to be, and should not be, used by anyone other than the specified parties.

[Service auditor's signature]
[Service auditor's city and state]
[Date of the service auditor's report]

Multiple Choice

AUD 4-Q21 through AUD 4-Q28

C. Accounting and Review Service Engagements

> *Hint:* Quick reference summary for accounting and review service engagements:
> 1. **Preparation**
>   - Accountant prepare financial statements from client records.
>   - Understand applicable financial reporting framework.
>   - No report -- each page marked "no assurance provided."
>
> 2. **Compilations** (no assurance) (Assist management in presenting financial information).
>   - Do not deal with internal control
>   - Read financial statements for logic.
>   - May omit substantially all disclosures required by GAAP, but must add an extra paragraph to the report
>   - Cite measurement GAAP departures in an extra paragraph in the report
>
> 3. **Reviews** (limited or negative assurance):
>   - Do not deal with internal control.
>   - Inquiry and analytical procedures.
>   - Cite measurement and/or disclosure GAAP departure in an extra paragraph in report ("known departures")

> **Hint:** The main sources of professional guidance that serve as the basis for this review are obtained from the following:
> AR-C 60, *General Principles for Engagements Performed in Accordance with Statements on Standards for Accounting and Review Services* (see Statements on Standards for Accounting and Review Services (SSARS) No. 21, *Statements on Standards for Accounting and Review Services: Clarification and Recodification*), AICPA.
> AR-C 70, *Preparation of Financial Statements* (see SSARS No. 21), AICPA.
> AR-C 80, *Compilation Engagements* (see SSARS No. 21), AICPA.
> AR-C 90, *Review of Financial Statements* (see SSARS No 21), AICPA.

Similar to the auditing standards, the AICPA undertook a project to clarify the professional standards relating to accounting and review engagements. Statement on Standards for Accounting and Review Services (SSARS) No. 21 supersedes all outstanding SSARSs through No. 20, except SSARS No. 14, *Compilation of Pro Forma Financial Information*, as amended (AR sec. 120). SSARS No. 14 is currently being redrafted (as of September 2015) and will be issued as a separate SSARS when finalized. SSARS No. 21 is effective for engagements for periods ending on or after December 15, 2015. Early implementation is permitted for all sections.

Accounting and review engagements refer to compilations and reviews of financial statements. The professional standards for compilations and reviews of financial statements are called **Statements on Standards for Accounting and Review Services** (SSARS) and are issued by the Accounting and Review Services Committee of the AICPA.

Compilations and reviews provide less assurance than audits and the relationships between type of service, level of assurance, and evidence requirements are summarized in the following table.

	Compilation	Review	Audit
Evidence Requirements	Minimal	Significant	Extensive
Assurance	None	Limited	Reasonable

1) Defining Professional Responsibilities in SSARSs
   SSARSs use the following two categories of professional requirements, identified by specific terms, to describe the degree of responsibility they impose on accountants:
   - **Unconditional requirements**. The accountant must comply with an unconditional requirement in all cases in which such requirement is relevant. SSARSs use the word **"must"** to indicate an unconditional requirement.
   - **Presumptively mandatory requirements**. The accountant must comply with a presumptively mandatory requirement in all cases in which such a requirement is relevant, except in rare circumstances. SSARSs use the word **"should"** to indicate a presumptively mandatory requirement. Whether the accountant performs the procedure or action is based upon the outcome of the accountant's consideration and the accountant's professional judgment.

1. Preparation engagements [AR-C 70]

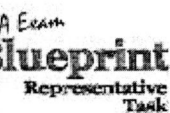

Identify the factors that an accountant should consider when performing a preparation engagement.

The main source of professional guidance that serves as the basis for this subsection is obtained from AR-C 70, *Preparation of Financial Statements*.

Generally, AR-C 70 applies when an accountant in public practice is engaged to prepare financial statements, but he or she **does not** perform a compilation, review, or audit of the financial statements. AR-C 70 does not apply to financial statements used for:
- submission to taxing authorities,
- inclusion in written personal financial plans prepared by the accountant,
- in conjunction with litigation services that involve pending or potential legal or regulatory proceedings, or
- in conjunction with business valuation services.

Factors that should be considered when performing a preparation engagement:

1) Independence is not required.

	Preparation	Compilation	Review
Independence Requirements	Not required	Not required, must disclose	Required

2) No opinion or conclusion presented, thus no requirement to verify accuracy or completeness.
3) Terms of the engagement should be agreed upon with management or those charged with governance.
4) The accountant should have the appropriate knowledge of the entity and its financial reporting framework.
5) The accountant should prepare the financial statements using the records, documents, explanations, and other information provided by management.
6) A statement that "no assurance is provided" should be included on each page of the financial statements.
7) When preparing financial statements in accordance with a **special purpose framework**, the accountant should include a description of the financial reporting framework on the face of the financial statements or in a note to the financial statements.
8) If financial statements contain a known departure or departures from the applicable financial reporting framework (including inadequate disclosure), the accountant should disclose the material misstatement or misstatements in the financial statements.

9) If financial statements omit substantially all disclosures required by the applicable financial reporting framework, the accountant should disclose such omission in the financial statements.
10) The accountant should not prepare financial statements that omit substantially all disclosures required by the financial reporting framework **if the accountant becomes aware that the omission of substantially all disclosures was undertaken with the intention of misleading users of such financial statements.**

a. **Documentation in a preparation engagement**
Per AR-C 70.21: The accountant should prepare documentation in connection with each preparation engagement in sufficient detail to provide a clear understanding of the work performed which, at a minimum, includes the following:
- The engagement letter or other suitable form of written documentation with management, and
- A copy of the financial statements that the accountant prepared

> **Hint:** SSARS 22, *Compilation of Pro-Forma Information*, **was eligible for testing starting in Q3 2017.** Previously, pro forma engagements were part of SSAE, but SSAE (attestation engagements) do not include compilations, so this was moved to SSARS. SSARS applies only to non-issuers. Note, "pro forma" means "as if" – so, if an entity engages in a major transaction early in the new year, the pro forma would show how that transaction may have affected financial statements if it had occurred before the prior year end.

> **Hint**: SSARS 23, Omnibus Statement on Standards for Accounting and Review Services—2016, expands the coverage SSARS standards to engagements performed on a subject matter other than financial statements. Changes include:
> - SSARS engagements must have a written understanding with the client signed by both the accountant and the client.
> - SSARS may apply to prospective financial information (forecasts or projections) and must include management's assumptions.
> - Cannot use a review engagement for pro forma (as-if) financial information.
> - Supplementary information (that is, in addition to the financial statements and notes) should be addressed in an "other matter" paragraph of the accountant's report or a separate accountant's report.
>
> **SSARS 23 was eligible for testing in starting in Q3 2017.**

2. Compilation reports [AR-C 80]

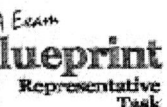

> **Identify the factors that an accountant should consider when reporting on an engagement to compile an entity's financial statements, including the proper form and content of the compilation report.**

The main source of professional guidance that serves as the basis for this subsection is obtained from AR-C 80, *Compilation Engagements*.

A compilation engagement is one in which accountants assist management in the presentation of financial statements without providing any assurance about those statements.

The accountant should agree upon the terms of the engagement with management or those charged with governance, as appropriate. The agreed-upon terms of the engagement should be documented in an engagement letter or other suitable form of written agreement. The engagement letter or other suitable form of written agreement should be signed by the accountant or the accountant's firm and management or those charged with governance, as appropriate.

a. Compilation procedures
The accountant should read the financial statements in light of the accountant's understanding of the applicable financial reporting framework and the significant accounting policies adopted by management and consider whether such financial statements appear to be appropriate in form and free from obvious material misstatements.

If, in the course of the engagement, the accountant becomes aware that the records, documents, explanations, or other information, including significant judgments, provided by management, are incomplete, inaccurate, or otherwise unsatisfactory, the accountant should bring that to the attention of management and request additional or corrected information.

If the accountant becomes aware during the course of the engagement that:
- the financial statements do not adequately refer to or describe the applicable financial reporting framework;
- revisions to the financial statements are required for the financial statements to be in accordance with the applicable financial reporting framework; or
- the financial statements are otherwise misleading then, the accountant should propose the appropriate revisions to management.

The accountant should withdraw from the engagement and inform management of the reasons for withdrawing if:
- the accountant is unable to complete the engagement because management has failed to provide records, documents, explanations, or other information, including significant judgments, as requested, or
- management does not make appropriate revisions that are proposed by the accountant, or does not disclose such departures in the financial statements, and the accountant determines to not disclose such departures in the accountant's compilation report.

b. Documentation
The accountant should prepare documentation in connection with each compilation engagement in sufficient detail to provide a clear understanding of the work performed which, at a minimum, includes the following:
- The engagement letter or other suitable form of written documentation with management.
- A copy of the financial statements.
- A copy of the accountant's report.

c. Reporting when the accountant is not independent
When the accountant is not independent with respect to the entity, the accountant should indicate the accountant's lack of independence in a final paragraph of the accountant's compilation report.

If the accountant elects to disclose a description about the reasons the accountant's independence is impaired, the accountant should include all such reasons in the description.

> **Prepare a draft report for an engagement to compile an entity's financial statements, starting with a report example (e.g., an illustrative report from professional standards).**

d. Reporting
1) The accountant's compilation report
The accountant's compilation report should be in writing and
- include a statement that management (owners) is (are) responsible for the financial statements.
- identify the financial statements that have been subjected to the compilation engagement.
- identify the entity whose financial statements have been subjected to the compilation engagement.
- specify the date or period covered by the financial statements.
- include a statement that the accountant performed the compilation engagement in accordance with SSARSs promulgated by the Accounting and Review Services Committee of the AICPA.
- include a statement that the accountant did not audit or review the financial statements nor was the accountant required to perform any procedures to verify the accuracy or completeness of the information provided by management and, accordingly, does not express an opinion, a conclusion, nor provide any assurance on the financial statements.
- include the signature of the accountant or the accountant's firm.
- include the city and state where the accountant practices.
- include the date of the report, which should be the date that the accountant has completed the procedures required by this section.

i. Example compilation report – standard framework
An Accountant's Compilation Report on Comparative Financial Statements Prepared in Accordance with Accounting Principles Generally Accepted in the United States of America.

THE REPORT
Management is responsible for the accompanying financial statements of XYZ Company, which comprise the balance sheets as of December 31, 20X2 and 20X1 and the related statements of income, changes in stockholders' equity, and cash flows for the years then ended, and the related notes to the financial statements in accordance with accounting principles generally accepted in the United States of America. I (We) have performed compilation engagements in accordance with Statements on Standards for Accounting and Review Services promulgated by the Accounting and Review Services Committee of the AICPA. I (We) did not audit or review the financial statements nor was (were) I (we) required to perform any procedures to verify the accuracy or completeness of the information provided by management. Accordingly, I (we) do not express an opinion, a conclusion, nor provide any form of assurance on these financial statements.

[Signature of accounting firm or accountant, as appropriate]
[Accountant's city and state]
[Date of the accountant's report]

2) The accountant's compilation report on financial statements prepared in accordance with a special purpose framework

   Unless the entity elects to omit substantially all disclosures, the accountant should modify the compilation report when that accountant becomes aware that the financial statements do not include
   - a description of the special purpose framework.
   - a summary of significant accounting policies.
   - an adequate description about how the special purpose framework differs from GAAP. The effects of these differences need not be quantified.
   - informative disclosures similar to those required by GAAP when the financial statements contain items that are the same as, or similar to, those in financial statements prepared in accordance with GAAP.

   The accountant's compilation report on financial statements prepared in accordance with a special purpose framework should
   - make reference to management's responsibility for determining that the applicable financial reporting framework is acceptable in the circumstances when management has a choice of financial reporting frameworks in the preparation of such financial statements.
   - describe the purpose for which the financial statements are prepared or refer to a note in the financial statements that contains that information when the financial statements are prepared in accordance with a regulatory- or contractual-basis of accounting.

   The accountant's compilation report on financial statements prepared in accordance with a special purpose framework should include a separate paragraph that
   - indicates that the financial statements are prepared in accordance with the applicable special purpose framework,
   - refers to the note to the financial statements that describes the framework, if applicable, and
   - states that the special purpose framework is a basis of accounting other than GAAP.

   i. Example compilation Report – special purpose framework
   An Accountant's Compilation Report on Comparative Financial Statements Prepared in Accordance with the Tax-Basis of Accounting, and Management Has Elected to Omit Substantially All Disclosures Ordinarily Included in Financial Statements Prepared in Accordance With the Tax-Basis of Accounting

   THE REPORT
   Management is responsible for the accompanying financial statements of XYZ Partnership, which comprise the statements of assets, liabilities, and partners' capital—tax-basis as of December 31, 20X2 and 20X1 and the related statements of revenue and expenses—tax-basis, and changes in partners' capital—tax-basis for the years then ended in accordance with the tax-basis of accounting, and for determining that the tax-basis of accounting is an acceptable financial reporting framework. I (We) have performed compilation engagements in accordance with Statements on Standards for Accounting and Review Services promulgated by the Accounting and Review Services Committee of the AICPA. I (We) did not audit or review the financial statements nor was (were) I (we) required to perform any procedures to verify the accuracy or completeness of the information provided by management. Accordingly, I (we) do not express an opinion, a conclusion, nor provide any form of assurance on these financial statements.

The financial statements are prepared in accordance with the tax-basis of accounting, which is a basis of accounting other than accounting principles generally accepted in the United States of America.

Management has elected to omit substantially all the disclosures ordinarily included in financial statements prepared in accordance with the tax-basis of accounting. If the omitted disclosures were included in the financial statements, they might influence the user's conclusions about the company's assets, liabilities, equity, revenue, and expenses. Accordingly, the financial statements are not designed for those who are not informed about such matters.

[Signature of accounting firm or accountant, as appropriate]
[Accountant's city and state]
[Date of the accountant's report]

3) Reporting on financial statements that omit substantially all the disclosures required by the applicable financial reporting framework

The accountant should <u>not</u> issue an accountant's compilation report on financial statements that omit substantially all disclosures required by the applicable financial reporting framework, unless the omission of substantially all disclosures is not, to the accountant's knowledge, undertaken with the intention of misleading those who might reasonably be expected to use such financial statements.

ii. Example compilation report – known departures from applicable accounting framework
An Accountant's Compilation Report on Comparative Financial Statements, and the Accountant Is Aware of Departures from Accounting Principles Generally Accepted in the United States of America.

THE REPORT
Management is responsible for the accompanying financial statements of XYZ Company, which comprise the balance sheets as of December 31, 20X2 and 20X1 and the related statements of income, changes in stockholders' equity, and cash flows for the years then ended, and the related notes to the financial statements in accordance with accounting principles generally accepted in the United States of America. I (We) have performed compilation engagements in accordance with Statements on Standards for Accounting and Review Services promulgated by the Accounting and Review Services Committee of the AICPA. I (We) did not audit or review the financial statements nor was (were) I (we) required to perform any procedures to verify the accuracy or completeness of the information provided by management. Accordingly, I (we) do not express an opinion, a conclusion, nor provide any form of assurance on these financial statements.

Accounting principles generally accepted in the United States of America require that land be stated at cost. Management has informed me (us) that XYZ Company has stated its land at appraised value and that if accounting principles generally accepted in the United States of America had been followed, the land account and stockholders' equity would have been decreased by $500,000.

[Signature of accounting firm or accountant, as appropriate]
[Accountant's city and state]
[Date of the accountant's report]

Multiple Choice

AUD 4-Q29

3. Review reports [AR-C 90]

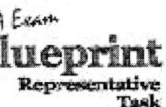

> **Identify the factors that an accountant should consider when reporting on an engagement to review an entity's financial statements, including the proper form and content of the review report.**

The main source of professional guidance that serves as the basis for this subsection is obtained from AR-C 90, *Review of Financial Statements*.

A review of financial statements requires an accountant to obtain limited assurance as a basis for reporting whether the accountant is aware of any material modifications that should be made to the financial statements for them to be in accordance with the applicable financial reporting framework (often GAAP), primarily through the performance of inquiry and analytical procedures.

a. Independence
The accountant **must be independent** of the entity when performing a review of financial statements in accordance with SSARSs. If, during the performance of the review engagement, the accountant determines that the accountant's independence is impaired, the accountant should withdraw from the review engagement.

b. Agreement on engagement terms and engagement letter
The accountant should agree upon the terms of the engagement with management or those charged with governance, as appropriate. The engagement letter, or other suitable form of written communication, should be signed by:
- the accountant or the accountant's firm and
- management or those charged with governance, as appropriate.

c. Review procedures
1) Understanding of the Industry
To perform the review engagement, the accountant should possess or obtain an understanding of the industry in which the entity operates, including the accounting principles and practices generally used in the industry, sufficient to enable the accountant to review financial statements that are appropriate for an entity operating in that industry.

2) Knowledge of the Entity
The accountant should obtain knowledge about the entity, including an understanding of the entity's business and the accounting principles and practices used by the entity that are sufficient to identify areas in the financial statements where there is a greater likelihood that material misstatements may arise and to be able to design procedures to address those areas.

In obtaining the understanding of the entity's accounting policies and practices, the accountant should be alert to accounting policies and procedures that, based on the accountant's knowledge of the industry, are unusual.

3) Designing and Performing Review Procedures
The accountant should design and perform analytical procedures, make inquires, and perform other procedures, as appropriate, in order to obtain limited assurance as a basis for reporting, whether the accountant is aware of any material modifications that should be made to the financial statements in order for the statements to be in accordance with the applicable financial reporting framework based on the accountant's understanding of the industry, knowledge of the entity, and awareness of the risk that the accountant may

unknowingly fail to modify the accountant's review report on financial statements that are materially misstated.

The accountant should focus the analytical procedures and inquiries in those areas where the accountant believes there are increased risks of material misstatements.

4) Analytical Procedures
The accountant should apply analytical procedures to the financial statements to identify and provide a basis for inquiry about the relationships and individual items that appear to be unusual and that may indicate a material misstatement.

Such analytical procedures should include the following:
- Comparing the financial statements with comparable information for the prior period, giving consideration to knowledge about changes in the entity's business and specific transactions.
- Considering plausible relationships among both financial and, when relevant, nonfinancial information.
- Comparing recorded amounts or ratios developed from recorded amounts to expectations developed by the accountant through identifying and using relationships that are reasonably expected to exist, based on the accountant's understanding of the entity and the industry in which the entity operates.
- Comparing disaggregated revenue data, as applicable.

When designing and performing analytical procedures, the accountant should do the following:
- determine the suitability of particular analytical procedures;
- consider the reliability of data from which the accountant's expectation of recorded amounts or ratios is developed, taking into account the source, comparability, and nature and relevance of information available;
- develop an expectation of recorded amounts or ratios and evaluate whether the expectation is sufficiently precise to provide the accountant with limited assurance that a misstatement will be identified that, either individually or when aggregated with other misstatements, may cause the financial statements to be materially misstated; and
- determine the amount of any difference of recorded amounts from expected values that is acceptable without further investigation (i.e., inquiry and other review procedures) and compare the recorded amounts, or ratios developed from recorded amounts, with the expectations.

5) Investigating Results of Analytical Procedures
If analytical procedures identify fluctuations or relationships that are inconsistent with other relevant information, or that differ from expected values by a significant amount, the accountant should investigate such differences by
- inquiring of management and
- performing other review procedures if considered necessary in the circumstances.

6) Inquiries of Members of Management Who Have Responsibility for Financial and Accounting Matters
The accountant should inquire of members of management who have responsibility for financial and accounting matters concerning the financial statements about the following:
  i. whether the financial statements have been prepared and fairly presented in accordance with the applicable financial reporting framework consistently applied.

    ii. unusual or complex situations that may have an effect on the financial statements.
    iii. significant transactions occurring or recognized during the period, particularly those in the last several days of the period.
    iv. the status of uncorrected misstatements identified during the previous review (that is, whether adjustments had been recorded subsequent to the periods covered by the prior review and, if so, the amounts recorded and period in which such adjustments were recorded).
    v. matters about which questions have arisen in the course of applying the review procedures.
    vi. events subsequent to the date of the financial statements that could have a material effect on the fair presentation of such financial statements.
    vii. its knowledge of any fraud or suspected fraud affecting the entity involving
        a) management,
        b) employees who have significant roles in internal control, or
        c) others, when the fraud could have a material effect on the financial statements.
    viii. whether management is aware of allegations of fraud or suspected fraud affecting the entity communicated by employees, former employees, regulators, or others.
    ix. whether management has disclosed to the accountant all known instances of noncompliance or suspected noncompliance with laws and regulations whose effects should be considered when preparing financial statements.
    x. significant journal entries and other adjustments.
    xi. communications from regulatory agencies, if applicable.
    xii. related parties and significant new related party transactions.
    xiii. any litigation, claims, and assessments that existed at the date of the balance sheet being reported on and during the period from the balance sheet date to the date of management's response to the accountant's inquiry.
    xiv. whether management believes that significant assumptions used by it in making accounting estimates are reasonable.
    xv. any actions taken at meetings of stockholders, the board of directors, committees of the board of directors, or comparable meetings that may affect the financial statements.
    xvi. any other matters that the accountant may consider necessary.

The accountant should consider the reasonableness and consistency of management's responses in light of the results of other review procedures and the accountant's knowledge of the entity's business. **However, the accountant is not required to corroborate management's responses with other evidence.**

7) Reading the Financial Statements
The accountant should read the financial statements and consider whether any information has come to the accountant's attention to indicate that such financial statements do not conform to the applicable financial reporting framework.

8) Using the Work of Other Accountants
If other accountants have issued a report on the financial statements of significant components, such as subsidiaries and investees, the accountant should obtain and read reports from such other accountants.

9) Reconciling the Financial Statements to the Underlying Accounting Records
The accountant should obtain evidence that the financial statements agree or reconcile with the accounting records.

d. Evaluating evidence obtained from the procedures performed
The accountant should accumulate misstatements, including inadequate disclosure, identified by the accountant in performing the review procedures, or brought to the accountant's attention during the performance of the review.

The accountant should evaluate, individually and in the aggregate, misstatements to determine whether material modification should be made to the financial statements for them to be in accordance with the applicable financial reporting framework.

If, during the performance of review procedures, the accountant becomes aware that information coming to the accountant's attention is incorrect, incomplete, or otherwise unsatisfactory, the accountant should
- request that management consider the effect of those matters on the financial statements and communicate the results of its consideration to the accountant and
- consider the results communicated to the accountant by management and whether such results indicate that the financial statements may be materially misstated.

If the accountant believes that the financial statements may be materially misstated, the accountant should perform additional procedures deemed necessary to obtain limited assurance that there are no material modifications that should be made to the financial statements in order for the statements to be in accordance with the applicable financial reporting framework.

The accountant should evaluate whether sufficient appropriate review evidence has been obtained from the procedures performed and, if not, the accountant should perform other procedures judged by the accountant to be necessary in the circumstances to be able to form a conclusion on the financial statements.

e. Written representations
Written representations are necessary information that the accountant requires in connection with a review of the entity's financial statements. Accordingly, similar to responses to inquiries, written representations are review evidence.

f. Review documentation
The accountant should prepare review documentation that is sufficient to enable an experienced accountant, having no previous connection to the review, to understand the following:
- the nature, timing, and extent of the review procedures performed to comply with SSARSs;
- the results of the review procedures performed and the review evidence obtained; and
- significant findings or issues arising during the review, the conclusions reached thereon, and significant professional judgments made in reaching those conclusions.

In addition to the requirements listed above, the review documentation should include the following:
- The engagement letter or other suitable form of written documentation with management.
- Communications to management and others regarding fraud or noncompliance with laws and regulations.
- Communications with management regarding the accountant's expectation to include an emphasis-of-matter or other-matter paragraph in the accountant's review report.
- Communications with other accountants that have audited or reviewed the financial statements of significant components.
- The representation letter.
- A copy of the reviewed financial statements and the accountant's review report thereon.

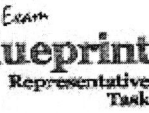

> **Prepare a draft report for an engagement to review an entity's financial statements, starting with a report example (e.g., an illustrative report from professional standards).**

    g. Reports
       The accountant's review report should be in writing.

        1) Accountant's review report
           The written review report should include:
- a title that includes the word *independent* to clearly indicate that it is the report of an independent accountant.
- an addressee, as appropriate for the circumstances of the engagement.
- an introductory paragraph that
- a section with the heading "Management's Responsibility for the Financial Statements"
- a section with the heading "Accountant's Responsibility" that includes the following statements:
    - a) The accountant's responsibility is to conduct the review engagement in accordance with SSARSs promulgated by the Accounting and Review Services Committee of the AICPA.
    - b) The accountant believes that the review evidence the accountant has obtained is sufficient and appropriate to provide a basis for the accountant's conclusion.
- a concluding section with an appropriate heading that includes a statement about whether the accountant is aware of any material modifications.
- the manual or printed signature of the accountant's firm.
- the city and state where the accountant practices.
- the date of the review report, which should be dated no earlier than the date on which the accountant completed procedures sufficient to obtain limited assurance as a basis for reporting whether the accountant is aware of any material modifications that should be made to the financial statements for them to be in accordance with the applicable financial reporting framework.

i. Example review report – standard framework

An Accountant's Review Report on Single Year Financial Statements Prepared in Accordance with Accounting Principles Generally Accepted in the United States of America.

Circumstances include the following:
- Review of a complete set of financial statements (single year).
- The financial statements are prepared in accordance with accounting principles generally accepted in the United States of America.

Independent Accountant's Review Report

[Appropriate Addressee]

I (We) have reviewed the accompanying financial statements of XYZ Company, which comprise the balance sheet as of December 31, 20XX, and the related statements of income, changes in stockholders' equity, and cash flows for the year then ended, and the related notes to the financial statements. A review includes primarily applying analytical procedures to management's (owners') financial data and making inquiries of company management (owners). A review is substantially less in scope than an audit, the objective of which is the expression of an opinion regarding the financial statements as a whole. Accordingly, I (we) do not express such an opinion.

Management's Responsibility for the Financial Statements
Management (Owners) is (are) responsible for the preparation and fair presentation of these financial statements in accordance with accounting principles generally accepted in the United States of America; this includes the design, implementation, and maintenance of internal control relevant to the preparation and fair presentation of financial statements that are free from material misstatement whether due to fraud or error.

Accountant's Responsibility
My (Our) responsibility is to conduct the review engagement in accordance with Statements on Standards for Accounting and Review Services promulgated by the Accounting and Review Services Committee of the AICPA. Those standards require me (us) to perform procedures to obtain limited assurance as a basis for reporting whether I am (we are) aware of any material modifications that should be made to the financial statements for them to be in accordance with accounting principles generally accepted in the United States of America. I (We) believe that the results of my (our) procedures provide a reasonable basis for my (our) conclusion.

Accountant's Conclusion
Based on my (our) review, I am (we are) not aware of any material modifications that should be made to the accompanying financial statements in order for them to be in accordance with accounting principles generally accepted in the United States of America.

[Signature of accounting firm or accountant, as appropriate]
[Accountant's city and state]
[Date of the accountant's review report]

2) Accountant's Review Report on Financial Statements Prepared in Accordance with a Special Purpose Framework

The accountant should modify the review report when the accountant becomes aware that the financial statements do not include:
- a description of the special purpose framework.
- a summary of significant accounting policies.
- an adequate description about how the special purpose framework differs from GAAP. The effects of these differences need not be quantified.

- informative disclosures similar to those required by GAAP when the financial statements contain items that are the same as, or similar to, those in financial statements prepared in accordance with GAAP.

In the case of financial statements prepared in accordance with a contractual-basis of accounting, the accountant should modify the review report if the financial statements do not adequately describe any significant interpretations of the contract on which the financial statements are based.

The accountant's review report on financial statements prepared in accordance with a special purpose framework should

- make reference to management's responsibility for determining that the applicable financial reporting framework is acceptable in the circumstances when management has a choice of financial reporting frameworks in the preparation of such financial statements.
- describe the purpose for which the financial statements are prepared or refer to a note in the financial statements that contains that information when the financial statements are prepared in accordance with a regulatory- or contractual-basis of accounting.

The accountant's review report on financial statements prepared in accordance with a special purpose framework should include an emphasis-of-matter paragraph, under an appropriate heading, that

- indicates that the financial statements are prepared in accordance with the applicable special purpose framework,
- refers to the note to the financial statements that describes the framework, and
- states that the special purpose framework is a basis of accounting other than GAAP.

The accountant's review report on special purpose financial statements should include an other-matter paragraph, under an appropriate heading, that restricts the use of the accountant's review report when the special purpose financial statements are prepared in accordance with

- a contractual-basis of accounting,
- a regulatory-basis of accounting, or
- an other-basis of accounting when require (see discussion of **Alert That Restricts the Use of the Accountant's Review Report**).

ii. Example review report – special purpose framework
An Accountant's Review Report on Single Year Financial Statements Prepared in Accordance with the Tax-Basis of Accounting.

Independent Accountant's Review Report

[Appropriate Addressee]

I (We) have reviewed the accompanying financial statements of XYZ Partnership, which comprise the statement of assets, liabilities, and partners' capital—tax-basis as of December 31, 20XX, and the related statements of revenue and expenses—tax-basis, and partners' capital—tax-basis for the year then ended, and the related notes to the financial statements. A review includes primarily applying analytical procedures to management's (partners') financial data and making inquiries of partnership management (owners). A review is substantially less in scope than an audit, the objective of which is the expression of an opinion regarding the financial statement as a whole. Accordingly, I (we) do not express such an opinion.

Management's Responsibility for the Financial Statements
Management (Partners) is (are) responsible for the preparation and fair presentation of these financial statements in accordance with the basis of accounting the partnership uses for income tax purposes; this includes determining that the basis of accounting the partnership uses for income tax purposes is an acceptable basis for the preparation of financial statements in the circumstances. Management (Partners) is (are) also responsible for the design, implementation, and maintenance of internal control relevant to the preparation and fair presentation of financial statements that are free from material misstatement, whether due to fraud or error.

Accountant's Responsibility
My (Our) responsibility is to conduct the review engagement in accordance with Statements on Standards for Accounting and Review Services promulgated by the Accounting and Review Services Committee of the AICPA. Those standards require me (us) to perform procedures to obtain limited assurance as a basis for reporting whether I am (we are) aware of any material modifications that should be made to the financial statements for them to be in accordance with the basis of accounting the partnership uses for income tax purposes. I (We) believe that the results of my (our) procedures provide a reasonable basis for my (our) conclusion.

Accountant's Conclusion
Based on my (our) review, I am (we are) not aware of any material modifications that should be made to the accompanying financial statements in order for them to be in accordance with the basis of accounting the partnership uses for income tax purposes.

Basis of Accounting
I (We) draw attention to Note X of the financial statements, which describes the basis of accounting. The financial statements are prepared in accordance with the basis of accounting the partnership uses for income tax purposes, which is a basis of accounting other than accounting principles generally accepted in the United States of America. Our conclusion is not modified with respect to this matter.

[Signature of accounting firm or accountant, as appropriate]
[Accountant's city and state]
[Date of the accountant's review report]

h. Other reporting issues
  1) Reporting When One Period Is Audited
  When the prior period financial statements were audited and the auditor's report on the prior period financial statements is not reissued, the review report on the current period financial statements should include an other-matter paragraph indicating
   a. that the financial statements of the prior period were previously audited;
   b. the date of the auditor's report on the prior period financial statements;
   c. the type of opinion issued on the prior period financial statements;
   d. if the opinion was modified, the substantive reasons for the modification; and
   e. that no auditing procedures were performed after the date of the previous report.

  2) Emphasis-of-Matter and Other-Matter Paragraphs in the Accountant's Review Report
   i. **Emphasis-of-Matter Paragraphs in the Accountant's Review Report**
   If the accountant considers it necessary to draw users' attention to a matter appropriately presented or disclosed in the financial statements that, in the accountant's professional judgment, is of such importance that it is fundamental to users' understanding of the financial statements, the accountant should include an emphasis-of-matter paragraph in the accountant's review report, provided that the accountant does not believe that the financial statements may be materially misstated.

Such a paragraph should refer only to information presented or disclosed in the financial statements.

When the accountant includes an emphasis-of-matter paragraph in the accountant's review report, the accountant should
- include it immediately after the accountant's conclusion paragraph in the accountant's review report,
- use the heading "Emphasis of a Matter" or other appropriate heading,
- include in the paragraph a clear reference to the matter being emphasized and to where relevant disclosures that fully describe the matter can be found in the financial statements, and
- indicate that the accountant's conclusion is not modified with respect to the matter emphasized.

ii. *Other-Matter Paragraphs in the Accountant's Review Report*
If the accountant considers it necessary to communicate a matter other than those that are presented or disclosed in the financial statements that, in the accountant's professional judgment, is relevant to the users' understanding of the review, the accountant's responsibilities, or the accountant's review report, the accountant should do so in a paragraph in the accountant's review report with the heading "Other Matter" or other appropriate heading. The accountant should include this paragraph immediately after the accountant's conclusion paragraph and any emphasis-of-matter paragraph.

3) Known Departures from the Applicable Financial Reporting Framework
When the accountant becomes aware of a departure from the applicable financial reporting framework (including inadequate disclosure) that is material to the financial statements and if the financial statements are not revised, the accountant should consider whether modification of the standard report is adequate to disclose the departure.

If the accountant concludes that modification of the standard report is adequate, the departure should be disclosed in a separate paragraph of the report under the heading "Known Departures From the [*identify the applicable financial reporting framework*]," including disclosure of the effects of the departure on the financial statements if such effects have been determined by management or are known to the accountant as the result of the accountant's procedures.

If the effects of the departure have not been determined by management or are not known to the accountant as a result of the accountant's procedures, the accountant is not required to determine the effects of a departure; however, in such circumstances, the accountant should state in the report that such determination has not been made.

If the accountant believes that modification of the standard report is *not adequate* to indicate the deficiencies in the financial statements as a whole, the accountant should *withdraw* from the review engagement.

The accountant should *not modify* the standard report to include a statement that the financial statements are not in accordance with the applicable financial reporting framework.

4) **Alert That Restricts the Use of the Accountant's Review Report**
   An accountant's review report should include an alert, in a separate paragraph, that restricts its use when the subject matter of the accountant's review report is based on
   - measurement or disclosure criteria that are determined, by the accountant, to be suitable only for a limited number of users who can be presumed to have an adequate understanding of the criteria or
   - measurement or disclosure criteria that are available only to the specified parties.

   The alert that restricts the use of the accountant's review report should
   - state that the accountant's review report is intended solely for the information and use of the specified parties.
   - identify the specified parties for whom use is intended.
   - state that the accountant's review report is not intended to be, and should not be, used by anyone other than the specified parties.

5) **The Accountant's Consideration of an Entity's Ability to Continue as a Going Concern**
   i. ***Consideration of Conditions or Events That Indicate That There Could Be an Uncertainty about the Entity's Ability to Continue as a Going Concern***
   The accountant should consider whether, during the performance of review procedures, evidence or information came to the accountant's attention indicating that there could be an uncertainty about the entity's ability to continue as a going concern for a reasonable period of time.

   A reasonable period of time is the same period of time required of management to assess going concern when specified by the applicable financial reporting framework. If the applicable financial reporting framework does not specify a period of time for management, a reasonable period is one year from the date of the issued.

   The following is an illustration of an emphasis-of-matter paragraph the accountant may include in the accountant's review report when the accountant concludes that management has adequately disclosed an uncertainty about the entity's ability to continue as a going concern for a reasonable period of time, and determines to include an emphasis-of-matter paragraph with respect to the going concern uncertainty:

   Emphasis of Matter
   The accompanying financial statements have been prepared assuming that the Company will continue as a going concern. As discussed in Note X to the financial statements, the Company has suffered recurring losses from operations and has a net capital deficiency that raises an uncertainty about its ability to continue as a going concern. Management's plans in regard to these matters are also described in Note X. The financial statements do not include any adjustments that might result from the outcome of this uncertainty. Our conclusion is not modified with respect to this matter.

6) **Reference to the Work of Other Accountants in an Accountant's Review Report**
   If other accountants audited or reviewed the financial statements of significant components, such as consolidated and unconsolidated subsidiaries and investees, and the accountant of the reporting entity decides **not to assume responsibility** for the audit or review performed by the other accountants, the accountant of the reporting entity should make reference to the review or audit of such other accountants in the accountant's review report. In that instance, the accountant should clearly indicate, in the accountant's review report, that the accountant used the work of other accountants and should include the magnitude of the portion of the financial statements audited or reviewed by the other accountants.

Regardless of whether the accountant of the reporting entity decides to make reference to the review or audit of other accountants, the accountant of the reporting entity should communicate with the other accountants and ascertain the following:
- that the other accountants are aware, that the financial statements of the component that the other accountants have audited or reviewed, are to be included in the financial statements on which the accountant of the reporting entity will report, and that the other accountants' report thereon will be relied upon (and, where applicable, referred to) by the accountant of the reporting entity.
- that the other accountants are familiar with the applicable financial reporting framework and with SSARSs or auditing standards generally accepted in the United States of America, as applicable, and will conduct the review or audit in accordance therewith.
- that a review will be made of matters affecting elimination of intercompany transactions and accounts and, if appropriate in the circumstances, the uniformity of accounting practices among the components included in the financial statements.

Multiple Choice

AUD 4-Q30 through AUD 4-Q74

D. Reporting on Compliance

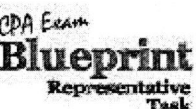

Identify the factors that an auditor should consider when reporting on compliance with aspects of contractual agreements or regulatory requirements in connection with an audit of an entity's financial statements.

Hint: The main sources of professional guidance that serve as the basis for this review are obtained from the following:

AU-C 806, *Reporting on Compliance with Aspects of Contractual Agreements or Regulatory Requirements in Connection with Audited Financial Statements* (AICPA)

A compliance audit is when an auditor is asked to report on an entity's compliance with aspects of contractual agreements or regulatory requirements, insofar as they relate to accounting matters, in connection with an audit of financial statements. Such a report is commonly referred to as a **by-product report**.

a. Reports on compliance – an example
Entities may be required by contractual agreements, such as certain bond indentures and loan agreements, or regulatory agencies, to provide an auditor's report on compliance. For example, loan agreements may impose a variety of obligations on borrowers involving matters such as payments into sinking funds, payments of interest, maintenance of current ratios, and restrictions of dividend payments. Loan agreements may also require the borrower to provide annual financial statements that have been audited. In some instances, the lenders or their trustees, may request the auditor to report that the borrower has complied with certain covenants of the agreement relating to accounting matters. The auditor may satisfy this request by issuing a report on compliance in accordance with the requirements of this section.

An auditor can be engaged to report on an entity's compliance in connection with an audit of financials statements or as a separate attest engagement:

What standard applies? AU-C 806 / AU-C 935 / AT 601	
IF, reporting on an entity's compliance with aspects of contractual agreements or regulatory requirements *in connection with an audit of financial statements*.	**AU-C 806** *Reporting on Compliance with Aspects of Contractual Agreements or Regulatory Requirements in Connection with Audited Financial Statements*
IF, engaged to perform a compliance audit in accordance with **all** of the following: • generally accepted auditing standards (GAAS) • the standards for financial audits under *Government Auditing Standards* • a **governmental audit** requirement that requires the auditor to express an opinion on compliance with applicable compliance requirements	**AU-C 935** *Compliance Audits*
IF, the auditor is engaged to perform a *separate attest engagement* on (*a*) an entity's compliance with requirements of specific laws, regulations, rules, contracts, or grants or (*b*) the effectiveness of an entity's internal control over compliance with specified requirements	**AT Section 601** *Compliance Attestation*

b. **AU-C 935, *Compliance Audits* (AICPA)**
   1) Government Auditing Standards Perspective
   Under ***Government Auditing Standards*** (GAO 2011) compliance audits relate to auditing compliance with applicable compliance requirements relating to one or more government programs.

   Compliance audit objectives relate to an assessment of compliance with criteria established by provisions of laws, regulations, contracts, or grant agreements, or other requirements that could affect the acquisition, protection, use, and disposition of the entity's resources and the quantity, quality, timeliness, and cost of services the entity produces and delivers. Compliance requirements can be either financial or nonfinancial.

   Compliance objectives include determining whether:
   - the purpose of the program, the manner in which it is to be conducted, the services delivered, the outcomes, or the population it serves, is in compliance with provisions of laws, regulations, contracts or grant agreements, or other requirements;
   - government services and benefits are distributed or delivered to citizens based on the individual's eligibility to obtain those services and benefits;
   - incurred or proposed costs are in compliance with applicable laws, regulations, contracts, or grant agreements; and
   - revenues received are in compliance with applicable laws, regulations, contracts or grant agreements.

   i. **Compliance Requirements Applicable to Federal Financial Assistance Programs**
   Compliance requirements applicable to federal financial assistance programs are usually one of two types:
   - General
   - Specific

      a) **General requirements** – involve national policy and apply to all or most federal financial assistance programs.

      b) **Specific requirements** – apply to a particular federal program and generally arise from statutory requirements and regulations. The OMB's Compliance Supplements set forth general and specific requirements for many of the federal programs awarded to state and local governments and to not-for-profit organizations, as well as suggested audit procedures to test for compliance with the requirements.

   For program-specific audits, the auditor should consult federal grantor agency audit guides to identify general requirements that are statutory and regulatory requirements pertaining to certain federal programs, specific requirements for a particular program, and suggested audit procedures to test for compliance with the requirements.

   Generally, the auditor is required to determine whether the recipient has complied with the general and specific requirements. The form of the report and the required level of assurance to be provided in the report may vary, depending on the requirements of a particular agency or program. For example, if reporting on compliance requirements, the auditor may be required to report findings relating to compliance with those requirements, or the auditor may be required to express an opinion on whether the recipient has complied with the requirements applicable to its major federal financial assistance programs. (See PCAOB AS 6110.)

Compliance audits usually are performed in conjunction with a financial statement audit.

> **Hint**: AT section 601, *Compliance Attestation*, is applicable to an examination of an entity's compliance with **specified requirements**.
>
> AT section 101, *Attest Engagements*, is applicable to an examination of an entity's **internal control over compliance**.

If the entity is required to undergo a compliance audit and an examination of internal control over compliance, then
- AU-C 935 is applicable to performing and reporting on the compliance audit, and
- AT section 101 is applicable to performing and reporting on the examination of internal control over compliance.

2) Management's Responsibilities
A compliance audit is based on the premise that management is responsible for the entity's compliance with compliance requirements. Management's responsibility for the entity's compliance with compliance requirements includes the following:
- Identifying the entity's government programs and understanding and complying with the compliance requirements.
- Establishing and maintaining effective controls that provide reasonable assurance that the entity administers government programs in compliance with the compliance requirements.
- Evaluating and monitoring the entity's compliance with the compliance requirements.
- Taking corrective action when instances of noncompliance are identified, including corrective action on audit findings of the compliance audit.

3) Auditor Objectives
The auditor's objectives in a compliance audit are to
- obtain sufficient appropriate audit evidence to form an opinion and report at the level specified in the governmental audit requirement on whether the entity complied in all material respects with the applicable compliance requirements; and
- identify audit and reporting requirements specified in the governmental audit requirement that are supplementary to GAAS and *Government Auditing Standards*, if any, and perform procedures to address those requirements.

c. Audit procedures
1) Establishing Materiality Levels
The auditor should establish and apply materiality levels for the compliance audit based on the governmental audit requirement.

Generally, the auditor's consideration of materiality is in relation to the government program taken as a whole. However, the governmental audit requirement may specify a different level of materiality for one or more of these purposes.

The auditor's determination of materiality usually is influenced by the needs of the grantors. However, in a compliance audit, the auditor's judgment about matters that are material to users of the auditor's report also is based on consideration of the needs of users as a group, including grantors.

2) Identifying Government Programs and Applicable Compliance Requirements
A compliance audit is based on the premise that management is responsible for identifying the entity's government programs and understanding and complying with the compliance requirements.

The auditor should determine which of those government programs and compliance requirements to test (that is, the applicable compliance requirements) in accordance with the governmental audit requirement.

3) Performing Risk Assessment Procedures
For each of the government programs and applicable compliance requirements selected for testing, the auditor should perform risk assessment procedures to obtain a sufficient understanding of the applicable compliance requirements and the entity's internal control over compliance with the applicable compliance requirements.

In performing risk assessment procedures, the auditor should inquire of management about whether there are findings and recommendations in reports or other written communications resulting from previous audits, attestation engagements, and internal or external monitoring, that directly relate to the objectives of the compliance audit.

The auditor should gain an understanding of management's response to findings and recommendations that could have a material effect on the entity's compliance with the applicable compliance requirements (for example, taking corrective action). The auditor should use this information to assess risk and determine the nature, timing, and extent of the audit procedures for the compliance audit, including determining the extent to which testing the implementation of any corrective actions is applicable to the audit objectives.

4) Assessing the Risks of Material Noncompliance
The auditor should assess the risks of material noncompliance, whether due to fraud or error, for each applicable compliance requirement and should consider whether any of those risks are pervasive to the entity's compliance because they may affect the entity's compliance with many compliance requirements.

5) Performing Further Audit Procedures in Response to Assessed Risks
If the auditor identifies risks of material noncompliance that are pervasive to the entity's compliance, the auditor should develop an overall response to such risks. AU-C 330, *Performing Audit Procedures in Response to Assessed Risks and Evaluating the Audit Evidence Obtained*, provides guidance that may be adapted when developing an overall response to the risks of material noncompliance.

The auditor should design and perform further audit procedures, including tests of details (which may include tests of transactions) to obtain sufficient appropriate audit evidence about the entity's compliance with each of the applicable compliance requirements in response to the assessed risks of material noncompliance.

Risk assessment procedures, tests of controls, and analytical procedures alone are not sufficient to address a risk of material noncompliance.

A compliance audit includes designing procedures to detect both intentional and unintentional material noncompliance.

The use of analytical procedures to gather substantive evidence is generally less effective in a compliance audit than it is in a financial statement audit.

Some governmental audit requirements, for example, OMB Circular A-133, require tests of the operating effectiveness of controls identified as likely to be effective, even if the auditor believes that such testing would be inefficient.

The auditor should design and perform further audit procedures in response to the assessed risks of material noncompliance. These procedures should include performing tests of controls over compliance if
- the auditor's risk assessment includes an expectation of the operating effectiveness of controls over compliance related to the applicable compliance requirements;
- substantive procedures alone do not provide sufficient appropriate audit evidence; or
- such tests of controls over compliance are required by the governmental audit requirement.
- If any of these conditions are met, the auditor should test the operating effectiveness of controls over each applicable compliance requirement to which the conditions apply in each compliance audit.

d. Written representations
The auditor should request, from management, written representations that are tailored to the entity and the governmental audit requirement.

e. Evaluating the sufficiency and appropriateness of the audit evidence and forming an opinion
The auditor should evaluate the sufficiency and appropriateness of the audit evidence obtained.

In determining whether an entity has materially complied with the applicable compliance requirements, the auditor may consider the following factors:
- The frequency of noncompliance with the applicable compliance requirements identified during the compliance audit.
- The nature of the noncompliance with the applicable compliance requirements identified.
- The adequacy of the entity's system for monitoring compliance with the applicable compliance requirements and the possible effect of any noncompliance on the entity.
- Whether any identified noncompliance with the applicable compliance requirements resulted in likely questioned costs that are material to the government program.

The auditor should form an opinion, at the level specified by the governmental audit requirement, on whether the entity complied in all material respects with the applicable compliance requirements, and report appropriately.

f. Documentation
The auditor should document the risk assessment procedures performed, including those related to gaining an understanding of internal control over compliance.

The auditor should document the auditor's responses to the assessed risks of material noncompliance, the procedures performed to test compliance with the applicable compliance requirements, and the results of those procedures, including any tests of controls over compliance.

The auditor should document materiality levels and the basis on which they were determined.

The auditor should document how the auditor complied with the specific governmental audit requirements that are supplementary to GAAS and *Government Auditing Standards*.

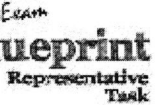

> **Identify the factors that a practitioner should consider when reporting on an attestation engagement related to an entity's compliance with the requirements of specified laws, regulations, rules, contracts or grants, including reports on the effectiveness of internal controls over compliance with the requirements.**

AT 601, *Compliance Attestation*, provides guidance for engagements related to either (*a*) an entity's compliance with requirements of specified laws, regulations, rules, contracts, or grants or (*b*) the effectiveness of an entity's internal control over compliance with specified requirements. Compliance requirements may be either financial or nonfinancial in nature. A practitioner may be engaged to report on compliance with agreed-upon procedures or an examination.

To obtain an understanding of the specified compliance requirements, a practitioner should consider the following:
- Laws, regulations, rules, contracts, and grants that pertain to the specified compliance requirements, including published requirements.
- Knowledge about the specified compliance requirements obtained through prior engagements and regulatory reports.
- Knowledge about the specified compliance requirements obtained through discussions with appropriate individuals within the entity (for example, the chief financial officer, internal auditors, legal counsel, compliance officer, or grant or contract administrators).
- Knowledge about the specified compliance requirements, obtained through discussions with appropriate individuals outside the entity (for example, a regulator or a third-party specialist).

g. Scope of services
   1) Agreed-Upon Procedures – The practitioner may be engaged to perform agreed-upon procedures to assist users in evaluating the following subject matter (or assertions related thereto)
      - The entity's compliance with specified requirements.
      - The effectiveness of the entity's internal control over compliance.
      - Both the entity's compliance with specified requirements and the effectiveness of the entity's internal control over compliance.

      Requirements to perform agreed-upon procedure engagement:
      - The responsible party accepts responsibility for the entity's compliance with specified requirements and the effectiveness of the entity's internal control over compliance.
      - The responsible party evaluates the entity's compliance with specified requirements or the effectiveness of the entity's internal control over compliance.

      <u>Scope Restriction:</u>
      When circumstances impose ***restrictions on the scope of an agreed-upon procedures engagement***, the practitioner should attempt to obtain agreement from the users for modification of the agreed-upon procedures. When such agreement cannot be obtained (for example, when the agreed-upon procedures are published by a regulatory agency that will not modify the procedures), the practitioner should describe such restrictions in his or her report or withdraw from the engagement.

The practitioner has no obligation to perform procedures beyond the agreed-upon procedures. However, if noncompliance comes to the practitioner's attention by other means, such information ordinarily should be included in his or her report.

2) Examination – The practitioner also may be engaged to examine the entity's compliance with specified requirements or a written assertion thereon.

Requirements to perform examination engagement:
- The responsible party accepts responsibility for the entity's compliance with specified requirements and the effectiveness of the entity's internal control over compliance.
- The responsible party evaluates the entity's compliance with specified requirements.
- Sufficient evidential matter exists or could be developed to support management's evaluation.

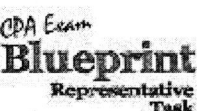

Prepare a draft compliance report for an attestation engagement to report on an entity's compliance with the requirements of specified laws, regulations, rules, contracts or grants starting with a report example (e.g., an illustrative report from professional standards).

h. Reports
  1) Agreed-Upon Procedures Reports
  The practitioner's report on agreed-upon procedures on an entity's compliance with specified requirements (or the effectiveness of an entity's internal control over compliance) ***should be in the form of procedures and findings***.

  The practitioner's report should contain the following elements:
  - A title that includes the word *independent*.
  - Identification of the specified parties.
  - Identification of the subject matter of the engagement (or management's assertion thereon), including the period or point in time addressed and a reference to the character of the engagement.
  - An identification of the responsible party.
  - A statement that the subject matter is the responsibility of the responsible party.
  - A statement that the procedures, which were agreed to by the specified parties identified in the report, were performed to assist the specified parties in evaluating the entity's compliance with specified requirements or the effectiveness of its internal control over compliance.
  - A statement that the agreed-upon procedures engagement was conducted in accordance with attestation standards established by the American Institute of Certified Public Accountants.
  - A statement that the sufficiency of the procedures is solely the responsibility of the specified parties and a disclaimer of responsibility for the sufficiency of those procedures.
  - A list of the procedures performed (or reference thereto) and related findings (The practitioner should not provide negative assurance).
  - Where applicable, a description of any agreed-upon materiality limits.
  - A statement that the practitioner was not engaged to and did not conduct an examination of the entity's compliance with specified requirements (or the effectiveness of an entity's internal control over compliance), a disclaimer of

opinion thereon, and a statement that if the practitioner had performed additional procedures, other matters might have come to his or her attention that would have been reported.
- A statement restricting the use of the report to the specified parties.
- Where applicable, reservations or restrictions concerning procedures or findings.
- Where applicable, a description of the nature of the assistance provided by the specialist.
- The manual or printed signature of the practitioner's firm
- The date of the report

i. **Example Agreed-Upon Procedure Reports**
   a) *Report on an Entity's Compliance with Specified Requirements*
      The following is an illustration of an agreed-upon procedures report on an entity's compliance with specified requirements in which the procedures and findings are enumerated rather than referenced.

      Independent Accountant's Report on Applying Agreed-Upon Procedures
      We have performed the procedures enumerated below, which were agreed to by [list specified parties], solely to assist the specified parties in evaluating [name of entity]'s compliance with [list specified requirements] during the [period] ended [date]. Management is responsible for [name of entity]'s compliance with those requirements. This agreed-upon procedures engagement was conducted in accordance with attestation standards established by the American Institute of Certified Public Accountants. The sufficiency of these procedures is solely the responsibility of those parties specified in this report. Consequently, we make no representation regarding the sufficiency of the procedures described below either for the purpose for which this report has been requested or for any other purpose.

      [Include paragraphs to enumerate procedures and findings.]

      We were not engaged to and did not conduct an examination, the objective of which would be the expression of an opinion on compliance. Accordingly, we do not express such an opinion. Had we performed additional procedures, other matters might have come to our attention that would have been reported to you.

      This report is intended solely for the information and use of [list or refer to specified parties] and is not intended to be and should not be used by anyone other than these specified parties.

      [Signature]
      [Date]

   b) *Report on an Entity's Internal Control over Compliance*
      The following is an illustration of an agreed-upon procedures report on the effectiveness of an entity's internal control over compliance in which the procedures and findings are enumerated rather than referenced.

      Independent Accountant's Report on Applying Agreed-Upon Procedures
      We have performed the procedures enumerated below, which were agreed to by [list specified parties], solely to assist the specified parties in evaluating the effectiveness of [name of entity]'s internal control over compliance with [list specified requirements] as of [date]. Management is responsible for [name of entity]'s internal control over compliance with those requirements. This agreed-upon procedures engagement was conducted in accordance with attestation standards established by the American Institute of Certified Public Accountants. The sufficiency of these procedures is solely the responsibility of those parties specified in this report. Consequently, we make no

representation regarding the sufficiency of the procedures described below either for the purpose for which this report has been requested or for any other purpose.

[Include paragraphs to enumerate procedures and findings.]

We were not engaged to and did not conduct an examination, the objective of which would be the expression of an opinion on the effectiveness of internal control over compliance. Accordingly, we do not express such an opinion. Had we performed additional procedures, other matters might have come to our attention that would have been reported to you.
This report is intended solely for the information and use of [list or refer to specified parties] and is not intended to be and should not be used by anyone other than these specified parties.

[Signature]
[Date]

2) Examination Reports
   i. **Examination Report on Compliance**
   The practitioner's examination report on compliance, which is ordinarily addressed to the entity, should include the following:
   - A title that includes the word *independent*.
   - Identification of the specified compliance requirements, including the period covered, and of the responsible party.
   - A statement that compliance with the specified requirements is the responsibility of the entity's management.
   - A statement that the practitioner's responsibility is to express an opinion on the entity's compliance with those requirements based on his or her examination.
   - A statement that the examination was conducted in accordance with attestation standards established by the American Institute of Certified Public Accountants and, accordingly, included examining, on a test basis, evidence about the entity's compliance with those requirements and performing such other procedures as the practitioner considered necessary in the circumstances.
   - A statement that the practitioner believes the examination provides a reasonable basis for his or her opinion.
   - A statement that the examination does not provide a legal determination on the entity's compliance.
   - The practitioner's opinion on whether the entity complied, in all material respects, with specified requirements based on the specified criteria.
   - A statement restricting the use of the report to the specified parties (see the fourth reporting standard) under the following circumstances:
   - When the criteria used to evaluate compliance are determined by the practitioner to be appropriate only for a limited number of parties who either participated in their establishment or can be presumed to have an adequate understanding of the criteria.
   - When the criteria used to evaluate compliance are available only to the specified parties
   - The manual or printed signature of the practitioner's firm.
   - The date of the examination report.

a) Example examination report on compliance
   The following is the form of report a practitioner should use when he or she is expressing an opinion on an entity's compliance with specified requirements during a period of time.

   Independent Accountant's Report

   [Introductory paragraph]
   We have examined [name of entity]'s compliance with [list specified compliance requirements] during the [period] ended [date]. Management is responsible for [name of entity]'s compliance with those requirements. Our responsibility is to express an opinion on [name of entity]'s compliance based on our examination.

   [Scope paragraph]
   Our examination was conducted in accordance with attestation standards established by the American Institute of Certified Public Accountants and, accordingly, included examining, on a test basis, evidence about [name of entity]'s compliance with those requirements and performing such other procedures as we considered necessary in the circumstances. We believe that our examination provides a reasonable basis for our opinion. Our examination does not provide a legal determination on [name of entity]'s compliance with specified requirements.
   [Opinion paragraph]
   In our opinion, [name of entity] complied, in all material respects, with the aforementioned requirements for the year ended December 31, 20XX.

   [Signature]
   [Date]

ii. **Examination Report on an Entity's Assertion About Compliance with Specified Requirements**
   The practitioner's examination report on an entity's assertion about compliance with specified requirements, which is ordinarily addressed to the entity, should include the following:
   - A title that includes the word *independent*.
   - Identification of the responsible party's assertion about the entity's compliance with specified requirements, including the period covered by the responsible party's assertion, and of the responsible party (When the responsible party's assertion does not accompany the practitioner's report, the first paragraph of the report should also contain a statement of the responsible party's assertion.).
   - A statement that compliance with the requirements is the responsibility of the entity's management.
   - A statement that the practitioner's responsibility is to express an opinion on the responsible party's assertion on the entity's compliance with those requirements based on his or her examination.
   - A statement that the examination was conducted in accordance with attestation standards established by the American Institute of Certified Public Accountants and, accordingly, included examining, on a test basis, evidence about the entity's compliance with those requirements and performing such other procedures as the practitioner considered necessary in the circumstances.
   - A statement that the practitioner believes the examination provides a reasonable basis for his or her opinion.

- A statement that the examination does not provide a legal determination on the entity's compliance.
- The practitioner's opinion on whether the responsible party's assertion about compliance with specified requirements is fairly stated in all material respects based on the specified criteria.
- A statement restricting the use of the report to the specified parties (see the fourth reporting standard) under the following circumstances:
    1. When the criteria used to evaluate compliance are determined by the practitioner to be appropriate only for a limited number of parties who either participated in their establishment or can be presumed to have an adequate understanding of the criteria
    2. When the criteria used to evaluate compliance are available only to the specified parties
- The manual or printed signature of the practitioner's firm.
- The date of the examination report.

b) <u>Example examination report on an entity's assertion about compliance with specified requirements</u>
The following is the form of report that a practitioner should use when expressing an opinion on management's assertion about compliance with specified requirements.

Independent Accountant's Report

[Introductory paragraph]
We have examined management's assertion, included in the accompanying [title of management report], that [name of entity] complied with [list specified compliance requirements] during the [period] ended [date]. Management is responsible for [name of entity]'s compliance with those requirements. Our responsibility is to express an opinion on management's assertion about [name of entity]'s compliance based on our examination.

[Scope paragraph]
Our examination was conducted in accordance with attestation standards established by the American Institute of Certified Public Accountants and, accordingly, included examining, on a test basis, evidence about [name of entity]'s compliance with those requirements and performing such other procedures as we considered necessary in the circumstances. We believe that our examination provides a reasonable basis for our opinion. Our examination does not provide a legal determination on [name of entity]'s compliance with specified requirements.

[Opinion paragraph]
In our opinion, management's assertion that [name of entity] complied with the aforementioned requirements during the [period] ended [date] is fairly stated, in all material respects.

[Signature]
[Date]

iii. Report Modifications

The practitioner should modify the standard reports described above, if any of the following conditions exist.

- There is material noncompliance with specified requirements.
- There is a restriction on the scope of the engagement (see AT 101).
- The practitioner decides to refer to the report of another practitioner as the basis, in part, for the practitioner's report (see AT 501).

a) <u>Material Noncompliance</u>

A material noncompliance results in a qualified opinion or adverse opinion (analogous to financial statement auditing – the noncompliance is material (qualified) versus pervasively material (adverse).

Qualified Opinion – The report has the same Introductory and Scope paragraphs. An Explanatory paragraph is added (after the scope) and the Opinion is modified to include '*except for*' language. The Explanatory paragraph and modified Opinion paragraph are illustrated below:

Independent Accountant's Report

[Same Introductory paragraph as Unmodified Report]
[Same Scope paragraph as Unmodified Report]

[Explanatory paragraph]
Our examination disclosed the following material noncompliance with [type of compliance requirement] applicable to [name of entity] during the [period] ended [date]. [Describe noncompliance.]

[Opinion paragraph]
In our opinion, except for the material noncompliance described in the third paragraph, [name of entity] complied, in all material respects, with the aforementioned requirements for the [period] ended [date].

[Signature]
[Date]

Adverse Opinion – The report has the same Introductory and Scope paragraphs. An Explanatory paragraph is added (after the scope) and the Opinion is modified to include the adverse opinion language. The Explanatory paragraph and modified Opinion paragraph are illustrated below:

Independent Accountant's Report

[Same Introductory paragraph as Unmodified Report]
[Same Scope paragraph as Unmodified Report]

[Explanatory paragraph]
Our examination disclosed the following material noncompliance with [type of compliance requirement] applicable to [name of entity] during the [period] ended [date]. [Describe noncompliance.]

[Opinion paragraph]
In our opinion, because of the effect of the noncompliance described in the third paragraph, [name of entity] has not complied with the aforementioned requirements for the [period] ended [date].

[Signature]
[Date]

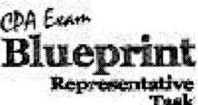

> Prepare a draft compliance report when reporting on compliance with aspects of contractual agreements or regulatory requirements in connection with an audit of an entity's financial statements starting with a report example (e.g., an illustrative report from professional standards).

i. AU-C 806 reports
The auditor's report on compliance should include a statement that nothing came to the auditor's attention that caused the auditor to believe that the entity failed to comply with specified aspects of the contractual agreements or regulatory requirements, insofar as they relate to accounting matters, only when
- the auditor has not identified any instances of noncompliance,
- the auditor has expressed an unmodified or qualified opinion on the financial statements to which the applicable covenants of such contractual agreements or regulatory requirements relate, and
- the applicable covenants or regulatory requirements relate to accounting matters that have been subjected to the audit procedures applied in the audit of financial statements.

When the auditor has identified one or more instances of noncompliance, the report on compliance should describe such noncompliance.

The report on compliance should be in writing and should be provided, either in a separate report, or in one or more paragraphs included in the auditor's report on the financial statements.

1) Separate Report on Compliance with Aspects of Contractual Agreements or Regulatory Requirements
When the auditor reports on compliance in a separate report, the report should include the following:
- A title that includes the word *independent* to clearly indicate that it is the report of an independent auditor.
- An appropriate addressee.
- A paragraph that states that the financial statements were audited in accordance with generally accepted auditing standards and an identification of the United States of America as the country of origin of those standards (for example, auditing standards generally accepted in the United States of America or U.S. generally accepted auditing standards) and the date of the auditor's report on those financial statements.
- If the auditor expressed a modified opinion on the financial statements, a statement describing the nature of the modification.
- When no instances of noncompliance are identified by the auditor, a reference to the specific covenants or paragraphs of the contractual agreement or regulatory requirement and a statement that nothing came to the auditor's attention that caused the auditor to believe that the entity failed to comply with specified aspects of the contractual agreements or regulatory requirements, insofar as they relate to accounting matters.
- When instances of noncompliance are identified by the auditor, a reference to the specific covenants or paragraphs of the contractual agreement or regulatory requirement, insofar as they relate to accounting matters, and a description of the identified instances of noncompliance.
- A statement that the report is being provided in connection with the audit of the financial statements.
- A statement that the audit was not directed primarily toward obtaining knowledge regarding compliance, and accordingly, had the auditor performed additional procedures, other matters may have come to the auditor's attention regarding

noncompliance with the specific covenants or paragraphs of the contractual agreement or regulatory requirement, insofar as they relate to accounting matters.
- A paragraph that includes a description and the source of significant interpretations, if any, made by the entity's management relating to the provisions of the relevant contractual agreement or regulatory requirement.
- A paragraph that includes an appropriate alert in accordance with AU-C 905, *Alert That Restricts the Use of the Auditor's Written Communication*.
- The manual or printed signature of the auditor's firm and the city and state where the auditor practices.
- The date of the report, which should be the same date as the auditor's report on the financial statements.

i. Example Report on Compliance with Aspects of Contractual Agreements or Regulatory Requirements

A Report on Compliance with Aspects of Contractual Agreements Provided in a Separate Report When No Instances of Noncompliance Are Identified.

<u>Independent Auditor's Report</u>

[Appropriate Addressee]

We have audited, in accordance with auditing standards generally accepted in the United States of America, the financial statements of XYZ Company, which comprise the balance sheet as of December 31, 20X2, and the related statements of income, changes in stockholders' equity, and cash flows for the year then ended, and the related notes to the financial statements, and have issued our report thereon dated February 16, 20X3.

In connection with our audit, nothing came to our attention that caused us to believe that XYZ Company failed to comply with the terms, covenants, provisions, or conditions of sections XX to YY, inclusive, of the Indenture dated July 21, 20X0, with ABC Bank, insofar as they relate to accounting matters. However, our audit was not directed primarily toward obtaining knowledge of such noncompliance. Accordingly, had we performed additional procedures, other matters may have come to our attention regarding the Company's noncompliance with the above-referenced terms, covenants, provisions, or conditions of the Indenture, insofar as they relate to accounting matters.

This report is intended solely for the information and use of the board of directors and management of XYZ Company and ABC Bank and is not intended to be and should not be used by anyone other than these specified parties.

[Auditor's signature]
[Auditor's city and state]
[Date of the auditor's report]

ii. Example compliance report with aspects of contractual agreements or regulatory requirements included in the auditor's report
A Report on Compliance with Aspects of Contractual Agreements Given in a Combined Report, and No Instances of Noncompliance Were Identified.

<u>Independent Auditor's Report</u>

[Appropriate Addressee]

Report on the Financial Statements
We have audited the accompanying financial statements of ABC Company, which comprise the balance sheet as of December 31, 20X1, and the related statements of income, changes in stockholders' equity, and cash flows for the year then ended, and the related notes to the financial statements.

Management's Responsibility for the Financial Statements
Management is responsible for the preparation and fair presentation of these financial statements in accordance with accounting principles generally accepted in the United States of America; this includes the design, implementation, and maintenance of internal control relevant to the preparation and fair presentation of financial statements that are free from material misstatement, whether due to fraud or error.

Auditor's Responsibility
Our responsibility is to express an opinion on these financial statements based on our audit. We conducted our audit in accordance with auditing standards generally accepted in the United States of America. Those standards require that we plan and perform the audit to obtain reasonable assurance about whether the financial statements are free from material misstatement.

An audit involves performing procedures to obtain audit evidence about the amounts and disclosures in the financial statements. The procedures selected depend on the auditor's judgment, including the assessment of the risks of material misstatement of the financial statements, whether due to fraud or error. In making those risk assessments, the auditor considers internal control relevant to the entity's preparation and fair presentation of the financial statements in order to design audit procedures that are appropriate in the circumstances, but not for the purpose of expressing an opinion on the effectiveness of the entity's internal control. Accordingly, we express no such opinion. An audit also includes evaluating the appropriateness of accounting policies used and the reasonableness of significant accounting estimates made by management, as well as evaluating the overall presentation of the financial statements.

We believe that the audit evidence we have obtained is sufficient and appropriate to provide a basis for our audit opinion.

Opinion
In our opinion, the financial statements referred to above present fairly, in all material respects, the financial position of ABC Company as of December 31, 20X1, and the results of its operations and its cash flows for the year then ended in accordance with accounting principles generally accepted in the United States of America.

Other Matter
In connection with our audit, nothing came to our attention that caused us to believe that ABC Company failed to comply with the terms, covenants, provisions, or conditions of sections XX to YY, inclusive, of the Indenture dated July 21, 20X0 with XYZ Bank, insofar as they relate to accounting matters. However, our audit was not directed primarily toward obtaining knowledge of such noncompliance. Accordingly, had we performed additional procedures, other matters may have come to our attention regarding the Company's noncompliance with the above-referenced terms, covenants, provisions, or conditions of the Indenture, insofar as they relate to accounting matters.

Restricted Use Relating to the Other Matter
The communication related to compliance with the aforementioned Indenture described in the Other Matter paragraph is intended solely for the information and use of the boards of directors and management of ABC Company and XYZ Bank and is not intended to be and should not be used by anyone other than these specified parties.

Report on Other Legal and Regulatory Requirements
[Form and content of this section of the auditor's report will vary depending on the nature of the auditor's other reporting responsibilities.]

[Auditor's signature]
[Auditor's city and state]
[Date of the auditor's report]

j. AU-C 935 reports
Regardless of the auditor's opinion on compliance, federal audit regulations may require him or her to report any instances of noncompliance found and any resulting questioned (unsupported) costs. In reporting instances of noncompliance, the auditor should follow the provisions of *Government Auditing Standards*. For purposes of reporting questioned costs, the auditor is not required to report likely questioned costs; rather, the auditor should report only known questioned costs without adequate supporting documentation.

i. **Example Report on Internal Control over Compliance**
Illustrative Combined Report on Compliance with Applicable Requirements and Internal Control over Compliance – (Unmodified Opinion on Compliance, No Material Weaknesses or Significant Deficiencies in Internal Control over Compliance Identified)

The following is an illustrative combined report on compliance with applicable requirements and internal control over compliance that contains the elements above. This illustrative report contains an unmodified opinion on compliance with no material weaknesses or significant deficiencies in internal control over compliance identified. The AICPA Audit Guide Government Auditing Standards and Circular A-133 Audits contains illustrative language for other types of reports, including reports containing qualified or adverse opinions on compliance with either material weaknesses in internal control over compliance, significant deficiencies in internal control over compliance, or both identified.

<u>Independent Auditor's Report</u>

[Addressee]
Compliance
We have audited Example Entity's compliance with the [identify the applicable compliance requirements or refer to the document that describes the applicable compliance requirements] applicable to Example Entity's [identify the government program(s) audited or refer to a separate schedule that identifies the program(s)] for the year ended June 30, 20X1.

Management's Responsibility
Compliance with the requirements referred to above is the responsibility of Example Entity's management.

Auditor's Responsibility
Our responsibility is to express an opinion on Example Entity's compliance based on our audit. We conducted our audit of compliance in accordance with auditing standards generally accepted in the United States of America; the standards applicable to financial audits contained in Government Auditing Standards issued by the Comptroller General of the United States; and [insert the name of the governmental audit requirement or program-specific audit guide]. Those standards and [insert the name of the governmental audit requirement or program-specific audit

guide] require that we plan and perform the audit to obtain reasonable assurance about whether noncompliance with the compliance requirements referred to above that could have a material effect on [identify the government program(s) audited or refer to a separate schedule that identifies the program(s)] occurred. An audit includes examining, on a test basis, evidence about Example Entity's compliance with those requirements and performing such other procedures as we considered necessary in the circumstances. We believe that our audit provides a reasonable basis for our opinion. Our audit does not provide a legal determination of Example Entity's compliance with those requirements.

Opinion
In our opinion, Example Entity complied, in all material respects, with the compliance requirements referred to above that are applicable to [identify the government program(s) audited] for the year ended June 30, 20X1.

Internal Control over Compliance
Management of Example Entity is responsible for establishing and maintaining effective internal control over compliance with the compliance requirements referred to above. In planning and performing our audit, we considered Example Entity's internal control over compliance to determine the auditing procedures for the purpose of expressing our opinion on compliance, but not for the purpose of expressing an opinion on the effectiveness of internal control over compliance. Accordingly, we do not express an opinion on the effectiveness of Example Entity's internal control over compliance.

A deficiency in internal control over compliance exists when the design or operation of a control does not allow management or employees, in the normal course of performing their assigned functions, to prevent, or detect and correct, noncompliance on a timely basis. A material weakness in internal control over compliance is a deficiency, or combination of deficiencies in internal control over compliance, such that there is a reasonable possibility that material noncompliance with a compliance requirement will not be prevented, or detected and corrected, on a timely basis.

Our consideration of internal control over compliance was for the limited purpose described in the first paragraph of this section and was not designed to identify all deficiencies in internal control that might be deficiencies, significant deficiencies, or material weaknesses in internal control over compliance. We did not identify any deficiencies in internal control over compliance that we consider to be material weaknesses, as defined above.

The purpose of this report on internal control over compliance is solely to describe the scope of our testing of internal control over compliance and the results of that testing based on the [insert the name of the governmental audit requirement or program-specific audit guide]. Accordingly, this report is not suitable for any other purpose.

[Signature]
[Date]

1) Modified reports
   The auditor should modify the auditor's opinion on compliance in accordance with AU-C 705, *Modifications to the Opinion in the Independent Auditor's Report*, if any of the following conditions exist:
   - The compliance audit identifies noncompliance with the applicable compliance requirements that the auditor believes has a material effect on the entity's compliance.
   - A restriction on the scope of the compliance audit.

Multiple Choice

AUD 4-Q75 through AUD 4-Q76

E. Other Reporting Considerations
1. Comparative statements and consistency between periods

> **Identify the factors that would affect the comparability or consistency of financial statements, including a change in accounting principle, the correction of a material misstatement and a material change in classification.**

> *Hint*: The main sources of professional guidance that serve as the basis for this review are obtained from the following:
> AU-C 708, *Consistency of Financial Statements (AICPA)*.
> AS 2820, *Evaluating Consistency of Financial Statements* (PCAOB).
>
> Generally, the AICPA requirements and the PCAOB requirements are the same or similar.

   a. Objectives
   The objectives of the auditor are to:
   - evaluate the consistency of the financial statements for the periods presented and
   - communicate appropriately in the auditor's report when the comparability of financial statements between periods has been materially affected by a change in accounting principle or by adjustments to correct a material misstatement in previously issued financial statements.

   b. Requirements
   1) Evaluating consistency
   When evaluating consistency, an auditor is determining if financial statements are comparable year over year. Two specific areas of evaluation include a change in accounting principle or adjustment to correct a prior material misstatement.

   i. Periods to evaluate
   The periods included in the auditor's evaluation of consistency depend on the periods covered by the auditor's opinion on the financial statements.

Reporting period	Consistency Evaluation
Current period only	Is the current period consistent with the preceding period?
Comparative statements (2 or more periods)	Is there consistency between the periods being reported on? Is there consistency between the periods being reported on AND the preceding period?

   Example: Assume a company changes auditor. In the first year, the successor auditor evaluates consistency between the year on which he or she reports and the immediately preceding year. In the second year, the successor auditor would evaluate consistency between the two years on which he or she reports and between those years and the earliest year presented (when three periods are presented).

   2) Change in accounting principle
   The auditor should evaluate a change in accounting principle to determine whether
   i. the newly adopted accounting principle is in accordance with the applicable financial reporting framework,
   ii. the method of accounting for the effect of the change is in accordance with the applicable financial reporting framework,
   iii. the disclosures related to the accounting change are appropriate and adequate, and

iv. the entity has justified that the alternative accounting principle is preferable.

(These criteria are the same as AS 2820.07, but the PCAOB refers to GAAP, instead of applicable financial reporting framework.)

If the auditor concludes that the 4 criteria above have been met, and the change in accounting principle has a material effect on the financial statements, the auditor should include an **emphasis-of-matter paragraph** in the auditor's report that describes the change in accounting principle and provides a reference to the entity's disclosure.

If the 4 criteria above are not met, the auditor should evaluate whether the accounting change results in a material misstatement and whether the auditor should modify the opinion accordingly. This is a departure from GAAP.

The auditor should include an emphasis-of-matter paragraph relating to a change in accounting principle in reports on financial statements in the period of the change, and in subsequent periods, until the new accounting principle is applied in all periods presented.

If the change in accounting principle is accounted for by retrospective application to the financial statements of all prior periods presented, the emphasis-of-matter paragraph is needed only in the period of such change.

The auditor should evaluate and report on a **change in accounting estimate that is inseparable from the effect of a related change in accounting principle** like other changes in accounting principle, as just discussed.

When a **change in the reporting entity** results in financial statements that, in effect, are those of a different reporting entity, the auditor should include an emphasis-of-matter paragraph in the auditor's report that describes the change in the reporting entity and provides a reference to the entity's disclosure, unless the change in reporting entity results from a transaction or event.

If an entity's financial statements contain an investment accounted for by the equity method, the auditor's evaluation of consistency should include consideration of the investee. If the investee makes a change in accounting principle that is material to the investing entity's financial statements, the auditor should include an emphasis-of-matter paragraph in the auditor's report to describe the change in accounting principle.

Opinion modification	Emphasis-of-matter paragraph
• Change in accounting principle criteria **not met**, material misstatement	• Change in accounting principle criteria **met**, material misstatement • Change is reporting entity • Investee change in accounting principle

3) Correction of a Material Misstatement in Previously Issued Financial Statements
When there are adjustments to correct a material misstatement in previously issued financial statements, the auditor should include an emphasis-of-matter paragraph in the auditor's report, during the period of correction. The paragraph is not required in subsequent periods.

The emphasis-of-matter paragraph should include:
i. a statement that the previously issued financial statements have been restated for the correction of a material misstatement in the respective period and
ii. a reference to the entity's disclosure of the correction of the material misstatement.

If the financial statement disclosures relating to the restatement to correct a material misstatement in previously issued financial statements are not adequate, the auditor should address the inadequacy of disclosure as described in AU-C 705, *Modifications to the Opinion in the Independent Auditor's Report.*

4) Change in Classification
The auditor should evaluate a material change in financial statement classification and the related disclosure to determine whether such a change is also either a change in accounting principle or an adjustment to correct a material misstatement in previously issued financial statements.

The PCAOB's requirement is the same [PCAOB AS 2820.11].

Multiple Choice

AUD 4-Q77 through AUD 4-Q83

2. Other information in documents with audited statements

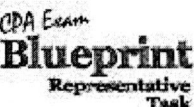

> **Understand the auditor's responsibilities related to other information included in documents with audited financial statements.**

AU-C 720 addresses the auditor's responsibility with respect to other information in documents containing audited financial statements and the auditor's report thereon.

In the absence of any separate requirement in the particular circumstances of the engagement, the auditor's opinion on the financial statements does not cover other information, and the auditor has no responsibility for determining whether such information is properly stated.

AU-C 720 requires the auditor to read the other information of which the auditor is aware because the credibility of the audited financial statements may be undermined by material inconsistencies between the audited financial statements and other information.

In this section, *documents containing audited financial statements* refers to annual reports (or similar documents) that are issued to owners (or similar stakeholders) and annual reports of governments and organizations for charitable or philanthropic purposes that are available to the public that contain audited financial statements and the auditor's report thereon.

a. Requirements

1) **Read All Other Information**
   The auditor should read the other information of which the auditor is aware in order to identify material inconsistencies, if any, with the audited financial statements.

   The auditor should communicate with those charged with governance the auditor's responsibility with respect to the other information, any procedures performed relating to the other information, and the results.

2) **Material Inconsistencies**
   If, on reading the other information, the auditor identifies a material inconsistency, the auditor should determine whether the audited financial statements or the other information needs to be revised.

3) **Material Inconsistencies Identified Prior to the Date of the Auditor's Report That Require Revision of the Audited Financial Statements**
   When the auditor identifies a material inconsistency prior to the date of the auditor's report that requires revision of the audited financial statements and management refuses to make the revision, the auditor should modify the auditor's opinion in accordance with AU-C 705, *Modifications to the Opinion in the Independent Auditor's Report*.

4) **Material Inconsistencies Identified after the Date of the Auditor's Report but Prior to the Report Release Date That Require Revision of the Audited Financial Statements**
   When the auditor identifies a material inconsistency after the date of the auditor's report but prior to the report release date that requires revision of the audited financial statements, the auditor should apply the relevant requirements in AU-C 560, *Subsequent Events and Subsequently Discovered Facts*.

5) **Material Inconsistencies Identified Prior to the Report Release Date That Require Revision of the Other Information**
   When the auditor identifies a material inconsistency prior to the report release date that requires revision of the other information and **management refuses to make the revision**, the auditor should communicate this matter to those charged with governance and
   - include in the auditor's report an other-matter paragraph describing the material inconsistency, in accordance with section 706, *Emphasis-of-Matter Paragraphs and Other-Matter Paragraphs in the Independent Auditor's Report*;
   - withhold the auditor's report; or
   - when withdrawal is possible under applicable law or regulation, withdraw from the engagement.

6) **Material Inconsistencies Identified Subsequent to the Report Release Date**
   When revision of the audited financial statements is necessary as a result of a material inconsistency with other information and the auditor's report on the financial statements has already been released, the auditor should apply the relevant requirements in AU-C 560, *Subsequent Events and Subsequently Discovered Facts.*

   When revision of the other information is necessary after the report release date and **management agrees to make the revision**, the auditor should carry out the procedures necessary under the circumstances

   When revision of the other information is necessary after the report release date but **management refuses to make the revision**, the auditor should notify those charged with governance of the auditor's concerns regarding the other information and take any further appropriate action.

7) **Material Misstatements of Fact**
   If, on reading the other information for the purpose of identifying material inconsistencies, the auditor becomes aware of an apparent material misstatement of fact, the auditor should discuss the matter with management.

   When, following such discussions, the auditor still considers that there is an apparent material misstatement of fact, the auditor should request management to consult with a qualified third party, such as the entity's legal counsel, and the auditor should consider the advice received by the entity in determining whether such matter is a material misstatement of fact.

   When the auditor concludes that there is a material misstatement of fact in the other information that management refuses to correct, the auditor should notify those charged with governance of the auditor's concerns regarding the other information and take any further appropriate action.

Multiple Choice

AUD 4-Q84 through AUD 4-Q87

3. Review of interim financial information

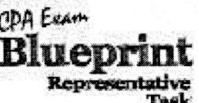

Identify the factors an auditor should consider when reporting on an engagement to review interim financial information.

Hint: The main sources of professional guidance that serve as the basis for this review are obtained from the following:
   AU-C 930, *Interim Financial Information* (AICPA).
   AS 4105, *Reviews of Interim Financial Information* (PCAOB).

Generally, the AICPA requirements and the PCAOB requirements are the same of similar.

   a. Applicability
AU-C 930 applies to a review of interim financial information when
- the entity's latest annual financial statements have been audited by the auditor or a predecessor auditor;
- the auditor either has been engaged to audit the entity's current year financial statements, or audited the entity's latest annual financial statements, and in situations in which it is expected that the current year financial statements will be audited, the engagement of another auditor to audit the current year financial statements is not effective prior to the beginning of the period covered by the review;
- the entity prepares its interim financial information in accordance with the same financial reporting framework as that used to prepare the annual financial statements; and
- all of the following conditions are met if the interim financial information is condensed:
  a) The condensed interim financial information purports to be prepared in accordance with an appropriate financial reporting framework, which includes appropriate form and content of interim financial information.
  b) The condensed interim financial information includes a note that the financial information does not represent complete financial statements and is to be read in conjunction with the entity's latest audited annual financial statements.
  c) The condensed interim financial information accompanies the entity's latest audited annual financial statements, or such audited annual financial statements are made readily available by the entity.

Statements on Standards for Accounting and Review Services (SSARS) provide guidance for review engagements for which this section is not applicable.

   b. Objective
The objective of the auditor when performing an engagement to review interim financial information is to obtain a basis for reporting whether the auditor is aware of any material modifications that should be made to the interim financial information for it to be in accordance with the applicable financial reporting framework through performing limited procedures.

      1) Agreement on engagement terms
The auditor should agree upon the terms of the engagement with management or those charged with governance, as appropriate.

The agreed-upon terms of the engagement should be recorded in an engagement letter or other suitable form of written agreement and should include the following:
- The objectives and scope of the engagement.
- The responsibilities of management.
- The responsibilities of the auditor.

- The limitations of a review engagement.
- Identification of the applicable financial reporting framework for the preparation of the interim financial information.

c. Procedures for a review of interim financial information
   1) Understanding the Entity and Its Environment, Including Its Internal Control
   To plan and conduct the engagement, the auditor should have an understanding of the entity and its environment, including its internal control as it relates to the preparation and fair presentation of both annual and interim financial information, sufficient to be able to
   - identify the types of potential material misstatements in the interim financial information and consider the likelihood of their occurrence.
   - select the inquiries and analytical procedures that will provide the auditor with a basis for reporting whether the auditor is aware of any material modifications that should be made to the interim financial information, for it to be in accordance with the applicable financial reporting framework.

   To update or, in the case of an auditor who has not yet performed an audit of the entity's annual financial statements, obtain the understanding of the entity and environment, the auditor should perform the following procedures:
   - Read available documentation of the preceding year's audit, the of reviews of the prior interim period(s) of the current year and the corresponding interim period(s) of the prior year to the extent necessary, based on the auditor's judgment, to enable the auditor to identify matters that may affect the current period interim financial information. In reading such documents, the auditor should specifically consider the nature of any
     a) corrected material misstatements;
     b) matters identified in any summary of uncorrected misstatements;
     c) identified risks of material misstatement due to fraud, including the risk of management override of controls; and
     d) significant financial accounting and reporting matters that may be of continuing significance, such as significant deficiencies and material weaknesses.
   - Read the most recent annual and comparable prior interim period financial information.
   - Consider the results of any audit procedures performed with respect to the current year's financial statements.
   - Inquire of management about changes in the entity's business activities.
   - Inquire of management about the identity of, and nature of transactions with, related parties.
   - Inquire of management about whether significant changes in internal control, as it relates to the preparation and fair presentation of interim financial information, have occurred subsequent to the preceding annual audit or prior review of interim financial information, including changes in the entity's policies, procedures, and personnel, as well as the nature and extent of such changes.

   2) Analytical procedures, inquiries, and other review procedures
      i. **Analytical procedures**
      The auditor should apply analytical procedures to the interim financial information to identify and provide a basis for inquiry about the relationships and individual items that appear to be unusual and that may indicate a material misstatement. Such analytical procedures should include the following:

- Comparing the interim financial information with comparable information for the immediately preceding interim period, if applicable, and with the corresponding period(s) in the previous year, giving consideration to knowledge about changes in the entity's business and specific transactions.
- Considering plausible relationships among both financial and, when relevant, nonfinancial information.
- Comparing recorded amounts or ratios developed from recorded amounts to expectations developed by the auditor through identifying and using relationships that are reasonably expected to exist, based on the auditor's understanding of the entity and the industry in which the entity operates.
- Comparing disaggregated revenue data.

ii. ***Inquiries and Other Review Procedures***

The auditor should make the following inquiries and perform the following other review procedures when conducting a review of interim financial information:
- Read the available minutes of meetings of stockholders, directors, and appropriate committees.
- Obtain reports from component auditors, if any.
- Inquire of management about the following:
    a) whether the interim financial information has been prepared and fairly presented in accordance with the applicable financial reporting framework consistently applied.
    b) unusual or complex situations that may have an effect on the interim financial information.
    c) significant transactions
    d) the status of uncorrected misstatements identified during the previous audit and interim review
    e) events subsequent to the date of the interim financial information
    f) knowledge of any fraud or suspected fraud
    g) significant journal entries and other adjustments.
    h) communications from regulatory agencies.
    i) significant deficiencies and material weaknesses in the design or operation of internal control as it relates to the preparation and fair presentation of both annual and interim financial information.
    j) changes in related parties or significant new related party transactions.
- Obtain evidence that the interim financial information agrees or reconciles with the accounting records.

The PCAOB requires the following additional procedures (see AS 4105, *Reviews of Interim Financial Information*):
- Reading other information that accompanies the interim financial information and is contained in reports (1) to holders of securities or beneficial interests or (2) filed with regulatory authorities under the Securities Exchange Act of 1934 (such as Form 10-Q or 10-QSB), to consider whether such information, or the manner of its presentation is materially inconsistent with the interim financial information. If the accountant concludes that there is a material inconsistency, or becomes aware of information that he or she believes is a material misstatement of fact, the action taken will depend on his or her judgment in the particular circumstances.
- Evaluating management's quarterly certifications about internal control over financial reporting by performing the following procedures –

- a) Inquiring of management about significant changes in the design or operation of internal control over financial reporting, as it relates to the preparation of annual as well as interim financial information that could have occurred subsequent to the preceding annual audit or prior review of interim financial information;
- b) Evaluating the implications of misstatements identified by the auditor as part of the auditor's other interim review procedures, as they relate to effective internal control over financial reporting; and
- c) Determining, through a combination of observation and inquiry, whether any change in internal control over financial reporting has materially affected, or is reasonably likely to materially affect, the company's internal control over financial reporting.

iii. ***Inquiry Concerning Litigation, Claims, and Assessments***
If information comes to the auditor's attention regarding litigation, claims, or assessments that leads the auditor to question if the interim financial information has been prepared in accordance with the applicable financial reporting framework, the auditor should inquire of the company's legal counsel.

iv. ***Inquiry Concerning an Entity's Ability to Continue as a Going Concern***
The auditor should inquire of management about its plans for dealing with the adverse effects of the conditions and events, and consider the adequacy of the disclosure about such matters in the interim financial information.

v. ***Consideration of Management's Responses and Extension of Interim Review Procedures***
The auditor should consider the reasonableness and consistency of management's responses in light of the results of other review procedures and the auditor's knowledge of the entity's business and its internal control. However, the auditor is not required to corroborate management's responses with other evidence.

d. Evaluating the results of interim review procedures
The auditor should accumulate misstatements, including inadequate disclosure, identified by the auditor in performing the review procedures, or brought to the auditor's attention during the performance of the review.

The auditor should evaluate, individually and in the aggregate, misstatements, including inadequate disclosure, to determine whether material modification should be made to the interim financial information for it to be in accordance with the applicable financial reporting framework.

e. Written representations from management
For all interim financial information presented and for all periods covered by the review, the auditor should request management to provide written representations, as of the date of the auditor's review report:
- that management has fulfilled its responsibility for the preparation and fair presentation of the interim financial information, in accordance with the applicable financial reporting framework, as set out in the terms of the engagement.
- that management acknowledges its responsibility for designing, implementing, and maintaining internal control relevant to the preparation and fair presentation of interim financial statements, including its responsibility to prevent and detect fraud.
- that management has disclosed to the auditor all significant deficiencies and material weaknesses in the design or operation of internal control of which management is aware as

it relates to the preparation and fair presentation of both annual and interim financial information.
- that management has provided the auditor with all relevant information and access, as agreed upon in the terms of the engagement.
- that all transactions have been recorded and are reflected in the interim financial information.
- that management has disclosed to the auditor the results of its assessment of the risk that the interim financial information may be materially misstated as a result of fraud.
- that management has disclosed to the auditor its knowledge of fraud or suspected fraud affecting the entity involving management, employees who have significant roles in internal control, or others, when the fraud could have a material effect on the interim financial information.
- that management has disclosed to the auditor its knowledge of any allegations of fraud or suspected fraud affecting the entity's interim financial information, communicated by employees, former employees, regulators, or others.
- that management has disclosed to the auditor all known instances of noncompliance or suspected noncompliance with laws and regulations, whose effects should be considered when preparing interim financial information.
- about whether management believes that the effects of uncorrected misstatements are immaterial, individually and in the aggregate, to the interim financial information as a whole. A summary of such items should be included in, or attached to, the written representation.
- that management has disclosed to the auditor all known actual or possible litigation and claims whose effects should be considered when preparing the interim financial information, and it has appropriately accounted for, and disclosed, such litigation and claims in accordance with the applicable financial reporting framework.
- about whether management believes that significant assumptions used by it in making accounting estimates are reasonable.
- that management has disclosed to the auditor the identity of the entity's related parties and all the related party relationships and transactions of which it is aware, and it has appropriately accounted for and disclosed such relationships and transactions.
- that all events occurring subsequent to the date of the interim financial information, and for which the applicable financial reporting framework requires adjustment or disclosure, have been adjusted or disclosed.

When management does not provide the written representations described above, the auditor should withdraw from the engagement to review the interim financial information.

    f. Communications with management and those charged with governance
        1) Matters affecting the completion of the review
If the auditor cannot complete the review, the auditor should communicate to the appropriate level of management and those charged with governance
- the reason why the review cannot be completed;
- that an incomplete review does not provide a basis for reporting and, accordingly, that the auditor is precluded from issuing a review report; and
- any material modifications of which the auditor has become aware that should be made to the interim financial information for it to be in accordance with the applicable financial reporting framework.

The auditor should communicate to the appropriate level of management, as soon as practicable, matters that come to the auditor's attention during the conduct of the review that cause the auditor to believe that
- material modification should be made to the interim financial information for it to be in accordance with the applicable financial reporting framework, or

- the entity issued the interim financial information before the completion of the review.

If, in the auditor's judgment, management does not respond appropriately to the auditor's communication within a reasonable period of time, the auditor should inform those charged with governance of the matters as soon as practicable.

If, in the auditor's judgment, those charged with governance do not respond appropriately to the auditor's communication within a reasonable period of time, the auditor should consider whether to withdraw (*a*) from the engagement to review the interim financial information and (*b*) if applicable, from serving as the entity's auditor.

2) Other matters
If the auditor becomes aware that fraud may have occurred, the auditor should communicate the matter as soon as practicable to the appropriate level of management.

If the fraud involves senior management or results in a material misstatement of the interim financial information, the auditor should communicate the matter directly to those charged with governance.

If the auditor becomes aware of matters involving identified, or suspected, noncompliance with laws and regulations whose effects should be considered when preparing interim financial information, the auditor should communicate the matters to those charged with governance, other than when the matters are clearly inconsequential.

The auditor should communicate relevant matters of governance interest arising from the review of interim financial information to those charged with governance, including significant deficiencies or material weaknesses in internal control as it relates to the preparation and fair presentation of annual and interim financial information.

g. Documentation
The auditor should prepare documentation in connection with a review of interim financial information that will enable an experienced auditor, having no previous connection to the review, to understand
- the nature, timing, and extent of the review procedures performed;
- the results of the review procedures performed and the evidence obtained; and
- significant findings or issues arising during the review, the conclusions reached thereon, and significant professional judgments made in reaching those conclusions.

h. Reporting
1) The Auditor's Report on a Review of Interim Financial Information
The auditor's review report should be in writing. The auditor should determine that management has clearly marked as unaudited each page of the interim financial information accompanying the review report.

i. Example review report on interim financial information
   Circumstances include the following:
   A review of interim financial information presented as a complete set of financial statements, including disclosures.

THE REPORT - AICPA

Independent Auditor's Review Report
[Appropriate Addressee]

Report on the Financial Statements
We have reviewed the accompanying [describe the interim financial information or statements reviewed] of ABC Company and subsidiaries as of September 30, 20X1, and for the three-month and nine-month periods then ended.

Management's Responsibility
The Company's management is responsible for the preparation and fair presentation of the interim financial information in accordance with [identify the applicable financial reporting framework; for example, accounting principles generally accepted in the United States of America]; this responsibility includes the design, implementation, and maintenance of internal control sufficient to provide a reasonable basis for the preparation and fair presentation of interim financial information in accordance with [identify the applicable financial reporting framework; for example, accounting principles generally accepted in the United States of America].

Auditor's Responsibility
Our responsibility is to conduct our review in accordance with auditing standards generally accepted in the United States of America applicable to reviews of interim financial information. A review of interim financial information consists principally of applying analytical procedures and making inquiries of persons responsible for financial and accounting matters. It is substantially less in scope than an audit conducted in accordance with auditing standards generally accepted in the United States of America, the objective of which is the expression of an opinion regarding the financial information. Accordingly, we do not express such an opinion.

Conclusion
Based on our review, we are not aware of any material modifications that should be made to the accompanying interim financial information for it to be in accordance with [identify the applicable financial reporting framework; for example, accounting principles generally accepted in the United States of America].

[Auditor's signature]
[Auditor's city and state]
[Date of the auditor's report]

Report of Independent Registered Public Accounting Firm (PCAOB)

To the shareholders and the board of directors of ABC Company,

Results of Review of Interim [Financial Information or Statements]
We have reviewed the accompanying [describe the interim financial information or statements reviewed] of ABC Company (the "Company") and consolidated subsidiaries as of September 30, 20X1, and for the three-month and nine-month periods then ended, and the related notes [and schedules] (collectively referred to as the "interim financial information or statements"). Based on our review, we are not aware of any material modifications that should be made to the accompanying interim financial information (statements) for it (them) to be in conformity with accounting principles generally accepted in the United States of America.

Basis for Review Results
This (These) interim financial information (statements) is (are) the responsibility of the Company's management. We conducted our review in accordance with the standards of the Public Company Accounting Oversight Board (United States) ("PCAOB"). A review of interim financial information consists principally of applying analytical procedures and making inquiries of persons responsible for financial and accounting matters. It is substantially less in scope than an audit conducted in accordance with the standards of the PCAOB, the objective of which is the expression of an opinion regarding the financial statements taken as a whole. Accordingly, we do not express such an opinion.

[Signature]
[City and State or Country]
[Date]

    ii. Modification of the auditor's review report
When the interim financial information has **not** been prepared in accordance with the applicable financial reporting framework in all material respects, the auditor should consider whether modification of the auditor's review report on the interim financial information is sufficient to address the departure from the applicable financial reporting framework.

If the auditor concludes that modification of the standard review report is sufficient to address the departure, the auditor should **modify** the review report. The modification should describe the nature of the departure and, if practicable, should state the effects on the interim financial information. If the departure is due to inadequate disclosure, the auditor should, if practicable, include the information in the report that the auditor believes is necessary for adequate disclosure in accordance with the applicable financial reporting framework.

If the auditor believes that modification of the review report is not sufficient to address the deficiencies in the interim financial information, the auditor should **withdraw** from the review engagement and provide no further services with respect to such interim financial information.

i. Subsequent discovery of facts existing at the date of the auditor's review report
If, subsequent to the date of the auditor's review report, the auditor becomes aware that facts existed at the date of the review report that might have affected the auditor's review report had the auditor then been aware of those matters, the auditor should apply the requirements and guidance, adapted as necessary, in section 560, *Subsequent Events and Subsequently Discovered Facts* (see review of Topic G of chapter AUD 3).

j. Other information related to a review of interim financial information
    1) Analytical Procedures the Auditor May Consider Performing When Conducting a Review of Interim Financial Information

Examples of analytical procedures that an auditor may consider performing in a review of interim financial information include the following:
- Comparing current interim financial information with the interim financial information of the immediately preceding interim period, the interim financial information of the corresponding interim period of the preceding financial year, and the most recent audited annual financial statements.
- Comparing current interim financial information with anticipated results, such as budgets or forecasts (for example, comparing tax balances and the relationship

between the provision for income taxes and pretax income in the current interim financial information, with corresponding information in (a) budgets, using expected rates, and (b) financial information for prior periods). Caution is necessary when comparing and evaluating current interim financial information with budgets, forecasts, or other anticipated results, because of the inherent lack of precision in estimating the future, and the susceptibility of such information to manipulation and misstatement by management to reflect desired interim results.
- Comparing current interim financial information with relevant nonfinancial information.
- Comparing ratios and indicators for the current interim period with expectations based on prior periods (for example, performing gross profit analysis by product line and operating segment using elements of the current interim financial information and comparing the results with corresponding information for prior periods). Examples of key ratios and indicators are the current ratio, receivable turnover or number of days sales outstanding, inventory turnover, depreciation to average fixed assets, debt to equity, gross profit percentage, net income percentage, and plant operating rates.
- Comparing ratios and indicators for the current interim period with those of entities in the same industry.
- Comparing relationships among elements in the current interim financial information with corresponding relationships in the interim financial information of prior periods (for example, expense by type as a percentage of sales, assets by type as a percentage of total assets, and percentage of change in sales to percentage of change in receivables).
- Comparing disaggregated data. The following are examples of how data may be disaggregated:
  a) By period (for example, interim financial information items disaggregated into quarterly, monthly, or weekly amounts)
  b) By product line or operating segment
  c) By location (for example, subsidiary, division, or branch)

Analytical procedures may include such statistical techniques as trend analysis or regression analysis and may be performed manually or with the use of computer-assisted techniques (CAATs).

2) Unusual or complex situations to be considered by the auditor when conducting a review of interim financial information

The following are examples of situations about which the auditor may inquire of management:
- Business combinations
- New or complex revenue recognition methods
- Impairment of assets
- Disposal of a segment of a business
- Use of derivative instruments and hedging activities
- Sales and transfers that may call into question the classification of investments in securities, including management's intent and ability with respect to the remaining securities classified as held to maturity
- Adoption of new stock compensation plans or changes to existing plans
- Restructuring charges taken in the current and prior quarters
- Significant, unusual, or infrequently occurring transactions
- Changes in litigation or contingencies

- Changes in major contracts with customers or suppliers
- Application of new accounting principles
- Changes in accounting principles or the methods of applying them
- Trends and developments affecting accounting estimates, such as allowances for bad debts and excess or obsolete inventories, provisions for warranties and employee benefits, and realization of unearned income and deferred charges
- Compliance with debt covenants
- Changes in related parties or significant new related party transactions
- Material off-balance-sheet transactions, special purpose entities, and other equity investments
- Unique terms for debt or capital stock that could affect classification

---

Hint:

Review of Interim Financial Statements Summary

1. Obtain engagement letter
2. Obtain understanding of entity and internal control
3. Apply analytical procedures
4. Make inquires and other review procedures
5. Inquiry concerning litigation, claims assessments
6. Inquiry concerning going concern
7. Evaluate results
8. Obtain written representations from management (withdraw from engagement if not provided)
9. Communicate results

4. Supplementary information

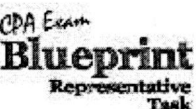

Identify the factors an auditor should consider when reporting on supplementary information included in or accompanying an entity's financial statements.

Auditors may have to deal with two types of supplementary information:
- Required Supplementary Information
- Supplementary Information

a. Required supplementary information (AU-C 730)
The objectives of the auditor, when a designated accounting standards setter requires information to accompany an entity's basic financial statements, are to perform specified procedures in order to
- describe, in the auditor's report, whether required supplementary information is presented and
- communicate therein when some or all of the required supplementary information has not been presented in accordance with guidelines established by a designated accounting standards setter, or when the auditor has identified material modifications that should be made to the required supplementary information in order for it to be in accordance with guidelines established by the designated accounting standards setter.

1) Procedures
The auditor should apply the following procedures to required supplementary information:
- Inquire of management about the methods of preparing the information, including, whether:
    a) it has been measured and presented in accordance with prescribed guidelines,
    b) methods of measurement or presentation have been changed from those used in the prior period and the reasons for any such changes, and
    c) there were any significant assumptions or interpretations underlying the measurement or presentation of the information.
- Compare the information for consistency with (i) management's responses to the foregoing inquiries, (ii) the basic financial statements, and (iii) other knowledge obtained during the audit of the basic financial statements.
- Obtain written representations from management (i) that it acknowledges its responsibility for the required supplementary information; (ii) about whether the required supplementary information is measured and presented in accordance with prescribed guidelines; (iii) about whether the methods of measurement or presentation have changed from those used in the prior period and, if so, the reasons for such changes; and (iv) about any significant assumptions or interpretations underlying the measurement or presentation of the required supplementary information

If the auditor is unable to complete the procedures listed above, the auditor should consider whether management contributed to the auditor's inability to complete the procedures. If the auditor concludes that the inability to complete the procedures was due to significant difficulties encountered in dealing with management, the auditor should inform those charged with governance.

2) Reporting
The auditor should include an ***other-matter paragraph*** in the auditor's report on the financial statements to refer to the required supplementary information in accordance with AU-C 706, *Emphasis-of-Matter Paragraphs and Other-Matter Paragraphs in the Independent Auditor's Report*.

The other-matter paragraph should include language to explain the following circumstances, as applicable:
- The required supplementary information is included, and the auditor has applied the procedures listed above.
- The required supplementary information is omitted.
- Some required supplementary information is missing and some is presented in accordance with the prescribed guidelines.
- The auditor has identified material departures from the prescribed guidelines.
- The auditor is unable to complete the procedures listed above.
- The auditor has unresolved doubts about whether the required supplementary information is presented in accordance with prescribed guidelines.

If **all of the required supplementary information is omitted**, the other-matter paragraph should include the following elements:
- A statement that management has omitted [*description of the missing required supplementary information*] that [*identify the applicable financial reporting framework (for example, accounting principles generally accepted in the United States of America)*] require to be presented to supplement the basic financial statements
- A statement that such missing information, although not a part of the basic financial statements, is required by [*identify designated accounting standards setter*], who considers it to be an essential part of financial reporting for placing the basic financial statements in an appropriate operational, economic, or historical context
- A statement that the auditor's opinion on the basic financial statements is not affected by the missing information

b. PCAOB requirements (AS 2705, Required Supplementary Information)
The PCAOB requirements are similar with respect to procedures. The PCAOB requirements differ regarding reporting on required supplementary information and the differences are summarized below.

1) Reporting on Required Supplementary Information
Since the supplementary information is not audited and is **not** a required part of the basic financial statements, the auditor need **not add an explanatory paragraph** to the report on the audited financial statements to refer to the supplementary information or to his or her limited procedures, *except in any of the following circumstances*:
- the supplementary information that GAAP requires to be presented in the circumstances is omitted
- the auditor has concluded that the measurement or presentation of the supplementary information departs materially from prescribed guidelines
- the auditor is unable to complete the prescribed procedures
- the auditor is unable to remove substantial doubts about whether the supplementary information conforms to prescribed guidelines.

Since the required supplementary information does not change the standards of financial accounting and reporting used for the preparation of the entity's basic financial statements, the circumstances described above do not affect the auditor's opinion on the fairness of presentation of such financial statements in conformity with generally accepted accounting principles.

If the entity includes, with the supplementary information, an indication that the auditor performed any procedures regarding the information without also indicating that the auditor does **not** express an opinion on the information presented, the auditor's report on the audited financial statements should be expanded to include a disclaimer on the information or, if appropriate, an opinion on whether the information is fairly stated in all material respects in relation to the financial statements taken as a whole.

In order to report on whether supplementary information is fairly stated, in all material respects, in relation to the financial statements as a whole, the auditor should determine that all of the following conditions are met:
- The supplementary information was derived from, and relates directly to, the underlying accounting and other records used to prepare the financial statements.
- The supplementary information relates to the same period as the financial statements.
- The auditor issued an audit report on the financial statements that contained neither an adverse opinion nor a disclaimer of opinion.
- The supplementary information will accompany the entity's audited financial statements, or such audited financial statements will be made readily available by the entity.

The auditor has no responsibility for the consideration of *subsequent events* with respect to the supplementary information.

c. Supplementary information (AU-C 725)
The AICPA and PCAOB (AS 2701: *Auditing Supplemental Information Accompanying Audited Financial Statements*) requirements (procedures and reporting) are essentially the same.

1) Reporting
   i. Supplementary information presented with the financial statements
   When the entity presents the supplementary information with the financial statements, the auditor should report on the supplementary information in either:
   - an other-matter paragraph or
   - in a separate report on the supplementary information

   When the audited financial statements are not presented with the supplementary information, the auditor should report on the supplementary information in a separate report. When reporting separately on the supplementary information, the report should include, in addition to the elements just listed, a reference to the report on the financial statements, the date of that report, the nature of the opinion expressed on the financial statements, and any report modifications.

2) Adverse opinion or disclaimer of opinion on the audited financial statements
   When the auditor's report on the audited financial statements contains an adverse opinion or a disclaimer of opinion and the auditor has been engaged to report on whether supplementary information is fairly stated, in all material respects, in relation to such financial statements as a whole, **the auditor is precluded from expressing an opinion on the supplementary information**.

   When permitted by law or regulation, the auditor may withdraw from the engagement to report on the supplementary information. If the auditor does not withdraw, the auditor's report on the supplementary information should state that because of the significance of the matter disclosed in the auditor's report, it is inappropriate to, and the auditor does not, express an opinion on the supplementary information.

3) Material misstatement in the supplementary information
If the auditor concludes, on the basis of the procedures performed, that the supplementary information is materially misstated in relation to the financial statements as a whole, the auditor should discuss the matter with management and propose appropriate revision of the supplementary information. If management does not revise the supplementary information, the auditor should either
- modify the auditor's opinion on the supplementary information and describe the misstatement in the auditor's report, or
- if a separate report is being issued on the supplementary information, withhold the auditor's report on the supplementary information.

4) Report Date
The date of the auditor's report on the supplementary information, in relation to the financial statements as a whole, should not be earlier than the date on which the auditor completed the required procedures.

Multiple Choice

AUD 4-Q88 through AUD 4-Q90

5. Single statements

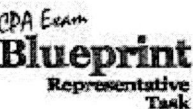

> Identify the factors an auditor should consider when reporting on the audit of a single financial statement.

> *Hint*: All relevant auditing standards are applicable to the audit of a single financial statement.

a. Objective
The objective of the auditor, when applying generally accepted auditing standards (GAAS) in an audit of a single financial statement or of a specific element, account, or item of a financial statement, is to address appropriately the special considerations that are relevant to
- the acceptance of the engagement;
- the planning and performance of that engagement; and
- forming an opinion and reporting on the single financial statement or the specific element, account, or item of a financial statement.

b. Requirements
1) Understanding
The auditor should obtain an understanding of
- the purpose for which the single financial statement or specific element of a financial statement is prepared,
- the intended users, and
- the steps taken by management to determine that the application of the financial reporting framework is acceptable in the circumstances.

2) Interrelated items
In the case of an audit of a single financial statement or a specific element of a financial statement, the auditor should perform procedures on interrelated items as necessary to meet the objective of the audit.

> *Example:* In the case of an audit of a specific element is based upon stockholders' equity, the auditor should perform procedures necessary to obtain sufficient appropriate audit evidence to enable the auditor to express an opinion about financial position, excluding matters related to classification or disclosure that are not relevant to the audit of the specific element.

3) Materiality
AU-C 320, *Materiality in Planning and Performing an Audit*, requires the auditor to determine, when establishing the overall audit strategy, materiality for the financial statements as a whole. In the case of an audit of a single financial statement, the auditor should determine materiality for the single financial statement being reported on, rather than for the complete set of financial statements.

c. Reporting

If, in conjunction with an engagement to audit the entity's complete set of financial statements, the auditor undertakes an engagement to audit a single financial statement or a specific element of a financial statement, the auditor should

- issue a separate auditor's report and express a separate opinion for each engagement.
- indicate in the report on a specific element of a financial statement the date of the auditor's report on the complete set of financial statements and the nature of opinion expressed on those financial statements under an appropriate heading.

An audited single financial statement, or an audited specific element of a financial statement, may be published together with the entity's audited complete set of financial statements, **provided that the presentation of the single financial statement, or the specific element, is sufficiently differentiated from the complete set of financial statements**. The auditor should also differentiate the report on the single financial statement, or the specific element of a financial statement, from the report on the complete set of financial statements.

If the auditor concludes that the presentation of the audited single financial statement, or the audited specific element, **does not differentiate it sufficiently** from the complete set of financial statements, the auditor should ask management to remedy the situation. The auditor should not release the auditor's report containing the opinion on the single financial statement, or the specific element of a financial statement, until satisfied with the differentiation.

1) Modified opinion, emphasis-of-matter paragraph, or other-matter paragraph in the auditor's report on the entity's complete set of financial statements

If the opinion in the **auditor's report on an entity's complete set of financial statements is modified**, the auditor should determine the effect that this may have on the auditor's opinion on a single financial statement, or a specific element of those financial statements, in accordance with AU-C 705, *Modifications to the Opinion in the Independent Auditor's Report*.

In the case of an audit of a specific element of a financial statement, if the auditor's modified opinion on the entity's complete set of financial statements as a whole, is relevant to the audit of the specific element, the auditor should

- express an adverse opinion on the specific element when the modification of the auditor's opinion on the complete set of financial statements as a whole arises from a material misstatement in such financial statements (i.e., **GAAP violation**).
- disclaim an opinion on the specific element when the modification of the auditor's opinion on the complete set of financial statements as a whole arises from an inability to obtain sufficient appropriate audit evidence (i.e., **scope restriction**).

If the **auditor concludes that it is necessary to express an adverse opinion or disclaim an opinion on the entity's complete set of financial statements as a whole**, an unmodified opinion on a specific element in the same auditor's report would contradict the adverse opinion, or disclaimer of opinion, on the entity's complete set of financial statements as a whole, and would be tantamount to expressing a piecemeal opinion.

In the context of a separate audit of a specific element that is included in those financial statements, when the auditor nevertheless considers it appropriate to express an unmodified opinion on that specific element, the auditor should only do so if
- that opinion is expressed in an auditor's report that is neither published together with nor otherwise accompanies the auditor's report containing the adverse opinion or disclaimer of opinion and
- the specific element does not constitute a major portion of the entity's complete set of financial statements or the specific element is not, or is not based upon, the entity's stockholders' equity or net income or the equivalent.

A single financial statement is deemed to constitute a major portion of a complete set of financial statements. Therefore, the auditor should not express an unmodified opinion on a single financial statement of a complete set of financial statements if the auditor has expressed an adverse opinion or disclaimed an opinion on the complete set of financial statements as a whole, even if the auditor's report on the single financial statement is neither published together with nor otherwise accompanies the auditor's report containing the adverse opinion or disclaimer of opinion.

If the auditor's report on an entity's complete set of financial statements includes an emphasis-of-matter paragraph or an other-matter paragraph that is relevant to the audit of the single financial statement, or the specific element, the auditor should include a similar emphasis-of-matter paragraph or an other-matter paragraph in the auditor's report on the single financial statement, or the specific element, in accordance with AU-C 706, *Emphasis-of-Matter Paragraphs and Other-Matter Paragraphs in the Independent Auditor's Report*.

2) Reporting on an incomplete presentation but one that is otherwise in accordance with generally accepted accounting principles (GAAP)
   When the auditor reports on an incomplete presentation but one that is otherwise in accordance with GAAP, the auditor should include an emphasis-of-matter paragraph in the auditor's report that
   - states the purpose for which the presentation is prepared and refers to a note in the financial statements that describes the basis of presentation, and
   - indicates that the presentation is not intended to be a complete presentation of the entity's assets, liabilities, revenues, or expenses.

Multiple Choice

AUD 4-Q91 through AUD 4-Q94

6. Special-purpose and other country frameworks

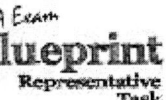

> **Identify the factors an auditor should consider when reporting on the audit of financial statements prepared in accordance with a financial reporting framework generally accepted in another country, when the financial statements are intended for use outside of the United States.**

   a. Performance
   When auditing financial statements prepared in accordance with a financial reporting framework generally accepted in another country that are **intended for use only outside the United States**, the auditor should comply with GAAS (except for requirements related to the form and content of the report).

   The auditor should determine whether the application of GAAS requires special consideration in the circumstances of the engagement.

   If the auditor is engaged to audit financial statements prepared in accordance with a financial reporting framework generally accepted in another country, and the agreed-upon terms of engagement require the auditor to apply either the auditing standards of that country or International Standards on Auditing (ISAs), the auditor should obtain an understanding of and apply those relevant auditing standards.

   b. Reporting
   1) **Reporting – use only outside the United States**
      If the auditor is reporting on financial statements prepared in accordance with a financial reporting framework generally accepted in another country that are intended for use only outside the United States, the **auditor should report using**
      - **either** a **U.S. form of report** that reflects that the financial statements being reported on have been prepared in accordance with a financial reporting framework generally accepted in another country, to include, both
        a) the elements required by AU-C 700 and
        b) a statement that refers to the note to the financial statements that describes the basis of presentation of the financial statements on which the auditor is reporting, including identification of the country of origin of the accounting principles,
      - **or** the report **form and content of the other country** (or, if applicable, as set forth in the ISAs), provided that
        a) such a report would be issued by auditors in the other country in similar circumstances,
        b) the auditor understands and has obtained sufficient appropriate audit evidence to support the statements contained in such a report, and
        c) the auditor has complied with the reporting standards of that country and identifies the other country in the report.

2) **Reporting – use in the United States**
   If financial statements prepared in accordance with a financial reporting framework generally accepted in another country are also intended for use in the United States, the auditor should report using the U.S. form of report.

   In addition, the auditor should include in the auditor's report an emphasis-of-matter paragraph that
   - identifies the financial reporting framework used in the preparation of the financial statements,
   - refers to the note to the financial statements that describes that framework, and
   - indicates that such framework differs from accounting principles generally accepted in the United States of America.

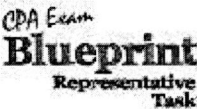

> **Identify the factors an auditor should consider when reporting on the audit of financial statements prepared in accordance with a special-purpose framework, including cash basis, tax basis, regulatory basis, contractual basis or other basis.**

> *Hint*: The AICPA refers to a financial reporting framework other than GAAP as a **special purpose framework.** A special purpose framework is one of the following bases of accounting: Cash basis, Tax basis, Regulatory basis, Contractual basis, and Other-basis. The cash basis, tax basis, regulatory basis, and other basis of accounting are commonly referred to as *other comprehensive bases of accounting* (term used by the PCAOB).

c. Requirements
   The auditor should determine the acceptability of the financial reporting framework applied in the preparation of the financial statements.

   In an audit of special purpose financial statements, the auditor should obtain an understanding of the following:
   - the purpose for which the financial statements are prepared,
   - the intended users, and
   - the steps taken by management to determine that the applicable financial reporting framework is acceptable in the circumstances.

   In an audit of special purpose financial statements, the auditor should obtain the agreement of management that it acknowledges and understands its responsibility to include all informative disclosures that are appropriate for the special purpose framework used to prepare the entity's financial statements, which include
   - a description of the special purpose framework, including a summary of significant accounting policies, and how the framework differs from GAAP, the effects of which need not be quantified.
   - informative disclosures similar to those required by GAAP, in the case of special purpose financial statements that contain items that are the same as, or similar to, those in financial statements prepared in accordance with GAAP.
   - a description of any significant interpretations of the contract on which the special purpose financial statements are based, in the case of special purpose financial statements prepared in accordance with a contractual basis of accounting.
   - additional disclosures beyond those specifically required by the framework that may be necessary for the special purpose financial statements to achieve fair presentation.

In planning and performing an audit of special purpose financial statements, the auditor should adapt and apply all AU-C sections relevant to the audit as necessary in the circumstances of the engagement.

d. Reporting

AU-C 700 addresses the form and content of the auditor's report. The auditor's report should also describe the purpose for which the financial statements are prepared, or refer to a note in the special purpose financial statements that contains that information, when the financial statements are prepared in accordance with
- a regulatory or contractual basis of accounting or
- an other-basis of accounting, and the auditor is required to restrict use of the auditor's report.

1) Alerting readers in an emphasis-of-matter paragraph that the financial statements are prepared in accordance with a special purpose framework

    Except for general use regulatory basis financial statements, the auditor's report on special purpose financial statements should include an emphasis-of-matter paragraph, under an appropriate heading, that does the following:
    - indicates that the financial statements are prepared in accordance with the applicable special purpose framework,
    - refers to the note to the financial statements that describes that framework, and
    - states that the special purpose framework is a basis of accounting other than GAAP.

    If the special purpose financial statements are prepared in accordance with a regulatory basis of accounting intended for general use, the auditor should not include the emphasis-of-matter or other-matter paragraphs.

2) Auditor's Report Prescribed by Law or Regulation

    If the auditor is required by law or regulation to use a specific layout, form, or wording of the auditor's report, the auditor's report should refer to GAAS only if the auditor's report includes, at a minimum, each of the following elements:
    - A title.
    - An addressee.
    - An introductory paragraph that identifies the special purpose financial statements audited.
    - A description of the responsibility of management for the preparation and fair presentation of the special purpose financial statements.
    - A reference to management's responsibility for determining that the applicable financial reporting framework is acceptable in the circumstances.
    - A description of the purpose for which the financial statements are prepare.
    - A description of the auditor's responsibility to express an opinion on the special purpose financial statements and the scope of the audit, that includes
        a) A reference to GAAS and, if applicable, the law or regulation.
        b) A description of an audit in accordance with those standards.
    - An opinion paragraph containing an expression of opinion on the special purpose financial statements and a reference to the special purpose framework used to prepare the financial statements (including identifying the origin of the framework) and, if applicable, an opinion on whether the special purpose financial statements are presented fairly, in all material respects, in accordance with GAAP when they are general use regulatory basis financial statements
    - **An emphasis-of-matter paragraph that indicates that the financial statements are prepared in accordance with a special purpose framework.**

- **An other-matter paragraph that restricts the use of the auditor's report when required.**
- The auditor's signature.
- The auditor's city and state.
- The date of the auditor's report.

If the prescribed specific layout, form, or wording of the auditor's report is not acceptable or would cause an auditor to make a statement that the auditor has no basis to make, the auditor should reword the prescribed form of report or attach a separate report.

Multiple Choice

AUD 4-Q95 through AUD 4-Q99

7. Letter for underwriters and filings with the SEC

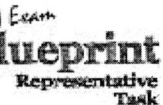

> **Identify the factors an auditor should consider when engaged to issue a comfort letter in connection with an entity's financial statements that are included in a securities offering.**

AS 6101, *Letters for Underwriters and Certain Other Requesting Parties* [PCAOB] and AU-C 920, *Letters for Underwriters and Certain Other Requesting Parties* [AICPA] are substantially the same. AS 6101 is somewhat more detailed.

a. Scope
Comfort letters are letters from auditors regarding nonissuer entity's financial statements included in registration statements filed with the Securities and Exchange Commission (SEC) under the Securities Act of 1933 (the 1933 Act) and other securities offerings. For example, inclusion of the nonissuer entity's financial statements may be required by either Rule 3-05 or 3-09 of Regulation S-X.

Comfort letters exist because underwriters, among others, could be liable if any part of a registration statement contains material omissions or misstatements per Section 11 of the 1933 Act. An affirmative defense for an underwriter is to demonstrate that, after a reasonable investigation, the underwriter has reasonable grounds to believe that no material omissions or misstatements existed in a securities offering. Consequently, underwriters may request auditors to assist them in developing a record of reasonable investigation. What constitutes a "reasonable investigation" of unaudited financial information, sufficient to satisfy an underwriter's purposes, has never been authoritatively established.

An auditor's responsibilities when engaged to issue comfort letters:
- Auditors can only comment on matters to which their professional expertise is substantially relevant.
- Comfort letters provide, at most, negative assurance about any significant matters affecting the financial information.

The subjects that may be covered in a comfort letter include:
- the independence of the auditor.
- whether the audited financial statements included in the securities offering comply regarding form, in all material respects, with the applicable accounting requirements of the 1933 Act and the related rules and regulations adopted by the SEC.
- unaudited financial statements, condensed interim financial information, capsule financial information, pro forma financial information, financial forecasts, management's discussion and analysis (MD&A), and changes in selected financial statement items during a period subsequent to the date and period of the latest financial statements included in the securities offering.
- tables, statistics, and other financial information included in the securities offering.
- negative assurance about whether certain nonfinancial statement information included in the securities offering complies regarding form, in all material respects, with Regulation S-K.

b. Format and contents of comfort letters
1) Dating
The letter ordinarily is dated on or shortly before the effective date (that is, the date on which the registration statement becomes effective).

On rare occasions, letters have been requested to be dated at or shortly before the filing date (that is, the date on which the registration statement is first filed with the SEC).

The underwriting agreement ordinarily specifies the date, often referred to as the "cutoff date," to which certain procedures described in the letter are to relate (for example, a date five days before the date of the letter). The letter should state that the inquiries and other procedures described in the letter did not cover the period from the cutoff date to the date of the letter.

2) Addressee
The letter should be addressed only to the requesting party, or both the requesting party and the entity, and should not be provided to any other parties.

3) Introductory paragraph
The letter should contain an introductory paragraph that identifies the financial statements and the securities offering.

4) Auditor's report
In the letter, the auditor should reference the report on the audited financial statements included in the securities offering.

When the auditor's report on the audited financial statements included in the securities offering contains an emphasis-of-matter or other-matter paragraph addressing matters other than consistency of application of accounting policies, the auditor should refer to that fact in the comfort letter and discuss the subject matter of the paragraph.

The auditor should not provide negative assurance regarding the auditor's report or regarding financial statements that have been audited and are reported on in the securities offering by other auditors. The auditor should not imply that he or she is assuming reasonability for the sufficiency of the procedures for the requesting party's purposes.

5) Independence
The auditor should state in the comfort letter that the auditor is independent, or the date through which the auditor was independent, and identify the applicable independence rules.

6) Compliance with SEC Requirements
If requested, the auditor can include an opinion on whether the financial statements covered by the auditor's report comply (in form) with the pertinent accounting requirements adopted by the SEC. The auditor's opinion should refer to compliance as to form, in all material respects, with the applicable accounting requirements adopted by the SEC (i.e., rules of 1933 Act).

If a material departure from the pertinent rules and regulations adopted by the SEC exists, the auditor should disclose the departure in the comfort letter.

The auditor should express an opinion on compliance as to form only with respect to financial statements that the auditor has audited. When the financial statements or financial statement schedules have not been audited, the auditor is limited to providing negative assurance on compliance as to form.

The auditor should not comment in a comfort letter on compliance as to form of MD&A with rules and regulations adopted by the SEC.

7) Commenting in a Comfort Letter on Information Other Than Audited Financial Statements
    i. *General*
       When commenting in a comfort letter on information other than audited financial statements, the auditor should
       - describe the procedures performed by the auditor.
       - describe the criteria specified by the requesting party.
       - state that the procedures performed, with respect to interim periods, may not disclose matters of significance regarding certain matters about which negative assurance is requested.

       The auditor should not, in the comfort letter
       - make any statements, or imply, that the auditor has applied procedures that the auditor determined to be necessary or sufficient for the requesting party's purposes.
       - use terms of uncertain meaning (such as *general review*, *limited review*, *reconcile*, *check*, or *test*) in describing the work unless the procedures encompassed by these terms are described in the comfort letter.
       - make a statement that nothing else has come to the auditor's attention that would be of interest to the requesting party as a result of carrying out the specified procedures.

       When the report on the audited financial statements in the securities offering is a modified report, the auditor should consider the effect on providing negative assurance in the comfort letter, regarding subsequent interim financial information included in the securities offering, or regarding an absence of specified subsequent changes.

    ii. *Knowledge of Internal Control*
        The auditor should obtain an understanding of the entity's internal control over financial reporting for both annual and interim periods when commenting in a comfort letter on
        - unaudited interim financial information, including unaudited condensed interim financial information;
        - capsule financial information;
        - a financial forecast when historical financial statements provide a basis for one or more significant assumptions for the forecast; or
        - subsequent changes in specified financial statement items.

    iii. *Unaudited Interim Financial Information*
         The auditor should provide negative assurance on unaudited interim financial information, included in the securities offering, only if the auditor has conducted a review of the interim financial information in accordance with GAAS applicable to reviews of interim financial information.

         If the auditor has not conducted a review in accordance with GAAS applicable to reviews of interim financial information, the auditor is limited to reporting procedures performed and findings obtained.

         The negative assurance provided regarding such unaudited interim financial information should be about whether
         - any material modifications should be made to the unaudited interim financial information for it to be in accordance with the applicable financial reporting framework, and

- the unaudited interim financial information complies, as to form, in all material respects with the applicable accounting requirements of the 1933 Act and the related rules and regulations adopted by the SEC, if applicable.

If the auditor states in the comfort letter he or she has issued a review report on the unaudited interim financial information, the auditor should attach the review report to the letter.

The auditor should specifically identify any unaudited interim financial information indicating when interim financial information was not audited in accordance with GAAS and, the auditor does not express an opinion concerning such information.

iv. *Capsule Financial Information*
The auditor should not provide negative assurance regarding whether the selected capsule financial information is in accordance with the applicable financial reporting framework unless
- the auditor has performed a review of the financial statements, underlying the capsule financial information, in accordance with GAAS applicable to reviews of interim financial information, and
- the selected capsule financial information, is in accordance with minimum disclosure requirements of the applicable financial reporting framework for interim financial information.

If these conditions have not been met, the auditor is limited to reporting procedures performed and findings obtained.

The auditor should not provide negative assurance on selected capsule financial information regarding whether the dollar amounts were determined on a basis substantially consistent with that of the corresponding amounts in the audited financial statements, unless the auditor has performed a review of the financial statements underlying the capsule financial information, in accordance with GAAS applicable to reviews of interim financial information. Otherwise, the auditor is limited to reporting procedures performed and findings obtained.

When the auditor is requested by the requesting party to provide negative assurance on unaudited condensed interim financial information, or information extracted therefrom, for a period ending after the latest financial statements included in the securities offering, the requirements for negative assurance discussed above. When the auditor provides negative assurance on such information, a copy of the unaudited interim financial information should be attached to the comfort letter.

v. *Pro Forma Financial Information*
The auditor should not comment in a comfort letter on pro forma financial information unless the auditor has an appropriate level of knowledge of the accounting and financial reporting practices of the entity.

The auditor should not provide negative assurance in a comfort letter on pro forma financial information, including negative assurance on
- the application of pro forma adjustments to historical amounts,
- the compilation of pro forma financial information, or
- whether the pro forma financial information complies as to form in all material respects with the applicable accounting requirements of Rule 11-02 of Regulation S-X, or with the pro forma bases as described in the pro forma

financial information, as applicable, unless the auditor has obtained the required knowledge of the accounting and financial reporting practices of the entity and has performed an audit of the annual financial statements, or a review of the interim financial information, in accordance with GAAS applicable to reviews of interim financial information.

vi. *Financial Forecasts*
When performing procedures agreed to with the requesting party on a financial forecast and commenting thereon in a comfort letter, the auditor should
- obtain an understanding of the entity's internal control over financial reporting for both annual and interim periods, as previously described;
- perform procedures required by AT section 301, *Financial Forecasts and Projections*, for reporting on the compilation of a forecast;
- issue a report on the compilation of prospective financial information in accordance with AT section 301 and attach the report thereon to the comfort letter; and
- perform additional procedures as requested by the requesting party and report the findings in the comfort letter.

The auditor should not provide negative assurance on the results of procedures performed on a financial forecast.

The auditor should not provide negative assurance with respect to compliance of the financial forecast with Rule 11-03 of Regulation S-X unless the auditor has performed an examination of the financial forecast in accordance with AT section 301.

If a financial forecast that the auditor has not examined is included in the securities offering, the auditor should not issue a comfort letter unless the financial forecast is accompanied by an indication that the auditor has not examined the financial forecast and, therefore, does not express an opinion on it.

vii. *Subsequent Changes*
The auditor should provide negative assurance in the comfort letter regarding subsequent changes in specified financial statement items only as of a date less than 135 days from the end of the most recent period for which the auditor has performed an audit or a review.

When the requesting party requests negative assurance regarding subsequent changes in specified financial statement items as of a date 135 days or more from the end of the most recent period for which the auditor has performed an audit or a review, the auditor is limited to reporting procedures performed and findings obtained.

In commenting on subsequent changes, the auditor should not characterize subsequent changes using ambiguous terms, such as referring to the change as "adverse." The auditor should note in the comfort letter if there has been a change in the application of the requirements of the applicable financial reporting framework.

The auditor should comment only on the occurrence of subsequent changes in specified financial statement items that are not disclosed in the securities offering. Accordingly, the auditor should include the phrase *except for changes, increases, or decreases that the securities offering discloses have occurred or may occur* in the comfort letter when it has come to the auditor's attention that a change, increase, or decrease has occurred during the change period, and the amount of such change, increase, or decrease is disclosed in the securities offering. This phrase need not be included in the letter when no changes, increases, or decreases in the specified financial statement items are disclosed in the securities offering.

The auditor should identify, in the comfort letter in both draft and final form, the dates as of which, and periods for which, data at the cut-off date and data for the change period are to be compared, whether or not specified in the underwriting agreement.

viii. *Tables, Statistics, and Other Financial Information*
The auditor should not comment in a comfort letter on tables, statistics, and other financial information appearing in the securities offering unless the information
- is expressed in dollars (or percentages derived from such dollar amounts) and has been obtained from accounting records that are subject to internal control over financial reporting, or
- has been derived directly from such accounting records by analysis or computation.

The auditor should not comment, in a comfort letter, on quantitative information that has been obtained from accounting records, unless the information is subject to the same controls over financial reporting as the dollar amounts.

The auditor should not comment in a comfort letter on tables, statistics, and other financial information relating to an unaudited period unless the auditor has
- performed an audit of the entity's financial statements for a period including, or immediately prior to, the unaudited period or completed an audit for a later period, or
- otherwise obtained knowledge of the entity's internal control over financial reporting.

The auditor should not use the term *presents fairly* in comments concerning tables, statistics, and other financial information and should not comment on
- information subject to legal interpretation, such as beneficial share ownership;
- nonfinancial data presented in MD&A, unless the auditor has conducted an examination or review of MD&A in accordance with AT 701, *Management's Discussion and Analysis*; or
- matters merely because the auditor is capable of reading, counting, measuring, or performing other functions that might be applicable.

The auditor's comments in the comfort letter concerning tables, statistics, and other financial information included in the securities offering should include
- a clear identification of the specific information commented on;
- a description of the procedures performed; and
- the findings, expressed in terms of agreement between items compared.

With respect to the acceptability of methods of allocation used in deriving the figures commented on, the auditor should comment only to the extent to which such allocation is made in, or can be derived directly by analysis or computation from, the entity's accounting records. Such comments, if made, should make clear that
- such allocations may be, to a substantial extent, arbitrary.
- the method of allocation used is not the only acceptable method.

- other acceptable methods of allocation might produce significantly different results.

The comfort letter should state that the auditor makes no representations regarding
- any matter of legal interpretation;
- the completeness or adequacy of disclosure; and
- the adequacy of the procedures followed, and that such procedures would not necessarily disclose material misstatements or omissions in the information to which the comments relate.

ix. *Compliance as to Form with Regulation S-K*
The auditor should not provide negative assurance about whether certain financial information in registration statements, included because of specific requirements of Regulation S-K, is in conformity with the disclosure requirements of Regulation S-K, unless the following conditions are met:
- The information is derived, directly, or by analysis or computation, from the accounting records subject to internal control over financial reporting.
- The information is capable of evaluation against reasonable criteria that have been established by the SEC.

The auditor should not express an opinion on conformity with the disclosure requirements of Regulation S-K.

x. *Concluding Paragraph*
The comfort letter should include a concluding paragraph restricting the use of the comfort letter for the information of the addressees and to assist the requesting parties in connection with the securities offering.

xi. *Disclosure of Subsequently Discovered Matters*
The auditor should inform the entity when the auditor has discovered matters that require mention in the final comfort letter but were not mentioned in the draft letter that has been furnished to the requesting party. If the entity decides that disclosure will not be made in the securities offering, the auditor should inform the entity that the matters will be mentioned in the comfort letter and should recommend that the requesting party be informed promptly.

Multiple Choice

AUD 4-Q100 through AUD 4-Q101

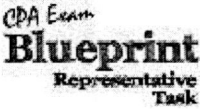

> **Identify the factors an auditor should consider in connection with audited financial statements of a nonissuer that are included in a registration statement.**

    c. Compliance with SEC requirements
The accountants may be requested to express an opinion on whether the financial statements covered by their report, comply as to form with the pertinent accounting requirements adopted by the SEC. This may be done substantially by including the following in the comfort letter:

In our opinion [include phrase "except as disclosed in the registration statement," if applicable], the [identify the financial statements and financial statement schedules] audited by us and included (incorporated by reference) in the registration statement comply as to form in all material respects with the applicable accounting requirements of the Act and the related rules and regulations adopted by the SEC.

If there is a material departure from the pertinent rules and regulations adopted by the SEC, the departure should be disclosed in the letter.

Accountants may provide positive assurance on compliance as to form with requirements under the rules and regulations adopted by the SEC only with respect to those rules and regulations applicable to the form and content of financial statements and financial statement schedules that they have audited.

Accountants are limited to providing **negative assurance** on compliance as to form when the financial statements or financial statement schedules have not been audited.

8. Alerts that restrict the use of written communication

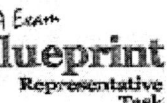

> **Identify the factors an auditor should consider when restricting the use of written communication by including an alert when the potential exists for the written communication to be misunderstood or taken out of context.**

a. Scope
AU-C 905, *Alert That Restricts the Use of the Auditor's Written Communication*, addresses the auditor's responsibility, when required or the auditor decides, to include in the auditor's report or other written communication issued by the auditor in connection with an engagement conducted in accordance with generally accepted auditing standards (GAAS) (referred to as auditor's written communication) ***language that restricts the use of the auditor's written communication***. This language is referred to as an alert.

In an auditor's report, such language is included in an other-matter paragraph.

The objective of the auditor is to restrict the use of the auditor's written communication by including an alert when the potential exists for the auditor's written communication to be misunderstood if taken out of the context in which the auditor's written communication is intended to be used.

b. Requirements
1) Alert That Restricts the Use of the Auditor's Written Communication
The auditor's written communication should include an alert, in a separate paragraph, that restricts its use when the subject matter of the auditor's written communication is based on
- measurement or disclosure criteria that are determined by the auditor to be suitable only for a limited number of users who can be presumed to have an adequate understanding of the criteria,
- measurement or disclosure criteria that are available only to the specified parties, or
- matters identified by the auditor during the course of the audit engagement when the identification of such matters is not the primary objective of the audit engagement (commonly referred to as a by-product report).

The alert that restricts the use of the auditor's written communication should
- state that the auditor's written communication is intended solely for the information and use of the specified parties.
- identify the specified parties for whom use is intended. Generally, the specified parties should only include management, those charged with governance, others within the entity, the parties to the contract or agreement, or the regulatory agencies to whose jurisdiction the entity is subject, as appropriate in the circumstances.
- state that the auditor's written communication is not intended to be and should not be used by anyone other than the specified parties.

2) Alert for Engagements Performed in Accordance with *Government Auditing Standards*
The alert language described above should not be used when
- the engagement is performed in accordance with *Government Auditing Standards*, and
- the auditor's written communication pursuant to that engagement is issued in accordance with
    a) AU-C 265, *Communicating Internal Control Related Matters Identified in an Audit*;

b) AU-C 806, *Reporting on Compliance with Aspects of Contractual Agreements or Regulatory Requirements in Connection with Audited Financial Statements;* or
c) AU-C 935, *Compliance Audits.*

Instead, the alert should
- describe the purpose of the auditor's written communication and
- state that the auditor's written communication is not suitable for any other purpose.

9. Additional requirements under Government Accountability Office Government Audit Standards

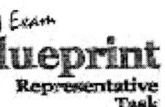

> **Identify requirements under Government Accountability Office Government Auditing Standards related to reporting on internal control over financial reporting and compliance with provisions of law, regulations, contracts and grant agreements that have a material effect on the financial statements.**

When providing an opinion or a disclaimer on financial statements, auditors should also report on internal control over financial reporting and on compliance with provisions of laws, regulations, contracts, or grant agreements that have a material effect on the financial statements.

Auditors report on internal control and compliance, regardless of whether or not they identify internal control deficiencies or instances of noncompliance.

Auditors should include, either in the same, or in separate report(s) a description of the scope of the auditors' testing of internal control over financial reporting and of compliance with provisions of laws, regulations, contracts, or grant agreements.

Auditors should also state in the reports whether the tests they performed provided sufficient, appropriate evidence to support opinions on the effectiveness of internal control and on compliance with provisions of laws, regulations, contracts, or grant agreements.

The objective of the GAGAS requirement for reporting on internal control over financial reporting differs from the objective of an examination of internal control in accordance with the AICPA Statement on Standards for Attestation Engagements (SSAE), which is to express an opinion on the design, or the design and operating effectiveness, of an entity's internal control, as applicable. To form a basis for expressing such an opinion, the auditor would need to plan and perform the examination to provide a high level of assurance about whether the entity maintained, in all material respects, effective internal control over financial reporting as of a point in time or for a specified period of time. If auditors issue an opinion on internal control, the opinion would satisfy the GAGAS requirement for reporting on internal control.

If auditors report separately (including separate reports bound in the same document) on internal control over financial reporting and on compliance with provisions of laws, regulations, contracts, and grant agreements, they should state, in the auditors' report on the financial statements, that they are issuing those additional reports. They should include a reference to the separate reports and also state that the reports on internal control over financial reporting and on compliance with provisions of laws, regulations, contracts, and grant agreements, are an integral part of a GAGAS audit in considering the audited entity's internal control over financial reporting and compliance.

When performing GAGAS financial audits, auditors should communicate in the report on internal control over financial reporting and compliance, based upon the work performed,
- significant deficiencies and material weaknesses in internal control;
- instances of fraud and noncompliance with provisions of laws or regulations that have a material effect on the audit and any other instances that warrant the attention of those charged with governance;
- noncompliance with provisions of contracts or grant agreements that has a material effect on the audit; and
- abuse that has a material effect on the audit.

a. Deficiencies in Internal Control
The AICPA requirements to communicate, in writing, significant deficiencies and material weaknesses identified during an audit, form the basis for reporting significant deficiencies and

material weaknesses in the GAGAS report on internal control over financial reporting when deficiencies are identified during the audit.

b. Fraud, Noncompliance with Provisions of Laws, Regulations, Contracts, and Grant Agreements, and Abuse

When performing a GAGAS financial audit, and auditors conclude, based on sufficient, appropriate evidence, that any of the following either has occurred or is likely to have occurred, they should include in their report on internal control and compliance the relevant information about the following:

- fraud and noncompliance with provisions of laws or regulations that have a material effect on the financial statements or other financial data significant to the audit objectives, and any other instances that warrant the attention of those charged with governance;
- noncompliance with provisions of contracts or grant agreements that has a material effect on the determination of financial statement amounts or other financial data significant to the audit objectives; or
- abuse that is material, either quantitatively or qualitatively.

When auditors detect instances of noncompliance with provisions of contracts or grant agreements or abuse that have an effect on the financial statements or other financial data, significant to the audit objectives that are less than material but warrant the attention of those charged with governance, they should communicate those findings in writing to audited entity officials.

When auditors detect any instances of fraud, noncompliance with provisions of laws, regulations, contracts or grant agreements, or abuse that do not warrant the attention of those charged with governance, the auditors' determination of whether and how to communicate such instances to audited entity officials is a matter of professional judgment.

When fraud, noncompliance with provisions of laws, regulations, contracts, or grant agreements, or abuse either have occurred or are likely to have occurred, auditors may consult with authorities or legal counsel about whether publicly reporting such information would compromise investigative or legal proceedings. Auditors may limit their public reporting to matters that would not compromise those proceedings, and for example, report only on information that is already a part of the public record.

c. Presenting Findings in the Auditors' Report

When performing a GAGAS financial audit and presenting findings such as deficiencies in internal control, fraud, noncompliance with provisions of laws, regulations, contracts, or grant agreements, or abuse, auditors should develop the elements of the findings to the extent necessary, including findings related to deficiencies from the previous year that have not been remediated.

Clearly developed findings assist management or oversight officials of the audited entity in understanding the need for taking corrective action, and assist auditors in making recommendations for corrective action. If auditors sufficiently develop the elements of a finding, they may provide recommendations for corrective action.

Auditors should place their findings in perspective by describing the nature and extent of the issues being reported and the extent of the work performed that resulted in the finding. To give the reader a basis for judging the prevalence and consequences of these findings, auditors should, as appropriate, relate the instances identified to the population or the number of cases examined and quantify the results in terms of dollar value or other measures. If the results cannot be projected, auditors should limit their conclusions appropriately.

1) Developing Elements of a Finding
   In a financial audit, findings may involve deficiencies in internal control; noncompliance with provisions of laws, regulations, contracts, or grant agreements; fraud; or abuse.

   As part of a GAGAS audit, when auditors identify findings, auditors should plan and perform procedures to develop the elements of the findings that are relevant and necessary to achieve the audit objectives. The elements of a finding are discussed below.

   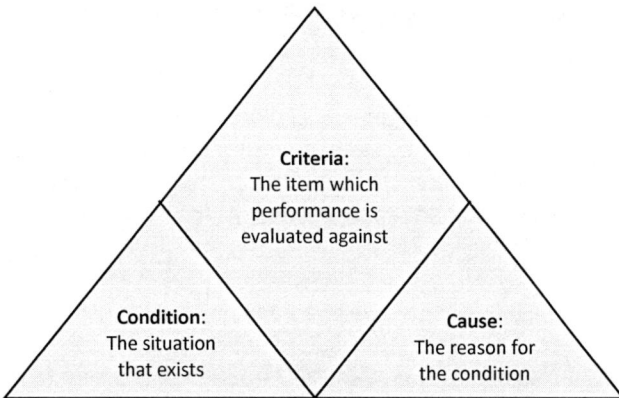

   Criteria: The laws, regulations, contracts, grant agreements, standards, measures, expected performance, defined business practices, and benchmarks against which performance is compared or evaluated. Criteria identify the required or desired state or expectation with respect to the program or operation. Criteria provide a context for evaluating evidence and understanding the findings.

   Condition: Condition is a situation that exists. The condition is determined and documented during the audit.

   Cause: The cause identifies the reason or explanation for the condition or the factor or factors responsible for the difference between the situation that exists (condition) and the required or desired state (criteria), which may also serve as a basis for recommendations for corrective actions. Common factors include poorly designed policies, procedures, or criteria; inconsistent, incomplete, or incorrect implementation; or factors beyond the control of program management. Auditors may assess whether the evidence provides a reasonable and convincing argument for why the stated cause is the key factor or **factors contributing to the difference between the condition and the criteria.**

   Effect or potential effect: The effect is a clear, logical link to establish the impact or potential impact of the difference between the situation that exists (condition) and the required or desired state (criteria). The effect or potential effect identifies the outcomes or consequences of the condition. When the audit objectives include identifying the actual or potential consequences of a condition that varies (either positively or negatively) from the criteria identified in the audit, "effect" is a measure of those consequences. Effect or potential effect may be used to demonstrate the need for corrective action in response to identified problems or relevant risks.

d. Reporting Findings Directly to Parties outside the Audited Entity
   Auditors should report known or likely fraud, noncompliance with provisions of laws, regulations, contracts, or grant agreements, or abuse directly to parties outside the audited entity in the following two circumstances.

- When entity management fails to satisfy legal or regulatory requirements to report such information to external parties specified in law or regulation, auditors should first communicate the failure to report such information to those charged with governance. If the audited entity still does not report this information to the specified external parties as soon as practicable after the auditors' communication with those charged with governance, then the auditors should report the information directly to the specified external parties.
- When entity management fails to take timely and appropriate steps to respond to known or likely fraud, noncompliance with provisions of laws, regulations, contracts, or grant agreements, or abuse that is **likely to have a material effect on the financial statements** and involves **funding received directly or indirectly from a government agency**, auditors should first report management's failure to take timely and appropriate steps to those charged with governance. If the audited entity still does not take timely and appropriate steps as soon as practicable after the auditors' communication with those charged with governance, then the auditors should report the entity's failure to take timely and appropriate steps directly to the funding agency.

The reporting described above is in addition to any legal requirements to report such information directly to parties outside the audited entity. Auditors should comply with these requirements even if they have resigned or been dismissed from the audit prior to its completion.

e. Reporting Confidential and Sensitive Information
When performing a GAGAS financial audit, if certain pertinent information is prohibited from public disclosure or is excluded from a report due to the confidential or sensitive nature of the information, auditors should disclose in the report that certain information has been omitted and the reason or other circumstances that make the omission necessary.

Certain information may be classified or may otherwise be prohibited from general disclosure by federal, state, or local laws or regulations. In such circumstances, auditors may issue a separate, classified, or limited use report containing such information and distribute the report only to persons authorized by law or regulation to receive it.

f. Distributing Reports
Distribution of reports completed in accordance with GAGAS depends on the relationship of the auditors to the audited organization and the nature of the information contained in the report. Auditors should document any limitation on report distribution. The following discussion outlines distribution for reports completed in accordance with GAGAS:
- **Audit organizations in government entities should distribute auditors' reports to those charged with governance, to the appropriate audited entity officials, and to the appropriate oversight bodies or organizations requiring or arranging for the audits.**
- **Internal audit organizations in government entities may also follow the Institute of Internal Auditors (IIA)** *International Standards for the Professional Practice of Internal Auditing*. **In accordance with GAGAS and IIA standards, the head of the internal audit organization should communicate results to the parties who can ensure that the results are given due consideration.**
- **Public accounting firms contracted to perform an audit in accordance with GAGAS should clarify report distribution responsibilities with the engaging organization. If the contracting firm is responsible for the distribution, it should reach agreement with the party contracting for the audit about which officials or** organizations will receive the report and the steps being taken to make the report available to the public.

Multiple Choice

AUD 4-Q102

Glossary: Forming Conclusions and Reporting

A

Analytical procedures – evaluations of financial information through analysis of plausible relationships among both financial and nonfinancial data

Applicable financial reporting framework – the financial reporting framework adopted by management and, when appropriate, those charged with governance in the preparation and fair presentation of the financial statements that is acceptable in view of the nature of the entity and the objective of the financial statements, or that is required by law or regulation

Audit of internal control over financial reporting (ICFR) – an audit of the design and operating effectiveness of an entity's internal control over financial reporting

B

Basic financial statements – financial statements presented in accordance with an applicable financial reporting framework as established by a designated accounting standards setter, excluding required supplementary information

C

Capsule financial information – unaudited summarized interim financial information for periods subsequent to the periods covered by the audited financial statements or unaudited interim financial information included in the securities offering

Carve-out method – method of addressing the services provided by a subservice organization, whereby management's description of the service organization's system identifies the nature of the services performed by the subservice organization, and excludes from the description and from the scope of the service auditor's engagement, the subservice organization's relevant control objectives and related controls

Change period – the period ending on the cut-off date and ordinarily beginning, for balance sheet items, immediately after the date of the latest balance sheet in the securities offering and, for income statement items, immediately after the latest period for which such items are presented in the securities offering

Closing date – the date on which the issuer of the securities or selling security holder delivers the securities in exchange for the proceeds of the offering

Comfort letter – a letter issued by an auditor in accordance with this section to requesting parties in connection with an entity's financial statements included in a securities offering

Comparative financial statements – a complete set of financial statements for one or more prior periods included for comparison with the financial statements of the current period

Comparative information – prior period information presented for purposes of comparison with current period amounts or disclosures that is not in the form of a complete set of financial statements

Comparison date and comparison period – the date as of which, and period for which, data at the cut-off date and data for the change period are to be compared

Complementary user entity controls – controls that management of the service organization assumes, in the design of the service provided by the service organization, will be implemented by user entities, and which, if necessary to achieve the control objectives stated in management's description of the service organization's system, are identified as such in that description

Condensed financial statements – historical financial information that is presented in less detail than a complete set of financial statements, in accordance with an appropriate financial reporting framework

Control objective – the aim or purpose of specified controls

Controls at a service organization – the policies and procedures at a service organization likely to be relevant to user entities' internal control over financial reporting

Controls at a subservice organization – the policies and procedures at a subservice organization likely to be relevant to internal control over financial reporting of user entities of the service organization

Criteria – the benchmarks used to measure or evaluate the subject matter

Current period – the most recent period upon which the auditor is reporting

Cut-off date – the date through which certain procedures described in the comfort letter are to relate.

D

Deficiency – a deficiency in internal control over financial reporting exists when the design or operation of a control does not allow management or employees, in the normal course of performing their assigned functions, to prevent or detect misstatements on a timely basis

Deficiency in design – exists when (a) a control necessary to meet the control objective is missing or (b) an existing control is not properly designed so that, even if the control operates as designed, the control objective would not be met

Deficiency in operation – exists when a properly designed control does not operate as designed, or when the person performing the control does not possess the necessary authority or competence to perform the control effectively.

Detective control – a control that has the objective of detecting and correcting errors or fraud that have already occurred that could result in a misstatement of the financial statements

E

Effective date – The date on which the securities offering becomes effective.

Emphasis-of-matter paragraph – a paragraph included in the auditor's report that is required by GAAS, or is included at the auditor's discretion, and that refers to a matter appropriately presented or disclosed in the financial statements that, in the auditor's professional judgment, is of such importance that it is fundamental to users' understanding of the financial statements

Engagement partner – the partner or other person in the firm who is responsible for the engagement and its performance and for the report that is issued on behalf of the firm and who, when required, has the appropriate authority from a professional, legal, or regulatory body

Engagement team – all accountants and staff performing the engagement and any individuals engaged by the firm who perform procedures on the engagement

Entity – the party whose financial statements are the subject of the engagement

Error – mistakes in the financial statements, including arithmetical or clerical mistakes, and mistakes in the application of accounting principles, including inadequate disclosures

F

Financial reporting framework – a set of criteria used to determine measurement, recognition, presentation, and disclosure of all material items appearing in the financial statements (e.g., accounting principles generally accepted in the United States of America [U.S. GAAP], International Financial Reporting Standards promulgated by the International Accounting Standards Board, or a special purpose framework)

Financial statements – a structured representation of historical financial information, including related notes, intended to communicate an entity's economic resources and obligations at a point in time, or the changes therein for a period of time in accordance with a financial reporting framework

Financial statements and related disclosures – a company's financial statements and notes to the financial statements as presented in accordance with generally accepted accounting principles ("GAAP")

Firm – a form of organization permitted by law or regulation, whose characteristics conform to resolutions of the Council of the AICPA and that is engaged in the practice of public accounting

Fraud – an intentional act that results in a misstatement in financial statements

G

General-purpose financial statements – Financial statements prepared in accordance with a general-purpose framework

General-purpose framework – a financial reporting framework designed to meet the common financial information needs of a wide range of users

H

Historical financial information – information expressed in financial terms regarding a particular entity, derived primarily from that entity's accounting system, about economic events occurring in past time periods or about economic conditions or circumstances at points in time in the past

I

Inclusive method – method of addressing the services provided by a subservice organization whereby management's description of the service organization's system includes a description of the nature of the services provided by the subservice organization as well as the subservice organization's relevant control objectives and related controls

Inconsistency – other information that conflicts with information contained in the audited financial statements. A material inconsistency may raise doubt about the audit conclusions drawn from audit evidence previously obtained and, possibly, about the basis for the auditor's opinion on the financial statements

Interim financial information – financial information prepared and presented in accordance with an applicable financial reporting framework that comprises either a complete or condensed set of financial statements covering a period or periods less than one full year or covering a 12-month period ending on a date other than the entity's fiscal year end

Internal audit function – the service organization's internal auditors and others, for example, members of a compliance or risk department, who perform activities similar to those performed by internal auditors

Internal control over financial reporting (ICFR) – a process designed by management to provide reasonable assurance regarding the preparation of reliable financial statements in accordance with the applicable financial reporting framework

J
K
L
M

Management – the person(s) with executive responsibility for the conduct of the entity's operations

Management's assessment about ICFR – management's conclusion about the effectiveness of the entity's internal control over financial reporting

Material weakness – a material weakness is a deficiency, or a combination of deficiencies, in internal control over financial reporting, such that there is a reasonable possibility that a material misstatement of the company's annual or interim financial statements will not be prevented or detected on a timely basis

Misstatement – a difference between the amount, classification, presentation, or disclosure of a reported financial item and the amount, classification, presentation, or disclosure that is required for the item to be presented fairly in accordance with the applicable financial reporting framework

Misstatement of fact – other information that is unrelated to matters appearing in the audited financial statements that is incorrectly stated or presented

Modified opinion – a qualified opinion, an adverse opinion, or a disclaimer of opinion

Negative assurance – a statement that, based on the procedures performed, nothing has come to the auditor's attention that caused the auditor to believe that specified matters do not meet specified criteria (e.g., that nothing came to the auditor's attention that caused the auditor to believe that any material modifications should be made to the unaudited interim financial information for it to be in accordance with generally accepted accounting principles).

Noncompliance – acts of omission or commission by the entity, either intentional or unintentional, which are contrary to the prevailing laws or regulations, does not include personal misconduct of management

O

Other information – financial and nonfinancial information (other than the financial statements and the auditor's report thereon) that is included in a document containing audited financial statements and the auditor's report thereon, excluding required supplementary information

Other-matter paragraph – a paragraph that refers to a matter other than those presented or disclosed in the financial statements that, in the accountant's professional judgment, is relevant to users' understanding of the engagement, the accountant's responsibilities, or the accountant's report

P

Pervasive – a term used in the context of misstatements to describe the effects on the financial statements of misstatements or the possible effects on the financial statements of misstatements, if any, that are undetected due to an inability to obtain sufficient appropriate audit evidence

Preventive control – a control that has the objective of preventing errors or fraud that could result in a misstatement of the financial statements

Q
R

Relevant assertion – a relevant assertion is a financial statement assertion that has a reasonable possibility of containing a single or multiple misstatements that would cause the financial statements to be materially misstated

Report release date – the date the accountant grants the entity permission to use the accountant's report in connection with the financial statements

Requesting party – one of the following specified parties requesting a comfort letter, which has negotiated an agreement with the entity such as an underwriter or other parties that are conducting a review process that is, or will be, substantially consistent with the due diligence process performed when the securities offering is, or was, being registered pursuant to the 1933 Act, as follows: a selling shareholder, sales agent, or other party with a statutory due diligence defense under Section 11 of the 1933 Act; a broker-dealer or other financial intermediary acting as principal or agent in a securities offering; or the buyer or seller in connection with acquisition transactions in which there is an exchange of stock

Required supplementary information – information that a designated accounting standards-setter requires to accompany an entity's basic financial statements

Review documentation – the record of review procedures performed, relevant review evidence obtained, and conclusions the accountant reached (terms such as working papers or workpapers are also sometimes used).

Review evidence – information used by the accountant to provide a reasonable basis for obtaining limited assurance

S

Securities offerings – one of the following types of securities offerings: a. Registration of securities with the SEC under the 1933 Act. b. Foreign offerings, including Regulation S, Eurodollar, and other offshore offerings. c. Transactions that are exempt from the registration requirements of Section 5 of the 1933 Act, including those pursuant to Regulation A, Regulation D, and Rule 144A. d. Offerings of securities issued or backed by governmental, municipal, banking, tax-exempt, or other entities that are exempt from registration under the 1933 Act. e. Acquisition transactions in which there is an exchange of stock.

Service auditor – a practitioner who reports on controls at a service organization

Service organization – an organization, or segment of an organization, that provides services to user entities, which are likely to be relevant to those user entities' internal control over financial reporting

Service organization's assertion – a written assertion about the matters referred to in part (b) of the definition of *Report on management's description of a service organization's system and the suitability of the design and operating effectiveness of controls*, for a type 2 report; and, for a type 1 report, the matters referred to in part (b) of the definition of *Report on management's description of a service organization's system and the suitability of the design of controls*.

Service organization's system – the policies and procedures designed, implemented, and documented, by management of the service organization to provide user entities with the services covered by the service auditor's report

Significant account or disclosure – an account or disclosure is a **significant account or disclosure** if there is a reasonable possibility that the account or disclosure could contain a misstatement that, individually or when aggregated with others, has a material effect on the financial statements, considering the risks of both overstatement and understatement

Significant deficiency – a deficiency, or a combination of deficiencies, in internal control over financial reporting that is less severe than a material weakness, yet important enough to merit attention by those responsible for oversight of the company's financial reporting

Special purpose financial statements – financial statements prepared in accordance with a special purpose framework

Special purpose framework – a financial reporting framework, other than GAAP, that is one of the following bases of accounting: **Cash basis.** A basis of accounting that the entity uses to record cash receipts and disbursements and modifications of the cash basis having substantial support (for example, recording depreciation on fixed assets). **Tax basis.** A basis of accounting that the entity uses to file its tax return for the period covered by the financial statements. **Regulatory basis.** A basis of accounting that the entity uses to comply with the requirements or financial reporting provisions of a regulatory agency to whose jurisdiction the entity is subject (for example, a basis of accounting that insurance companies use pursuant to the accounting practices prescribed or permitted by a state insurance commission). **Contractual basis.** A basis of accounting that the entity uses to comply with an agreement between the entity and one or more third parties other than the auditor. **Other basis.** A basis of accounting that uses a definite set of logical, reasonable criteria that is applied to all material items appearing in financial statements. The cash basis, tax basis, regulatory basis, and other basis of accounting are commonly referred to as *other comprehensive bases of accounting*.

Specified parties – the intended users of the auditor's written communication

Subsequent events – events occurring between the date of the financial statements and the date of the accountant's review report

Subsequently discovered facts – facts that become known to the accountant after the date of the accountant's review report that, had they been known to the accountant at that date, may have caused the accountant to revise the accountant's review report

Subservice organization – a service organization used by another service organization to perform some of the services provided to user entities that are likely to be relevant to those user entities' internal control over financial reporting

Supplementary information – information presented outside the basic financial statements, excluding required supplementary information, that is not considered necessary for the financial statements to be fairly presented in accordance with the applicable financial reporting framework

T

Test of controls – a procedure designed to evaluate the operating effectiveness of controls in achieving the control objectives stated in management's description of the service organization's system

Those charged with governance – the person(s) or organization(s) (for example, a corporate trustee) with responsibility for overseeing the strategic direction of an entity and the obligations related to the accountability of the entity

U

Underwriter – as defined in the 1933 Act: "any person who has purchased from an issuer with a view to, or offers or sells for an issuer in connection with, the distribution of any security, or participates or has a direct or indirect participation in any such undertaking, or participates or has a participation in the direct or indirect underwriting of any such undertaking; but such term shall not include a person whose interest is limited to a commission from an underwriter or dealer not in excess of the usual and customary distributors' or sellers' commission. As used in this paragraph, the term 'issuer' shall include, in addition to an issuer, any person directly or indirectly controlling or controlled by the issuer, or any person under direct or indirect common control with the issuer."

Unmodified opinion – the opinion expressed by the auditor when the auditor concludes that the financial statements are presented fairly, in all material respects, in accordance with the applicable financial reporting framework

Updated report – a report issued by a continuing accountant that takes into consideration information that the accountant becomes aware of during the accountant's current engagement and that re-expresses the accountant's previous conclusions or, depending on the circumstances, expresses different conclusions on the financial statements of a prior period reviewed by the accountant as of the date of the accountant's current report

User auditor – an auditor who audits and reports on the financial statements of a user entity

User entity – an entity that uses a service organization

V

W

Written representation – a written statement by management provided to the accountant to confirm certain matters or to support other review evidence; a written representation in this context do not include financial statements, the assertions therein, or supporting books and records

X

Y

Z

This page is intentionally left blank.

Multiple Choice – Questions

AUD 3-Q1 A17. Under which of the following circumstances would an auditor's expression of an unmodified opinion be inappropriate for a nonissuer?

A. The auditor is unable to obtain the audited financial statements of a significant subsidiary
B. The financial statements are prepared on the entity's income tax basis.
C. There are significant deficiencies in the design and operation of the entity's internal control.
D. Analytical procedures indicate that many year-end account balances are not comparable with the prior year's balances.

AUD 3-Q2 A934. In an integrated audit of a nonissuer, if an auditor concludes that a material weakness exists as of the date specified in management's assertion, the auditor should take which of the following actions?

A. Obtain written representations from management relating to such matters.
B. Communicate, in writing, to the entities outside legal counsel that the material weakness exists.
C. Issue an adverse opinion.
D. Disclaim an opinion.

AUD 4-Q3 A273. Under which of the following circumstances would the expression of a disclaimer of opinion be inappropriate?

A. The auditor is unable to obtain the audited financial statements of a consolidated investee.
B. Management does not provide reasonable justification for a change in accounting principles.
C. The company failed to make a count of its physical inventory during the year and the auditor was unable to apply alternative procedures to verify inventory quantities.
D. Management refuses to allow the auditor to have access to the company's canceled checks and bank statements.

AUD 4-Q4 A311. When qualifying an opinion because of an insufficiency of audit evidence, an auditor should refer to the situation in the

	Basis for qualified opinion paragraph	Notes to the financial statements
A.	Yes	Yes
B.	Yes	No
C.	No	Yes
D.	No	No

AUD 4-Q5 A141. A nonissuer's comparative financial statements include the financial statements of the prior year that were audited by a predecessor auditor whose report is not presented. If the predecessor's report was qualified, the successor should

A. Issue an updated comparative audit report indicating the division of responsibility.
B. Explain to the client that comparative financial statements may not be presented under these circumstances
C. Express an opinion only on the current year's financial statements and make no reference to the prior year's statements.
D. Indicate the substantive reasons for the qualification in the predecessor auditor's opinion.

AUD 4-Q6 A126. A client has capitalizable leases but refuses to capitalize them in the financial statements. Which of the following reporting options does an auditor have if the amounts pervasively distort the financial statements?

A. Qualified opinion.
B. Unqualified opinion.
C. Disclaimer opinion.
D. Adverse opinion.

AUD 4-Q7 A1406. If a non-issuer refuses to give permission to the auditor to communicate with its external legal counsel, then the auditor should modify which of the following?

A. The audit plan.
B. The management representation letter.
C. The attorney's letter of inquiry.
D. The opinion in the auditor's report.

AUD 4-Q8 A49. A principal auditor (group) decides not to refer to the audit of another CPA (component) who audited a subsidiary of the principal auditor's client. After making inquiries about the other CPA's professional reputation and independence, the principal auditor most likely would

A. Document in the engagement letter that the principal auditor assumes no responsibility for the other CPA's work.
B. Obtain written permission from the other CPA to omit the reference in the principal auditor's report.
C. Contact the other CPA and review the audit programs and working papers pertaining to the subsidiary.
D. Add an explanatory paragraph to the auditor's report indicating that the subsidiary's financial statements are not material to the consolidated financial statements.

AUD 4-Q9 A1207. Which of the following would cause an auditor of an entity's financial statements to issue either a modified opinion or a disclaimer of opinion?

A. Scope limitation involving a recorded uncertainty.
B. Inadequate disclosure of an uncertainty.
C. The use of inappropriate accounting principles.
D. Unreasonable accounting estimates.

AUD 4-Q10 A373. Jones, CPA, is the principal auditor who is auditing the consolidated financial statements of his client. Jones plans to refer to another CPA's audit of the financial statements of a subsidiary company but does not wish to present the other CPA's audit report. Both Jones and the other CPA's audit reports have noted no exceptions to generally accepted accounting principles. Under these circumstances the opinion paragraph of Jones' consolidated audit report should express

A. An unmodified opinion.
B. A disclaimer of opinion.
C. A modified opinion.
D. An adverse opinion.

AUD 4-Q11 A385. When an adverse opinion is expressed, the opinion paragraph should include a direct reference to

A. A footnote to the financial statements which discusses the basis for the opinion.
B. The scope paragraph which discusses the basis for the opinion rendered.
C. A separate paragraph which discusses the basis for the opinion rendered.
D. The consistency or lack of consistency in the application of the applicable financial reporting framework.

AUD 4-Q12 A410. The annual report of a publicly held company presents the prior year's financial statements which are clearly marked "unaudited" in comparative form with current year audited financial statements. The auditor's report should

A. Express an opinion on the audited financial statements and contain a separate paragraph describing the responsibility assumed for the financial statements of the prior period.
B. Disclaim an opinion on the unaudited financial statements, modify the consistency phrase, and express an opinion on the current year's financial statements.
C. State that the unaudited financial statements are presented solely for comparative purposes and express an opinion only on the current year's financial statements.
D. Express an opinion on the audited financial statements and state whether the unaudited financial statements were compiled or reviewed.

AUD 4-Q13 A412. When an independent CPA is associated with the financial statements of a publicly held entity, but has not audited or reviewed such statements, the appropriate form of report to be issued must include a (an)

A. Negative assurance.
B. Compilation opinion.
C. Disclaimer of opinion.
D. Explanatory paragraph.

AUD 4-Q14 A904. Which of the following would cause an auditor of an entity's financial statements to issue either a modified opinion or a disclaimer of opinion?

A. Scope limitation due to the destruction of accounting records due to a fire.
B. Inadequate disclosure of a fair value estimate.
C. Unreasonable accounting estimates.
D. The use of inappropriate accounting principles.

AUD 4-Q15 A73. An auditor has substantial doubt about the entity's ability to continue as a going concern for a reasonable period of time because of negative cash flows and working capital deficiencies. Under these circumstances, the auditor would be most concerned about the

A. Control environment factors that affect the organizational structure.
B. Correlation of detection risk and inherent risk.
C. Effectiveness of the entity's internal control activities.
D. Possible effects on the entity's financial statements.

AUD 4-Q16 A117. An auditor who is unable to form an opinion on a new client's opening inventory balances may issue an unmodified opinion on the current year's

A. Income statement only.
B. Statement of cash flows only.
C. Balance sheet only.
D. Statement of shareholders' equity only.

AUD 4-Q17 A1393. A report on an issuer's integrated audit must include each of the following statements, except:

A. The audit was conducted in accordance with AICPA standards.
B. The auditor believes the audit provides a reasonable basis for the issued opinion.
C. Management is responsible for maintaining effective internal control.
D. Internal control over financial reporting includes policies and procedures regarding the ability to report financial data consistent with management's assertions.

AUD 4-Q18 A216. A1392. In which of the following engagements would a practitioner provide limited assurance about the possible significant effects on the historical financial statements if a change in capitalization had occurred at an earlier date?

A. A compilation of a financial projection.
B. A review of pro forma financial information.
C. An examination of management's discussion and analysis.
D. An audit of condensed interim financial information.

AUD 4-Q19 A1359. A practitioner's report on agreed-upon procedures should contain which of the following statements?

A. The procedures performed were those agreed to by the specified parties identified in the report.
B. Sufficiency of procedures is the responsibility of the practitioner.
C. All classification codes appeared to comply with such performance documents.
D. Nothing came to my attention as a result of applying the procedures.

AUD 4-Q20 A103. Which of the following procedures should a user auditor include in the audit plan to create the most efficient audit when an audit client uses a service organization for several processes?

A. Review the service auditor's report on controls placed in operation.
B. Review the service auditor's report and outline the accounting system in a memo to the working papers in the audit workpapers.
C. Audit the service organization's controls, assess risk, and prepare the audit plan.
D. Audit the service organization's controls to test the work of the service auditor.

AUD 4-Q21 A101. A practitioner is engaged to express an opinion on management's assertion that the square footage of a warehouse offered for sale is 150,000 square feet. The practitioner should refer to which of the following sources for professional guidance?

A. Statements on Auditing Standards.
B. Statements on Standards for Attestation Engagements.
C. Statements on Standards for Accounting and Review Services.
D. Statements on Standards for Consulting Services

AUD 4-Q22 A136. According to the AICPA Statements on Standards for Attestation Engagements, a public accounting firm should establish quality control policies to provide assurance about which of the following matters related to agreed-upon procedures engagements?

A. Use of the report is not restricted.
B. The public accounting firm takes responsibility for the sufficiency of procedures.
C. The practitioner is independent from the client and other specified parties.
D. The practitioner sets the criteria to be used in the determination of findings.

AUD 4-Q23 A308. What type of evidence would provide the highest level of assurance in an attestation engagement?

A. Evidence secured solely from within the entity.
B. Evidence obtained from independent sources.
C. Evidence obtained indirectly.
D. Evidence obtained from multiple internal inquiries.

AUD 4-Q24 A338. Which of the following components is appropriate in a practitioner's report on the results of applying agreed-upon procedures?

A. A list of the procedures performed, as agreed to by the specified parties identified in the report.
B. A statement that management is responsible for expressing an opinion.
C. A title that includes the phrase "independent audit."
D. A statement that the report is unrestricted in its use.

AUD 4-Q25 A250. A practitioner has been engaged to apply agreed-upon procedures in accordance with Statements on Standards for Attestation Engagements (SSAE) to prospective financial statements. Which of the following conditions must be met for the practitioner to perform the engagement?

A. The prospective financial statement includes a summary of significant accounting policies.
B. The practitioner takes responsibility for the sufficiency of the agreed-upon procedures.
C. The practitioner and specified parties agree upon the procedures to be performed by the practitioner.
D. The practitioner reports on the criteria to be used in the determination of findings.

AUD 4-Q26 A288. Which of the following is a conceptual similarity between generally accepted auditing standards for an issuer and the attestation standards?

A. Both sets of standards require the CPA to report on the adequacy of disclosure in the financial statements.
B. All of the standards of fieldwork in generally accepted auditing standards are included in the attestation standards.
C. The requirement that the CPA be independent in mental attitude is included in both sets of standards.
D. Both sets of standards are applicable to engagements regarding financial forecasts and projections.

AUD 4-Q27 A78. Which of the following should a practitioner perform as part of an engagement for agreed-upon procedures in accordance with Statements on Standards for Attestation Engagements?

A. Issue a report on findings based on specified procedures performed.
B. Assess whether the procedures meet the needs of the parties.
C. Express negative assurance on findings of work performed.
D. Report the differences between agreed-upon and audit procedures.

AUD 4-Q28 A98. Which of the following statements should be included in a practitioner's report on the application of agreed-upon procedures?

A. A statement that the practitioner performed an examination of prospective financial statements.
B. A statement of scope limitation that will qualify the practitioner's opinion.
C. A statement referring to standards established by the AICPA.
D. A statement of negative assurance based on procedures performed.

AUD 4-Q29 A1391. If prior-period compiled financial statements have been restated and the predecessor accounting firm decides not to reissue its report, the successor accounting firm

A. May be engaged to reissue the prior-period report.
B. May not be engaged to reissue the prior-period report.
C. Must disclose the prior-period misstatements in the introductory paragraph of its current-year report.
D. Must issue a combined report of both the prior-period and current-period financial statements.

AUD 4-Q30 A1367. During a review of financial statements, an accountant decides to emphasize a matter in the review report. Which of the following is an example of a matter that the accountant would most likely want to emphasize?

A. Other entities in the same industry have recently changed from LIFO to FIFO.
B. The IRS has notified the entity that it intends to audit income tax returns for prior years.
C. The entity has had significant transactions with related parties.
D. The entity has had significant tax expenses as a result of a new tax law.

AUD 4-Q31 A114. An accountant compiles the financial statements of a nonissuer and issues the standard compilation report. Although not specifically stated in this report, it is implied that

A. The accountant has not audited or reviewed the financial statements.
B. Substantially all disclosures required by GAAP are included in the financial statements.
C. The financial statements should not be used to obtain credit from a lending institution.
D. The compilation is limited to presenting information that is the representation of management.

AUD 4-Q32 A51. The inability to complete which of the following activities most likely would prevent an accountant from accepting and completing an engagement for a review of financial statements performed in accordance with Statements on Standards for Accounting and Review Services?

A. Performing tests of details of major account balances.
B. Performing inquiries and analytical procedures.
C. Obtaining an understanding of internal control to assess control risk.
D. Having previous experience in the client's industry

AUD 4-Q33 A53. Which of the following procedures most likely would be performed in a review engagement of a nonissuer's financial statements in accordance with Statements on Standards for Accounting and Review Services?

A. Making inquiries of management.
B. Observing a year-end inventory count.
C. Assessing the internal control system.
D. Examining subsequent cash receipts

AUD 4-Q34 A68. An accountant was asked by a potential client to perform a compilation of its financial statements. The accountant is not familiar with the industry in which the client operates. In this situation, which of the following actions is the accountant most likely to take?

A. Request that management engage an independent industry expert to consult with the accountant
B. Accept the engagement and obtain an adequate level of knowledge about the industry.
C. Decline the engagement
D. Postpone accepting the engagement until the accountant has obtained an adequate level of knowledge about the industry.

AUD 4-Q35 A69. To compile financial statements of a nonissuer in accordance with Statements on Standards for Accounting and Review Services, an accountant should

A. Identify material misstatements in the financial statements.
B. Review bank statement reconciliations
C. Make inquiries of significant customers, vendors, and creditors
D. Obtain a general understanding of the client's business transactions.

AUD 4-Q36 A130. Which of the following activities is an accountant not responsible for in review engagements performed in accordance with Statements on Standards for Accounting and Review Services?

A. Performing basic analytical procedures.
B. Remaining independent.
C. Developing an understanding of internal control.
D. Providing any form of assurance.

AUD 4-Q37 A134. Which of the following procedures would be generally performed when evaluating the accounts receivable balance in an engagement to review financial statements in accordance with Statements on Standards for Accounting and Review Services?

A. Perform a reasonableness test of the balance by computing days' sales in receivables.
B. Vouch a sample of subsequent cash receipts from customers.
C. Confirm individually significant receivable balances with customers.
D. Review subsequent bank statements for evidence of cash deposits.

AUD 4-Q38 A171. General Retailing, a nonissuer, has asked Ford, CPA, to compile its financial statements that omit substantially all disclosures required by GAAP. Ford may comply with General's request provided the omission is clearly indicated in Ford's report and the

A. Distribution of the financial statements and Ford's report is restricted to internal use only.
B. Reason for omitting the disclosures is acknowledged in the notes to the financial statements.
C. Omitted disclosures are not significant
D. Omission is not undertaken with the intention of misleading the users of General's financial statements.

AUD 4-Q39 A179. A company hires one of its board members, a CPA, to issue accounting reports for the company. Assuming any required disclosures are made, which of the following reports may the CPA issue without violating independence rules?

A. Compilations.
B. Reviews.
C. Audits.
D. Agreed-upon procedures.

AUD 4-Q40 A186. When planning a review of an audit client's interim financial statements, which of the following procedures should the accountant perform to update the accountant's knowledge about the entity's business and its internal control?

A. Perform analytical procedures on selected accounts by comparing the interim amounts to the amounts for the previous audited fiscal year end.
B. Inquire of the entity's outside legal counsel about the status of any previous pending litigation and any new litigation involving the entity.
C. Select a sample of material revenue transactions occurring during the interim period and examine supporting documentation.
D. Consider the results of audit procedures performed with respect to the current-year's financial statements.

AUD 4-Q41 A188. In an accountant's review of interim financial information, the accountant typically performs each of the following, except

A. Reading the available minutes of the latest stockholders' meeting.
B. Applying financial ratios to the interim financial information.
C. Inquiring of the accounting department's management.
D. Obtaining corroborating external evidence.

AUD 4-Q42 A291. An accountant has been engaged to review a nonissuer's financial statements that contain several departures from GAAP. Management is unwilling to revise the financial statements, and the accountant believes that modification of the standard review report is inadequate to communicate the deficiencies. Under these circumstances, the accountant should

A. Determine the effects of the departures from GAAP and issue a special report on the financial statements.
B. Express a disclaimer of opinion on the financial statements and advise the board of directors that the financial statements should not be relied on.
C. Inform management that a review of the financial statements cannot be completed and request a change from a review to a compilation engagement.
D. Withdraw from the engagement and provide no further services concerning these financial statements.

AUD 4-Q43 A306. Before reissuing a compilation report on the financial statements of a nonissuer for the prior year, the predecessor accountant is required to

A. Make inquiries about actions taken at meetings of the board of directors during the current year.
B. Verify that the reissued report will not be used to obtain credit from a financial institution.
C. Review the successor accountant's working papers for matters affecting the prior year.
D. Compare the prior year's financial statements with those of the current year.

AUD 4-Q44 A307. Which of the following procedures would a CPA ordinarily perform when reviewing the financial statements of a nonissuer in accordance with Statements on Standards for Accounting and Review Services (SSARS)?

A. Apply year-end cutoff tests for the sales and purchasing functions.
B. Compare the financial statements with budgets or forecasts.
C. Obtain an understanding of the entity's internal control components.
D. Document whether control risk is assessed at or below the maximum level.

AUD 4-Q45 A312. An accountant compiled the financial statements of a nonissuer in accordance with Statements on Standards for Accounting and Review Services (SSARS). If the accountant has an ownership interest in the entity, which of the following statements is correct?

A. The accountant should refuse the compilation engagement.
B. A report need not be issued for a compilation of a nonissuer.
C. The accountant should include the disclaimer "I am an owner of the entity" in the report.
D. The accountant should include the statement "I am not independent with respect to the entity" in the compilation report.

AUD 4-Q46 A1408. If an accountant is performing a review engagement for a non-issuer and considers it necessary to communicate a matter that is not presented in the financial statements, then the accountant should include this information in which of the following paragraphs in the review report?

A. The opinion paragraph.
B. The introductory paragraph.
C. The other-matter paragraph.
D. The emphasis-of-matter paragraph.

AUD 4-Q47 A331. Which of the following is required of an accountant in reviewing a company's financial statements under Statements on Standards for Accounting and Review Services (SSARS)?

A. Obtain knowledge of the client's industry.
B. Send bank confirmations.
C. Test the effectiveness of internal controls
D. Observe client's physical inventory.

AUD 4-Q48 A336. Which of the following services, if any, may an accountant who is not independent provide?

A. Compilations, but not reviews.
B. Reviews, but not compilations.
C. Both compilations and reviews.
D. No services.

AUD 4-Q49 A337. Which of the following situations would preclude an accountant from issuing a review report on a company's financial statements in accordance with Statements on Standards for Accounting and Review Services (SSARS)?

A. The owner of a company is the accountant's father.
B. The accountant was engaged to review only the balance sheet.
C. Land has been recorded at appraisal value instead of historical cost.
D. Finished-goods inventory does not include any overhead amounts.

AUD 4-Q50 A242. Which of the following procedures is an accountant required to perform when reviewing the financial statements of a nonpublic entity in accordance with Statements on Standards for Accounting and Review Services (SSARS)?

A. Assess control risk.
B. Obtain a management representation letter.
C. Confirm account balances.
D. Perform a physical inventory observation.

AUD 4-Q51 A258. Independence is not required on which of the following types of engagements?

A. Audit.
B. Review.
C. Compilation.
D. Agreed-upon procedures.

AUD 4-Q52 A1200. When an accountant compiles the financial statements of a non-issuer in accordance with *Statements on Standards for Accounting and Review Services*, the accountant's report should include

A. A statement that the accountant is **not** aware of material modifications that should be made to the financial statements for them to be in conformity with the applicable financial reporting framework.
B. A statement regarding the accountant's assessment of fraud risk.
C. A statement that the accountant does **not** express an opinion on the financial statements.
D. A statement regarding the entity's compliance with laws and regulations.

AUD 4-Q53 A267. An accountant has been engaged to compile the financial statements of a nonpublic entity. The financial statements contain many departures from GAAP because of inadequacies in the accounting records. The accountant believes that modification of the compilation report is not adequate to indicate the deficiencies. Under these circumstances, the accountant should

A. Inform management that the engagement can proceed only if distribution of the accountant's report is restricted to internal use.
B. Withdraw from the engagement and provide no further service concerning these financial statements.
C. Quantify the effects of the departures from GAAP and describe the departures from GAAP in a special report.
D. Obtain written representations from management that the financial statements will not be used to obtain credit from financial institutions.

AUD 4-Q54 A194. Which of the following procedures is ordinarily performed by an accountant during an engagement to compile the financial statements of a nonissuer?

A. Make inquiries of the employees and senior management regarding transactions with related parties.
B. Determine whether there is substantial doubt about the entity's ability to continue as a going concern.
C. Scan the entity's records for the period just after the balance sheet date to identify subsequent events requiring disclosure.
D. Consider whether the financial statements are free from obvious material mistakes in the application of accounting principles.

AUD 4-Q55 A196. When providing limited assurance that the financial statements of a nonissuer require no material modifications to be in accordance with GAAP, the accountant should

A. Assess the risk of material misstatement in the financial statements due to fraud.
B. Perform tests of controls to evaluate the effectiveness of the controls.
C. Understand the accounting principles of the industry in which the entity operates.
D. Communicate with the audit committee regarding material weaknesses in internal control.

AUD 4-Q56 A202. In an engagement to review the financial statements of a nonissuer, the accountant most likely would perform which of the following procedures?
A. Physical inspection of inventory.
B. Vouching of inventory purchase transactions.
C. Analysis of inventory turnover.
D. Evaluation of internal control over inventory

AUD 4-Q57 A207. Which of the following statements is correct regarding a compilation report on financial statements issued in accordance with Statements on Standards for Accounting and Review Services (SSARS)?

A. The report should not be issued if the accountant is not independent from the entity.
B. The report should include a statement indicating that the information is the representation of the accountant.
C. The report should include a description of other procedures performed during the compilation.
D. The date on the report should be the date of completion of the compilation.

AUD 4-Q58 A211. An accountant is required to comply with the provisions of the Statements on Standards for Accounting and Review Services (SSARS) when performing which of the following tasks?
A. Preparing monthly journal entries.
B. Providing the client with software to generate financial statements.
C. Generating financial statements of a nonissuer.
D. Providing a blank financial statement format or template.

AUD 4-Q59 A212. Which of the following statements would be appropriate in an accountant's report on compiled financial statements of a nonissuer prepared in accordance with Statements on Standards for Accounting and Review Services (SSARS)?

A. We are not aware of any material modifications that should be made to the accompanying financial statements.
B. A compilation is substantially less in scope than an audit in accordance with generally accepted auditing standards (GAAS).
C. A compilation is limited to presenting in the form of financial statements information that is a representation of management.
D. A compilation is performed to obtain reasonable assurance about whether the financial statements are free from material misstatement.

AUD 4-Q60 A217. Which of the following statements is true regarding analytical procedures in a review engagement?

A. Analytical procedures are not required to be used.
B. Analytical procedures do not involve comparisons of recorded amounts to expected amounts.
C. Analytical procedures are required to be used in the final review stage.
D. Analytical procedures involve the use of both financial and nonfinancial data.

AUD 4-Q61 A218. In reviewing the financial statements of a nonissuer, an accountant is required to modify the standard review report for which of the following matters?

	Inability to assess the risk of material misstatement due to fraud	Discovery of significant deficiencies in the design of the entity's internal control
A.	Yes	Yes
B.	Yes	No
C.	No	Yes
D.	No	No

AUD 4-Q62 A936. Which of the following procedures regarding notes payable would an accountant most likely perform during a non-issuer's review engagement?

A. Confirming the year-end outstanding note payable balance with the lender.
B. Examining records indicating proper authorization of the notes payable.
C. Making inquiries of management regarding maturities, interest rate, and collateral.
D. Documenting control procedures for payment calculations of the notes' principal and interest.

AUD 4-Q63 A227. Before reissuing a compilation report on the financial statements of a nonissuer for the prior year, the predecessor accountant is required to

A. Obtain an updated management representation letter from the entity's management.
B. Compare the prior year's financial statements with those of the current year.
C. Review the successor accountant's working papers for matters affecting the prior year.
D. Make inquiries of the entity's lawyers concerning continuing litigation.

AUD 4-Q64 A228. Which of the following procedures would an accountant most likely perform during an engagement to review the financial statements of a nonissuer?

A. Review the predecessor accountant's working papers.
B. Inquire of management about related party transactions.
C. Corroborate litigation information with the entity's attorney.
D. Communicate internal control deficiencies to senior management.

AUD 4-Q65 A230. Which of the following actions should an accountant take when engaged to compile a company's financial statements in accordance with Statements on Standards for Accounting and Review Services (SSARS)?

A. Perform analytical procedures.
B. Express negative assurance on the financial statements.
C. Make management inquiries and examine internal controls.
D. Perform the engagement even though independence is compromised.

AUD 4-Q66 A231. Which of the following procedures would a CPA most likely perform when reviewing the financial statements of a nonissuer?

A. Verify that the accounting estimates that could be material to the financial statements have been developed.
B. Obtain an understanding of the entity's internal control components.
C. Make inquiries of client's attorney regarding pending litigation.
D. Make inquiries about actions taken at the board of directors' meetings.

AUD 4-Q67 A236. When an accountant is not independent with respect to an entity, which of the following types of compilation reports may be issued?

A. The standard compilation report may be issued, regardless of independence, with no reference to the accountant's independence.
B. A compilation report with negative assurance may be issued.
C. A compilation report with special wording that notes the accountant's lack of independence may be issued.
D. A compilation report may be issued if the engagement is upgraded to a review.

AUD 4-Q68 A6. Which of the following procedures does a CPA normally perform first in a review engagement in accordance with *Statements on Standards for Accounting and Review Services* (SSARS)?

A. Inquiry regarding the client's principles and practices and the method of applying them.
B. Inquiry concerning the effectiveness of the client's system of internal control.
C. Inquiry to identify transactions between related parties and management.
D. Inquiry of the client's professional advisors, including bankers, insurance agents, and consultants.

AUD 4-Q69 A8. Which of the following describes how the objective of a review of financial statements under SSARS differs from the objective of a compilation engagement?

A. The primary objective of a review engagement is to test the completeness of the financial statements prepared, but a compilation tests for reasonableness.
B. The primary objective of a review engagement is to provide positive assurance that the financial statements are fairly presented, but a compilation provides **no** such assurance.
C. In a review engagement, accountants provide limited assurance, but a compilation expresses **no** assurance.
D. In a review engagement, accountants provide reasonable or positive assurance that the financial statements are fairly presented, but a compilation provides limited assurance.

AUD 4-Q70 A75. An entity engaged an accountant to review its financial statements in accordance with Statements on Standards for Accounting and Review Services. The accountant determined that the entity maintained its accounts on a comprehensive basis of accounting other than generally accepted accounting principles (GAAP), also called special purpose framework. In this situation, the accountant most likely would have taken which of the following actions?

A. Withdrawn from the engagement because the entity has not been following GAAP.
B. Advised management to make the adjustments necessary for the account balances to conform to GAAP.
C. Modified the review report to reflect the fact that the financial statements were presented on another comprehensive basis of accounting.
D. Requested that management justify the use of the other comprehensive basis of accounting in the management representation letter.

AUD 4-Q71 A84. Which of the following is correct regarding a compilation of financial statements engagement in accordance with Statement on Standards for Accounting and Review Services?

A. If the accountant's independence is impaired, a qualified opinion must be issued.
B. The accountant may not base the report on information obtained from prior engagements with the same client.
C. The accountant is not required to make inquiries nor perform procedures to corroborate the information provided by the client.
D. The accountant should perform analytical procedures using the financial data.

AUD 4-Q72 A93. If requested to perform a compilation engagement for a nonissuer in which an accountant has an immaterial direct financial interest, the accountant is

A. Independent because the financial interest in the nonissuer is immaterial.
B. Not independent and, therefore, may not be associated with the financial statements.
C. Not independent and, therefore, may not issue a compilation report.
D. Not independent and, therefore, may issue a compilation report, but may not issue a review report.

AUD 4-Q73 A36. The standard report issued by an accountant after reviewing the financial statements of a nonpublic entity should state that

A. The auditor obtained an understanding of the Company's internal control.
B. A review consists of inquiries of company personnel and analytical procedures applied to financial data.
C. The accountant does not express an opinion or any other form of assurance on the financial statements.
D. The auditor assessed fraud risk.

AUD 4-Q74 A427. The objective of a review of the interim financial information of a publicly held company is to

A. Provide the accountant with the basis for the expression of an opinion.
B. Estimate the accuracy of financial statements based upon limited tests of accounting records.
C. Provide the accountant with a basis for reporting to the board of directors or stockholders.
D. Obtain corroborating evidential matter through inspection, observation and confirmation.

AUD 4-Q75 A1184. After performing compliance audit of an entity that received federal funds, what conclusion would the auditor draw if the entity does not have adequate documentation to support $5 million in operating expenses paid from federal program funds?

A. The entity spent $5 million in operating expenses that were not approved.
B. Questioned costs of $5 million for operating expenses have been identified.
C. The entity spent $5 million of government funds for services that were not required.
D. The entity submitted unauthorized invoices for expenses.

AUD 4-Q76 A1381. A practitioner has examined a client's compliance with debt covenants associated with a bank loan and is ready to issue a report. Which of the following standards apply to the report?

A. Internal control standards.
B. Compliance attestation standards.
C. Agreed-upon procedures standards.
D. Auditing standards of field work.

AUD 4-Q77 A166. How does an auditor make the following representations when issuing the standard auditor's report on comparative financial statements?

	Consistent application of accounting principles	Examination of evidence
A.	Implicitly	Explicitly
B.	Explicitly	Implicitly
C.	Implicitly	Implicitly
D.	Explicitly	Explicitly

AUD 4-Q78 A55. In which of the following should an auditor's report for a nonissuer refer to the lack of consistency when there is a change in accounting principle that is significant?

A. Management responsibility paragraph.
B. The opinion paragraph.
C. An emphasis of matter paragraph following the opinion paragraph.
D. An emphasis of matter before the opinion paragraph.

AUD 4-Q79 A94. When there has been a change in accounting principles, but the effect of the change on the comparability of the financial statements is not material, the auditor should

A. Not refer to the change in the auditor's report.
B. Refer to the note in the financial statements that discusses the change.
C. Refer to the change in an emphasis-of-matter paragraph.
D. Explicitly state, in the audit report, whether the change conforms with GAAP

AUD 4-Q80 A344. Which of the following, when materially affecting comparability, would ordinarily be referred to by an independent auditor reporting on the statement of cash flows?

A. Changing from a balanced to an unbalanced form of presentation.
B. Changes in terminology.
C. Changing from cash to accrual basis of accounting.
D. Changes in the content of working capital.

AUD 4-Q81 A362. A CPA's client has changed from straight-line depreciation to sum-of-the-years-digits depreciation. The effect on this year's income is immaterial but in the future the change, which is adequately disclosed in the notes to the financial statements, may be expected to result in materially different results. Based upon this fact, the auditor should express

A. An unmodified opinion.
B. A modified opinion.
C. A disclaimer.
D. An adverse opinion.

AUD 4-Q82 A363. In a first audit of a new company the auditor's report will

A. Remain silent with respect to consistency.
B. State that the accounting principles have been applied on a consistent basis.
C. State that accounting principles have been applied consistently during the period.
D. State that the consistency standard does not apply because the current year is the first year of audit.

AUD 4-Q83 A379. Which of the following requires recognition in the auditor's opinion as to consistency?

A. Changing the salvage value of an asset.
B. Changing the presentation of prepaid insurance from inclusion in "other assets" to disclosing it as a separate line item.
C. Division of the consolidated subsidiary into two subsidiaries which are both consolidated.
D. Changing from consolidating a subsidiary to carrying it on the equity basis.

AUD 4-Q84 A122. An auditor is engaged to report on selected financial data that are included in a client-prepared document containing audited financial statements. Under these circumstances, the report on the selected data should

A. State that the presentation is a comprehensive basis of accounting other than GAAP.
B. Restrict the use of the report to those specified users within the entity.
C. Be limited to data derived from the entity's audited financial statements.
D. Indicate that the data are subject to prospective results that may not be achieved.

AUD 4-Q85 A26. An auditor reads the letter of transmittal accompanying the comprehensive annual financial report and identifies a material inconsistency with the financial statements. The auditor determines that the financial statements do not require revision. Which of the following actions should the auditor first take?

A. Request that the client revise the letter of transmittal.
B. Include an explanatory paragraph in the auditor's report.
C. Consider withdrawing from the engagement.
D. Request a client representation letter acknowledging the inconsistency.

AUD 4-Q86 A383. Whenever special reports, filed on a printed form designed by authorities, call upon the independent auditor to make an assertion that the auditor believes is not justified, the auditor should

A. Submit a report in the form of procedures and findings.
B. Reword the form or attach a separate report.
C. Submit the report with questionable items clearly omitted.
D. Withdraw from the engagement.

AUD 4-Q87 A419. Which of the following should be recognized in the auditor's report, whether or not the item is fully disclosed in the financial statements?

A. A change in accounting estimate.
B. Correction of an error not involving a change in accounting principle.
C. A change from a non-accepted accounting principle to a generally accepted one.
D. A change in classification.

AUD 4-Q88 A13. An auditor determines that the entity is presenting certain supplementary financial disclosures of pension information that are required by the GASB. Under these circumstances, the auditor should

A. Add an explanatory paragraph to the auditor's report that refers to the required supplementary information.
B. State that the audit is not being performed in accordance with generally accepted auditing standards.
C. Document in the working papers that the required supplementary information is presented, but should not apply any procedures to the information.
D. Compare the required supplementary information for consistency with the audited financial statements.

AUD 4-Q89 A289. What is an auditor's responsibility for required supplementary information, such as disclosure of pension information, which is outside the basic financial statements but required by the GASB?

A. The auditor should engage a specialist, such as an actuary, to verify that management's assertions are reasonable.
B. The auditor's only responsibility for supplementary information is to determine that such information has not been omitted.
C. The auditor should perform tests of transactions to the supplementary information to verify that it is reasonably comparable to the prior-year's information.
D. The auditor should apply certain limited procedures to the supplementary information and report deficiencies in, or omissions of, such information.

AUD 4-Q90 A1383. The client's financial reporting includes supplementary financial information outside the basic financial statements but required by the Financial Accounting Standards Board (FASB). Which of the following statements is correct regarding the auditor's responsibility for this supplementary financial information?

A. The auditor should perform limited procedures.
B. The auditor should apply tests of details of transactions.
C. The auditor is not required to report omissions.
D. The auditor should read the supplementary financial information.

AUD 4-Q91 A339. An auditor may report on condensed financial statements that are derived from a complete set of audited financial statements only if the auditor

A. Expresses an unmodified opinion on the audited financial statements from which the condensed financial statements are derived.
B. Indicates whether the information is fairly stated in all material respects in relation to the complete financial statements.
C. Determines that the condensed financial statements include all the disclosures necessary for the complete set of financial statements.
D. Presents the condensed financial statements in comparative form with the prior-year's condensed financial statements.

AUD 4-Q92 A167. As a condition of obtaining a loan from First National Bank, Maxim Co. is required to submit an audited balance sheet but not the related statements of income, retained earnings, or cash flows. Maxim would like to engage a CPA to audit only its balance sheet. Under these circumstances, the CPA

A. May not audit only Maxim's balance sheet if the amount of the loan is material to the financial statements taken as a whole.
B. May not audit only Maxim's balance sheet if Maxim is a nonissuer.
C. May audit only Maxim's balance sheet if the CPA disclaims an opinion on the other financial statements.
D. May audit only Maxim's balance sheet if access to the information underlying the basic financial statements is not limited.

AUD 4-Q93 A1281. An auditor has been asked to report on the balance sheet of Kane Company but not on the other basic financial statements. The auditor will have access to all information underlying the basic financial statements. Under these circumstances, the auditor

A. May accept the engagement because such engagements merely involve limited reporting objectives.
B. May accept the engagement but should disclaim an opinion because of an inability to apply the procedures considered necessary.
C. Should refuse the engagement because there is a client-imposed scope limitation.
D. Should refuse the engagement because of a departure from generally accepted auditing standards.

AUD 4-Q94 A1365. Which of the following statements concerning a compilation of specific elements, accounts, or items of a financial statement is correct?

A. The accountant performing the compilation must be independent with regard to the client.
B. The compilation cannot be relied upon to disclose errors, fraud, or illegal acts.
C. The compilation involves compiling financial statements for different subsidiaries of the company.
D. The compilation must be performed in conformance with an accounting basis consistent with GAAP.

AUD 4-Q95 A254. Which of the following titles would be considered suitable for financial statements that are prepared on a cash basis?

A. Income statement.
B. Statement of operations.
C. Statement of revenues collected and expenses paid.
D. Statement of cash flows.

AUD 4-Q96 A290. Which of the following would be an appropriate title for a statement of revenues and expenses prepared using a special-purpose framework?

A. Statement of operations.
B. Statement of income--regulatory basis.
C. Income statement.
D. Statement of activities.

AUD 4-Q97 A131. Which of the following items should be included in an auditor's report for financial statements prepared in conformity with a special-purpose framework?

A. A sentence stating that the auditor is responsible for the financial statements.
B. A title that includes the word "independent."
C. The signature of the company controller.
D. A sentence stating that the audit was prepared with special-purpose framework guidelines.

AUD 4-Q98 A95. An entity prepares its financial statements on its income tax basis. A description of how that basis differs from GAAP should be included in the

A. Notes to the financial statements.
B. Auditor's engagement letter.
C. Management representation letter.
D. Report on financial statements paragraph of the auditor's report.

AUD 4-Q99 A358. An auditor is reporting on cash-basis financial statements. These statements are best referred to in his opinion by which one of the following descriptions?

A. Financial position and results of operations arising from cash transactions.
B. Assets and liabilities arising from cash transactions, and revenue collected and expenses paid.
C. Balance sheet and income statement resulting from cash transactions.
D. Cash balance sheet and the source and application of funds.

AUD 4-Q100 A14. Comfort letters ordinarily are

	Addressed to the client's	Signed by the client's
A.	Audit committee	Independent auditor
B.	Underwriter of securities	Senior management
C.	Audit committee	Senior management
D.	Underwriter of securities	Independent auditor

AUD 4-Q101 A210. When issuing letters for underwriters, commonly referred to as comfort letters, an accountant may provide negative assurance concerning

A. The absence of any significant deficiencies in internal control.
B. The conformity of the entity's unaudited condensed interim financial information with generally accepted accounting principles (GAAP).
C. The results of procedures performed in compiling the entity's financial forecast.
D. The compliance of the entity's registration statement with the requirements of the Securities Act of 1933.

AUD 4-Q102 A1366. An independent auditor is issuing an audit report for a governmental entity and plans to issue separate reports on internal control over financial reporting and compliance with laws and regulations. The auditor should do which of the following?

A. Report to the governing authority that separate reports will be issued.
B. Issue the same opinion in each report.
C. State in the audit report that separate reports will be issued.
D. Obtain permission from the audit committee to issue separate reports.

This page is intentionally left blank.

Multiple Choice – Solutions

AUD 3-Q1 A17. Choice A is correct because failure to obtain a material piece of evidence (such as audited financials from a significant subsidiary) would cause a scope limitation and hence cause the auditor to issue a qualified or disclaimer of opinion.

Choice B is incorrect as an unmodified opinion may be issued if the entity prepares its financial statements on the income tax basis of accounting.

Choice C is incorrect because even if there are significant deficiencies, an auditor may perform additional substantive procedures (and less controls testing) to compensate for the deficiencies.

Choice D is incorrect as the auditor may perform alternative procedures to compensate.

AUD 3-Q2 A934. Answer C is correct because the existence of a material weakness results in an adverse opinion.

Answer A is incorrect because no such written representation need be obtained.

Answer B is incorrect because, ordinarily, outside counsel need not be contacted.

Answer D is incorrect because a disclaimer of opinion is not issued in this situation.

AUD 4-Q3 A273. Choice B is correct. If management does not provide reasonable justification for a change in accounting principle, then an adverse or qualified opinion would be issued. (GAAP departure)

Choice A, C, and D are incorrect. In these situations, a disclaimer opinion would be appropriate as they are scope limitations.

AUD 4-Q4 A511. Choice B is correct. The auditor should refer to the insufficiency of evidence in the scope paragraph but not the notes to the financial statements.

Choices A, C, and D are incorrect per the above.

AUD 4-Q5 A141. Choice D is correct. When the predecessor's audit report is not presented, the auditor should indicate the reasoning for the qualification in the predecessor's audit report as well as the type of opinion that the predecessor auditor issued.

Choice A is incorrect as there is no requirement that the auditor issue an updated comparative report.

Choice B is incorrect as there is no requirement as a CPA is able to issue comparative financial statements.

Choice C is incorrect as the successor auditor may make a reference to the prior year's financial statements but must include the reason for the qualification that the predecessor had.

AUD 4-Q6 A126. Choice D is correct. When a material and unjustified departure from GAAP pervasively distorts the financial statement, this would cause an adverse opinion to be used.

Choice A is incorrect as a significant departure from GAAP would cause an adverse opinion – not a qualified opinion.

Choice B is incorrect as an unmodified opinion would mean that their financial statements are fairly presented.

Choice C is incorrect as a disclaimer opinion is a result of a scope limitation.

AUD 4-Q7 A1406. The correct answer choice is D. The auditor should modify the opinion in the auditor's report if a non-issuer refuses to permit the auditor to communicate with its external legal counsel. The auditor would seek information from the external counsel on applicable matters such as litigations, claims, and assessments. If the auditor is unable to directly communicate with the client's external legal counsel, no basis for being able to express an opinion on legal matters can be established.

Choice A is incorrect because the audit plan should not be modified if a non-issuer refuses to permit the auditor to communicate with its external legal counsel. An audit plan details the nature, extent, and timing of the auditor's planned audit procedures.

Choice B is incorrect because the management representation letter should not be modified if a non-issuer refuses to permit the auditor to communicate with its external legal counsel. The management representation letter is used to ensure client management confirms the information given to the auditor is true and fair to the best of management's knowledge, and that no material omissions exist.

Choice C is incorrect because the attorney's letter of inquiry should not be modified if a non-issuer refuses to permit the auditor to communicate with its external legal counsel. The letter of inquiry serves as the auditor's request for management to authorize legal counsel to discuss applicable matters with the auditor.

AUD 4-Q8 A49. Choice C is correct. When the principal (group) auditor does not refer to the work of the component auditor, then the principal auditor has effectively assumed full responsibility of the work of the component auditor. As such, the principal auditor will need to review the relevant working papers to ensure that the audit was properly conducted.

Choice A is incorrect because when no reference to the component auditor is made, then the principal auditor assumes full responsibility of the component auditor's work.

Choice B is incorrect, as no written permission is needed if the auditor does not refer to the work of another CPA.

Choice D is incorrect because no explanatory paragraph is needed if the principal auditor does not make reference to the component auditor.

AUD 4-Q9 A1207. The correct answer is A. The type of opinion is a judgment call made by the auditor but scope limitations with a recorded uncertainty often get disclaimed however in limited situations a modified opinion may be issued.

Answer B is incorrect because an inadequate disclosure about an uncertainty would not cause a modified opinion or disclaimer of opinion.

Answer C is incorrect because departures from the applicable financial reporting standards would lead to an adverse opinion.

Answer D is incorrect because unreasonable accounting estimates would lead to an unmodified opinion with an explanatory paragraph.

AUD 4-Q10 A373. The correct answer is A. When the auditor decides to make reference to the report of another auditor as a basis, in part, for his opinion, he should disclose this fact in stating the scope of his audit and should refer to the report of the other auditor in expressing his opinion. These references indicate division of responsibility for performance of the audit. Although they are departures from the standard report language, they do not constitute a modification of the auditor's opinion.

Answers B, C and D are all wrong because the types of opinions are not expressed this way.

AUD 4-Q11 A385. The correct answer is C. When an adverse opinion is expressed, the opinion paragraph should include a direct reference to a separate paragraph that discloses the basis for the adverse opinion.

Answer A is wrong because the footnotes of financial statements are the responsibility of management.

Answer B is wrong because the opinion isn't given in the scope paragraph.

Answer D is wrong because the lack of consistency in applying the applicable financial reporting framework should be discussed in an explanatory paragraph.

AUD 4-Q12 A410. The correct answer is A. Where unaudited financial statements are presented in comparative form with audited financial statements in documents other than those filed with the SEC, either (a) the report on the prior period should be reissued... (b) or the report on the current period should include as a separate paragraph an appropriate description of the responsibility assumed for the financial statements of the prior period.

Answer B is incorrect because there is no consistency phrase.

Answer C is incorrect because the last year's financial statements may be misleading without making it clear that they are unaudited.

Answer D is incorrect because the service provided is an audit, not a review or compilation

AUD 4-Q13 A412. The correct answer is C. When an accountant is associated with financial statements of a public entity, but has not audited or reviewed such statements, the form of report to be issued... (should include a disclaimer of opinion). This disclaimer of opinion is the means by which the accountant complies with GAAS, when associated with unaudited financial statements in these circumstances.

Answer A is incorrect because negative assurance represents the level of assurance spelled out in an auditor's report to management relating to a review of interim financial information.

Answer B is incorrect because a "compilation" opinion only relates to non-public entities as per Statement on Standards for Accounting and Review Services.

Answer D is incorrect because an explanatory paragraph is used within a report to explain an inconsistency, a going concern problem, change in accounting principle and other explanations which are a judgment call for the auditor and the paragraph may be placed before the opinion paragraph or after the opinion paragraph.

AUD 4-Q14 A904. Answer A is correct because a scope limitation results in either a modified opinion or a disclaimer, depending upon the pervasiveness of the destruction of the accounting records involved in the audit.

Answers B, C and D are all incorrect because they represent inappropriate situations in which an applicable financial reporting framework departure exists. They would all result in either a modified opinion or adverse opinion.

AUD 4-Q15 A73. Choice D is correct. If the auditor has substantial doubt about an entity's ability to continue as a going concern, the auditor would be concerned with the effect on the financial statements.

Choice A is incorrect as the auditor would not be concerned with the control environment.

Choice B is incorrect as the auditor would not be concerned with this relationship.

Choice C is incorrect as the effectiveness of internal controls is not a primary concern when evaluating going concern.

AUD 4-Q16 A117. Choice C is correct. If an auditor is unable to gain assurance on the beginning inventory balance, the auditor may only issue an unmodified opinion on the balance sheet as the balance sheet would report the end of year, *not* the beginning of year inventory amounts. Note that if the balance sheet also reported balances for the previous period, the auditor would not be able to issue an unmodified opinion on the previous year's balance sheet.

Choice A is incorrect as cost of goods sold within the income statement is calculated using beginning inventory numbers. As such, because the auditor cannot rely on these numbers, the auditor is not able to issue an unmodified opinion on this financial statement.
Choice B is incorrect as the statement of cash flows uses beginning inventory numbers to calculate the change in inventory. As such, because the auditor cannot rely on these numbers, the auditor is not able to issue an unmodified opinion on this financial statement.

Choice D is incorrect as the statement of stockholder's equity is calculated using net income for the year. Net income relies on the accuracy of beginning inventory numbers. As such, because the auditor cannot rely on these numbers, the auditor is not able to issue an unmodified opinion on this financial statement.

AUD 4-Q17 A119. The correct answer choice is A. This statement is false. An audit is conducted in accordance with the applicable accounting framework (e.g., U.S. GAAP).

Choices B, C and D are all true statements.

AUD 4-Q18 A1392. The correct answer choice is B because a review is the level of service that provides limited or negative assurance.

Choice A is incorrect because a compilation service provides no assurance.

Choice C is incorrect because an examination is an attestation service and doesn't relate to the historical financial statements.

Choice D is incorrect because an audit provides a greater level of assurance.

AUD 4-Q19 A1359. The correct answer choice is A. This statement should be made in an agreed-upon procedures report to articulate and clarify the nature of the engagement.

Choice B is incorrect because this statement would not be made in the report.

Choice C is incorrect because this is not a statement that is made in the report.
Choice D is incorrect because this statement is a negative assurance statement used in a review report, not an agreed-upon procedures report.

AUD 4-Q20 A103. Choice A is correct. Reviewing the service auditor's report on controls placed in operation would be the most efficient procedure.

Choice B is incorrect as it would be more efficient to review the service auditor's report (and include that report in the audit workpapers).

Choice C is incorrect as choice A is a more efficient procedure.

Choice D is incorrect as choice A is a more efficient procedure.

AUD 4-Q21 A101. Choice B is correct. In an attestation engagement, a practitioner provides written communication expressing a conclusion about the reliability of an assertion by another party. In this situation, the practitioner is expressing a conclusion on the square footage of a warehouse.

Choice A is incorrect as these apply to the audits of financial statements

Choice C is incorrect as these standards only apply to accounting and review services.

Choice D is incorrect as these standards only apply to consulting services.

AUD 4-Q22 A136. Choice C is correct. The practitioner must be independent from the client and other specified parties in an agreed-upon procedures engagement.
Choice A is incorrect as an agreed-upon procedures report is restricted in use.

Choice B is incorrect as the public accounting firm does not take responsibility for the procedures.

Choice D is incorrect as both the client and the practitioner set the criteria.

AUD 4-Q23 A308. Choice B is incorrect as evidence obtained from independent sources would provide the highest level of assurance.

Choices A, C, and D are incorrect as choice B provides the highest level of assurance.

AUD 4-Q24 A338. Choice A is correct. A list of the procedures performed, as agreed to by the specific parties identified in the report, is included in the agreed upon procedures.

Choice B is incorrect as an opinion is not rendered in an agreed-upon procedures report.

Choice C is incorrect as an agreed-upon-procedures is not an "independent audit."

Choice D is incorrect as there need not be such a statement.

AUD 4-Q25 A250. Choice C is correct as the practitioner and the specified parties should agree on the procedures to be performed by the practitioner.

Choice A is incorrect as this is not part of the prospective financial statement.

Choice B is incorrect as the specified parties take responsibility for this.

Choice D is incorrect as there is no requirement that the practitioner report on such criteria.

AUD 4-Q26 A288. Choice C is correct. The requirement that a CPA be independent in mental attitude is included in both sets of standards.

Choice A is incorrect as the attestation standards do not require the CPA to report on the adequacy of disclosure.

Choice B is incorrect as this is not a true statement. Choice D is incorrect as only attestation standards apply to financial forecasts and projections.

AUD 4-Q27 A78. Choice A is correct. An agreed-upon procedure occurs when a practitioner performs specific procedures and issues a report based on specific findings.

Choice B is incorrect as the practitioner does not assess the sufficiency and appropriateness of the procedures.

Choice C is incorrect as the practitioner does not provide assurance when performing agreed upon procedures.

Choice D is incorrect as the practitioner does not report these differences.

AUD 4-Q28 A98. Choice C is correct. There should be a statement that refers to the standards that are established by the AICPA.

Choice A is incorrect because an agreed-upon procedures report is not an examination of subject matter.

Choice B is incorrect as there is no opinion rendered in an agreed-upon procedures report.

Choice D is incorrect as an agreed upon procedures report does not provide any assurance.

AUD 4-Q29 A1391. The correct answer choice is A. The auditor may be engaged to reissue the prior-period report because without reissuing the financial statements as a whole would be misleading.

Choice B is incorrect because the auditor may be engaged to reissue the prior-period report.

Choice C is incorrect because disclosure in the current year report is not a must.

Choice D is incorrect because a combined report is not required.

AUD 4-Q30 A1367. The correct answer choice is C. A significant related party transaction is something that the accountant should emphasize in the review report.

Choice A is incorrect because you wouldn't emphasize anything relating to other entities.

Choice B is incorrect because an IRS notification is unrelated to the scope of the review of financial statements.

Choice D is incorrect because changes in the environment (tax laws) do not get emphasized in a review report.

AUD 4-Q31 A114. Choice B is correct. A compilation report generally implies that all disclosures that are required by GAAP are included in the financial statements. If the disclosures are omitted from the financials, there will be a report modification stating that they are omitted.
Choice A is incorrect because a standard compilation report specifically states that the financial statements were not audited or reviewed.

Choice C is incorrect as the entity may use the report to obtain credit.

Choice D is incorrect as the compilation is limited to presenting the information that management provides to the accountant as this is management's responsibility, and this is stated in the report.

AUD 4-Q32 A51. Choice B is correct. According to SSARS, a review engagement is based on inquiry and analytical procedures. As such, if the accountant was unable to perform these procedures, then it would be difficult to obtain limited assurance over the financial statements.

Choices A and C are incorrect, as these are only requirements when performing an audit.

Choice D is incorrect because this is not a requirement for performing a review engagement. However, it would be helpful if the accountant had previous experience in the client's industry.

AUD 4-Q33 A53. Choice A is correct because a review engagement typically consists of internal inquiries and analytical procedures.

Choices B, C, and D are incorrect as these procedures are performed during an audit – not a review.

AUD 4-Q34 A68. Choice B is correct. There is no requirement that the auditor who performs a compilation have adequate knowledge about the client and the industry. As such, the auditor is able to accept the compilation engagement and then subsequently obtain the knowledge necessary to complete the engagement.

Choice A is incorrect as this procedure is not necessary when performing a compilation.

Choice C is incorrect as the auditor need not decline the compilation engagement as he/she can obtain the necessary knowledge prior to commencing the engagement.

Choice D is incorrect as there is no need to postpone the engagement if the auditor is able to obtain the necessary knowledge prior to commencing the engagement.

AUD 4-Q35 A69. Choice D is correct. When an auditor accepts a new compilation engagement, he/she should obtain a general understanding of the business of the client.
Choice A is incorrect as this procedure is only performed in an audit engagement.

Choice B is incorrect as this procedure is only performed in an audit engagement.

Choice C is incorrect as external inquiries are performed in an audit engagement. A review engagement only requires internal inquiries whereas external and internal inquiries are required in an audit engagement.

AUD 4-Q36 A130. Choice C is correct. A review engagement prepared in accordance with SSARS does not require that the accountant obtain an understanding of internal controls.
Choice A is incorrect as review engagements prepared in accordance with SSARS require an accountant to perform analytical procedures.

Choice B is incorrect as independence is required in review engagements.

Choice D is incorrect as review engagements provide limited assurance that the financial statements are not materially misstated.

AUD 4-Q37 A134. Choice A is correct. A review engagement consists of inquiries and analytical procedures. A reasonableness test is considered to be an analytical procedure.

Choices B, C, and D are incorrect as these are substantive audit procedures and are not performed in a review engagement.

AUD 4-Q38 A171. Choice D is correct. The CPA must disclose the fact that the disclosures are omitted and it is not undertaken with the intention of misleading the users of the financial statements.

Choice A is incorrect as this is not a requirement.

Choice B is incorrect. The reason for omitting the disclosure need not be included.

Choice C is incorrect as this is not a requirement.

AUD 4-Q39 A179. Choice A is correct. In a compilation report, a CPA need not be independent. However, the CPA must disclose this fact in the compilation report.

Choices B, C, and D are incorrect as a CPA needs to be independent when issuing a review, audit, or agreed-upon procedures

AUD 4-Q40 A186. Choice D is correct. When planning a review of financial information, an auditor would most likely consider the results of procedures performed with respect to current year financial statements.

Choice A is incorrect as this is not an interim procedure.

Choice B is incorrect as this is not done in a review engagement.

Choice C is incorrect as this is not performed in a review engagement.

AUD 4-Q41 A188. Choice D is correct. In a review engagement, obtaining corroborating external evidence is generally not required. Also, the word "corroborating" is an audit term.
Choices A, B, and C are incorrect as these are generally procedures performed in a review engagement.

AUD 4-Q42 A291. Choice D is correct. If the accountant believes that modification to the standard review report is insufficient enough to communicate the deficiencies, then the accountant should withdraw from the engagement and provide no further services.

Choice A is incorrect as these reports are not issued in a review engagement.

Choice B is incorrect as a disclaimer of opinion is not issued in a review engagement.

Choice C is incorrect as management's unwillingness to change the financial statements is not a reasonable basis for requesting a change in the engagement.

AUD 4-Q43 A306. Choice D is correct. Before reissuing a compilation report, the predecessor accountant is required to compare prior year's financial statements with those of the current year.

Choice A is incorrect as this is not a required procedure.

Choice B is incorrect as no verification is needed.

Choice C is incorrect as it is not required to review successor auditor working papers.

AUD 4-Q44 A307. Choice B is correct. When reviewing the financial statements of a nonissuer, the CPA would compare the financial statements with budgets or forecasts.

Choices A, C, and D are incorrect as these would be done in an audit – not a review.

AUD 4-Q45 A312. Choice D is correct. The accountant should include the phrase "I am not independent with respect to the entity."

Choices A is incorrect as the accountant may prepare the compilation report if he/she is not independent.

Choice B is incorrect as a report should be issued.

Choice C is incorrect as this phrase need not be included.

AUD 4-Q46 A1408. The correct answer choice is C. The other-matter paragraph is used to draw a user's attention to matters other than those presented or disclosed in the financial statements. The inclusion of the matter is based on the accountant's judgment that it is relevant to a user's understanding of the review, accountant's responsibilities, and/or the review report.

Choice A is incorrect because an opinion paragraph is found in an audit report and provides a statement referring to the financial statements identified in the introductory paragraph, an opinion as to the fair presentation of the overall financial statements, and a statement identifying the applicable financial framework.

Choice B is incorrect because an introductory paragraph is found in an audit report and identifies the entity (client) that is being evaluated, the financial statements that have been evaluated, and the timeframe for the evaluation.

Choice D is incorrect because the emphasis-of-matter paragraph is used to refer to a matter that is already appropriately presented or disclosed in the financial statements.

AUD 4-Q47 A331. Choice A is correct. When performing a review engagement, the accountant is required to obtain knowledge of the client's industry.

Choices B, C, and D are incorrect as these are only required in an audit engagement.

AUD 4-Q48 A336. Choice A is correct. An accountant who is not independent of the client may provide compilation services – not review services to the client. The lack of independence must then be disclosed.

Choices B, C, and D are incorrect per the above explanation.

AUD 4-Q49 A337. Choice A is correct. If an accountant lacks independence, then the accountant may not issue a review report.

Choices B, C, and D are incorrect as these would not preclude the accountant from issuing a review report.

AUD 4-Q50 A242. Choice B is correct as obtaining a management representation letter is required when performing a review of financial statements.

Choices A, C, and D are incorrect as these are only required in an audit.

AUD 4-Q51 A258. Choice C is correct. Independence is not required when performing a compilation report but must be disclosed.

Choices A, B, and D are incorrect as independence is required when performing these types of engagements.

AUD 4-Q52 A1200. The correct answer is C. The distinction on level of service is important and a requirement in a compilation report.

Answer A is incorrect because the accountant doesn't state they are unaware of material modifications that should be made to the financial statements.

Answer B is incorrect because no assessment of fraud risk is performed. Should fraud come to the accountant's attention, they should notify those charged with governance (management and audit committee).

Answer D is incorrect because an entity's compliance with laws and regulations is under government auditing standards and not a part of a compilation report.

AUD 4-Q53 A267. Choice B is correct. If the accountant believes that this is the case, the accountant should withdraw from the engagement and provide no further services to the client.

Choice A is incorrect as it would not be appropriate to restrict the response in this circumstance.

Choice C is incorrect as a compilation report cannot be tailored in this way.

Choice D is incorrect as choice B would be a more appropriate response for an accountant.

AUD 4-Q54 A194. Choice D is correct. In a compilation engagement, an accountant should read the financial statements to ensure that there are no obvious mistakes or errors in the financial statements.

Choice A is incorrect as an accountant is not required to make such inquiries in a compilation engagement.

Choice B is incorrect. There is no requirement to perform going concern procedures in a compilation engagement. However, if an accountant comes across any information that would indicate substantial doubt about an entity's ability to continue as a going concern, then the accountant should indicate that to management and potentially affect the compilation report.

Choice C is incorrect. Subsequent events procedures are not performed in a compilation engagement.

AUD 4-Q55 A196. Choice C is correct. In a review engagement, an accountant is required to obtain an understanding of the entity and the major accounting principles that apply to the entity.

Choice A is incorrect as this is not required to be assessed in a review engagement – only in an audit engagement.

Choices B and D are incorrect as in a review engagement, there are no internal controls testing performed.

AUD 4-Q56 A202. Choice C is correct. In a review engagement, typically inquiry and analytical procedures are performed. Ratios are analytical procedures.

Choice A and B are incorrect as audit procedures are not required to be performed in a review engagement.

Choice D is incorrect as internal control procedures are not required to be performed in a review engagement.

AUD 4-Q57 A207. Choice D is correct. In accordance with SSARS, the date of the compilation report should be the completion date.

Choice A is incorrect as an accountant may issue this report even if the accountant is not independent – but must state so in the report.

Choice B is incorrect as the information is representation of management.

Choice C is incorrect as this is not something that is included on the compilation report.

AUD 4-Q58 A211. Choice C is correct. An accountant is required to comply with Statement on Standards for Accounting and Review Services when generating financial statements of a nonissuer.

Choice A, B, and D are incorrect as SSARS do not apply to these tasks.

AUD 4-Q59 A212. Choice C is correct. A compilation is limited to presenting in the form of financial statements information that is a representation of management.

Choice A is incorrect as there is no opinion expressed in a compilation.
Choice B is incorrect as this statement is not included in the compilation report.

Choice D is incorrect as this is true in an audit – not a compilation.

AUD 4-Q60 A217. Choice D is correct. Analytical procedures involve the use of both financial and nonfinancial data.

Choice A is incorrect as in a review engagement, analytical procedures are required to be used.

Choice B is incorrect as analytical procedures *do* involve comparison of recorded amounts to expected amounts.

Choice C is incorrect as analytical procedures are *not* required to be used in the final review stage. Note that the term *final review stage* is an audit term.

AUD 4-Q61 A218. Choice D is correct. In a review engagement, there is no requirement to assess the risk of material misstatement due to fraud nor to test internal controls.

Choices A, B, and C are incorrect per the above.

AUD 4-Q62 A936. Answer C is correct because a review consists primarily of such inquiries, analytical procedures and obtaining written representations from management.

Answer A is incorrect because confirming accounts is not ordinarily a part of a review engagement.

Answer B is incorrect because a non-issuer review does not ordinarily include such tests of controls.

Answer D is incorrect because such documentation is not required.

AUD 4-Q63 A227. Choice B is correct. Before reissuing a compilation report, the predecessor accountant is required to compare the prior years' financial statement with those of the current year.

Choice A is incorrect as there is no requirement to obtain a management representation letter in a compilation engagement.

Choice C is incorrect as this a recommended, not a required procedure.

Choice D is incorrect as this is not a required procedure in a compilation report.

AUD 4-Q64 A228. Choice B is correct as a review engagement consists of inquiries and analytical procedures, so an accountant would most likely inquire of management about related party transactions.

Choice A is incorrect as the accountant may be the continuing accountant.

Choice C is incorrect as this is not a required procedure in a review engagement.

Choice D is incorrect as this is not a required procedure in a review engagement.

AUD 4-Q65 A230. Choice D is correct. An accountant may perform a compilation if independence is compromised but must disclose this in the compilation report.

Choice A is incorrect as analytical procedures are not required in a compilation.

Choice B is incorrect as there is no assurance in a compilation report.

Choice C is incorrect as internal controls are not required in a compilation report.

AUD 4-Q66 A231. Choice D is correct. When reviewing the financial statements of a nonissuer, the CPA should make inquiries about actions taken at board of directors' meetings.

Choice A is incorrect as this is not an appropriate procedure in a review engagement.

Choice B is incorrect as internal control is not tested in a review engagement.

Choice C is incorrect as this is an external inquiry whereas review engagements only require internal inquiries.

AUD 4-Q67 A236. Choice C is correct. When issuing a compilation report, if the accountant is not independent, the accountant must disclose the lack of independence in the compilation report.

Choice A is incorrect as there needs to be disclosure of the lack of independence.

Choice B is incorrect as there is no assurance provided in a compilation report.

Choice D is incorrect as a review report would have to be issued. (Highest level of service performed.)

AUD 4-Q68 A6. Choice A is correct. According to *Statements on Standards for Accounting and Review Services* (SSARS), an auditor is first required to understand the client's principles and practices.

Choice B is incorrect because an accountant need not address internal control in a review.

Choice C is incorrect because the identification of related party transactions is not the first step in a review engagement.

Choice D is incorrect because inquiry of the client's legal council is not normally required in an audit.

AUD 4-Q69 A8. Choice C is correct. The objective of a review engagement is to provide limited assurance that the financial statements are not materially misstated and compilations provide no assurance that financial statements are fairly stated.

Choice A is incorrect because the standard does not distinguish between completeness and the reasonableness.

Choices B and D are incorrect as review engagements provide limited assurance and compilation engagements provide no assurance that the financial statements are fairly stated.

AUD 4-Q70 A75. Choice C is correct. An entity is permitted to present financial statements based on Other Comprehensive Basis of Accounting (OCBOA) so long as:
1. Financial statement titles are different than GAAP based financial statements and
2. The notes to the financial statements should disclose the differences between OCBOA and GAAP

Choice A is incorrect as there is no need to withdraw from the engagement as entities are permitted to prepare their financial statements based on OCBOA.

Choice B is incorrect as no changes are required since entities are permitted to prepare their financial statements based on OCBOA.

Choice D is incorrect as management does not need to justify using OCBOA.

AUD 4-Q71 A84. Choice C is correct. An accountant is not required to corroborate information received in a compilation engagement. This is only required in an audit engagement.

Choice A is incorrect as there is no opinion issued in a compilation engagement.

Choice B is incorrect as an accountant may base the report on information received from prior engagements.

Choice D is incorrect as analytical procedures are only required in a review or audit engagement.

AUD 4-Q72 A93. Choice D is correct. Even if there is an immaterial direct financial interest, the accountant is not considered independent and may only issue a compilation report as no independence is required in a compilation (but this must be disclosed in the compilation report). However, a review report requires the accountant to be independent.

Choice A is incorrect because even an immaterial direct financial interest is considered to affect independence.

Choices B and C are incorrect because an accountant need not be independent if issuing a compilation.

AUD 4-Q73 A36. Choice B is correct. According to AR 90, a review engagement consists of performing procedures such as inquiry, observation, and analytical procedures to provide limited assurance that there are no material modifications needed to the financial statements.

Choice A is incorrect because in a review engagement, the auditor does not obtain an understanding of the Company's internal control – this is only done in an audit.

Choice C is incorrect because in a review engagement, the auditor provides limited assurance that no material modifications are needed to the financial statements.

Choice D is incorrect because in a review engagement, the auditor does not assess fraud risk.

AUD 4-Q74 A427. The correct answer is C. Reviews of interim financial information are undertaken to help management of a publicly held company meet their reporting responsibilities to regulatory agencies. The Securities and Exchange Commission requires quarterly financial information as part of the quarterly 10-Q. reports. Such statements need not be audited and the CPA firm's name need not be associated with the financial statements disclosing quarterly financial information. Generally, the statements would be labeled as "unaudited."

Answer A is incorrect because a complete audit must be performed in order to express an opinion.

Answer B is incorrect; estimating the accuracy is not the objection of a review.

Answer D is incorrect because no substantive testing needs to be performed in a review engagement typically minor analytical testing is done.

AUD 4-Q75 A1184. The correct answer is B. Costs that are not adequately supported with documentation are referred to as questioned costs.

Answer A is incorrect. The costs may or may not have been properly approved.

Answer C is incorrect. The services may or may not have been required.

Answer D is incorrect. There is no indication of submission of unauthorized invoices.

AUD 4-Q76 A1381. The correct answer choice is B as examination on compliance is a within the category of attestation and would require the practitioner to apply attestation standards.

Choice A is incorrect because internal control standards relate closer to audits than attestation.

Choice C is incorrect because agreed upon procedures are not related to compliance examinations.

Choice D is incorrect because auditing standards do not govern compliance examinations.

AUD 4-Q77 A166. Choice A is correct. The consistent application of accounting principles is implicitly (not directly stated) in the audit report. However, the examination of evidence on a test basis is stated directly within the audit report.

Choices B, C, and D are incorrect per the above explanation.

AUD 4-Q78 A55. Choice C is correct. According to AU-C 708.07-.08, when there a change in accounting principle that meets a "four test rule," the auditor should include an emphasis-of-matter paragraph after the opinion paragraph of the audit report.

Choices A, B, and D are incorrect per the guidance of AU-C 708.

AUD 4-Q79 A94. Choice A is correct. When the effect of a change in accounting principle is immaterial, the auditor should not refer to this change in the audit report. The auditor would only refer to the change if the effect of the change is material.

Choice B is incorrect because the notes to the financial statements are not the appropriate place for the auditor to disclose the effect of the change in accounting principle.

<u>Remember</u>: The notes and financial statements belong to the client – *not* the auditor.

Choice C is incorrect because an emphasis of matter paragraph is only needed if the effect of the change is material.

Choice D is incorrect because this would be documented in the auditor's workpapers and not stated in the audit report.

AUD 4-Q80 A344. The correct answer is C. Variation between periods in terms used to express changes in cash flows, such as changing from cash to accrual, constitute a change in the application of accounting principles, and involve consistency. When such a change occurs and the independent auditor deems it to be material, he should express in his report a lack of consistency. None of the other answer choices would represent a change in accounting principle and require a modified opinion due to lack of consistency.

AUD 4-Q81 A362. The correct answer is A. In future years, the auditor will not have to refer to the change. The auditor's report need not refer to a change in accounting principle and restatement made in conformity with the applicable financial reporting framework if the statements for the year ot change are reported all together with the financial statements for a year subsequent to the year of the change. Additionally, the auditor need NOT refer to the change in the current year because its effect is immaterial. The auditor may issue an unmodified opinion.

AUD 4-Q82 A363. The correct answer is A. Consistency is not mentioned in the audit report. The consistency of the financial statements is implicit in the report.

AUD 4-Q83 A379. The correct answer is D. The consistency standard is applicable to this type of change and requires recognition in the auditor's opinion as to consistency. A change in the reporting entity is a special type of change in accounting principle, the consistency standard is applicable. Changing the basis of accounting for an investment (i.e., from consolidation to carrying it on the equity basis) is a change in the reporting entity.

Answer A is wrong because it represents a change in estimate and does NOT require modification of the auditor's opinion.

Answer B is wrong because it represents a change in classification and also does NOT require a consistency exception.

Answer C is wrong because it is not considered a change in reporting entity.

AUD 4-Q84 A122. Choice C is correct. The report should be limited to data derived from the entity's audited financial statements.

Choice A is incorrect as the presentation of data is not on a comprehensive basis of accounting other than GAAP.

Choice B is incorrect as this report need not be restricted.

Choice D is incorrect as the report is not prospective.

AUD 4-Q85 A26. Choice A is correct. If the auditor notices this discrepancy, the auditor should first request that the client revise the letter of transmittal since the financial statements do not require any changes.

Choice B is incorrect because an explanatory paragraph is only required if the client does not revise the letter of transmittal.

Choice C is incorrect because it would take an extreme circumstance for an auditor to withdraw from the engagement.

Choice D is incorrect because client representation letters are not used for these situations.

AUD 4-Q86 A383. The correct answer is B. Some report forms can be made acceptable by inserting additional wording; others can be made acceptable only by complete revision. When a printed report calls upon an independent auditor to make an assertion that he believes he is not justified in making, he should reword the form or attach a separate report.

Answer A is wrong because a report submitted in the form of procedures and findings is used for engagements with agreed-upon procedures.

Answer C is wrong because omitting questionable items would fail to meet GAAS.

Answer D is wrong because withdrawing from the engagement is likely not appropriate in given the above fact pattern.

AUD 4-Q87 A419. The correct answer is C. A change from an accounting principle that is not generally accepted to one that is generally accepted, including the correction of a mistake in the application of a principle, is a correction of an error. Although this type of change in accounting principle should be accounted for as the correction of an error, the change requires recognition in the auditor's opinion as to consistency.

Answer A is incorrect because a change in accounting estimate doesn't need to be recognized in the auditor's report.

Answer B is incorrect because a correction of an error not involving a change in accounting principle is not required to be recognized in the auditor's report.

Answer D is incorrect because a change in classification is not required to be recognized in the auditor's report.

AUD 4-Q88 A13. Choice D is correct. According to GASB, an auditor should perform limited procedures on supplementary information that accompany the financial statements. Comparing the required supplementary information to the financial statements for consistency serves this purpose.

Choice A is incorrect because normally there is no requirement to include an explanatory paragraph regarding the supplementary information unless there was something wrong with the supplementary information.

Choice B is incorrect because the audit should be performed following generally accepted auditing standards.

Choice C is incorrect because the auditor must perform limited procedures on the supplementary information.

AUD 4-Q89 A289. Choice D is correct. The auditor should only apply certain limited procedures to the supplementary information and report deficiencies in, or omissions of, such information.

Choice A is incorrect as the auditor is not required to engage a specialist.

Choice B is incorrect as the auditor is required to read the supplementary information to determine if there is a material departure from the required supplementary information.

Choice C is incorrect as the auditor is not required to perform such procedures on supplementary information.

AUD 4-Q90 A1383. The correct answer choice is A. The auditor should perform limited procedures in addition to reading the supplementary financial information to determine if any clues exist that would suggest either misleading the information users or material misstatements on the financial statements.

Choice B is incorrect because test of details of transactions is a substantive audit procedure performed during the field work.

Choice C is incorrect because the auditor should notify management of omissions in the supplementary information.

Choice D is incorrect because only reading the supplementary financial information is not enough and is not considered due diligence under professional responsibilities.

AUD 4-Q91 A339. Choice B is correct. An auditor may report on a condensed set of financial statements that are derived from a complete set if the information is fairly stated in all material respects in relation to the complete financial statements.

Choice A is incorrect as the auditor is not limited to issuing an unmodified opinion.

Choice C is incorrect as condensed financial statements do not include all the disclosures.

Choice D is incorrect as there is no such requirement.

AUD 4-Q92 A167. Choice D is correct. A CPA may accept an engagement to audit only the balance sheet so long as access to the underlying financial information to audit the balance sheet is not limited.

Choice A is incorrect as this is not a requirement when only auditing the balance sheet.

Choice B is incorrect as there is no such requirement.

Choice C is incorrect as there is no requirement to disclaim an opinion unless the client limits access to information needed to audit the financial statements.

AUD 4-Q93 A1281. The correct answer is A. The auditor may be asked to report on one basic financial statement and not on the others. These engagements do not involve scope limitations if the auditor's access to the information underlying the basic financial statements is not limited and if he applies all the procedures he considers necessary in the circumstances; rather, such engagements involve limited reporting objectives.

Answer B is incorrect because disclaiming an opinion wouldn't be appropriate under the circumstances.

Answer C is incorrect because this is not a scope limitation.

Answer D is incorrect because this situation is not a departure from generally accepted auditing standards.

AUD 4-Q94 A1365. The correct answer choice is B. A compilation is the lowest level of service and provides no assurance.

Choice A is incorrect because the accountant performing the compilation may not be independent so long as that is disclosed along with the reason for the lack of independence.

Choice C is incorrect because only the consolidated financials would be complied, not all of the financial statements for the different subsidiaries.

Choice D is incorrect because the compilation may be performed under other comprehensive basis of accounting, not just generally accepted accounting principles (GAAP).

AUD 4-Q95 A254. Choice C is correct. This would be an appropriate title.

Choices A, B, and D are incorrect as these titles are suitable for GAAP basis financial statement prepared on the accrual basis of accounting (and not to be used on cash basis financial statements).

AUD 4-Q96 A290. Choice B is correct. Regulatory basis financial statements may be prepared using a special-purpose framework. As such, this would be an appropriate title.

Choices A and C are incorrect as these are appropriate titles for revenues and expenses prepared in accordance with US GAAP.

Choice D is incorrect as this would an appropriate title for a not-for-profit entity.

AUD 4-Q97 A131. Choice B is correct. The title of the report should state that the auditor is independent. Choice A is incorrect as the management, not the auditor, is responsible for the financial statements.

Choice C is incorrect as the auditor – not the Company's controller, signs the audit report.

Choice D is incorrect as there is no such thing as special-purpose framework guidelines. Auditors follow generally accepted auditing standards (GAAS) as a guidance on how to plan and perform the audit.

AUD 4-Q98 A95. Choice A is correct. The notes to the financial statements (generally the first note) describe the differences in the basis of the financial statements.

Choice B is incorrect. The differences in the basis of financial statements are not typically described in the auditor's engagement letter.
Choice C is incorrect. The management representation letter typically states management's representations asserting the fair presentation of the financial statements in accordance with the reporting framework.

Choice D is incorrect as the report on financial statements paragraph identifies the financial statements audited and does not describe the differences in reporting basis.

AUD 4-Q99 A358. The correct answer is B. Terms such as 'balance sheet,' statement of financial position,' statement of income,' or similar unmodified titles are generally understood to be applicable only to financial statements that are intended to present financial position in conformity with GAAP. Consequently, the auditor should consider whether the financial statements he is reporting on are suitably titled. For example, a cash-basis financial statement might be titled 'statement of assets and liabilities arising from cash transactions'.

AUD 4-Q100 A14. Choice D is correct. Comfort letters are letters prepared by the client's auditors to a third party. Management does not prepare the letters and the receipt of the comfort letter is someone outside the client's organization (an underwriter).

AUD 4-Q101 A210. Choice B is correct. When issuing letters to underwriters, the accountant may provide negative assurance regarding the conformity of the unaudited condensed internal financial information with GAAP.

Choice A is incorrect as comfort letters are not used for internal controls issues.

Choice C is incorrect as accountants may not provide negative assurance regarding the results of procedures performed in compiling the entity's financial forecast.

Choice D is incorrect as this type of situation would not require negative assurance.

AUD 4-Q102 A1366. The correct answer choice is C. Stating in the audit report that separate reports will be issued, one for the internal controls over financial reporting and another for compliance with laws and regulation, is appropriate.

Choice A is incorrect because reporting directly to the governing authority is not appropriate.

Choice B is incorrect because the opinion may be different between internal control over financial reporting and with compliance with laws and regulations.

Choice D is incorrect because getting permission is not a requirement.

This page is intentionally left blank.

AUD 5 – Task-based Simulations

Task-based Simulation – Questions   5-2 – 5-12

    AUD 5-SIMQ1 SIM27   2

    AUD 5-SIMQ2 SIM28   4

    AUD 5-SIMQ3 SIM133   5

    AUD 5-SIMQ4 SIM29   7

    AUD 5-SIMQ5 SIM931   8

    AUD 5-SIMQ6 DRS2   9

    AUD 5-SIMQ7 SIM33   12

Task-based Simulation – Solutions   5-13 – 5-20

    AUD 5-SIMQ1 SIM27   13

    AUD 5-SIMQ2 SIM28   14

    AUD 5-SIMQ3 SIM133   15

    AUD 5-SIMQ4 SIM29   16

    AUD 5-SIMQ5 SIM931   17

    AUD 5-SIMQ6 DRS2   18

    AUD 5-SIMQ7 SIM33   20

Task-based Simulation – Questions

Remember: The icons and buttons below are *not* functional. The formatting in this chapter mirrors the CPA exam. It is intended to familiarize you with the look and feel of the exam.

AUD 5-SIMQ1 SIM27

✏ Evidence Accumulation & Evaluation   Help   Authoritative Literature    Submit Testlet

For each of the account balances and associated assertions below, double-click on the associated shaded cell and select from the list provided the procedure that provides the most appropriate audit evidence for the assertion with respect to the account.

Account Balance	Assertion	Procedure
1. Accounts Receivable	Completeness	Select
2. Inventory	Valuation and Allocation	Select
3. Fixed Assets	Rights and Obligations	Select
4. Accounts Payable	Completeness	Select
5. Cash	Existence	Select

Accounts Receivable
Select Item
Review confirmation of accounts receivable balances and agree to accounts receivable subledger.
Review list of accounts written off during year.
Review schedule of bad debt expense.
Trace individual customer account transactions to sales invoice.
Trace sales invoice and shipping documents just before year end to customer account transactions.

OK   Cancel

Inventory
Select Item
Examine invoices from suppliers.
Examine invoices paid subsequent to year end and trace to subsidiary ledger.
Select items from inventory listing and locate the items in the warehouse.
Select items located in the inventory warehouse and trace to inventory listing.
Trace sales invoice and shipping documents just before year end to customer accounts.

OK   Cancel

Fixed Assets
Select Item
Interview plant managers regarding fixed asset additions during the year.
Recalculate partial year depreciation for fixed asset acquisitions.
Trace fixed asset item to fixed asset master control listing.
Vouch fixed asset acquisitions to purchase invoices.
Vouch fixed asset acquisitions to related cash disbursements.

OK | Cancel

Accounts Payable
Select Item
Compare aging of accounts payable to prior periods.
Confirm accounts payable balance with suppliers.
Examine invoices paid subsequent to year end and trace to subsidiary ledger.
Trace individual payable transaction to purchase order.
Vouch invoices for the purchase of supplies to receiving documents.

OK | Cancel

Cash
Select Item
Agree bank statement to the subsidiary ledger.
Agree cash balance per the bank reconciliation to the year-end bank statement.
Agree cash balance to online year-end bank statement.
Recalculate bank statement balance, including interest receivable.
Trace deposits per the bank statement to the cash subsidiary ledger.

OK | Cancel

⚑ = Reminder   Directions | 1 | 2 | 3 | 4 | 5 | 6 | 7 | 8   ◀ Previous | Next ▶

Remember: The icons and buttons below are **not** functional. The formatting in this chapter mirrors the CPA exam. It is intended to familiarize you with the look and feel of the exam.

AUD 5-SIMQ2 SIM28

 Evidence Accumulation & Evaluation | Help    Authoritative Literature    Submit Testlet

During the audit of a dealership selling only new luxury automobiles, the auditors calculated the year 2 and year 1 ratios in the table below. Double-click on the associated shaded cells and select from the list provided the most reasonable explanation the controller will provide for the change. An explanation may be used once, more than once, or not at all. Consider each ratio independently.

	Ratios	Year 2	Year 1	Explanations
1.	Days in accounts receivable	32	20	Select
2.	Inventory turnover	4.01	6.32	Select
3.	Debt to equity	3.2	4.3	Select
4.	Return on assets	10.5%	12%	Select
5.	Net fixed assets to equity	19%	23.2%	Select

Select Item

Due to an economic downturn, buyers have shifted to economy cars.
In October of year 1, the company hired additional collection clerks.
In year 1, the company removed some fully depreciated machinery from its books.
In year 2, the board of directors decided to begin a buyback of company stock.
In year 2, the company began accounting for inventory using the last in, first out method from the first in, first out.
In year 2, the company increased the annual dividend to shareholders.
In year 2, the company instituted more stringent collection policies.
In year 2, the company made a required principal payment on its long-term debt.
In year 2, the company reclassified its international production factories to held-for-sale.
Positive consumer reviews have caused increased movements of cars.
Sales managers are recording fraudulent sales to receive larger commissions.

OK   Cancel

Remember: The icons and buttons below are *not* functional. The formatting in this chapter mirrors the CPA exam. It is intended to familiarize you with the look and feel of the exam.

AUD 5-SIMQ3 SIM133

Physical Inventory Results | Help | Authoritative Literature

Smith, the senior audit associate in charge of the audit of Raymond's Mfg. observed the client's physical inventory count held on the last day of the company's fiscal year, August 31, year 1.

The results of the test counts are listed below. For each variance identified, double-click in the associated shaded cell and select from the list provided the auditor's most likely response. A response may be used once, more than once, or not at all.

Test count number	Inventory item	Client inventory quantity	Auditor's test count	Variance	Explanation	Audit Response
1	AB-6123	484	434	(50)	Inventory in transit shipped f.o.b. shipping point; received September 2, year 1	Select
2	HJ-0990	11,222	11,000	(222)	Inventory sold to customer f.o.b destination; not received by customer until September 2, year 1	Select
3	CO-8013	203	197	(6)	Payments Made in advance for items received September 2, year 1	Select
4	CO-8012	786	800	14	Inventory received August 30, year 1; vendor shipment receipt not recorded	Select
5	WI-5491	663	600	(63)	Inventory was separated for a September 1 sale; held on dock for customer pickup	Select
6	MQ-6403	127	150	23	Additional items identified as damaged and will be returned to vendor	Select

See following page for audit response menu.

AUD 5-5
Auditing and Attestation (AUD)
Copyright © 2018 Yaeger CPA Review. All rights reserved.

Select Item

Inspect supporting documents and agree quantities received to purchase order.

Inspect supporting purchase documents for proper shipping terms and receiving information to verify exclusion from inventory count.

Inspect supporting purchase documents for proper shipping terms and receiving information to verify inclusion in inventory count.

Inspect supporting sale and shipping documentation for proper shipping terms for exclusion from inventory count.

Inspect supporting sale and shipping documentation for proper shipping terms for inclusion in inventory count.

Obtain the scrap inventory log and agree to general ledger.

Request that client make appropriate correction to record additional inventory.

Request that client make appropriate correction to reduce inventory.

Review return shipment documentation to verify exclusion from inventory count.

Review return shipment documentation to verify inclusion in inventory count.

OK   Cancel

Remember: The icons and buttons below are **not** functional. The formatting in this chapter mirrors the CPA exam. It is intended to familiarize you with the look and feel of the exam.

AUD 5-SIMQ4 SIM29

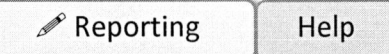  

During audits of internal controls over financial reporting of various issuers, the auditors encountered the independent situations below. For each situation, double-click the associated shaded cell and select from the list provided the appropriate audit response.

A response may be selected once, more than once, or not at all.

	Situation	Response
1.	The client did not furnish adequate evidence for the auditor to evaluate the internal controls over inventory. All other evidence was provided.	Select
2.	The auditors examined the client's internal controls over cash receipts and concluded that they are operating exactly as designed. However, the design of the controls does not include control procedures to prevent misstatements and the potential omission of cash receipts.	Select
3.	The auditors concluded that the ineffectiveness of the design of controls over accounts payable and cash disbursements represents a material weakness in internal control even though the financial statements are not materially misstated.	Select
4.	Management has not provided assurance that there are no material weaknesses in controls. Subsequent tests revealed no material weaknesses.	Select
5.	The auditor's prior year report on internal control included an adverse opinion. The client has since modified internal controls. No material weaknesses were found in the current year.	Select

Select Item

Assess control risk as low for the purpose of the financial statement audit.
Consult legal counsel to explore reducing auditor liability.
Determine if the control deficiency is a material weakness by obtaining further evidence.
Disclose in the notes to the financial statements that there are material weaknesses.
Express an adverse opinion on the internal controls.
Express an unqualified opinion on the internal controls.
Express an unqualified opinion on the internal controls and add a paragraph on whether a previously reported material weakness in internal control continues to exist.
Insist that management's assessment of internal control includes a description
Issue a disclaimer of opinion.
Issue a Report on Internal Controls stating that no deficiencies were noted.
Issue a separate report on the client's internal control.
Modify the Report on Internal Controls for significant deficiencies.
Report matter only to the board of directors.

OK   Cancel

Remember: The icons and buttons below are **not** functional. The formatting in this chapter mirrors the CPA exam. It is intended to familiarize you with the look and feel of the exam.

AUD 5-SIMQ5 SIM931

  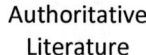 

Authoritative Literature   Submit Testlet

The auditors of Green Pen, Inc. obtained the journal entries below as part of the year 2 audit. For each of the journal entries, double-click the associated shaded cell and select from the list provided the most appropriate audit procedure to perform or action to take regarding the transaction represented by the journal entry. A procedure or action may be selected once, more than once, or not at all.

Situation	Response
1. A journal entry was made by the controller on December 31, year 2: Dr. Salaries and wages expense Cr. Accrued liabilities To account for compensation for year 2 to be paid in year 3.	Select
2. A journal entry was made by the fixed asset manager on December 31, year 2: Dr. Accumulated depreciation Cr. Depreciation expense To adjust machine's depreciation expense.	Select
3. A journal entry was made by the controller on December 30, year 2: Dr. Investments held for trading purposes Cr. Investments held-to-maturity Change in asset classification.	Select
4. A journal entry was made by the controller on January 1, year 2: Dr. Repairs and maintenance Cr. Accounts payable To record the proposed audit adjustments from year 1.	Select
5. A journal entry was made by the controller on December 31, year 2: Dr. Investment in stock Cr. Investment income Record subsidiary income for year 2.	Select

Select Item
Confirm with controller any changes in estimates.
Discuss with human resources and obtain employees' permanent file to verify hire date and recalculate year 1 and 2 salaries.
Obtain current market values of subsidiary's stock.
Obtain financial statement of subsidiary.
Obtain management's bonus plan and eligible employee list and recalculate expense.
Physically examine the asset to verify existence.
Propose adjusting entry to debit prior-year retained earnings.
Propose an entry to record assets at historical cost.
Review board minutes for change in classification of long-lived assets.
Review board minutes for change in accounting policies for long-lived assets.
No exception, no further audit work deemed necessary.
OK   Cancel

⚐ = Reminder   Directions | 1 | 2 | 3 | 4 | 5 | 6 | 7 | 8   ◀ Previous | Next ▶

AUD 5-SIMQ6 DRS2

Document Review | Help | Authoritative Literature | Submit Testlet

Scroll down to complete all parts of the task.

The audit of Forest Corporation's financial statements for the year ended December 31, 20X1 is being performed by Snyder & Smith, CPAs. Forest is an issuer (public company). As part of the review of subsequent events, the auditors performed various audit procedures including: inquires of management, reading available minutes of board of director meetings, and obtaining a client letter of representation. As a result of these procedures, a member of the audit staff of Snyder & Smith drafted a summary document of Forest's subsequent events and recommended accounting treatment on March 4, 20X2, which is prior to the issuance of the audited financial statements. The target date for issuing the financial statements and audit report is March 6, 20X2. The partner in charge of the Forest audit has asked you to review the summary document and make any necessary corrections.

To revise the document, click on each segment of underlined text below and select the best choice for needed correction, if any, from the list provided. If the underlined text is already correct in the context of the document, select [Original text] from the list. If removal of the entire underlined text is the best revision to the document as a whole, select [Delete text] from the list.

Summary of Forest Corporation's Subsequent Events and Recommended Accounting Treatment
Year-ended December 31, 20X1
March 4, 20X2 (DRAFT)

The following are the subsequent events and recommended accounting treatment prior to issuing the audited financial statements for Forest Corporation in connection with the annual audit of the financial statements for the year-ended December 31, 20X1.

On January 2, 20X2, Forest declared a dividend payable of $0.10 per share on its common stock. Dividends amounting to $150,000 are payable on February 15, 20X2 to common stock shareholders of record as of the close of business on February 4, 20X2.
Recommended accounting treatment: No adjustments to the December 31, 20X1 financial statements are required.

1. Choose an option below:
○ [Original text] No adjustments to the December 31, 20X1 financial statements are required.
○ [Delete text]
○ The December 31, 20X1 financial statements must be adjusted to reflect an estimate of the amount of dividends that will be paid.
○ A footnote disclosure is required on the December 31, 20X1 financial statements.

On January 6, 20X2, Forest sold 10% of its inventory for $9,300,000, which is $500,000 below cost.
Recommended accounting treatment: The December 31, 20X1 financial statements only need to have footnote disclosure indicating the $500,000 difference.

2. Choose an option below:
○ [Original text] The December 31, 20X1 financial statements only need to have footnote disclosure indicating the $500,000 difference.
○ [Delete text]
○ No adjustments to the December 31, 20X1 financial statements are required.
○ The December 31, 20X1 financial statements must be adjusted because the net realizable value was lower than the cost, resulting in an overstatement of inventory at the balance sheet.

On January 12, 20X2, Forest completed an acquisition of Timber Company for cash consideration of $4,000,000, consisting of $3,000,000, which was paid on January 12, 20X2, and up to $1,000,000 is payable based upon an earn-out period of 24 months.
Recommended accounting treatment: No adjustments to the December 31, 20X1 financial statements are required.

3. Choose an option below:
- [Original text] No adjustments to the December 31, 20X1 financial statements are required.
- [Delete text]
- No adjustments to the December 31, 20X1 financial statements are required however, if the event would cause the financial statements to be misleading, a footnote disclosure should be made indicating the nature of the event and an estimate of the financial impact.
- The December 31, 20X1 financial statements must be adjusted to reflect the $3,000,000 amount paid for the acquisition and the $1,000,000 payable, in addition to footnote disclosures.

On February 3, 20X2, Forest entered into an agreement to sublease additional office space for its world headquarters. The amounts related in the sublease will total approximately $7,200,000 over the six-year term of the agreement, beginning in the second quarter of 20X2.
Recommended accounting treatment: The December 31, 20X1 financial statements must be adjusted to reflect the amount of $7,200,000 liability.

4. Choose an option below:
- [Original text] The December 31, 20X1 financial statements must be adjusted to reflect the amount of $7,200,000 liability.
- [Delete text]
- A footnote disclosure is required on the December 31, 20X1 financial statements.
- No adjustments to the December 31, 20X1 financial statements are required.

On February 5, 20X2, Forest issued 3,700,000 shares of additional common stock.
Recommended accounting treatment: No adjustments to the December 31, 20X1 financial statements are required.

5. Choose an option below:
- [Original text] No adjustments to the December 31, 20X1 financial statements are required.
- [Delete text]
- The December 31, 20X1 financial statements must be adjusted to reflect the amount of additional common stock.
- A footnote disclosure is required on the December 31, 20X1 financial statements.

At December 31, 20X1, Forest wrote-off 50% of the $200,000 accounts receivable due from Pine, Inc., a major customer, because Forest became aware that Pine was possibly on the verge of bankruptcy. On February 12, 20X2, Forest received notification that Pine went bankrupt and determined that the accounts receivable is uncollectible.
Recommended accounting treatment: Write off Pine's remaining accounts receivable of $100,000 in the December 31, 20X1 financial statements.

6. Choose an option below:
- [Original text] Write off Pine's remaining accounts receivable of $100,000 in the December 31, 20X1 financial statements.
- [Delete text]
- A footnote disclosure is required on the December 31, 20X1 financial statements.
- No adjustments to the December 31, 20X1 financial statements are required.

On February 14, 20X2, Forest became aware the company was a defendant in a lawsuit brought on by one of their customers over the quality of their products. Forest's attorney estimated the payment, if Forest lost the suit would range between $300,000 and $500,000, but the more likely amount would be $350,000. On February 22, 20X2, Forest paid $315,000 to the customer to settle the lawsuit.

Recommended accounting treatment: A footnote disclosure is required on the December 31, 20X1 financial statements describing the lawsuit and the $315,000 settlement.

7. Choose an option below:
- [Original text] A footnote disclosure is required on the December 31, 20X1 financial statements describing the lawsuit and the $315,000 settlement.
- [Delete text]
- No adjustments to the December 31, 20X1 financial statements are required.
- The December 31, 20X1 financial statements must be adjusted to reflect the amount of the $315,000 settlement payment.

On February 24, 20X2, Forest increased the quarterly dividend on common stock from $0.10 to $0.12 per share. On an annualized basis, the dividend increased from $0.40 to $0.48 per share. The next quarterly will be payable on May 13, 20X2 to shareholders of record as of March 31, and 20X2.

Recommended accounting treatment: No adjustments to the December 31, 20X1 financial statements are required.

8. Choose an option below:
- [Original text] No adjustments to the December 31, 20X1 financial statements are required.
- [Delete text]
- The December 31, 20X1 financial statements must be adjusted to reflect an estimate of the amount of dividends that will be paid.
- A footnote disclosure is required on the December 31, 20X1 financial statements.

On February 25, 20X2, one of the three factories owned by Forest caught fire and was destroyed with an estimated loss of $3,125,000. The other two operating factories were reconfigured to accommodate approximately 40% of the production that was performed at the factory that was destroyed.

Recommended accounting treatment: A footnote disclosure is required on the December 31, 20X1 financial statements.

9. Choose an option below:
- [Original text] A footnote disclosure is required on the December 31, 20X1 financial statements.
- [Delete text]
- The loss is not recognized in the December 31, 20X1 financial statements however, if the event would cause the financial statements to be misleading, a footnote disclosure should be made indicating the nature of the event and an estimate of the financial impact.
- The December 31, 20X1 financial statements must be adjusted to reflect the amount of dividends the will be paid.

Remember: The icons and buttons below are not functional. The formatting in this chapter mirrors the CPA exam. It is intended to familiarize you with the look and feel of the exam.

AUD 5-SIMQ7 SIM33

  Authoritative Literature  Submit Testlet

When an auditor is examining financial statements prepared in accordance with a special purpose framework, one of the ways the financial statements may be prepared is under the cash basis. The cash basis is a basis of accounting that the entity uses to record cash receipts and disbursements and modifications of the cash basis having substantial support (for example, recording depreciation and fixed assets). Search the Statements on Auditing Standards and Interpretations, and enter the exact section, paragraph and sub-paragraph in the boxes below related to this particular circumstance.

Enter your response in the answer fields below. Guidance on correctly structuring your response appears above and below the answer fields.

Choose a title from the list.

Type the paragraph here.
Correctly formatted AU-C paragraphs are 1, 2, or 3 digits, preceded in some cases by an uppercase letter.

[ ] ▼ § [ ] . [ ] [ ]

Type the section here.
Correctly formatted AU-C sections are 3 or 4 digits.

Type the sub-paragraph here.
Correctly formatted AU-C sections are lower case letters (e.g., a, b, c).

● Some examples of correctly formatted AU-C responses are AU-C§123.45, AU-C §123.456, AU-C §123.A45, AU-C §123.45a

⚑ = Reminder   Directions | 1 | 2 | 3 | 4 | 5 | 6 | 7 | 8   ◀ Previous | Next ▶

Task-based Simulation – Solutions

AUD 5-SIMQ1 SIM27

Account Balance	Assertion	Procedure
6. Accounts Receivable	Completeness	Trace sales invoice and shipping documents just before year end to customer account transactions.
7. Inventory	Valuation and Allocation	Examine invoices from suppliers.
8. Fixed Assets	Rights and Obligations	Vouch fixed asset acquisitions to purchase invoices.
9. Accounts Payable	Completeness	Examine invoices paid subsequent to year end and trace to subsidiary ledger.
10. Cash	Existence	Agree cash balance per the bank reconciliation to the year-end bank statement.

Explanations:

1. As a sales cutoff test, the tracing of shipping documents immediately just before year end should be performed with a focus on any FOB shipping point and FOB destination issues.

2. This is done to vouch recorded purchases to the documentation, such as invoices, so that a determination can be made if the inventory is valued properly.

3. In order to assert the rights and obligations of fixed assets, inspection of source documents such as, purchase invoices, lease agreements and title documents, are performed.

4. This is done to help determine if the balances contain transactions for the period. As a purchases cutoff test, it asserts that proper recording occurred for shipments in which title has passed or not passed, with a focus is on FOB shipping point and FOB destination issues.

5. Performing a bank reconciliation verifies that the cash bank balance exists.

AUD 5-SIMQ2 SIM28

	Ratios	Year 2	Year 1	Explanations
1.	Days in accounts receivable	32	20	Sales managers are recording fraudulent sales to receive larger commissions.
2.	Inventory turnover	4.01	6.32	Due to an economic downturn, buyers have shifted to economy cars.
3.	Debt to equity	3.2	4.3	In year 2, the company made a required principal payment on its long-term debt.
4.	Return on assets	10.5%	12%	Due to an economic downturn, buyers have shifted to economy cars.
5.	Net fixed assets to equity	19%	23.2%	In year 2, the company reclassified its international production factories to held-for-sale.

Explanations:
1. Accounts receivable turnover equals net credit sales divided by average net receivables. Number of days sales in accounts receivable equals 365 divided by accounts receivable turnover. An increase in days sales in accounts receivable could be an indication that fraudulent sales are being recorded, where there is no settlement of the accounts receivable.

2. Inventory turnover = cost of goods sold / average inventory. The inventory turnover decreased, which could indicate an excess inventory of less fuel-efficient cars and additional inventory of economy cars due to satisfy demand from the economic downturn.

3. Debt to equity ratio equals total debt (all liabilities) divided by total stockholders' equity. The debt to equity ratio decreased. A principal payment on long debt would reduce the ratio as a result of fewer liabilities in the numerator.

4. Return on assets equals net income after interest and tax divided by average total assets. Return on assets decreased. This could be an indication of excess inventory in less fuel-efficient cars and additional inventory of economy cars due to satisfy demand from the economic downturn, which would increase the denominator of the ratio.

5. Net fixed asset to equity equals total net fixed assets divided by total stockholders' equity. Net fixed assets to equity decreased, which could indicate that the international production facilities were removed from fixed assets when they were reclassified to held-for-sale, resulting in a lower numerator.

AUD 5-SIMQ3 SIM133

Test count number	Inventory item	Client inventory quantity	Auditor's test count	Variance	Explanation	Audit Response
1	AB-6123	484	434	(50)	Inventory in transit shipped f.o.b. shipping point; received September 2, year 1	Inspect supporting purchase documents for proper shipping terms and receiving information to verify inclusion in inventory count.
2	HJ-0990	11,222	11,000	(222)	Inventory sold to customer f.o.b destination; not received by customer until September 2, year 1	Inspect supporting sale and shipping documentation for proper shipping terms for inclusion in inventory count.
3	CO-8013	203	197	(6)	Payments Made in advance for items received September 2, year 1	Inspect supporting purchase documents for proper shipping terms and receiving information to verify inclusion in inventory count.
4	CO-8012	786	800	14	Inventory received August 30, year 1; vendor shipment receipt not recorded	Request that client make appropriate correction to record additional inventory.
5	WI-5491	663	600	(63)	Inventory was separated for a September 1 sale; held on dock for customer pickup	Inspect supporting sale and shipping documentation for proper shipping terms for inclusion in inventory count
6	MQ-6403	127	150	23	Additional items identified as damaged and will be returned to vendor	Review return shipment documentation to verify exclusion from inventory count.

AUD 5-SIMQ4 SIM29

	Situation	Response
1.	The client did not furnish adequate evidence for the auditor to evaluate the internal controls over inventory. All other evidence was provided.	Issue a disclaimer of opinion.
2.	The auditors examined the client's internal controls over cash receipts and concluded that they are operating exactly as designed. However, the design of the controls does not include control procedures to prevent misstatements and the potential omission of cash receipts.	Determine if the control deficiency is a material weakness by obtaining further evidence.
3.	The auditors concluded that the ineffectiveness of the design of controls over accounts payable and cash disbursements represents a material weakness in internal control even though the financial statements are not materially misstated.	Express an adverse opinion on the internal controls.
4.	Management has not provided assurance that there are no material weaknesses in controls. Subsequent tests revealed no material weaknesses.	Express an unqualified opinion on the internal controls.
5.	The auditor's prior year report on internal control included an adverse opinion. The client has since modified internal controls. No material weaknesses were found in the current year.	Express an unqualified opinion on the internal controls.

Explanations:
1. If an auditor is unable to obtain adequate evidence because the client did not furnish sufficient information and documentation, a disclaimer of opinion is appropriate.

2. The auditor would obtain additional evidence in order to determine if the control deficiency was a material weakness.

3. An adverse opinion is used when a material weakness exists.

4. Even though no material weakness exists and an unqualified opinion may be issued, management must provide the auditors with a written representation letter.

5. Because the material weakness from the prior year was corrected with modifications to internal controls, an unqualified opinion may be used for the current year.

AUD 5-SIMQ5 SIM931

	Situation	Response
1.	A journal entry was made by the controller on December 31, year 2: Dr. Salaries and wages expense Cr. Accrued liabilities *To account for compensation for year 2 to be paid in year 3.*	Obtain management's bonus plan and eligible employee list and recalculate expense.
2.	A journal entry was made by the fixed asset manager on December 31, year 2: Dr. Accumulated depreciation Cr. Depreciation expense *To adjust machine's depreciation expense.*	Confirm with controller any changes in estimates.
3.	A journal entry was made by the controller on December 30, year 2: Dr. Investments held for trading purposes Cr. Investments held-to-maturity *Change in asset classification.*	Review board minutes for change in classification of long-lived assets.
4.	A journal entry was made by the controller on January 1, year 2: Dr. Repairs and maintenance Cr. Accounts payable *To record the proposed audit adjustments from year 1.*	Propose adjusting entry to debit prior-year retained earnings.
5.	A journal entry was made by the controller on December 31, year 2: Dr. Investment in stock Cr. Investment income *Record subsidiary income for year 2.*	Obtain financial statement of subsidiary.

AUD 5-SIMQ6 DRS2

Subsequent events represent activity which occurred after the balance sheet date, but prior to the issuance of the financial statements. There are two types of subsequent events:
1) Those events in which <u>conditions existed at the balance sheet</u> date and would affect the financial information inherent in financial statement as of the balance sheet date. These events must be recognized in the financial statement as of the balance sheet date.
2) Those events in which <u>conditions did not exist at the balance sheet date</u>, but occurred after the balance sheet date. However, if the event would cause the financial statements to be misleading, a footnote disclosure should be made indicating the nature of the event and an estimate of the financial impact.

Summary of Forest Corporation's Subsequent Events and Recommended Accounting Treatment
Year-ended December 31, 20X1
March 4, 20X2 (DRAFT)

The following are the subsequent events and recommended accounting treatment prior to issuing the audited financial statements for Forest Corporation in connection with the annual audit of the financial statements for the year-ended December 31, 20X1.

1. On January 2, 20X2, Forest declared a dividend payable of $0.10 per share on its common stock. Dividends amounting to $150,000 are payable on February 15, 20X2 to common stock shareholders of record as of the close of business on February 4, 20X2.
   Recommended accounting treatment: <u>No adjustments to the December 31, 20X1 financial statements are required.</u>

   ⊙ *[Original text]* **No adjustments to the December 31, 20X1 financial statements are required.**

2. On January 6, 20X2, Forest sold 10% of its inventory for $9,300,000, which is $500,000 below cost.
   Recommended accounting treatment: ~~The December 31, 20X1 financial statements only need to have footnote disclosure indicating the $500,000 difference.~~

   ⊙ **The December 31, 20X1 financial statements must be adjusted because the net realizable value was lower than the cost, resulting in an overstatement of inventory at the balance sheet.**

3. On January 12, 20X2, Forest completed an acquisition of Timber Company for cash consideration of $4,000,000, consisting of $3,000,000, which was paid on January 12, 20X2, and up to $1,000,000 is payable based upon an earn-out period of 24 months.
   Recommended accounting treatment: ~~No adjustments to the December 31, 20X1 financial statements are required.~~

   ⊙ **No adjustments to the December 31, 20X1 financial statements are required however, if the event would cause the financial statements to be misleading, a footnote disclosure should be made indicating the nature of the event and an estimate of the financial impact.**

4. On February 3, 20X2, Forest entered into an agreement to sublease additional office space for its world headquarters. The amounts related in the sublease will total approximately $7,200,000 over the six-year term of the agreement, beginning in the second quarter of 20X2.
   Recommended accounting treatment: ~~The December 31, 20X1 financial statements must be adjusted to reflect the amount of $7,200,000 liability.~~

   ⊙ **No adjustments to the December 31, 20X1 financial statements are required.**

5. On February 5, 20X2, Forest issued 3,700,000 shares of additional common stock.
   Recommended accounting treatment: ~~No adjustments to the December 31, 20X1 financial statements are required.~~

   - ⊙ *[Original text]* **No adjustments to the December 31, 20X1 financial statements are required.**

6. At December 31, 20X1, Forest wrote-off 50% of the $200,000 accounts receivable due from Pine, Inc., a major customer, because Forest became aware that Pine was possibly on the verge of bankruptcy. On February 12, 20X2, Forest received notification that Pine went bankrupt and determined that the accounts receivable is uncollectible.
   Recommended accounting treatment: ~~Write off Pine's remaining accounts receivable of $100,000 in the December 31, 20X1 financial statements.~~

   - ⊙ *[Original text]* **Write off Pine's remaining accounts receivable of $100,000 in the December 31, 20X1 financial statements.**

7. On February 14, 20X2, Forest became aware the company was a defendant in a lawsuit brought on by one of their customers over the quality of their products. Forest's attorney estimated the payment, if Forest lost the suit would range between $300,000 and $500,000, but the more likely amount would be $350,000. On February 22, 20X2, Forest paid $315,000 to the customer to settle the lawsuit.
   Recommended accounting treatment: ~~A footnote disclosure is required on the December 31, 20X1 financial statements describing the lawsuit and the $315,000 settlement.~~

   - ⊙ **No adjustments to the December 31, 20X1 financial statements are required.**

8. On February 24, 20X2, Forest increased the quarterly dividend on common stock from $0.10 to $0.12 per share. On an annualized basis, the dividend increased from $0.40 to $0.48 per share. The next quarterly will be payable on May 13, 20X2 to shareholders of record as of March 31, and 20X2.
   Recommended accounting treatment: ~~No adjustments to the December 31, 20X1 financial statements are required.~~

   - ⊙ *[Original text]* **No adjustments to the December 31, 20X1 financial statements are required.**

9. On February 25, 20X2, one of the three factories owned by Forest caught fire and was destroyed with an estimated loss of $3,125,000. The other two operating factories were reconfigured to accommodate approximately 40% of the production that was performed at the factory that was destroyed.
   Recommended accounting treatment: ~~A footnote disclosure is required on the December 31, 20X1 financial statements.~~

   - ⊙ **The loss is not recognized in the December 31, 20X1 financial statements however, if the event would cause the financial statements to be misleading, a footnote disclosure should be made indicating the nature of the event and an estimate of the financial impact.**

AUD 5-SIMQ7 SIM33

AU-C § 800 . 07 a

Keywords: Cash basis

Auditing and Attestation – CRAM
Quick Reference Guide

Players	
GAAP (Private Sector)	FASB [ASC]
	IASB [IFRS] (Previously IAS for IASC)
	GASB
	FASAB
	SASB
AICPA	SAS (Non-issuers) [AU-C]
	SSAE [AT]
	SSARS [AR]
	ET, QC, PFP, CS
U.S. Government	SEC
	SOX – PCAOB (Issuers) [AS]
	GAO
	DOL
IFAC	IAASB [ISA]
	IESBA

Independence **required**: audits, reviews, attestations

Independence **not required**: compilations (must disclose if not independent), tax, consulting

1. Generally accepted auditing standards (GAAS)
2. New client
    a. Decision to accept
        i. Evaluate independence and ability to handle
        ii. Evaluate communications with predecessor auditor – permission of client
    b. If accepted, understand the client and industry
        i. Engagement letter
        ii. Determine materiality levels [qualitative and quantitative]
        iii. Evaluate risk: AR = IR x CR x DR [RMM x DR]
        iv. Must do risk assessment procedures and further audit procedures (test of controls, substantive tests)
3. Auditor's responsibility
    a. Errors and fraud – reasonable assurance
    b. Direct effect laws and regulations
    c. Other laws and regulations

Reference: AUD 1A-1

1. Internal control
   a. Definition -- <u>process</u> effected by <u>people</u> to achieve entity's <u>objectives</u>
   b. Components-- environment, risk assessment, control activities, information and communication, monitoring
   c. Control activities -- [R I P S] Reviews, Information processing, physical controls, segregation of duties (authorization, recording, custody)
   d. Basic requirements -- Risk assessment procedures [document -- narrative, questionnaire, flowchart]
   e. Tests of controls
      - To test operating effectiveness of controls
      - Done ONLY if you wish to rely on controls
      - Includes -- Inquire Observe Inspect Reperform

2. Cycles
   Sales/Accounts Receivable/Cash Receipts
   - Sales order
   - Credit approval
   - Ship - bill of lading
   - Bill/Collect cash
   - Records - aging schedule, bad debts, sales returns

   Purchases/Accounts Payable/Cash Disbursements
   - Requisition
   - Purchase order
   - Receive goods
   - Approve for payment/Pay

   Personnel/Payroll
   - Authorization - personnel (human resource management)
   - Recording - payroll accounting
   - Custody - paycheck distribution

3. Control deficiencies -- communications
   - Required to the extent that they come to your attention
   - Must be **written** to management **and** those charged with governance
   - Show significant deficiencies and material weaknesses **and** potential effects on the financial statements
   - Not required to give recommendations
   - Cannot write that "no significant deficiencies found" but may write "no material weaknesses found"
   - Other communications to management about other deficiencies noted (other than significant deficiencies or material weaknesses) -- may be written or oral

4. Internal auditors
   - Competence
   - Objectivity - To whom do they answer in the client entity?

Reference: 2C-1

CRAM 2
Auditing and Attestation (AUD)
Copyright © 2018 Yaeger CPA Review. All rights reserved.

Fraudulent financial reporting and misappropriation of assets
1. Characteristics of fraud:
    - incentive (pressure)
    - opportunity
    - rationalize (attitude)
2. Discussion among engagement personnel (brainstorming)
3. Identify risks that may lead to material misstatement due to fraud:
    - interviews
    - brainstorming
    - fraud risk factors
    - analytical procedures
    - client acceptance/continuance
    - entity's programs and controls
    - revenue recognition/management estimates/inventory quantities
4. Respond to identified risks
    - overall (personnel, predictability)
    - specific (nature, timing, extent)
    - test journal entries
    - management override of controls
5. Communicate to management and audit committee (i.e., those charged with governance)
6. Document

Reference: 2D-1

Auditing and IT [definitions, internal control, substantive tests]:
1. EDP department -- Control clerks, Operator, Programmer, Analyst, Librarian [C O P A L]
2. General and application controls
3. Batch vs. on-line real-time processing
4. Auditing around the computer (without using the computer)
5. Auditing through the computer
    - Test data
    - Integrated test facility
    - Parallel simulation

6. Computers in auditing
    - Spreadsheet
    - Sampling
    - Audit through computer - computer assisted audit techniques -- CAATS
    - Manage engagement
    - Word processing

7. Electronic evidence
    - Electronic data interchange (EDI) may reduce or eliminate traditional paper trail
    - Auditor may need more test of controls in these environments
    - Auditor may need to do work at interim dates when electronic evidence exists at a certain point in time before this evidence may become non-retrievable (affect nature, timing, extent of tests)

8. IT Advantages
    - Speed/accuracy
    - Minimize redundancy
    - Improve communications
    - Remain competitive
    - Facilitate additional analysis of data
    - Backup/recovery

9. IT Disadvantages
    - Cost
    - Specialized personnel
    - Backup/recovery
    - Compatibility
    - Loss of confidentiality
    - Rely on others
    - Audit trail
    - Legal issues

10. Internal control implications
    - General vs application controls
    - Access codes/passwords
    - Backup/recovery
    - Security over data
    - Test for accurate processing of data
    - Documentation

Reference: 2C-6

Analytical procedures
   What? Does the number make sense? Includes comparisons, ratios, budgets, nonfinancial data
   When? Required for planning and overall review. May be used during the audit as a substantive test.
   Why? Usually very efficient (more than effective)

Reference: 3C-1

Management assertions [PERCV]
   1. Presentation and disclosure
   2. Existence and occurrence
   3. Rights and obligations
   4. Completeness
   5. Valuation or allocation

Audit evidence
   1. Evidence
      a. Sufficient - quantity
      b. Appropriate - quality
         - observe
         - external -- directly to auditor or held by client
         - internal
         - oral
   2. Substantive tests
      - Trace/vouch
      - Reconcile
      - Analytical procedures
      - Confirm
      - Examine

Directional testing

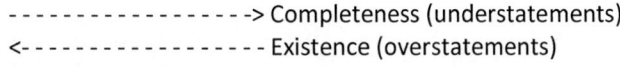

- - - - - - - - - - - - - - - - - -> Completeness (understatements)
<- - - - - - - - - - - - - - - - - - Existence (overstatements)

Reference: 2E-4

Examine	A reasonably detailed study of a document or record to determine specific facts about it.
Scan	A less detailed examination of a document or record to determine whether there is something unusual warranting further investigation.
Read	An examination of written information to determine facts pertinent to the audit.
Compute	A calculation done by the auditor independent of the client. **Re-compute:** When the auditor tests a client computation by performing it again.
Foot	Addition of a column of numbers to determine whether the total is the same as the client's.
Count	A determination of assets on hand at a given time. This term should be associated with the type of evidence defined as physical examination.
Vouch	The use of documents to verify recorded transactions or amounts.
Trace	An instruction normally associated with documentation or re-performance. The instruction should state what the auditor is tracing and where it is being traced from and to. Often, an audit procedure that includes the term *trace* will also include a second instruction, such as *compare* or *recalculate*.
Compare	A comparison of information in two different locations. The instructions should state which information is being compared in as much detail as practical.

Reference: 2E-27

Audit procedures
   Balance sheet accounts
   Balances -- cash, AR, inventory, AP
   Transactions -- PPE, LT debt, investments, capital stock [beg bal + additions - subtractions = end bal]

Fair Value
- Review and test management's process
- Independently develop an estimate
- Review subsequent events

Reference: 2H-3

Subsequent discovery of facts
- Would it have affected report?
- Is it addressed with other procedures?
- Can you get client's permission to do work?
- Are statements misstated?
    - Encourage client to recall statements and adjust and reissue.
- If client refuses, you notify all known users of financial statements that they cannot rely on your report.

Reference: 3G-1

Group audits
1. Group consists of more than one component
2. Component -- entity or business activity for which group or component management prepares financial information to be included in the group financial statements
3. Component auditor -- performs work on the financial information of a component to be used as audit evidence for the group audit. A component auditor may be part of the group engagement partner's firm, a network firm of the group engagements partner's firm, or an unrelated firm.
4. Group financial statements -- include financial information of more than one component, including consolidated or combined financial statements
5. Group engagement partner is responsible for the direction, supervision and performance for the group audit

Cash flow statement (CFS) audits
1. Foot
2. Trace to other financial statements
3. Classification -- operating, investing, financing
4. Schedules for various accounts
5. Disclosures

Audit Sampling
1. Terminology
    - Risk of assessing control risk too low -- overreliance
    - Risk of assessing control risk too high -- under reliance
    - Incorrect acceptance
    - Incorrect rejection
    - Error, exception, deviation

2. Attribute sampling -- sample size factors
    - Tolerable rate -- inverse
    - Expected population error rate -- direct
    - Risk of assessing control risk too low -- inverse (compliment of confidence level)

    Formula: (**Sample error rate + Allowance for sampling risk**) < **Tolerable error rate**

3. Variables sampling -- sample size factors
    - Confidence level (reliability) - direct
    - Precision - direct
    - Variability within the population - direct
    - Tolerable misstatement - inverse

4. Sampling plans
    - Determine objective of test
    - Define population and deviation
    - Determine sample size
    - Select sampling technique
    - Perform sampling plan
    - Evaluate results/Document

Reference: 3B-1

Audit reports
(You must know when they're issued and how they're worded.)
1. Qualified -- "except for"
    Major GAAP departure (Material) *OR*
    Major scope limitation (Material)
2. Disclaimer -- no opinion
    Very major scope limitation (Pervasive)
3. Adverse - "not present fairly"
    Very major GAAP departure (Pervasive)
4. Emphasis of Matter (opinion still unmodified)
    Going concern -- substantial doubt
    Inconsistency
    Others at auditor's discretion
5. Other Matter
    Restrict distribution, if applicable

Headings for audit reports (subtitles) of nonissuers

Unmodified	Qualified	Adverse	Disclaimer
Report on F/S	Report on F/S	Report on F/S	Report on F/S
Mgt's Respon	Mgt's Respon	Mgt's Respon	Mgt's Respon
Auditors Resp	Auditors Resp	Auditors Resp	Auditors Resp
------	Basis for Q Op	Basis for A Op	Basis for D Op
Opinion	Qualified Opin	Adverse Opin	Disclaimer of Opin
Emphasis of Matter	Emphasis of Matter	Emphasis of Matter	Emphasis of Matter
Other Matter	Other Matter	Other Matter	Other Matter

Report on other legal & regulatory requirements

General parts of a report
1. Title (for audits, reviews, and agreed-upon procedures)
2. Address
3. Service type
4. What we worked on
5. Date of #4 (what we worked on)
6. Responsibilities of parties
7. Professional standards followed
8. Description of procedures - general
9. Conclusion
10. Inherent Limitations - if any
11. Restrict distributions - if applicable
12. Sign and date

Special purpose frameworks
1. Types
    a. Cash basis
    b. Tax basis
    c. Regulatory basis
    d. Contractual basis
2. Description
    a. Use different names for financial statements (not GAAP names) / Disclosures

Special considerations
1. Specific elements, accounts, or items of a financial statement **OR** a single financial statement (general purpose or special purpose framework)
2. Incomplete presentation of a financial statement (but following GAAP)
    a. Include emphasis-of-matter paragraph in the audit report

Reference: 4A-1

CRAM 8
Auditing and Attestation (AUD)
Copyright © 2018 Yaeger CPA Review. All rights reserved.

Negative assurance
1. Review
2. Comfort letter
3. Compliance with contract as part of audit

Restrict distribution
1. Control deficiencies --------------------/ BY-
2. Auditor communications --------------------/ PRODUCT
3. Compliance with contract as part of audit --------------------/ REPORT
4. Agreed-upon procedures
5. Regulatory basis
6. Contractual basis

Government auditing standards (Yellow Book)
1. Must follow all of GAAS and issue report on financial statements
2. Must issue written report on internal controls
3. Must issue written report on compliance with laws and regulations
4. Must issue additional reports for A-I 33 audits

Attestations
1. Report on a subject matter or an assertion about the subject matter that is the responsibility of another party.
2. Used for anything other than historical financial statement(s) taken as a whole (may be nonfinancial data)
3. Levels -- examination, review, agreed-upon procedures (AUP)
4. AUP -- CPA, client, and third party agree on procedures to be used. Third party must assume responsibility for sufficiency of procedures. Report on findings based on specific procedures performed on subject matter.
5. Forecasts and projections
   a. Forecast - based on conditions expected to exist
   b. Projection - hypothetical assumptions
   c. General use - used by anyone (not projections)
   d. Limited use - users deal directly with preparer
   e. Accounting services - examination, compilation, AUP
   f. "May differ from actual"
   g. "No responsibility to update"

Reference: 4A-2

1. **Preparation**
   - Accountant prepare financial statements from client records.
   - Understand applicable financial reporting framework.
   - No report -- each page marked "no assurance provided".

2. **Compilations** (no assurance) (Assist management in presenting financial information).
   - Do not deal with internal control
   - Read financial statements for logic.
   - May omit substantially all disclosures required by GAAP, but must add an extra paragraph to the report
   - Cite measurement GAAP departures in an extra paragraph in the report

3. **Reviews** (limited or negative assurance):
   - Do not deal with internal control.
   - Inquiry and analytical procedures.
   - Cite measurement and/or disclosure GAAP departure in an extra paragraph in report (known departures")

Reference: 4C-1

General comments

Internal control
1. May be task-based simulation
2. May be flowcharts or questionnaires
3. To identify weaknesses in internal control or to design a questionnaire, use control activities [R I P S]

Evidence
1. May be task-based simulation
2. Objectives of auditing various accounts developed from assertions [P E R C V]
3. Task-based simulation

Use **PERCV** and the following table:
- **P** Inquire; Inspect documents
- **E** Vouch; Observe; Confirm
- **R** Inspect documents; Inquire; Confirm
- **C** Cut-off; Analytical procedures; Trace
- **V** Reconcile; Recalculate; Analytical procedures

Summary

Internal Control	Dollar Amounts
Tests of controls	Substantive tests
Attributes	Variables
Over/under reliance	Incorrect acceptance/rejection
CR (control risk)	DR (detection risk)
Sampling	Sampling
Discovery	PPS Mean per unit Difference estimation Ratio estimation

AICPA Code of Conduct – applies to all professional engagements
Look at other rules also (GAO, DOL, State law)

Sections:
- Preface – All Members
- Part 1 – Members in Public Practice
- Part 2 – Members in Business
- Part 3 – Other Members

Framework:
Threats – potential violation of any part of the Code
(adverse interest, familiarity, management participation, self-interest, self-review, undue influence)

Safeguards – bring threat to an *acceptable level*
- Created by profession, legislation, or regulation
- Implemented by client (Cannot rely solely on these)
- Implemented by the Firm

Covered member:
- Attest engagement team
- Someone in a position to influence the engagement
- Partner or manager who provides more than 10 hours of non-attest service
- Partner in same office as lead engagement partner
- Firm's employee benefit plan
- Entity whose policies can be controlled by any of the above (subsidiary)

Reference: 1B-1

Immediate family – spouse or spousal equivalent, dependents

Close relatives – parents, siblings, nondependent children

Direct financial interest – under direct control of the investor
      e.g., owning equity or debt securities of an audit client

Indirect financial interest – not under control of the investor (mutual fund)

Non-attest services as part of attest engagement
      (tax, bookkeeping, financial statement preparation)

Gifts/Entertainment

Contingent fees – prohibited where the firm performs a service for which accountant must be independent or prepare original/amended tax return

PCAOB:
    Registered public accounting firm is not independent of its audit client if firm provides any tax service to someone in a financial reporting oversight role at that client entity

Reference: 1B-1